GED

success

2005

TEST PREP

THOMSON

PETERSON'S

Australia • Canada • Mexico • Singapore • Spain • United Kingdom • United States

About Thomson Peterson's

Thomson Peterson's (www.petersons.com) is a leading provider of education information and advice, with books and online resources focusing on education search, test preparation, and financial aid. Its Web site offers searchable databases and interactive tools for contacting educational institutions, online practice tests and instruction, and planning tools for securing financial aid. Thomson Peterson's serves 110 million education consumers annually.

Petersons.com/publishing

Check out our Web site at www.petersons.com/publishing to see if there is any new information regarding the test and any revisions or corrections to the content of this book. We've made sure the information in this book is accurate and up-to-date; however, the test format or content may have changed since the time of publication.

For more information, contact Thomson Peterson's, 2000 Lenox Drive, Lawrenceville, NJ 08648; 800-338-3282; or find us on the World Wide Web at www.petersons.com/about.

© 2004 Thomson Peterson's, a part of The Thomson Corporation
Thomson Learning™ is a trademark used herein under license.

Previous editions © 1997, 2002, 2003

Acknowledgments: American BookWorks Corporation would like to thank the following individuals for their assistance in the development of this title: Larry Elowitz, Aart Hoogenboom, James Liptack, James Lucey, Barbara Maynard, Sharon Sharonson, and Lawrence Trivieri.

Science: Christopher Bender, Richard Bleil, Gordon Chenery, Gordon Gonyea, Gloria Dyer, Gabriel Lombardi
Mathematics: Mark Weinfeld
Writing: Jo Palmore, Elaine Silverstein
Reading: Elaine Bender, Bruce Thaler, Heidi Thompson
Social Studies: Masuda Floyd

Editor: Wallie Walker Hammond; Production Editor: Farah Pedley; Manufacturing Manager: Judy Coleman; Composition Manager: Gary Rozmierski; Cover and Interior Design: Allison Sullivan.

ISBN 0-7689-1509-0

Printed in the United States of America

10 9 8 7 6 5 4 3 2 1   06 05 04

Fourth Edition

Contents

CONTENTS

www.petersons.com

Introduction to the GED Tests

How have adults who have prepared for and passed the GED Tests described their experience? As a major life achievement. A milestone. A turning point.

This introduction will give you general information about the GED Tests and answer some basic questions you may have, such as:

- What are the GED Tests?

- What do the GED Tests look like?

- What does it take to pass the GED Tests?

- How can this book help me to pass the GED Tests?

What Are the GED Tests?

The Tests of General Educational Development (GED) are developed and administered by the GED Testing Service of the American Council on Education. Each year, they provide more than one million adults the opportunity to earn a certificate or diploma that is widely recognized as the equivalent of a high school diploma. Since 1942, when the GED program began, more than 14 million adults have earned GED credentials.

Because the GED credential is recognized and accepted by more than 95 percent of businesses, industries, schools, and colleges, it is often a step toward further achievements. Perhaps most importantly, the GED credential proves to those who have earned it that they are indeed achievers with potential for further success.

The GED Tests are five separate exams: Language Arts, Writing; Social Studies; Science; Language Arts, Reading; and Mathematics. A GED certificate or diploma is earned by obtaining a passing score based on the results of all five exams.

What Does It Take to Pass the GED Tests?

In general, you will need to show that you have the skills of an average graduating high school senior to pass the GED Tests. You will be tested on your knowledge of broad concepts and generalizations—not on how well you can remember exact details or facts. Your ability to use knowledge, information, and skills to solve problems is the key to passing the tests. A good test-preparation tip is to read as much as you can of everything that interests you—general and specific. Studies show that GED

What Do the GED Tests Look Like?

The GED Tests are made up entirely of multiple-choice questions, except for the Writing Test, which includes an essay section.

Test Number	Test Name	Number of Test Items	Time	Content Areas
Test 1	Language Arts, Writing: Part I Part II	50 items 1 essay topic	75 min. 45 min.	Sentence Structure: 30% Usage: 30% Mechanics: 25% Organization: 15%
Test 2	Social Studies	50 items	70 min.	History: 45% Geography: 15% Civics and Government: 20% Economics: 20%
Test 3	Science	50 items	80 min.	Life Sciences: 50% Physical Sciences: 50%
Test 4	Language Arts, Reading	40 items	65 min.	Literary: 75% Nonfiction: 25%
Test 5	Mathematics	50 items	90 min.	Arithmetic: 50% Algebra: 30% Geometry: 20%

candidates who read more tend to do better on the tests. Read books, newspapers, and magazines—whatever you enjoy reading. Just read!

To earn a GED credential, you need to earn a minimum passing score on each of the five tests as well as a passing average score overall. If you do not achieve a passing score on any one test or an overall passing score on all five tests, it is possible to retake one or more of the individual tests. By retaking a test, you can improve individual test scores, and that will increase your overall average score.

You probably already have many of the skills you need and know much of what you need to know to pass the GED Tests. Getting ready for the tests means finding out what you already know and what you need to work on, choosing a study plan for self-improvement, and spending the necessary time to follow through on your plan.

Note: You will want to find out more about the requirements of the GED Tests where you live. Each state, U.S. territory, and Canadian province sets its own specific requirements for taking and passing the GED Tests. This region-specific information is available by contacting a local adult education center, community college, or library or simply by calling the toll-free number 1-800-62-MYGED.

What Are the Changes to the GED?

MATHEMATICAL TEST ALTERNATE FORMAT QUESTIONS

As we have already discussed, the GED contains 50 math questions. Of these, 40 will be in the standard multiple-choice format. There will be five answer choices and you will be asked to select the correct one. The remaining ten questions are special, alternate-format questions. In these questions, you will not be given any answer choices, but instead will have to determine your own answer and code it on the answer grid in the correct way.

There are two different types of alternate-format questions. In one type, you will be asked a geometry question, the answer to which will be a point on the coordinate plane. Instead of simply writing the point down, you will be asked to shade it in on a coordinate plane grid. As an example, if you determine the answer to a particular problem to be (2,3), you will need to shade that point in on a grid similar to the one following:

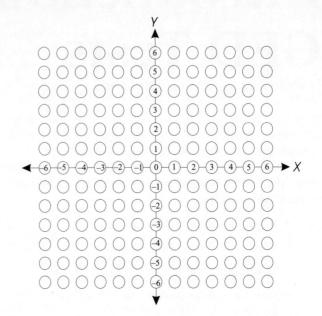

That is, in order to answer the question, you will need to shade in the grid as shown below:

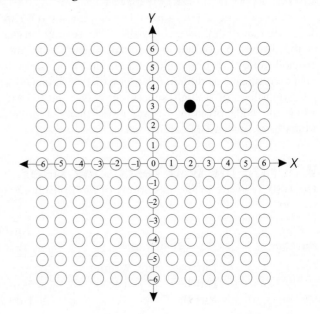

How Do I Use This Book?

This book has been written to help you prepare for the five subject areas of the GED Test. There is a logical approach to each section of study. Take a minute now to become familiar with the features and format of this book.

PRETEST

This book begins with a full-length practice GED Test. This pretest is similar in content to the test you will eventually take. The purpose of the pretest is to help you diagnose your strengths and weaknesses. With this information, you can plan how best to use your time to prepare for the actual test. If you score worse than you would like in a particular subject area, you can allot more time to studying for that subject. Likewise, if you do very well in a subject area, you may choose to spend less time on that subject.

Following the pretest are detailed answers and explanations for each item. Carefully review the explanation for any items you may have answered incorrectly. Once you have completed the pretest, you are ready to go on to the subject area reviews.

REVIEW SECTION

Each of the five subject review sections begins with an introduction to the question types you will be asked to answer in that subject area test. You will also find information about what content areas will be covered. In this introduction, you will see an example of each question type and how best to approach it.

Next, you will be given a review for each content area. After every one or two pages of information, you will have a chance to practice answering sample GED Test questions about the material. As you answer the multiple-choice questions, read all the choices carefully. You are asked to choose the one best answer to each item. Although an answer choice may contain facts from the material you have read, only choose it if it is the best answer for that particular item.

POSTTEST

After you review the five subject areas, you are ready to take the posttest. The posttest is a full-length practice GED Test. As you take the test, approximate the testing conditions. Choose a quiet place to work. Set a timer. If you do not finish in the allotted time, mark your place and then continue to answer the questions. If you finish early, go back and review your work. Working under timed conditions will help you adjust to the pacing of the actual test.

Next, check your answers to the posttest. Carefully study the explanations for the items you missed. If you had trouble with a particular subject area, review that section of the book. Then proceed to the Practice Tests.

PRACTICE TESTS

The five full-length Practice Tests contain the same question types and cover the same content areas that you will find on the GED Test. Read the instructions for each test carefully. These are the same instructions you will see on the actual test. By reading and understanding the instructions now, you will save time when you take the GED Test. Again, approximate the testing conditions. Choose a quiet place to work. Time your work. If possible, complete all five Practice Tests in the same day, allowing short breaks between tests as needed. Use the answer sheets printed in the book and fill in the ovals with a No. 2 pencil.

When you have completed all five tests, check your answers. Carefully study the explanations for any items you may have missed. At the end of each set of explanations, use the chart to find out which areas of content and question types you may still need to review. Review pages as indicated on the chart. Your performance on the Practice Tests will help you determine whether you are ready for the GED Tests.

Now, it's time to get to work! Begin with the Pretest and go on to review each subject area. The material in this book will help you develop the test-taking skills you need to do well on the GED Test. Make sure you carefully read and answer each exercise in the book. The exercises and sample tests will give you all the practice you need to take the GED Tests with confidence.

Good Luck!

PRETESTS

ANSWER SHEETS

- Use a No. 2 pencil.
- Mark one numbered space beside the number that corresponds to each question you are answering.
- Erase errors cleanly and completely.

Pretest 1: Language Arts, Writing
Part I

1. ①②③④⑤
2. ①②③④⑤
3. ①②③④⑤
4. ①②③④⑤
5. ①②③④⑤
6. ①②③④⑤
7. ①②③④⑤
8. ①②③④⑤
9. ①②③④⑤
10. ①②③④⑤
11. ①②③④⑤
12. ①②③④⑤
13. ①②③④⑤

14. ①②③④⑤
15. ①②③④⑤
16. ①②③④⑤
17. ①②③④⑤
18. ①②③④⑤
19. ①②③④⑤
20. ①②③④⑤
21. ①②③④⑤
22. ①②③④⑤
23. ①②③④⑤
24. ①②③④⑤
25. ①②③④⑤
26. ①②③④⑤

27. ①②③④⑤
28. ①②③④⑤
29. ①②③④⑤
30. ①②③④⑤
31. ①②③④⑤
32. ①②③④⑤
33. ①②③④⑤
34. ①②③④⑤
35. ①②③④⑤
36. ①②③④⑤
37. ①②③④⑤
38. ①②③④⑤

39. ①②③④⑤
40. ①②③④⑤
41. ①②③④⑤
42. ①②③④⑤
43. ①②③④⑤
44. ①②③④⑤
45. ①②③④⑤
46. ①②③④⑤
47. ①②③④⑤
48. ①②③④⑤
49. ①②③④⑤
50. ①②③④⑤

Pretest 2: Social Studies

1. ①②③④⑤
2. ①②③④⑤
3. ①②③④⑤
4. ①②③④⑤
5. ①②③④⑤
6. ①②③④⑤
7. ①②③④⑤
8. ①②③④⑤
9. ①②③④⑤
10. ①②③④⑤
11. ①②③④⑤
12. ①②③④⑤
13. ①②③④⑤

14. ①②③④⑤
15. ①②③④⑤
16. ①②③④⑤
17. ①②③④⑤
18. ①②③④⑤
19. ①②③④⑤
20. ①②③④⑤
21. ①②③④⑤
22. ①②③④⑤
23. ①②③④⑤
24. ①②③④⑤
25. ①②③④⑤
26. ①②③④⑤

27. ①②③④⑤
28. ①②③④⑤
29. ①②③④⑤
30. ①②③④⑤
31. ①②③④⑤
32. ①②③④⑤
33. ①②③④⑤
34. ①②③④⑤
35. ①②③④⑤
36. ①②③④⑤
37. ①②③④⑤
38. ①②③④⑤

39. ①②③④⑤
40. ①②③④⑤
41. ①②③④⑤
42. ①②③④⑤
43. ①②③④⑤
44. ①②③④⑤
45. ①②③④⑤
46. ①②③④⑤
47. ①②③④⑤
48. ①②③④⑤
49. ①②③④⑤
50. ①②③④⑤

Pretest 3: Science

1. ① ② ③ ④ ⑤
2. ① ② ③ ④ ⑤
3. ① ② ③ ④ ⑤
4. ① ② ③ ④ ⑤
5. ① ② ③ ④ ⑤
6. ① ② ③ ④ ⑤
7. ① ② ③ ④ ⑤
8. ① ② ③ ④ ⑤
9. ① ② ③ ④ ⑤
10. ① ② ③ ④ ⑤
11. ① ② ③ ④ ⑤
12. ① ② ③ ④ ⑤
13. ① ② ③ ④ ⑤

14. ① ② ③ ④ ⑤
15. ① ② ③ ④ ⑤
16. ① ② ③ ④ ⑤
17. ① ② ③ ④ ⑤
18. ① ② ③ ④ ⑤
19. ① ② ③ ④ ⑤
20. ① ② ③ ④ ⑤
21. ① ② ③ ④ ⑤
22. ① ② ③ ④ ⑤
23. ① ② ③ ④ ⑤
24. ① ② ③ ④ ⑤
25. ① ② ③ ④ ⑤
26. ① ② ③ ④ ⑤

27. ① ② ③ ④ ⑤
28. ① ② ③ ④ ⑤
29. ① ② ③ ④ ⑤
30. ① ② ③ ④ ⑤
31. ① ② ③ ④ ⑤
32. ① ② ③ ④ ⑤
33. ① ② ③ ④ ⑤
34. ① ② ③ ④ ⑤
35. ① ② ③ ④ ⑤
36. ① ② ③ ④ ⑤
37. ① ② ③ ④ ⑤
38. ① ② ③ ④ ⑤

39. ① ② ③ ④ ⑤
40. ① ② ③ ④ ⑤
41. ① ② ③ ④ ⑤
42. ① ② ③ ④ ⑤
43. ① ② ③ ④ ⑤
44. ① ② ③ ④ ⑤
45. ① ② ③ ④ ⑤
46. ① ② ③ ④ ⑤
47. ① ② ③ ④ ⑤
48. ① ② ③ ④ ⑤
49. ① ② ③ ④ ⑤
50. ① ② ③ ④ ⑤

Pretest 4: Language Arts, Reading

1. ① ② ③ ④ ⑤
2. ① ② ③ ④ ⑤
3. ① ② ③ ④ ⑤
4. ① ② ③ ④ ⑤
5. ① ② ③ ④ ⑤
6. ① ② ③ ④ ⑤
7. ① ② ③ ④ ⑤
8. ① ② ③ ④ ⑤
9. ① ② ③ ④ ⑤
10. ① ② ③ ④ ⑤

11. ① ② ③ ④ ⑤
12. ① ② ③ ④ ⑤
13. ① ② ③ ④ ⑤
14. ① ② ③ ④ ⑤
15. ① ② ③ ④ ⑤
16. ① ② ③ ④ ⑤
17. ① ② ③ ④ ⑤
18. ① ② ③ ④ ⑤
19. ① ② ③ ④ ⑤
20. ① ② ③ ④ ⑤

21. ① ② ③ ④ ⑤
22. ① ② ③ ④ ⑤
23. ① ② ③ ④ ⑤
24. ① ② ③ ④ ⑤
25. ① ② ③ ④ ⑤
26. ① ② ③ ④ ⑤
27. ① ② ③ ④ ⑤
28. ① ② ③ ④ ⑤
29. ① ② ③ ④ ⑤
30. ① ② ③ ④ ⑤

31. ① ② ③ ④ ⑤
32. ① ② ③ ④ ⑤
33. ① ② ③ ④ ⑤
34. ① ② ③ ④ ⑤
35. ① ② ③ ④ ⑤
36. ① ② ③ ④ ⑤
37. ① ② ③ ④ ⑤
38. ① ② ③ ④ ⑤
39. ① ② ③ ④ ⑤
40. ① ② ③ ④ ⑤

Pretest 5: Mathematics
Part I

1. ① ② ③ ④ ⑤

2. ① ② ③ ④ ⑤

3. ① ② ③ ④ ⑤

4. ① ② ③ ④ ⑤

5. ① ② ③ ④ ⑤

6.

7. ① ② ③ ④ ⑤

8. ① ② ③ ④ ⑤

9.

10.

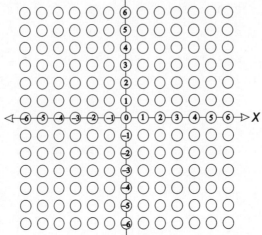

11. ① ② ③ ④ ⑤

12. ① ② ③ ④ ⑤

13. ① ② ③ ④ ⑤

14. ① ② ③ ④ ⑤

15.

16. ① ② ③ ④ ⑤

17. ① ② ③ ④ ⑤

18. ① ② ③ ④ ⑤

19. ① ② ③ ④ ⑤

20. ① ② ③ ④ ⑤

21. ① ② ③ ④ ⑤

22.

23.

24.

25. ① ② ③ ④ ⑤

Part II

1. ① ② ③ ④ ⑤

2. ① ② ③ ④ ⑤

3. ① ② ③ ④ ⑤

4. ① ② ③ ④ ⑤

5. ① ② ③ ④ ⑤

6. ① ② ③ ④ ⑤

7. ① ② ③ ④ ⑤

8. ① ② ③ ④ ⑤

9. ① ② ③ ④ ⑤

10. ① ② ③ ④ ⑤

11.

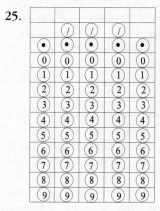

12. ① ② ③ ④ ⑤

13. ① ② ③ ④ ⑤

14. ① ② ③ ④ ⑤

15. ① ② ③ ④ ⑤

16.

	/	/	/	
•	•	•	•	•
0	0	0	0	0
1	1	1	1	1
2	2	2	2	2
3	3	3	3	3
4	4	4	4	4
5	5	5	5	5
6	6	6	6	6
7	7	7	7	7
8	8	8	8	8
9	9	9	9	9

17. ① ② ③ ④ ⑤

18. ① ② ③ ④ ⑤

19. ① ② ③ ④ ⑤

20. ① ② ③ ④ ⑤

21. ① ② ③ ④ ⑤

22. ① ② ③ ④ ⑤

23. ① ② ③ ④ ⑤

24. ① ② ③ ④ ⑤

25.

	/	/	/	
•	•	•	•	•
0	0	0	0	0
1	1	1	1	1
2	2	2	2	2
3	3	3	3	3
4	4	4	4	4
5	5	5	5	5
6	6	6	6	6
7	7	7	7	7
8	8	8	8	8
9	9	9	9	9

Pretest 1

LANGUAGE ARTS, WRITING
PART I: MULTIPLE CHOICE

75 Minutes ❖ **50 Questions**

Directions: Choose the one best answer for each item.

Items 1–10 refer to the following paragraphs.

(1) *The process of glassblowing to create beautiful crystal, and ornate glassware is an art mastered by only a few.* (2) *Usually no solitary individual completes all of the necessary stages by himself; rather several people are involved.* (3) *Which has been in existence for about two thousand years.*

(4) *Glass is essentially made from three ingredients sand, soda, and lime.* (5) *The first step in making glass involves melting these raw materials by subjecting them to intense heat.* (6) *A number of different processes to shape the molten glass are possible depending on the kind of glassware being made.* (7) *Fine crystal, for instance, is typically created by blowing.*

(8) *Glassblowing is a skill that requires patience and mastery.* (9) *The glassblower gently dips a blowpipe into molten glass, and begins to blow as he twirls the pipe.* (10) *Then the heated glass as it bulges out can be shaped by squeezing, by stretching, by twirling, and cutting.* (11) *Other methods of creating glassware are molding, casting, and pressing.*

(12) *The final stages in the glassblowing process are typically done by hand as well to work the glass into it's final shape.* (13) *Completed glass products can range in size from miniatures to larger items such as vases, pitchers, bowls, and really large commemorative pieces.* (14) *If a design has been drawn by another craftsperson on the cooled glass, some crystal glassware is carefully cut with sandstone or carborundum.* (15) *Once the cutting is completed, the finished product is meticulously buffed and sanded to remove any sharp edges or imperfections.* (16) *Often creating intricate designs such as those available from Water-*

ford Crystal. (17) *Many times master crystal cutters will sign there work.* (18) *If you visit the Waterford factory in Ireland, you can watch this glassware being made.*

1. Sentence 1: **The process of glassblowing to create beautiful crystal, and ornate glassware is an art mastered by only a few.**

   What correction should be made to this sentence?

   (1) Change <u>glassblowing to create</u> to <u>glassblowing is used to create</u>
   (2) Insert a comma after <u>glassware</u>
   (3) Remove the comma after <u>crystal</u>
   (4) Insert a comma after <u>beautiful</u>
   (5) No correction is necessary

2. Sentence 3: **Which has been in existence for about two thousand years.**

   What correction should be made to this sentence?

   (1) A process which has been in existence for about two thousand years.
   (2) This process had been in existence for about two thousand years.
   (3) This process was in existence for about two thousand years.
   (4) This process has been in existence for about two thousand years.
   (5) No correction is necessary

3. Sentence 4: **Glass is essentially made from three ingredients sand, soda, and lime.**

   What correction should be made to this sentence?

   (1) Reverse <u>essentially</u> and <u>made</u>
   (2) Change <u>is made</u> to <u>was made</u>
   (3) Insert a colon after <u>ingredients</u>
   (4) Remove <u>and</u> after <u>soda</u>
   (5) No correction is necessary

4. Sentence 9: **The glassblower gently dips a blowpipe into molten glass, and begins to blow as he twirls the pipe.**

What correction should be made to this sentence?

(1) Remove the comma after glass
(2) Change dips to dipped
(3) Change into molten glass to in molten glass and move it to the beginning of the sentence
(4) Change as he twirls the pipe to after he twirls the pipe
(5) No correction is necessary

5. Which sentence should be removed from the third paragraph?

(1) The first sentence
(2) The second sentence
(3) The third sentence
(4) The fourth sentence
(5) No sentence should be removed

6. Sentence 10: **Then the heated glass as it bulges out can be shaped by squeezing, by stretching, by twirling, and cutting.**

What correction should be made to the underlined portion of this sentence?

(1) Insert by after and
(2) Arrange the processes alphabetically
(3) Remove the second and third instance of by
(4) Following cutting add into many different shapes
(5) No correction is necessary

7. Sentence 12: **The final stages in the glassblowing process are typically done by hand as well to work the glass into it's final shape.**

What correction should be made to the underlined portion of this sentence?

(1) Change as well to work to as well as to work
(2) Change to work the glass into to to work the glass in
(3) Insert a comma after as well
(4) Remove the apostrophe from it's
(5) No correction is necessary

8. Sentence 14: **After a design has been drawn by another craftsperson on the cooled glass, some crystal glassware is carefully cut with sandstone or carborundum.**

What correction should be made to the underlined potion of this sentence?

(1) Change has been drawn to was drawn
(2) Move on the cooled glass to follow has been drawn
(3) Change the underlined portion to After another craftsman on the cooled glass has drawn a design
(4) Move on the cooled glass to introduce the sentence
(5) No correction is necessary

9. Sentence 16: **Often creating intricate designs such as those available from Waterford Crystal.**

What correction should be made to this sentence?

(1) Change creating to having created
(2) Change Often creating intricate designs to Which often create intricate designs
(3) omit from Waterford Crystal
(4) Change Often creating to Often these masters create
(5) No correction is necessary

10. Sentence 17: **Many times master crystal cutters will sign there work.**

What correction should be made to this sentence?

(1) Change master crystal cutters to Master Crystal Cutters
(2) Change work to job
(3) Change there to their
(4) Add because they are paid by the piece.
(5) No correction is necessary

Items 11–20 refer to the following paragraphs.

(1) *Parents who have young children with full-time employment discover that choosing a day care center for their child can be a challenge.* (2) *More and more people are facing this task every year.* (3) *Characteristics to look for when a parent visits a prospective day care center include the following.* (4) *Number and qualifications of staff, cleanliness of facilities, licensure by the appropriate state agency, kinds of playground equipment, number of other children at the center, kinds of structured activities, presence of teaching and reading materials, behavior and demeanor of children on site, and kinds of snacks and drinks served.*

(5) *If at all possible parents should talk with the director of the center and ask questions about these qualities.* (6) *Meeting the staff is another good idea, but another important aspect is the behavior and demeanor of the children currently at the center.* (7) *Do they look happy?* (8) *Check to see what kind of toys and activities are provided.* (9) *Do the children engage in some kind of hands-on activity like finger-painting or building with blocks or Legos?* (10) *How often are they read to?* (11) *Do these children spend much time watching television?* (12) *Are educational videos or tapes of popular children's movies such as* The Little Mermaid *or* The Muppet Movie *available?* (13) *How is nap time managed successfully?* (14) *What standards does the center have for children who are ill?*

(15) *Even after visiting locations that meet parents' standards, another serious problem may occur.* (16) *The center may not have any openings and therefore cannot except another child for some time.* (17) *Openings in really good child care centers fill rapidly when registration is held in late summer.* (18) *Unless a parent all ready has one child enrolled, success in registering a new child is sometimes unlikely.* (19) *The best way to deal with this issue is to apply at several day care centers in the hope that at least one center will accept the child.*

11. Sentence 1: **Parents who have young children with full-time employment discover that choosing a day care center for their child can be a challenge.**

What correction should be made to this sentence?

(1) Insert a comma after employment
(2) Move with full-time employment to follow Parents
(3) Change choosing to chosing
(4) Insert a comma after discover
(5) No correction is necessary

12. Sentence 2: **More and more people are facing this task every year.**

What correction should be made to this sentence?

(1) Change every year to ever year
(2) Change more and more to most
(3) Change are facing to were facing
(4) Insert a comma between more and and
(5) No correction is necessary

13. Sentence 3: **Characteristics to look for when a parent visits a prospective day care center include the following.**

What correction should be made to this sentence?

(1) Insert a comma after center
(2) Change include to includes
(3) Insert features after following
(4) Change day care center to Day Care Center
(5) No correction is necessary

14. Sentence 4: **Number and qualifications of staff, cleanliness of facilities, licensure by the appropriate state agency, kinds of playground equipment, number of other children at the center, kinds of structured activities, presence of teaching and reading materials, behavior and demeanor of children on site, and kinds of snacks and drinks served.**

What correction should be made to this sentence?

(1) Change Number to number
(2) Insert are all important factors after drinks served
(3) Connect this construction to Sentence 3 with a comma
(4) Replace Number and qualifications to Number the qualifications
(5) No correction is necessary

15. Sentence 5: **If at all possible parents should talk with the director of the center and ask questions about these qualities.**

What correction should be made to this sentence?

(1) Insert a comma after If at all
(2) Insert a comma after center
(3) Replace possible with necessary
(4) Insert a comma after possible
(5) No correction is necessary

16. Sentence 8: **Check to see what kind of toys and activities are provided.**

What correction should be made to this sentence?

(1) Replace kind with kinds
(2) Change what to the
(3) Add for my child to play with after are provided
(4) Insert a comma after toys
(5) No correction is necessary

17. Sentences 11 and 12: (11) **Do these children spend much time watching television?** (12) **Are educational videos or tapes of popular children's movies such as *The Little Mermaid* or *The Muppet Movie* available?**

The best way to combine these two sentences is:

(1) If children watch television, are the programs age appropriate and educational?
(2) If children watch much television, which programs do they see?
(3) Do the children watch video versions of *The Little Mermaid* and *The Muppet Movie*?
(4) How much television of any type do the children watch?
(5) Do these children spend much time watching television, and are educational videos or tapes of popular children's movies such as *The Little Mermaid* or *The Muppet Movie* available?

18. Sentence 15: **Even after visiting locations that meet parents' standards, another serious problem may occur.**

What correction should be made to this sentence?

(1) Change Even after visiting locations that meet parents' standards to Even after parents have visited qualified locations
(2) Change another serious problem may occur to another serious problem might occur
(3) Remove the apostrophe after parents'
(4) Move the apostrophe after parents' to parent's
(5) No correction is necessary

19. Sentence 16: **The center may not have any openings and therefore cannot except another child for some time.**

What correction should be made to this sentence?

(1) Change may not have to does not have
(2) Insert a comma after openings
(3) Insert a semicolon after openings
(4) Change except to accept
(5) No correction is necessary

20. Sentence 17: **Openings in really good child care centers fill rapidly when registration is held in late summer.**

What correction should be made to this sentence?

(1) Change really to real
(2) Change fill to have been filled
(3) Insert a comma after rapidly
(4) Change is held to has been held
(5) No correction is necessary

Items 21–29 refer to the following document.

May 27, 2001

Ms. Rose White
Post-Adoption Unit
Department of Human Services
Box 365
Nashville, TN 37100

Dear Ms. White:

(A)

(1) *At birth I was surrendered by my birthmother to the Tennessee Department of Human Services.* (2) *After being in a foster home for six months, I was adopted when my birthfather surrendered his parental rights, and I was then placed with my adoptive parents.*

(B)

(3) *My adoptive parents support me completely in my search for information about my heritage.* (4) *Since I have recently been diagnosed as diabetic, I am particularly eager to learn health facts about my biological parents and relatives.* (5) *I have very little information about these people.* (6) *It is important to me to discover any relevant information that may explain this recent diagnosis or prepare me for any other possible medical condition.*

(C)

(7) *I have only a few facts about my background, but I do have a legitimate Tennessee birth certificate; however, it has been amended to identify my adoptive parents as my birth parents, which is a common practice.* (8) *I was born in Columbus, Tennessee, at Maycomb County Hospital on August 17, 1978.* (9) *After several months in foster care, I was eligible for adoption through the Department of Human Services Adoption Unit.* (10) *My adoptive parents applied to Human Services for adopt a child, and shortly after their application was approved, I was placed with them in 1980.*

(D)

(11) *My foster family recorded some details about my development and health, but I don't hardly know anything about my biological family.* (12) *I want to find out if I have any brothers or sisters, for instance.* (13) *I would also like to see photographs of relatives.* (14) *Whether I will be able to meet any of these birth relatives is another of my questions.*

(E)

(15) *Since the courts have recently ruled that Tennessee adoption records will no longer be closed to adoptees above the age of 21.* (16) *I am exercising my right as an adult adoptee to seek information from formally closed files.* (17) *Please tell me what I must do to access these records.* (18) *You can contact me as follows: 511 Harpeth Hollow, Hillview, TN 37423 or at 931-282-7003 or samsun@aol.com.* (19) *Thank you for your assistance.*

Sincerely,

Samuel Sunderson

21. Which sentence would be most effective if placed at the beginning of paragraph A?

    (1) I am writing to apply for access to my adoption records.
    (2) This letter requests information about how to discover my background information.
    (3) As per this request please provide the information I seek.
    (4) I hardly know how to start this letter, which may be one of the most important of my life.
    (5) You have probably received many letters like this one.

22. Which sentence in paragraph B is not relevant to the information expressed in this paragraph and should be removed?

    (1) Sentence 3
    (2) Sentence 4
    (3) Sentence 5
    (4) Sentence 6
    (5) No revision is necessary

23. Sentence 7: How can this sentence be revised to be more concise?

    (1) Change however, it has been amended to identify my adoptive parents as my birth parents, which is a common practice to On these my adoptive parents are listed as my birth parents as is common practice
    (2) Change however, it has been amended to identify my adoptive parents as my birth parents, which is a common practice to They changed it so my adoptive parents are given as my birth parents. This change is typical
    (3) Change however, it has been amended to identify my adoptive parents as my birth parents, which is a common practice to It has been modified to register my adoptive parents as birth parents, a common practice
    (4) Change however, it has been amended to identify my adoptive parents as my birth parents, which is a common practice to But my birth certificate presently records my adoptive parents as birth parents, a procedure that is typical in adoptions today
    (5) No correction is necessary

24. Sentence 10: **My adoptive parents applied to Human Services for adopt a child, and shortly after their application was approved, I was placed with them in 1980.**

    What correction should be made to this sentence?

    (1) Change I was placed with them to some people put me with them
    (2) Change parents applied to Human Services to parents applied from Human Services
    (3) Change their application was approved to they approved their application
    (4) Change for adopt a child to to adopt a child
    (5) No correction is necessary

25. Sentence 11: **My foster family recorded some details about my development and health, but I don't hardly know anything about my biological family.**

    What correction should be made to this sentence?

    (1) Change family recorded some details to family has recorded some details
    (2) Change I don't hardly know to I hardly know
    (3) Change development and health, but I to development and health, and I
    (4) Change I don't hardly know to I won't hardly know
    (5) No correction is necessary

26. Sentence 14: **Whether I will be able to meet any of these birth relatives is another of my questions.**

    What correction should be made to this sentence?

    (1) Change will be able to to would be able
    (2) Change is another to was another
    (3) Change Whether I will be able to meet any of these birth relatives to Whether meeting any of these birth relatives
    (4) Change Whether I will be able to meet any of these birth relatives to Meeting any of these birth relatives
    (5) No correction is necessary

27. Sentence 15: **Since the courts have recently ruled that Tennessee adoption records will no longer be closed to adoptees above the age of 21.**

What correction should be made to this sentence?

(1) Change <u>Since the courts</u> to <u>Because the courts</u>

(2) Change <u>Since the courts have recently ruled</u> to <u>The courts have recently ruled</u>

(3) Change <u>will no longer be closed</u> to <u>were no longer closed</u>

(4) Change <u>courts have recently ruled</u> to <u>courts would have recently ruled</u>

(5) No correction is necessary

28. Sentence 16: **I am exercising my right as an adult adoptee to seek information from formally closed files.**

What correction should be made to this sentence?

(1) Change <u>right</u> to <u>rite</u>

(2) Change <u>exercising</u> to <u>exorcising</u>

(3) Change <u>formally</u> to <u>formerly</u>

(4) Change <u>closed</u> to <u>hidden</u>

(5) No correction is necessary

29. Sentence 19: **You can contact me as follows: 511 Harpeth Hollow, Hillview, TN 37423 or at 931-282-7003 or samsun@aol.com.**

What correction should be made to this sentence?

(1) Remove the comma after <u>Hillview</u>

(2) Insert a comma after <u>TN</u>

(3) Insert a comma after <u>37423</u>

(4) Delete the email address

(5) No correction is necessary

Items 30–40 refer to the following paragraphs.

(1) *The famous Covered Bazaar in Istanbul, the largest covered market in the world, is often a traveler's first and favorite shopping place. (2) With millions of products for sale ranging from spices to carpets. (3) The Grand Bazaar, or Kapali Carsi, as it is also known, has been in existence for hundreds of years since Istanbul was conquered by the Ottomans around 1450. (4) It is constructed on the remains of a Byzantine covered market. (5) Originally Oriental in appearance, this Turkish shopping mecca under a number of connected hemispherical roofs is actually a vast collection of over four thousand shops joined by a maze of sixty roads, streets, and alleys. (6) Though lacking a proper shape, it has hundreds of silver plated domes with many windows. (7) The names of the many streets recall the days when each trade had their own street: the carpet sellers' street, the goldsmiths' street, the leather workers' street, etc.*

(8) *Bazaar merchants watch the passers-by carefully to gauge what the shopper seeks. (9) If a shopper evinces even the least interest in an object, often a merchant may rush out of his shop to invite the potential customer to have some tea while examining the shop's wares. (10) Another merchant may quickly scale a wall to retrieve something on display such as a ceramic or brass item that seems to intrigue a possible buyer.*

(11) *Almost anything a tourist will seek can be found for sale in the Covered Bazaar. (12) The Bazaar has faced at least twelve strong earthquakes and nine major fires, but with restorations that followed in the nineteenth century, it has enlarged to have the appearance it has today. (13) Somehow the merchants have developed some kind of "sixth sense" of selling that helps them spot potential customers as well as employ persuasive sales techniques and offer attractive prices, frequently they are willing to bargain to make a sale. (14) The Covered Bazaar is the original shopping mall with something to suit every taste and pocket. (15) Turkish crafts, the world-renowned carpets, brilliant hand painted ceramics, copperware, brass ware, and meerschaum pipes make charming souvenirs and gifts. (16) The gold jewelry in brilliantly lit cases dazzles the window shoppers. (17) Leather and suede goods of excellent quality made a relatively inexpensive purchase. (18) Whether a customer searches for a splendid Oriental carpet, beautiful ceramics with distinct Turkish designs, aromatic spices, fine embroidered cloth, or gleaming brass items, he can be sure to find plenty of appealing choices at the Grand Bazaar in Istanbul.*

30. Sentence 2: **With millions of products for sale ranging from spices to carpets.**

What correction should be made to this sentence?

(1) Change millions of to a variety of
(2) Change ranging from to from
(3) Omit for sale
(4) Connect the entire construction to Sentence 1
(5) No correction is necessary

31. What is the best way to combine Sentences 4 and 5?

(1) Constructing on the remains of a Byzantine covered market and originally Oriental in appearance . . .
(2) Constructed on the remains of a Byzantine covered market and originally Oriental in appearance . . .
(3) It is constructed on the remains of a Byzantine covered market, originally Oriental in appearance, this Turkish shopping mecca . . .
(4) Originally Oriental in appearance, this Turkish shopping mecca constructed on the remains of a Byzantine covered market under a number of connected hemispherical roofs joined by a maze of sixty roads, streets, and alleys.
(5) A vast collection of over four thousand shops joined by a maze of sixty roads, streets, and alleys, constructed on the remains of a Byzantine covered market, originally Oriental in appearance, this Turkish shopping mecca under a number of connected hemispherical roofs.

32. Sentence 7: **The names of the many streets recall the days when each trade had their own street: the carpet sellers' street, the goldsmiths' street, the leather workers' street, etc.**

What correction should be made to this sentence?

(1) Change trade had their own street to trade had its own street
(2) Change carpet sellers' to carpet seller's
(3) Place a period after leather workers' street
(4) Change own street: the carpet sellers' street to own streets
(5) No correction is necessary

33. Sentence 8: **Bazaar merchants watch the passers-by carefully to gauge what the shopper seeks.**

What correction should be made to this sentence?

(1) Change gauge to guage
(2) Change passers-by to passerby
(3) Change the shopper seeks to the shoppers seek
(4) Change watch to watches
(5) No correction is necessary

34. Sentence 9: **If a shopper evinces even the least interest in an object, often a merchant may rush out of his shop to invite the potential customer to have some tea while examining the shop's wares.**

What correction should be made to this sentence?

(1) Move while examining the shop's wares to follow a merchant
(2) Omit the comma after an object
(3) Change a merchant may rush to a merchant might rush
(4) Insert a comma after his shop
(5) No correction is necessary

35. Which of the following sentences in the third paragraph should be moved to the first paragraph?

(1) Sentence 11
(2) Sentence 12
(3) Sentence 13
(4) Sentence 15
(5) Sentence 16

36. Which of the following sentences in the third paragraph should be moved to the second paragraph?

(1) Sentence 13
(2) Sentence 14
(3) Sentence 15
(4) Sentence 16
(5) Sentence 17

37. Sentence 12: **The Bazaar has faced at least twelve strong earthquakes and nine major fires, but with restorations that followed in the nineteenth century, it has enlarged to have the appearance it has today.**

Which of the following choices is the most logical revision of this sentence?

(1) Enlarging to have the appearance it has today, the Bazaar has faced at least twelve strong earthquakes and nine major fires, but with restorations following in the nineteenth century.

(2) Facing at least twelve strong earthquakes and nine major fires, restorations in the nineteenth century enlarged the Bazaar to have today's appearance.

(3) The Bazaar has faced at least twelve strong earthquakes and nine major fires, but restorations following in the nineteenth century enlarged it to its modern appearance.

(4) The appearance the Bazaar has today has been the result of restorations in the nineteenth century because of at least twelve strong earthquakes and nine major fires.

(5) Nineteenth-century restorations both repaired damage from at least twelve strong earthquakes and nine major fires and enlarged the Bazaar to its modern appearance.

38. Sentence 13: **Somehow the merchants have developed some kind of "sixth sense" of selling that helps them spot potential customers as well as employ persuasive sales techniques and offer attractive prices, frequently they are willing to bargain to make a sale.**

What correction should be made to this sentence?

(1) Change the comma after prices to because
(2) Change employ to employing
(3) Change sale to sell
(4) Change Somehow to Some how
(5) No correction is necessary

39. Sentence 14: **The Covered Bazaar is the original shopping mall with something to suit every taste and pocket.**

Which of the following is **not** a logical revision of this sentence?

(1) The Covered Bazaar, the original shopping mall with something to suit every taste and pocket.

(2) With something to suit every taste and pocket, the Covered Bazaar is the original shopping mall.

(3) The Covered Bazaar, the original shopping mall, has something to suit every taste and pocket.

(4) The original shopping mall, the Covered Bazaar has something to suit every taste and pocket.

(5) The original shopping mall, the Covered Bazaar, has something to suit every taste and pocket.

40. Sentence 17: **Leather and suede goods of excellent quality made a relatively inexpensive purchase.**

What correction should be made to this sentence?

(1) Change relatively to relative
(2) Change made to make
(3) Omit goods
(4) Insert a comma after quality
(5) No correction is necessary

Items 41–50 refer to the following document.

Rules for Employee Behavior at Rustlers' Restaurant

1. All employees must report for work timely, cleanly and with appropriate dress. If you are unable to come to work, phone the manager on duty.
2. All employees must wear black pants and black shoes with the red Rustler's polo shirt. Cooks will also wear white aprons.
3. Facial hair is limited to neatly trimmed mustaches, beards, and sideburns. If your hair is longer than your collar you must tie your hair back—both males and females. More than four earrings per ear is prohibited. Cleanliness is essential.
4. Employees must clock in and out personally. Do not clock in or out someone else. Keep a record of your time is your responsibility.
5. Paychecks are delivered every other Friday.
6. Employees may have a 10-minute break every 2 hours. Learn to rotate the break schedule with coworkers. Smoking must take place outside the back door of the kitchen.
7. Don't forget to wash your hands thoroughly after visiting the restroom or smoking.
8. No drinking or eating are allowed in the food preparation area.
9. Every employee has a specific job to complete theirself.
    *   If you are a host or hostess, greet people warmly when they arrive. Keep an accurate list of customers names, the number in their party, and their smoking preference to seat them as quickly as possible.
    *   If you are a busboy, your job is clearing the tables, setting up for the next customers, and clean the chairs as well as the table.
    *   If you are a server, pay attention to customers in your area and respond promptly when they are seated; likewise, continue to check with them on the quality of the food or to see if they have other requests. Do not forget to offer dessert. Present their bill in a timely fashion, but don't never hesitate to continue offering drink refills. We do not want guests to feel rushed.
    *   Dishwashers are responsible for following state health guidelines as well to guarantee good health. Be sure to follow specific guidelines for washing, rinsing, drying, and reshelving dishes and glasses.
    *   Cooks must read orders and follow it carefully. Maintain clean preparation and cooking surfaces. Be sure to store foods at proper temperatures.

10. Above all, remember it is your job to welcome customers and make they're dining experience pleasant. If they have complaints, offer to send a manager to they're table. Only a manager is authorized to offer free desserts, coupons for future visits, or free meals.
11. Finally, the secret to success in the restaurant business is to repeat the customers. Everything you can to make diners comfortable, happy, and well-fed so they will eat with us again.

41. Rule 1: **All employees must report for work timely, cleanly and with appropriate dress.**

    What kind of correction is needed for the underlined portion of this sentence?

    (1) On time, cleanly, and appropriate dress
    (2) Timely, cleanly, and appropriately dressed
    (3) On time, clean, and dressed appropriately
    (4) Timely, clean, and dressed appropriately
    (5) No correction is necessary

42. Rule 2: **All employees must wear black pants and black shoes with the red Rustler's polo shirt.**

    What correction should be made to this sentence?

    (1) Change employees to employers
    (2) Insert a comma after pants
    (3) Change employees to employee's
    (4) Change Rustler's to Rustlers'
    (5) No correction is necessary

43. Rule 4: **Employees must clock in and out personally. Do not clock in or out someone else. Keep a record of your time is your responsibility.**

    What correction should be made to these sentences?

    (1) Change Do not clock in or out to Do not be clocking in or out
    (2) Change must clock in or out personally to must clock in or out for theirselves
    (3) Change Keep a record to Keeping a record
    (4) Combine the first two sentences by inserting a comma after personally, adding and and attaching the second sentence
    (5) No correction is necessary

19

44. Rule 8: **No drinking or eating are allowed in the food preparation area.**

What correction should be made to this sentence?

(1) Change in the food preparation area to the place where the food is prepared and cooked
(2) Change are to is
(3) Insert a comma after drinking
(4) Change or to nor
(5) No correction is necessary

45. Rule 9: **Every employee has a specific job to complete theirself.**

What correction should be made to this sentence?

(1) Omit theirself
(2) Change theirself to himself
(3) Change has to had
(4) Insert a comma after job
(5) No correction is necessary

46. Rule 9: **If you are a busboy, your job is clearing the tables, setting up for the next customers, and clean the chairs also.**

What correction should be made to this sentence?

(1) Omit the comma after busboy
(2) Change clean to cleaning
(3) Change clearing to to clear
(4) Change is to was
(5) No correction is necessary

47. Rule 9: **If you are a server, pay attention to customers in your area and respond promptly when they are seated; likewise, continue to check with them on the quality of the food or to see if they have other requests. Do not forget to suggest dessert. Present their bill in a timely fashion, but don't never hesitate to continue offering drink refills. We do not want guests to feel rushed.**

What correction should be made to this item?

(1) Change dessert to desert
(2) Omit on the quality of the food or to see if they have other requests
(3) Insert a comma after fashion
(4) Omit don't never hesitate to
(5) No correction is necessary

48. Rule 9: **Dishwashers are responsible for following state health guidelines as well to guarantee good health. Be sure to follow specific guidelines for washing, rinsing, drying, and reshelving dishes and glasses.**

What correction should be made to this item?

(1) Change to guarantee good health to guaranteeing good health
(2) Change are responsible for to must respond to
(3) Insert a comma after guidelines
(4) Change dishes and glasses to dish's and glass's
(5) No correction is necessary

49. Rule 9: **Cooks must read orders and follow it carefully. Maintain clean preparation and cooking surfaces. Be sure to store foods at proper temperatures.**

What correction should be made to this item?

(1) Change Maintain to Maintaining
(2) Change Be sure to Making sure
(3) Change follow it to follow them
(4) Combine the sentences in this manner: Cooks must read orders and follow it carefully, maintain clean preparation and cooking surfaces, and store foods at proper temperatures.
(5) No correction is necessary

50. Rule 10: **Above all, remember it is your job to welcome customers and make they're dining experience pleasant. If they have complaints, offer to send a manager to their table. Only a manager is authorized to offer free desserts, coupons for future visits, or free meals.**

What correction should be made to this sentence?

(1) Change your job to you're job
(2) Change they're dining experience to there dining experience
(3) Change they're dining experience to their dining experience
(4) Combine the second and third sentence by changing the period after table to a comma
(5) No correction is necessary

PART II: ESSAY

45 Minutes

Directions: In your state there is a controversy surrounding whether it should be declared illegal for a driver of a vehicle to use a cell phone while driving. Some citizens favor the proposition because they contend that many more accidents are occurring because drivers on cell phones are distracted and make steering mistakes, while those who oppose the proposal maintain that the cell phone has become an integral part of communication today. Cell phones are necessary to stay connected to business and family. With which of these two positions do you agree?

Write an essay of 200 to 250 words to the editor of your local newspaper, stating your opinion. Give reasons and examples to support your opinions.

SCORED 4-3-2-1

SCORE = 4

The use of cell phones today has grown so rapidly that it seems we have come to depend on a device that makes us accessible at virtually all times and almost always able to contact others. As a result of such widespread use, cell phones are the topic of a controversy about whether the driver of a vehicle should be allowed to use the phone while driving. The rate of accidents for drivers using cell phones has increased alarmingly because many accidents occur while the driver is using a cell phone. Sometimes steering is difficult while the driver is dialing a number or answering the phone, or a driver may shift attention away from watching the road. For these reasons the use of cell phones causes so many problems that it should be illegal to use cell phones in a car. Although a driver has to contend with other kinds of distractions such as changing a radio station or changing a tape or CD, it seems more logical for a driver to pull off the road, stop, and then use the phone to avoid making mistakes that cause accidents. Of course, others may point out that drivers make these same kind of mistakes because they try to read, apply makeup, or eat and drink while they are driving. But the number of accidents has grown since cell phones became popular. The best way to eliminate these kinds of accidents is to make use of cell phones illegal. Heavy fines and confiscation of phones will help to enforce the law.

SCORE = 3

Cell phones are causing many problems on the highways today. Often drivers who are on their cell phones are distracted from watching the road and driving carefully. Many accidents have occurred because drivers who were using their cell phones had to reach for the phone to answer it or looked away from the road while they dialed a number. I think that in most cases a cell phone call is not an emergency and could wait until the driver stops the car. I have seen so many drivers using cell phones on their way to and from work that I wonder what is so important that cannot wait until these drivers reach their destination. Passing a law to make using cell phones while driving a car against the law is a good way to reduce accidents. People will think twice before using their cell phones if they know they will be fined or arrested.

SCORE = 2

People who want to make using cell phones while you drive are making a mistake. Cell phones are a necessary part of communication today. Instead of being cut off from everyone while you drive, with a cell phone you stay connected all the time. If you need to call home or call for help, you can use the cell phone. Why would using it be illegal? Using a cell phone is no different than changing a tape or a CD while you are driving. People say using cell phones cause accidents, but I don't think so. We have more serious problems to solve than cell phones. What about people who race through yellow traffic lights? They cause accidents, too. Drivers who try to fuss at their children in the back seat lose control sometimes. Also people with pets in their laps while they are driving are sometimes careless. So I don't think we need to penalize people with cell phones.

SCORE = 1

I do not really know much about cell phones, but I have seen a lot of people using them whenever they are driving. It seems to me that it has to be hard to steer the car with one hand and hold the cell phone with the other. And when you have to dial a number, that takes two hands. I guess it just depends on how much practice a driver has as a driver and as a cell phone user. Making cell phones illegal is too drastic. If you follow the laws of the road, you can use a cell phone as long as you are careful.

Pretest 2

SOCIAL STUDIES

75 Minutes ❖ 50 Questions

Directions: Choose the one best answer for each item.

Items 1 and 2 refer to the following passage.

Operant conditioning occurs when you learn from the consequences of your behavior. For example, if you park your car in a handicapped-designated parking space and receive a parking ticket, you probably will not park your car in a handicapped space again.

1. According to the passage, which of the following statements is true?

   (1) Your behavior "operates" on the outside world to produce a consequence.
   (2) Operant conditioning is only a theory.
   (3) Your behavior has no effect on operant conditioning.
   (4) Only handicapped persons are to use handicapped parking spaces.
   (5) People change their actions depending on the consequences of their previous actions.

2. In the example given in the passage, the stimulus, or the factor that influences your change in behavior, is

   (1) the handicapped parking space.
   (2) the car that you parked.
   (3) the parking ticket.
   (4) the fact that you got caught.
   (5) your reaction to the ticket.

Items 3 and 4 refer to the following information.

Economist: one who studies production, distribution, and consumption of wealth and ways of supplying the material wants of people.

Psychologist: one who studies behavior and the human mind in their many aspects, operations, powers, and functions.

Sociologist: one who studies human society and social phenomena, the progress of civilization, and the laws controlling human institutions and functions.

Historian: one who studies and explains the record of past events.

Geographer: one who studies the planet Earth, including its climate, products, natural features, and inhabitants.

3. John Maynard Keynes, who wrote *The General Theory of Employment, Interest, and Money*, was a(n)

   (1) economist.
   (2) psychologist.
   (3) sociologist.
   (4) historian.
   (5) geographer.

4. Someone who examines the effects of poverty on preschool children living in urban areas of the American Southwest is a(n)

   (1) economist.
   (2) psychologist.
   (3) sociologist.
   (4) historian.
   (5) geographer.

Items 5 and 6 refer to the following information.

The Eastern Woodland peoples of North America lived in what is now the northeastern part of the United States. The Mohawk, Oneida, Seneca, and other groups lived by hunting, farming corn and squash, fishing, and gathering berries. By contrast, peoples of the Northwest, including Nootka, Tillamook, and Coos, survived by fishing for salmon, cod, herring, and halibut in the crowded streams and coastal waters and by using the trees of the huge forests of the area for many of their needs.

5. Salmon was a staple in the diet of the

   (1) Tillamook.
   (2) Seneca.
   (3) Mohawk.
   (4) Oneida.
   (5) peoples of the Northeast.

6. The passage indicates that a native people's way of living depended on the

   (1) fish available in the region.
   (2) proximity of streams and coastal waters.
   (3) crops and berries that grew in the region.
   (4) geography and resources of the region.
   (5) proximity of large forests.

Items 7 and 8 refer to the following information.

Unemployment of qualified workers has three basic causes:

1. Cyclical unemployment is caused by slowdowns in the economy. Businesses sell fewer goods and thus need fewer workers. These same workers often are rehired when business picks up again.
2. Seasonal unemployment occurs in industries such as farming that need many workers during some seasons but not during others.
3. Structural unemployment takes place when businesses move from one location to another or when skills of certain workers become obsolete or are no longer needed for some reason.

Occasionally, unemployment can be caused by more than one of these situations at a time.

7. Peter is a ski instructor in Colorado. When the economy is slow, fewer people ski, but Peter is still hired by the ski resort. Every year, though, he has trouble finding someone who will hire him for about five months when there is no skiing.

Peter's unemployment is

   (1) cyclical.
   (2) seasonal.
   (3) structural.
   (4) cyclical and seasonal.
   (5) seasonal and structural.

8. Critics of the North American Free Trade Agreement (NAFTA) argue that many Americans' jobs will be lost as companies take advantage of opportunities to move their operations to Mexico. The fear is that workers will experience which type of unemployment?

   (1) Cyclical
   (2) Seasonal
   (3) Structural
   (4) Cyclical and seasonal
   (5) Cyclical and structural

Items 9 and 10 refer to the time-zone map below.

TIME ZONES IN THE 48 CONTIGUOUS STATES

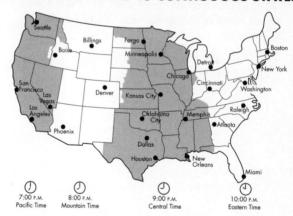

9. When it is 1 a.m. in Atlanta, what time is it in Los Angeles?

   (1) Midnight
   (2) 2 a.m.
   (3) 1 p.m.
   (4) 11 p.m.
   (5) 10 p.m.

10. When it is 2 p.m. in Seattle, what time is it in San Francisco?

   (1) Noon
   (2) 1 p.m.
   (3) 2 a.m.
   (4) 2 p.m.
   (5) 11 a.m.

Items 11 and 12 refer to the following graph.

Items 13 and 14 refer to the cartoon.

COST OF AN AVERAGE TRADITIONAL WEDDING

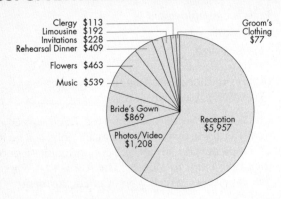

Clergy $113
Limousine $192
Invitations $228
Rehearsal Dinner $409
Flowers $463
Music $539
Bride's Gown $869
Photos/Video $1,208
Reception $5,957
Groom's Clothing $77

11. According to the graph, which two categories cost less than the limousine?

   (1) Invitations and clergy
   (2) Music and the flowers
   (3) Clergy and groom's clothing
   (4) Rehearsal dinner and invitations
   (5) Groom's and bride's clothing

12. The average traditional wedding shown in the graph costs slightly more than $10,000. About what portion of that amount is the cost of the reception?

   (1) Less than 10 percent
   (2) About 90 percent
   (3) About 30 percent
   (4) A little less than half
   (5) About 60 percent

13. Which statement best summarizes the point of this 1990 cartoon?

   (1) Farmers in the Soviet Union were sometimes able to raise bumper crops.
   (2) Despite huge resources, the Soviet system managed to produce practically nothing.
   (3) The Soviet Union used a highly centralized distribution system.
   (4) People in the Soviet Union had to endure a low standard of living.
   (5) By the 1990s, machinery in the Soviet Union was quite antiquated by Western standards.

14. With which statement would the cartoonist be most likely to agree?

   (1) Communism provided a decent living to its citizens.
   (2) Few people believed that communism would fail so completely in the Soviet Union.
   (3) People who lived in the Soviet Union got what they deserved.
   (4) Communism was a system that took advantage of the people forced to endure it.
   (5) The Soviet Union had many lazy workers.

15. In the first years of the existence of the United States, the right to vote was limited to white male landowners aged 21 or over. Since then there has been a gradual extension of this right to include women, minorities, and people aged 18 and over, regardless of economic status. Which statement best describes why this extension of rights has taken place?

  (1) The great growth in overall population has been the major cause of the extension of voting rights.
  (2) The idea has grown that all people are equal and should be treated as such.
  (3) The westward movement of white settlers in the 1800s led to the need for more voters west of the Mississippi River.
  (4) The elimination of slavery in 1865 was the main reason for this extension of rights.
  (5) More people today feel qualified to elect responsible leaders.

16. Which of the following men is best known as the leader of the American civil rights movement of the 1960s?

  (1) W. E. B. Du Bois
  (2) Jesse Jackson
  (3) Martin Luther King Jr.
  (4) Booker T. Washington
  (5) Marcus Garvey

Items 17 and 18 refer to the globe.

LATITUDE AND LONGITUDE

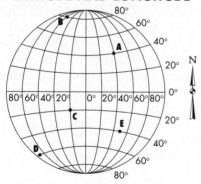

17. Which point on the globe can be found at 80 degrees north, 60 degrees west?

  (1) Point A
  (2) Point B
  (3) Point C
  (4) Point D
  (5) Point E

18. A traveler going from point B to point E would travel in which direction?

  (1) North
  (2) West
  (3) Southeast
  (4) Southwest
  (5) Northwest

Items 19 and 20 refer to the following information.

To help America recover from the Great Depression, President Franklin Delano Roosevelt's administration got Congress to enact laws that created the following programs:

Rural Electrification Administration, which provided low-cost electricity to isolated rural areas.

Civilian Conservation Corps, which provided jobs for young, single men on conservation projects for the federal government.

Works Progress Administration, which created as many jobs as possible as quickly as possible, from electrician to violinist, and paid wages with government funds.

Banking Act of 1935, which created a seven-member board of public officials to regulate the nation's money supply and interest rates on loans.

Tennessee Valley Authority, which developed natural resources of the Tennessee Valley.

19. Today's powerful Federal Reserve Board, which sets interest rates charged by the Federal Reserve Bank, is an outgrowth of which legislative initiative of the 1930s?

  (1) Rural Electrification Administration
  (2) Civilian Conservation Corps
  (3) Works Progress Administration
  (4) Banking Act of 1935
  (5) Tennessee Valley Authority

20. A farmer in rural Oregon was probably most interested in which of the five government initiatives?

  (1) Rural Electrification Administration
  (2) Civilian Conservation Corps
  (3) Works Progress Administration
  (4) Banking Act of 1935
  (5) Tennessee Valley Authority

21. From 1919 to 1933, Americans lived with a constitutional amendment that forbade the making, selling, or transporting of intoxicating liquors for drinking purposes. During that time, now often referred to as the Roaring Twenties, a great deal of liquor was illegally manufactured, transported, sold, and consumed. Large, well-organized groups of violent criminals made huge profits on this illegal activity. Which of the following people may cite that national experience to support his or her point of view today?

    (1) Someone who favors the decriminalization of drugs
    (2) Someone who wants to increase the number of government drug inspectors at major seaports and airline terminals
    (3) Someone who works for a liquor manufacturer today
    (4) Someone who believes there is too much violence on TV
    (5) Someone who wants much higher "sin taxes" on items such as liquor and tobacco products

Items 22 and 23 refer to the following information.

The collapse of the Soviet Union in the early 1990s led to a drastic fall in the birth rate across Russia. The birth rate fell from 2.1 children per woman in 1988 to 1.4 children per woman in 1993. At the same time, the death rate soared. In 1993, there were 800,000 more deaths than births.

22. If this trend continues, you can safely predict that Russia's population will

    (1) decrease by half by the year 2010.
    (2) increase when the country achieves economic stability.
    (3) decrease sharply in the coming years.
    (4) decrease sharply, then increase after the year 2000.
    (5) follow the same patterns as other countries in the former Soviet Union.

23. What is the most likely reason for the falling birth rate?

    (1) The large number of women compared to men after World War II
    (2) A national problem of alcoholism
    (3) The large percentage of the population that is already over age 65
    (4) Uncertainty about the future as a result of economic and political chaos
    (5) An increase in the suicide rate

24. George Washington was chosen president of the Constitutional Convention in 1787 and was then overwhelmingly elected to serve as the first president of the new republic in 1789 and 1792. Washington is associated with which of the following wars?

    (1) French and Indian War
    (2) Revolutionary War
    (3) War of 1812
    (4) Civil War
    (5) Spanish-American War

25. With which act of government is President Abraham Lincoln most closely associated?

    (1) Monroe Doctrine
    (2) Louisiana Purchase
    (3) Emancipation Proclamation
    (4) Roosevelt Corollary
    (5) Truman Doctrine

Item 26 refers to the following passage.

In the early 1800s, the decision to send a child to school was a private one. By the middle of the century, a change was brought about by reformers such as Horace Mann of Massachusetts, who believed that education promoted inventiveness and economic growth and allowed workers to increase their incomes. More and more states began to use tax money to pay for public schools. By 1870, about 57 percent of the nation's children were enrolled in public school and by 1920, 75 percent of American children were in school.

26. During the 1800s, education became not a privilege for the few but a(n)

    (1) obligation for everyone.
    (2) tax burden on society.
    (3) right for everyone.
    (4) economic decision.
    (5) business decision.

27. The southern colonies were favored with fertile land and a warm climate—perfect conditions for growing tobacco, cotton, rice, and other cash crops or crops grown for profit. To grow these cash crops, large farms, or plantations, were developed. Plantations, with their need for tremendous numbers of workers, gave rise to a "peculiar institution" in the colonies and then in the United States. This institution was

   (1) democracy.
   (2) colonialism.
   (3) land development.
   (4) cash crop economy.
   (5) slavery.

Items 28 and 29 refer to the following passage.

The removal of Native Americans from land desired by white settlers began long before Americans crossed the Mississippi River. The Indian Removal Act of 1830 gave the U.S. government authority to relocate the native peoples of the South and Northwest to Indian Territory, an area set aside west of the Mississippi. There they would "cast off their savage habits and become an interesting, civilized, and Christian community," said President Jackson. During the forced migration, disease, severe weather, and hardships on the trail took their toll; thousands of Native Americans died. The Cherokee had a particularly hard time. Of about 20,000 removed from their homes, 4,000 died on the journey, which came to be known as the "Trail of Tears."

28. The Indian Removal Act was a justification of the American policy of

   (1) Manifest Destiny.
   (2) expansion.
   (3) "civilizing" Native Americans.
   (4) Native American relocation.
   (5) settlement west of the Mississippi River.

29. The Cherokees' name for their journey, "Trail of Tears," suggests that they

   (1) were forced to migrate against their will.
   (2) were not as civilized as other tribes.
   (3) planned to hurt the people responsible for their move.
   (4) wept constantly on the trail.
   (5) viewed the journey with bitterness and sorrow.

Items 30 and 31 refer to the following passage.

The railroad changed the way Americans viewed time. Before, most people used the sun to set their clocks. Because the sun appears to move across the sky from east to west, a city a little to the east of a neighboring town marked noon a few minutes earlier. In the early days of the railroad, each city and each railroad had its own time. The main terminal in Buffalo, New York, had four clocks, one for each railroad using the train station and one on "Buffalo time." In 1883, an association of railroad managers ended the confusion with Standard Railway Time. They divided the nation into time zones, and every community within a time zone was on the same time. An Indianapolis newspaper noted, "The sun is no longer [the boss]. People—55,000,000 people—must now eat, sleep, and work, as well as travel by railroad time." In 1918, Standard Railway Time became federal law.

30. Standard Railway Time most likely had the effect of

   (1) placing all cities in the same time zone.
   (2) confusing the public.
   (3) establishing two main time zones.
   (4) improving railroad efficiency.
   (5) making trains run faster.

31. The Indianapolis newspaper viewed railroad time as

   (1) a great innovation.
   (2) a dangerous move.
   (3) an example of the power of the railroad.
   (4) unnecessary.
   (5) unnatural.

Items 32 and 33 refer to the following information.

Other factors besides latitude may affect the climate of a region.

Ocean currents can warm or cool shorelines as they pass.

Oceans and large lakes, which do not lose or gain heat as quickly as land does, may cause milder temperatures nearby.

Mountains affect rainfall by forcing clouds to rise up and over them. As air rises, it cools. Since cold air cannot hold as much moisture as warm air, the clouds drop their moisture as they rise.

32. Inland areas, away from the coast, are likely to be

    (1) colder in winter than places near a coast.
    (2) warmer in winter than places near a coast
    (3) rainier than places near a coast.
    (4) drier than places near a coast.
    (5) similar in temperature and rainfall to places near a coast.

33. Although Valdez, a port in Alaska, lies near the Arctic Circle, it is free of ice all year long. The most likely explanation is that

    (1) winds that blow over water are warmer than winds that blow over land.
    (2) mountains block the cold winds.
    (3) Valdez is warmed by an ocean current.
    (4) the ocean does not gain or lose heat as quickly as land.
    (5) Valdez is affected by prevailing winds.

34. For which of the following activities would knowledge of relative location be more helpful than information about longitude and latitude?

    (1) Piloting a plane
    (2) Driving a car
    (3) Sailing on the ocean
    (4) Surveying a state's borders
    (5) Laying out a new city

Item 35 refers to the circle graph below.

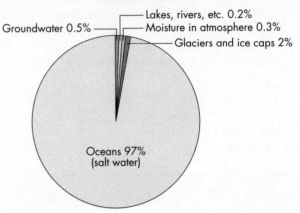

WATER SUPPLY

35. The graph suggests that people could increase their fresh water supply significantly if they could find an inexpensive way to

    (1) melt the glaciers.
    (2) reach aquifers and other sources of groundwater.
    (3) turn salt water into fresh water.
    (4) channel water from places that have too much water to those that have too little.
    (5) clean polluted rivers and lakes.

36. All of the following are checks on the judicial branch EXCEPT

    (1) the president appoints federal judges.
    (2) congressional committees exercise oversight on the judiciary.
    (3) the Senate can withhold approval of presidential appointments to the judiciary.
    (4) Congress can decrease or withhold appropriations for the judicial branch.
    (5) Congress can create additional courts.

Items 37 and 38 refer to the cartoon.

"Isn't it about time we issued some new guidelines about something?"

37. To what federal government group or segment does the cartoon refer?

(1) The judicial system
(2) Lobbyists
(3) The bureaucracy
(4) Special districts
(5) State government

38. With which of the following statements would the cartoonist most likely agree?

(1) Government is needlessly complex and confusing because there are too many local special districts.
(2) The bureaucracy creates too many rules that aren't really necessary.
(3) The bureaucracy is an efficient system when properly controlled by the executive and legislative branches of government.
(4) The judicial system meddles in citizens' lives too much and should step back from trying to set policy for the government.
(5) Lobbyists have too much influence at all levels of government.

39. The New Deal programs of the 1930s changed the role of government in citizens' lives. Social Security and other programs had some success in helping Americans recover from the Great Depression. As a result, many Americans now believe the government

(1) has an obligation to help individual citizens.
(2) should stay out of people's private lives.
(3) does not care about individual citizens.
(4) caused the Great Depression.
(5) has become too big.

40. The Supreme Court's reversals of some of its earlier rulings demonstrate that

(1) the Court changes the meaning of laws when it wants to.
(2) the Court is flexible and recognizes the need to interpret a 200-year-old document in terms of modern life.
(3) the Court doesn't take its decision-making role seriously.
(4) the justices don't think carefully enough about the possible results of their decisions.
(5) Supreme Court justices should be forced to retire at age seventy.

Items 41 and 42 refer to the following information.

The Constitution provides for changing times with a process for amendment or change. Today, the Constitution includes 27 amendments. The first 10 amendments, called the Bill of Rights, are outlined below.

BILL OF RIGHTS

First Amendment: religious and political freedom

Second Amendment: the right to bear arms

Third Amendment: the right to refuse to house soldiers in peacetime

Fourth Amendment: protection against unreasonable search and seizure

Fifth Amendment: the right of accused persons to due process of the law

Sixth Amendment: the right to a speedy and public trial

Seventh Amendment: the right to a jury trial in civil cases

Eighth Amendment: protection against cruel and unusual punishment

Ninth Amendment: the rights of the people to powers that may not be spelled out in the Constitution

Tenth Amendment: the rights of the people and the states to powers not otherwise given to the federal government, states, or people

41. Which two amendments provide for changes over time in the circumstances and realities of American life?

(1) First and Second Amendments
(2) Fifth and Sixth Amendments
(3) Third and Fourth Amendments
(4) Ninth and Tenth Amendments
(5) Seventh and Eighth Amendments

42. A family that was forced by the U.S. Army to provide housing and food for a group of soldiers could appeal to the courts based on which amendment to the Constitution?

(1) Sixth Amendment
(2) Third Amendment
(3) Second Amendment
(4) Ninth Amendment
(5) Tenth Amendment

43. Which choice best describes the meaning of the word "democracy"?

(1) Multiple branches of government
(2) Rule by the few
(3) Freedom for all
(4) Rule by the people
(5) Balance of power

44. Economics is concerned with the distribution of goods and services. It deals with all of the following EXCEPT

(1) the best ways to make money.
(2) the allocation of limited resources.
(3) scarcity, the condition in which wants exceed resources.
(4) the demand for goods and services.
(5) the production of goods and services.

Items 45 and 46 refer to the following passage.

When people make economic decisions, they must often give up something; for example, they give up taking a vacation in order to save for a car. The value of the thing given up is called opportunity cost. In another example, Maria is trying to decide whether to take a part-time night job that pays $200 per week or take courses for credit at the local community college. Her uncle will pay for her tuition and books if she decides to go to college. In addition, he will give her $100 per week.

45. What is Maria's opportunity cost of going to college?

(1) $100 per week
(2) College credits
(3) The $200-per-week job
(4) Payment for tuition and books
(5) Working too slowly toward her degree

46. Why does Maria's decision involve opportunity cost?

(1) She doesn't want her uncle to pay her college costs.
(2) She wants both to work and to go to school.
(3) Her resources (her uncle's money) are endless, so she can choose to take classes.
(4) Her resources (time and money) are limited, so she must make a choice.
(5) She would rather go to college than work at night.

47. In recent years, mail-order catalog sales have increased substantially over previous years. What is the best explanation for this increase?

(1) People are too lazy to shop in stores.
(2) People respond favorably to lower prices in catalogs and the convenience of ordering by mail.
(3) People respond favorably to lower catalog prices.
(4) People like the convenience of ordering by mail.
(5) People are effectively persuaded to buy from catalogs.

Item 48 refers to the following graph.

NEW HOME SALES
Seasonally Adjusted Annual Rate, Thousands of Units

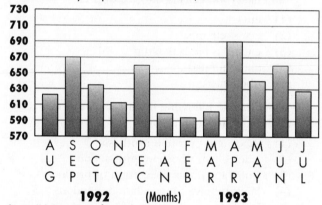

Source: U.S. Department of Commerce

48. Which is the best description of the market for new homes shown in the graph?

(1) The market is on a decreasing trend.
(2) The market is on an increasing trend.
(3) Compared to 1991, the market is good.
(4) There doesn't seem to be an overall trend in the market for the time period shown.
(5) Sales of between 600,000 and 700,000 houses are pretty good for the time period shown.

49. Which of the following does not describe a cultural change that has occurred in America over the past twenty to thirty years?

(1) Men in America earn more pay than women in the same jobs.
(2) Many men in America share the responsibilities of housework and child-rearing with their wives.
(3) African Americans and Hispanic Americans are being elected to political office.
(4) Many women in America have both families and careers.
(5) Divorce and remarriage are increasingly accepted in America.

Item 50 refers to the following passage.

In 1993, Michael Jordan's father was fatally wounded as he slept in his car on the side of a North Carolina road. Two eighteen-year-olds were charged with the murder. Both boys, who grew up in very poor families in the area, had lengthy police records that included violent crimes.

50. Many people believe that we can prevent such crimes only by teaching youngsters new values and by showing them that these values work. These people think that crime can be prevented through

(1) diffusion, or the spread of values from one culture to another through contact between societies.
(2) cultural transmission, or the sharing of information about what works in a certain situation.
(3) enculturation, or the transmission of knowledge and values from one generation to another.
(4) trial-and-error learning, or the type of learning that occurs when a person tries out a behavior without first knowing whether or not it will work.
(5) internal conflict, or the struggle within society resulting from opposing ideas, needs, wishes, or drives.

Pretest 3

SCIENCE

85 Minutes ❖ **50 Questions**

Directions: Choose the one best answer for each item.

Items 1–3 refer to the following illustration of the human heart.

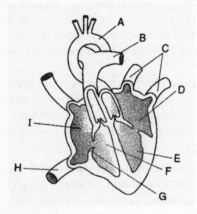

1. The aorta is labeled
   (1) A
   (2) B
   (3) C
   (4) G
   (5) H

2. Blood that leaves the lungs after being oxygenated will enter which area next?
   (1) H
   (2) I
   (3) B
   (4) D
   (5) E

3. Which of the following shows the correct order of blood flow?
   (1) C→D→E→A→I
   (2) B→A→I→C→D
   (3) H→F→I→A→E
   (4) C→I→F→E→A
   (5) C→I→F→E→B

4. One of the major differences between prokaryotic and eukaryotic cells is the size of their
   (1) nuclei.
   (2) cytoskeletons.
   (3) endoplasmic reticulum.
   (4) mitochondria.
   (5) ribosomes.

5. Which of the following organelles is not correctly matched with its function?
   (1) Ribosome : protein synthesis
   (2) Nucleolus : ribosome production
   (3) Golgi apparatus : secretion of products
   (4) Microtubules : muscular contractions
   (5) Lysosomes : digestion

6. The following list includes events that occur during mitosis.

   (A) Attachment of double-stranded chromosomes to the spindle apparatus
   (B) Formation of single-stranded chromosomes, which are moved to opposite ends of the cell
   (C) Disintegration of the nuclear membrane
   (D) Nuclear membrane formation around each set of chromosomes, forming two nuclei
   (E) Synthesis of a spindle fiber

   Which sequence represents the correct order of these events?
   (1) A→B→C→D→E
   (2) B→D→A→C→E
   (3) A→D→E→B→C
   (4) C→E→A→B→D
   (5) B→D→A→E→C

Item 7 refers to the following diagram and information.

The U-shaped tube pictured below has a semipermeable membrane (designated by the arrow). Side A contains a 0.5 molar sugar solution, while side B contains water. The membrane has holes in it that are too small to allow the sugar to pass through.

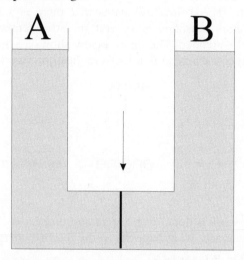

7. Which statement about this apparatus is correct?

   (1) The membrane will eventually allow the sugar through because of water pressure.
   (2) The volume on side A will become higher than the volume on side B.
   (3) The two sides will remain equal for at least 24 hours.
   (4) The sugar will be evenly distributed within 24 hours.
   (5) None of the above statements is correct.

8. Which statement about the change of state of water is correct?

   (1) It requires the same amount of energy to go from solid to liquid as from liquid to gas.
   (2) It requires more energy to go from solid to liquid than from liquid to gas.
   (3) It requires more energy to go from liquid to gas than from solid to liquid.
   (4) It requires the same amount of energy to go from gas to solid as from liquid to gas.
   (5) It requires less energy to go from liquid to gas than from solid to liquid.

Item 9 refers to the following graph.

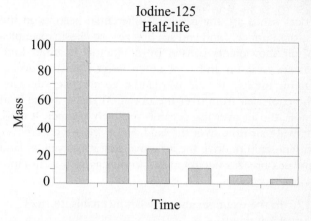

9. The half-life of iodine-125 is 60 days. If you start with 100g of iodine-125, how many days would it take to have only 10g left?

   (1) 6 days
   (2) 10 days
   (3) 120 days
   (4) 180 days
   (5) 220 days

10. Consider the following equation:

    $$CH_4 + O_2 = CO_2 + H_2O$$

    To balance this equation, one should place a 2 in front of the

    (1) methane and the oxygen.
    (2) oxygen and the carbon dioxide.
    (3) carbon dioxide and the water.
    (4) oxygen and the water.
    (5) methane and the water.

11. At what temperature are the centigrade and the Fahrenheit scales the same?

    (1) 212°
    (2) 100°
    (3) 32°
    (4) −20°
    (5) −40°

33

Items 12 and 13 are based on the following paragraph.

Local winds are the result of differential heating on the earth's surface. Land and sea breezes are classic examples of air movements caused by differential heating. Land masses heat up and cool down faster than the ocean. During the day, the air over land heats and rises, drawing the cooler air from over the ocean. At night, as the land cools, the air over the ocean is relatively warmer. It rises, drawing air from over the land. Since relative differences in temperature drive the air movement, this cycle of land and sea breezes occurs in the tropics as well as in more temperate zones.

12. In the example above, what mechanism drives local winds?

(1) Uniform heating from solar radiation
(2) Differential heating of land and sea
(3) Lack of sunlight over the ocean
(4) Reflection of heat into the atmosphere
(5) Waves transferring ocean heat to land

13. Mountain and valley breezes also result from differential heating. What is the most likely reason for differential heating in this case?

(1) Warm air flows up the mountainside during the day and down at night.
(2) Valley floors are heavily insulated by snow and ice.
(3) Mountain air is less dense due to the increased elevation.
(4) Lakes in the valley absorb substantial heat energy.
(5) Mountainsides absorb sunlight during the day and radiate heat at night.

Items 14–16 refer to the following information.

The laws of thermodynamics describe how matter exchanges heat for work. The First Law, an expression of conservation of energy, states that heat added, minus work done, equals the change in the internal energy of a system. The Second Law states that heat cannot be entirely converted to work; some heat must be rejected as waste. The Third Law states that there is a lowest temperature, absolute zero, and that this temperature cannot be attained. The figure below shows a schematic diagram of a machine that converts heat into work.

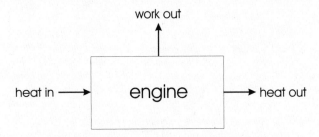

14. If work is done by a system and no heat is removed, what happens to the internal energy?

(1) It decreases.
(2) It increases.
(3) It remains the same.
(4) It increases or decreases depending on the amount of work done.
(5) This cannot be determined.

15. The laws of thermodynamics involve the relationship of matter with

(1) heat and temperature.
(2) work and temperature.
(3) heat and work.
(4) energy and heat.
(5) energy and work.

16. "A heat engine cannot convert all input heat into work." This statement follows from the

(1) First Law.
(2) Second Law.
(3) Third Law.
(4) First and Second Laws.
(5) First and Third Laws.

Item 17 refers to the following information and illustration.

A pendulum is a mass at the end of a string, as shown in the figure below. The time it takes for a pendulum to swing back and forth (the period) depends on the length of the string and the acceleration due to gravity.

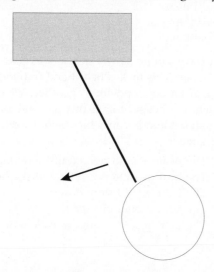

17. Which of the following would change the period of a pendulum?

  (1) Decreasing the amplitude of the swing
  (2) Increasing the amplitude of the swing
  (3) Increasing the mass at the end of the string
  (4) Decreasing the mass at the end of the string
  (5) Taking the pendulum to the moon

18. Electric charges produce magnetic fields only when they are in motion. Magnetic fields do not affect charges unless they are in motion. If two electric charges are moving toward each other, how can the magnetic force between them be eliminated?

  (1) Decrease the distance between the charges.
  (2) Make the charges move away from each other.
  (3) Make the charges move parallel to each other.
  (4) Stop either charge.
  (5) Increase the distance between the charges.

Item 19 refers to the following illustration.

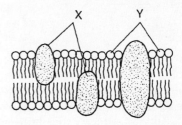

19. The diagram above represents the fluid mosaic model of a plasma membrane. What do letters X and Y represent?

  (1) pores; cellulose
  (2) phospholipids; proteins
  (3) proteins; phospholipids
  (4) nuclei; ribosomes
  (5) lipids; phospholipids

20. A researcher isolated mitochondria and placed them in a buffered pH 4 solution. After several hours, he replaced the solution with a buffered pH 8 solution. A test revealed more ATP 30 minutes after transfer to the second solution than after placement in the first solution. What is the most likely explanation?

  (1) Mitochondria produce more ATP synthase at higher pHs.
  (2) Hydrogen ions were flowing through ATP synthase at higher pHs.
  (3) Mitochondria have an optimum pH of 8.
  (4) ATP synthase has a competitive inhibitor whose optimum pH is 8.
  (5) The electron transport chain is more active at pH 8.

21. Glycolysis is the breakdown of glucose. At the end of glycolysis, each molecule of glucose has yielded

  (1) lactic acid, NADH, and ATP.
  (2) ethanol, NAD^+, and ATP.
  (3) pyruvate, NADH, and ADP.
  (4) pyruvate, NAD^+, and ADP.
  (5) pyruvate, NADH, and ATP.

22. If 6 molecules of oxygen are released during photosynthesis, how many molecules of carbon dioxide are fixed?

(1) 1
(2) 3
(3) 6
(4) 12
(5) 24

23. In gray squirrels, gray fur color is dominant over red, and straight hair is dominant over curly. A gray male squirrel with straight hair and a red female with straight hair had 8 pups: 3 with gray straight fur, 3 with red straight fur, 1 with gray curly fur, and 1 with red curly fur.

The genotypes of the parents are

(1) GgSs × GgSs.
(2) GgSs × ggSs.
(3) GgSs × Ggss.
(4) ggSs × ggSs.
(5) Ggss × Ggss.

24. A male with normal color vision marries a woman whose father was red-green color-blind but who can see colors herself. If this is a sex-linked trait, what is the chance that their first child will be a color-blind boy?

(1) 0%
(2) 25%
(3) 50%
(4) 75%
(5) 100%

25. The number of times you would expect the restriction enzyme BAM HI, which cuts the sequence CAT AC, to cut the 3 million base pair sequence of *E. coli* is about

(1) 2
(2) 20
(3) 70
(4) 700
(5) 2,000

26. Falling objects accelerate at a constant rate: the velocity increases the same amount for each equal time interval. If the speed of a falling object increases from 0 to 10 meters per second in the first second of falling, what will the speed be after the third second?

(1) 3 m/s
(2) 10 m/s
(3) 30 m/s
(4) 100 m/s
(5) 300 m/s

27. Light travels more slowly in water or glass than it does in air. This makes light bend (refract) when it travels from one medium to another. What would happen to a beam of light that left one material and entered another in which light traveled at the same speed?

(1) The beam would refract at the boundary.
(2) The beam would not refract at the boundary.
(3) The light would slow down.
(4) The light would change frequency.
(5) The light would change wavelength.

Items 28 and 29 refer to the following diagram.

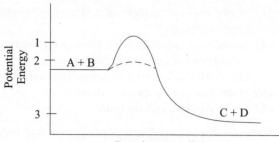

Reaction Coordinate

28. In the diagram above, A and B represent reactants, and C and D represent products. Which of the following statements is correct?

(1) There is more energy bound up in the reactants than in the products; therefore, the reaction is exothermic.

(2) There is more energy bound up in the products than in the reactants; therefore, the reaction is exothermic.

(3) There is more energy bound up in the reactants than in the products; therefore, the reaction is endothermic.

(4) There is more energy bound up in the products than in the reactants; therefore, the reaction is endothermic.

(5) There is more energy required to cause the reaction than is given off in the reaction.

29. The numbers on the *y*-axis represent different energy levels corresponding to the curve, so that 1 represents the top of the curve, 2 is the top of the dotted line, and 3 is the energy level of the products. Which of the following statements is not correct?

(1) The difference between 2 and 3 is the activation energy.

(2) The difference between 2 and 3 could be caused by a catalyst.

(3) The difference between 2 and 3 could be caused by an enzyme.

(4) The difference between 1 and 3 is the activation energy for the reverse reaction.

(5) The reactants have more energy than the products.

Items 30–32 refer to the following information and illustration.

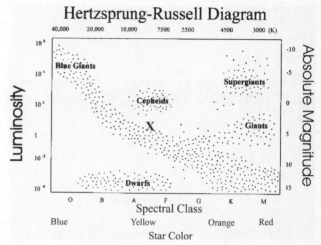

The Hertzsprung-Russell (H-R) diagram is used by astronomers to categorize stars based on luminosity and temperature. Colors represented in the diagram correspond to the observed color of the stars. The temperature plotted in a H-R diagram refers to the outer layers of the star (photosphere), where its spectrum is formed. Historically, stars were ordered in a sequence reflecting highest temperatures and assigned a letter class. For example, our Sun is a G-type star with a photosphere of around 6000-K. As shown in the illustration, luminosity and temperature are related but not identical. Temperature is a measure of molecular energy, while luminosity takes into account the surface area from which the energy is emitted. Plotting of all the nearby stars reveals that most fall in a narrow band called the main sequence. Main sequence stars are plotted from upper left to lower right in the illustration.

30. Based on the diagram, which statement is correct?

(1) Giant stars are all the same temperature.

(2) Color has no relation to star temperature.

(3) The sun has high absolute magnitude.

(4) Magnitude is higher for hotter stars.

(5) All dwarf stars are dim.

31. According to the text and the diagram, our sun is located in what group of stars?

(1) Dwarfs

(2) Giants

(3) Supergiants

(4) Main sequence

(5) Cepheids

32. According to the diagram, which spectral class of stars contains those of both the highest and lowest luminosity?

- **(1)** O
- **(2)** A
- **(3)** G
- **(4)** M
- **(5)** F

Items 33–35 refer to the following illustration.

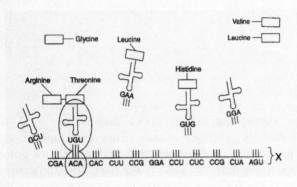

33. The synthesis of structure X occurred in the

- **(1)** nucleus.
- **(2)** cytoplasm.
- **(3)** lysosome.
- **(4)** vacuole.
- **(5)** endoplasmic reticulum.

34. The amino acid that would be transferred to the position of codon CAC would be

- **(1)** leucine.
- **(2)** histidine.
- **(3)** valine.
- **(4)** glycine.
- **(5)** arginine.

35. The biochemical process represented in the diagram is most closely associated with which cell organelle?

- **(1)** Nucleolus
- **(2)** Chloroplast
- **(3)** Ribosome
- **(4)** Mitochondrion
- **(5)** Medichlorion

36. All of our cells contain proto-oncogenes, which may turn into oncogenes, which are cancer genes. The best explanation for the existence of proto-oncogenes is that they

- **(1)** came into our cells from a viral infection of our ancestors.
- **(2)** arose from plasmids that have been inserted into bacteria and now reside in us.
- **(3)** are junk DNA with no known function.
- **(4)** turn into oncogenes as we age.
- **(5)** help regulate cell division.

37. Darwin's finches are a group of sparrow-like birds inhabiting the Galapagos Islands. Which of the following statements is most likely true?

- **(1)** Darwin's finches are good examples of convergent evolution because they look so similar.
- **(2)** Darwin's finches are good examples of convergent evolution because they are so closely related.
- **(3)** Darwin's finches are good examples of adaptive radiation because they come from a relatively recent ancestor.
- **(4)** Darwin's finches have had 100 million years to become so different in appearance.
- **(5)** Darwin's finches are good examples of the long periods required for punctuated equilibrium.

38. Four-o'clocks are flowers that exhibit incomplete dominance in their petal color. There are red and white homozygous flowers, but the heterozygote is pink. If you pollinated one four-o'clock that was red with one that was pink, what percentage of the offspring would be expected to be pink?

- **(1)** 0%
- **(2)** 25%
- **(3)** 50%
- **(4)** 75%
- **(5)** 100%

39. Runoff and erosion would probably be greatest on a land area that is

- **(1)** sloping and contour plowed.
- **(2)** sloping and barren of vegetation.
- **(3)** gently sloping and covered with grass.
- **(4)** flat and highly covered with vegetation.
- **(5)** fertile and above sea level.

40. Which characteristic of metamorphic rocks indicates that they were formed deep within the earth's crust?

 (1) The absence of elements commonly found on the earth's surface
 (2) Inclusion of bits of material from the earth's core
 (3) Presence of minerals that form under high temperature and pressure
 (4) Marked bedding, a characteristic not developed at a shallow depth
 (5) The presence of strata, or layers

Items 41–43 refer to the following illustration.

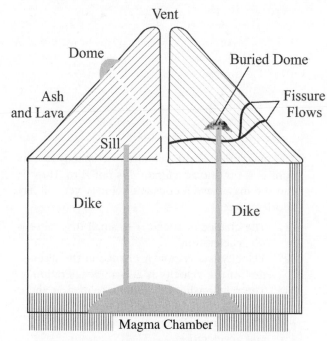

41. Pyroclastics are rock debris discharged from the cone of a volcano during an eruption. Pyroclastics found near a volcano would suggest that the volcano

 (1) had previously erupted violently.
 (2) had previously erupted quietly.
 (3) had not recently erupted.
 (4) was likely to erupt soon.
 (5) was now extinct.

42. Alternating layers of ash and lava would likely mark the volcano as a(n)

 (1) shield cone.
 (2) cinder cone.
 (3) composite cone.
 (4) island volcano.
 (5) extinct volcano.

43. The Hawaiian Islands are volcanic in origin. Through a weak spot in the Pacific plate, molten rock has leaked through the ocean floor. Over millions of years, the resulting seamounts have formed the Hawaiian Islands. Several active volcanoes in Hawaii currently produce steady streams of lava that flow into the Pacific Ocean. The description of this eruption style would mark these volcanoes as examples of

 (1) cinder cones.
 (2) shield cones.
 (3) composite cones.
 (4) caldera cones.
 (5) rift zone volcanoes.

Items 44 and 45 refer to the following equation, which represents the production of oxygen in the laboratory.

$$2KClO_3 \rightarrow 2KCl + 3O_2$$

The molar mass of K is 39.1, Cl is 35.4, and O is 16.

44. How much $KClO_3$ would be required to make 4 grams of oxygen (O_2) at STP?

 (1) 10.2g
 (2) 20.4g
 (3) 20.6g
 (4) 30.6g
 (5) 32.0g

45. If a student collected 5.6 liters of oxygen at STP by doing the above reaction in the laboratory, how many grams of oxygen did she collect?

 (1) 2
 (2) 4
 (3) 6
 (4) 8
 (5) 10

46. If one planted 6 red and 4 white four-o'clocks in a garden, and there was random cross pollination, what percentage of the next generation would be pink?

   (1) 100%
   (2) 0%
   (3) 36%
   (4) 48%
   (5) 52%

47. In the name *Canis lupus*, the term *Canis* represents the

   (1) race.
   (2) species.
   (3) genus.
   (4) family.
   (5) order.

Items 48 and 49 refer to the following illustration.

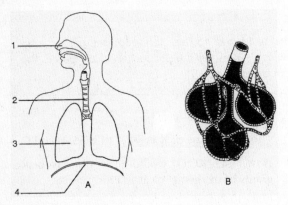

48. Diagram B represents the functional unit of which structure represented in diagram A?

   (1) 1
   (2) 2
   (3) 3
   (4) 4
   (5) None of the above

49. Which of the following statements is incorrect?

   (1) Number 2 represents the esophagus and divides into bronchi.
   (2) Number 2 represents the trachea and has cilia lining it.
   (3) Number 4 represents the diaphragm, which by contraction lowers the pressure in the lungs.
   (4) Number 3 contains many tubules called bronchioles.
   (5) All of the above statements are false.

50. A mass is going around a circle at constant speed while tethered with a string to a post, as shown in the figure below.

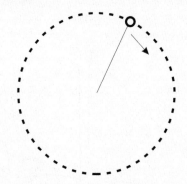

The magnitude of the velocity (the speed) is constant, but the acceleration is not zero. How can the mass have a constant velocity yet still have acceleration?

   (1) The change in speed is so small that there is no acceleration.
   (2) Velocity is a vector. A change in the direction of the velocity is also an acceleration.
   (3) The relationship between acceleration and speed breaks down for circular motion.
   (4) There is no relationship between velocity and acceleration.
   (5) If the speed is constant, there cannot be acceleration.

Pretest 4

LANGUAGE ARTS, READING

65 Minutes ❖ **40 Questions**

Directions: Each excerpt from a longer work is followed by multiple-choice questions about the reading material. Read each excerpt and then answer the questions that follow. Choose the one best answer for each question. Refer to the reading material as often as necessary in answering the questions.

Each excerpt is preceded by a "purpose question." The purpose question gives a reason for reading the material. Use these purpose questions to help focus your reading. You are not required to answer these purpose questions. They are given only to help you concentrate on the ideas presented in the reading materials.

Items 1–5 refer to the following excerpt from a novel.

WHAT ARE THESE CHARACTERS FEELING?

Line I don't want Joe to find me on my knees, buffing the kitchen floor with an old cotton turtleneck, but he does, and says, "Mom! What are you doing? Relax!"

5 I sit back on my heels and say, "It's only six-thirty. What's with you?"

But I know. We both know. He crosses the kitchen and pours himself his first cup of coffee. He drinks them three at a time, I've noticed this
10 summer, hot and with lots of milk and sugar. Now he turns away from the coffeemaker, and the cup is half empty before he sits at the table. He is grinning. Michael will be here today. Michael, Joe's identical twin, has been teaching mathemat-
15 ics in a secondary school in Banares, India for two years. That is why I am buffing the floor, why neither of us can relax.

The floor is pegged maple, about seventy-five years old. The boards vary in width, from two
20 inches to five, and are laid diagonally. In the last fifteen minutes, I have worked my way from the pantry to the back door, into a long bronze leaf of sunlight that colors my forearm and turns my hands muscular with shadows. I like this floor,
25 troublesome as it is: caring for it, I remind myself of my mother, and this city, in spite of all its trees, seems rather like Nebraska, where I grew up. The long, rhythmic motions with the rag are soothing and productive at the same time.

30 Joe says, "I think I'll leave for the airport about nine." He is bouncing in his chair. I smile and say, "Why don't you leave now?"

"I'm relaxed, Mom. What makes you think I'm not relaxed?" His expression is almost mania-
35 cal. They are twenty-five, and they have not seen each other in two years. "You, woman, get up and have a cup of tea or something." And so I do, simply for the pleasure of sitting at the kitchen table with my son. I let him make me toast and
40 peel me an orange, and pour milk on my Rice Krispies.

—From *Ordinary Love*, by Jane Smiley

1. The reason that neither the narrator nor Joe can relax is that
   (1) Michael is leaving for India.
   (2) they cannot get to the airport in time.
   (3) they have not seen Michael in two years.
   (4) necessary chores have not been done.
   (5) they had to get up very early to meet Michael.

2. What is the overall mood of this passage?
   (1) Tense but comfortable
   (2) Tense and worried
   (3) Angry and tense
   (4) Moody and troubled
   (5) Carefree but unhappy

3. The author's purpose in describing the kitchen floor is to give background information about

(1) the plot.
(2) Joe and Michael's relationship.
(3) setting.
(4) the narrator.
(5) Michael's trip.

4. Based on this excerpt, this novel is most likely to be about

(1) religious conflict.
(2) cultural change.
(3) educational methods.
(4) personal history.
(5) family relationships.

5. Why does the narrator provide these details about Joe in lines 11–14?

"He drinks them three at a time, I've noticed this summer, hot and with lots of milk and sugar."

(1) They show his similarity to Michael.
(2) They illustrate his nervousness.
(3) They show his affection for his mother.
(4) They make him seem like a lifelike character.
(5) They make him seem angry and impatient.

Items 6–9 refer to the following excerpt from a book review.

WHAT MAKES THIS NOVEL SO INTERESTING?

Line   Crime novel fans, check out the current crop of
thrillers written by women about women crime
solvers. A new breed of sleuth has burst on the
scene. She's professional, disciplined, and dedi-
5   cated. A hot date matters less to her than a hot
clue. She's also more ethical and humane than her
male counterparts—in fact, all-around nicer—and
must contend not only with the killer but with the
hostility she arouses in those who are threatened
10   by her strength.
Patricia D. Cornwell produces such a heroine
in *Cruel & Unusual*. Kay Scarpetta is the chief
medical examiner of Virginia, which means that
her typical workday involves carving up some
15   hapless crime victim with a Stryker saw and
sorting through organs . . .
The pace is unrelenting; the suspense
nerve-jangling; the dialogue scalpel-sharp. Characters are deftly drawn. The workaholic Kay has a
20   tragic love affair in her past ("Mark's death had left
a tear in her soul"). Her sidekick, Marino, a police
lieutenant, is both gruff and lovable. Kay's
precocious niece, Lucy, helps track the killer with

her computer savvy. The "love interest" in this
25   book is not romantic, but between the middle-
aged Kay and Lucy, a kind of surrogate daughter.
Throughout, you're showered with info on
high-tech methods of crime detection, as in a
sequence in which Kay and colleagues return to
30   the scene of a ten-year-old murder and reenact it
through the latest chemical potions. I was
particularly moved by Kay's confrontation with a
former law school professor, whom she has
always resented. He browbeat her, he confesses,
35   because he didn't want her to lose herself in love.
"I was determined that you would not waste gifts
and give away your power." Cornwell's Kay
Scarpetta is a woman functioning at the peak of
her powers. She is truly a heroine of our times.

—From "Female Suspicions" by Erica Abeel

6. Based on lines 1–3, which of the following works is most similar to *Cruel & Unusual*?

(1) A TV show about a police lieutenant and his niece
(2) A documentary about female artists, produced by a woman
(3) A novel about a gruff law school professor
(4) A movie written and directed by a woman
(5) A magazine article about women's changing roles

7. According to the reviewer, the dialogue in *Cruel & Unusual* is

(1) sappy and emotional.
(2) tired and dull.
(3) unrealistic and outdated.
(4) direct and concise.
(5) graphic and gruesome.

8. According to the review, which of the following is not a part of this novel's plot?

(1) Crime reenactment
(2) Crime detection
(3) Relationships at work
(4) Family relationships
(5) Romantic love

9. Which of the following best restates the professor's explanation in lines 36–37?

(1) "I wanted you to become a professor."
(2) "I wanted you to get married and have a family."
(3) "You worked too hard in school."
(4) "I knew you would never fall in love."
(5) "I wanted you to achieve your full potential."

Items 10–13 refer to the following excerpt from a publisher's instructions to textbook authors.

HOW SHOULD CO-AUTHORS WORK TOGETHER?

Line If you're writing a text along with one or more
authors, the following steps will help you achieve
a consistent result:

1. Agree in advance on issues of style and
5   format. Then create a style sheet that will
        govern everyone's work.
2. Exchange chapters on a regular basis. Read
    each other's material carefully to make sure
    that the writing has the same tone, style,
10   degree of detail, and conceptual complexity.
3. If the book has many different contributors,
    choose one author to act as the coordinating
    author. He or she will make the final
    decisions on content and style.

15 Coordinating authors have an extremely important
role in the book's development. They tie together
the pieces of the book through the introduction
and part openers and make sure that all the
contributors know exactly what they must do.
20 Coordinating authors work with acquisitions
editors to decide on a final table of contents, and
help contributors decide the length of each
chapter and chapter due dates. They also read all
drafts before they are sent to the acquisitions
25 editor and work with the editor to decide how to
handle reviewers' comments. Most important,
coordinating authors are the final arbiters in
disputes about text content, and they are responsible for getting the manuscript to us on time.

—HarperCollins Author's Guide

10. According to the passage, which task is not part of the coordinating author's responsibilities?

(1) Writing introductions and part openers
(2) Deciding on a final table of contents
(3) Deciding on the length of each chapter
(4) Deciding how much to pay authors
(5) Reading all authors' drafts

11. Why has the publisher made so many suggestions about ways for authors to work together?

(1) To help authors write chapters that are similar in style
(2) To make sure authors submit chapters on time
(3) To make sure that a competent coordinating author is chosen
(4) To help authors decide on a final table of contents
(5) To make sure that each draft is read several times

12. The coordinating author of a textbook should be the author who

(1) knows the acquisitions editor the best.
(2) knows the most about the book's overall content.
(3) wants to be paid the most for his or her work.
(4) is the best writer.
(5) is the most famous.

13. According to the passage, the role of a coordinating author is most like that of a

(1) cheerleader.
(2) drill sergeant.
(3) team captain.
(4) midwife.
(5) acquisitions editor.

Items 14–18 refer to the following excerpt from a speech.

WHY IS THE WORD NO IMPORTANT TO THIS SPEAKER?

Line Brief, solid, affirmative as a hammer blow, this is
the virile word, which must enflame lips and save
the honor of our people, in these unfortunate days
of anachronistic imperialism . . .
5   We do not know how to say "no," and we
are attracted, unconsciously, like a hypnotic
suggestion, by the predominant *si* of the word on
thought, of the form of essence—artists and weak
and kindly, as we have been made by the beauty
10 and generosity of our land. Never, in general
terms, does a Puerto Rican say, nor does he know
how to say "no": "We'll see," "I'll study the
matter," "I'll decide later,"; when a Puerto Rican
uses these expressions, it must be understood that
15 he does not want to; at most, he joins *si* with the
no. . . .

We have to learn to say "no," raise our lips, unburden our chest, put in tension all our vocal muscles and all our will power to fire this *o* of *no*,
20 which will resound perhaps in America and the world, and will respond in the heavens with more efficacy than the rolling of cannons.

—From "No" by José De Diego

14. Based on this passage, you can infer that the speaker's heritage is

(1) African American.
(2) Puerto Rican.
(3) Haitian.
(4) Mexican.
(5) European.

15. According to this speaker, in what manner does the Puerto Rican citizen say "no"?

(1) In a tone of voice that cannot be misunderstood
(2) With faith that justice will be done
(3) In a tone of voice that might offend others
(4) With expressions that might sound like "yes" to others
(5) With a firm, resounding voice that cannot be questioned

16. The speaker wishes that his people would learn to say "no" so that they might

(1) find better jobs.
(2) be stricter parents.
(3) save their environment.
(4) help end political oppression.
(5) increase their exports.

17. Based on lines 8-10, the speaker believes that his homeland is

(1) cruel.
(2) unattractive.
(3) nurturing.
(4) forgotten.
(5) hopeless.

18. "We have to learn to say no, . . . to fire this *o* of *no* . . ." (lines 17-19)

The speaker compares the sound of the word *no* to gunfire in order to

(1) stress that war is imminent.
(2) encourage the Puerto Rican people to revolt.
(3) support gun control.
(4) show that he is not afraid.
(5) emphasize the power of this word.

Items 19–23 refer to the following excerpt from an essay.

HOW ARE THE FORESTS PLANTED?

Line Yes, these dense and stretching oak forests, whose withered leaves now redden and rustle on the hills for many a New England mile, were all planted by the labor of animals. For after some weeks of close
5 scrutiny I cannot avoid the conclusion that our modern oak woods sooner or later spring up from an acorn, not where it has fallen from the tree, for that is the exception, but where it has been dropped or placed by an animal.

10 Consider what a vast work these forest planters are doing! So far as our noblest hardwood forests are concerned, the animals, especially squirrels and jays, are our greatest and almost only benefactors. It is to them that we owe this gift. It
15 is not in vain that a squirrel lives in almost every forest tree or hollow log or wall or heap of stones.

Thus, one would say that our oak forests, vast and indispensable as they are, were produced by a kind of accident, that is, by the failure of
20 animals to reap the fruits of their labors. Yet who shall say that they have not a dim knowledge of the value of their labors?—that the squirrel when it plants an acorn, and the jay when it lets one slip from under its foot, has not sometimes a transient
25 thought for its posterity, which at least consoles it for its loss?

But what is the character of our gratitude to these squirrels—to say nothing of the others—these planters of forests, these exported dukes of
30 Athol of many generations, which have found out how high the oak will grow on many a mountain, how low in many a valley, and how far and wide in all our plains? Are they on our pension list? Have we in any way recognized their services? We
35 regard them as vermin.

—From Henry David Thoreau, *Faith in a Seed*

19. "Yes, these dense and stretching oak forests, whose withered leaves now redden and rustle on the hills for many a New England mile . . ."

What primary effect does the author create with these words?

(1) He shows the extent of the animals' activities.
(2) He shows how he feels about the animals.
(3) He shows the insignificance of human activity.
(4) He paints a word picture of the forest.
(5) He shows how others feel about the animals.

20. The author bases his opinion that the forests are planted by animals on

(1) the farmers' observations.
(2) books about forestry.
(3) books about ecology.
(4) Native-American lore.
(5) his own observations.

21. "There is value in any experience that reminds us of our dependency on the soil-plant-animal-human food chain, and of the fundamental organization of the biota."

Which idea from the passage is most closely related to the above statement?

(1) Forests were produced by the failure of animals to reap the fruits of their labor.
(2) Who shall say that they have not a dim knowledge of the value of their labors?
(3) Our modern oak woods sooner or later spring up from an acorn.
(4) What is the character of our gratitude to these squirrels—we regard them as vermin.
(5) A squirrel lives in almost every forest tree or hollow log.

22. In the third paragraph, the author states that oak forests were produced "by the failure of animals to reap the fruit of their labor." This means that

(1) animals sometimes do not use the food they store.
(2) farmers sometimes steal animals' food stores.
(3) farmers destroy animals before they use their food stores.
(4) animals steal the acorns that people plant.
(5) some trees grow from acorns that fall from trees.

23. Which is the best statement of the main idea of this passage?

(1) People are relative newcomers to the New England forest.
(2) The lives of squirrels and oak trees are interconnected.
(3) Oaks are the most important hardwood tree of New England.
(4) Close observation is the best way to learn about nature.
(5) Squirrels are common animals in New England forests.

Items 24–29 refer to the following excerpt from a play.

WHAT WILL HAPPEN TO THESE CHARACTERS?

Act 1, Scene 1

Line *Thursday night.*
       A sandy bank of the Salinas River sheltered with willows—one giant sycamore right, upstage. The stage is covered with dry leaves. The
5   *feeling of the stage is sheltered and quiet.*
       Stage is lit by a setting a setting sun.
       Curtain rises on an empty stage. A sparrow is singing. There is a distant sound of ranch dogs barking aimlessly and one clear quail call. The
10   *quail call turns to a warning call and there is a beat of the flock's wings. Two figures are seen entering the stage in single file, with George, the short man, coming in ahead of Lennie. Both men are carrying blanket rolls. They approach the*
15   *water. The small man throws down his blanket roll, the large man follows and then falls down and drinks from the river, snorting as he drinks.*

GEORGE [*irritably*]. Lennie, for God's sake, don't drink so much. [*Leans over and shakes Lennie.*]
20   Lennie, you hear me! You gonna be sick like you was last night.

LENNIE [*dips his whole head under, hat and all. As he sits upon the bank, his hat drips down the back*]. That's good. You drink some, George. You
25   drink some too.

GEORGE [*kneeling and dipping his finger in the water*]. I ain't sure it's good water. Looks kinda scummy to me.

LENNIE [*imitates, dipping his finger also*]. Look
30   at them wrinkles in the water, George. Look what I done.

GEORGE [*drinking from his cupped palm*]. Tastes all right. Don't seem to be running much, though. Lennie, you oughtn't to drink water when it ain't
35 running. [*Hopelessly.*] You'd drink water out of a gutter if you was thirsty. [*He throws a scoop of water into his face and rubs it around with his hand, pushes himself back and embraces his knees. Lennie, after watching him, imitates him*
40 *in every detail.*]

—From John Steinbeck, *Of Mice and Men*

24. When the audience hears a quail's warning call and "the beat of the flock's wings," they will have a feeling of

(1) peacefulness.
(2) natural beauty.
(3) imminent danger.
(4) the seasons changing.
(5) sleepiness.

25. Based on this excerpt, what is the relationship between Lennie and George?

(1) Both men admire each other and stick together in good times and bad.
(2) George looks after Lennie, and Lennie obeys George without question.
(3) Both men travel together but think and act independently.
(4) George looks after Lennie, but Lennie frequently ignores his advice.
(5) Lennie is more thoughtful and creative, and George looks up to him.

26. When George says, "You gonna be sick like you was last night," the audience discovers that Lennie

(1) likes to copy George's actions.
(2) is thoughtful and considerate.
(3) is extremely thirsty and hungry.
(4) is weak and frequently sickly.
(5) does not learn from experience.

27. How does Lennie's imitation of George dipping his finger in the water (lines 29-31) differ from the original action?

(1) The imitation is playful rather than purposeful.
(2) The imitation is thoughtful rather than heedless.
(3) The imitation is impulsive rather than careful.
(4) The imitation is hasty rather than deliberate.
(5) The imitation is noisy rather than quiet.

28. Which statement of George's is an attempt to teach something to Lennie?

(1) "Lennie, for God's sake, don't drink too much."
(2) "You gonna be sick like you was last night."
(3) "Don't seem to be running much, though."
(4) "You oughtn't to drink water when it ain't running."
(5) "You'd drink water out of a gutter if you was thirsty."

29. The overall effect of this scene on the audience is to suggest that

(1) Lennie will learn from his experiences and become ennobled.
(2) George will be unable to prevent tragedy from striking Lennie.
(3) George and Lennie will encounter a series of comic characters.
(4) George and Lennie will soon strike it rich together.
(5) Lennie will get sick and die from poisoned drinking water.

Items 30–35 refer to the following short poems by William Carlos Williams.

CAN YOU SEE THESE WOMEN CLEARLY?

Proletarian Portrait

Line A big young bareheaded woman
In an apron

Her hair slicked back standing
On the street

5 One stockinged foot toeing
The sidewalk

Her shoe in her hand. Looking
intently into it

She pulls out the paper insole
10 To find the nail

That has been hurting her

To a Poor Old Woman

Line munching a plum on
     the street a paper bag
     of them in her hand
     They taste good to her
5   They taste good
     to her. They taste
     good to her

     You can see it by
     the way she gives herself
10   to the one half
     sucked out in her hand

     Comforted
     a solace of ripe plums
     seeming to fill the air
15   They taste good to her

30. What was the poet's purpose in writing these two poems?

   (1) To convey complex ideas
   (2) To describe powerful emotions
   (3) To give detailed descriptions
   (4) To use powerful metaphors
   (5) To narrate a story

31. What central idea do these two poems share?

   (1) Ordinary details of daily life are important.
   (2) Women have difficult lives.
   (3) Poverty and hardship are ennobling.
   (4) Food and clothing are basic human needs.
   (5) All humans suffer pain.

32. "Proletarian Portrait" is most like a

   (1) color documentary.
   (2) lengthy essay.
   (3) limerick.
   (4) Impressionist portrait.
   (5) black-and-white snapshot.

33. In the second poem, what impression is conveyed by the repetition in lines 4–7 and 15?

   (1) Poverty
   (2) Sadness
   (3) Pleasure
   (4) Anger
   (5) Decline

34. What is the old woman in the second poem doing?

   (1) Eating plums she has found in the garbage
   (2) Eating a plum from a paper bag of plums
   (3) Begging for fruit from a fruit stand
   (4) Removing a nail from inside her shoe
   (5) Trying to find someone to fix her shoe

35. When the poet says that the old woman "gives herself to" eating the plum, he means that she

   (1) spends all her money on it.
   (2) dies after eating it.
   (3) remembers her youth.
   (4) enjoys it completely.
   (5) forgets about it quickly.

Items 36–40 refer to the following excerpt from a short story.

WHAT KIND OF PLACE IS THIS?

Line In winter the glazed bunchgrass and wild oats tuft
     the roadsides and edges of fields. In spring the
     exhausted grass will be there still, a blond
     whiskering to the green. Through summer the dry
5   stalks of last year's grass memorialize winter, the
     pale of the dead fringing the alive in this place
     that has become Jim Blood's country. In the heat
     of summer, it takes a powerful leap of the
     imagination to remember the snow that covered
10   the fields. So it is. Usually, the winters in eastern
     Washington are kind enough, but not too many
     years ago the cold came early. A northerly from
     the Gulf of Alaska found a trough between
     mountain ranges to howl down. For a solid month
15   record low temperatures were broken daily.
     Before it was done Jim found cause for the first
     time in years to reflect upon the small
     Saskatchewan town he'd come from.
        That was a hard place. He remembered it as
20   crystalline and white. He remembered voices
     ringing in the cold like metal. How two-year-old
     sister had died there. He remembered the bright
     sound the tiny coffin made when it struck the ice
     at the bottom of the grave. He remembered his
25   parents in the graveyard, and how his father, the
     only minister for miles around, had conducted the
     service himself. He remembered how his father
     seemed to stand straight against this trouble, while
     his mother bent under it. That was then. He'd
30   been a boy to whom the many common and
     uncommon things in life were equal in their
     power to astonish him.

Now, he lived here with his wife, Diane, and their three sons. They were trying to start up a
35 ranch. They'd moved out to the place late last spring to finish building a house. They had few neighbors. By their driveway, the distance from the house to the county road was nearly a mile, and when they drove out they emerged from the
40 woods onto a rise from which they could look northward to the Lanattos' place across the fields, and then the Hollisters' place, the two houses and network of outbuildings that went with a dairy.

—From "The Chasm," by John Keeble

36. Jim Blood's ranch can best be described as

  (1) dangerous.
  (2) pretty.
  (3) isolated.
  (4) cold.
  (5) luxurious.

37. "Through summer the dry stalks of last year's grass memorialize winter, the pale of the dead fringing the alive in this place that has become Jim Blood's country." This sentence suggests that

  (1) past and present are mixed together for Jim.
  (2) Jim has sad memories, but the present is good.
  (3) the past winter was a very hard one.
  (4) it is often difficult to remember the past.
  (5) winters are harder in Saskatchewan than in eastern Washington.

38. Based on the second paragraph, Jim's memories of his childhood are primarily

  (1) vague.
  (2) bleak.
  (3) carefree.
  (4) joyous.
  (5) peaceful.

39. In this story, the most important element is

  (1) action.
  (2) character.
  (3) conflict.
  (4) setting.
  (5) dialogue.

40. Based on the excerpt, what is Jim's attitude toward memories of the past?

  (1) Jim remembers the past vividly and uses it to understand the present.
  (2) Jim is always looking for things that remind him of childhood.
  (3) Jim focuses on the present and remembers the past only reluctantly.
  (4) Jim wishes to relive the past and blot out the hardships of the present.
  (5) Jim seldom remembers the past, but his memories are all happy ones.

Pretest 5

MATHEMATICS FORMULAS

Use the following formulas to answer questions in the following pretest.

AREA of a:

square	Area = side^2
rectangle	Area = length × width
parallelogram	Area = base × height
triangle	Area = $\dfrac{1}{2}$ × base × height
trapezoid	Area = $\dfrac{1}{2}$ × (base$_1$ + base$_2$) × height
circle	Area = π × radius^2; π is approximately equal to 3.14

PERIMETER of a:

square	Perimeter = 4 × side
rectangle	Perimeter = 2 × length + 2 × width
triangle	Perimeter = side$_1$ + side$_2$ + side$_3$

CIRCUMFERENCE of a circle — Circumference = π × diameter; π is approximately equal to 3.14

VOLUME of a:

cube	Volume = edge^3
rectangular solid	Volume = length × width × height
square pyramid	Volume = $\dfrac{1}{3}$ × (base edge)^2 × height
cylinder	Volume = π × radius^2 × height; π is approximately equal to 3.14
cone	Volume = $\dfrac{1}{3}$ × π × radius^2 × height; π is approximately equal to 3.14

COORDINATE GEOMETRY

distance between points =

$$\sqrt{(x_2 - x_1)^2 + (y_2 - y_1)^2}; (x_1, y_1) \text{ and } (x_2, y_2) \text{ are two points in a plane.}$$

Slope of a line = $\dfrac{y_2 - y_1}{x_2 - x_1}$; (x_1, y_1) and (x_2, y_2) are two points on the line.

PYTHAGOREAN RELATIONSHIP — $a^2 + b^2 = c^2$; a and b are legs and c the hypotenuse of a right triangle.

TRIGONOMETRIC RATIOS

$$\sin = \frac{\text{opposite}}{\text{hypotenuse}} \quad \cos = \frac{\text{adjacent}}{\text{hypotenuse}} \quad \tan = \frac{\text{opposite}}{\text{adjacent}}$$

MEASURES OF CENTRAL TENDENCY

mean = $\dfrac{x_1 + x_2 + \ldots + x_n}{n}$, where the x's are the values for which a mean is desired, and n is the total number of values for x.

median = the middle value of an odd number of _ordered_ scores, and halfway between the two middle values of an even number of _ordered_ scores.

SIMPLE INTEREST — interest = principal × rate × time

DISTANCE — distance = rate × time

TOTAL COST — total cost = (number of units) × (price per unit)

49

Pretest 5

MATHEMATICS
PART 1

45 Minutes ❖ **25 Questions** ❖ **Calculator Permitted**

1. Jim buys three apples for $0.34 and 5 pears for $0.27 to make a fruit salad. If he pays for these fruits with a five-dollar bill, how much change will he receive?

   (1) $2.37
   (2) $2.63
   (3) $3.65
   (4) $3.98
   (5) $4.39

2. A discount store takes 20% off of any item they have in their store. For their post-Christmas blowout sale, they take an additional 25% off of any sporting good. If someone buys a baseball mitt that is marked as costing $57, how much will he pay at the checkout stand?

   (1) $45.60
   (2) $42.75
   (3) $34.20
   (4) $31.35
   (5) $2.85

3. 1 yard is equivalent to 36 inches. 1 meter is equivalent to 1.094 yards. Using these facts, how many inches are equivalent to 1 kilometer (1000 meters)?

   (1) 30.389
   (2) 39.384
   (3) 32,907
   (4) 36,000
   (5) 39,384

4. Kim is baking cakes for a party. According to her recipe, the cake mix requires 3 ounces of butter. Another mix for the icing requires 1 ounce of butter. For the cake shell, 2 ounces of butter are needed. Kim has determined that for 2 large cakes, she needs to make 3 times the batter, 4 times the shell, and 2 times the icing than the recipe suggests. How much butter, in ounces, does Kim need?

   (1) 6
   (2) 9
   (3) 15
   (4) 19
   (5) 54

5. It takes a publisher 3 hours to print 100 copies of a book. If a bookstore has ordered 1250 copies of the book, how long will it take for the publisher to print all the copies of the books?

   (1) 38
   (2) 37.5
   (3) 34.5
   (4) 12.5
   (5) 3.75

6. Bob is looking for a box to consolidate all of his baseball cards. He knows that he can fit 100 cards for every 3 cubic inches of space he has in his box. If he finds a box that has a capacity of 36 cubic inches, how many cards will he be able to store in it?

   Answer this question on the standard grid on your answer sheet on page 8.

7. Jim lives in Boonieville, UT, where he must pay for his Internet access at an hourly usage rate. It costs him $3.44 an hour to surf the Internet during the daytime and $2.37 to surf the Internet during the night. Last month, Jim spent 13 hours logged on during the daytime and another 22 hours logged on during the nighttime. How much more did he spend last month for his nightly usage compared to his daily usage?

(1) $203.35
(2) $98.86
(3) $54.14
(4) $44.72
(5) $7.42

8. Alice used $3\frac{1}{4}$ lbs. of flour for a loaf of bread.

Afterwards, she used another $4\frac{1}{4}$ lbs. of flour to make a cake. Later, she measured her bag of flour and found that it contains $22\frac{3}{4}$ lbs. of flour in it. How much flour did the bag contain before she made the bread or the cake?

(1) $15\frac{1}{4}$

(2) 26

(3) 27

(4) $30\frac{1}{4}$

(5) Not enough information is given.

9. An experimenter measured the voltage and the current through a resistor for a few values of voltage. The chart below is what he found:

Voltage   1.0   1.5   2.0   2.5
Current   2   3   4   5

If the current was rising steadily with voltage during the experiment, what was the current when the voltage reached 1.75?

Answer this question in the standard grid on your answer sheet on page 8.

10. The town Johnny lives in is much like a coordinate plane. This town numbers its blocks using an ordered pair with the town hall existing on block (0,0). Johnny lives in block (3,−2). He has forgotten on what block his friend lives. He remembers that he has to go three blocks right and two blocks down to reach his friend's block from his own block. On the coordinate grid, mark the point where his friend lives.

Answer this question in the coordinate plane grid provided on your answer sheet on page 8.

Items 11–15 refer to the following graph. This is a graph showing from where the profits of a department store come.

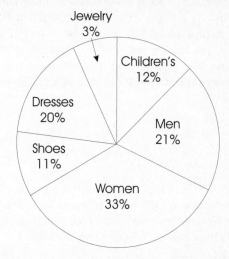

11. How much of every dollar comes from the women, dresses, and jewelry sections?

(1) $0.44
(2) $0.53
(3) $0.56
(4) $0.83
(5) Not enough information is given.

12. This department store makes $15,000 a month. How much of that profit comes from the shoes section?

(1) $4,950
(2) $3,150
(3) $3,000
(4) $1,800
(5) $1,650

13. This department store makes $15,000 a month. How much is made in the children's section?

(1) $4,950
(2) $3,150
(3) $3,000
(4) $1,800
(5) $1,650

14. If the jewelry section brings in $150 in one month, what is the store's total profit for that month?

(1) $714.29
(2) $750.00
(3) $1,250.00
(4) $1,363.64
(5) $5,000.00

15. If the store makes $7,500 a month, at most how much could have possibly come from earrings?

Answer this question in the standard grid on your answer sheet on page 8.

16. Joel went to a local general store to buy some candy. He bought 2 lbs of Jawbreakers at $0.69 per lb. and bought another 3 lbs of Jelly Beans at $0.46 per lb. The owner of the general store knows Joel's parents, so he gave Joel a 15% discount on his candy. How much did Joel have to pay?

   (1) $0.41
   (2) $0.98
   (3) $1.15
   (4) $2.35
   (5) $2.76

17. The local golf club has 8 players. They all played the 18 hole "experts only" course and got the following scores: 3 under par, 2 under, 1 under, 5 under, 2 under, 3 under, 7 under, and 6 under. On the average, how far under par were the players of the club?

   (1) 3
   (2) 3.625
   (3) 4
   (4) 29
   (5) Not enough information is given.

18. An experimenter is studying the reproduction of bacteria. When the bacteria reproduces, it splits into two, creating two new bacteria at the expense of destroying the parent bacteria. If the experiment starts with 250 bacteria, after 10 such separations, how many bacteria will be in the experiment?

   (1) 512,000
   (2) 256,000
   (3) 128,000
   (4) 2,500
   (5) 250

Items 19 and 20 refer to the following figure.

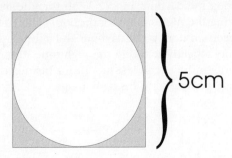

19. In the figure, the square has a length of 5cm on one side and the circle is inscribed in the square. What is the area of the circle?

   (1) 15.7
   (2) 19.625
   (3) 31.4
   (4) 39.25
   (5) 78.5

20. What is the area of the shaded region?

   (1) 25
   (2) 19.625
   (3) 9.3
   (4) 6.4
   (5) 5.375

21. In right triangle ABC, sin A is $\frac{7}{25}$. What is cos A?

   (1) $\frac{7}{24}$

   (2) $\frac{24}{25}$

   (3) $\frac{25}{24}$

   (4) $\frac{24}{7}$

   (5) $\frac{25}{7}$

22. Roseanne has an insatiable appetite. She ate 35 lbs of food on a week when she was on a hunger strike. How much did she munch through in a day?

Answer this question in the standard grid on your answer sheet on page 8.

23. Arda invests money in electronics stocks at a return of 22%. To be safe, she invests another sum of money in blue chip stocks that return 10%. She invested $450 more in the electronics than she did in the blue chips. If she made $1,253 in annual return, how much did she invest in total? Round answer to the nearest dollar.

Answer this question in the standard grid on your answer sheet on page 8.

24. Mr. Spencer has an outstanding bar bill of $625. The bartender has told him that he will sue him if he doesn't pay within the week. Mr. Spencer makes $6.25 an hour for the first 40 hours he works. He then gets paid time and a half for the next 20 hours. After that, he gets double time. How long does Mr. Spencer have to work at a minimum to make enough to pay off his bar bill?

Answer this question in the standard grid on your answer sheet on page 8.

Item 25 refers to the following information.

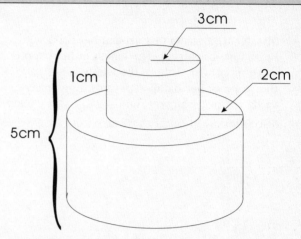

25. This container is inserted in a car to hold brake fluid. It consists of two cylinders, one on top of the other. The top cylinder has a radius of 3cm, and the bottom cylinder is 2cm larger than the top in radius. The top is 1cm high, and the entire structure is 5cm in height. How many cubic centimeters of brake fluid can the container hold?

  (1) 28.26
  (2) 50.24
  (3) 78.5
  (4) 314
  (5) 342.26

PART II

25 Questions ❖ 45 Minutes ❖ Calculator *Not* Permitted

---

1. Mrs. Nguyen wants to surround her patio with a decorative brick wall. The length of her patio is 2 yards more than 3 times the width of her patio. If the width of her patio is 15 yards, how many yards of brick wall will she have to lay to enclose her yard?

   15 yd [rectangle diagram]

   (1) 30
   (2) 34
   (3) 90
   (4) 120
   (5) 124

2. There are 12 inches in a foot, and three feet in a yard. How many inches are there in a yard?

   (1) 4
   (2) 9
   (3) 15
   (4) 18
   (5) 36

3. Charlotte got $10 for Christmas. She decided that she would use half and would give the rest equally to her four other siblings who only got a lump of coal. How much did each of Charlotte's siblings get?

   (1) $7.50
   (2) $5.00
   (3) $2.50
   (4) $1.25
   (5) $1.00

4. Two campers are sitting at a picnic table. They notice that a 3-inch drink can is casting a 5-inch shadow. If a 6-inch super size drink can were there instead, how could the length of its shadow be calculated for?

   (1) $\dfrac{1}{5} = \dfrac{6}{x}$

   (2) $\dfrac{3}{5} = \dfrac{x}{6}$

   (3) $\dfrac{53}{3} = \dfrac{6}{x}$

   (4) $3 \times 5 = 6x$

   (5) $\dfrac{3}{6} = \dfrac{x}{5}$

5. Which one is NOT the same as $112(233 - 121)$?

   (1) $112(233) - 112(121)$
   (2) $(233 - 121)112$
   (3) $233(121) - 112(121)$
   (4) $233(112) - 121(112)$
   (5) $-112(121 - 233)$

6. Mark spends 10 minutes reading a Web page. If he spends 12 hours browsing the Web, how many Web pages could he have read?

   (1) 1
   (2) 12
   (3) 72
   (4) 120
   (5) 720

Items 7–10 refer to the following graph, which represents the density of a few materials with respect to temperature.

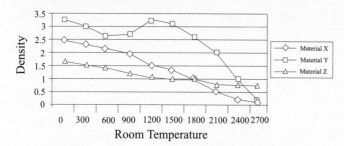

7. According to the graph, approximately what is the highest density that Material Y reaches?

(1) 0.25
(2) 2
(3) 2.75
(4) 3
(5) 3.25

8. What is the difference between the densities of Materials X and Y at room temperature (300 K)?

(1) 0.1
(2) 0.6
(3) 1.6
(4) 1.7
(5) 3.15

9. What is the difference between the highest and lowest density of Material Z?

(1) 3.0
(2) 2.4
(3) 0.9
(4) 0.5
(5) 0.3

10. 5 times a number is 3 less than twice the sum of the number and 2. If x is used to denote the number, which equation can be used to solve for the number?

(1) $5x - 3 = 2x - 2$
(2) $5x + 3 = 2x + 2$
(3) $5x - 3 = 2(x - 2)$
(4) $5x + 3 = 2(x + 2)$
(5) $5x + 3 = 2(x - 2)$

11. A rectangle has a diagonal of length 5. If one of its points lie on the origin, its sides are parallel to the axes, and it is longer on the x-axis than it is on the y-axis, mark on the coordinate grid where the point farthest from the origin will lie.

Answer this question in the coordinate plane grid provided on your answer sheet on page 9.

12. A supersonic jet is traveling at 1,200m/s. The pilot is training for low altitude flight. His radar picks up a tree in front of him that is 0.6km away. How long does the pilot have to pull up before he hits the tree? There are 1,000 meters in one kilometer. Give your answer in seconds.

(1) 0.5
(2) 1.5
(3) 2.5
(4) 5.0
(5) 6.5

13. If $x^2 - 3x - 54 = 0$, then $x =$

(1) +6 and +9
(2) −6 and −9
(3) +6 and −9
(4) −6 and +9
(5) +9 only

14. What is the length of the largest rod that can fit into the object shown?

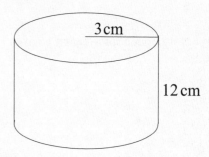

(1) 12
(2) $3\sqrt{17}$
(3) $6\sqrt{5}$
(4) 6π
(5) $6\pi\sqrt{5}$

15. Before the market slump, Bill Gates had a net worth of approximately $122 billion. Afterward, he only had about $64 billion left. How much money did he lose to the market slump?

(1) $186 billion
(2) $62 billion
(3) $60 billion
(4) $58 billion
(5) $31 billion

16. The following data set was collected via a poll that inquired what was the yearly profit of several first year small businesses (in thousands of dollars). What was the mode income?

1.6 2.1 2.0 1.6 1.5 1.8 1.0 2.3 1.5 1.4 1.7 1.8
1.1 1.2 1.5 1.4 1.8 1.6 2.2 2.0 2.5 2.3 0.9 1.1
1.4 1.7 1.7 1.3 1.9 1.2 0.5 1.9 1.6 1.4 1.8 1.2
1.3 1.7 2.5 2.0 1.5 2.6 1.8 1.1 1.6 2.0 1.1 1.4
1.1 1.6 2.8 2.7 3.4 2.1 1.6 1.8 1.5 1.5 1.3 1.2

Answer this question in the standard grid on your answer sheet on page 9.

17. Sue has a 108-foot roll of twine. She wants to make 12 smaller rolls out of it. How many feet of twine will each of the smaller rolls have?

   (1) 6
   (2) 9
   (3) 12
   (4) 15
   (5) 18

18. Yuri was playing games one day. He played for 10 hours during which he played Descent: Freespace and Starcraft. He also has Star Trek: Elite Force. How long did he play Star Trek: Elite Force (in hours)?

   (1) 2
   (2) 3
   (3) 5
   (4) 7
   (5) Not enough information is given.

19. Shahla wants to put up wallpaper in her bedroom. The wallpaper comes in a package of 3-foot-by-25-foot roll. How many rolls will she need in order to cover all the walls of her room? (See picture below.)

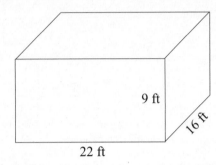

9 ft

16 ft

22 ft

   (1) 9
   (2) 9.12
   (3) 10
   (4) 19
   (5) 43

20. For the 4th of July, Nathan wants to have a barbecue. In order to make enough burgers for everyone, he needs $2\frac{1}{2}$ lbs. of ground beef. The supermarket has ground beef for $2.50 per lb. How much will Nathan have to pay?

   (1) $7.50
   (2) $6.25
   (3) $5.00
   (4) $1.25
   (5) $0.10

21. 675 students are enrolled in an undergraduate-level physics class. If the number of men exceeds the number of women 3 to 2, which one of the following equations can solve for the number of women?

   (1) $3M + 2W = 675$

   (2) $W + \frac{3}{2}W = 675$

   (3) $W + \frac{2}{3}W = 675$

   (4) $2W + 3W = 675$

   (5) Not enough information is given.

22. A farmer is granted an irregularly shaped plot of land to cultivate. If he can make $1.50 per sq ft of land he cultivates, how much money can he make off of this plot? (See figure below.)

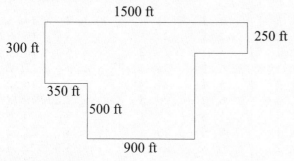

(1) $591,667
(2) $887,500
(3) $1,200,000
(4) $1,331,250
(5) $1,800,000

23. An assorted bag of potatoes has two types of potatoes in it. One type weighs $\frac{1}{2}$ lb, and the other weighs $\frac{1}{4}$ lb. If a bag of 100 potatoes weighs 47 lb, how can we find out how many $\frac{1}{4}$ lb potatoes are in the bag?

(1) $\frac{1}{4}x + \frac{1}{2}x = 47$

(2) $\frac{1}{4}x + \frac{1}{2}(47 - x) = 0$

(3) $\frac{1}{4}x = 47 + \frac{1}{2}x$

(4) $47 + \frac{1}{4}x + \frac{1}{2}x = 0$

(5) $\frac{1}{2}x + \frac{1}{4}(100 - x) = 47$

Items 24 and 25 refer to the following graph. The following data shows graphically the number of books a publishing company sold for 6 years.

Book Sales (× 1,000)

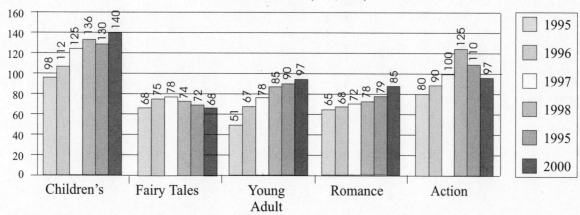

24. Of the books sold in 1998, what genre was sold most?

(1) Children's
(2) Fairy Tales
(3) Young Adult
(4) Romance
(5) Action

25. How many more thousand children's books were sold in 2000 than action books in 1995?

Answer this question in the standard grid on your answer sheet on page 9.

QUICK-SCORE ANSWERS

LANGUAGE ARTS, WRITING PART I		SOCIAL STUDIES		SCIENCE		LANGUAGE ARTS, READING		MATHEMATICS, PART I	
1. 3	26. 5	1. 5	26. 3	1. 1	26. 3	1. 3	21. 4	1. 2	14. 5
2. 4	27. 2	2. 3	27. 5	2. 4	27. 2	2. 1	22. 1	2. 3	15. $225
3. 3	28. 3	3. 1	28. 2	3. 1	28. 1	3. 4	23. 2	3. 5	16. 4
4. 1	29. 5	4. 3	29. 5	4. 5	29. 1	4. 5	24. 3	4. 4	17. 2
5. 4	30. 4	5. 1	30. 4	5. 4	30. 5	5. 4	25. 4	5. 2	18. 2
6. 3	31. 2	6. 4	31. 3	6. 4	31. 4	6. 2	26. 5	6. 1,200	19. 2
7. 4	32. 1	7. 2	32. 1	7. 2	32. 4	7. 4	27. 1	7. 5	20. 5
8. 2	33. 3	8. 3	33. 3	8. 3	33. 1	8. 5	28. 4	8. 4	21. 2
9. 4	34. 5	9. 5	34. 2	9. 5	34. 2	9. 5	29. 2	9. 3.5	22. 5
10. 3	35. 2	10. 4	35. 3	10. 4	35. 3	10. 4	30. 3	10. 6,-4	23. $7,663
11. 2	36. 1	11. 3	36. 2	11. 5	36. 5	11. 1	31. 1	11. 3	24. 75
12. 5	37. 5	12. 5	37. 3	12. 2	37. 3	12. 2	32. 5	12. 5	25. 5
13. 3	38. 1	13. 2	38. 2	13. 5	38. 3	13. 3	33. 3	13. 4	
14. 2	39. 1	14. 4	39. 1	14. 1	39. 2	14. 2	34. 2		
15. 4	40. 2	15. 2	40. 2	15. 3	40. 3	15. 4	35. 4	MATHEMATICS, PART II	
16. 1	41. 3	16. 3	41. 4	16. 2	41. 1	16. 4	36. 3		
17. 1	42. 4	17. 2	42. 2	17. 5	42. 3	17. 3	37. 1	1. 5	14. 3
18. 1	43. 3	18. 3	43. 4	18. 4	43. 2	18. 5	38. 2	2. 5	15. 4
19. 4	44. 2	19. 4	44. 1	19. 3	44. 1	19. 1	39. 4	3. 4	16. 1.6
20. 5	45. 1	20. 1	45. 3	20. 2	45. 4	20. 5	40. 3	4. 5	17. 2
21. 1	46. 2	21. 1	46. 4	21. 5	46. 4			5. 3	18. 5
22. 1	47. 4	22. 3	47. 2	22. 3	47. 3			6. 3	19. 3
23. 3	48. 1	23. 4	48. 4	23. 2	48. 3			7. 5	20. 2
24. 4	49. 3	24. 2	49. 1	24. 2	49. 1			8. 2	21. 2
25. 2	50. 3	25. 3	50. 3	25. 4	50. 2			9. 3	22. 4
								10. 4	23. 5
								11. 4,3	24. 1
								12. 1	25. 60
								13. 4	

PART II

Turn to page 64.

FILLED-IN STANDARD GRIDS AND COORDINATE PLANE GRIDS

Part I

6.

1	2	0	0	
	/	/	/	
•	•	•	•	•
0	0	●	●	0
●	1	1	1	1
2	●	2	2	2
3	3	3	3	3
4	4	4	4	4
5	5	5	5	5
6	6	6	6	6
7	7	7	7	7
8	8	8	8	8
9	9	9	9	9

15.

2	2	5		
	/	/	/	
•	•	•	•	•
0	0	0	0	0
1	1	1	1	1
●	●	2	2	2
3	3	3	3	3
4	4	4	4	4
5	5	●	5	5
6	6	6	6	6
7	7	7	7	7
8	8	8	8	8
9	9	9	9	9

23.

7	6	6	3	
	/	/	/	
•	•	•	•	•
0	0	0	0	0
1	1	1	1	1
2	2	2	2	2
3	3	3	●	3
4	4	4	4	4
5	5	5	5	5
6	●	●	6	6
●	7	7	7	7
8	8	8	8	8
9	9	9	9	9

9.

3	.	5		
	●	/	/	
•		•	•	•
0	0	0	0	0
1	1	1	1	1
2	2	2	2	2
●	3	3	3	3
4	4	4	4	4
5	5	●	5	5
6	6	6	6	6
7	7	7	7	7
8	8	8	8	8
9	9	9	9	9

22.

5				
	/	/	/	
•	•	•	•	•
0	0	0	0	0
1	1	1	1	1
2	2	2	2	2
3	3	3	3	3
4	4	4	4	4
●	5	5	5	5
6	6	6	6	6
7	7	7	7	7
8	8	8	8	8
9	9	9	9	9

24.

7	5			
	/	/	/	
•	•	•	•	•
0	0	0	0	0
1	1	1	1	1
2	2	2	2	2
3	3	3	3	3
4	4	4	4	4
5	●	5	5	5
6	6	6	6	6
●	7	7	7	7
8	8	8	8	8
9	9	9	9	9

10.

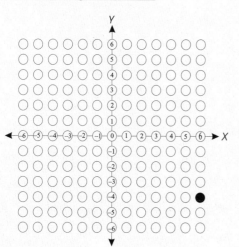

Part II

11.

16.

1	.	6		

25.

6	0			

ANSWERS AND EXPLANATIONS

Pretest 1: Language Arts, Writing

1. **The correct answer is (3).** No comma is needed to separate the parts of this compound direct object because there are only two parts. Commas are typically used for three or more items in a series. Choice (1) does not correct the error. Choice (2) would create a comma error because no comma is needed after this object. Choice (4) would also create a comma error by separating an adjective from the word it modifies.

2. **The correct answer is (4).** The original sentence is a sentence fragment, not a complete sentence. Therefore, choice (1) does not correct the mistake because it is also a fragment. Choices (2), (3), and (4) look like good possibilities, but you must read carefully to determine the differences among these choices. Choice (2) is incorrect because of the use of past perfect tense in *had been*; this tense refers to an action completed in the past. Glassmaking, however, continues today. In choice (3), the use of past tense, *was*, offers a similar error. The mistake is corrected by choice (4) because it eliminates the sentence fragment and uses the proper tense for an action that began in the past but continues into the present.

3. **The correct answer is (3).** The colon is needed because it sets up a list. Choice (1) does not correct the error; rather it presents an unnecessary change. Choice (2) incorrectly changes the tense, and choice (4) creates another mistake by removing *and*.

4. **The correct answer is (1).** A comma is not needed to separate the two parts of the predicate. Choice (2) incorrectly changes the tense to indicate an action that happened in the past. The error in choice (3) involves the difference between *into* and *in*; *into* is used to show movement as in *We went into the room*. On the other hand, *in* is used to indicate placement as in *We were in the room when the door closed*. Choice (4) changes *as* to *after* and thereby changes the sequence of actions needed in the glassmaking process.

5. **The correct answer is (4).** This sentence does not pertain directly to the process of *glassblowing*. The other sentences describe steps in glassblowing, not other methods of creating glassware.

6. **The correct answer is (3).** This choice will maintain parallel construction. This kind of grammatical expression refers to consistency in writing form. Unless the preposition *by* is repeated prior to each of the gerunds *squeezing, stretching, twirling,* and *cutting,* only one instance of *by* is called for. Choice (1) is incorrect because it would create an illogical construction. Choice (2) is a mistake because there is no need to arrange processes alphabetically. Choice (4) is an error because the addition of that prepositional phrase *into many different shapes* is unnecessary.

7. **The correct answer is (4).** *It's* is a contraction for *it is*. The possessive pronoun *its* is needed instead. Choice (1) offers a needless *as* that sets up an uncalled for comparison. Choice (2) offers a different preposition, but the change here is unnecessary. *NOTE: See explanation for question 6 above for clarification.* Choice (3) introduces an unnecessary comma that separates the infinitive phrase from the remainder of the sentence.

8. **The correct answer is (2).** Moving the prepositional phrase *on the cooled glass* to follow *has been drawn* avoids the misplaced modifier. In the original sentence, the *craftsperson* appears to be *on the cooled glass*. Choice (1) incorrectly changes the tense. While choice (3) changes from passive to active voice, the modifier is still misplaced. Finally, choice (4) illogically moves the modifier to precede the introductory clause. Reread the entire sentence carefully.

9. **The correct answer is (4).** It eliminates the sentence fragment. Choice (1) does not correct the fragment but instead unnecessarily changes the tense from present to past present. Choice (2) looks like a good possible answer, but *Which* merely sets up another sentence fragment. Choice (3) offers needless removal of detail.

10. **The correct answer is (3).** The possessive pronoun form is used here. *There* can be used as an adverb as in *There are my books on the floor* or as an expletive that has no function in a sentence except to introduce it as in *There are ten other players on my team*. Choice (1) needlessly changes capitalization, and choice (2) changes the idea of a finished product to the process of making the glass. Choice (4) unnecessarily adds a clause not relevant to the sentence.

11. **The correct answer is (2).** The phrase *with full-time employment* describes the parents, not the *young children*. Choice (1) is not correct because there is no need to separate a subject and predicate with a comma, choice (3) offers an incorrectly spelled word, and choice (4) needlessly separates a predicate and direct object.

12. **The correct answer is (5).** This sentence has no error. Choice (1) offers a change in spelling, but *every* is used properly as an adjective here; *ever* is an adverb. Choice (2) changes the meaning of the sentence by shifting from comparative to superlative forms; *more* and *most* refer to different numbers of people, with *most* indicating a majority. Choice (3) changes the tense from present to past, but the action referred to was not completed in the past. Choice (4) incorrectly inserts a comma between parts of a compound adjective.

13. **The correct answer is (3).** This sentence is setting up a list of details, and the word *features* clarifies that point. Choice (1) offers an unnecessary comma separating the subject and predicate, while choice (2) incorrectly changes the predicate from the plural form, which agrees with *characteristics*, to singular. Choice (4) needlessly makes *day care center* a proper noun.

14. **The correct answer is (2).** The sentence fragment must be corrected, and this choice provides a predicate. Choice (1) incorrectly removes the necessary capitalization for the beginning of the sentence. Choice (3) attempts to connect the two constructions with only a comma when a colon is the needed punctuation to set up the list of details provided in sentence 4. Choice (4) seems to provide a predicate for the sentence fragment, but this choice of verb, *number*, does not logically complete the sentence.

15. **The correct answer is (4).** The insertion of a comma in this place eliminates confusion between *If at all* possible and *possible parents*. Choice (1) sets up that confusing construction, while choice (2) needlessly separates the subject and predicate. Changing *possible* to *necessary*, in choice (3), makes no sense because of the clash between possibility (*if*) and necessity.

16. **The correct answer is (1).** The plural form *kinds* is needed because of *toys* and *activities*, which are also plural forms. Choice (2) seems to offer a logical choice, but it does not correct *kind*. Choice (3) shifts from second person (you) implied in the imperative form *check* to first person (*my*). The comma inserted by choice (4) is unnecessary because it separates a compound object of preposition.

17. The correct answer is (1). It questions whether the children watch television as well as whether what they watch is age-appropriate. Choice (2) offers a question that can be answered with a list that would not necessarily indicate how much television the children watch. Choice (3) limits the question to two popular videos; this question does not ask how much television the children watch. On the other hand, choice (4) is too broad because parents also want to know what kinds of programs the children see. Finally, choice (5) offers only two approaches that will not indicate what parents truly want to know. Asking how much time the children watch television and whether these two videos are available does not sufficiently address the parents' concerns.

18. The correct answer is (1). It takes care of the dangling modifier, *Even after visiting locations that meet parents' standards.* This construction should refer to *parents,* and choice (1) creates a dependent adverb clause to eliminate the modifier problem. Choice (2) needlessly changes from present to past tense, while choice (3) incorrectly removes the apostrophe from the possessive form of *parents,* but choice (3) does not address the error with the modifier. Choice (4) also wrongly focuses attention on the possessive form.

19. The correct answer is (4). The sentence needs the verb *accept,* not the preposition *except.* Choice (1) unnecessarily changes the verb form and thereby changes the sense of the sentence from the possibility of *may* to finality of *does.* Insertion of a comma after *openings* separates the parts of the compound predicate in choice (2). The semicolon suggested in choice (3) is also wrong because it, too, separates the parts of the compound predicate.

20. The correct answer is (5). This sentence is correct as written. Choice (1) offers a change from the adverb *really* to the adjective *real,* but *really* is the correct form because it modifies the adjective *good.* Choice (2) needlessly shifts tense from present to present perfect, passive voice; the action has not yet been completed. Insertion of a comma after *rapidly* in choice (3) unnecessarily separates the adverb clause from the independent clause. Choice (4) offers another needless tense shift from present to present perfect, passive voice.

21. The correct answer is (1). This sentence clearly states the purpose of the letter. Choice (2) does not state the purpose as concisely, while choice (3) sounds stiff and awkward. Choice (4) may express the writer's feelings, but it is not an appropriate way to begin the letter. Choice (5) does not indicate the purpose of the letter.

22. The correct answer is (1). This sentence is not relevant to the rest of the paragraph, which focuses attention on his concern about health. Choice (2) is appropriate because it indicates what may have prompted the writer's request. Choice (3) reinforces his need for information, and choice (4) stresses concerns about other health issues.

23. The correct answer is (3). This choice expresses the idea more concisely by dividing the lengthy sentence 7 into two parts. In choice (1) *these* has no antecedent, or word that the pronoun replaces. The same error occurs in choice (2) because there is no antecedent for *they.* Choice (4) provides no real change in that it is still a long sentence; it also uses *presently,* which means *soon,* instead of *currently,* which means *now.*

24. The correct answer is (4). It eliminates the awkward expression *for adopt* with *to adopt.* Choice (1) provides no substantial change; including *some people* is confusing as well. In choice (2), the correct preposition *to* is already in place. The change from passive to active voice verb in choice (3) may seem to be a good choice, but *they* has no antecedent, no word to which it can refer.

25. The correct answer is (2). It eliminates the double negative *don't hardly.* Choice (1) incorrectly changes the tense from past to present perfect, which would indicate that the record keeping continues to the present. The change from *but* to *and* in choice (3) loses the essential contrast between what the writer already knows and what he would like to know. Choice (4) is just a variation of the double negative corrected in choice (2).

26. The correct answer is (5). The sentence is correct as written. Choice (1) offers an unnecessary tense change that does not agree with the present tense of *is.* Choice (2) makes essentially the same mistake in tense. On the other hand, choice (3) shortens the first part of the sentence so much that meaning is lost, and choice (4) takes away the idea of a question.

27. The correct answer is (2). The construction is not a complete sentence. Removal of the subordinate conjunction *since* is essential. Choice (1) offers no real change; *since* and *because* can mean the same, and this answer does not correct the sentence fragment. Choice (3) provides an incorrect tense shift, and choice (4) with its change from *have recently ruled* to *would have recently ruled* sets up a shift in mood.

28. The correct answer is (3). The words *formally* and *formerly* can easily be confused. You must be able to recognize the differences in meaning by the difference in spelling. *Formally* means *politely* or *ceremonially,* while *formerly* means *past* or *previously.* Choice (1) also offers a choice of spelling, but *right,* meaning *prerogative,* is the correct word. *Rite* refers to a service or ceremony. In choice (2), *exercising* means *utilizing* or *implementing,* but *exorcizing* means freeing from an evil spirit. Choice (4) changes the meaning of the sentence.

29. The correct answer is (5). The sentence is correct as written. In choice (1), the comma between *Hillview* and *TN* is needed to separate city and state. Choice (2) wrongly inserts a comma between state and zip code, while choice (3) incorrectly inserts a comma after the zip code. Finally, there is no reason to delete the email address, choice (4), because this information is widely accepted as another legitimate means by which to contact someone.

30. The correct answer is (4). The construction is a sentence fragment because it lacks a predicate or verb. Connecting the phrase to the previous sentence provides a verb. None of the other choices supplies a verb.

31. The correct answer is (2). This choice changes the verb in sentence 4 to a past participle that logically modifies *mecca.* Choice (1) offers a present participle of the same predicate, but that construction is not logical here because the *mecca* is not *constructing.* Choice (3) uses a comma to connect the sentences and thereby creates a comma splice, which is a serious error. This kind of mistake can be remedied by adding a conjunction. Choices (4) and (5) do not have complete predicates.

32. The correct answer is (1). Because *trade* is singular, the pronoun referring to it must also be singular (*its*). Choice (2) incorrectly makes a plural possessive noun to a singular possessive noun because of the placement of the apostrophe. Choice (3) needlessly ends the sentence when the writer clearly indicates other kinds of trades. Choice (4) also overlooks the need for the singular form of *street.*

33. The correct answer is (3). Choice (1) misspells *gauge.* Choice (2) also offers an incorrect spelling of *passers-by.* Since *passers-by* is plural, then *shoppers* supplied in choice (3) is the correct choice. In choice (4), *watches* is a singular form of the verb, but the plural is needed to agree with *merchants.*

34. The correct answer is (5). No correction is necessary. Choice (1) moves the elliptical clause *while examining the shop's wares* illogically to modify *merchants.* Choice (2) removes a needed comma following an introductory adverb clause, while choice (3) incorrectly changes from present to past tense. Choice (4) improperly inserts a comma in a series of phrases.

35. **The correct answer is (2).** Sentence (12) provides historical information about the structure of the Covered Bazaar. The other choices pertain to the variety of goods for sale.

36. **The correct answer is (1).** This option relates to the actual sale of goods and the merchants talents in selling. The other choices pertain to the variety of goods for sale.

37. **The correct answer is (5).** The primary problems with the other choices are tenses or modifiers. In choice (1), *Enlarging to have the appearance it has today* is used incorrectly to modify *the Bazaar*. A similar modifier problem occurs in choice (2) because *Facing at least twelve strong earthquakes and nine major fires* improperly modifies *restorations*. In choice (3), *has faced*, the present perfect tense, incorrectly indicates an action that occurred in the past and continues into the present. The predicate in choice (4) also is in the wrong tense; *has been* once again indicates an event that happened in the past but continues into the present.

38. **The correct answer is (1).** This option eliminates the comma splice caused by using a comma to connect two independent clauses. Choice (2) looks good, but *employ* is in the proper form to be parallel, or the same form, as *spot*, an understood infinitive. In choice (3), changing *sale* to *sell* amounts to substituting a verb when you need a noun. Choice (4) misspells *somehow*.

39. **The correct answer is (1).** This choice contains no predicate so it is merely a phrase, not a sentence. Choice (2) appropriately moves the prepositional phrase at the end of the sentence to the beginning where it can also logically modify the predicate. The other choices rely primarily on the use of appositive phrases to eliminate the need for the predicate noun *the original shopping mall*.

40. **The correct answer is (2).** This answer maintains the present tense used in the essay. Choice (1) incorrectly changes to an adjective the adverb that modifies an adjective *inexpensive*. Choice (3) needlessly eliminates a key word from the sentence because the *leather and suede* have been fashioned into a variety of goods; they are not mere pieces. Choice (4) incorrectly separates the subject from its verb.

41. **The correct answer is (3).** *Cleanly* is misused for the adjective *clean* describing the employee's appearance. *Timely* is actually an adjective even though it has the typical *-ly* ending of adverbs, so its form must be changed to *on time*. Choice (1) is also incorrect because *appropriate dress* has no logical function in the sentence. Choice (2) incorrectly uses *timely* and *cleanly*, while choice (4) also misuses *timely*.

42. **The correct answer is (4).** Review the title for the passage again. Sometimes you can find a correct answer somewhere else on a test. The plural possessive form of *rustler* is needed here. Choice (1) changes the meaning of the sentence. Choice (2) incorrectly separates parts of a compound direct object. Choice (3) needlessly offers a possessive form of the noun.

43. **The correct answer is (3).** *Keep . . . is your responsibility* is illogical. The gerund form *Keeping* is needed. Choice (1) improperly changes the verb to a form of progressive, while choice (2) exchanges *personally* to an incorrect pronoun form *theirselves*. Choice (4) combines the sentences in an illogical way as well.

44. **The correct answer is (2).** The singular form of the verb is required. The conjunction *or* makes the subject singular. Choice (1) is a needless change. Choice (3) improperly separates the parts of the subject, while choice (4) creates a double negative with *no* and *nor*.

45. **The correct answer is (1).** *Theirself* is an incorrect form of pronoun. *Themselves* is the corrected form, but since the antecedent for this pronoun is singular (*employee*), the singular form of the pronoun is needed. In choice (2), however, *himself* is gender-specific language, which you should try to avoid. Choice (3) mistakenly changes the tense from present to past, and choice (4) inserts an unnecessary comma that separates an infinitive phrase and the word it modifies.

46. **The correct answer is (2).** It maintains parallel construction: *clearing*, *setting up*, and *cleaning*. Choice (1) incorrectly omits the comma needed after the introductory adverb clause. Choice (3) creates an error with parallelism by changing the gerund *clearing* to an infinitive form. All three parts of this compound predicate noun must be in the same form. Choice (4) wrongly changes the tense from present to past.

47. **The correct answer is (4).** *Don't never hesitate to* is a double negative; removing it from the sentence does not change the meaning. Choice (1) is suggesting a misspelling of *dessert;* to remember the difference between *dessert* and *desert*, try to associate something with one of the words, like **s**imply **s**crumptious (ss) with *dessert*. Choice (2) omits important information, and choice (3) separates the parts of the predicate by inserting an unnecessary comma.

48. **The correct answer is (1).** Again, parallel form is necessary; *guaranteeing* must appear in the same form as *following*. Choice (2) offers an illogical option. Choice (3) incorrectly separates a word from the prepositional phrase modifying it. Choice (4) uses the singular possessive form of the nouns instead of the plural form.

49. **The correct answer is (3).** The error involves agreement of pronoun and antecedent again. Since *orders* is plural, the pronoun that refers to it must also be in plural form: *them*. Choice (1) creates a sentence fragment as does choice (3). Choice (4) repeats the error with pronoun-antecedent agreement.

50. **The correct answer is (3).** The sentence calls for the possessive form of the pronoun. Confusion about spelling these three sound-alike words can be eliminated by understanding a few basic rules: (a) *they're* is a contraction of *they are*, (b) *their* is a possessive pronoun (see the word *heir* within *their*? Maybe that will remind you of ownership), and (c) *there* is usually an adverb indicating place where it can also be used, however, as an expletive to begin a sentence, as in *There* are fifty-five questions on this test. Choice (4) creates a comma splice by attempting to connect two sentences with merely a comma.

Part II: Essay

The scoring information below will help you estimate a score for your essay. If you can, ask an instructor to read and score your essay. To help you decide which skills you need to work on, make a list of its strengths and weaknesses based on the checklist below.

With 6 as the top score and 1 at the bottom, rank your essay for each item on the checklist. Put a check in the box that you think reflects the quality of that particular part of your essay.

Does my essay . . .	1	2	3	4	5	6
discuss the topic?						
have a clear, controlling idea that is developed throughout?						
have a clear structure (introduction, body, and conclusion)?						
tell the reader in the introduction what the topic is and what I am going to say about it?						
use details and examples to support each point?						
sum up the essay in the conclusion?						
have few or no errors in sentence structure, usage, or punctuation?						

Pretest 2: Social Studies

1. **The correct answer is (5). (Analysis)** The consequence of receiving a ticket will probably decrease or completely eliminate the behavior that caused you to get the ticket.

2. **The correct answer is (3). (Application)** The parking ticket will probably influence your decision not to park in handicapped spaces in the future.

3. **The correct answer is (1). (Application)** Keynes was an economist, as indicated by the title of his most famous book.

4. **The correct answer is (3). (Application)** Someone who studies the social effects of circumstances on a group is a sociologist.

5. **The correct answer is (1). (Comprehension)** The Tillamook group lived in the Northwest, where the tribes fished for salmon.

6. **The correct answer is (4). (Comprehension)** The passage shows that the native peoples in both areas of the country relied on locally available game and plants (such as fish and berries) for food and on geographic characteristics, such as forests, for their other needs.

7. **The correct answer is (2). (Application)** Peter's temporary unemployment is seasonal. According to the passage, he always has a job during ski season, even when the economy is slow. He has difficulty finding employment only during the months when the ski slopes are not open.

8. **The correct answer is (3). (Application)** When companies change locations, their employees are subject to structural unemployment.

9. **The correct answer is (5). (Application)** As the map shows, the later times are in the east, and the time difference is three hours from east coast to west coast.

10. **The correct answer is (4). (Application)** A time zone covers all of one north-to-south area (a vertical strip on the map). Seattle and San Francisco both lie on the Pacific Ocean and therefore are in the same time zone.

11. **The correct answer is (3). (Comprehension)** According to the circle graph, the clergy costs $113 and the groom's clothing costs $77, which are both less than $192, the cost of the limousine.

12. **The correct answer is (5). (Analysis)** If the wedding cost about $10,000 and the cost of the reception was just under $6,000, then a little more than half, or about 60 percent, of the total cost was for the reception.

13. **The correct answer is (2). (Analysis)** The cartoon shows huge resources being turned into tiny results.

14. **The correct answer is (4). (Evaluation)** Nothing in the cartoon supplies evidence for support of choices (2), (3), or (5). Choice (1) is completely denied by the image of the cartoon. Choice (4) is correct because the tiny image of the citizen in relation to the huge state apparatus can be seen as evidence of victimization of the people.

15. **The correct answer is (2). (Evaluation)** A growing belief in the essential equality of all people is the core factor that has led to an extension of voting rights.

16. **The correct answer is (3). (Application)** Martin Luther King Jr. was the great leader of the 1960s American civil rights movement. Choices (1), (4), and (5) are African-American leaders of the early 1900s, and choice (2) is a leader of today.

17. **The correct answer is (2). (Comprehension)** Point B is at about 80 degrees north latitude and 60 degrees west longitude.

18. **The correct answer is (3). (Application)** A traveler would move in a southeasterly direction when going from point B to point E.

19. **The correct answer is (4). (Analysis)** The 1935 Banking Act created a group to regulate the money supply and interest rates, very much as the Federal Reserve Board does today.

20. **The correct answer is (1). (Analysis)** The nationwide spread of cheap electricity to rural areas probably would have held the most interest for an Oregon farmer, so choice (1) is correct. Choice (2) might have been involved in conservation projects nearby, but there is nothing to indicate an even national spread. Choices (3) and (4) would have had no more effect on a rural farmer than on any other person in the nation, and choice (5) was for a specific geographic region of which Oregon was not a part.

21. **The correct answer is (1). (Evaluation)** The similarity of crime today because of illegal drug sales to the crime caused in the 1920s by illegal liquor sales could be cited as a possible reason to change drug laws by someone who favors such a decriminalization.

22. **The correct answer is (3). (Evaluation)** The passage provides enough information to predict that the population will decline, but not enough information to predict either choice (1) or choice (2). Nothing in the passage suggests that choice (4) is true, and while choice (5) may be true, there is no information in the passage to support it.

23. **The correct answer is (4). (Analysis)** The tremendous problems now facing Russia have caused many couples to wonder how well they could provide for a family in such circumstances. Therefore, some have decided against having children.

24. **The correct answer is (2). (Application)** George Washington was a general and commander-in-chief of the colonial armies in the American Revolution. The dates of his presidency are clues you can use to arrive at the correct answer (the Revolution was fought between 1775 and 1783). The French and Indian War was earlier in the eighteenth century (1754–1763), while the remaining three wars were fought in the nineteenth century.

25. **The correct answer is (3). (Application)** Abraham Lincoln issued the Emancipation Proclamation in 1865. Choices (1), (4), and (5) all include the names of other presidents, which should tell you that these choices are incorrect, even if the specific action or stance is not well known. The Louisiana Purchase, choice (2), made by President Thomas Jefferson in 1803, more than doubled the size of the United States at that time.

26. **The correct answer is (3). (Analysis)** The growth of publicly funded education suggests that an education became a citizen's right regardless of status or ability to pay. The other choices are not incorrect, but choice (3) is the best answer.

27. **The correct answer is (5). (Application)** Plantations could not have existed without slavery. Democracy, choice (1), and colonialism, choice (2), were discussed in the text, but they were not associated with plantations. Land development, choice (3), and a cash crop economy, choice (4), were associated with the plantation system, but they were not caused by it, as slavery was.

28. **The correct answer is (2). (Analysis)** The information in Lesson 2 and in the passage indicates that white settlers wanted more land. This passage shows that the U.S. government pursued a policy of helping the settlers take the land from the native peoples. Manifest Destiny, choice (1), was a sentiment, not a policy. The government was interested in land, not Native American civilization, choice (3), and Native American relocation, choice (4), was an effect of the policy of expansion. Settlement west of the Mississippi, choice (5), was not an issue in 1830.

29. **The correct answer is (5). (Comprehension)** The Cherokees viewed their forced migration, choice (1), with great bitterness. There is no evidence in the passage that they actually wept, choice (4), or planned to hurt people, choice (3). Their level of civilization, choice (2), was not related to their hardships.

30. **The correct answer is (4). (Analysis)** The passage strongly implies that different times caused confusion and standard time lessened the confusion. The fact that the entire country adopted Standard Railway Time indicates that the new standard time had improved efficiency.

31. **The correct answer is (3). (Comprehension)** The writer complained that railroad time controlled 55 million people—an example of the railroad's power.

32. **The correct answer is (1). (Application)** The passage refers to the effect of large bodies of water on temperature. It suggests that such bodies of water have a moderating effect on temperatures. Therefore, places inland are likely to be colder in winter and warmer in summer than places near a coast.

33. **The correct answer is (3). (Analysis)** As a port, Valdez lies along an ocean, so choice (2) is incorrect. Choices (1) and (4) are incorrect because they explain only why Valdez might have more moderate temperatures than places inland. They do not explain why those temperatures are above freezing. Choice (5) is incorrect because prevailing winds can bring warm or cold temperatures to a place.

34. **The correct answer is (2). (Analysis)** Drivers rely on landmarks to find their way. The other activities require a knowledge of absolute location.

35. **The correct answer is (3). (Evaluation)** The graph shows that most of the world's water is salt water.

36. **The correct answer is (2). (Comprehension)** Any one branch of government is prevented from growing too powerful by the system of checks and balances.

37. **The correct answer is (3). (Application)** The bureaucracy, which is mostly responsible for creating policies and guidelines to implement new laws, is the target of this cartoon.

38. **The correct answer is (2). (Evaluation)** The devil-may-care attitude of the two government workers in the cartoon implies that they don't think the job they do is entirely worthwhile or necessary.

39. **The correct answer is (1). (Application)** Most people now believe that the government has some obligation to help citizens in need.

40. **The correct answer is (2). (Analysis)** The ability to be flexible is vital to the role of the Supreme Court. Without this ability, the justices would not be able to play a positive role in a nation that has changed greatly since the Constitution was written more than two centuries ago.

41. **The correct answer is (4). (Analysis)** The Ninth and Tenth Amendments give powers not otherwise described to the people and to the states.

42. **The correct answer is (2). (Application)** The Third Amendment protects citizens from having to house and feed troops during peacetime.

43. **The correct answer is (4). (Comprehension)** The best way to describe "democracy" is with the phrase "rule by the people."

44. **The correct answer is (1). (Comprehension)** Although economic reasoning can help a person make money, the study of economics is not about how to do so.

45. **The correct answer is (3). (Application)** By choosing to attend college, Maria gives up the opportunity of earning $200 per week.

46. **The correct answer is (4). (Analysis)** Maria's decision involves a choice between the part-time job and college classes. Because she can't be in two places at once or pay her college costs, choosing one means giving up the other.

47. **The correct answer is (2). (Analysis)** While people may like lower prices (3) and convenience (4), a combination of these reasons is a better explanation.

48. **The correct answer is (4). (Analysis)** Home sales are up one month and down the next, meaning that there is no discernible trend in this market.

49. **The correct answer is (1). (Evaluation)** Choice (1) does not constitute a cultural change, because men have always made more money than women who do the same work. Choices (2) to (5) describe cultural changes that have occurred in America recently.

50. **The correct answer is (3). (Application)** People who believe that we can prevent violent crimes by teaching young people our values and showing them that these values work are espousing enculturation.

Pretest 3: Science

1. **The correct answer is (1). (Fundamental understandings)** The aorta arises from the largest chamber of the heart, the left ventricle.

2. **The correct answer is (4). (Fundamental understandings)** The left atrium receives the blood that is ready to be pumped out in the systemic circulation.

3. **The correct answer is (1). (Fundamental understandings)** C represents the pulmonary arteries, through which oxygenated blood is carried to the lungs.

4. **The correct answer is (5). (Fundamental understandings)** Both have ribosomes, but prokaryotes lack the other organelles.

5. **The correct answer is (4). (Fundamental understandings)** Microtubules serve a support function and movement function in mitosis and meiosis. This question is a good illustration of using the process of elimination in choosing your answer. Be careful not to confuse microtubules with microfilaments.

6. **The correct answer is (4). (Unifying concepts and principals)** Mitosis begins with the disintegration of the nuclear membrane, the condensation of the chromosomes, and the synthesis of the spindle apparatus, which define prophase.

7. **The correct answer is (2). (Unifying concepts and processes)** Since there are more water molecules on side B, they will diffuse to the A side. Water always diffuses (osmoses) from a higher to a lower concentration.

8. **The correct answer is (3). (Fundamental understandings)** The heat of vaporization (liquid to gas) is almost seven times greater than the heat of fusion (melting) for water. Each substance has its own characteristic properties, and the heats of fusion and vaporization will vary.

9. **The correct answer is (5). (Science as inquiry)** The half-life is 60 days, and by the graph, that is at least three full time periods, or 180 days. But it takes longer than 180 days, since at that point 12.5 grams would be left.

10. **The correct answer is (4). (Fundamental understandings)** There is no need to place any number in front of the methane, since the carbons are in a 1:1 ratio. Since the reactant side contains 4 hydrogen atoms, put a 2 in front of the water molecule on the product side. This results in a total of 4 oxygen atoms on the product side, so a 2 is needed in front of the oxygen.

11. **The correct answer is (5). (Unifying concepts and processes)** The answer cannot be a positive number, since 0° centigrade is the same as 32° Fahrenheit. Any movement up from that point cannot diverge on the same number. If you multiply degrees Fahrenheit by 1.8 and then add 32, you will get degrees centigrade.

12. **The correct answer is (2). (Unifying concepts and processes)** A variety of factors cause land and ocean to heat at different rates. Warm air over land is less dense and rises as it heats. Cool air over the ocean moves to fill the area vacated by the rising air, creating breezes.

13. **The correct answer is (5). (Unifying concepts and processes)** As choice (5) states, the mountainsides, which are made of rock, absorb solar heat during the day and radiates heat at night, causing temperature differences. The difference in heating rate causes valley breezes in the morning and mountain breezes in the afternoon.

14. **The correct answer is (1). (Fundamental understandings)** The change in the internal energy of a system is the heat added minus the work done. Since no heat is added, the internal energy change is negative.

15. **The correct answer is (3). (Fundamental understandings)** Thermodynamics describes how matter interacts with heat or work. Temperature is a parameter used in thermodynamics, but it is not a fundamental quantity. Heat and work are both forms of energy, so choices (4) and (5) are incomplete.

16. **The correct answer is (2). (Fundamental understandings)** The Second Law limits how much heat can be converted to work by a heat engine.

17. **The correct answer is (5). (Fundamental understandings)** The acceleration of gravitational acceleration on the moon is much lower than on Earth. According to the question, the period of the pendulum does not depend on the mass or amplitude.

18. **The correct answer is (4). (Unifying concepts and processes)** Both charges must be moving for there to be a magnetic force between them. It is only necessary to stop one charge for the force to be zero. While changing the distance between the charges will change the magnitude of the force, it will not reduce it to zero.

19. **The correct answer is (3). (Fundamental understandings)** As the fluid mosaic model explains, the embedded proteins in the phospholipid bilayer may move about among the phospholipids.

20. **The correct answer is (2). (Science as inquiry)** ATP is produced by hydrogen ions, which have been concentrated in the intermembrane space, flowing down a concentration gradient. The ions moved because of diffusion.

21. **The correct answer is (5). (Unifying concepts and principals)** In addition to making a net of 2 ATP, energy is also stored temporarily in NADH, because the hydrogens and electrons will be used later in the electron transport chain.

22. **The correct answer is (3). (Fundamental understandings)** There is a 1:1 ratio in photosynthesis.

23. **The correct answer is (2). (Fundamental understandings)** Taking one trait at a time, to have half gray and half red, the parents had to be Gg × gg. Since three-fourths of the offspring were straight, Ss × Ss would be the genotypes for straight/curly.

24. **The correct answer is (2). (Fundamental understandings)** The mother is a carrier for the gene. She has the color-blind allele from her father, but she doesn't express it. The dad is normal and is going to contribute his Y to the boy. Therefore, half of the mother's sons will be color-blind (and half of the couple's children will be boys).

25. **The correct answer is (4). (History and nature of science)** Restriction enzymes cut DNA at specific sites. The likelihood of finding any base in a DNA sequence is 1 in 4 or $\frac{1}{4}$. The probability of finding 6 specific bases is $\left(\frac{1}{4}\right)^6$, or $\frac{1}{4096}$. Therefore, 3 million divided by 4096 is 732.

26. **The correct answer is (3). (Fundamental understandings)** The speed increases by the same amount each second. After 1 second, the speed is 10 m/s; after 2 seconds, the speed is 20 m/s; after 3 seconds, the speed is 30 m/s.

27. **The correct answer is (2). (Fundamental understandings)** Since the speed is the same in both materials, there is no refraction. The frequency and wavelength would not be affected.

28. **The correct answer is (1). (Fundamental understandings)** Since the energy dropped when going from the reactants to the products, some energy had to be given off. When energy is given off, the reaction is said to be exothermic, as opposed to endothermic.

29. **The correct answer is (1). (Fundamental understandings)** The activation energy is the difference between the energy of the reactants and the height of the line, either 1 or 2, depending on whether a catalyst was used.

30. **The correct answer is (5). (Unifying concepts and processes)** Due to their small relative size, dwarf stars often have an absolute magnitude of 10 or more.

31. **The correct answer is (4). (Fundamental understandings)** According to the text, the Sun is a class G star with a surface temperature of about 6000°K and a luminosity of 1. Finding the point on the diagram where these properties intersect places the Sun along the main sequence.

32. The correct answer is (4). (Fundamental understandings) Red stars include giants and supergiants (high luminosity), but there are also red dwarf stars (low luminosity) too. None of the other classes listed contain both giant and dwarf stars.

33. The correct answer is (1). (Fundamental understandings) Structure X represents a strand of RNA that is transcribed in the nucleus.

34. The correct answer is (2). (Fundamental understandings) The transfer RNA (t-RNA) that translates the m-RNA strand does so by Watson-Crick base pairing rules. The complement of CAC is GUG, and the amino acid that is transferred by GUG is histidine.

35. The correct answer is (3). (Fundamental understandings) The biochemical process represented is translation, the making of proteins from the information found in RNA. The central dogma of modern biology is that DNA is *transcribed* into RNA, which is *translated* into protein. This translation happens at the ribosome.

36. The correct answer is (5). (Fundamental understandings) Cancer genes are cell division genes gone awry. They may be suppressor genes or activator genes, either of which can cause cancer.

37. The correct answer is (3). (Fundamental understandings) The question revolves around adaptive radiation versus convergent evolution. Adaptive radiation begins with organisms that are closely related but differentiate into different niches and become dissimilar. Convergent radiation begins with organisms that are not closely related but, because of the environment, come to look similar.

38. The correct answer is (3). (Fundamental understandings) The red is *rr* and the pink is *rw*. The possible combinations give half red and half pink.

39. The correct answer is (2). (Fundamental understandings) Gravity and moving water are significant agents of erosion. The steeper the slope, the greater the effects of gravity and the greater the velocity of water runoff. In addition, a hillside without vegetation would have little to hold soil in place. The combined factors make choice (2) the best answer.

40. The correct answer is (3). (Fundamental understandings) Metamorphic rock is rock that has undergone a change as a result of heat and pressure.

41. The correct answer is (1). (Fundamental understandings) Pyroclastics are driven into the air during violent eruptions. Quiet eruptions are characterized by flowing lava and the lack of projectiles during eruption. The discovery of pyroclastics is evidence of eruption but not a prediction of further eruptions or a guide to a timeline of past eruptions.

42. The correct answer is (3). (Fundamental understandings) The hallmark of a composite cone is the variable eruption types, based on the mineral and water vapor content of the magma. When magma is high in water vapor and silica, violent eruptions are likely, with deposition of layers of ash. Low water vapor and silica content in the magma are associated with quiet eruptions and flows of lava down the cone.

43. The correct answer is (2). (Fundamental understandings) Hawaii is covered with shield cones. Flowing lava is a characteristic of shield cones.

44. The correct answer is (1). (Unifying concepts and processes) Convert 4 grams of oxygen to moles of oxygen (0.125), multiply by the ratio of moles of $KClO_3$ to moles of O_2 (2/3), and then multiply by grams of $KClO_3$/mole (122.5).

45. The correct answer is (4). (Unifying concepts and processes) A mole of any gas at STP occupies 22.4 liters. Therefore, change 5.6 liters to moles (0.25 moles) and multiply by the molar mass of oxygen gas (32).

46. The correct answer is (4). (Fundamental understandings) The gene frequency for red is 0.6 and for white its 0.4. To find the next generation of pinks, use the Hardy-Weinberg rule: $p^2 + 2pq + q^2 = 1$, where p^2 is red, $2pq$ is pink, and q^2 is white.

47. The correct answer is (3). (Fundamental understandings) The scientific name for a species includes both the genus (capitalized) and the species (lower case).

48. The correct answer is (3). (Fundamental understandings) Diagram B represents an alveolus, a cluster of air sacs at the end of the smallest bronchioles.

49. The correct answer is (1). (Fundamental understandings) Number 2 is the trachea, and the esophagus is behind or dorsal to it.

50. The correct answer is (2). (Fundamental understandings) Acceleration is a change in velocity. When the direction of velocity changes, there is acceleration. Speed can be a constant while the direction of motion is changing.

Pretest 4: Language Arts, Reading

What Are These Characters Feeling?

1. The correct answer is (3). (Comprehension) The passage states that Michael's return is the reason that neither character can relax.

2. The correct answer is (1). (Synthesis) In spite of the fact that both characters are aware of each other's nervousness, the overall mood is comfortable. This shows up in such details as the narrator's memories of her mother's kitchen and her pleasure when Joe makes breakfast for her.

3. The correct answer is (4). (Analysis) Although the kitchen floor is certainly part of the setting, the best answer is choice (4). When she describes the kitchen floor, the narrator also tells the reader about her childhood, her mood, and her feelings for her current home.

4. The correct answer is (5). (Analysis) The situation described in the excerpt concerns the narrator's relationship with Joe and Joe and Michael's relationship, so the novel is most likely to focus on family relationships.

5. The correct answer is (4). (Analysis) These particular details tell what Joe is like in general, not about his relationship to Michael or his mother or his mood at the moment.

What Makes This Novel So Interesting?

6. The correct answer is (2). (Application) One of the reviewer's central points is that this novel was written by a woman about a female detective, so a female-produced documentary about female artists is most similar. Though this novel contains a young niece and a law school professor, they are only supporting characters, so choices (1) and (3) can be eliminated. Choice (4) would be logical only if the movie's subject matter was about a female. Choice (5) could be logical only if the article was also written by a woman.

7. The correct answer is (4). (Comprehension) The dialogue is described as "scalpel sharp," which means it is direct and concise. Choices (1), (2), and (3) do not suggest crisp, razor-edged dialogue. Although Scarpetta's work might sometimes be described as "graphic and gruesome," it would be inappropriate to apply the term to the dialogue, so choice (5) can be eliminated.

8. The correct answer is (5). (Comprehension) Lines 24–25 state, "The 'love interest' in the book is not romantic . . . ." All of the other choices are directly stated as elements in *Cruel & Unusual*. Choice (1) is mentioned is lines 29–31, choice (2) is mentioned in line 28 and elsewhere, choice (3) is referred to in line 29, and choice (4) is mentioned in line 23.

9. The correct answer is (5). (Comprehension) The professor did not want Kay to "lose herself"—and her abilities—in love and not reach her full potential as an individual. Choice (2) is the opposite of what the professor wanted for Kay. There is no support for the other choices in the passage.

How Should Co-Authors Work Together?

10. The correct answer is (4). (Comprehension) All of the other tasks listed are mentioned in the excerpt as among those done by the coordinating author.

11. **The correct answer is (1). (Application)** Choice (1)—consistency—is mentioned throughout the chapter. Choices (2), (3), and (5) are mentioned as specific tasks of the coordinating editor, but they are not overall goals. Choice (4) cannot be correct because the excerpt states that not all books have coordinating editors.

12. **The correct answer is (2). (Application)** The excerpt states that the coordinating author is the final arbiter in disputes about text content; therefore, he or she should be familiar with the content of all the chapters. There is no support for the other choices in the text.

13. **The correct answer is (3). (Application)** The coordinating author is most like a team captain, who takes part in the action while guiding the other players. There is no support for the other choices in the passage.

Why Is the Word *No* Important to This Speaker?

14. **The correct answer is (2). (Analysis)** In lines 5 and 12-14, the speaker says that "We" do not know how to say "no" and that "Puerto Ricans" do not know how to say "no." By identifying himself with those who do not know how to say "no," he is also identifying himself with Puerto Ricans. Based on these associations, the other choices are incorrect.

15. **The correct answer is (4). (Analysis)** According to the speaker, Puerto Ricans may say "We'll see," but mean "no." To many people, this expression may sound like "yes." Because this confusion exists, choices (1) and (5) are incorrect. The tone of voice described is accommodating, not offensive, so choice (3) is incorrect. There is no evidence for choice (2).

16. **The correct answer is (4). (Comprehension)** In lines 1-5, the speaker explains that the word "no" is necessary to end "anachronistic imperialism," or an outdated system in which a country is ruled by outsiders. Though the speaker might want his people to find better jobs, save the environment, or increase exports, these goals are not the most direct result of the powerful word "no." The other choices are not explained in this passage.

17. **The correct answer is (3). (Synthesis)** The speaker describes his homeland as full of beauty and generosity. Of the choices, nurturing is closest to this description. Choices (1), (2), and (5) are negative descriptions, and the speaker's devotion to Puerto Rico means that the land is not forgotten, as choice (4) suggests.

18. **The correct answer is (5). (Analysis)** To the speaker, the sound of the *o* in *no* is as sharp and powerful as gunfire, so choices (1), (2), and (3) are incorrect. He is trying to motivate his people, not prove he is brave; therefore, choice (4) can be eliminated.

How Are the Forests Planted?

19. **The correct answer is (1). (Analysis)** The answer choice is supported by the repetition of the idea of extent: dense, stretching, many a mile. Choice (4) is also supported by the text, but painting a picture of the forest is not a primary goal. Choices (2), (3), and (5) are not supported by the text.

20. **The correct answer is (5). (Comprehension)** The author states in the first paragraph that his conclusion is based on several weeks of close scrutiny, or observation. The other choices are not supported by the text.

21. **The correct answer is (4). (Synthesis)** The idea of the quoted sentence is that we should be aware of our dependency on nature; the idea of this answer choice is that we sometimes are not—these statements are therefore opposite sides of the same coin. The other choices, all statements from the excerpt, are statements of details that are not concerned with this main idea.

22. **The correct answer is (1). (Analysis)** This answer is implied by the passage, which states that trees are planted when animals drop or purposely store acorns. Although choices (3) and (5) are also implied by the passage, they are not the meaning of the quoted phrase. Choices (2) and (4) are not supported by the passage.

23. **The correct answer is (2). (Synthesis)** This option best states the passage's main idea. Choices (4) and (5) are details of the passage, not the main idea. Choices (1) and (3) are unsupported by the passage.

What Will Happen to These Characters?

24. **The correct answer is (3). (Application)** The sound effects suggest that the originally peaceful scene will be marred by danger. Although choices (1) and (2) are suggested by the general scene, they are not suggested by the warning call. Choices (4) and (5) are not supported by the text.

25. **The correct answer is (4). (Synthesis)** Choice (2) is partially supported by the text, as shown by Lennie's imitations of George's actions, but Lennie does not obey George without question. Choices (1), (3), and (5) are not supported by the text.

26. **The correct answer is (5). (Analysis)** Choices (2) and (4) are not supported by the text. Choices (1) and (3) are true, but we do not specifically discover these traits by means of this action.

27. **The correct answer is (1). (Analysis)** The text makes clear that George's action is purposeful and deliberate, whereas Lennie's is merely playful and childlike. The other choices are not supported by the text.

28. **The correct answer is (4). (Comprehension)** This statement conveys a general principle that George wants Lennie to learn. The other choices are admonitions or corrections.

29. **The correct answer is (2). (Synthesis)** The ominous opening sound effects, and Lennie's inability to learn from his experiences, suggest that tragedy will strike. The other choices are not supported by the passage.

Can You See These Women Clearly?

30. **The correct answer is (3). (Synthesis)** The poems use ordinary, concrete, yet detailed language and are lacking in metaphor or narrative. None of the other choices are supported by the poems.

31. **The correct answer is (1). (Synthesis)** Both poems present ordinary details in plain, ordinary language. The other choices are not supported by the poems.

32. **The correct answer is (5). (Synthesis)** Choice (1) is incorrect because the poem is primarily a still image, not a moving one, and certainly not a lengthy color one like a documentary. Choice (2) is incorrect because the poem is very brief. Choice (3) is incorrect because although the poem is short like a limerick, it is not humorous. Choice (4) is incorrect because Impressionist portraits do not convey photographic realism.

33. **The correct answer is (3). (Analysis)** The repetition of "They taste good to her," with varying stress resulting from the changing position of the words in the lines, creates emphasis. This creates an overwhelming sense of the old woman's enjoyment of a simple pleasure. Choices (1) and (2) are appropriate to the poem in general, although not to these particular lines. The other choices are not supported by the poem.

34. **The correct answer is (2). (Analysis)** The old woman is described as eating a plum and holding a paper bag full of plums. The other choices are not supported by the poem.

35. **The correct answer is (4). (Analysis)** The poem's repetition of the words "They taste good to her" suggests enjoyment. She gives herself over completely to the taste. The other choices are not supported by the poem.

What Kind of Place Is This?

36. **The correct answer is (3). (Analysis)** The last paragraph of the excerpt emphasizes the ranch's isolation from its neighbors. Although the second paragraph mentions that the area can be cold, as stated in choice (4), the opening paragraph mentions the hot summers. The other choices are not supported by the excerpt.

37. **The correct answer is (1). (Analysis)** The way that the dead grass, lingering through summer, reminds you of winter, means that past and present are always intermingled. Choice (2) is wrong because we don't yet know whether the present is good for Jim. Choices (3) and (5) are literally true, but they do not help interpret the sentence. Choice (4) is not supported by the text.

38. **The correct answer is (2). (Synthesis)** The descriptive terms used in the second paragraph are bleak rather than sad. Choice (1) is wrong because Jim's memories are very clear, not at all vague. Choices (3), (4), and (5) are not supported by the text.

39. **The correct answer is (4). (Analysis)** Each of the three paragraphs in the excerpt is about setting: the first, about the general setting, the second, about the setting of Jim's childhood, and the third, about the specific human setting. The other choices are not supported by the text.

40. **The correct answer is (3). (Synthesis)** In the first paragraph, the narrator states that Jim "found cause for the first time in years to reflect upon the small Saskatchewan town he'd come from." Later on, Jim dismisses an unhappy memory with the phrase, "that was then." The suggestion is that Jim remembers only reluctantly and is unwilling to link the past with the present.

Pretest 5: Mathematics

Part I

1. **The correct answer is (2).** 3 apples for $0.34 each cost a total of $1.02 and 5 pears for $0.27 each cost a total of $1.35, which all add up to a total of $2.37. The change from a $5.00 bill is $5.00 − $2.37 = $2.63.

2. **The correct answer is (3).** A 20% discount means you would pay 80%, so $0.8 \times 57 = $45.60. Now take another 25% off of $45.60, which is $0.25 \times 45.60 = $11.40. So the person pays $45.60 − $11.40 = $34.20.

3. **The correct answer is (5).** $1{,}000 \text{ meter} \times 1.094 \frac{\text{yard}}{\text{meter}} \times 36 \frac{\text{inch}}{\text{yard}} = 39{,}384$. Note the units divide out and you are left with inches.

4. **The correct answer is (4).** $3(3) + 2(4) + 1(2) = 19$

5. **The correct answer is (2).** Use a proportion:
$$\frac{3 \text{ hour}}{x \text{ hour}} = \frac{100 \text{ books}}{1{,}250 \text{ books}}$$
$3 \times 1{,}250 = 100x$ of $100x = 3{,}750$
Therefore, $x = 37.5$ hours.

6. **The correct answer is 1,200.** We need to determine how many times 3 cu. in. divides 36 cu. in. $36 \div 3$ cu. in. For every 12 spots he can fit $12 \times 100 = 1{,}200$ cards. See page 59 for filled-in answer grid.

7. **The correct answer is (5).** For the daytime surfing at the day rate he pays $3.44 \times 13 = 44.72$. For the nighttime surfing at the night rate he pays $2.37 \times 22 = 52.14$. The difference between the two is $52.14 − 44.72 = 7.42$.

8. **The correct answer is (4).** The total amount she used plus what was left over in the bag *is* what she had originally, so
$$3\frac{1}{4} + 4\frac{1}{4} + 22\frac{3}{4} = 30\frac{1}{4}.$$

9. **The correct answer is 3.5.** Make a proportion: For every $1.5 − 1 = 0.5$ rise in voltage the current rises by $3 − 2 = 1$. So we write the proportion:

Voltage	Current
0.5	1
1.75	x

so we have $\frac{0.5}{1.75} = \frac{1}{x}$ or $0.5 \times x = 1.75$. Therefore, $x = \frac{1.75}{0.5} = 3.5$.

See page 59 for filled-in answer grid.

10. **The correct answer is (6,-4).** First mark where Johnny lives (3,-2). Then using that as your reference and move 3 units to the right arriving at 6 and then move 2 units down ending up at (6,-4) where his friend lives. See page 59 for filled-in answer grid.

11. **The correct answer is (3).** Add up the different portions: $3 + 20 + 33 = 56\% = \$0.56$.

12. **The correct answer is (5).** 11% of $15,000 is $0.11 \times 15{,}000 = \$1{,}650$.

13. **The correct answer is (4).** 12% of $15,000 is $0.12 \times 15{,}000 = \$1{,}800$.

14. **The correct answer is (5).** Use a proportion:
$$\frac{3}{100} = \frac{150}{x}$$
or $3x = 15{,}000$
Therefore, $x = \$5{,}000$.

15. **The correct answer is $225.** Earrings fall under jewelry. Since the question asks for *at most* and earrings are a form of jewelry, earrings cannot make more profit than the entire jewelry department. Therefore, 3% of $7,500 or $0.3 \times 7{,}500 = \$225$. See page 59 for filled-in answer grid.

16. **The correct answer is (4).** The price before the discount was $2(0.69) + 3(0.46) = \$2.76$. His discount was 15%, so he paid $100\% − 15\% = 85\%$ of the original price. Therefore, $0.85(2.76) = 2.346 \approx \$2.35$.

17. **The correct answer is (2).** To find the mean (average) we add all the values and divide by the total number of values.
$$\frac{3 + 2 + 1 + 5 + 2 + 3 + 7 + 6}{8} = \frac{29}{8} = 3.625.$$

18. **The correct answer is (2).** The first time (Time 1) it splits into 2, then the second time (Time 2) each of those split into 2 again giving us $2 \times 2 = 2^2 = 4$ splits, which in turn the third time (Time 3) will each split into 2 again giving us $2 \times 2 \times 2 = 2^3 = 8$ and so on. Notice the pattern. The fourth time it should be $2 \times 2 \times 2 \times 2 = 2^4$. So we can predict on the 10th time it will be $2^{10} \times 250 = 256{,}000$.

19. **The correct answer is (2).** The radius of the circle is $r = \frac{5}{2} = 2.5$ Therefore, Area $= \pi r^2 = 3.14(2.5)^2 = 19.625$.

20. **The correct answer is (5).** The area of the shaded region is the difference between the areas of the square and the circle. Area of the square is $5 \times 5 = 25$. Therefore, Area$_{\text{Shaded Region}} = 25 − 19.625 = 5.375$.

21. **The correct answer is (2).** $AC = \sqrt{25^2 − 7^2} = 24$. Therefore, $\cos A = \frac{24}{25}$.

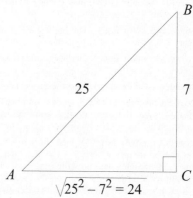

22. **The correct answer is (5).** $35 \div 7 = 5$. See page 59 for filled-in answer grid.

23. The correct answer is $7,663.

	Electronics	Blue Chip	Total
Amount Invested	$x + 450$	x	
Interest	0.22	0.10	1,253

Therefore, $0.10x + 0.22(x + 450) = 1,253$

$$0.10x + 0.22x + 99 = 1,253$$
$$0.32x = 1,154$$
$$x = \frac{1,154}{0.32} = \$3,606.25 \text{ Blue chip}$$

Therefore, Electronics: $3,606.25 + 450 = \$4,056.25$
Her total investment is $3,606.25 + 4056.25 = 7662.50 \approx \$7,663$.
See page 59 for filled-in answer grid.

24. The correct answer is 75. The first 40 hours he gets paid $40 \times 6.25 = 250$. For the next 20 hours he is paid time and a half:

$$20 \times \left(6.25 + \frac{6.25}{2}\right) = 187.50.$$ Now he has earned $250 + 187.50$
$= 437.50$. He still owes $625 - 437.50 = 187.50$. He can earn this at a double time rate, which is $6.25 \times 2 = 12.50$ an hour. So he needs to work another $187.50 \div 12.50 = 15$ hours. In total, he has to work $40 + 20 + 15 = 75$ hours. See page 59 for filled-in answer grid.

25. The correct answer is (5). We need to find the sum of the volumes of the two cylinders:

$V = \pi r^2 h$, $r_{Top} = 3$, $r_{Bottom} = (3 + 2) = 5$, $h_{Top} = 1$,
$h_{Bottom} = (5 - 1) = 4$
$V_{Top} + V_{Bottom} = 3.14(3)^2(1) + 3.14(5)^2(4) = 342.26$

Part II

1. The correct answer is (5). Length is $l = 2 + 3w, l = 2 + 3 \times 15$ $= 47$ width is 15. So perimeter is $2 \times 15 + 2 \times 47 = 124$.

2. The correct answer is (5).

$$\frac{12 \text{ inch}}{1 \text{ foot}} \times \frac{3 \text{ foot}}{1 \text{ yard}} = \frac{36 \text{ inch}}{1 \text{ yard}} = 36 \text{ inches/yard}$$

3. The correct answer is (4). $\frac{1}{2} \times 10 = 5$, $10 - 5 = 5$, $5 \div 4 =$ $\$1.25$

4. The correct answer is (5). Use a proportion:

Can	Shadow	
3	5	Therefore, $\frac{3}{6} = \frac{5}{x}$ or rearrange $\frac{3}{5} = \frac{6}{x}$
6	x	

5. The correct answer is (3). The distributive law has been incorrectly applied: $233(121) - 112(121)$.

6. The correct answer is (3). First change hours to minutes then divide $12 \times 60 = 720$, $720 \div 10 = 72$.

7. The correct answer is (5). The highest point in the y direction is 3.25.

8. The correct answer is (2). Find the difference of the y-value at $x = 300$, $3 - 2.4 = 0.6$.

9. The correct answer is (3). Find the range $1.6 - 0.7 = 0.9$.

10. The correct answer is (4). 5 times a number is $5x$ (=), 3 less than (-3) twice the sum of the number and 2 $2(x + 2)$. Therefore, $5x = 2(x + 2) - 3$ or $5x + 3 = 2(x + 2)$.

11. The correct answer is (4,3). First, find the length of the two sides of the rectangle, where 5 is the diagonal. Using the 3-4-5 ratio for right triangles we know the other sides are 3 and 4 units long. We move 4 units to the right on the x-axis (longer side) and 3 up. Point is (4,3). See page 60 for filled-in answer grid.

12. The correct answer is (1). Use the formula: $d = r \times t$, $r = 1200m/s$, $d = 0.6km = (0.6 \times 1000) = 600m$

$$600 = 1200t, \text{ therefore, } t = \frac{600}{1200} = 0.5 \text{ seconds.}$$

13. The correct answer is (4). Factor and solve:

$x^2 - 3x - 54 = 0$ $x + 6 = 0$ or $x - 9 = 0$
$(x + 6)(x - 9) = 0$ $x = -6$ or $x = 9$

14. The correct answer is (3). The largest rod that can fit into the cylinder cannot have a length any larger than the diagonal of the cylinder.

height = 12, radius = 3, therefore, diameter = $3 \times 2 = 6$
$(\text{diagonal})^2 = (\text{height})^2 + (\text{diameter})^2$
diagonal $= \sqrt{144 + 36} = 6\sqrt{5}$

15. The correct answer is (4). Calculate the range (difference between highest and lowest) $122 - 64 = \$58$ billion.

16. The correct answer is 1.6. Mode is the most frequently occurring number in your data set: 1.6 shows up seven times in the table. See page 60 for filled-in answer grid.

17. The correct answer is (2). $108 \div 12 = 9$ rolls

18. The correct answer is (5). No information has been given on Star Trek: Elite Force.

19. The correct answer is (3). First we find the area of the four walls. Remember she will not be wall-papering the ceiling and the floor! Then divide that by the area of the wallpaper rolls. $2(32 \times 9) + 2(16 \times 9) = 684$ is the area of the four walls. $3 \times 25 = 75$ is the area of each wallpaper roll. Now $684 \div 75 = 9.12$. She needs to buy 10 rolls because they come in complete packages.

20. The correct answer is (2). 1 lb $\Rightarrow$ \$2.50; therefore,

$2\frac{1}{2}$lb $\Rightarrow 2.50 \times 2\frac{1}{2} = \$6.25$.

21. The correct answer is (2). Let W be the number of women. The ratio of men to women is 3 to 2 which means for every 1 woman there is $\frac{3}{2}$ men. Therefore, the total is $W + \frac{3}{2}W = 675$.

22. The correct answer is (4). Break the plot up into three distinct rectangles, find each of their areas and add them to find the total area of the plot.

$(300 \times 350) + [(300 + 500) \times 900] + \{[1500 - (350 + 900)] \times 250\} = 887,500$ sq ft

Now we multiply to find his earnings $887,500 \times \$1.50 = \$1,331,250$.

23. The correct answer is (5). There are x lb of half-pound weight potatoes.

	$\frac{1}{2}$lb-weight potatoes	$\frac{1}{4}$lb-weight potatoes	Total
# of potatoes	x	$100 - x$	
Weight of bag	$\frac{1}{2}x$	$\frac{1}{4}(100 - x)$	47

Therefore, the equation is $\frac{1}{2}x + \frac{1}{4}(100 - x) = 47$

24. The correct answer is (1). In such problems you would simply add up sales for each genre and compare. However, in this problem it is visually explicit that the correct answer is children's books.

25. The correct answer is 60. 140 thousand children's books were sold in 2000. 80 thousand action books were sold in 1995. So the difference is $140 - 80 = 60$. See page 60 for filled-in answer grid.

PART I

LANGUAGE ARTS, WRITING

What Will I Find on the Language Arts, Writing Test?

The GED Language Arts, Writing Test is Test One of the GED Tests. It measures your knowledge of written English and your ability to write. The GED Language Arts, Writing Test is an opportunity for you to demonstrate how well you read and that you can think logically and express yourself clearly. It is *not* a measure of how many grammar rules you know.

Part I

Part I of the GED Language Arts, Writing Test measures your ability to use the conventions of standard written English. These conventions include sentence structure, usage, and mechanics.

All items in Part I are multiple-choice questions. Each question has five answer choices. You are first asked to read a paragraph or two. Then, you respond to a series of questions that focus on certain sentences within those paragraphs.

Three types of multiple-choice questions appear on the test: sentence correction questions (45 percent of all items), sentence revision questions (35 percent), and construction shift questions (20 percent).

SENTENCE CORRECTION QUESTIONS

These questions ask you to find what is wrong with a sentence and to determine how it can be corrected. Here is a sample:

1. Sentence 2: **Dorothy and her assistant evaluates 20 applications every day.**

   What correction should be made to this sentence?

   (1) Insert a comma after Dorothy
   (2) Insert a comma after assistant
   (3) Change the spelling of assistant to assistent
   (4) Change evaluates to evaluate
   (5) No correction is necessary

The correct answer is (4). To find the correct answer to this sample, you need to know something about commas, spelling, and verbs because those are the kinds of changes covered by the choices. If you know when and why to use commas, you will know that choices (1) and (2) are not correct. Choice (3) has a misspelled word. Looking back at the sample sentence, you can see that

the verb doesn't agree in number with the subject. Choice (4), therefore, is the correct answer. The plural verb *evaluate* agrees with the plural subject *Dorothy and her assistant.*

Note: *If you are offered an answer choice that says no correction is necessary, do not assume that it is the correct choice. Occasionally it will be, but it will not always. You must consider all answer choices as possibilities.*

SENTENCE REVISION QUESTIONS

These questions have a specific portion of a sentence underlined. Your task is to choose the answer that best improves the underlined portion:

2. Sentence 4: **After they attended the technology workshop the accounting clerks felt more confident about using computers.**

   Which of the following is the best way to write the underlined portion of the sentence? If you think the original is the best way, choose option (1).

   (1) workshop the accounting clerks felt
   (2) workshop, the accounting clerks felt
   (3) workshop the Accounting Clerks felt
   (4) workshop the accounting clerks will feel
   (5) workshop. The accounting clerks felt

The correct answer is (2). To find the correct answer to this sample, you need to know something about punctuation, capitalization, and verb tense because those are the kinds of changes offered by the choices. The correct answer is choice (2). It inserts a comma after the dependent clause that introduces the sentence.

CONSTRUCTION SHIFT QUESTIONS

These questions ask you to choose a better way to write a sentence that contains no mechanical errors but may be awkwardly written. The same idea must be expressed in a clearer, smoother way, or you may be asked to combine two sentences more effectively. Either way, to find the correct answer, you must understand the meaning of the original sentence (or sentences). Here is a sample:

3. Sentence 5: **Schools all across America are seeking ways to address the needs of children who have a wide range of ethnic backgrounds, which is a major problem that educators struggle to solve.**

If you rewrote sentence 5 beginning with American educators seek ways to, the next word should be

(1) struggle.
(2) need.
(3) help.
(4) separate.
(5) employ.

The correct answer is (3). Here, the original sentence tells you that *educators want to find ways to meet the needs of students with varying ethnic backgrounds.* The answer that most closely expresses this idea is choice (3): *help.*

Note: *It is in your best interest to answer every question on the test whether or not you know the answer. There is no penalty for guessing. When you are stuck, relax and then make your best guess.*

Part II

Part II of the GED Language Arts, Writing Test measures your ability to state an opinion on a given topic or to explain something. You will need to write an essay that clearly states ideas and supports them effectively with detailed reasons and examples. Your essay will be evaluated on how clear, well organized, and free of mechanical errors it is. It will need to be about 250 words in length.

You will not have a choice of topics. You will make decisions, however, on how to respond to the topic that is given to you. Notice in the example that follows that the GED essay topic has two parts. The first part introduces the topic by giving you some background information about it. The second part tells what the topic is; that is, it tells you what you must write about.

SAMPLE ESSAY TOPIC

More and more homes have electronic devices like compact disc players, computerized games, and personal computers. One of the most popular electronic inventions is the videocassette recorder (VCR). In an essay of 250 words, discuss the advantages, disadvantages, or both of owning a VCR. Be sure to support your ideas with details and examples.

For this sample topic, you might choose to discuss as advantages the convenience of recording television shows to watch later and the wide choice of movies a VCR owner can watch comfortably at home.

Unit 1

SENTENCE STRUCTURE

Avoiding Sentence Fragments

When we speak to each other, we don't worry about complete sentences. Even if we hear only pieces or fragments of sentences, the situation in which we hear the words fills in for the sentence's missing words.

When we write, complete sentences help our readers understand us.

A **complete sentence** must meet three requirements:

1. It must *have a subject.*

2. It must *have a complete verb.*

3. It must *express a complete thought.*

A **fragment** is a word group that may *look like* a sentence because it begins with a capital letter and ends with a period. However, a fragment is not a sentence because it lacks either a subject, a verb, or a verb part or because it does not express a complete thought.

Usually, if you read a word group out loud, you can tell if it's not a complete sentence because it won't sound finished. Something will be missing, and you will have questions like Who? or What? or What about it?

Being late to work.

What about being late to work? To complete the sentence, we have to answer the question: *Being late to work can cost you your job.*

It's true that we often can figure out what a fragment means because of the preceding sentence or sentences. But a complete sentence must have meaning on its own, regardless of what the sentences before and after it say.

A fragment may lack a subject. The following words look like a sentence:

Fell off the horse.

However, the words make no sense because we can't tell who or what fell off the horse. There's no subject. The **subject** of a sentence tells us who or what the sentence is about. To correct this fragment, add a subject:

The *jockey* fell off the horse.

When you're looking for the subject of a sentence, look for the doer or the actor. Ask yourself who or what is doing something in the sentence. If you can't find an answer, there probably is no subject, and you're probably looking at a sentence fragment.

Here is another word group that looks like a sentence but isn't:

Five dogs in our neighborhood.

These words don't make sense because you don't know anything about the five dogs. You don't know who they are or what they are doing because there is no **verb.** The verb in a sentence tells what the subject *does* or what it *is.*

Action verbs show that the subject is *doing* something. To correct this fragment, add a verb.

Five dogs in our neighborhood growled.

Linking verbs show no action, but they tell what the subject *seems like,* what it *is,* or how it *feels.*

The five dogs in our neighborhood *seem* ferocious. Actually, they *are* harmless unless they *feel* threatened.

Sometimes fragments occur because the verb is not complete.

Music blaring outside my window.

Because *blaring* expresses an action, you may see it as a verb. But it really is only part of a verb, and without the other part, the word group doesn't make sense. To correct this fragment, complete the verb by adding *is.*

Music is blaring outside my window.

Exercise 1

Directions: Choose the one best answer for each item.

Items 1–3 refer to the following paragraph.

(1) *AIDS is a devastating disease that the medical profession has trouble.* (2) *Understanding or treating.* (3) *The name is an abbreviation for* acquired immuno-deficiency syndrome. (4) *People with AIDS suffer a breakdown.* (5) *In their bodies' immune systems.* (6) *In a healthy body, a certain type of white blood cell attacks foreign substances that enter it.* (7) *That type of cell protects us from disease.* (8) *Scientists believe that AIDS is caused by a virus that kills this particular type of blood cell.* (9) *Leaving the AIDS victim defenseless against infection and tumors.* (10) *Researchers hope to produce a vaccine against AIDS.*

1. Sentences 1 and 2: **AIDS is a devastating disease that the medical profession has trouble. Understanding or treating.**

   Which of the following is the best way to write the underlined portion of these sentences? If you think the original is the best way, select choice (1).

   (1) trouble. Understanding or
   (2) trouble. To understand or
   (3) trouble understanding or
   (4) trouble understanding. Or
   (5) trouble. With understanding or

2. Sentences 4 and 5: **People with AIDS suffer a breakdown. In their bodies' immune systems.**

   Which of the following is the best way to write the underlined portion of these sentences? If you think the original is the best way, select choice (1).

   (1) breakdown. In their
   (2) breakdown in their
   (3) breakdown in. Their
   (4) breakdown. That's in
   (5) breakdown that's also in

3. Sentence 9: **Leaving the AIDS victim defenseless against infection and tumors.**

   What correction should be made to this sentence?

   (1) Change Leaving to Leaves
   (2) Replace Leaving with This leaves
   (3) Replace victim defenseless with victim. Defenseless
   (4) Insert is after victim
   (5) Replace defenseless against with defenseless. Against

Directions: Choose the one best answer for each item.

Items 4 and 5 refer to the following paragraph.

(1) *After becoming concerned about the environment, many people have decided to try recycling.* (2) *Most commonly, newspapers, glass, and aluminum cans.* (3) *However, automotive oil, cardboard, and plastic can be recycled too.* (4) *In most communities, several recycling centers taking these materials.* (5) *Some are private operations, and others are public.*

4. Sentence 2: **Most commonly, newspapers, glass, and aluminum cans.**

   What correction should be made to this sentence?

   (1) Insert they before newspapers
   (2) Insert collect before newspapers
   (3) Insert they collect before newspapers
   (4) Insert collecting before newspapers
   (5) Insert collected before newspapers

5. Sentence 4: **In most communities, several recycling centers taking these materials.**

   What correction should be made to this sentence?

   (1) Replace communities, several with communities. Several
   (2) Replace centers taking with centers. Taking
   (3) Remove taking
   (4) Change taking to take
   (5) No correction is necessary

Check your answers on page 128.

CLAUSES

A **clause** is a group of words containing a subject and a verb.

Independent clauses

Independent clauses can stand alone. They can also be combined with other clauses to make longer sentences.

Example: I have a headache.

Dependent Clauses

Some clauses have no meaning by themselves.

Example: Whenever I drink milk.

They *depend* on another word group for their meaning and, therefore, are called **dependent clauses.**

Example: When the lions entered the circus ring.

A dependent clause is a sentence fragment. One way to correct this kind of fragment is to attach the dependent clause to an independent clause:

The crowd roared with excitement when the lions entered the circus ring.

Another way is to eliminate the word that makes the clause dependent:

The lions entered the circus ring.

These words often begin a dependent clause:

after	even though	until
although	if	when
as	since	whenever
because	though	where
before	unless	wherever

Exercise 2

Directions: Choose the one best answer for each item.

Items 1–3 refer to the following paragraph.

(1) *While she prepares to become an American citizen.* (2) *Kimiko attends a class once a week.* (3) *In the class, students from all over the world.* (4) *Studying U.S. government.* (5) *Kimiko will be ready to pass the naturalization examination after completing the class.* (6) *It will be a proud day for her and the others when they receive their U.S. citizenship.*

1. Sentences 1 and 2: **While she prepares to become an American citizen. Kimiko attends a class once a week.**

   Which of the following is the best way to rewrite the underlined portion of these sentences? If you think the original is the best way, select choice (1).

   (1) American citizen. Kimiko
   (2) American citizen, Kimiko
   (3) American citizen: Kimiko
   (4) American citizen Kimiko
   (5) American citizen; Kimiko

2. Sentences 3 and 4: **In the class, students from all over the world. Studying U.S. government.**

   Which of the following is the best way to write the underlined portion of these sentences? If you think the original is the best way, select choice (1).

   (1) world. Studying
   (2) world studying
   (3) world that studying
   (4) world are studying
   (5) world have studying

3. Sentence 5: **Kimiko will be ready to pass the naturalization examination after completing the class.**

   If you rewrote sentence 5 beginning with After she completes the class, the next word should be

   (1) they.
   (2) everyone.
   (3) Kimiko.
   (4) students.
   (5) citizens.

Check your answers on page 128.

AVOIDING RUN-ON SENTENCES AND COMMA SPLICES

A **run-on sentence** is simply a string of two or more sentences written as a single sentence.

Incorrect: Charles worked late last night he didn't get enough sleep he fell asleep in class today.

Correct: Charles worked late last night, and he didn't get enough sleep. He fell asleep in class today.

When you write, if you have more than one complete thought to express, you must take care to separate the thoughts with proper punctuation and connecting words. Sometimes writers try to avoid run-ons by inserting commas after each complete thought. Then it becomes a list of ideas rather than a sentence.

A series of complete thoughts separated by commas only is called a **comma splice**.

Incorrect: The lawn mower made too much noise in the early morning, it annoyed Dorothy, she asked the neighbor to mow the lawn later in the day, the neighbor agreed, Dorothy felt better, it was quiet for a while.

Correct: The lawn mower made too much noise in the early morning, and it annoyed Dorothy. She asked the neighbor to mow the lawn later in the day. The neighbor agreed. Dorothy felt better. It was quiet for a while.

To correct a run-on or comma splice:

- Write the thoughts as separate sentences.

- Separate closely related thoughts using a semicolon.

- Connect the thoughts using a comma and a conjunction. Some common conjunctions are and, or, but, for, yet, and so.

- Connect the thoughts using a semicolon and a transitional word or phrase followed by a comma.

Incorrect: The movie was sold out, we didn't get in.

Corrections: The movie was sold out. We didn't get in.

The movie was sold out; we didn't get in.

The movie was sold out, so we didn't get in.

The movie was sold out; as a result, we didn't get in.

If either of the independent clauses in a run-on already contains commas, you should always use a semicolon to separate the independent clauses.

Akemi, Maria, Lucas, and Tom enjoyed the movie; but Sumio, Mario, and Irene didn't like it.

Exercise 3

Directions: Choose the one best answer for each item.

Items 1–3 refer to the following paragraph.

(1) *Although the reunification of Germany and the breakdown of the Soviet Union held out hope for a more peaceful world, the ending of the Cold War has had a serious economic impact on Americans.* (2) *As the defense industry cut back, many people found themselves unemployed highly skilled workers suddenly faced an uncertain future.* (3) *Military personnel no longer felt secure about their career choice.* (4) *The government closed bases at home and abroad this affected service people and also hurt the civilians who worked on these bases.* (5) *We must find ways to turn defense industries to peaceful endeavors it's tragic to waste the skills of former defense workers.*

1. Sentence 2: **As the defense industry cut back, many people found themselves unemployed highly skilled workers suddenly faced an uncertain future.**

    What correction should be made to this sentence?

    (1) Replace back, many with back. Many
    (2) Replace people found with people. Found
    (3) Rremove many
    (4) Insert a semicolon after unemployed
    (5) Insert a semicolon after workers

2. Sentence 4: **The government closed bases at home and abroad this affected service people and also hurt the civilians who worked on these bases.**

    Which of the following is the best way to write the underlined portion of this sentence? If you think the original is the best way, select choice (1).

    (1) home and abroad this affected
    (2) home and abroad. This affected
    (3) home. And abroad this affected
    (4) home and abroad this affecting
    (5) home and abroad affected

3. Sentence 5: **We must find ways to turn defense industries to peaceful endeavors it's tragic to waste the skills of former defense workers.**

If you rewrote sentence 5 beginning with Because it's tragic to waste the skills of former defense workers, the next word would be

(1) skills.
(2) peaceful.
(3) endeavors.
(4) we.
(5) there.

Items 4–6 refer to the following paragraph.

---

(1) *"Doves" and "hawks" are terms that came into use during the Vietnam War.* (2) *Doves are birds that symbolize peace, but that became the name applied to people who opposed the war.* (3) *They wanted the United States to negotiate peace.* (4) *Hawks are more aggressive birds their name was applied to those who wanted to step up the fighting.* (5) *The terms continue to be used to identify people according to their attitudes toward global conflict.* (6) *For example, the media refers to those who advocate negotiated settlements as doves those who believe military force is the answer are called hawks.*

4. Sentence 2: **Doves are birds that symbolize peace, but that became the name applied to people who opposed the war.**

What correction should be made to this sentence?

(1) Remove the comma
(2) Replace peace, but with peace. But
(3) Replace the comma with a semicolon
(4) Replace but with yet
(5) Replace but with so

5. Sentence 4: **Hawks are more aggressive birds their name was applied to those who wanted to step up the fighting.**

Which of the following is the best way to write the underlined portion of this sentence? If you think the original is the best way, select choice (1).

(1) birds their
(2) birds, but their
(3) birds, so their
(4) birds; and their
(5) birds, their

6. Sentence 6: **For example, the media refers to those who advocate negotiated settlements as doves those who believe military force is the answer are called hawks.**

Which of the following is the best way to write the underlined portion of this sentence? If you think the original is the best way, select choice (1).

(1) doves those
(2) doves, because those
(3) doves, or those
(4) doves, those
(5) doves; those

Check your answers on page 128.

LINKING IDEAS OF EQUAL IMPORTANCE

A **simple sentence** contains one subject and one verb and expresses a complete thought, but a string of simple sentences is not very interesting to read. To make your writing more appealing, you should occasionally combine two or more ideas into one sentence.

Charles was thirsty. He poured a glass of juice.

Charles was thirsty, so he poured a glass of juice.

Both examples express the same ideas, but the second flows more smoothly.

When you combine independent clauses into single sentences, you're writing compound sentences. A **compound sentence** links ideas of equal importance. That is, each idea could stand by itself and make sense.

However, not all independent clauses can be combined effectively into compound sentences. Be sure to link only those ideas that are closely related.

The following two ideas, for example, would not make an effective compound sentence, since they have little to do with each other:

Armando borrowed three books from the library. Leah has always enjoyed browsing in libraries.

But the following two ideas are so closely related that it does make sense to link them into one sentence:

Armando borrowed three books from the library, but Leah was unable to find the books she wanted.

To clarify the relationship between two ideas, you must use connecting words.

To choose the proper connecting words, you must understand the relationship between the ideas in the two independent clauses. For example, it would be senseless to say:

> Milton was ill; however, he had to stay home from work.

The writer really means:

> Milton was ill; consequently, he had to stay home from work.

In this case, *however* is an inappropriate connector because it shows contrast between ideas. *Consequently* makes more sense because it shows that the second idea is the result of the first.

Some common connectors are *however, therefore, for example, furthermore,* and *then.*

Exercise 4

Directions: Choose the one best answer for each item.

Items 1–3 refer to the following paragraphs.

(1) *Some states charge a sales tax on food.* (2) *It seems like a fair tax because everyone has to buy food everyone pays the tax.* (3) *There are those, however, who think this kind of tax is unfair.* (4) *They point out that people with little money have to buy just as much food as people with lots of money.* (5) *These people spend a larger portion of their income on food, so they also pay a larger portion of their income on the taxes.*

(6) *Taxes that cost some people a higher proportion of their income than others are called regressive taxes.* (7) *Income taxes are called progressive taxes they increase proportionately as the taxpayer's income goes up.* (8) *Thus, a person earning $60,000 a year pays a higher tax than someone earning $18,000.* (9) *Because sales tax is regressive, many states do not apply it to food.* (10) *On the other hand, some states collect no state income tax they rely instead on other taxes, including sales tax on food.*

1. Sentence 2: **It seems like a fair tax because everyone has to buy food everyone pays the tax.**

   Which of the following is the best way to write the underlined portion of this sentence? If you think the original is the best way, select choice (1).

   (1) food everyone
   (2) food, everyone
   (3) food but everyone
   (4) food and everyone
   (5) food. Everyone

2. Sentence 7: **Income taxes are called progressive taxes they increase proportionately as the taxpayer's income goes up.**

   What correction should be made to this sentence?

   (1) Replace progressive taxes with progressive. Taxes
   (2) Insert a comma after the second taxes
   (3) Insert a semicolon after the second taxes
   (4) Replace proportionately as with proportionately. As
   (5) Remove as

3. Sentence 10: **On the other hand, some states collect no state income tax they rely instead on other taxes, including sales tax on food.**

   What correction should be made to this sentence?

   (1) Replace hand, some with hand. Some
   (2) Replace income tax they with income tax. They
   (3) Insert a comma after income tax
   (4) Remove they
   (5) Replace taxes, including with taxes. Including

Items 4–6 refer to the following paragraph.

(1) *Advertising is an essential feature of our economy.* (2) *Clever ads can entertain the public as they introduce them to goods and services.* (3) *Advertising gives consumers useful information on new products, so it also makes consumers want things they don't need.* (4) *Ads are everywhere; however, they appear on television, on the radio, in magazines, and in newspapers.* (5) *Some ads are misleading, so they cause people to spend money unwisely.* (6) *The wise consumer approaches advertising claims carefully.*

4. Sentence 3: **Advertising gives consumers useful information on new products, so it also makes consumers want things they don't need.**

What correction should be made to this sentence?

(1) Remove the comma after products
(2) Replace so with but
(3) Change products, so to products. So
(4) Replace so with then
(5) No correction is necessary

5. Sentence 4: **Ads are everywhere; however, they appear on television, on the radio, in magazines, and in newspapers.**

What correction should be made to this sentence?

(1) Replace however with for example
(2) Replace however with nevertheless
(3) Replace the comma after however with a semicolon
(4) Remove the comma after however
(5) No correction is necessary

6. Sentence 5: **Some ads are misleading, so they cause people to spend money unwisely.**

If you rewrote sentence 5 beginning with Misleading ads, the next word should be

(1) and.
(2) people.
(3) cause.
(4) prevent.
(5) help.

Check your answers on page 128.

LINKING IDEAS OF UNEQUAL IMPORTANCE

Besides combining two equally important ideas into one sentence, you can vary your sentence structure and make your writing more interesting with complex sentences.

Like a compound sentence, a **complex sentence** links two ideas into one sentence. However, in a complex sentence, one of the ideas is less important than the other and depends on the main idea for its meaning. The main idea appears in the independent clause.

Because he was late, Jeff decided not to stop at the cleaners on the way to work.

You see that, by itself, *Because he was late* doesn't make sense. When it's added to the independent clause *Jeff decided not to stop at the cleaners on the way to work* you understand it.

Dependent clauses may precede the main clause or they may follow it. If the dependent clause comes first, it is followed by a comma. If the dependent clause appears at the end of the sentence, a comma is not needed.

Because it was 102 degrees in the shade, they stayed in the house all day.

They stayed in the house all day because it was 102 degrees in the shade.

The connectors in complex sentences must accurately express the relationship between the ideas in the two clauses. Complex sentences relate ideas in several different ways.

- cause and effect
  Since the house was dark, they didn't ring the doorbell.

- contrast
  Leona turned down the invitation *despite the fact that* she loved parties.

- time
  They screamed *until* their throats hurt.

- place
  They put the key *where* no one would see it.

- condition
  If you work hard, you'll get good grades.

- similarity between the ideas in the two clauses
  Terry felt *as if* he could eat a horse.

Exercise 5

Directions: Choose the one best answer for each item.

Items 1–3 refer to the following paragraph.

(1) *The history of ice cream, perhaps America's favorite dessert, goes back to colonial times.* (2) *It was enjoyed by people like George Washington and Dolly Madison.* (3) *Although ice cream is delicious by itself.* (4) *It also forms the basis for other wonderful treats.* (5) *According to legend, in 1874 a businessman in Philadelphia combined ice cream with a carbonated beverage to create the ice-cream soda.* (6) *Laws were passed prohibiting the sale of ice-cream sodas on Sundays.* (7) *Because the drink was so sinfully delicious.* (8) *This led to a new creation.* (9) *A druggist in Illinois put noncarbonated syrup over ice cream and called it a Sunday.* (10) *The spelling changed over the years, and the ice-cream sundae became a favorite dessert.*

1. Sentences 3 and 4: **Although ice cream is delicious by itself. It also forms the basis for other wonderful treats.**

   Which of the following is the best way to write the underlined portion of these sentences? If you think the original is the best way, select choice (1).

   (1) itself. It
   (2) itself, it
   (3) itself, and it
   (4) itself, so it
   (5) itself because it

2. Sentence 5: **According to legend, in 1874 a businessman in Philadelphia combined ice cream with a carbonated beverage to create the ice-cream soda.**

   What correction should be made to this sentence?

   (1) Insert a period after legend
   (2) Insert a comma after Philadelphia
   (3) Insert a period after beverage
   (4) Insert a comma after create
   (5) No correction is necessary

3. Sentences 6 and 7: **Laws were passed prohibiting the sale of ice-cream sodas on Sundays. Because the drink was so sinfully delicious.**

   What correction should be made to these sentences?

   (1) Insert a semicolon after passed
   (2) Replace sodas on Sundays with sodas. On Sundays
   (3) Replace Sundays. Because with Sundays, but
   (4) Replace Sundays. Because with Sundays because
   (5) Insert a comma after drink

   Items 4 and 5 refer to the following paragraph.

   (1) *We can remember things more easily if we write them down.* (2) *Some people use calendars or appointment books, although others just use a piece of paper.* (3) *Then we have to remember to look at the reminder we wrote.* (4) *Jean forgot to look at her calendar.* (5) *She missed her dental appointment.*

4. Sentence 2: **Some people use calendars or appointment books, although others just use a piece of paper.**

   What correction should be made to this sentence?

   (1) Replace books, although with books. Although
   (2) Replace the comma with a semicolon
   (3) Remove the comma after books
   (4) Replace although with in order that
   (5) Replace although with whenever

5. Sentences 4 and 5: **Jean forgot to look at her calendar. She missed her dental appointment.**

   The most effective combination of sentences 4 and 5 would begin with which of the following words?

   (1) Unless
   (2) As soon as
   (3) Until
   (4) Because
   (5) Although

Check your answers on page 128.

USING MODIFIERS

A **modifier** is a word or word group that describes another word or word group in a sentence. Single-word modifiers (adjectives and adverbs) don't usually cause many problems with sentence structure, but it's important to be able to recognize them. **Adjectives** describe **nouns,** which are words that often represent people, places, or things (*angry* citizens). **Adverbs** describe verbs (meet *regularly*), adjectives (*very* angry), and other adverbs (*quite* regularly).

Prepositional phrases and verb phrases are the modifiers most likely to cause problems in writing.

When writers are careless about where they put modifiers, they confuse readers with unclear sentences.

The police officer spoke about heroic crime stoppers at the local high school.

The sentence suggests that the crime stoppers were from the local high school. The modifier *at the local high school* seems to be modifying *crime stoppers* because it appears next to it.

The police officer spoke at the local high school about heroic crime stoppers.

This time the modifier is next to *spoke,* the word it modifies.

81

Some sentences are unclear because of *dangling modifiers*. These phrases are confusing because there is nothing in the sentence they could logically modify.

> Diving into the pool, the tension was extreme.

Who was diving into the pool? Who was feeling the tension?

To correct dangling modifiers, you must change the main part of the sentence so that it includes something for the modifier to describe:

> Diving into the pool, *the athlete* felt extreme tension.

You may turn the modifier into a prepositional phrase:

> *Before diving into the pool,* the athlete felt extreme tension.

You may also turn the modifier into a dependent clause:

> The athlete felt extreme tension *before she dove into the pool.*

Exercise 6

Directions: Choose the one best answer for each item.

Items 1–3 refer to the following paragraph.

(1) *Counting on public transportation, schedules are very important.* (2) *People who ride buses count on them to be on time.* (3) *Most buses and commuter trains do stick closely to the advertised schedule.* (4) *Missing a bus is often the fault of the rider.* (5) *Carmela often gets last-minute phone calls at work that force her to miss her bus.* (6) *Tired from working late, missing the bus can be extremely annoying.* (7) *Carmela wonders whether it's any worse to be stuck in a traffic jam in her car.* (8) *Out of patience, another bus is seen coming down the street.* (9) *Once she boards the bus, she settles down and reads or naps.*

1. Sentence 1: **Counting on public transportation, schedules are very important.**

   If you rewrote sentence 1 beginning with For people who count on, the next word(s) should be

   (1) schedules.
   (2) public transportation.
   (3) work.
   (4) importance.
   (5) advertised.

2. Sentence 6: **Tired from working late, missing the bus can be extremely annoying.**

   If you rewrote sentence 6 beginning with Because Carmela is tired from working late, the next word should be

   (1) missing.
   (2) annoying.
   (3) working.
   (4) the.
   (5) while.

3. Sentence 8: **Out of patience, another bus is seen coming down the street.**

   Which of the following is the best way to write the underlined portion of this sentence? If you think the original is the best way, select choice (1).

   (1) another bus is seen coming
   (2) the bus is coming
   (3) the bus sees
   (4) Carmela sees another bus coming
   (5) Carmela is seen coming

Check your answers on page 128.

PARALLEL STRUCTURE

You've already learned about compound sentences, which contain two or more complete thoughts. Many sentences also contain compound elements. This means parts within the sentence are linked with connecting words, such as *and, but,* and *or.* To maintain clarity in your writing, it's important to put elements that play similar roles within a sentence into the same form. Consider the following sentences:

> Incorrect: JoAnn does billing for a dentist, a law firm, and one doctor's office also employs her.

> Correct: JoAnn does billing for a dental group, a law firm, and a doctor's office.

The sentence names three businesses for which JoAnn does billing, so all three play the same role in the sentence. They should be written in the same form, which we call **parallel structure**. As you can see, a sentence that lacks parallel structure does not flow smoothly.

Sometimes sentences lack parallel structure because the writer adds an entire clause when a single word is better. For example:

> Dogs require food, shelter, and you have to bathe them.

The sentence above tells us three things about dogs. Two of those things are expressed as nouns (*food* and *shelter*), but the third is expressed as a clause, with a subject (*you*) and a verb (*have*).

Parallel structure expresses each requirement as a noun and changes the sentence:

Dogs require food, shelter, and baths.

Sometimes sentences lack parallel structure because the writer switches subjects in midsentence. Think about this example:

At parks, people play baseball, toss Frisbees, and parks are good places to talk to friends.

This sentence has three word groups, but the third one changes subjects from *people* to *parks,* which spoils the parallel structure. A better sentence would be:

At parks, people play baseball, toss Frisbees, and talk to friends.

Exercise 7

Directions: Choose the one best answer for each item.

Items 1–3 refer to the following paragraphs.

(1) *The Peace Corps was established in 1961, during President John F. Kennedy's administration.* (2) *That year, about three thousand volunteers worked in Asia, in Africa, and countries in Latin America to help the natives improve their standard of living.* (3) *Peace Corps workers live among the natives, learn their language, and their standard of living is just like that of the natives.* (4) *Their pay, about $75 a month, is deposited for them in the United States, and they receive travel and living expenses.* (5) *Although most Peace Corps volunteers are young men and women, the age range is from eighteen to sixty.*

(6) *Not only has this program developed good will between the United States and underdeveloped countries, it has taught people in hundreds of communities to help themselves improve their lives.* (7) *Some people believe all Americans, when they reach the age of eighteen, should be required to serve for two years either at home or go to foreign countries.*

1. Sentence 2: **That year, about three thousand volunteers worked in Asia, in Africa, and countries in Latin America to help the natives improve their standard of living.**

   Which of the following is the best way to write the underlined portion of this sentence? If you think the original is the best way, select choice (1).

   (1) and countries in Latin America
   (2) and other countries in Latin America
   (3) and in Latin America
   (4) and the many countries of Latin America
   (5) and countries that are in Latin America

2. Sentence 3: **Peace Corps workers live among the natives, learn their language, and their standard of living is just like that of the natives.**

   Which of the following is the best way to write the underlined portion of this sentence? If you think the original is the best, select choice (1).

   (1) their standard of living is just like that of the natives
   (2) share their standard of living
   (3) their standard of living is the same
   (4) their standard of living matches that of the natives
   (5) standard of living goes down

3. Sentence 7: **Some people believe all Americans, when they reach the age of eighteen, should be required to serve for two years either at home or go to foreign countries.**

   What correction should be made to this sentence?

   (1) Replace of eighteen, should with of eighteen. Should
   (2) Replace years either with years. Either
   (3) Remove at
   (4) Replace go to with in
   (5) No correction is necessary

Items 4–9 refer to the following paragraph.

(1) *One way to give children a sense of family history is to share memories with them.* (2) *Through memories, children can learn about relatives they may not see often, such as aunts, uncles, cousins, or even grandparents.* (3) *It can be fun for parents to share family memories with their children.* (4) *They can do this through photographs, scrapbooks, and the children ask questions.* (5) *Modern technology makes it easier than ever to capture the past.* (6) *Many types of cameras help people record family events, capture vacation highlights, and remembering all kinds of things.* (7) *Cameras come in a wide range of prices and sophistication, from video cameras that record sound to disposable cameras that are used once and turned in with the film.* (8) *With the help of cameras, tape recorders, and by keeping diaries, parents can easily look back on their children's growing up.* (9) *Adults are often amused by their own childhood photos, drawings, report cards, and to remember special times from years back.* (10) *To record your children's growing up is giving them a precious gift for their later years.*

4. Sentence 2: **Through memories, children can learn about relatives they may not see often, such as aunts, uncles, cousins, or even grandparents.**

   What correction should be made to this sentence?

   (1) Replace relatives they with relatives. They
   (2) Replace often, such as with often. Such as
   (3) Insert including before cousins
   (4) Insert their before grandparents
   (5) No correction is necessary

5. Sentence 4: **They can do this through photographs, scrapbooks, and the children ask questions.**

   Which of the following is the best way to write the underlined portion of this sentence? If you think the original is the best way, select choice (1).

   (1) the children ask questions
   (2) when the children ask questions
   (3) children's questions
   (4) whenever the children ask questions
   (5) the parents answer questions

6. Sentence 6: **Many types of cameras help people record family events, capture vacation highlights, and remembering all kinds of things.**

   What correction should be made to this sentence?

   (1) Change record to recording
   (2) Insert to before capture
   (3) Change remembering to to remember
   (4) Change remembering to remember
   (5) No correction is necessary

7. Sentence 8: **With the help of cameras, tape recorders, and by keeping diaries, parents can easily look back on their children's growing up.**

   What correction should be made to this sentence?

   (1) Replace by keeping diaries with diaries
   (2) Replace With the help of with By
   (3) Remove can easily
   (4) Replace can easily look with by looking
   (5) No correction is necessary

8. Sentence 9: **Adults are often amused by their own childhood photos, drawings, report cards, and to remember special times from years back.**

   What correction should be made to this sentence?

   (1) Replace photos with pictures
   (2) Replace drawings with they drew pictures
   (3) Replace to remember with memories of
   (4) Remove report cards
   (5) Remove from years back

9. Sentence 10: **To record your children's growing up is giving them a precious gift for their later years.**

   What correction should be made to this sentence?

   (1) Replace To with Parents who
   (2) Replace To record with When you record
   (3) Insert like before giving
   (4) Change giving to to give
   (5) Remove their

Check your answers on page 128.

Unit 2

USAGE AND GRAMMAR

Subject-Verb Agreement

You already know that subjects and verbs are the basic components of a complete sentence. To do well on the GED Language Arts, Writing Test, you must also understand how to write those subjects and verbs in their correct forms.

Can you tell that something is wrong with the following sentence?

Lee and Melva lives in a mountain community 65 miles from the nearest city.

The problem is that the verb *lives* doesn't match the subject *Lee and Melva. And* is the key word here. In discussing language, when we talk about one thing, we call it **singular.**

A tree grows in the park.

This sentence contains two singular nouns: *tree* and *park.* One of those nouns, *tree,* is the subject of the sentence. We can say this sentence has a singular subject. But if there is more than one tree in the park, the subject would be **plural:**

Several trees grow in the park.

Subject-verb agreement means that singular subjects take singular verbs and plural subjects take plural verbs. In English, we usually make a noun plural by adding *s* or *es* to it: *tree* becomes *trees.* A plural verb, however, never ends in *s.*

Here is a sentence with a *singular* subject and verb:

He goes to night school.

This sentence has a *plural* subject and verb:

Mark and Hakeem go to night school.

Remember that *compound* subjects are two words linked by *and.* They always take plural verbs:

Naomi and Judson sell hot dogs from a corner stand.

If the sentence has one subject and two verbs, be sure both verbs agree with the subject:

Every month, a *firefighter speaks* to our club and *shows* slides.

Exercise 1

Directions: Choose the correct verb from the pair in each of the following sentences.

1. Bruce Lee (was/were) a good actor.
2. They (cheer/cheers) for different teams.
3. Flashing yellow lights (warn/warns) drivers of road hazards.
4. Four-way stops (confuse/confuses) some drivers.
5. Elsa (take/takes) the bus everywhere.

Directions: Correct the following sentences for subject-verb agreement. Some sentences may not contain errors.

6. Charles play card games with his friends and sometimes he win.
7. Michelle seem to win every time she play.
8. Carla enjoys her job at the hardware store.
9. Computers scare my mother.
10. Mr. Chan hate long lines and becomes impatient in them.

Directions: Choose the one best answer for each item.

Items 11–13 refer to the following paragraph.

(1) *Strikes is the most powerful weapon workers have against unfair treatment by employers.* (2) *Strikes usually occur over wages, but working conditions can also be a source of dissatisfaction for laborers.* (3) *When all negotiation attempts fails, labor union members may vote to strike.* (4) *This means they stop work so that the employer will lose money.* (5) *The hope are that this tactic will force the employer to meet their demands.* (6) *They gamble that the employer would rather give in to them than risk*

85

the financial ruin of the company. (7) Strikes can last for weeks or even months and can be a severe hardship to the striking workers as well as to the company they work for. (8) The economic impact of these battles of will between labor and management can be felt in communities or across the nation for a long time.

11. Sentence 1: **Strikes is the most powerful weapon workers have against unfair treatment by employers.**

   What correction should be made to this sentence?

   (1) Change is to are
   (2) Change weapon to weapons
   (3) Change have to has
   (4) Replace have against with have. Against
   (5) Replace treatment by with treatment. By

12. Sentence 3: **When all negotiation attempts fails, labor union members may vote to strike.**

   Which of the following is the best way to write the underlined portion of this sentence? If you think the original is the best way, select choice (1).

   (1) negotiation attempts fails
   (2) negotiation attempts fail
   (3) negotiation attempt fail
   (4) negotiations attempt to fail
   (5) negotiation fails to attempt

13. Sentence 5: **The hope are that this tactic will force the employer to meet their demands.**

   What correction should be made to this sentence?

   (1) Replace The with They
   (2) Replace The with Their
   (3) Change hope are to hopes is
   (4) Change are to is
   (5) No correction is necessary

Check your answers on page 129.

Recognizing Singular and Plural Subjects

There are some nouns that seem to be plural because they refer to groups of individuals. However, these words usually take a singular verb:

   The *team practices* daily.

Here are some other nouns that take a singular verb:

   group   congress   choir   audience

There are also nouns that appear to be plural because they end in *s*, but they are actually singular and require a singular verb:

   No *news is* good news.

Here are some other nouns that appear to be plural but take a singular verb:

   physics   measles   athletics   economics   series

When a sentence has two subjects that are connected by *either/or* or *neither/nor*, the verb must agree with the subject closest to it. Compare the following two sentences:

   Either the doctor or the *nurses answer* questions.

   Either the nurses or the *doctor answers* questions.

Personal pronouns (*I, we, you, he, she, they,* and *it*) have their own set of subject-verb agreement rules. *He, she,* and *it* take a singular verb, while all the others (including the singular *I* and the singular *you*) take a plural verb:

- He/she/it (singular) goes.
- They (plural) go.
- I (singular) go.
- We (plural) go.
- You (singular or plural) go.

Sometimes beginning writers have trouble with subject-verb agreement when they work with the verb *to be*. You must learn the correct forms of that verb to avoid problems.

   Incorrect: They be late again.

   Correct: They are late again.

Here are the personal pronouns with correct forms for the verb *to be*:

   I am   you are   he/she/it is   we/they are
   I was   you were   he/she/it was   we/they were

To learn other tricky singular and plural subjects, study the list below. These words always take *singular* verbs:

another	either	one	nothing
anyone	everybody	other	somebody
anybody	everyone	either	someone
anything	everything	nobody	something
each	much	no one	

Example: *Everything costs* too much these days.

These words always take *plural* verbs:

both	few	many	several

Example: *Few put* forth their best effort.

Exercise 2

Directions: Determine whether the subjects in the following sentences are singular or plural and choose the correct verb from each pair.

1. Congress (vote/votes) on every tax law.

2. You (go/goes) first.

3. Today's news (look/looks) good.

4. The city council (choose/chooses) the site for games.

5. They (ask/asks) too many questions.

Directions: Choose the correct verb form for the following sentences.

6. She (say/says) to hurry back from the store.

7. No one (know/knows) the park rules.

8. I (am/be) too tired for a movie tonight.

9. Most (run/runs) on regular gasoline.

Directions: Choose the one best answer for each item.

Items 10 and 11 refer to the following paragraph.

(1) *A three-day weekend is coming up.* (2) *No one wants to waste a weekend, but Holly and Kent has no particular plans.* (3) *Kent thinks about going to the beach for at least one day.* (4) *Holly fears bad weather, so she suggest staying home instead.* (5) *Kent doesn't mind, as long as they find something relaxing to do.*

10. Sentence 2: **No one wants to waste a weekend, but Holly and Kent has no particular plans.**

    What correction should be made to this sentence?

    (1) Change wants to want
    (2) Remove the comma
    (3) Replace has with be without
    (4) Change has to have
    (5) Change Kent has to Kent. Has

11. Sentence 4: **Holly fears bad weather, so she suggest staying home instead.**

    What correction should be made to this sentence?

    (1) Change fears to fear
    (2) Remove the comma
    (3) Change weather, so to weather. She
    (4) Change suggest to suggests
    (5) Replace staying with they stays

Check your answers on page 129.

When Subjects Are Separated from Their Verbs

Matching a verb to a plural or a singular subject isn't difficult if you know what the subject is. Occasionally, however, you may be confused by phrases that appear between the subject and the verb. For example, can you select the correct verb in the following sentence?

Millie, like her sisters and her mother, (has/have) small feet.

To choose the correct verb, you must first determine who or what the subject is. Is *Millie* the subject in this sentence? Or is it *Millie and her mother and sisters*?

Remember: Two or more words *must* be joined by *and* to be a plural subject. In the sentence above, only *Millie* is the subject. The verb form must be the singular, *has*. To take a plural verb, the subjects would have to be linked by *and:*

Millie, her sisters, *and* her mother have small feet.

Notice that in the original sentence, the interrupting words *like her sisters and her mother* are set off by commas. Sometimes, however, words that separate the subject and verb are not set apart by commas, so it's easier to mistake them for the subject. These interrupters are the prepositional phrases. One way to be certain of the subject is to identify the prepositional phrase and see how the sentence sounds without it. Try this sentence:

One of the dancers (is/are) especially graceful.

If you set aside the prepositional phrase *of the dancers,* you can see the subject next to the verb:

One . . . is.

Verb phrases can sometimes be subjects of sentences.

Studying for three straight hours (make/makes) me tired.

To identify the subject of this sentence, you might look at the verb and ask *who* or *what makes* me tired. You'll see that *studying,* not *hours,* is the subject of the sentence.

Exercise 3

Directions: Choose the one best answer for each item.

Items 1–3 refer to the following paragraphs.

(1) *Mr. Brewer wants his adult education students to learn math in the context of real life.* (2) *He feels it's not enough for them just to work problems from a book.* (3) *To show his class how math can really help them, he holds or has them enter several contests during the year.* (4) *The contests allow his students to have fun while they practice math and raises money.*

(5) *Once they filled a fishbowl with marbles, asked people to guess how many marbles there was, and awarded a free lunch to the winner.* (6) *Another time they entered and won a contest to guess how many soda cans the back of a pickup truck held.* (7) *To win, they had to practice their skills at estimating, multiplying, dividing, and measuring.* (8) *They used most of the prize money for an end-of-the-year field trip.* (9) *The class thinks the best thing about entering contests are winning.*

1. Sentence 4: **The contests allow his students to have fun while they practice math and raises money.**

   What correction should be made to this sentence?

   (1) Change allow to allows
   (2) Change fun while to fun. While
   (3) Change fun while to fun, while
   (4) Change practice to practices
   (5) Change raises to raise

2. Sentence 5: **Once they filled a fishbowl with marbles, asked people to guess how many marbles there was, and awarded a free lunch to the winner.**

   Which of the following is the best way to write the underlined portion of this sentence? If you think the original is the best way, select choice (1).

   (1) asked people to guess how many marbles there was
   (2) asked people to guess how many marbles was there
   (3) asked how many could guess the right number
   (4) asked people to guess how many marbles there were
   (5) asked people how many marbles there was

3. Sentence 9: **The class thinks the best thing about entering contests are winning.**

   What correction should be made to this sentence?

   (1) Change thinks to think
   (2) Remove entering
   (3) Change are to is
   (4) Change contests are to contests. Are
   (5) No correction is necessary

Check your answers on page 129.

When the Verb Comes before the Subject

As you have seen in this lesson, sometimes the structure of the sentence can make it difficult to spot errors in subject-verb agreement. This is especially true when the verb comes before the subject.

In sentences that begin with *There* or *Here*, the verb comes before the subject: *Here come the clowns.* The verb in the preceding sentence is *come*, but when we ask who or what comes, we see the subject is *the clowns*, which appears after the verb. As always, the subject must agree with the verb. It would be incorrect to write *Here comes the clowns* because that would put a singular verb with a plural subject.

Questions pose an additional problem for subject-verb agreement because they often split the verb into two parts with the subject in between: *Does Judith have her shoes?* The singular verb, *does*, must agree with the singular subject, *Judith*. It would be incorrect to write: *Do Judith have her shoes?*

Both the subject and the verb sometimes appear at the ends of sentences, which can cause some confusion:

In the backyard are two peach trees.

The subject of the sentence above, *peach trees,* is plural, so it must take a plural verb: *are.* If you think *back yard* is the subject, you will use a singular verb, which would be incorrect. *Backyard* is part of the prepositional phrase.

Follow these tips to ensure subject-verb agreement:

- Find the verb.

- Ask *who* or *what* is performing the action.

- Make the verb agree in number (*singular* or *plural*) with the subject.

Exercise 4

Directions: Choose the correct verb from the pairs in the sentences below.

1. There (is/are) too many leaves to rake in one afternoon.

2. (Does/Do) both of them want to go to the game?

3. In the cupboard (is/are) all the things you need to bake a cake.

4. Upstairs (is/are) two more bedrooms.

5. Here (is/are) the information you asked for.

Directions: Choose the one best answer for each item.

Items 6–11 refer to the following paragraph.

(1) *Many people hate to cook, but others find cooking is a good way to relax.* (2) *There is many ways to learn to cook.* (3) *One of the best ways are watching other people do it.* (4) *This can be done in an actual kitchen, in a cooking class, or by watching cooking programs on television.* (5) *There are all kinds of cooks.* (6) *Some people follow recipes carefully, measuring and counting with precision.* (7) *Others prefers to create as they go, tasting and testing along the way.* (8) *Cooks, especially when modifying recipes, has to use some basic math skills, such as estimating amounts.* (9) *In a well-stocked kitchen is many kinds of ingredients.* (10) *A creative cook must also be familiar with them all.* (11) *Otherwise, it would be difficult to know which herbs and spices goes best with different foods.* (12) *The kitchen is a place where creative people can experiment and expand their talents.*

6. Sentence 2: **There is many ways to learn to cook.**

    What correction should be made to this sentence?

    (1) Replace There with Here
    (2) Change is to are
    (3) Replace to learn with for learn
    (4) Change learn to learning
    (5) Change cook to cooking

7. Sentence 3: **One of the best ways are watching other people do it.**

    What correction should be made to this sentence?

    (1) Change are to is
    (2) Change are to be
    (3) Insert to before watching
    (4) Change watching to to watch
    (5) Change do to did

8. Sentence 7: **Others prefers to create as they go, tasting and testing along the way.**

    What correction should be made to this sentence?

    (1) Replace Others with Other people
    (2) Change prefers to prefer
    (3) Replace to create with creating
    (4) Insert they are before tasting
    (5) Insert everything before along

9. Sentence 8: **Cooks, especially when modifying recipes, has to use some basic math skills, such as estimating amounts.**

    If you rewrote sentence 8 beginning with When modifying recipes, cooks, the next word should be

    (1) has.
    (2) uses.
    (3) use.
    (4) estimates.
    (5) modify.

10. Sentence 9: **In a well-stocked kitchen is many kinds of ingredients.**

    Which of the following is the best way to write the underlined portion of this sentence? If you think the original is the best way, select choice (1).

    (1) In a well-stocked kitchen is many kinds
    (2) In a well-stocked kitchen many kinds
    (3) A well-stocked kitchen have many kinds
    (4) A well-stocked kitchen has many kinds
    (5) Many kinds of well-stocked kitchens

11. Sentence 11: **Otherwise, it would be difficult to know which herbs and spices goes best with different foods.**

What correction should be made to this sentence?

(1) Remove would
(2) Change to know to knowing
(3) Replace know which with know. Which
(4) Change goes to go
(5) Insert kinds of after different

Check your answers on page 129.

Using Verb Phrases

Understanding subject-verb agreement is important for clear writing. Verbs tell us not only *what* the subject does or is, but also *when*—past, present, or future. The form of the verb changes to show an action's place in time. Those forms indicate **verb tense**.

Notice that some tenses require more than one word in the verb form:

The relatives *have arrived* for the wedding.

A verb form with more than one word is called a **verb phrase,** containing a helping verb *(have)* and some form of the main verb *(arrive).*

To see how verb phrases affect meaning, look at the two sentences below:

Jake and Brigitte have gone to the store.

Jake and Brigitte went to the store.

From the first sentence we learn that the action (going to the store) happened at some unclear time in the past, but it was not too long ago. They are probably still at the store. That is, the action began in the past and continues into the present. Notice that the verb form includes two words, or a *verb phrase.*

The second sentence tells us something slightly different. We learn from that sentence that Jake and Brigitte went to the store at a particular time in the past, perhaps *this morning*, and the action is complete. (Presumably, they are back.) This verb form is in the simple past tense and uses only one word *(went).*

In the first sentence, the word *gone* is a **participle**. Because the action started in the past, it is a past participle. Participles may not be used alone as verbs. They must appear with a helping verb, such as *have*.

Participles can also be used to show action taking place in the present:

Ruth *is mowing* the lawn.

When we add *-ing* to a verb to show action that is occurring in the present, we form a present participle. This form of the verb also requires a helping verb, like *is*.

Gerunds are present participles that are used in sentences as nouns rather than as parts of verb phrases.

Her *dancing* on the table shocked everyone.

Compare the following sentences:

Their *working* extra hours impressed the boss.

Because of the new project, they are *working* extra hours this month.

In the first sentence, *working* is a gerund that is the subject of the sentence. The verb is *impressed*. In the second sentence *working* is part of a verb phrase. *They* is the subject of the sentence; *are working* is the verb.

Exercise 5

Directions: Identify the participles in the following sentences, paying attention to the meaning of the sentence, and determine whether the participle is past or present.

1. Jill and Evan are planning a party for next week.

2. Maurice had helped with the presentation.

3. The boss is sitting at Eva's table.

Directions: Choose the one best answer for each item.

Items 4–6 refer to the following paragraph.

(1) *Although much of the country suffers from crippling snowstorms, Californians usually have to drive to the mountains to see snow.* (2) *The California Highway Patrol knows that many people will be plan trips to the snow during wet winters.* (3) *The authorities warn people to prepare well for trips to the mountains.* (4) *A sudden storm could close roads and tie up traffic for hours.* (5) *Traveling without tire chains, good windshield wipers, plenty of gasoline, and antifreeze in your radiator is foolish.* (6) *Start out on a mountain drive without blankets and extra food and water could also be regrettable.* (7) *If you get stuck in the snow, you'll know you should have pay attention to the highway patrol's advice.*

4. Sentence 2: **The California Highway Patrol knows that many people will be plan trips to the snow during wet winters.**

What correction should be made to this sentence?

(1) Change knows that to knows. That
(2) Change plan to planning
(3) Change plan to planned
(4) Change snow during to snow. During
(5) No correction is necessary

5. Sentence 6: **Start out on a mountain drive without blankets and extra food and water could also be regrettable.**

What correction should be made to this sentence?

(1) Change Start to Starting
(2) Change drive to driven
(3) Insert take before blankets
(4) Change be to been
(5) Change regrettable to regretting

6. Sentence 7: **If you get stuck in the snow, you'll know you should have pay attention to the highway patrol's advice.**

Which of the following is the best way to write the underlined portion of this sentence? If you think the original is the best way, select choice (1).

(1) you should have pay attention
(2) you should have paying attention
(3) you should have been pay attention
(4) you should have attention
(5) you should have paid attention

Check your answers on page 129.

Using the Correct Verb Form

For most verbs in English, the past participle looks exactly like the simple past tense form of the verb. We merely place a helper in front of it:

The ponies *trotted* around the track.

The ponies *have trotted* around the track many times before.

Here are some frequently used regular verbs.

Present Tense (Today I . . .)	Past Tense (Yesterday I . . .)	Past Participle (Many times I have . . .)
sit	sat	sat
walk	walked	walked
play	played	played

Unfortunately, English contains numerous *irregular verbs* that have past participles that differ from their past-tense forms. There is, for example, the *I, A, U* group of verbs:

sing, sang, sung

ring, rang, rung

But watch out for these exceptions:

bring, brought, brought

swing, swung, swung

Because there are so many irregular verbs in English, you must listen and read carefully to become alert to them. The chart below shows you the forms of some frequently used irregular verbs.

Present Tense (Today I . . .)	Past Tense (Yesterday I . . .)	Past Participle (Many times I have . . .)
am	was	been
bring	brought	brought
choose	chose	chosen
come	came	come
do	did	done
eat	ate	eaten
forget	forgot	forgotten
go	went	gone
know	knew	known
see	saw	seen
take	took	taken
throw	threw	thrown
write	wrote	written

Be careful not to use participles alone, as if they were complete verbs. *"I seen you at the restaurant"* is incorrect. The writer means either *"I saw you at the restaurant"* (past tense) or *"I have seen you at the restaurant"* (verb phrase).

One other verb form to consider is the **infinitive**—a verb form with *to* in front of it: *to go, to stare, to study*. Infinitives function as nouns in sentences. It is important not to *split* an infinitive (separate its parts) in a sentence.

Incorrect: She didn't mean *to rudely stare* at the woman's unusual hat.

Correct: She didn't mean *to stare rudely* at the woman's unusual hat.

Exercise 6

Directions: Choose the one best answer for each item.

Items 1–3 refer to the following paragraph.

(1) *Not long ago, people thought the way to lose weight was to cutting out starchy foods like potatoes, pasta, and bread.* (2) *Believing that protein was better for them than carbohydrates, weight-conscious individuals ate extra meat.* (3) *High-protein diets made the dieters feel hungry and frustrated with their failed efforts to lose weight.* (4) *They would give up counting calories and go on eating binges, which caused them to gain back whatever pounds they had lose.* (5) *Nutritionists now understand the best way to reach and maintain a healthful weight is to cut fat rather than carbohydrates out of the diet.* (6) *It had not been the bread, potatoes, and pasta that caused weight problems.* (7) *Actually, it had been the butter, sour cream, and rich sauces that people were put on them.* (8) *Pasta and fresh vegetables has become one of the most popular meals among health-conscious people.*

1. Sentence 1: **Not long ago, people thought the way to lose weight was to cutting out starchy foods like potatoes, pasta, and bread.**

   What correction should be made to this sentence?

   (1) Change thought to thinked
   (2) Change thought to thinking
   (3) Change lose to losing
   (4) Change lose to lost
   (5) Change cutting to cut

2. Sentence 4: **They would give up counting calories and go on eating binges, which caused them to gain back whatever pounds they had lose.**

   If you rewrote sentence 4 beginning with Any weight they had, the next word should be

   (1) lose.
   (2) losing.
   (3) lost.
   (4) gained.
   (5) eaten.

3. Sentence 7: **Actually, it had been the butter, sour cream, and rich sauces that people were put on them.**

   What correction should be made to this sentence?

   (1) Change been to being
   (2) Replace had been with be
   (3) Remove had
   (4) Change put to putting
   (5) Change put to putten

Check your answers on page 130.

Using Verb Tenses

When you use verbs, their tense tells your reader when the action in a sentence or paragraph takes place. It is important to know whether an event happened in the past, is happening right now, happens all the time, or will happen later. Verb tense affects a reader's reaction to information.

When you write, you must be careful not to change tenses in midsentence or midparagraph. The following sentence is confusing because it changes from past to future tense:

The crowd *went* wild when the team *will enter* the stadium.

Does the writer mean the crowd *will go* wild or that the team *entered* the stadium?

The verb tense that uses a present tense helping verb with a past participle *(has gone)* is called present perfect. It may mean the action occurred over a period of time in the past, or that it occurred in the past but continues into the present.

A past tense helping verb with a past participle *(had gone)* is called past perfect, and it indicates that an action was completed in the past after another past action occurred:

By the time the sun came up, the street cleaners had finished their work.

Sometimes verbs use a past participle with the verb *to be* rather than *to have*. We call these verbs *passive*. They occur in sentences where the subject doesn't perform the action:

The ladder was placed against the fence.

In the sentence above, we don't see the actor—whoever placed the ladder against the fence. We see only the ladder that someone has placed against the fence. In passive sentences, the subject doesn't perform action; it receives it. Compare the following two sentences.

The telephone pole was hit hard.

The truck hit the telephone pole hard.

In the first sentence, no actor is apparent. Instead, the subject *(the telephone pole)* receives action. In the second sentence, the subject *(the truck)* appears and performs an action *(hits the telephone pole)*. Good writing tends most often to use active, rather than passive, verb structure.

Exercise 7

> **Directions:** Circle the time clues in the following sentences and then choose the correct verb tense.

1. When she heard thunder, the kitten (will crawl/crawled) under the chair.

2. Whenever it rains, I (feel/felt) cold all over.

3. By the time his roommate arrived, Guy (walks/had walked) home.

4. Now Jonathan loves cross-country skiing, but last year he (refuses/refused) to try it.

5. Currently, we (receive/received) only one newspaper, but next fall we will subscribe to two.

6. Now that school has started, I (am/was) ready to study.

7. Last year, Ken and Lucille (will have/had) a long vacation.

> **Directions:** Choose the one best answer for each item.

> Items 8–10 refer to the following passage.

(1) *Schools are frequently under attack for not teaching basic reading, writing, and math skills.* (2) *But even those children who do acquire basic skills in school may be poorly prepared for the world of work.* (3) *Included among workplace skills are being able to listen, speak, and work well with others.* (4) *A successful worker needs critical thinking skills, too.* (5) *Knowing how to handle information and modern technology also will help in the workplace.* (6) *Equally important were a sense of personal responsibility.* (7) *Business and labor are working with educators to close the skills gap between the classroom and the job.*

8. Sentence 3: **Included among workplace skills are being able to listen, speak, and work well with others.**

   If you rewrote sentence 3 beginning with Workplace skills, the next word should be

   (1) will.
   (2) had.
   (3) meant.
   (4) include.
   (5) were.

9. Sentence 5: **Knowing how to handle information and modern technology also will help in the workplace.**

   What correction should be made to this sentence?

   (1) Change Knowing to Know
   (2) Change handle to handling
   (3) Change will help to helps
   (4) Change will help to helped
   (5) Change help in to help. In

10. Sentence 6: **Equally important were a sense of personal responsibility.**

    What correction should be made to this sentence?

    (1) Change important were to important. Were
    (2) Change were to is
    (3) Change were to are
    (4) Change were to was
    (5) No correction is necessary

Check your answers on page 130.

Keeping Verb Tense Consistent Throughout a Paragraph

Within paragraphs, the clue for tense in one sentence often comes from the other sentences. This is an important concept to know for the multiple-choice section of the GED Language Arts, Writing Test. For example, if the first three sentences in a paragraph are written in the present tense, the fourth sentence should also be in the present tense. In the paragraph below, you can see what happens when tense changes unnecessarily:

> Kim's parents watch the news every evening. They like to keep up with current events. Kim watches with them, but she preferred game shows.

The sudden shift to past tense in the last sentence is incorrect and confusing. The writer probably meant that Kim *prefers* game shows.

There are times, however, when one sentence in a paragraph could require a different tense from the others. When this is the case, there will be a clue, as in the following example:

Last year the school parking lot *was* a disaster. Cars *parked* in no-parking zones, *blocked* driveways, and *hemmed* in other cars. No one *paid* attention to signs or directions. People *came* in and *went* out the same driveways, and there *were* several accidents. Finally, the police *were called* in to direct traffic and give tickets to illegally parked cars. *This year,* our parking lot *is* easy to use.

All the italicized clues call for past-tense verbs except for the last one, which calls for a present-tense verb.

Exercise 8

Directions: Write the word *present, past,* or *future* to indicate which verb tense would follow each of the clues below.

1. yesterday
2. when I get old
3. the other day
4. next summer
5. right now
6. when I was at my brother's house
7. whenever I hear loud noises
8. at this time tomorrow
9. for the next three months
10. last time

Directions: Correct the following paragraph for appropriate verb tense. All the verbs appear in *italics*. Not all the verbs are incorrect.

11. Last summer, the Orangerie Produce Co. *had* an employee picnic. The picnic *is* a great success, thanks to the Planning Committee. The committee members *will work* for weeks by the time picnic day *arrived*. The employees *had played* games, *danced, swam,* and *ate* hot dogs and apple pie by the end of the day. Everyone *will hope* there *was* another picnic next year.

Directions: Choose the *one best answer* for each item.

Items 12–15 refer to the following paragraphs.

(1) *For generations, the United States has been a haven for people from vastly different cultures.* (2) *The first wave of immigrants, who came primarily from Europe, poured into the country, learned American ways, and become part of the huge American "melting pot."* (3) *The idea of a melting pot suggests that everyone became the same, adopting the same attitudes, language, and customs.*

(4) *A new wave of immigration in the 1970s and 1980s has change this view of America.* (5) *While people continue to seek freedom and opportunity in the United States, they clung with pride to the culture of their homelands.* (6) *No longer wanting to be like everyone else, American citizens are taking renewed pride in their heritage.* (7) *It's common to hear a variety of languages in American schools.* (8) *Restaurants and food stores offer many kinds of ethnic foods.* (9) *Cultural fairs and festivals gave Americans an opportunity to learn about the music, stories, and costumes of one another's native countries.*

12. Sentence 2: **The first wave of immigrants, who came primarily from Europe, poured into the country, learned American ways, and become part of the huge American "melting pot."**

    Which of the following is the best way to write the underlined portion of this sentence? If you think the original is the best way, select choice (1).

    (1) poured into the country, learned American ways, and become part of
    (2) pour into the country, learn American ways, and become part of
    (3) poured into the country, learned American ways, and became part of
    (4) poured into the country, learn American ways, and become part of
    (5) pour into the country, learn American ways, and became part of

13. Sentence 4: **A new wave of immigration in the 1970s and 1980s has change this view of America.**

    What correction should be made to this sentence?

    (1) Replace has change with is changing
    (2) Replace has change with has changed
    (3) Change has to had
    (4) Remove has
    (5) No correction is necessary

14. Sentence 5: **While people continue to seek freedom and opportunity in the United States, they clung with pride to the culture of their homelands.**

    Which of the following is the best way to write the underlined portion of this sentence? If you think the original is the best way, select choice (1).

    (1) they clung with pride to
    (2) they clinged with pride to
    (3) they clang with pride to
    (4) they cling with pride to
    (5) they were proud of

15. Sentence 9: **Cultural fairs and festivals gave Americans an opportunity to learn about the music, stories, and costumes of one another's native countries.**

    What correction should be made to this sentence?

    (1) Change gave to give
    (2) Change gave to had given
    (3) Replace to with for
    (4) Remove to
    (5) Replace to with and

Check your answers on page 130.

Using Pronouns

Writing stays both interesting and clear when we use pronouns. **Pronouns** are words used to refer to nouns, where otherwise we would have to repeat the noun. Without them, both speech and writing would not only sound ridiculous but would be difficult to understand.

This is what would happen if we eliminated pronouns from our writing:

> Jason and Peter were longtime friends, Jason and Peter worked together in construction, and Jason and Peter shared Jason's and Peter's tools.

Three repetitions of the subjects' names would confuse the reader and sound very strange. Here's how pronouns improve writing:

> Jason and Peter were longtime friends who worked together in construction and shared their tools.

English has a variety of pronouns for several different purposes. The most common group of pronouns refers to specific people or things:

I	you	he	she
it	me	him	her
we	they	us	them

Example: The lifeguard said *we* can swim today.

Another group of pronouns refers to nonspecific people or things; that is, nouns that are not specified elsewhere in the sentence:

anyone	everybody	no one	anything
each	one	both	nothing
many	others	one	

Example: *Many* disagreed.

Some pronouns suggest ownership:

yours	his	hers	its
mine	theirs	ours	

Example: Joel said to keep *your* hands off *his* car.

Others are used for emphasis or to reflect back on the noun:

myself	ourselves	yourself	itself
himself	herself	themselves	

Examples: The children can tie their shoes by *themselves.* I, *myself,* wouldn't do that.

Exercise 9

Directions: Choose the one best answer for each item.

Items 1–4 refer to the following paragraph.

(1) *About 35 million Americans suffer from an illness called Seasonal Affective Disorder.* (2) *These 35 million Americans lack energy and feel sad and hopeless during the long nights and dreary days of winter.* (3) *Victims of SAD, as the disorder is called by psychiatrists, often overeat, gain weight, lose interest in his jobs, and have trouble with their relationships.* (4) *Children and adolescents, who suffer from SAD just like adults, exhibit disruptive behavior in school, have short attention spans, and lack interest in learning.* (5) *The illness affects more women than men.* (6) *Researchers think the dim light of winter causes a reduction in certain brain chemicals and that people who are sensitive to this deprivation feel the symptoms of SAD.* (7) *It's possible to buy special lights that are twenty times brighter than ordinary indoor lights.* (8) *To control the symptoms for many people.* (9) *Anyone who suffers from SAD should consult a physician for advice and treatment.*

1. Sentence 2: **These 35 million Americans lack energy and feel sad and hopeless during the long nights and dreary days of winter.**

   Which of the following is the best way to write the underlined portion of this sentence? If you think the original is the best way, select choice (1).

   (1) These 35 million Americans
   (2) Everyone
   (3) Because they
   (4) Sometimes
   (5) They

2. Sentence 3: **Victims of SAD, as the disorder is called by psychiatrists, often overeat, gain weight, lose interest in his jobs, and have trouble with their relationships.**

   What correction should be made to this sentence?

   (1) Change called to call
   (2) Change psychiatrists, often to psychiatrists. Often
   (3) Change overeat to overeats
   (4) Change gains to gained
   (5) Change his to their

3. Sentence 8: **To control the symptoms for many people.**

   Which of the following is the best way to write the underlined portion of this sentence? If you think the original is the best way, select choice (1).

   (1) To control the symptoms
   (2) They control the symptoms
   (3) Their control the symptoms
   (4) Its control of the symptoms
   (5) They themselves control the symptoms

4. Sentence 9: **Anyone who suffers from SAD should consult a physician for advice and treatment.**

   What correction should be made to this sentence?

   (1) Replace Anyone with They
   (2) Change suffers to suffer
   (3) Change consult to consulted
   (4) Change physician for to physician. For
   (5) No correction is necessary

Check your answers on page 130.

Choosing the Correct Pronoun

The form of personal pronouns, those that substitute for specific people, is determined by the role the pronoun plays in the sentence in which it appears. That means if the pronoun is the actor in the sentence, it must be in the subject form (*we, he, she, they*). If it's the receiver of the action, it must be in the object form (*us, him, her, them*).

Just as verbs must agree with the nouns they go with in a sentence, pronouns must agree with the nouns they replace. The noun that is replaced by a pronoun is called an **antecedent,** and pronouns must agree with their antecedents in two ways.

First, the pronoun and antecedent must agree in number. That is, if the noun is plural, the pronoun must be plural, and if the noun is singular, the pronoun must be singular. The most common mistake with pronoun agreement in number is to confuse *their* with *his* or *her* and *them* with *him* or *her.*

Incorrect: Each applicant must turn in their cards.

This sentence is incorrect because the antecedent, *applicant*, is singular, but the pronoun, *their*, is plural. The sentence should read:

Correct: Each applicant must turn in his or her card.

You can make the pronoun and antecedent agree in number in the above sentence by rewriting it and by changing the antecedent:

Correct: All applicants must turn in their cards.

This construction actually is preferable because it avoids the awkwardness of using *his or her*.

The following table shows that pronouns and antecedents must also agree by person.

Type of Pronoun	Pronoun
First-person pronouns (refer to *me*)	I, we, me, us, my, mine, our, ours, myself, and ourselves
Second-person pronouns (refer to *you*)	you, your, yourself, and yourselves
Third-person pronouns (refer to everyone and everything other than *me* or *you*)	he, she, it, they, him, her, them, his, hers, its, theirs, himself, herself, and themselves

If you write one part of a sentence or a paragraph in the third person, it would be incorrect to shift suddenly to first- or second-person pronouns. For example, if you're talking about *Marjorie* (third person), do not shift to *you* for the pronoun:

Incorrect: Marjorie knows that if she wants to win, *you* must practice every day.

Correct: Marjorie knows that if she wants to win, *she* must practice every day.

Exercise 10

Directions: Correct the pronouns in the following sentences, making sure they agree with the nouns and are in the proper form.

1. Manuel and Umeki agreed to share one's study notes with each other.

2. A baby seal can swim by themselves right away.

3. The basketball team lost their third game in a row.

Directions: Choose the one best answer for each item.

Items 4–6 refer to the following paragraph.

(1) *If you're looking for a bargain, many people love to shop in consignment stores.* (2) *For low prices, these stores sell used clothing and other items that are in good condition.* (3) *It's possible to find wonderful bargains and hidden treasures.* (4) *One might find great clothing for yourself and gifts for your friends.* (5) *Consignment items might come from people who need new clothes because they have gained or lost weight.* (6) *Some people just get tired of their perfectly good clothes and want to sell them.* (7) *After selling an item, the owner of the store gives a portion of the money to the original owner and keeps the rest.* (8) *They make money, and you get our bargain.*

4. Sentence 1: **If you're looking for a bargain, many people love to shop in consignment stores.**

   Which of the following is the best way to write the underlined portion of this sentence? If you think the original is the best way, select choice (1).

   (1) many people love to shop
   (2) they love to shop
   (3) you might like to shop
   (4) everyone loves to shop
   (5) I would prefer to shop

5. Sentence 4: **One might find great clothing for yourself and gifts for your friends.**

   What correction should be made to this sentence?

   (1) Replace One with I
   (2) Replace One with We
   (3) Replace One with They
   (4) Replace One with You
   (5) Replace One with It

6. Sentence 8: **They make money, and you get our bargain.**

   What correction should be made to this sentence?

   (1) Replace They with We
   (2) Replace They with You
   (3) Replace you with we
   (4) Replace you with they
   (5) Replace our with your

Check your answers on page 130.

97

Does the Pronoun Fit the Rest of the Sentence?

In some GED Writing Skills Test items, you will need to correct the use of pronouns and their antecedents. You've seen how confusing it can be when pronouns do not agree with their antecedents in number and person. Sometimes, antecedents are so unclear that readers can't tell whether or not the pronouns agree with them. Can you tell what all the pronouns refer to in the following passage?

A group of us had hoped to go fishing over the weekend. We had gathered several times at one person's house to plan the trip. We agreed that some of us would have to go to the store to purchase supplies, while the others would get the boat and fishing gear ready. The day before the trip, when it was time to buy the food, they were so tired that we decided to forget it.

The last sentence above raises a few questions: Who are *they?* Are they the people who were going on the trip? Are they the people who sold supplies? What is *it* they decided to forget? Is it shopping for supplies, or is it the entire fishing trip?

When you use pronouns, you must make sure the antecedents are clear. Otherwise, the reader can't tell what the pronoun refers to and probably won't be able to understand what you mean.

Unclear pronoun references usually occur for one of three reasons:

1. There are two possible antecedents for a single pronoun.

   Mario told Albert *he* was wrong.

Because either *Mario* or *Albert* could be the antecedent for the pronoun *he*, the reader can't tell who was wrong.

2. The antecedent is placed too far away from the pronoun.

   At the bottom of the hill was a huge forest. Hundreds of trees crowded together to hide the sky. Pine needles covered up the paths, and overgrown shrubs and vines blocked the view. Hiking to the other side was difficult. The campers were frightened by *it.*

The pronoun *it* is so far from its antecedent *forest* that a reader might wonder what *it* is.

3. There is no antecedent.

   Patricia always loved school, which made her want to become a teacher.

The pronoun *which* doesn't refer to any particular noun. You might rewrite the sentence to read: *The fact that Patricia always loved school made her want to become a teacher.*

Exercise 11

Directions: Choose the one best answer for each item.

Items 1–3 refer to the following paragraph.

(1) *Historians and sociologists study periods of time and attach labels to them.* (2) *Some decades, for example, carry names that suggest their main characteristics.* (3) *We refer to the last decade of the 1800s as the Gay Nineties because of its general prosperity.* (4) *These were years when people had jobs.* (5) *They were industrially productive.* (6) *The Roaring Twenties suggests a time of wild behavior, when women cut her hair short and smoked cigarettes.* (7) *Wild dances like the Charleston were popular, and young people drove fast cars and partied a great deal.* (8) *Student protest, the sexual revolution, and feminism characterize the radical '60s and '70s.* (9) *The 1980s are seen as a time of greed, when selfish pursuit of money is what drove them.*

1. Sentences 4 and 5: **These were years when people had jobs. They were industrially productive.**

   The most effective combination of sentences 4 and 5 would include which of the following groups of words?

   (1) Although people had jobs
   (2) Although they were industrially productive
   (3) During these industrially productive years
   (4) Despite their productivity
   (5) Even though most people had jobs

2. Sentence 6: **The Roaring Twenties suggests a time of wild behavior, when women cut her hair short and smoked cigarettes.**

   What correction should be made to this sentence?

   (1) Replace her with our
   (2) Replace her with their
   (3) Replace her with its
   (4) Replace her with hers
   (5) No correction is necessary

3. Sentence 9: **The 1980s are seen as a time of greed, when selfish pursuit of money is what drove them.**

Which of the following is the best way to write the underlined portion of this sentence? If you think the original is the best way, select choice (1).

(1) selfish pursuit of money is what drove them
(2) they were driven by selfish pursuit of money
(3) selfish pursuit of money motivated them
(4) people selfishly pursued money
(5) they were selfish and drove big cars

Check your answers on page 130.

Using Relative Pronouns

Relative pronouns are a special kind of pronoun; they don't actually replace a noun but refer to it.

| who | whom | which |
| whoever | whomever | that |

Relative pronouns give you another way to combine ideas into a single sentence.

Simple sentence with a relative pronoun clause: People *who want muscular bodies* work out regularly.

When we refer to animals or things, we use *that* or *which*, but when we refer to people, we use *who* or *whom*.

The birds *that* sing all morning have built a nest in our tree.

The people *who* sing in the choir have nice voices.

Many people are troubled by *who* and *whom* because they can't figure out which one to use. You can solve this problem by remembering that *who* is used in the subject or actor position in a sentence or clause, and *whom* is used in the object or receiver position.

In the sentence below, the relative pronoun *who* is used as the subject of a clause. *Is going* is the verb.

Give a ticket to everyone *who* is going.

In the following sentence, the relative pronoun *whom* is used as an object:

The man *whom* the police suspected was proved innocent.

When you're not sure whether to use *who* or *whom*, look only at the words in the clause. Mentally substitute *he* or *him* for the pronoun, and if *he* fits, use who; if *him* fits, use whom.

The officer told the jury (*who/whom*) was at the scene of the crime.

Make the *he/him* substitution, and you find that only *he* makes sense:

The officer told the jury (*he/who*) was at the scene of the crime.

Exercise 12

Directions: Choose the correct relative pronouns in the following sentences.

1. All the dogs (who/that) went to obedience school can perform tricks.

2. Everyone (who/that) asked received an announcement.

3. Mrs. Doak, (who/which) lives next door, travels every summer.

4. (Who/Whom) shall I ask to help?

5. They finally fixed the car (who/that) had broken down four times.

6. (Whoever/Whomever) wants to come is welcome.

Directions: Choose the one best answer for each item.

Items 7–11 refer to the following paragraph.

(1) Because of their convenience, more and more people are running businesses out of their homes. (2) A home-based business is good for anyone who can discipline themselves. (3) Some companies allow employees to work at home, so they can have a home office without owning their own business. (4) People that work at home might miss the company of other workers and become lonely. (5) However, some people do very well on your own. (6) Working at home means one must be careful not to get caught up in the distractions of family, housework, or watching television instead of working; it can be a problem. (7) Some people who work at home find they snack all day long and gain weight. (8) Some home-based workers work late into the night and fail to get enough sleep, but others find the quiet of night hours the most appealing part of working in a home office.

7. Sentence 1: **Because of their convenience, more and more people are running businesses out of their homes.**

Which of the following is the best way to write the underlined portion of this sentence? If you think the original is the best way, select choice (1).

(1) Because of their convenience,
(2) Because they find it convenient,
(3) Being convenient,
(4) For your convenience,
(5) Because of your convenience,

8. Sentence 2: **A home-based business is good for anyone who can discipline themselves.**

What correction should be made to this sentence?

(1) Replace anyone with someone
(2) Replace anyone with people
(3) Replace anyone with a person
(4) Change themselves to themself
(5) No correction is necessary

9. Sentence 4: **People that work at home might miss the company of other workers and become lonely.**

What correction should be made to this sentence?

(1) Replace People with Someone
(2) Replace People with Anyone
(3) Replace that with whom
(4) Replace that with who
(5) Replace that with which

10. Sentence 5: **However, some people do very well on your own.**

What correction should be made to this sentence?

(1) Replace your with his or her
(2) Replace your with our
(3) Replace your with their
(4) Replace your with one's
(5) No correction is necessary

11. Sentence 6: **Working at home means one must be careful not to get caught up in the distractions of family, housework, or watching television instead of working; it can be a problem.**

If you rewrote sentence 6 beginning with Home-based workers must beware of, the next word should be

(1) working.
(2) them.
(3) it.
(4) him or her.
(5) distractions.

Check your answers on page 131.

Unit 3

MECHANICS

Capitalization

When you refer to general items, like *cities*, you don't capitalize the word. But if you refer to a specific city, like *Dallas*, you must capitalize its name.

Examples of specific and general names appear in the table below.

Names of Specific People, Places, and Things	People, Places, and Things in General
Governor Pataki will speak.	The governor will speak.
We live at 2511 Oak Street.	Our street is shady.
I'm reading *War and Peace*.	There could be a war.
They went rafting on the Colorado River.	They went rafting on the river.
He lives in the West.	She lives on the west side of the street.
They enjoyed *Gone with the Wind*.	They enjoyed last night's movie.

The following paragraph, which contains no capitalization errors, shows the distinction between general and specific words:

> When Jim decided to open a bank account with some money his aunt had given him, he looked for a bank that was both open on Saturdays and located close to his home. Looking in the phone book's yellow pages, he discovered First Continental Bank had a branch near his house on Olive Street. His Aunt Millie's check was large enough for him to open the account and still have some extra cash to buy *A Tale of Two Cities,* the book he needed for his class on the French Revolution. At the bank, he was assisted by Mr. Collier, an account clerk.

You see that words that name specific people or places are capitalized, while more general words are not.

We learn that Jim received money from his *aunt,* which could be any of his aunts. Later in the paragraph, we learn that the money came from *Aunt Millie*. In this instance, *Aunt* is part of someone's name. It refers to a specific person, so it must be capitalized. Jim was assisted by *an account clerk*, which could be any unnamed account clerk. But the writer could have said, "Jim was assisted by Account Clerk Collier." In this case, *Account Clerk* is capitalized because it is someone's title.

Exercise 1

Directions: Some of the specific names in the following sentences lack capitalization. Correct the sentences by capitalizing those words. Not all the sentences contain errors.

1. The notice says dr. Juanita Moreno will speak tonight.

2. We heard a deputy sheriff at the july meeting.

3. The governor answered questions for more than an hour.

4. Ryan likes old movies; his favorite is *casablanca*.

5. Chidori speaks several languages, including japanese, english, and french.

Directions: Choose the one best answer for each item.

Items 6 and 7 refer to the following paragraph.

(1) *Our legislator is senator Sperling.* (2) *He shows a genuine interest in his constituents.* (3) *Every month he sends out a newsletter and a questionnaire to survey voters' opinions on several issues.* (4) *He occasionally holds meetings at a public library.* (5) *Last month he spoke about health care at the Brownsville public library.* (6) *This is one politician who understands the need for voters to be informed.* (7) *He wants to keep in touch with the people.*

6. Sentence 1: **Our legislator is senator Sperling.**

   What correction should be made to this sentence?

   (1) Change Our to our
   (2) Change legislator to Legislator
   (3) Change senator to Senator
   (4) Change Sperling to sperling
   (5) No correction is necessary

7. Sentence 5: **Last month he spoke about health care at the Brownsville public library.**

What correction should be made to this sentence?

(1) Change month to Month
(2) Change health to Health
(3) Change Brownsville to brownsville
(4) Change public library to Public Library
(5) No correction is necessary

Check your answers on page 131.

Some Words Are *Always* Capitalized

Distinguishing between the general and the specific helps you determine when to capitalize many words. Certain words, however, always need to be capitalized. The best way to recognize them is to learn the following rules of capitalization.

Always capitalize:

1. Names of people and places

    Shirley Chisholm, John F. Kennedy, Lincoln Center, Museum of Modern Art, Grand Canyon

2. Titles of works (books, movies, paintings) Note: Do not capitalize *and, or, the, a, an,* or prepositions of fewer than five letters in titles unless they are the first or last word of the title.

    For Whom the Bell Tolls, The Witches of Eastwick, Jurassic Park, Leonardo da Vinci's *The Last Supper*

3. Names of streets, cities, states, and countries

    They live in the United States, at 555 Elm Street, Montgomery, Alabama.

4. Titles of people

    Doctor (Dr.) Hobart, Mayor Wallace, Princess Diana, Aunt Ethel, the President of the United States

    A person may serve up to eight years as President of the United States.

5. Days of the week, months, and holidays (but not seasons)

    The third Saturday in August is when we begin our vacation every summer, and we return after Labor Day.

6. Historic eras or events

    the Renaissance, World War II, the Stone Age

7. Languages or nationalities

    He speaks Spanish and loves Mexican food.

8. Direction words when used as the name of a place

    They moved to the West. Our cousins live in Northern Ireland.

    Do *not* capitalize directions when they are used to describe something:

    The southern side of the house needs shade.

    Their house faces east.

Exercise 2

Directions: Choose the one best answer for each item.

Items 1–5 refer to the following paragraph.

(1) *The United States has almost fifty National Parks ranging from the western edge of the continent to the eastern edge.* (2) *Some, like yellowstone, cover territory in more than one state.* (3) *Each park boasts something beautiful and special.* (4) *For example, the Great Smoky Mountains are the largest eastern Mountain Range.* (5) *California's Yosemite national park is famous for having the nation's highest waterfall.* (6) *Mammoth cave in Kentucky has 144 miles of underground passages.* (7) *Our national parks preserve the scenic wonders of our land.*

1. Sentence 1: **The United States has almost fifty National Parks ranging from the western edge of the continent to the eastern edge.**

    What correction should be made to this sentence?

    (1) Change United States to united states
    (2) Change National Parks to national parks
    (3) Change western to Western
    (4) Change continent to Continent
    (5) Change eastern to Eastern

2. Sentence 2: **Some, like yellowstone, cover territory in more than one state.**

What correction should be made to this sentence?

(1) Change Some to some
(2) Change yellowstone to Yellowstone
(3) Change territory to Territory
(4) Change state to State
(5) No correction is necessary

3. Sentence 4: **For example, the Great Smoky Mountains are the largest eastern Mountain Range.**

What correction should be made to this sentence?

(1) Change example to Example
(2) Change Great Smoky Mountains to great smoky mountains
(3) Change largest to Largest
(4) Change eastern to Eastern
(5) Change Mountain Range to mountain range

4. Sentence 5: **California's Yosemite national park is famous for having the nation's highest waterfall.**

What correction should be made to this sentence?

(1) Change Yosemite to yosemite
(2) Change national park to National Park
(3) Change nation's to Nation's
(4) Change highest to Highest
(5) Change waterfall to Waterfall

5. Sentence 6: **Mammoth cave in Kentucky has 144 miles of underground passages.**

What correction should be made to this sentence?

(1) Change Mammoth to mammoth
(2) Change cave to Cave
(3) Change Kentucky to kentucky
(4) Change underground to Underground
(5) Change passages to Passages

Check your answers on page 131.

Punctuation

In writing, punctuation is essential to make the meaning clear. Periods, question marks, and exclamation points appear at the ends of sentences and rarely present problems.

Commas, on the other hand, are used internally in sentences for a variety of reasons. They indicate pauses in thought, and they show relationships among the ideas in a sentence.

Linking Ideas into One Sentence

To add variety to your writing, you will sometimes join two or more ideas together into one sentence.

You must use a comma between independent clauses when you join the clauses with the connecting words (conjunctions) *and, so, but,* and *or.* The connecting word in compound sentences always appears in between the two clauses.

> Late movies on television put me to *sleep, so* I don't watch them.

Certain connecting words in compound sentences take a semicolon and a comma. The semicolon precedes the connector, and the comma follows:

> Movies on television put me to *sleep; however,* I never fall asleep in a movie theater.

These connectors are usually preceded by a semicolon and followed by a comma:

however	nevertheless	otherwise	on the other hand
finally	instead	likewise	moreover
besides	furthermore	in addition	consequently
thus	therefore	as a result	for example

Writing complex sentences is another way to link ideas into a single sentence. In complex sentences, one of the ideas will have a connecting word attached to it that makes it dependent upon the rest of the sentence for its meaning. That dependent clause, with the connecting word attached, can appear at the beginning or at the end of the sentence.

If the dependent clause appears at the beginning, before the independent clause, you must follow it with a comma:

> *Whenever I drink tea,* I put lemon in it.

If the dependent clause appears at the end, after the independent clause, you do not use a comma:

> I add lemon *whenever I drink tea.*

Exercise 3

Directions: Choose the one best answer for each item.

Items 1–4 refer to the following paragraph.

(1) *Enormous parking lots near shopping malls, hospitals, business districts, supermarkets, and movie theaters attest to the vast numbers of cars in America and the amount of time people spend in them.* (2) *Once people buck traffic jams to get to these parking lots they face the problem of finding a convenient parking place.* (3) *Because physical disabilities make it truly difficult for some people to walk long distances a few spaces for the disabled are often reserved close to the buildings.* (4) *Parking in these spots requires a special license plate.* (5) *It's not uncommon to find these spaces illegally occupied.* (6) *Parking in these spaces illegally carries a heavy fine.* (7) *Law enforcement officers have little time to patrol parking lots, but some communities have solved that problem with volunteers.* (8) *These volunteers cite illegally parked cars, inform the driver and report the car to the authorities.*

1. Sentence 2: **Once people buck traffic jams to get to these parking lots they face the prob-lem of finding a convenient parking place.**

   Which of the following is the best way to write the underlined portion of this sentence? If you think the original is the best way, select choice (1).

   (1)   to get to these parking lots they face
   (2)   to get to these parking lots. They face
   (3)   to get to these, parking lots they face
   (4)   to get to these parking lots, they face
   (5)   to get, to these parking lots they face

2. Sentence 3: **Because physical disabilities make it truly difficult for some people to walk long distances a few spaces for the disabled are often reserved close to the buildings.**

   What correction should be made to this sentence?

   (1)   Insert a comma after <u>difficult</u>
   (2)   Insert a comma after <u>distances</u>
   (3)   Insert a comma after <u>spaces</u>
   (4)   Insert a comma after <u>disabled</u>
   (5)   No correction is necessary

3. Sentences 4 and 5: **Parking in these spots requires a special license plate. It's not uncommon to find these spaces illegally occupied.**

   The most effective combination of sentences 4 and 5 would include which of the following groups of words?

   (1)   Parking is not uncommon
   (2)   Illegally parked cars occupy
   (3)   Even though spaces are illegal
   (4)   Special license plates require
   (5)   Cars without spaces

4. Sentence 8: **These volunteers cite illegally parked cars, inform the driver and report the car to the authorities.**

   What correction should be made to this sentence?

   (1)   Insert a comma after <u>volunteers</u>
   (2)   Remove the comma after <u>cars</u>
   (3)   Insert a comma after <u>driver</u>
   (4)   Insert a comma after <u>and</u>
   (5)   Insert a comma after <u>report</u>

Check your answers on page 131.

Using Commas to Set Off Parts of Sentences

Commas help readers understand your writing. Commas can indicate a pause in thought, or they may tell the reader that some information is set apart from the main part of the sentence.

Single words or word *groups* (called **phrases**) sometimes appear at the beginning of sentences to give the reader additional information. Introductory words, phrases, and clauses must be followed by a comma:

Across town, crowds watched the Fourth of July parade.

Hoping for a miracle, Louis searched the house for his lost keys.

Eagerly, Yolanda opened the letter from her brother.

Before the car started, the passengers fastened their seat belts.

When addressing someone directly in a sentence, you use a comma:

Mother, please don't tell me what to wear.

Occasionally a word or a phrase interrupts the main thought. If you remove the word or phrase, you still have a sentence that makes sense.

> Roy attended night school, exhausting himself in the process, to become a car mechanic.

The main idea of the sentence is that Roy attended school at night to become a car mechanic. The fact that he was exhausting himself in the process is informative, but it is not necessary to make the sentence clear.

Another kind of interrupter describes a noun in the sentence:

> Dmitri, *a Russian immigrant*, was eager to master English.

Common interrupters that are set off by commas include such expressions as *for example* and *I believe*, as well as people's names:

> Consider, *for example*, yesterday's discussion.

> Their favorite cousins, *Jeff and Lee*, were coming to visit.

You must not use commas to set apart information in the middle of a sentence if that information is *essential* to the meaning of the sentence. If you're tempted to set off some words or phrases with commas, try reading the sentence without those words to be sure it still makes sense. Remember, the commas mean you can omit the words between them without changing the meaning of the sentence.

Exercise 4

Directions: Choose the one best answer for each item.

Items 1–3 refer to the following paragraph.

(1) *One of the most famous English writers of the last century was Charles Dickens, a novelist who lived from 1812 to 1870.* (2) *When he was alive his novels appeared in magazines in serial form.* (3) *People read the stories in monthly installments, and had to wait for the next issue to find out about the next plot twist.* (4) *Acclaimed during his lifetime, Dickens remains a popular novelist whose offbeat characters and satiric plots are well known to people around the world.* (5) *Among his books are the well-known titles,* David Copperfield, Oliver Twist, A Tale of Two Cities, *and* A Christmas Carol.

1. Sentence 2: **When he was alive his novels appeared in magazines in serial form.**

   What correction should be made to this sentence?

   (1) Change was to were
   (2) Insert a comma after alive
   (3) Change appeared to will appear
   (4) Change the spelling of magazines to magisines
   (5) No correction is necessary

2. Sentence 3: **People read the stories in monthly installments, and had to wait for the next issue to find out about the next plot twist.**

   Which of the following is the best way to write the underlined portion of this sentence? If you think the original is the best way, select choice (1).

   (1) monthly installments, and had to wait
   (2) monthly installments, and have to wait
   (3) monthly installments, and will wait
   (4) monthly installments and had to wait
   (5) Monthly Installments, and had to wait

3. Sentence 5: **Among his books are the well-known titles, *David Copperfield, Oliver Twist, A Tale of Two Cities,* and *A Christmas Carol.***

   What correction should be made to this sentence?

   (1) Insert a comma after are
   (2) Change titles to Titles
   (3) Remove the comma after titles
   (4) Change *of* to *Of*
   (5) Remove the comma after *Cities*

Check your answers on page 131.

Overcoming Spelling Problems

A good essay can be marred by misspelled words. You will need to know some basic rules, memorize exceptions to the rules, and practice. Study the list on pages 114–117. A dictionary can also help you with difficult words.

It's easier to spell words if you divide them into **syllables**. A syllable is a part of a word that is pronounced as a single unit: go + ing = going; fe + ver + ish = feverish. Say the word first, to hear how many syllables there are, and spell each one as you write. Notice that each syllable contains at least one vowel.

> con + cen + trate = concentrate

> op + por + tu + ni + ty = opportunity

ADDING *-ING* OR *-ED* TO A VERB

When you change verb tense or use verb phrases, you change the form of the verb, frequently by adding *-ed* or *-ing* to the main part of the verb.

1. If the verb ends in *e*, drop the *e* before adding *-ing*:

   use becomes *using*

   ride becomes *riding*

2. If the verb has *one syllable and a single consonant preceded by a single vowel*, double the final consonant before adding *-ed* or *-ing*:

   let becomes *letting*

   hit becomes *hitting*

3. If the word does not meet these criteria, do not double the consonant:

   listen becomes *listened*

   sleep becomes *sleeping*

WORDS WITH *IE* AND *EI*

1. If the vowel sound is *ee*, put the *i* first, except after *c*:

   believe, thief, niece, receive

Exceptions to this rule include *seize, either, neither, leisure, weird*.

2. If the vowel sound is *a* or *i*, put the *e* before the *i:*

   neighbor, freight, height

WORDS THAT END IN *-CEDE, -SEDE, -CEED*

1. Only one word ends in *-sede*:
   supersede

2. Only three words end in *-ceed*:
   exceed, proceed, succeed

3. All the others end in *-cede*:
   precede, recede, secede, concede

Exercise 5

Directions: Choose the one best answer for each item.

Items 1–3 refer to the following paragraph.

(1) *To encourage recycling, some service stations and oil-changing facilities are beginning to accept used motor oil from people who change the oil in their own cars.* (2) *Stations that recieve used oil have to pass government standards to obtain certification to recycle it.* (3) *Oil must not be contaminated, and there must be arrangements with waste-oil haulers to take the oil to recycling plants.* (4) *Many people, unsure of how to dispose of their used motor oil, pour it down storm drains, into garbage cans, or directly into the ground.* (5) *Each gallon of oil has the potential to damage one million gallons of groundwater, but it is important that oil be disposed of properly.*

1. Sentence 1: **To encourage recycling, some service stations and oil-changing facilities are begining to accept used motor oil from people who change the oil in their own cars.**

   What correction should be made to this sentence?

   (1) Change begining to beginning
   (2) Change accept to acept
   (3) Change facilities to facillities
   (4) Replace people with people's
   (5) Change people to People

2. Sentence 2: **Stations that recieve used oil have to pass government standards to obtain certification to recycle it.**

   What correction should be made to this sentence?

   (1) Change recieve to reccieve
   (2) Change recieve to receive
   (3) Replace obtain with obtains
   (4) Change certification to certafication
   (5) No correction is necessary

3. Sentence 5: **Each gallon of oil has the potential to damage one million gallons of groundwater, but it is important that oil be disposed of properly.**

What correction should be made to this sentence?

(1) Change has to had
(2) Remove to
(3) Change damage to damaged
(4) Replace but with or
(5) Replace but with so

Check your answers on page 132.

Changing Nouns: Singular to Plural

If you write that Lorenzo drives *a truck*, you are using a singular noun. But if Lorenzo drives *several trucks*, you change the noun to plural.

You change words from singular to plural all the time, both in speaking and in writing. In English, nouns change to their plural form in several ways, so the trick is to spell the plural correctly. The following six rules will help you.

1. Most nouns can be made plural by adding *s*. If the noun ends in *s*, *x*, *ch*, or *sh*, make it plural by adding *es*:

   loss becomes *losses*

   fox becomes *foxes*

   wrench becomes *wrenches*

   lash becomes *lashes*

2. Nouns that end in a consonant plus *y* become plural by changing the *y* to *i* and adding *es*:

   city becomes *cities*

   penny becomes *pennies*

   party becomes *parties*

   doily becomes *doilies*

3. Some nouns that end in a consonant plus *o* add *es*:

   hero becomes *heroes*

   potato becomes *potatoes*

   tomato becomes *tomatoes*

   halo becomes *haloes*

4. Some nouns that end in *f* change the *f* to *v* and add *es* for the plural:

   leaf becomes *leaves*

   wolf becomes *wolves*

   calf becomes *calves*

   half becomes *halves*

5. Some nouns that end in *fe* change the *f* to *v* and add *s*:

   knife becomes *knives*

   wife becomes *wives*

   life becomes *lives*

6. Some nouns don't change at all when they become plural:

   The *deer* were hiding among the trees.

   I saw a *deer* by the side of the road.

   On a trip to Alaska, several *moose* crossed the street in front of us.

   To see a *moose* up close is an amazing sight.

Exercise 6

Directions: Circle and correct the misspelled words in the sentences that follow.

1. They had hopped to find more clues at the scene of the crime.

2. Some adults think there are no heros for youngsters to admire.

3. Guido's directions were so good, we found both address in less than an hour.

4. There were too many boxs to fit into the back of the car.

5. Marguerita planted tomatos and carrots in her garden.

6. After three trys, Madeline got the basketball through the hoop.

107

Directions: Choose the one best answer for each item.

Items 7–9 refer to the following paragraph.

(1) *With a weak economy and a high rate of unemployment, people seek ways to save money.* (2) *Several books and articles have been written to help people save money and change bad spending habits.* (3) *There are even classes available for helpping people reduce their debts.* (4) *Some people have started newsletters that show how to save money.* (5) *Among a variety of ways to avoid exorbitent prices, they suggest cutting out coupons, buying food in bulk, making your own bread, and growing vegetables in a home garden.* (6) *Newspapers and magazines also publish ideas for saving money; there are plenty of tips for anyone who is serious about financiel cutbacks.*

7. Sentence 3: **There are even classes available for helpping people reduce their debts.**

What correction should be made to this sentence?

(1) Change classes to class's
(2) Change the spelling of helpping to helping
(3) Change their to thier
(4) Change the spelling of debts to debtes
(5) No correction is necessary

8. Sentence 5: **Among a variety of ways to avoid exorbitent prices, they suggest cutting out coupons, buying food in bulk, making your own bread, and growing vegetables in a home garden.**

What correction should be made to this sentence?

(1) Change the spelling of variety to vareity
(2) Change the spelling of exorbitent to exorbitant
(3) Change the spelling of making to makeing
(4) Change the spelling of vegetables to vegetabels
(5) No correction is necessary

9. Sentence 6: **Newspapers and magazines also publish ideas for saving money; there are plenty of tips for anyone who is serious about financiel cutbacks.**

What correction should be made to this sentence?

(1) Change the spelling of magazines to magezines
(2) Insert a comma after ideas
(3) Replace the semicolon with a comma
(4) Change who to whom
(5) Change the spelling of financiel to financial

Check your answers on page 132.

Adding Suffixes

A **suffix** is one or more letters or syllables added to the end of a word. You have already learned the common suffixes *-ed* and *-ing*.

Some words change their spelling when a suffix is added to them; others don't. A few rules will help you correctly spell words that have suffixes.

1. When a word ends in a consonant and the suffix begins with a consonant, just add the suffix:

   fear + ful = fearful; mind + less = mindless

2. When a word ends with the letter *e* and the suffix begins with a consonant, just add the suffix:

   care + ful = careful; sense + less = senseless

   Exceptions include *truly, argument, ninth, wholly,* and *judgment.*

3. When a word ends with the letter *e* and the suffix begins with a vowel, drop the final *e*:

   value + able = valuable; confuse + ion = confusion

   Words that end in *ce* or *ge* are often exceptions to this rule:

   advantageous, replaceable, courageous, noticeable

4. Add *-ly* and *-ness* without changing the spelling of the main word:

   final + ly = finally; eager + ly = eagerly; careless + ness = carelessness

5. If a word ends in *y* following a consonant, change the *y* to *i* before adding a suffix:

   silly + er = sillier; forty + eth = fortieth

6. Don't change the *y* before adding *-ing*:

   cry + ing = crying

7. If a word ends in *y* following a vowel, do not change the *y*:

pay + ment = payment; annoy + ed = annoyed

Exceptions include *paid* and *said.*

Exercise 7

Directions: Choose the one best answer for each item.

Items 1–3 refer to the following paragraph.

(1) *Medical technology is so far advanced that it's possible for a team of surgeons to operate on an unborn baby with out removing it from the mother's body.* (2) *If doctors see that a fetus is not developing normaly, they may be able to fix it surgically.* (3) *If, for example, a fetus's organs are not in the proper location, doctors can relocate the organs within the tiny body of the fetus.* (4) *Fetal surgery involves operating on the mother, too.* (5) *To reach the fetus, the surgeons have to make one incision in the mother to reach the womb, and then they have to open the womb to reach the fetus.* (6) *After the fetal operation, they seal the uterus with staples and a material like glue.* (7) *Then they stitch the mother's incision.* (8) *It takes couragous parents and highly skilled doctors to give babies this chance at a healthy life.*

1. Sentence 1: **Medical technology is so far advanced that it's possible for a team of surgeons to operate on an unborn baby with out removing it from the mother's body.**

What correction should be made to this sentence?

(1) Change possible to posible
(2) Change the spelling of operate to oporate
(3) Change with out to without
(4) Change the spelling of removing to remove-ing
(5) No correction is necessary

2. Sentence 2: **If doctors see that a fetus is not developing normaly, they may be able to fix it surgically.**

What correction should be made to this sentence?

(1) Change the spelling of developing to developeing
(2) Change the spelling of normaly to normally
(3) Remove the comma after normaly
(4) Change the spelling of surgically to surgicaly
(5) No correction is necessary

3. Sentence 8: **It takes couragous parents and highly skilled doctors to give babies this chance at a healthy life.**

What correction should be made to this sentence?

(1) Change couragous to courageous
(2) Change couragous to courrageous
(3) Change highly to highlly
(4) Change skilled to skilld
(5) No correction is necessary

Check your answers on page 132.

Using Apostrophes

The **apostrophe** is the punctuation mark that looks like a comma but appears at the top of a word ('). Apostrophes are used in only two situations: to form contractions and to show possession.

A **contraction** combines two words into one by omitting one or more letters. The apostrophe takes the place of the missing *letter* or *letters*.

are + *not* becomes *aren't*

it + *is* becomes *it's*

The second reason to use an apostrophe is to show that one thing belongs to another:

the *soldier's* weapon

the *truck's* front wheel

Note, however, that we use apostrophes to show possession *only with nouns*. Pronouns that show possession (*yours, hers, his, theirs, ours, its, whose*) do not take apostrophes:

Her house is around the corner.

Their values are different from *ours.*

To show possession with a singular noun, add an *apostrophe* + *s*:

Marci's coat looks warm.

The *boss's* car was stolen yesterday.

With nouns that become plural by adding *s* or *es*, put the apostrophe after the *s*:

> The *bosses'* privileges seemed more numerous than ours.

The sentence above shows that there was more than one boss.

With nouns that become plural in other ways, add *apostrophe + s* to show possession:

> *Women's* fashions change more dramatically than *men's* fashions.

> The *oxen's* strength made them essential on farms before tractors were invented.

Exercise 8

Directions: Place apostrophes in the contractions in the following sentences. Identify the missing letters.

1. Being late so often, youre going to have trouble keeping the job.

2. Itll be hard to find any place open at this hour.

3. They arent selling that item any longer.

4. He hasnt missed a single game all season.

5. Youll have to wait until the report is published.

6. Sam saw that theyd been there already.

7. Shes completely dependable.

8. Take whatever theyll give you.

9. It really isnt hard to understand.

10. By now, its too late to get tickets.

Directions: Choose the one best answer for each item.

Items 11–13 refer to the following paragraph.

(1) *Nutritionists agree that snacks are an important part of our food intake.* (2) *Snacks keep us from feeling hungry before the next meal.* (3) *It's also fun to eat.* (4) *However, most people who work all day depend on vending machines for snacks, and there more likely to buy candy bars than a more healthful snack like pretzels.* (5) *Apparently, its necessary to bring something from home if we want a healthful snack during the workday.*

11. Sentence 3: **It's also fun to eat.**

    What correction should be made to this sentence?

    (1) Change It's to Its
    (2) Change It's to They're
    (3) Insert a comma after fun
    (4) Change fun to to fun. To
    (5) No correction is necessary

12. Sentence 4: **However, most people who work all day depend on vending machines for snacks, and there more likely to buy candy bars than a more healthful snack like pretzels.**

    What correction should be made to this sentence?

    (1) Remove the comma after However
    (2) Remove the comma after snacks
    (3) Change there to they're
    (4) Change there to theyr'e
    (5) Change the spelling of healthful to healthfull

13. Sentence 5: **Apparently, its necessary to bring something from home if we want a healthful snack during the workday.**

    What correction should be made to this sentence?

    (1) Remove the comma after Apparently
    (2) Change its to its'
    (3) Change its to it's
    (4) Insert a comma after home
    (5) Change snack during to snack. During

Directions: Choose the one best answer for each item.

Items 14–17 refer to the following paragraph.

(1) *A college computer students' project led to a fascinating discovery about jump rope rhymes.* (2) *While watching some children jumping rope on a school playground, the student decided to research the origins of their jingles.* (3) *Children who jump rope and chant jingles while they jump usually think they invented the rhymes.* (4) *Their older brothers and sisters claim the rhymes are their's.* (5) *However, the project revealed that the same or similar rhymes are sung by rope-jumping children all over the world.* (6) *Not only do the rhymes cross national boundaries, they cross generations.* (7) *They're the same rhymes that have been sung by children for decade's.* (8) *The projects conclusions not only led to information about jump rope rhymes, but show the similarity among people, no matter where they live or when they lived.*

14. Sentence 1: **A college computer students' project led to a fascinating discovery about jump rope rhymes.**

What correction should be made to this sentence?

(1) Change students' to students
(2) Change students' to student's
(3) Change the spelling of fascinating to fasinating
(4) Insert a comma after discovery
(5) No correction is necessary

15. Sentence 4: **Their older brothers and sisters claim the rhymes are their's.**

What correction should be made to this sentence?

(1) Change brothers to brother's
(2) Change sisters to sister's
(3) Change claim to claims
(4) Change their's to theirs
(5) Change their's to theirs'

16. Sentence 7: **They're the same rhymes that have been sung by children for decade's.**

What correction should be made to this sentence?

(1) Change They're to Theyre
(2) Change sung to sang
(3) Change sung to singed
(4) Change children to children's
(5) Change decade's to decades

17. Sentence 8: **The projects conclusions not only led to information about jump rope rhymes, but show the similarity among people, no matter where they live or when they lived.**

Which of the following is the best way to write the underlined portion of this sentence? If you think the original is the best way, select choice (1).

(1) the projects conclusions
(2) the projects' conclusions
(3) the project's conclusion
(4) the project's conclusions
(5) the projects conclusion's

Check your answers on page 132.

Homophones

One special class of words to look out for is **homophones**, pairs or groups of words that sound the same but have different meanings and usually different spelling. For example, the words *there*, *their*, and *they're* are pronounced exactly the same, but they mean very different things.

When you are writing, it is important to use the right homophone. For example, *they're* means "they are." In the sentence, "They're waiting for you in the cafeteria," you would not use *their* or *there*.

Here is a list of some common homophones. A longer list is on page 111.

They're is a contraction that means "they are."
There is an adverb that shows position ("over there").
Their is a possessive adjective.

It's is a contraction that means "it is."
Its is a possessive adjective.

One is a number.
Won is a past-tense verb.

Two is a number.
Too means "also."
To is a preposition.

Which is a pronoun.
Witch is a supernatural being.

Lose is the present tense of "lost."
Loose means "not tight."

Been is a form of the verb "to be."
Bean is a seed that you can eat.

There are many other homonyms in English, and you should watch for them in your writing.

COMMONLY CONFUSED HOMOPHONES

Word Pair	Meaning	Example
affect	verb meaning to have an impact	How did the exercise affect you?
effect	noun meaning a result	Did it have the effect you hoped for?
already	previously	He had already filled the gas tank.
all ready	entirely prepared	The class was all ready for the field trip.
altogether	entirely	She was altogether confused by the map.
all together	everyone or everything in the same place	The books were all together on the correct shelves.
capitol	the building in which government officials work	Pictures on the capitol walls show all of the governors.
capital	the city that serves as the seat of government; also wealth or money owned or used in business	The capital of the United States is Washington, DC.
desert	a dry, arid place	The desert blooms in the spring.
dessert	the last course of a meal	Ice cream is a popular dessert.
lead	a metal; the graphite in a pencil	A lead weight is hard to move.
led	past tense of the verb *to lead*	The captain led his team to victory.
passed	past tense of the verb *to pass*	She passed the exam easily.
past	time that has gone by	In the past, dress was more formal.
principal	head of a school; most important	The principal kept the school running smoothly. It was our principal demand.
principle	basic law or rule	He liked to study the principles of chemistry.
role	a part in a play	She wanted to play the role of the detective.
roll	to turn over and over; a single-serving loaf of bread; a list of names	The car would roll down the hill if the brake slipped. A roll and butter make a good snack. After roll call, the class started.
stationary	not moving	Riding a stationary bicycle is good exercise.
stationery	paper	She found note cards at the stationery store.
there	in that place	The ball is over there.
their	belonging to them	It's their problem.
they're	contraction of *they are*	They're able to solve it.
to	indicates direction	Turn to the left.
too	also; excessive	I'll go too. Too many movies are sad.
two	a number	Two people lost their cameras.
who's	contraction of *who is* or *who has*	Who's riding in the station wagon?
whose	possessive pronoun	Whose jacket is this?

Exercise 9

Directions: Choose the one best answer for each item.

Items 1–4 refer to the following paragraph.

(1) *My sixth-grade teacher, Mrs. Gastwirth, was one of the nicest teachers I have ever had.* (2) *I had a hard time that year, but Mrs. Gastwirth was always their for me.* (3) *I wanted to buy a yearbook like all the other sixth graders, but my family didn't have much money.* (4) *I couldn't effort the yearbook, and I was embarrassed.* (5) *Mrs. Gastwirth realized how I felt, and she told me in private that she would buy me the yearbook.* (6) *"Its a present in return for your excellent work in social studies," she said.* (7) *She made me feel really good.*

1. Sentence 1: **My sixth-grade teacher, Mrs. Gastwirth, was one of the nicest teachers I have ever had.**

   What correction should be made to this sentence?

   (1) Change sixth-grade to sixth grade
   (2) Delete the comma after teacher
   (3) Change one to won
   (4) Change nicest to nice
   (5) No correction is necessary

2. Sentence 2: **I had a hard time that year, but Mrs. Gastwirth was always their for me.**

   What correction should be made to this sentence?

   (1) Change had to been having
   (2) Delete the comma after year
   (3) Add a comma after Mrs. Gastwirth
   (4) Change their to there
   (5) No correction is necessary

3. Sentence 4: **I couldn't effort the yearbook, and I was embarrassed.**

   What correction should be made to this sentence?

   (1) Change couldn't to couldnt
   (2) Change effort to afford
   (3) Delete the comma after yearbook
   (4) Change embarrassed to embarassed
   (5) No correction is necessary

4. Sentence 6: **"Its a present in return for your excellent work in social studies," she said.**

   What correction should be made to this sentence?

   (1) Change "Its to "It's
   (2) Add a comma after in return
   (3) Change excellent to eccellent
   (4) Delete the comma after social studies
   (5) No correction is necessary

Check your answers on page 132.

Words to Watch Out For

Memory and practice are essential tools for mastering spelling. In this lesson, you'll find a list of word pairs or groups that sound the same but have different meanings and different spellings. Study the list and use it for reference.

Exercise 10

Directions: Choose the one best answer for each item.

Items 1–4 refer to the following paragraph.

(1) *The seen of the collision was a four-way-stop intersection.* (2) *It was hard to tell whose fault it was.* (3) *Three cars were involved, but their were no other witnesses to the accident.* (4) *Even after questioning the three drivers, the police were not sure what had happened.* (5) *One driver claimed neither of the other two applied the breaks.* (6) *Another driver said he was already to go when the other one ran the stop sign.*

1. Sentence 1: **The seen of the collision was a four-way-stop intersection.**

   What correction should be made to this sentence?

   (1) Change the spelling of seen to scene
   (2) Change collision to Collision
   (3) Change four-way to for-way
   (4) Change four-way to fore-way
   (5) Change intersection to inter section

2. Sentence 3: **Three cars were involved, but their were no other witnesses to the accident.**

What correction should be made to this sentence?

(1) Replace their with there
(2) Replace their with they're
(3) Replace no with know
(4) Replace to with too
(5) Replace to with two

3. Sentence 5: **One driver claimed neither of the other two applied the breaks.**

What correction should be made to this sentence?

(1) Replace one with won
(2) Change the spelling of neither to niether
(3) Replace two with to
(4) Replace breaks with brakes
(5) No correction is necessary

4. Sentence 6: **Another driver said he was already to go when the other one ran the stop sign.**

What correction should be made to this sentence?

(1) Insert a comma after said
(2) Change already to all ready
(3) Change ran to run
(4) Change stop sign to Stop Sign
(5) No correction is necessary

Check your answers on page 133.

Frequently Misspelled Words

Here is a list of commonly misspelled words. Some of these follow the spelling rules you have already learned, but some are exceptions to the rules and must simply be memorized. To find out which words on this list you need to study, ask someone to quiz you.

MASTER LIST OF FREQUENTLY MISSPELLED WORDS

a lot	affect	application	awful	buried
ability	affectionate	apply	awkward	bury
absence	again	appreciate	bachelor	bushes
absent	against	appreciation	balance	business
abundance	aggravate	approach	balloon	cafeteria
accept	aggressive	appropriate	bargain	calculator
acceptable	agree	approval	basic	calendar
accident	aisle	approve	beautiful	campaign
accommodate	all right	approximate	because	capital
accompanied	almost	argue	become	capitol
accomplish	already	arguing	before	captain
accumulation	although	argument	beginning	career
accuse	altogether	arouse	being	careful
accustomed	always	arrange	believe	careless
ache	amateur	arrangement	benefit	carriage
achieve	American	article	benefited	carrying
achievement	among	artificial	between	category
acknowledge	amount	ascend	bicycle	ceiling
acquaintance	analysis	assistance	board	cemetery
acquire	analyze	assistant	bored	cereal
across	angel	associate	borrow	certain
address	angle	association	bottle	changeable
addressed	annual	attempt	bottom	characteristic
adequate	another	attendance	boundary	charity
advantage	answer	attention	brake	chief
advantageous	antiseptic	audience	breadth	choose
advertise	anxious	August	breath	chose
advertisement	apologize	author	breathe	cigarette
advice	apparatus	automobile	brilliant	circumstance
advisable	apparent	autumn	building	citizen
advise	appear	auxiliary	bulletin	clothes
advisor	appearance	available	bureau	clothing
aerial	appetite	avenue	burial	coarse

MASTER LIST OF FREQUENTLY MISSPELLED WORDS—*continued*

coffee	criticize	dissipate	existence	height
collect	crystal	distance	exorbitant	heroes
college	curiosity	distinction	expense	heroine
column	cylinder	division	experience	hideous
comedy	daily	doctor	experiment	himself
comfortable	daughter	dollar	explanation	hoarse
commitment	daybreak	doubt	extreme	holiday
committed	death	dozen	facility	hopeless
committee	deceive	earnest	factory	hospital
communicate	December	easy	familiar	humorous
company	deception	ecstasy	fascinate	hurried
comparative	decide	ecstatic	fascinating	hurrying
compel	decision	education	fatigue	ignorance
competent	decisive	effect	February	imaginary
competition	deed	efficiency	financial	imbecile
compliment	definite	efficient	financier	imitation
conceal	delicious	eight	flourish	immediately
conceit	dependent	either	forcibly	immigrant
conceivable	deposit	eligibility	forehead	incidental
conceive	derelict	eligible	foreign	increase
concentration	descend	eliminate	formal	independence
conception	descent	embarrass	former	independent
condition	describe	embarrassment	fortunate	indispensable
conference	description	emergency	fourteen	inevitable
confident	desert	emphasis	fourth	influence
congratulate	desirable	emphasize	frequent	influential
conquer	despair	enclosure	friend	initiate
conscience	desperate	encouraging	frightening	innocence
conscientious	dessert	endeavor	fundamental	inoculate
conscious	destruction	engineer	further	inquiry
consequence	determine	English	gallon	insistent
consequently	develop	enormous	garden	instead
considerable	development	enough	gardener	instinct
consistency	device	entrance	general	integrity
consistent	dictator	envelope	genius	intellectual
continual	died	environment	government	intelligence
continuous	difference	equipment	governor	intercede
controlled	different	equipped	grammar	interest
controversy	dilemma	especially	grateful	interfere
convenience	dinner	essential	great	interference
convenient	direction	evening	grievance	interpreted
conversation	disappear	evident	grievous	interrupt
corporal	disappoint	exaggerate	grocery	invitation
corroborate	disappointment	exaggeration	guarantee	irrelevant
council	disapproval	examine	guess	irresistible
counsel	disapprove	exceed	guidance	irritable
counselor	disastrous	excellent	half	island
courage	discipline	except	hammer	its
courageous	discover	exceptional	handkerchief	it's
course	discriminate	exercise	happiness	itself
courteous	disease	exhausted	healthy	January
courtesy	dissatisfied	exhaustion	heard	jealous
criticism	dissection	exhilaration	heavy	judgment

MASTER LIST OF FREQUENTLY MISSPELLED WORDS—*continued*

journal	momentous	particular	precise	referred
kindergarten	monkey	partner	predictable	rehearsal
kitchen	monotonous	pastime	prefer	reign
knew	moral	patience	preference	relevant
knock	morale	peace	preferential	relieve
know	mortgage	peaceable	preferred	remedy
knowledge	mountain	pear	prejudice	renovate
labor	mournful	peculiar	preparation	repeat
laboratory	muscle	pencil	prepare	repetition
laid	mysterious	people	prescription	representative
language	mystery	perceive	presence	requirements
later	narrative	perception	president	resemblance
latter	natural	perfect	prevalent	resistance
laugh	necessary	perform	primitive	resource
leisure	needle	performance	principal	respectability
length	negligence	perhaps	principle	responsibility
lesson	neighbor	period	privilege	restaurant
library	neither	permanence	probably	rhythm
license	newspaper	permanent	procedure	rhythmical
light	newsstand	perpendicular	proceed	ridiculous
lightning	niece	perseverance	produce	right
likelihood	noticeable	persevere	professional	role
likely	obedient	persistent	professor	roll
literal	obstacle	personal	profitable	roommate
literature	occasion	personality	prominent	sandwich
livelihood	occasional	personnel	promise	Saturday
loaf	occur	persuade	pronounce	scarcely
loneliness	occurred	persuasion	pronunciation	scene
loose	occurrence	pertain	propeller	schedule
lose	ocean	picture	prophet	science
losing	o'clock	piece	prospect	scientific
loyal	offer	plain	psychology	scissors
loyalty	often	playwright	pursue	season
magazine	omission	pleasant	pursuit	secretary
maintenance	omit	please	quality	seize
maneuver	once	pleasure	quantity	seminar
marriage	operate	pocket	quarreling	sense
married	opinion	poison	quart	separate
marry	opportune	policeman	quarter	service
match	opportunity	political	quiet	several
material	optimist	population	quite	severely
mathematics	optimistic	portrayal	raise	shepherd
measure	origin	positive	realistic	sheriff
medicine	original	possess	realize	shining
million	oscillate	possession	reason	shoulder
miniature	ought	possessive	rebellion	shriek
minimum	ounce	possible	recede	siege
miracle	overcoat	post office	receipt	sight
miscellaneous	paid	potatoes	receive	signal
mischief	pamphlet	practical	recipe	significance
mischievous	panicky	prairie	recognize	significant
misspelled	parallel	precede	recommend	similar
mistake	parallelism	preceding	recuperate	similarity

MASTER LIST OF FREQUENTLY MISSPELLED WORDS—*continued*

sincerely	striking	temperament	twelve	village
site	studying	temperature	tyranny	villain
soldier	substantial	tenant	undoubtedly	visitor
solemn	succeed	tendency	United States	voice
sophomore	successful	tenement	university	volume
soul	sudden	therefore	unnecessary	waist
source	superintendent	thorough	unusual	weak
souvenir	suppress	through	useful	wear
special	surely	title	usual	weather
specified	surprise	together	vacuum	Wednesday
specimen	suspense	tomorrow	valley	week
speech	sweat	tongue	valuable	weigh
stationary	sweet	toward	variety	weird
stationery	syllable	tragedy	vegetable	whether
statue	symmetrical	transferred	vein	which
stockings	sympathy	treasury	vengeance	while
stomach	synonym	tremendous	versatile	whole
straight	technical	tries	vicinity	wholly
strength	telegram	truly	vicious	whose
strenuous	telephone	twelfth	view	wretched
stretch				

Unit 4

ORGANIZATION

Organization in writing means a logical flow of ideas. A piece of writing is well organized if the ideas flow clearly and the writer's argument is easy to follow. Writers make their organization clear by incorporating transitional words and phrases, by marking divisions within their work, by including clear topic sentences, and by making the sequence of ideas flow clearly.

Transitions within Paragraphs

Transitions are links between ideas. Transitional words and phrases show how the ideas in a paragraph are related to one another. They help the writer and the reader move smoothly from the main idea of a paragraph to the details that support it.

The most important type of paragraph structure is the *main idea and supporting details*. In a paragraph of this type, the writer usually begins by stating a topic sentence, or main idea, and then states details that support this main idea. Here is an example of this type of paragraph. Notice the transition words the author has used to connect the ideas:

There are several things you can do to make a good first impression on a job interview. Probably the most important is to be on time. Another tactic is to be well prepared for the job by finding out about the company and the specific opening ahead of time. You should always carry a copy of your resume, in case the interviewer has lost it. And finally, you should dress appropriately, be well-groomed, and wear a confident and natural smile.

The main idea of this paragraph is stated in the first sentence. All the other sentences state details that support the main idea.

Writers use many words and phrases to signal transition. Probably the most common is *for example*, which tells you that something is a supporting detail. Other such words and phrases are *in addition*, *similarly*, *such as*, *for instance*, *because*, and *therefore*. Number words, such as *first*, *second*, *then*, *next*, and *finally*, signal that the writer is providing a list of details.

Exercise 1

Directions: Choose the one best answer for each item.

Items 1–4 refer to the following paragraph.

(1) *Solving math problems is not difficult if you follow a logical sequence of steps.* (2) *The first thing you should always due is read the problem carefully.* (3) *Ask yourself, "What do I have to find?"* (4) *Next, ask yourself, "How do I find the answer?"* (5) *After that, find the numbers given in the problem that you need to find the answer write them in the form of an equation.* (6) *Solve the equation, and you're done!*

1. All of the sentences in this paragraph state supporting details EXCEPT for
   (1) Sentence 1.
   (2) Sentence 2.
   (3) Sentence 3.
   (4) Sentence 4.
   (5) Sentence 6.

2. Sentence 2: **The first thing you should always due is read the problem carefully.**

   What correction should be made to this sentence?
   (1) Add a comma after the first thing
   (2) Change due to do
   (3) Change read to red
   (4) Add for example to the end of the sentence
   (5) No correction is necessary

3. Sentence 3: **Ask yourself, "What do I have to find?"**

   What correction is necessary to this sentence?
   (1) Add Then at the beginning of the sentence
   (2) Delete the comma after yourself
   (3) Add a comma after I
   (4) Change find to fined
   (5) No correction is necessary

4. Sentence 5: **After that, find the numbers given in the problem that you need to find the answer write them in the form of an equation.**

What correction should be made to this sentence?

(1) Delete the comma after that
(2) Add a comma after need
(3) Change need to knead
(4) Change answer write to answer. Write
(5) No correction is necessary

Check your answers on page 133.

Marking Divisions within a Work

Marking divisions within a work is another way that writers make the organization of their writing clear. The most important way that writers do this is by including appropriate **headings** within a chapter or section. Another way to mark divisions is to number the sections or paragraphs. For example, the chapter you are reading is divided into numbered units, each of which covers one important topic.

Topic Sentences

A **topic sentence** states the main idea of a paragraph or longer piece of writing. The topic sentence is usually the first sentence in a paragraph, but it may also come at the end to provide emphasis. Less commonly, the topic sentence is embedded within the paragraph. Find the topic sentence in the following paragraph:

Maymark Corporation offers tuition assistance to all employees and makes substantial efforts to promote from within the company. We provide a generous benefits package, including company-paid health insurance. Child-care facilities are available at selected locations. Finally, we fund a generous 401(K) plan. All of these benefits make Maymark an excellent place to work.

As you probably realized, the last sentence is the topic sentence of this paragraph. All of the other sentences are details that support this main idea.

Exercise 2

Directions: Choose the one best answer for each item.

Items 1–3 refer to the following paragraph.

(1) *An old saying goes, "Dress for the job you want, not the job you have."* (2) *In other words, dress like an executive, and someday you may be one.* (3) *Of course, in today's business world, it's sometimes hard to tell whose the boss.* (4) *Everyone, supervisors and workers alike, tends to dress casually.* (5) *But there are occasions, such as meetings with important clients, when executives still dress quite formally.* (6) *Those are the occasions on which you should take pains to emulate your boss's style of dress.* (7) *Your sharp appearance may just work in you're favor at your next performance review.*

1. Which sentence in the paragraph is the topic sentence?

   (1) Sentence 1
   (2) Sentence 3
   (3) Sentence 4
   (4) Sentence 5
   (5) Sentence 7

2. Sentence 3: **Of course, in today's business world, it's sometimes hard to tell whose the boss.**

   What correction is necessary in this sentence?

   (1) Change Of course to for example
   (2) Delete the apostrophe in today's
   (3) Change it's to its
   (4) Change whose to who's
   (5) No correction is necessary

3. Sentence 7: **Your sharp appearance may just work in you're favor at your next performance review.**

   What correction is necessary in this sentence?

   (1) Add For example to the beginning of the sentence
   (2) Change you're to your
   (3) Add a comma after favor
   (4) Change your to you're
   (5) No correction is necessary

Check your answers on page 133.

Coherence

When writing is **coherent**, it is clear. The ideas flow logically with no extraneous or tangential material. For example, one of the sentences in the following paragraph does not belong there. Can you find it?

> When the dogwood berries ripen in early fall, birds seem to come from miles around to gobble them up. The bright-red, football-shaped berries are high in fat and therefore provide excellent nutrition for migrating birds. Sassafras berries, which are purple, are also highly nutritious for birds. When the dogwood berries ripen, the foliage turns red, providing a visual marker that helps birds find the tree and its healthful berries.

You probably guessed that the sentence about the sassafras berries is a **tangent**, an unrelated idea that does not belong in the paragraph.

Coherent writing has a logical structure. As we have seen, one of the most important kinds of structures is the main idea and supporting details. Other structures of coherent writing include comparison-contrast, chronological (time) order, cause and effect, or visual description. Whatever structure the author chooses, coherent writing is logical and contains no unnecessary details.

Exercise 3

Directions: Choose the one best answer for each item.

Items 1–4 refer to the following paragraph.

(1) *Choosing a career is one of the most important decisions a person will ever make. (2) Although it is possible to change careers later in life, this often requires retraining and lost income, so it is a good idea to choose carefully. (3) A careful choice should be based on your aptitudes, or likes and dislikes. (4) A person who hates details and record keeping should probably not choose to become a nurse! (5) My mother is a nurse, and I have great respect for this noble profession. (6) You can determine your aptitudes by thinking about the things you like to do and do well. (7) You can obtain a formal evaluation of your aptitudes by seeing a vocational counselor, a*

professional whose services may be available at your school. (8) Conversely, you should also consider tasks you absolutely hate, and which you are probably not good at. (9) Your choice should be feasible within your allowances of time and money. (10) For example, if you need to support yourself right away, you should probably not plan on becoming a concert violinist, which requires many years of study and practice. (11) You might, however, earn your living as a musician by playing at weddings and other events. (12) Considering both your aptitudes and the circumstances of your life will allow you to find the career that is right for you.

1. The organization of this paragraph would be improved by
   - (1) placing sentence 1 at the end.
   - (2) placing sentence 2 after sentence 3.
   - (3) placing sentence 7 after sentence 8.
   - (4) placing sentence 9 after sentence 10.
   - (5) No correction is necessary.

2. The structure of this paragraph is
   - (1) main idea and supporting details.
   - (2) comparison and contrast.
   - (3) chronological order.
   - (4) cause and effect.
   - (5) visual description.

3. Deleting which sentence would improve the organization of the paragraph?
   - (1) Sentence 1
   - (2) Sentence 3
   - (3) Sentence 5
   - (4) Sentence 8
   - (5) Sentence 10

4. Sentence 9: **Your choice should be feasible within your allowances of time and money.**

   Which correction should be made to this sentence?
   - (1) Add In addition to the beginning of the sentence
   - (2) Add Similarly to the beginning of the sentence
   - (3) Change Your to You're
   - (4) Add a comma after allowances
   - (5) No correction is necessary

Check your answers on page 133.

Unit 5

ESSAY WRITING

In Part II of the GED Langugage Arts, Writing Test, you are given 45 minutes to write an essay approximately 250 words in length. An **essay** is a written argument or discussion. Its purpose is to say something about an issue or a topic in a clear, logical way so that the reader understands the writer's points and is convinced that they make sense.

Like the sample in Figure 1, your GED essay needs a clear beginning, middle, and end. You can achieve this by planning four or five paragraphs. The first paragraph is the **introduction**. The middle two or three paragraphs are the **body** of the essay. The last paragraph contains the **conclusion**.

Each paragraph in your essay serves only one purpose. The introduction tells the reader what your essay will do. It introduces the main idea of your essay and each of your main supporting points. Each paragraph of the body discusses one of those supporting points and gives details and examples. Finally, the concluding paragraph briefly sums up the discussion to end the essay.

Look at the sample essay in Figure 1. The introduction briefly states three ways in which animals are useful to people. Notice that no specific examples or details are given in the introduction.

The second paragraph opens with a topic sentence, or a general statement, about animals as friends. Then the entire paragraph illustrates this point. The next two paragraphs begin in a similar way, each with a topic sentence (one about animals that assist disabled people and the other about animals as workers). Each goes on to discuss only that one main idea.

The fifth paragraph is the conclusion. It ties together everything in the essay. Like the introduction, it is general. Examples and details appear only in the body of the essay.

Use Your Time Well

In order to write a good essay in 45 minutes, you will need to use your time well. The following time frame is suggested:

5 Minutes
> Think about your essay.
> Understand the essay topic.
> Brainstorm ideas.

5 Minutes
> Organize your ideas.
> Group your ideas.
> Create a brief outline.

30 Minutes
> Write your essay.
> Introduce the subject in the first paragraph.
> Develop the body.
> Tie up your ideas in the conclusion.

5 Minutes
> Revise and edit your work.
> Check your sentence structure.
> Make grammar, spelling, capitalization, and punctuation corrections.

Understanding the Topic

In Part II of the GED Language Arts, Writing Test, a series of paragraphs, called the *prompt*, will give you a topic on which you must write your essay. GED essay prompts contain two parts:

- The *topic* itself

- Some *instructions* on how to write the essay

Here's an example of the kind of prompt you'll see:

Many adults worry about the amount of violence on television. They think television is a bad influence on young people, who spend far too much time watching it. Others take a different view, believing that television has many good features for children under the age of 18.

Write an essay of about 250 words in which you discuss the positive effects television has on young people. Be sure to use examples.

FIGURE 1. SAMPLE ESSAY

Introduction	Some people spend large amounts of money and time on animals. They do this because animals can bring them friendship if they're lonely and aid if they're disabled. Animals also help people with their work.
Body	People who live alone might count on a pet for company. An eager dog wagging its tail might welcome them home from a tiring day at work. A warm kitten might snuggle up and keep them company while they read or watch television.
	For the physically disabled, an animal can make life easier. Guide dogs help blind people get around. Highly skilled dogs and chimpanzees can turn lights on and off and get food for people who are paralyzed.
	Some people depend on animals in their work. The police rely on dogs to catch criminals. Scientists use dolphins and other animals to study behavior. People who work in the wilderness can use pack animals, such as horses and llamas, to provide transportation or carry heavy loads.
Conclusion	Animals serve as friends, as helpers, and as workers. That's why people are willing to spend time and money caring for them.

This sample meets all the criteria for a good essay.

First you might assume the essay topic is *violence on television* because that's the topic of the first sentence you read. But, in this prompt, violence on television is background to the topic. The topic is *the positive effects television has on young people*. If you don't read everything in the prompt, you could mistakenly write about the wrong topic, and even if your essay were otherwise perfect, you'd get no credit because you didn't write about the assigned topic.

Use these guidelines to find the topic when you read a GED essay prompt:

- Look for a statement that tells you to do something.

- Look for a question that you must answer.

Organizing Your Ideas

After you read a prompt and understand the topic, you need to decide what to say about it. Start with the topic and brainstorm some ideas that would support it. If you are asked by the topic to take a position on an issue, choose your position and brainstorm main ideas to support it. To **brainstorm** means to write down every idea about the topic that comes to your mind.

Consider the topic—the positive effects of television on young people. You might brainstorm these main ideas:

- Television provides entertainment.

- Television stars may provide good role models.

- Television provides information.

- Television models family relationships.

- Television shows people at work, which helps children make career goals.

Now narrow your ideas to no more than three main points. If some ideas are closely related, you can perhaps combine them. Eliminate ideas that seem short, dull, or inappropriate. Suppose you have chosen these three main points.

    I. Television provides entertainment.
   II. Television provides information.
  III. Television helps young people choose life goals.

From these ideas, you can now create an **outline** for the body of your essay. An outline is a plan to get you from the beginning of your essay to the end. It helps you stick to the subject of each paragraph and keeps your essay organized and under control.

Remember, as you write the body of your essay, you will need to support each point with details and specific examples. Your details and examples should reinforce the main idea of the paragraph. An outline keeps you on track.

You can use any method you like to write your outline. You may simply choose to make a list of points and examples or you may choose to use a formal numbering system. You will not be scored on your outline. Its only purpose is to organize your writing. To see how an outline works, look at this possible outline for the second paragraph of the essay on the positive effects of television.

II. Television provides information.
- A. Current events
  1. News
  2. Elections
  3. Talk shows (concerns of society)
- B. School subjects
  1. Documentaries
  2. Children's programs (*Sesame Street*)
- C. Commercials
  1. Consumer products (cars, toys, food)
  2. Services (credit cards, telephone companies)

At the outline stage, you may find that you have too much material for a 250-word essay. If so, you can eliminate one or two subgroups as you write. But, remember, it's always better to go into the writing stage knowing you won't be at a loss for something to say.

Writing Your Essay

Your essay's first paragraph, the introduction, tells the reader two things: (a) what the topic is and (b) what you are going to say about that topic. Stated in a single sentence, these ideas form a **thesis statement**. Your thesis statement is the central idea of your entire essay and clarifies your position as the writer of the essay.

Here is a possible thesis statement for an essay on the positive effects of television on young people: *Although adults worry that television is bad for children, television provides entertainment and information for young people and helps them set goals.*

Combined with another general sentence, you have a well-written introduction:

Although adults worry that television is bad for children, television provides entertainment and information for young people and helps them set goals. Used wisely, television is a positive influence on young people.

Notice what the introductory paragraph does *not* do:

- **It doesn't announce what it will say.** It doesn't say *"In this essay, I will show...."* If you have a clearly stated thesis, you don't need to *tell* the reader what you are going to say, you *just say it.*

- **It doesn't apologize for not being a good essay.** It doesn't say *"I'll do the best I can, but this is a hard topic."*

- **It doesn't wander away from the topic.** It doesn't say *"We have two television sets in our house, but my sister and I still fight over what to watch. I wouldn't spend 5 minutes watching the stuff she likes. I don't even like the same music she listens to. And I can't stand her clothes. Even her friends are hard to take."*

- **It doesn't contain specific details or examples.** The introduction must be general; examples will come later.

Exercise 1

Directions: Read the following GED essay prompt.

America is facing a health-care crisis. Many politicians and health-care professionals believe we can keep medical costs down only if we take better care of ourselves and try to prevent illness.

Write a 250-word essay in which you show how people can accept responsibility for their own health care.

Your topic: Show how people can accept responsibility for their own health to keep medical costs down.

Your main points:

- People must become informed.

- People must pay attention to diet and exercise.

- People must create a safe home environment.

Now use this information to write an introduction. When you have written your introduction, check for the following:

- Will the opening grab the reader's attention?

- Will the reader know what the topic is?

- Will the reader know what you intend to say about the topic?

In other words, is your thesis clear?

Check your answer on page 133.

Developing the Body and Conclusion

Once you've written the introduction, you're ready to develop the body of the essay. These middle paragraphs are the most complicated paragraphs in your essay because they contain details and supporting examples. Your job now is to expand your outline into sentence and paragraph form. Supporting details and examples should offer some new level of information; they can't be just a restatement of the introduction.

Each paragraph in the body should begin with a topic sentence. Here's a possible topic sentence:

> One reason television is a positive experience for young children is that it delivers complex information in a way that they can easily understand.

Notice that the sentence not only makes a point, but also reminds the reader that the entire essay is about the positive effects of television on children. Based on our earlier outline, the rest of the paragraph might read:

> Through the use of graphics and sound, news shows help children to understand current events. Maps and graphs help children to understand election reports. Talk shows explore human relationships and the concerns of society. Documentaries and other educational programs aim to deliver actual academic content in interesting, engaging ways. Even commercials inform as they introduce children to the products and services they may someday choose as consumers.

You may end a paragraph, if it seems complete, before you've included everything on your outline, or you may add new ideas if they fit the topic sentence.

As you know, the last paragraph of an essay will always be a conclusion. Regardless of what the topic is, a conclusion, like an introduction, does two things:

- It restates the thesis or the ideas contained in the thesis.

- It contains a closing thought, something the reader can think about after reading the essay.

Here's one possible conclusion to the essay on the positive effects of television.

> Television enriches the lives of young people in many ways. Not only does it entertain, but it also teaches. Through the depiction of people from every walk of life, children identify models of behavior for life in the family and on the job. No other artistic medium has a greater opportunity to affect the lives of young people in such a positive way.

Notice that the first sentence reminds the reader of the essay's topic. The paragraph also lists the main points of the thesis (that television entertains, informs, and helps children set goals). The last sentence strengthens the argument and ties the ideas together.

Notice, too, what the concluding paragraph does not do:

- **It doesn't report what you have just said.** It doesn't say, *"In this essay, I talked about the positive effects of television on young people."*

- **It doesn't apologize for not being a good essay.** It doesn't say, *"This probably isn't very clear, but I hope you understand it."*

- **It doesn't change the subject at the very end.** It doesn't say, *"When I was a child, I watched only cartoons, which are very violent."*

Exercise 2

Directions: Write a possible conclusion for an essay that asks you to consider why people enjoy horror movies. The essay has the following thesis statement: *Horror movies help me forget my problems, entertain me with special effects, and let me enjoy fantastic drama.*

Be sure your conclusion

- restates the thesis.

- contains a closing thought.

- does not change the subject.

If possible, try out different conclusions on a friend or family member to see which have the most impact. Read the possibilities and ask what works and what doesn't, or why one ending seems more effective than another.

Check your answer on page 133.

Revising and Editing Your Work

Before you submit your GED essay, take 5 minutes and revise and edit your work. If you find a mistake, draw a single line through the words you want to omit or change and write any correction neatly and clearly above. You may want to change some words or phrases to add variety and interest. You can improve the sophistication of your writing by choosing accurate words. For example, instead of writing *a lot*, try phrases like *several dozen*, *countless*, or *more than a thousand*.

Use these questions to help you revise and edit your work:

- Did you write about the topic?

- Did you stick to the subject?

- Does your essay have a clear structure?

- Did you use clear and interesting examples?

- Did you choose the best words?

- Are the sentences complete?

- Is the essay free of spelling, capitalization, and punctuation errors?

- Have you followed the rules of grammar?

Exercise 3

Directions: Write an essay based on the following sample GED prompt.

Topic

In our culture, it is impossible to escape the influence of advertising. Advertising is a multi-billion dollar industry that bombards consumers with information about countless products and services.

In an essay of 250 words, discuss some ways advertisers influence the buying public. Be sure to use examples to support your ideas.

Check your essay on 134.

Glossary

action verb: a verb that shows the subject doing something

adjective: a word that changes or alters a noun

adverb: a word that modifies a verb, adjective, or another adverb

antecedent: the noun that a pronoun substitutes for or replaces

apostrophe: a punctuation mark used to indicate either ownership or that a letter has been omitted

body: the middle two or three paragraphs of an essay

brainstorm: to write down *every* idea about a topic that comes to your mind

clause: a word group that contains a subject and a verb but is not necessarily a complete thought

coherent: clear and logical

comma splice: two or more complete sentences separated only by commas

complete sentence: a sentence that contains a subject and a complete verb that expresses a complete thought

complex sentence: a sentence containing a closely related independent clause and a dependent clause

compound sentence: a sentence that contains two or more independent clauses

conclusion: the last paragraph of an essay

contraction: a word formed by combining two words; one or more letters are omitted and an apostrophe is put in their place

dependent clause: a clause that depends on the rest of the sentence for its meaning

essay: a written argument or discussion

fragment: a word group that may look like a sentence but lacks a subject, a verb, or part of a verb, or is not a complete thought

gerund: present participle used in a sentence as a noun

headings: titles within a chapter or section

homophones: words that are pronounced the same but spelled differently

independent clause: a clause that includes a subject and a verb and has meaning on its own (a complete sentence)

infinitive: form of the verb that consists of the word *to* followed by the present tense form of the verb

introduction: the first paragraph of an essay

linking verb: a verb that shows what the subject is, seems, or feels

modifier: a word or group of words that describes another word or group of words in a sentence

noun: a word for a person, place, or thing

outline: a brief plan or list that guides you in writing an essay

parallel structure: putting similar elements in a sentence into the same form

participle: a form of the main verb that follows a helping verb in a verb phrase

phrase: a word group that does not contain a subject and verb; a phrase often appears at the beginning of a sentence as introductory material

plural: more than one

pronoun: a word that replaces or refers to a noun

relative pronoun: does not replace a noun but refers to it

run-on sentence: two or more complete sentences not separated by punctuation

simple sentence: a sentence containing one complete thought

singular: one

subject: the person or thing that performs the action in a sentence and tells who or what the sentence is about

subject-verb agreement: singular subjects take singular verbs; plural subjects take plural verbs

suffix: one or more letters added to the end of a word

syllable: a part of a word that is pronounced as a single unit; a syllable always contains a vowel

tangent: an unrelated idea that does not belong in a paragraph

thesis statement: the introduction of an essay that tells the reader two things: what the topic is and what you are going to say about that topic

topic sentence: sentence that states the main idea of a paragraph

transitions: links between ideas

verb: the word in a sentence that shows what the subject is or what it does

verb phrase: a verb form with more than one word: a helping verb and some form of the main verb

verb tense: form of the verb that indicates the time of the action

ANSWERS AND EXPLANATIONS

Unit 1: Sentence Structure

Exercise 1 (page 75)

1. **The correct answer is (3): trouble understanding or** Removing the period corrects the fragment by attaching it to the rest of a complete sentence. The other choices create different fragments.

2. **The correct answer is (2): breakdown in their** Removing the period corrects the fragment by attaching it to the rest of a complete sentence. Choice (3) creates different fragments. Choices (4) and (5) change the meaning of the sentence.

3. **The correct answer is (2): Change Leaving to This leaves.** Choice (2) creates a sentence that makes sense. The other choices create more fragments.

4. **The correct answer is (3): Insert they collect before newspapers.** Choice (3) gives the sentence a subject and a verb. The other choices do not correct the fragment.

5. **The correct answer is (4): Change taking to take.** The verb must be complete to complete the sentence. The other choices create different fragments.

Exercise 2 (page 76)

1. **The correct answer is (2): American citizen, Kimiko** When a dependent clause precedes the main clause, it takes a comma. The other choices use incorrect punctuation.

2. **The correct answer is (4): world are studying** Choice (4) completes the verb. The other choices do not complete the verb.

3. **The correct answer is (3): Kimiko** Kimiko is the subject of the sentence. The other choices don't make sense.

Exercise 3 (page 77)

1. **The correct answer is (4): Insert a semicolon after unemployed.** *Unemployed* marks the end of the first complete thought. A semicolon is the appropriate punctuation. Choices (1), (2), and (5) create fragments. Choice (3) doesn't correct the run-on.

2. **The correct answer is (2): home and abroad. This affected** *Abroad* marks the end of the first complete thought. A period or semicolon is the appropriate punctuation. Choice (3) forms two complete sentences but the intended meaning is changed in the second sentence. The other choices do not correct the run-on.

3. **The correct answer is (4): we** The other choices don't make sense in this sentence.

4. **The correct answer is (5): Replace but with So.** *So* is a more appropriate connecting word than either the original *but* or *yet*, which is given in choice (4). The other choices punctuate incorrectly.

5. **The correct answer is (3): birds, so their** Choice (3) uses the best connecting word and punctuates correctly.

6. **The correct answer is (5): doves; those** Choice (5) uses a semicolon to separate two independent clauses. Choice (1) is a run-on sentence. Choices (2) and (3) link the two independent clauses with a comma and a connecting word, but the connecting words are inappropriate. Choice (4) is punctuated incorrectly.

Exercise 4 (page 79)

1. **The correct answer is (5): food. Everyone** The first independent clause ends with *food*. The two clauses are not closely connected, so a period should be used to separate them. The other choices do not correct the run-on.

2. **The correct answer is (3): Insert a semicolon after the second taxes.** Because of the close connection between the clauses, a semicolon is the best way to link them into one sentence. However, making two separate sentences would also work. Choice (1) creates two complete sentences, but the second one contains an extra word. Choice (4) creates a fragment. Choices (2) and (5) don't correct the run-on.

3. **The correct answer is (2): Replace income tax they with income tax. They.** *Income tax* marks the end of the first complete thought. The other choices either create fragments or do not correct the run-on.

4. **The correct answer is (2): Replace so with but.** The connector *but* shows the correct relationship between the two ideas. Choice (1) creates a run-on. Choices (3) and (4) show the wrong relationship between the ideas.

5. **The correct answer is (1): Replace however with for example.** Choice (1) provides the proper connecting word. Choice (2) uses the wrong connecting word. Choices (3) and (4) incorrectly punctuate a compound sentence.

6. **The correct answer is (3): cause** Choice (3) provides an appropriate verb for the sentence. Choices (1) and (2) don't make sense, and choices (4) and (5) change the meaning of the sentence.

Exercise 5 (page 80)

1. **The correct answer is (2): itself, it** A dependent clause at the beginning of the sentence should be followed by a comma. Choice (1) creates a fragment. The other choices don't make sense.

2. **The correct answer is (5): No correction is necessary.**

3. **The correct answer is (4): Replace Sundays. Because with Sundays because.** A dependent clause that follows the main clause should not be separated from the main clause by a comma. The other choices don't make sense.

4. **The correct answer is (3): Remove the comma after books.** When the dependent clause follows the main clause, there is no need for a comma. Choice (1) creates a fragment; choice (2) uses incorrect punctuation, and choices (4) and (5) use inappropriate connecting words.

5. **The correct answer is (4): Because** The relationship is cause and effect. The other choices use inappropriate connecting words.

Exercise 6 (page 82)

1. **The correct answer is (2): public transportation** Choice (2) doesn't change the sentence's meaning and it clarifies the modifier. The other choices change the meaning of the sentence.

2. **The correct answer is (1): missing** The main part of the sentence doesn't need to change. The other choices change the meaning of the sentence.

3. **The correct answer is (4): Carmela sees another bus coming** Choice (4) puts the modifier next to the word it modifies. Choice (5) changes the meaning of the sentence, and the other choices do not correct the dangling modifier.

Exercise 7 (page 83)

1. **The correct answer is (3): and in Latin America** Choice (3) is the only choice that maintains parallel structure.

2. **The correct answer is (2): share their standard of living** Choice (2) is the only choice that maintains parallel structure.

3. **The correct answer is (4): Replace go to with in.** Choice (4) is the only choice that maintains parallel structure.

4. **The correct answer is (5): No correction is necessary.**

5. **The correct answer is (3): children's questions** Choice (3) is the only choice that maintains parallel structure.

6. **The correct answer is (4): Change remembering to remember.** Choice (4) is the only choice that maintains parallel structure.

7. **The correct answer is (1): Replace by keeping diaries with diaries.** Choice (1) is the only choice that maintains parallel structure.

8. **The correct answer is (3): Replace to remember with memories of.** Choice (3) is the only choice that maintains parallel structure.

9. **The correct answer is (4): Change giving to to give.** Choice (4) is the only choice that maintains parallel structure.

Unit 2: Usage and Grammar

Exercise 1 *(page 85)*

1. was
2. cheer
3. warn
4. confuse
5. takes
6. Charles *plays* card games with his friends and sometimes he *wins. Charles* is singular, so the verbs must be singular.
7. Michelle *seems* to win every time she *plays. Michelle* is a singular subject and takes singular verbs.
8. Correct
9. Correct
10. Mr. Chan *hates* long lines and becomes impatient in them. *Mr. Chan* is a singular subject and takes a singular verb.
11. **The correct answer is (1): Change is to are.** Choice (1) has a plural subject *(strikes)* that requires a plural verb. Choices (2) and (3) do not correct for subject-verb agreement. Choices (4) and (5) create fragments.
12. **The correct answer is (2): negotiation attempts fail** Choice (2) has a plural subject *(attempts)* that requires a plural verb. Choices (1) and (3) do not correct for subject-verb agreement; choices (4) and (5) change the meaning of the sentence.
13. **The correct answer is (4): Change are to is.** Choice (4) has a singular subject *(hope)* that requires a singular verb. The other choices don't correct for subject-verb agreement.

Exercise 2 *(page 87)*

1. votes
2. go
3. looks
4. chooses
5. ask
6. says
7. knows
8. am
9. run
10. **The correct answer is (4): Change has to have.** Choice (4) matches a plural verb *(have)* with a plural subject *(Holly and Kent)*. Choice (1) does not correct for subject-verb agreement. Choice (2) is incorrect punctuation for a compound sentence. Choice (3) is an incorrect verb form, and choice (5) creates sentence fragments.
11. **The correct answer is (4): Change suggest to suggests.** Choice (4) matches the singular verb *(suggests)* with a singular subject *(Holly)*. Choice (2) is incorrect punctuation for a compound sentence. Choices (1), (3), and (5) don't correct for subject-verb agreement.

Exercise 3 *(page 88)*

1. **The correct answer is (5): Change raises to raise.** Choice (5) uses a plural verb *(raise)* to agree with a plural subject *(they)*. Choices (1) and (4) lack subject-verb agreement; choice (2) creates a fragment, and choice (3) inserts a comma before a dependent clause.

2. **The correct answer is (4): asked people to guess how many marbles there were** Choice (4) uses a plural verb *(were)* to agree with a plural subject *(marbles)*. Choices (1), (2), and (5) lack subject-verb agreement, and choice (3) changes the meaning of the sentence.

3. **The correct answer is (3): Change are to is.** Choice (3) uses a singular verb *(is)* to agree with a singular subject *(thing)*. Choice (1) lacks subject-verb agreement; choice (2) doesn't correct for subject-verb agreement, and choice (4) creates a fragment.

Exercise 4 *(page 89)*

1. There *are* too many leaves to rake in one afternoon. (subject = leaves)
2. *Do* both of them want to go to the game? (subject = both)
3. In the cupboard *are* all the things you need to bake a cake. (subject = things)
4. Upstairs *are* two more bedrooms. (subject = bedrooms)
5. Here *is* the information you asked for. (subject = information)
6. **The correct answer is (2): Change is to are.** Choice (2) uses a plural verb to agree with the plural subject *(ways)*. Choice (1) changes the meaning of the sentence. Choices (3), (4), and (5) do not correct for subject-verb agreement.
7. **The correct answer is (1): Change are to is.** Choice (1) uses a singular verb to agree with a singular subject *(one)*. Choice (2) uses *be* alone as a verb; choice (3) is not a correct infinitive form; choice (4) doesn't correct for subject-verb agreement, and choice (5) shifts to past tense.
8. **The correct answer is (2): Change prefers to prefer.** Choice (2) matches a plural verb to a plural subject *(others)*. The other choices do not affect subject-verb agreement.
9. **The correct answer is (3): use** Choice (3) uses a plural verb form to agree with a plural subject *(cooks)*. Choices (1), (2), and (4) do not correct for subject-verb agreement, and choice (5) changes the meaning of the sentence.
10. **The correct answer is (4): A well-stocked kitchen has many kinds** Choice (4) restructures the sentence to put the subject and verb closer to the beginning. Choices (1) and (3) lack subject-verb agreement; choice (2) lacks a verb, and choice (5) changes the meaning of the sentence.
11. **The correct answer is (4): Change goes to go.** Choice (4) matches a plural verb with a plural subject *(herbs and spices)*. Choice (1) incorrectly uses *be* by itself; choice (3) creates a fragment, and the other choices do not affect subject-verb agreement.

Exercise 5 *(page 90)*

1. planning—present
2. helped—past
3. sitting—present
4. **The correct answer is (2): Change plan to planning.** Choice (2) uses a present participle to complete the verb and to show future action. Choices (1) and (4) create fragments, and choice (3) incorrectly uses a past participle.
5. **The correct answer is (1): Change Start to Starting.** Choice (1) uses a gerund as the subject of the sentence so that the sentence makes sense. Choice (2) changes the meaning of the sentence; choices (3) and (4) use incorrect verb forms, and choice (5) changes an adjective to a verb.

6. **The correct answer is (5): you should have paid attention** Choice (5) uses a past participle to complete the verb. Choices (1), (2), and (3) use incorrect verb forms, and choice (4) omits the participle.

Exercise 6 *(page 92)*

1. **The correct answer is (5): Change cutting to cut.** Choice (5) uses the correct infinitive form. Choice (1) is an incorrect verb form; choice (2) uses a participle by itself, and choices (3) and (4) are incorrect infinitive forms.

2. **The correct answer is (3): lost** Choice (3) is the correct past participle of *to lose*. Choices (1) and (2) are not past participle forms, and choices (4) and (5) change the meaning of the sentence.

3. **The correct answer is (4): Change put to putting.** Choice (4) uses the correct participle. Choice (1) is not the correct participle; choice (2) is an incorrect verb form, choice (3) eliminates the required helper in a verb phrase, and choice (5) does not use the correct form of the past participle of *to put*.

Exercise 7 *(page 93)*

1. she heard/crawled
2. Whenever it rains/feel
3. by the time/had walked
4. last year/refused
5. Currently/receive
6. Now/am
7. Last year/had
8. **The correct answer is (4): include** Choice (4) uses a present-tense verb, which is consistent with the rest of the paragraph. The other choices use incorrect tenses.
9. **The correct answer is (3): Change will help to helps.** Choice (3) uses a present-tense verb, which is consistent with the rest of the paragraph. Choice (1) removes the gerund that serves as the subject of the sentence; choice (2) uses an incorrect infinitive form; choice (4) uses the past tense, and choice (5) creates a fragment.
10. **The correct answer is (2): Change were to is.** Choice (2) uses a present-tense singular verb to agree with the singular subject *(sense)*. Choice (1) creates a fragment; choice (3) lacks subject-verb agreement, and choice (4) uses the past tense.

Exercise 8 *(page 94)*

1. past
2. future
3. past
4. future
5. present
6. past
7. present
8. future
9. future
10. past
11. Last summer, the Orangerie Produce Co. had an employee picnic. The picnic was a great success, thanks to the Planning Committee. The committee members had worked for weeks by the time picnic day arrived. The employees had played games, danced, swum, and eaten hot dogs and apple pie by the end of the day. Everyone hopes there will be another picnic next year.
12. **The correct answer is (3): poured into the country, learned American ways, and became part of** Choice (3) maintains past tense throughout the sentence. The tenses of the other choices are inconsistent.

13. **The correct answer is (2): Replace has change with has changed.** Choice (2) uses the correct past participle for *to change*. Choices (1) and (3) switch tense, and choice (4) lacks subject-verb agreement.

14. **The correct answer is (4): they cling with pride to** Choice (4) maintains the present tense that is used throughout the second paragraph. Choices (1) and (5) switch to past tense, and the other choices use incorrect verb forms.

15. **The correct answer is (1): Change gave to give.** Choice (1) maintains the present tense that is used throughout the paragraph. Choice (2) shifts tense, and choices (3), (4), and (5) are incorrect infinitive forms.

Exercise 9 *(page 96)*

1. **The correct answer is (5): They** Choice (5) is the appropriate pronoun to match the antecedent. Choice (1) repeats the lengthy subject. Choice (2) is not the appropriate pronoun and does not agree with the verb. Choices (3) and (4) create sentence fragments.

2. **The correct answer is (5): Change his to their.** Choice (5) uses a plural pronoun *(their)* to agree with a plural subject *(victims)*. Choice (1) is not a participle; choice (2) creates a fragment; choice (3) lacks subject-verb agreement, and choice (4) shifts to the past tense.

3. **The correct answer is (2): They control the symptoms** Choice (2) corrects the fragment by giving the sentence a subject. Choice (1) is a fragment; choice (3) doesn't make sense, and choices (4) and (5) change the meaning of the sentence.

4. **The correct answer is (5): No correction is necessary.**

Exercise 10 *(page 97)*

1. Manuel and Umeki agreed to share *their* study notes with each other.
2. A baby seal can swim by *itself* right away.
3. The basketball team lost *its* third game in a row.
4. **The correct answer is (3): you might like to shop** Choice (3) maintains the pronoun *you* that already has been used in the sentence. Choice (1) switches from second person to an indefinite pronoun. Choices (2) and (4) switch from second person to third person. Choice (5) shifts to first person.
5. **The correct answer is (4): Replace One with You.** Choice (4) maintains second-person pronoun consistency in the sentence. The other choices shift from second person.
6. **The correct answer is (5): Replace our with your.** Choice (5) maintains second person in the sentence. The other choices change the meaning of the sentence and do not correct the mismatched pronoun *our*.

Exercise 11 *(page 98)*

1. **The correct answer is (3): During these industrially productive years** Choice (3) corrects the pronoun *(they)*, which lacks a clear antecedent. The other choices change the meaning of the sentence.

2. **The correct answer is (2): Replace her with their.** Choice (2) correctly provides a plural third-person pronoun *their* to fit the plural antecedent *women*. The other choices do not fit the antecedent.

3. **The correct answer is (4): people selfishly pursued money** Choice (4) uses a noun *(people)* instead of the pronoun *them*, which has no clear antecedent. The other choices lack clear antecedents.

Exercise 12 *(page 99)*

1. **The correct answer is that**—The pronoun has a nonhuman antecedent.

2. **The correct answer is who**—The pronoun has a human antecedent.

3. **The correct answer is who**—The pronoun has a human antecedent.

4. **The correct answer is whom**—The pronoun is used in object position (substitute *him*).

5. **The correct answer is that**—The pronoun has a nonhuman antecedent.

6. **The correct answer is whoever**—The pronoun is used in actor position (substitute *he*).

7. **The correct answer is (2): Because they find it convenient,** Choice (2) is correct because it clears up the vague pronoun reference. Choice (1) is incorrect because the reader can't tell what *their* refers to. Choice (3) changes the meaning of the sentence; choices (4) and (5) are incorrect because there is no antecedent for *your*.

8. **The correct answer is (2): Replace anyone with people.** Choice (2) provides a plural antecedent to go with a plural pronoun *(themselves)*. Choices (1) and (3) do not correct the pronoun problem, and choice (4) is incorrect because *themself* is not an accepted English word.

9. **The correct answer is (4): Replace that with who.** Choice (4) is correct because *who* is the pronoun to use for people. Choices (1) and (2) use singular subjects *(Someone* and *Anyone)* with a plural verb *(work)*. Choice (3) uses the object form of the pronoun, and choice (5) assumes a nonhuman antecedent.

10. **The correct answer is (3): Replace your with their.** Choice (3) is correct because *their* agrees with the antecedent *people*. The other choices use pronouns that do not agree with the antecedent.

11. **The correct answer is (5): distractions** Choice (5) expresses the meaning of the original sentence: workers must be aware of distractions (such as family, housework, etc.). Choice (1) changes the meaning of the sentence; choices (2), (3), and (4) use pronouns without antecedents.

Unit 3: Mechanics

Exercise 1 *(page 101)*

1. **The correct answer is *Dr.***

2. **The correct answer is *July.***

3. **The correct answer is *Correct.***

4. **The correct answer is *Casablanca.***

5. **The correct answer is *Japanese, English, and French.***

6. **The correct answer is (3): Change senator to Senator.** In this sentence, *Senator* must be capitalized because it is a title used as part of someone's name. Choice (1) is incorrect because the first word in a sentence must be capitalized. Choice (2) is incorrect because *legislator* is a general term, and choice (4) is incorrect because a person's name must be capitalized.

7. **The correct answer is (4): Change public library to Public Library.** Choice (4) capitalizes both words because in this sentence they are part of the name of a specific public library. The other choices either capitalize general words or fail to capitalize specific names.

Exercise 2 *(page 102)*

1. **The correct answer is (2): Change National Parks to national parks.** Choice (2) is correct because the writer is speaking of national parks in general, so there is no need for capital letters. Choice (1) is incorrect because the name of a country must be capitalized. Choice (3) is incorrect because we do not capitalize directions unless they are used as the name of a place. There is no reason to capitalize the nouns in choices (4) and (5).

2. **The correct answer is (2): Change yellowstone to Yellowstone.** Choice (2) capitalizes the name of a specific national park. Choice (1) is incorrect because the first word of a sentence must be capitalized. There's no reason to capitalize the words in choices (3) and (4).

3. **The correct answer is (5): Change Mountain Range to mountain range.** Choice (5) is correct because there is no need to capitalize when speaking of mountain ranges in general. There is no reason to capitalize the words in choices (1), (3), and (4). Choice (2) is incorrect because the entire name of a specific mountain range must be capitalized.

4. **The correct answer is (2): Change national park to National Park.** Choice (2) capitalizes all the words that are part of a name. Choice (1) fails to capitalize all the words in a name, and there is no reason to capitalize the words in choices (3), (4), and (5).

5. **The correct answer is (2): Change cave to Cave.** Choice (2) capitalizes the name of a particular cave. Choice (1) is incorrect because the first word of a sentence and the name of a particular place must be capitalized. Choice (3) fails to capitalize the name of a state, and there is no reason to capitalize the words in choices (4) and (5).

Exercise 3 *(page 104)*

1. **The correct answer is (4): to get to these parking lots, they face** Choice (4) places a comma after the dependent clause at the beginning of the sentence. Choice (1) omits the comma; choice (2) creates a fragment, and choices (3) and (5) put the comma in the wrong places.

2. **The correct answer is (2): Insert a comma after distances.** Choice (2) places a comma after the dependent clause at the beginning of the sentence. The other choices put commas in the wrong places.

3. **The correct answer is (2): Illegally parked cars occupy** Choice (2) is the only choice that maintains the meaning of the original sentence.

4. **The correct answer is (3): Insert a comma after driver.** Choice (3) places a comma before the last item in a series. There's no reason for the comma in the other choices.

Exercise 4 *(page 105)*

1. **The correct answer is (2): Insert a comma after alive.** Choice (2) inserts a comma after a dependent clause. Choice (1) lacks subject-verb agreement; choice (3) shifts to the future tense, and choice (4) introduces a misspelling.

2. **The correct answer is (4): monthly installments and had to wait** Choice (4) removes the comma that separates the two parts of a compound verb. Choice (1) separates the parts of the compound verb with a comma; choice (2) shifts to the present tense; choice (3) shifts to the future tense, and choice (5) capitalizes general words.

3. **The correct answer is (3): Remove the comma after titles.** Choice (3) removes the comma before the beginning of the items in a series. There's no reason for the comma in choice (1); choice (2) capitalizes a general word; choice (4) capitalizes a two-letter preposition in a title, and choice (5) removes the comma before the last item in a series.

Exercise 5 *(page 106)*

1. **The correct answer is (1): Change beginning to beginning.** Choice (1) shows the correct spelling of *beginning*. Choices (2) and (3) show incorrect spellings. Choice (4) shows an incorrect use of the possessive. Choice (5) shows an incorrect use of capitalization.

2. **The correct answer is (2): Change recieve to receive.** Choice (2) shows the correct spelling of *receive*. Choices (1) and (4) show incorrect spellings. Choice (3) shows an incorrect use of present tense.

3. **The correct answer is (5): Replace but with so.** Choice (5) uses the correct connecting word to show contrast. Choice (1) shifts to the past tense; choice (2) omits part of a verb; choice (3) uses a past participle as part of the infinitive, and choice (4) uses an inappropriate connecting word.

Exercise 6 *(page 107)*

1. The correct answer is *hoped*.
2. The correct answer is *heroes*.
3. The correct answer is *addresses*.
4. The correct answer is *boxes*.
5. The correct answer is *tomatoes*.
6. The correct answer is *tries*.
7. **The correct answer is (2): Change the spelling of helpping to helping.** Choice (2) is correct because the consonant is doubled before *ing* is added to a one-syllable verb only if the consonant is preceded by a vowel. Choice (1) incorrectly changes a plural noun to a possessive. Choice (3) reverses the *ei* in *their*. Choice (4) adds *es* to a noun that becomes plural simply by adding *s*.

8. **The correct answer is (2): Change the spelling of exorbitent to exorbitant.** Choices (1) and (4) misspell words by reversing letters, and choice (3) fails to drop the *e* before adding *ing*.

9. **The correct answer is (5): Change the spelling of financiel to financial.** Choice (1) is a misspelling. There is no reason for the comma in choice (2). Choice (3) is incorrect because a comma between independent clauses requires a connecting word. Choice (4) is the incorrect form of the relative pronoun.

Exercise 7 *(page 109)*

1. **The correct answer is (3): Change with out to without.** Do not separate prefixes and suffixes from the main word even if the suffix or prefix is a complete word. Choices (1) and (2) are misspellings, and choice (4) fails to drop the final *e* before adding *ing*.

2. **The correct answer is (2): Change the spelling of normaly to normally.** Choice (2) adds the suffix *ly* without changing the spelling of the main word. Choice (1) fails to drop the final *e* before adding *ing*. Choice (3) removes the comma after a dependent clause in a compound sentence, and choice (4) changes the spelling of the main word before adding the suffix *ly*.

3. **The correct answer is (1): Change couragous to courageous.** Choice (1) correctly spells *courageous*. Choices (2), (3), and (4) misspell words.

Exercise 8 *(page 110)*

1. Being late so often, *you're* going to have trouble keeping the job. *a*
2. *It'll* be hard to find any place open at this hour. *wi*
3. They *aren't* selling that item any longer. *o*
4. He *hasn't* missed a single game all season. *o*
5. *You'll* have to wait until the report is published. *wi*
6. Sam saw that *they'd* been there already. *ha*
7. *She's* completely dependable. *i*

8. Take whatever *they'll* give you. *wi*
9. It really *isn't* hard to understand. *o*
10. By now, *it's* too late to get tickets. *i*
11. **The correct answer is (2): Change It's to They're.** Choice (2) uses a plural pronoun (*they*) to agree with a plural antecedent (*snacks*). Choice (1) removes an apostrophe from a contraction, choice (3) uses a comma for no reason, and choice (4) creates a fragment.

12. **The correct answer is (3): Change there to they're.** In choice (3) the wrong word *there* becomes a contraction meaning *they are*. Choices (1) and (2) remove necessary commas; choice (4) puts the apostrophe in the wrong place, and choice (5) misspells *healthful*.

13. **The correct answer is (3): Change its to it's.** Choice (3) makes a contraction out of *it is*. Choice (1) removes a comma after an introductory word, and choice (2) misplaces the apostrophe. Choice (4) places a comma before a dependent clause, and choice (5) creates a fragment.

14. **The correct answer is (2): Change students' to student's.** Choice (2) places the apostrophe to indicate that the possessive noun is singular. Choice (1) fails to use an apostrophe for a possessive noun. Choice (3) misspells *fascinating*, and there's no reason for the comma in choice (4).

15. **The correct answer is (4): Change their's to theirs.** Possessive pronouns do not use apostrophes. Choices (1) and (2) change plural words to singular possessives; choice (3) lacks subject-verb agreement, and choice (5) uses an apostrophe with a possessive pronoun.

16. **The correct answer is (5): Change decade's to decades.** Choice (5) removes the apostrophe from a word that is neither possessive nor a contraction. Choice (1) removes the apostrophe from a contraction; choices (2) and (3) use incorrect past participles, and choice (4) makes a noun possessive for no reason.

17. **The correct answer is (4): the project's conclusions** Choice (4) uses the apostrophe for the possessive and leaves it out of the plural word. Choice (1) has no possessive; choice (2) places the apostrophe after the *s* in a singular possessive; choice (3) changes a noun from plural to singular and will result in faulty subject-verb agreement (*conclusion show*), and choice (5) reverses the plural and the possessive words.

Exercise 9 *(page 113)*

1. **The correct answer is (5): No correction is necessary.** Choice (1) is incorrect because the hyphen is necessary. Choice (2) is incorrect because a comma is needed before the appositive. Choice (3) is incorrect because the number "one" is needed here. Choice (4) is wrong because the comparative adjective is needed here.

2. **The correct answer is (4): Change their to there.** Choice (1) is incorrect because the verb form used in the sentence is correct. Choice (2) is incorrect because the comma is needed before the introductory clause. Choice (3) is incorrect because a comma should not be placed between the subject and verb.

3. **The correct answer is (2): Change effort to afford.** Choice (1) is incorrect because the contraction is spelled correctly. Choice (3) is incorrect because the comma is needed to separate the two clauses of a compound sentence. Choice (4) is incorrect because the word is spelled correctly.

4. **The correct answer is (1): Change "Its to "It's.** Choice (2) is incorrect because a comma is not needed after a prepositional phrase. Choice (3) is incorrect because the word is already spelled correctly. Choice (4) is incorrect because a comma is needed at the end of a quotation.

Exercise 10 *(page 113)*

1. **The correct answer is (1): Change the spelling of seen to scene.** There's no reason to capitalize *collision*, as in choice (2). Choices (3) and (4) use the wrong sound-alike words, and choice (5) is incorrect because there's no reason to separate the prefix from the main word.

2. **The correct answer is (1): Replace their with there.** Choice (1) uses *there* to indicate place. The other choices use the wrong sound-alike words.

3. **The correct answer is (4): Replace breaks with brakes.** Choice (4) uses *brakes,* which stop cars. Choices (1) and (3) use the wrong sound-alike words, and choice (2) is incorrect because *neither* is an exception to the *ie* rule.

4. **The correct answer is (2): Change already to all ready.** *Already* means *previously,* and *all ready* means *entirely ready.* Choice (1) is incorrect because we use a comma only before a quotation. Choice (3) is the wrong verb tense, and there is no reason to capitalize the words in choice (4).

Unit 4: Organization

Exercise 1 *(page 118)*

1. **The correct answer is (1): Sentence 1** Sentence 1 clearly states the writer's main idea. All of the other sentences in the paragraph are supporting details.

2. **The correct answer is (2): Change due to do.** Choice (1) is incorrect because a comma is not necessary after this phrase. Choice (3) is incorrect because *red* refers to a color. Choice (4) is incorrect because the sentence is not an example but rather one in a series of steps.

3. **The correct answer is (1): Add Then at the beginning of the sentence.** Although this correction is not absolutely necessary, it does highlight the paragraph's organization. Choice (2) is incorrect because the comma is necessary before a quotation. Choice (3) is incorrect because a comma is never placed between the subject and verb of a sentence. Choice (4) is incorrect because *find* means "locate" and *fined* means "penalized."

4. **The correct answer is (4): Change answer write to answer. Write.** This is a run-on sentence; correct it by changing it to two complete sentences. Choice (1) is incorrect because the comma is needed after this introductory phrase. Choice (2) is incorrect because a comma is never used between a verb and its object. Choice (3) is incorrect because *need,* which means "require," is the correct choice in this sentence.

Exercise 2 *(page 119)*

1. **The correct answer is (1): Sentence 1** This sentence clearly states the main idea of the paragraph. Although Sentence 7, choice (5), recaps the main idea, Sentence 1 is clearly the best choice.

2. **The correct answer is (4): Change whose to who's.** Whose, a possessive, is incorrect here, where the meaning is "who is." Choice (1) is incorrect here because this sentence is not an example; therefore, this transitional phrase is not needed. Choice (2) is incorrect because the apostrophe is needed in this possessive form. Choice (3) is incorrect because *it's,* which means "it is," clearly fits the meaning here.

3. **The correct answer is (2): Change you're to your.** A possessive is needed here, not a contraction that means "you are." Choice (1) is incorrect because this sentence is not an example but rather a restatement of the sentence's main idea. Choice (3) is incorrect because no comma is needed before this phrase. Choice (4) is incorrect because, as with the correct answer, a possessive is needed here.

Exercise 3 *(page 120)*

1. **The correct answer is (3): placing sentence 7 after sentence 8** Sentence 7, as placed, disrupts the flow of the argument, since sentence 8 is a negative example of the point made in sentence 6.

2. **The correct answer is (1): main idea and supporting details** The paragraph has two main supporting details, that you should consider your likes and dislikes, and that you should consider your circumstances. Each sentence in the paragraph concerns either the main idea or one of these details.

3. **The correct answer is (3): Sentence 5** This sentence is a tangent, a sentence that is unrelated to the main idea of the paragraph.

4. **The correct answer is (1): Add In addition to the beginning of the sentence.** This sentence marks a new subtopic, or detail, related to the main idea. Therefore, a transition phrase that marks a new topic is needed. Choice (2) is incorrect because this idea is not similar to the one that preceded it. Choice (3) is incorrect because the word needed here is the possessive adjective, not the contraction. Choice (4) is incorrect because this change would make the sentence structure incorrect.

Unit 5: Essay Writing

Exercise 1 *(page 123)*

Answers will vary. Answer these questions to check your work:

- Is your introduction one paragraph?
- Does it start with a hook?
- Does it contain your thesis?

If you can answer *yes* to each of these questions, you have done the work correctly. Here's one possible introduction:

> Many Americans are worried about the rising cost of health care, and they want the government to do something about it. To keep medical costs down, however, people must accept responsibility for their own health. They need to stay informed about the latest health trends and take a look at their diet and exercise habits. They should also create a safe home environment to prevent injury.

The first sentence is the hook. The rest of the paragraph is the thesis.

Exercise 2 *(page 124)*

Answers will vary. Answer these questions to check your work:

- Do your conclusions restate the thesis?
- Do they contain a closing thought?
- Do they stick to the subject of the essay?

If you can answer *yes* to each of these questions, you have done the work correctly. Here is one possible conclusion for this essay:

> If I can forget my own problems and be thrilled by terrifying special effects, I will always enjoy horror movies. I like the fun of a good scare when I know I can't really be harmed. People who don't go to horror movies are missing a great escape.

The first two sentences restate the thesis. The last sentence is the closing thought.

A SAMPLE 3 ESSAY

Hook and thesis with two subtopics

Wherever we turn, we see advertisements. Ads are on television, on the radio, in the papers, everywhere. Sometimes they try to get us to buy products by pretending to be scientific. Other times they try to make us think we'll change for the better if we have the product, sometimes they just pressure us with time limits.

Weak development, confusing sentence structure

Sometimes advertisers try to get us to buy products by they'll pretend to be real science. They use charts and make it look like they're in a laboratory or a doctors office or something like that.

Example is developed, but writing contains too many errors

Some ads try to make us think we'll be better if we have the product. For example, sleep on a certain kind of mattress, the ad says you did a better job at work or school the next day. Another is use the right car for a happy picnic in the woods or some place.

Example needs more explanation

Some ads just pressure us with time limits. They say a special price is over by some date pretty soon. They'll say hurry, don't wait, and they make you feel like you better run right out this very minute or you'll be sorry.

Thesis is restated, but sentence structure is weak

Pressure, pretend science, and promising to change us is how advertisements influence consumers.

This essay is a 3 because the support is weak and there are errors in sentence structure and mechanics. However, it does develop a thesis with a clear structure.

Exercise 3 (page 125)

Your GED essay will be given a ranking on a scale of 1 through 4. The essay score, together with your score on Part I of the test, becomes your GED Language Arts, Writing Test score. The merging of the two scores is done on a special grid used by the GED test scorers.

If your essay makes a point, has a clear structure, uses logical examples, and is relatively free from errors in sentence structure, usage, and mechanics, it will fall in the upper half of the point range with a score of 3 to 4. An essay that is not legible or not clearly related to the topic will receive no points.

Essay Scoring Guide

- A *4 essay* develops ideas clearly, uses particularly sophisticated and vivid examples, flows smoothly, and has almost no errors.

- A *3 essay* develops ideas adequately, but the writing is a bit more awkward, the examples less extensive and less effective, and the essay has noticeably more errors than the 4 essay.

- A *2 essay* shows some evidence of planning, but the examples are weak or underdeveloped. It also contains repeated errors in sentence structure, usage, and mechanics.

- A *1 essay* lacks structure, purpose, and control. It contains many errors.

Use the following sample essays to evaluate the essay you have written.

A SAMPLE 4 ESSAY

Hook and thesis, with three subjects stated

Advertisers spend billions of dollars each year persuading consumers to buy their products. To sell products, they exploit human desires to be healthy, to save money, and to be happy.

First subtopic, example

Explanation

It's pretty hard to resist a product that promises health and long life. Actors posing as doctors appear in advertisements to sell cold medicines, headache remedies, and even health insurance. These actors look authentic and authoritative, so we pay attention to what they say. They use charts and graphs, along with testimonials from "ordinary people," to convince us that one product is more beneficial to our health than another.

Second subtopic, example
Explanation

Just as we all want to be healthy, most of us also want to save money. With free samples, coupons, and low prices, advertisers urge us to try a product. If it costs less, we might try it. Then we might continue to buy it, get used to it, and keep buying it even if the price goes up a little.

Third subtopic
Example, and explanation

When an ad shows people having fun or falling in love, it suggests that a particular product brings happiness. Advertisers would like us to believe that the right toothpaste, drink, car, perfume, or aftershave is all that is needed to find true love and happiness.

Conclusion, with thesis implied

As consumers, we must be careful shoppers if we are to avoid the awesome power and influence of advertisers.

A 4 essay has a clear structure, develops the topic with excellent examples, and concludes neatly. The conclusion does not repeat the three-point thesis but implies it in the closing sentence.

A SAMPLE 2 ESSAY

Television is where most advertising is on. Kids programs, sports, news, everything has it. Then kids nag there parents all day to buy the stuff they seen on television this just gets parents mad and the kids wont get anything. Which serve them right if they act bratty like that.

Sports is another thing. You cant even watch a football or baseball without too many commercals. Why do they have to ruin a perfectly good ballgame with those dumb commercals. Then they use the same guys to brake into other programs, I mean sport guys who get millions of dollars I bet just to tell you to buy some kind of razer and you cant even see them play there game. Because the ads ruin the game right in the middle.

So in conclusion, I think there's too many commercials in the cartoons and the sports. News, too.

This essay is a 2 because it lacks a clear thesis, the support details wander from the topic, the conclusion doesn't match the thesis, and there are many errors.

A SAMPLE 1 ESSAY

I think advertising is horrible. Because they lie and you waist your hard earned money. I can't think of any place where you dont see ads there everywhere and all they do is lie and tell you to buy stuff you don't need and you cant aford to anyway so it's kind of rotten to do that. Besides that stuff isnt ture anybody knows that.

So how do they do it? Well, there is alot of ways. Television for example. People just leave the room when the comershal come on, because it gets loud and its like their yelling at you to buy something. Who wants to listen to stuff like that. That why remote controls are good. Because you can just change the chanel or turn off the sound. The best thing is to go get something to eat, and it probly wont even be what they advertise. Which shows you that the ads just lie anyway.

This essay is a 1 because the ideas are jumbled together. It lacks a clear thesis, subtopics, and examples to support them. The writer has no control over the topic.

PART II
SOCIAL STUDIES

What Will I Find on the Social Studies Test?

The GED Social Studies Test is not a measurement of how much you know about specific social studies facts and concepts. Most questions will ask you to think logically about a passage or illustration related to a social studies topic.

CONTENT AREAS

Social Studies is Test 2 of the GED Tests and consists of five content areas. The percent for each area is given in parentheses.

History: (40 percent) The study of the American past, including major formative experiences such as the Civil War and national issues like slavery.

Geography: (15 percent) The study of location, physical environment, the earth and its people, geographic regions, and major themes such as agriculture.

Civics and Government: (25 percent) The ways citizens interact with one another as well as an examination of the federal, state, and local governments.

Economics: (20 percent) The study of production and consumption of goods, foreign trade, and labor.

TYPES OF QUESTIONS

When you take the GED Social Studies Test, you will have 85 minutes to answer 64 multiple-choice questions. Each question or set of questions will refer to a written passage or an illustration. To answer these questions, you will need to comprehend, apply, analyze, or evaluate the information presented. Of the social studies questions, 30 percent will be application questions, 30 percent will be analysis questions, 20 percent will be comprehension questions, and 20 percent will be evaluation questions.

Comprehension questions ask you to identify, restate, or summarize information and ideas that are stated directly or indirectly in a passage, drawing, or chart. The following question is an example of a comprehension question that asks you to summarize information.

1.

Which of the following best summarizes the cartoonist's meaning?

(1) The original concept of the U.S. presidency has stayed pretty much the same for more than 200 years.

(2) The executive branch is one of the three branches of the federal government.

(3) Too many people in the executive branch have held their jobs for too long and aren't keeping up with the times.

(4) The current powers of the executive branch have greatly outgrown the original concept of the U.S. presidency.

(5) People in the judicial and legislative branches are jealous of the powers of the executive branch.

The correct answer is (4).

Application questions ask you to use information from a passage, drawing, or chart to solve a problem or to use data in a different situation. The following application question asks you to use the information given to solve a problem.

2. The three branches of the federal government are executive, legislative, and judicial. Each branch has specific duties, as set out in the Constitution of the United States. Which one of the following people is a part of the judicial branch of the federal government?

   (1) A law clerk for an associate justice of the Supreme Court
   (2) The legal counsel to the President
   (3) A congressman from Ohio
   (4) The legal counsel to a Senatorial subcommittee
   (5) The lawyer for a large corporation who argues a case before the Supreme Court

The correct answer is (1).

Analysis questions ask you to determine causes and effects, distinguish facts from opinions, and draw conclusions. The analysis question below asks you to distinguish facts from opinions.

In 1918 and 1919, about 2 billion people came down with an especially lethal strain of flu virus. Between 20 million and 40 million died. This pandemic, or international epidemic, killed as many people in one year as the Black Death (bubonic plague) did between 1347 and 1351. Today, many people feel that flu vaccines have made the disease basically harmless. Some scientists worry, however, that available treatments might be useless against a particularly virulent flu.

3. Which of the following statements is an opinion, not a fact?

   (1) The 1918-1919 flu epidemic caused widespread death.
   (2) A pandemic is a worldwide epidemic.
   (3) About 2 billion people were affected by the flu in 1918 and 1919.
   (4) Modern medicine could easily defeat even an especially strong strain of flu virus today.
   (5) Scientists don't know exactly how many people died in the pandemic of 1918-1919.

The correct answer is (4).

Evaluation questions ask you to judge the accuracy of information, recognize the role of values in decision making, assess documentation or proof, and recognize logical fallacies. The evaluation question below asks you to determine the role that values play in beliefs.

The failure of communism led to the breakup of the Soviet Union into fifteen separate nations, including Russia, Ukraine, and Belarus. All fifteen adopted a system of democracy and capitalism, but soon began to have economic troubles. The new nations argued over ownership of the Black Sea Navy Fleet and the Crimean Peninsula, as well as disputing who would pay which debts of the old Soviet Union.

4. Which would be the point of view held by someone in one of the fifteen new nations who believes that the old Soviet Union should be restored?

   (1) Ukraine and Belarus are causing all the problems.
   (2) Restoring communism will make the Soviet Union great again.
   (3) The West is not giving enough help to democratic leaders such as Russia's Boris Yeltsin.
   (4) Russia should give the Black Sea Fleet and the Crimea to Ukraine.
   (5) The breakup of the Soviet Union was its own fault because communism was an unworkable and unjust system.

The correct answer is (2).

Unit 1

HISTORY

Building a Nation

Between 1492 and 1763, Spain, France, the Netherlands, and England fought for control of North America. All four nations sought wealth from the untapped resources of the so-called New World. Many Europeans also wanted to convert the native inhabitants to Christianity or to make important new discoveries of territory to claim for their countries. By 1763, the English had won the prize. Through war, they took over territory claimed by the Dutch and the French. The Spanish, with their interests spread throughout Central and South America and parts of Europe, posed little threat to the English colonies along the eastern seaboard. With English rule firmly established, the seeds of American democracy were planted in the colonies.

Early Democracies

The first English settlers believed strongly in individual liberty, religious freedom, and self-government. The colonists' beliefs were based in part on English law, which granted citizens certain rights and provided for a **representative government**.

The first successful English settlement, Jamestown, was established in 1607 in what would become Virginia. After several rocky years, the settlement began to profit from a valuable new crop, tobacco. In 1619, the Jamestown colonists began to govern themselves through the House of Burgesses, the first representative assembly in America.

A second group of English colonists, arriving in Massachusetts in 1620, was the Pilgrims, who were religious dissenters, or protesters. On their ship the *Mayflower*, before landing, they developed the May-flower Compact, a plan of self-rule, which served as the basis for the colony's government. The compact contained the fundamental democratic principle that a government's power depends on the consent of the governed.

Were the colonial governments truly representative? Participation in government was reserved for men, usually landowners. Native Americans had no say in the settlement or affairs of Europeans. Enslaved Africans were considered property and therefore had no rights as citizens. Thus, we can see today that the colonial governments did not represent everyone who lived in the colonies.

Exercise 1

> **Directions:** Choose the one best answer for each item.

> Items 1 and 2 refer to the following paragraph and map.

The colonies were founded primarily for religious or economic purposes. That is, the founders wanted to provide a haven for a specific religious group or for all worshippers, or they wanted to develop land, make money for a company, or develop trade with Indians. Sometimes, colonies were founded for a combination of economic and religious reasons. The map shows the thirteen colonies and the primary reason for the founding of each one.

THE 13 COLONIES: PRIMARY REASONS FOR FOUNDING

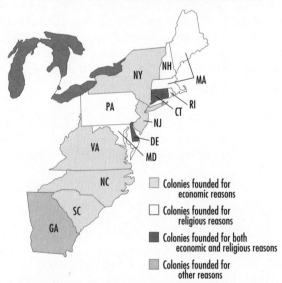

- ☐ Colonies founded for economic reasons
- ☐ Colonies founded for religious reasons
- ■ Colonies founded for both economic and religious reasons
- ▨ Colonies founded for other reasons

1. According to the map, the colonies founded for both religious and economic reasons were

   (1) Connecticut, Delaware, and Georgia.
   (2) New Jersey, Delaware, and Pennsylvania.
   (3) Connecticut and Delaware.
   (4) New Jersey and New York.
   (5) Massachusetts, New Hampshire, Rhode Island, and Maryland.

140

2. Which of the following conclusions could be drawn from the map?

   (1) Economic colonies were most successful in the South.

   (2) People living in religious colonies preferred to live in the North.

   (3) Colonies founded for both religious and economic reasons were the smallest ones.

   (4) Colonies founded for economic reasons tended to be large and located in the South.

   (5) Colonies were founded for two main reasons regardless of their size or location.

3. Read the following statement, made by John Winthrop, first governor of Massachusetts:

"As for the Natives in New England, they inclose noe Land, neither have any setled habytation, nor any tame Cattle to improve the Land by, and soe have noe . . . Right to those Countries."

Winthrop's statement reflects a common viewpoint held by New Englanders. Which item best summarizes this viewpoint?

   (1) Because Native Americans did not own land, they could not be represented in colonial governments.

   (2) Without improvements to the land, the Native Americans were not able to establish settlements.

   (3) Because Native Americans did nothing to show ownership of the land, they had no right to claim it.

   (4) Native Americans could claim any land they wanted, as long as they did not enclose it, settle on it, or graze cattle on it.

   (5) Because Native Americans had left the land as they found it—without fences or settlements—they had a greater claim to it than did the New Englanders.

Check your answers on page 179.

Revolution and Independence

Prior to 1776, each colony had developed in its own distinct way, and the independent-minded citizens preferred to maintain their differences. Events between 1754 and 1776, however, drew the colonies toward union with one another.

In 1754, conflict broke out between French and English settlers in areas north and west of the colonies. The conflict developed into a full-scale war—the French and Indian War—between France and Great Britain. In its hard-won victory in 1763, Britain gained virtually all French territory in North America—but at great cost.

To pay its debts and maintain control of the area, the British government began a series of restrictive measures. Colonists were required to pay taxes on imported goods, such as sugar, and were prevented from printing their own money. Under the Stamp Act, every paper document in the colonies was required to carry a stamp purchased from a government agent. The colonists protested with **boycotts** of English products. The colonists' outrage led to the First Continental Congress, a meeting of colonists, in 1774. In April 1775, the war now known as the American Revolution broke out and lasted until 1781, five years after the colonies had declared themselves free and independent of England. The Second Continental Congress began in May 1775. On July 4, 1776, Congress declared the colonies to be "free and independent States." You'll read more about the Declaration of Independence in Unit 3, Exercise 1.

Conflict and Compromise

During the first years of the new American nation, creating a national government was a matter of enormous conflict. Americans argued over issues such as states' rights, slavery, and the power of government as they worked out the details of running their country. After their experience with English rule, American citizens were determined to avoid a powerful, centralized government with broad powers over individuals and states. They believed in strong representation and individual freedoms.

The first national plan of government, the Articles of Confederation, provided a loose structure of union but made the federal government weak and ineffective. In 1787, a Constitutional Convention met for the purpose of revising the Articles. After nearly four months of debate and compromise, the United States Constitution was completed. It was not without flaws, but the framers thoughtfully provided a way to change it through **amendments** that can revise parts of the original document or add new provisions.

The next struggle was over **ratification**, or approval, by the states. In order to take effect, the Constitution had to be ratified by nine of the thirteen states. The nation divided itself into two opposing camps. The Federalists favored the Constitution and the strong central government it outlined. Anti-Federalists complained that it did not provide for individual rights and liberties. The Anti-Federalists were persuaded to support the Constitution only after they were promised that a bill of rights would be added.

The first ten amendments to the United States Constitution form the Bill of Rights. They guarantee certain rights and freedoms to individuals; for example, the freedom to worship as we please, the freedom to express our opinions, and the right to a fair trial. These liberties, born of conflict, now form the cornerstone of the American democratic system.

Exercise 2

> **Directions:** Choose the one best answer for each item.

1. Before 1774, the idea of a union of colonies was considered impossible. Which of the following is an objection the colonists would have had to a union?

   (1) They feared that the rights and freedoms of individuals would be overlooked.

   (2) They feared that their forms of self-government would be threatened.

   (3) They feared that their freedom to worship as they please would be lost.

   (4) They were afraid that a union would be easily overtaken by the British.

   (5) They were afraid that the Constitution could never be ratified.

2. In 1773, as colonial rebellion grew more daring, the British king said, "The colonies must submit or triumph." The British government passed strict, punishing laws intended to show the colonists that

   (1) they would not be allowed to raise their own taxes.

   (2) it would make them pay for the repeal of the Stamp Act.

   (3) Britain had complete authority over the colonies.

   (4) Britain would win the Revolutionary War.

   (5) the Declaration of Independence was null and void.

3. One possible disadvantage of a strong central government is that it may

   (1) give too many rights to states.

   (2) give too many rights to individuals.

   (3) limit the rights of individual citizens.

   (4) prevent representative assemblies.

   (5) limit the power of the Constitution.

4. Which of the following situations is not protected by the Bill of Rights, a guarantee of individual rights and freedoms?

   (1) A white supremacy organization wants to hold a rally in a city park.

   (2) Mr. B., an avid sportsman, owns a variety of weapons.

   (3) A suspected drug dealer is arrested without a warrant.

   (4) A woman wants to run for the office of U.S. Senator but has not reached the minimum age of thirty.

   (5) A Jewish man wishes to wear his yarmulke, a cap with religious significance, at work.

Check your answers on page 179.

GROWTH AND DIVISION

Was the Civil War fought over slavery? Historians are still debating that question. Before 1861, when the war began, the issue of slavery had already driven a wedge between the North and the South. As the nation expanded west of the Mississippi, the states argued over whether to extend slavery into the new territories. The adventure of moving west became linked with the fierce debate over slavery.

Slavery and Free Speech

During the early 1800s, more and more people began to demand that slavery be abolished. These **abolitionists** formed organizations to fight for the end of slavery. To them, slavery was morally wrong and had no place in a democracy. As this movement gained strength, southern political leaders feared that it would lead to slave rebellions and would threaten the southern way of life, which depended on slavery. In the South, abolitionist literature was seized and abolitionists were attacked. Abolitionists began to flood Congress with petitions demanding the end of slavery.

In 1836, under pressure from southern members, the U.S. House of Representatives passed a **"gag rule"** blocking all petitions and forbidding all discussion of the slavery issue. John Quincy Adams, a former U.S. president and now a state representative, devoted himself to the cause of repealing the gag rule. The rule, he said, violated Americans' right to petition their government and violated his own right of free speech. He encouraged citizens to send him their petitions, and he tirelessly presented them to Congress. Finally, in 1844, the gag rule was overturned.

Resentments in both North and South grew as the slavery debate intensified. In 1857, a case before the U.S. Supreme Court promised to resolve the debate once and for all. The case involved a man, originally a slave, named Dred Scott. With his master, Scott had spent four years living in the free state of Illinois and the free territory of Wisconsin. After his master's death, Scott sued for his freedom, saying that because he had lived on "free soil," he was now a free man.

The Supreme Court's ruling in *Dred Scott* v. *Sanford* included the following main points:

- Dred Scott, as an enslaved African American, was not a citizen and therefore could not sue in a federal court.

- Congress could not outlaw slavery in territories because that would deprive slaveholders of their property and thus violate the Fifth Amendment.

- Therefore, Congress could not forbid slave owners to take their slaves into free territory.

- Previous restrictions on slavery in the territories were unconstitutional.

The decision was a victory for southerners, who had been fighting to extend slavery to the territories, and a blow to abolitionists, who had hoped to stop the spread of slavery.

Exercise 3

Directions: Choose the one best answer for each item.

Items 1 and 2 refer to information in the text and the following map.

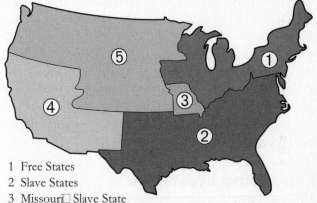

1 Free States
2 Slave States
3 Missouri⬜ Slave State
4 California (Free State) and Utah and New Mexico territories (open to slavery by inhabitant's choice)
5 Northern territories

1. What generalization about slavery can you make from the map?
   (1) Slavery was not permitted in New Mexico and Utah territories.
   (2) The compromises of 1820 and 1850 created many new states.
   (3) Slavery tended to be limited to the southern states and territories.
   (4) People in the northern territories did not want slavery.
   (5) The proslavery people were gaining more and more territory.

2. According to the Dred Scott decision, which of the following states or territories would be off-limits to you if you were a slave owner?
   (1) California
   (2) Missouri
   (3) Utah Territory
   (4) Texas
   (5) Unorganized territory

3. John Quincy Adams said that with the gag rule, the southern representatives had equated the wrong of slavery with the right of petition. He meant that the southerners were trying to hold onto slavery by

(1) disrupting Congress.
(2) denying free speech.
(3) only forbidding discussion.
(4) only blocking petitions.
(5) overturning the gag rule.

4. In *Dred Scott* v. *Sanford*, the Supreme Court ruled that slavery could be extended into territories. In effect, this ruling

(1) moved slavery from the states to the territories.
(2) forced slaves to move to the territories.
(3) allowed slavery anywhere in the United States.
(4) made slavery legal in the territories.
(5) forced slave owners to move to the territories.

Check your answers on page 179.

Expanding Westward

As soon as Americans had settled a country, they couldn't wait to explore it further. As if they were drawn by unseen forces, they began to pour over the Appalachians into the vast lands of the American West. During the first half of the nineteenth century, the United States expanded westward from the Mississippi River all the way to the Pacific Ocean. During these years, Americans believed they had a special mission to move into unexplored lands and "tame" them. In 1845, this mission was termed **"Manifest Destiny."**

GROWTH OF RAILROADS

Transportation was an essential part of westward expansion. Without a vast network of roads, canals, and railroads, Americans could not have reached the new lands so quickly and in such great numbers. In turn, the drive to move west spurred the rapid growth, development, and improvement of transportation systems.

Railroads in particular had a tremendous impact on westward expansion. The first steam-powered locomotives appeared in 1830, but railroad transportation did not boom for another twenty years. Between 1850 and 1860, the railroad network grew from 9,000 miles to 30,000 miles. Much of the new track connected the cities of the Northeast with the agricultural areas of the Middle West (the states along the Mississippi River). Manufactured goods from the Northeast and farm products from the West and Middle West could be shipped more easily and rapidly than ever before. Before 1860, people began to talk of a transcontinental railroad to link the vast resources of the West with the industrial centers of the East.

NATIVE AMERICANS: "YIELD OR PERISH"

After the Civil War ended in 1865, **migration** to the West increased. As waves of Americans crossed the Mississippi, seeking fortunes in the mines or homes on the prairies, they had a profound effect on the native peoples of the Great Plains and Far West. Railroad towns and farms took over the tribal homelands, which the Native Americans were expected to give up without protest. "The westward course of population is neither to be denied nor delayed for the sake of all the Indians that ever called this country their home," said a government report in 1873. "They must yield or perish."

Perhaps the most devastating effect of the railroad was the annihilation of the millions of buffalo that roamed the plains and served the Plains Nations' needs for food, shelter, and clothing. With the railroads came white hunters who killed the animals for food, clothing, and sport. The tracks split the herds and disrupted the Native Americans' hunting patterns. The end of the buffalo meant the end of the Plains Nations' way of life.

Exercise 4

Directions: Choose the one best answer for each item.

Item 1 refers to the following graph.

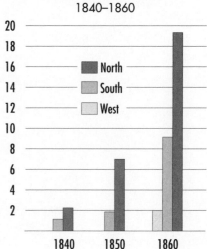

U.S. RAILROADS
1840–1860

1. What general conclusion can you draw from the graph?

    (1) The South showed very little railroad growth between 1840 and 1850.
    (2) Railroads grew at a phenomenal rate between 1840 and 1860.
    (3) Railroads did not appear in the West until 1860.
    (4) By 1860, the North had about 19,500 miles of railroads.
    (5) In spite of a boom in growth from 1850 to 1860, southern railroads could not catch up with northern railroads.

2. A person who believed in Manifest Destiny in the 1800s would most likely want to

    (1) preserve the natural environment.
    (2) respect the rights of others.
    (3) acquire more land and power.
    (4) rule foreign lands.
    (5) preserve peace at all costs.

3. In 1860, just before the Civil War began, the South had less than half the railroad mileage of the North. This deficiency placed the South at a disadvantage during the war. Which of the following items was not a disadvantage caused by a deficiency of railroad mileage?

    (1) Supplies and troops could not be transported quickly.
    (2) Many areas were not served by the railroad.
    (3) Railroad tracks in the South were wider than tracks in the North.
    (4) No alternate routes existed in case tracks were destroyed.
    (5) Many key cities had no direct connections.

4. Which of the following statements best summarizes the U.S. government's attitude toward Native Americans in the West?

    (1) They were no longer entitled to kill buffalo for food, shelter, and clothing.
    (2) They could live where they wanted as long as they did not interfere with settlers.
    (3) They were required to show the settlers how to live on the land.
    (4) They were a barrier to civilization and therefore had to move or be moved.
    (5) They were skillful buffalo hunters, but their towns were located on land desired by settlers.

Check your answers on page 179.

GROWTH OF INDUSTRIAL POWER

The period from 1870–1920, often known as the Industrial Revolution, was marked by tremendous economic growth, a boom in industry, and a flood of new inventions. These developments caused profound changes in American life. Locomotives, power looms, harvesting combines, and other machines turned factories and farms forever from small, home-based businesses into huge, profit-oriented companies. By 1900, the United States was the leading industrial nation in the world.

The Automobile Revolution

In finding a way to produce cars that the average person could afford, Henry Ford revolutionized American industry. To bring down the cost of building a car, Ford introduced a method of production, the assembly line, in 1913. As the chassis of a car passed by each worker, he or she performed a single, specialized job, repeating it as quickly as possible. Assembly-line methods cut production time for one car from 14 to 6 hours and allowed Ford to lower the price of a car from $600 in 1912 to $360 in 1916. At the same time, Ford doubled his employees' wages and reduced the working day from 9 hours to 8.

In other industries, standard business practice had been to keep wages as low as possible and prices as high as the market would allow. To the surprise of his critics, Henry Ford got rich by doing the opposite. By 1927, when the Model A replaced his original design, the Model T, Ford had sold 15 million cars.

Hard Times in the Factory

Those who lived with the reality of factory work saw a less pleasant side of the industrial boom. Profits ruled, and workers became commodities, like flour or cloth, to be bought at the cheapest price. Immigrants, pouring into the cities looking for jobs, provided an endless source of cheap labor. Most factory workers labored long hours for low pay at jobs that were repetitive and often dangerous.

Even worse than the factories were the tenement sweatshops. Entire families, including young children, made artificial flowers, rolled cigars, or sewed garments at home, working late into the night for very low pay.

These terrible working conditions gave rise to labor unions. Individuals believed that if they organized into groups, their complaints would be heard by company owners and managers. Labor unions did win many improvements for workers, such as shorter workdays, fair pay, and safety measures, but often workers were reluctant to join. Changing economic conditions, strikes and angry employers kept unions from gaining a firm hold until 1886, when the American Federation of Labor (AFL) was formed. The AFL was successful partly because it was a collection of separate unions, each one representing a craft or skill. Each union operated independently but worked with the AFL for the benefit of all workers.

Exercise 5

Directions: Choose the <u>one best answer</u> for each item.

1. A labor union would be concerned with all of the following items EXCEPT

   (1) regular inspection and repair of machinery.
   (2) number and duration of rest breaks.
   (3) vacation and insurance plans.
   (4) overhead lighting in the workplace.
   (5) how workers get to and from work.

Items 2 and 3 refer to the following circle graphs.

EMPLOYMENT BY OCCUPATION

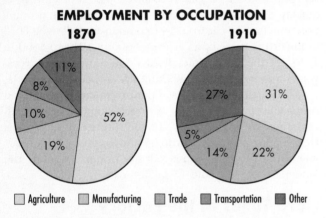

| 1870 | 1910 |

Agriculture · Manufacturing · Trade · Transportation · Other

2. Many of the people who moved to the cities worked in factories—sewing, assembling, sorting, and so on. These workers fit into which category?

   (1) Agriculture
   (2) Manufacturing
   (3) Trade
   (4) Other
   (5) Transportation

3. What trend do the two graphs together show for agricultural workers between 1870 and 1910?

   (1) Due to increasing urbanization, fewer agricultural workers were needed in 1910 than in 1870.
   (2) The proportion of agricultural workers dropped from about half of all workers in 1870 to less than one third in 1910.
   (3) Although the percentage of agricultural workers decreased between 1870 and 1910, the actual number increased.
   (4) In 1910, agricultural workers preferred to join the rush to the cities to work in trade and manufacturing jobs.
   (5) Agricultural workers were less in demand in 1910 than in 1870.

Check your answers on page 179.

Imperialism

"Remember the *Maine!*" In 1898, Cubans were in the midst of a rebellion against Spanish rule. The U.S.S. *Maine*, docked in the port of Havana to protect Americans in Cuba, exploded. Exaggerated rumors of Spanish atrocities against the rebels had angered Americans for several years. Now American lives had been lost. "This means war!" screamed newspaper headlines.

The three-month Spanish-American War began a period of American **imperialism**, or expanding the country's influence in foreign lands. American railroad builders, steel makers, and bankers had conquered the American West and established the United States as a major industrial power. Now they were looking beyond the country's borders for new opportunities—new trade markets, mineral wealth, land for cash crops, and cheap labor.

U.S. imperialist policy during this period was characterized by increasing **intervention**. Under Theodore Roosevelt, president from 1901 to 1909, the United States took on the role of a political police force to protect the Americas from European powers. The U.S. government had long relied on the Monroe Doctrine to maintain power in the Americas. In 1823, President Monroe had warned European nations not to try to establish colonies in the Americas. Gradually the doctrine also came to mean that European nations should avoid interfering in Latin-American independence movements. Under Roosevelt, the United States claimed the right to intervene in Latin American affairs.

The following political cartoon from 1901 depicts the United States as a protector of Latin-American countries. Would you say the cartoonist approved of or meant to criticize U.S. imperialism?

President Roosevelt pursued a policy called "Big Stick" diplomacy, which used the threat of military force to influence events in foreign nations. The U.S. government claimed to be maintaining regional stability, but many people believed these actions were more to protect American business interests in Latin-American countries. More and more, these nations resented American interference.

The years 1900–1917 are also referred to as the *Progressive Era*, during which significant economic, social, and political reform took place in the United States. Public disapproval of the growth of big business was widespread. A group of journalists, dubbed *muckrakers* by Roosevelt, wrote detailed accounts of corruption caused by big business.

Exercise 6

Directions: Choose the one best answer for each item.

1. The United States fought the Spanish-American War not just to help Cubans liberate themselves from Spanish rule but to break up Spain's worldwide empire as well. Which of the following facts best supports this statement?

    (1) Spain was having trouble holding onto its empire.
    (2) While attention was focused on Cuba, American forces attacked the Philippines, a Spanish holding in the Pacific.
    (3) President McKinley offered conditions to Spain for avoiding war.
    (4) The explosion of the battleship *Maine* was blamed on the Spanish, some say falsely.
    (5) Before helping the Cubans, the United States promised not to claim control over Cuba once it was free.

2. Politician Carl Schurz argued that U.S. expansion into foreign lands violated American democratic principles. Which democratic ideal in particular would be violated by imperialism, a policy that allows one country to interfere in the government and business of another country?

    (1) "All men are created equal."
    (2) All men and women possess "certain unalienable Rights, . . . among these are Life, Liberty and the pursuit of Happiness."
    (3) Governments draw their powers "from the consent of the governed."
    (4) "Whenever any Form of Government becomes destructive of these ends, it is the Right of the People to alter or to abolish it."
    (5) "The people have a right to institute a new Government [that will] effect their Safety and Happiness."

3. In the cartoon in the passage, what do the hens represent?

    (1) Latin-American countries
    (2) Latin-American countries under U.S. protection
    (3) Various U.S. imperialistic policies in Latin America
    (4) Latin-American colonies of European nations
    (5) Latin-American countries that refused U.S. protection

4. In the cartoon, what does the "European coop" marked "Monroe Doctrine" represent?

    (1) Latin-American countries being protected ("cooped up") from European nations
    (2) U.S. policies restricted ("cooped up") by European imperialism
    (3) European nations in closed-door meetings ("cooped up") about Latin-American independence movements
    (4) European countries restricted ("cooped up") by the Monroe Doctrine
    (5) European nations hiding in the chicken coop in fear of U.S. power

Check your answers on page 179.

CRISES AT HOME AND ABROAD

In 1933, the nation was in the depths of the Great Depression. Thirteen million people were out of work. Banks closed daily, taking people's life savings with them. The Depression ended only after the United States entered World War II. Despite its toll in lost lives and destruction, the war, with its plentiful jobs, provided a great boost to the nation's economy.

The New Deal

To help Americans recover from the depression, President Franklin D. Roosevelt promised a "new deal." His New Deal programs attacked the Depression on all fronts. For example, the Securities and Exchange Commission (SEC) regulated the sale of stocks, the Tennessee Valley Authority (TVA) managed the natural resources of a seven-state region, and the National Recovery Administration (NRA) set guidelines for fair competition in business.

Two programs that helped put people back to work were the Civilian Conservation Corps (CCC) and the Works Progress Administration (WPA). The CCC, also called Roosevelt's "Tree Army," employed over two million young men who planted trees, fought forest fires, and performed other conservation tasks. The WPA, formed in 1935, is best remembered for the jobs it provided for teachers, artists, and writers who lent their creative talents to many projects.

World War II: The Home Front

In 1939, war broke out in Europe, with Great Britain and France allied (joined) against Germany. Americans supported the Allies in spirit, but the United States remained uninvolved in the war until December 7, 1941, when Japanese bombers made a surprise attack on a U.S. base in Pearl Harbor, Hawaii. The United States declared war on Japan. Two days later, Japan's allies, Germany and Italy, declared war on the United States.

As U.S. soldiers fought overseas, the nation supported the war effort with massive production of airplanes, weapons, and supplies. Americans scrimped and saved, sharing a patriotic desire to help the cause of American victory. But Japanese Americans were seen as a threat to national security. As a result, more than 120,000 Japanese Americans, two thirds of them American citizens, were imprisoned in camps throughout the country.

The Cold War and the Cuban Missile Crisis

World War II ended in 1945 with the first use of atom bombs, causing the most destructive bomb blasts in history over Hiroshima and Nagasaki, Japan. World power was divided between the United States and the communist Soviet Union. The icy tensions between the two powers and their allies came to be known as the Cold War. Many Americans considered **communism** wrong because it denied economic and political freedom. They wanted communism kept as far away as possible, an idea referred to as **containment**.

On October 22, 1962, President Kennedy announced that Soviet missile bases were being built in Cuba. Kennedy planned a two-part approach: a naval blockade (a shutting off of a port by linking up ships) to prevent Soviet ships from reaching Cuba, and a demand that the Soviet Union dismantle and remove the bases.

American warships surrounded Cuba. The nation held its breath as Soviet ships carrying missiles approached. The first of the ships reached the blockade and abruptly turned back. After two days of secret negotiations, the Soviets agreed to remove the Cuban bases. In return, the United States promised not to invade Cuba. War had been narrowly avoided.

Exercise 7

Directions: Choose the one best answer for each item.

Item 1 refers to the following passage.

The Great Depression was brought about in part by reckless spending and wild speculation, or taking risks in hopes of quick profits. The wild mood of the 1920s was fueled by tremendous business growth and dreams of great wealth. Then, in the midst of plenty, the economy collapsed.

1. An example of speculation would be
   - (1) buying a car on a four-year credit plan.
   - (2) selling a used computer at a profit.
   - (3) moving a successful restaurant to a new, larger location.
   - (4) investing in an uncertain business venture with borrowed money.
   - (5) using a credit card.

2. In 1988, the U.S. government formally apologized to Japanese Americans and awarded the families of those who had been imprisoned modest monetary compensation for their losses. By this action, the United States acknowledged that
   - (1) Japanese Americans were citizens.
   - (2) Japanese Americans posed no security threat to the United States.
   - (3) the civil rights of Japanese Americans had been violated.
   - (4) the conditions in the detention camps were unsatisfactory.
   - (5) the property of Japanese Americans should have been protected.

3. Critics have said that Kennedy took a huge and terrible risk in the Cuban Missile Crisis. What did Kennedy risk?

    (1) Loss of America's lead in the arms race
    (2) A Soviet invasion of the United States
    (3) Destruction of the U.S. naval fleet
    (4) The possibility of nuclear war
    (5) The destruction of Cuba

Check your answers on page 179.

The Civil Rights Movement

Many people date the beginning of the civil rights movement—the fight for equal rights for people of all races—from the Montgomery, Alabama, bus boycott of 1955-1956. In the fight against **segregation**, or formal separation of the races, the Montgomery boycott had special significance. The boycott began after a woman, Rosa Parks, was arrested for refusing to give up her bus seat to a white man. At that time in many cities of the South, African Americans were forced to sit in the backs of buses or to stand.

In response to Mrs. Parks' arrest, Montgomery's bus-riding black citizens boycotted—refused to use—the bus system. In spite of constant harassment and acts of violence, they held on for more than a year. Finally, the U.S. Supreme Court ordered an end to segregated buses.

The Montgomery boycott mobilized African Americans into an organized resistance movement for the first time. From this movement emerged a leader who promoted peaceful means for protesting injustice—Dr. Martin Luther King Jr.

For the rest of the 1950s and through the 1960s, Americans fought for racial justice. Unfortunately, violence often erupted as civil rights groups became more demanding and racist resistance gained strength.

A Changing Population

For nearly two centuries, American culture was dominated by the values of whites of European descent, who held virtually every important position of political, economic, and social power. Since 1965, however, the American population has been shifting toward more ethnic diversity. By the end of the century, Americans with European ancestry were no longer a majority.

These population changes have been caused by shifts in immigration patterns. In the past, most immigrants came from Europe. Between 1924 and 1965, U.S. immigration policy favored entry by northern Europeans and set quotas, or limits, on entry by others. The Immigration Act of 1965, which ended the quota system, had a great impact on the future face of America. By the 1980s, only 17 percent of the immigrants were European; 75 percent were from Asian and Latin-American countries.

These immigrants have contributed enormous cultural diversity to the country. Their struggle to make a place for themselves in America has also provoked ten-

sions between minorities and the established population. Cultural differences can be barriers to understanding, and many Americans now resent the flood of immigrants entering the country. They argue that immigrants take away jobs or, even worse, they burden our welfare system. "Stem the tide of illegal immigration!" is the rallying cry of some Americans.

The United States—Global Cop?

The United Nations, or UN, was created after World War II as an international peacekeeping organization. Member nations voluntarily join and uphold its goals and ideals. In general, the organization has intervened only in situations with international implications, such as war involving two or more nations. The policy has been one of national **sovereignty**, or freedom from external control. A country could do whatever it wanted within its own borders. But since the end of the 1980s, the UN has had a new policy based on the idea that a country's internal problems are a threat to the global community. Intervention based on **humanitarianism**, or concern for human rights, is now considered a legitimate role of the UN. With the Cold War over, the UN has taken over the superpowers' role of enforcing peace and settling disputes.

Exercise 8

> **Directions:** Choose the <u>one best answer</u> for each item.

> Item 1 refers to the following map.

SCHOOL INTEGRATION: 1960

Dates indicate year desegregation began

- Del. 1953
- W.Va. 1954
- Va. 1954
- Md. 1956
- Mo. 1954
- Ky. 1955
- N.C. 1957
- Okla. 1955
- Ark. 1954
- Tenn. 1958
- S.C.
- Texas 1954
- Miss.
- Ala.
- Ga.
- La.
- Fla. 1959

☐ States with no integrated schools in 1960

1. The map shows that
   (1) most southerners did not believe in integration but were forced by law to integrate their schools.
   (2) five states in the Deep South closed their schools rather than integrate.
   (3) five states in the Deep South had no intention of ever integrating their schools.
   (4) five states in the Deep South had not begun to integrate their schools by 1960.
   (5) most southern states, except those in the Deep South, agreed to integrate schools.

2. For more than 100 years, the Statue of Liberty has been a beacon of hope and welcome to immigrants. The immigration restrictions of 1924 through 1965 reflected a view that
   (1) agreed totally with the statue's message.
   (2) completely contradicted the statue's message.
   (3) applied the statue's message to northern European immigrants.
   (4) applied the statue's message to Latin-American and Asian immigrants.
   (5) applied the statue's message to illegal immigrants only.

3. UN intervention in response to public outcry usually is based on
   (1) television coverage.
   (2) international peacekeeping.
   (3) concern for human rights.
   (4) national sovereignty.
   (5) the new code of international relations.

Check your answers on page 180.

Unit 2

GEOGRAPHY

Global Mapping

Every place on Earth has a unique location. The relative location of a place is its location in relation to other places. When you describe your town as a few miles south of another city or just beyond a bend in the river, you are describing its relative location. The absolute location of a place is its exact position on the planet. We find this position on a map by looking at a grid of lines that crisscross the surface of the globe to pinpoint the location of any place on Earth.

Mapmakers measure distances north and south by drawing parallels of **latitude** north and south of the equator. (Parallel lines never meet; they are always the same distance apart.) The **equator** is an imaginary line that circles the earth exactly halfway between the North Pole and the South Pole. Because the equator is the starting point for measuring latitude, it is labeled 0°. The North Pole, which is as far north as one can go on Earth, is exactly 90° north of the equator and is called 90° north latitude. All other parallels north of the equator lie between 0° and 90° north latitude.

A second set of lines measures **longitude**, distances east and west. These semicircular lines, which run between the North Pole and the South Pole, are known as meridians of longitude. The **prime meridian**, the starting point for measuring longitude, passes through an observatory in Greenwich, England. Mapmakers label each meridian as so many degrees east or west of the prime meridian until they reach the 180° meridian, which is halfway around the world from the prime meridian.

Every line of latitude or longitude can be thought of as a complete circle, which can be divided into 360 parts, or degrees, represented by the symbol °. Each degree can be divided into 60 minutes, represented by the symbol ′, and each minute into 60 seconds, represented by the symbol ″. The absolute location of Washington, DC, is at 38.5° north latitude and 77.0° west longitude.

Exercise 1

> **Directions:** For Item 1, fill in the blanks as instructed below. For Items 2–5, choose the <u>one best answer</u> for each item.

1. Write a **P** beside each sentence that describes parallels of latitude and an **M** beside each sentence that refers to meridians of longitude.

    _____ (a) These lines never meet.

    _____ (b) These lines meet at the North and South poles.

    _____ (c) These lines are always the same distance apart.

    _____ (d) These lines measure distances east and west.

    _____ (e) These lines measure distances north and south.

    _____ (f) These lines go no higher than 90°.

    _____ (g) These lines measure distances from the equator.

ROBINSON PROJECTION

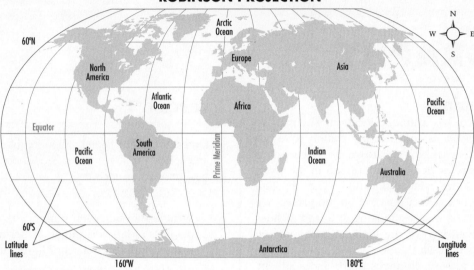

Items 2–4 refer to the map at the top of this page.

2. Where do the equator and the prime meridian cross?

   (1) Europe
   (2) The Arctic Ocean
   (3) Antarctica
   (4) Africa
   (5) The Atlantic Ocean

3. The longitude of the prime meridian is

   (1) 090° west.
   (2) 000°.
   (3) 180° west.
   (4) 090° east.
   (5) 090° north.

4. In what direction is North America from the prime meridian?

   (1) East
   (2) West
   (3) North
   (4) South
   (5) Southwest

5. To provide information about the absolute location of your seat at a ball game, you would

   (1) give the row number.
   (2) give the seat number.
   (3) give the row number and the seat number.
   (4) explain how far back the seat is from the playing field.
   (5) explain where the seat is in relation to the main gate.

Check your answers on page 180.

Latitude and Climate

Climate is the usual weather pattern found at a particular place on Earth. Temperature, wind, and rain are elements of climate, so are seasonal changes. Why do different places have different climates? The main reason is **latitude**—the distance north or south of the equator.

Exactly how much sunlight most places receive varies from season to season. As the earth makes its yearly journey around the sun, it is tilted. The northernmost latitude to receive direct sunlight is 23° 30′ north. This parallel is called the Tropic of Cancer. The sun is directly overhead at the Tropic of Cancer on June 21 or June 22. As you might expect, the southernmost latitude to receive the direct rays of the sun is 23° 30′ south. The sun is directly overhead at this parallel, known as the Tropic of Capricorn, on December 21 or 22. Places between the Tropic of Cancer and the Tropic of Capricorn are known as the **tropics**, or low latitudes, and they generally have warm climates.

The Arctic Circle is located at latitude 66° 30′ north, and the Antarctic Circle at latitude 66° 30′ south. The

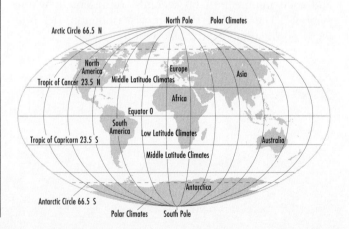

regions between the Arctic Circle and the North Pole and between the Antarctic Circle and the South Pole are called the **polar regions**, or high latitudes. These areas receive no sunshine for part of the year and only slanting rays the rest of the year. The climate is cold, with short summers.

Between the tropics and the polar regions are the middle latitudes. Here, the sun's rays reach the earth at a high angle for part of the year and at a lower angle (greater slant) for the remaining months. Average temperatures are cooler than in the tropics but warmer than in the polar regions. These regions of Earth, including the United States, are often called the **temperate zones**. Within these zones, temperatures vary greatly from place to place and from one season to another.

Geographers group areas with similar climate into regions. Temperature and rainfall in different regions are affected by features such as nearness to the ocean, wind patterns, and elevation, as well as latitude. Humid tropical climates, for example, exist in the low latitudes and can be either wet tropical (hot and very rainy all year) or wet-and-dry tropical (hot all year with wet and dry seasons). The rain forests of South America are wet tropical; the Caribbean Islands are wet-and-dry tropical.

Exercise 2

Directions: Choose the <u>one best answer</u> for each item.

1. June 21 or 22, when the sun shines directly on the Tropic of Cancer, marks the beginning of summer in the northern hemisphere (the half of the earth north of the equator). In the southern hemisphere, June 21 or 22 marks the

    (1) beginning of winter.
    (2) beginning of summer.
    (3) end of summer.
    (4) end of winter.
    (5) spring equinox.

2. Temperatures in the tropics are always hot, rarely falling below 70°F. Temperatures in the polar regions are always cold, rarely exceeding 30°F. Northern and southern temperate zones are found between the tropics and the polar regions. In these zones, temperatures are more moderate and usually fluctuate with the seasons. The continental United States lies within the

    (1) tropics.
    (2) northern polar zone.
    (3) southern polar zone.
    (4) northern temperate zone.
    (5) southern temperate zone.

3. The equator divides the earth into the northern and southern hemispheres. At the equator,

    (1) the average temperature is 0°C.
    (2) the latitude is 0°.
    (3) the longitude is 0°.
    (4) the temperate zones and the tropics meet.
    (5) the sun is directly overhead all year.

Item 4 refers to the following information.

This climate graph shows average rainfall and temperature for a region. The bar graph shows rainfall; the line graph shows temperature. Rainfall is shown in inches on the right; temperature is shown in degrees on the left. The months of the year are shown along the bottom.

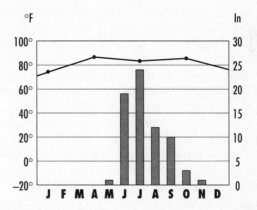

4. The graph above shows a place that is probably located between the

    (1) North Pole and the Arctic Circle.
    (2) Arctic Circle and the Tropic of Cancer.
    (3) Tropic of Cancer and the Tropic of Capricorn.
    (4) Tropic of Capricorn and the Antarctic Circle.
    (5) Antarctic Circle and the South Pole.

Check your answers on page 180.

NATURAL AND HUMAN-MADE RESOURCES

An environment is made up of all of the living and nonliving things in a place. People, plants, and animals all count on their environment for their survival. Plants and animals adapt physically to their environment. People adapt physically, but they also use technology to change their environment. Consequently, they can survive in almost any environment on Earth.

A **resource** is any part of the environment that people use to meet their wants and needs. Only a few resources, such as water, sunlight, and air, are used in their original forms. Most are changed before they can be used. Resources that can be made into a product are called **raw materials**. Trees, iron, and oil are all raw materials. For example, trees are used to make paper.

People's ideas about the value of resources often change as their way of life changes. Whales, for example, were an important resource in the early 1800s. Americans relied on whale oil to light their homes. By the late 1800s, however, whales were becoming harder to find, so people began to replace whale oil with kerosene, a by-product of oil. As a result, whales became a less important resource to Americans—many of whom now work to keep whales from dying out.

Electric lights replaced kerosene lamps, but the demand for oil continued to grow. Now it is used to heat homes, to lubricate machines, and to make fuel for automobile engines. In addition, oil has become an important source of chemicals for making plastics, dyes, and a variety of other products. Today so much oil is used that many fear that supplies will run out. Oil is a **nonrenewable resource**: once it is used up, it is gone forever. In contrast, trees are a **renewable resource**. As long as they are replanted, there will always be trees.

Is a field of corn a part of the natural environment? The answer is more tricky than you might expect. Unlike wheat, rice, and most other food crops, corn does not grow in the wild. It must be planted and tended. Corn originated more than 10,000 years ago in the highlands of Mexico, where farmers cross-cultivated two wild plants. Over the years, they improved the seeds so the plant produced more food. The natural environment, therefore, cannot always be separated from the environment we have made for ourselves.

As corn became more plentiful, it was traded throughout North and South America. By the time Columbus arrived in the Americas, corn was grown as far north as Canada and as far south as Argentina. Corn was taken to Europe after 1492 and spread throughout southern Europe and into northern Africa.

Most of the corn grown today is fed to livestock (farm animals). People eat only a tiny percentage of corn in its natural state. Much is processed into oils, syrups, and starches. Factories use corn by-products to make glue, shoe polish, fireworks, crayons, ink, batteries, aspirin, paint, and cosmetics. Corn may also help power your car. Ethanol, a fuel derived from cornstarch, is often combined with gasoline to reduce air pollution from car engines. Scientists can now also make a plastic-type film and packing material from cornstarch.

Exercise 3

Directions: For Item 1, fill in the blanks as instructed. For Items 2–5, choose the one best answer for each item.

1. Write an **R** beside each example of a renewable resource. Write an **N** beside each example of a nonrenewable resource.

   ____ (a) coal

   ____ (b) natural gas

   ____ (c) water

   ____ (d) corn

   ____ (e) iron

   ____ (f) wood

2. The text implies that some resources are more highly valued than others. This is probably because people tend to value resources that are

   (1) in scarce supply.
   (2) in plentiful supply.
   (3) nonrenewable.
   (4) a source of food as well as fuel.
   (5) of the greatest use to them at a given time.

3. What is the main advantage in substituting a renewable resource for a nonrenewable one?

   (1) It conserves supplies of the nonrenewable resource.
   (2) It conserves supplies of both resources.
   (3) It encourages recycling.
   (4) It protects the environment.
   (5) It guards against pollution.

4. Many people are interested in replacing plastic made from petroleum with plastic made from cornstarch because

   (1) corn is a plant created by people.
   (2) corn is a raw material and petroleum is not.
   (3) corn can be recycled and petroleum cannot.
   (4) corn is a renewable resource and petroleum is not.
   (5) petroleum is a renewable resource and corn is not.

5. The fact that corn is now used throughout the world can best be explained by the fact that

    (1) people need food.
    (2) useful products tend to be used widely.
    (3) corn is a nonrenewable resource.
    (4) corn had religious significance for Aztecs.
    (5) corn was used to feed African slaves.

Check your answers on page 180.

The Great American Desert

For generations, people from the United States regarded the Great Plains as the "Great American Desert." They saw only a flat land covered with shrubs and short grass. Hot, dry winds blow frequently across the plains during the summer months. In winter, sudden blizzards bury the region deep in snow.

The first people from the United States to settle on the Great Plains were ranchers. They herded their cattle and sheep on the grassy plains and shipped the animals to eastern markets. In the late 1800s, farmers also began to settle on the plains. By the 1920s, farms and ranches on the plains were booming. As more Americans moved to cities, the markets for beef, corn, and wheat reached increasingly high levels. Even the weather cooperated. Not realizing that rainfall on the plains comes in cycles, many farmers were convinced that "rain follows the plow."

In 1932, a drought began. Crops withered and died in the fields. That fall, farmers plowed and planted again. In doing so, they exposed more soil to the dry winds. With no plants to hold the soil in place, huge black billowing clouds of dust and dirt formed. These clouds settled and buried fields and farm buildings, blocked roadways, clogged water supplies, and killed animals.

Many people left the Great Plains during the dust storms, but some stayed on. Working with the federal government, they learned to practice **conservation—** careful and wise use of the environment. They repaired the damage they had done and slowly rebuilt the land around them. As a result, the Great Plains are more productive today than the most hopeful farmer could have imagined in the early 1900s.

THE WATER CYCLE

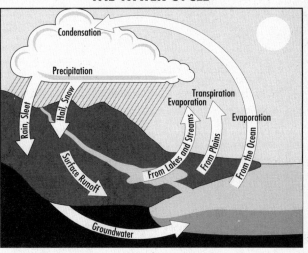

Water, Water Everywhere

There is as much water on Earth today as there ever was or ever will be. This is because water is a **recyclable resource**. That is, it is a resource that is continually reused. The diagram on the following page explains how.

Although the supply of water has not changed over the centuries, the demand for water has increased. Today the average American household uses between 140 and 168 gallons of water a day, or more than 50,000 gallons a year. But individuals are responsible for only about 10 percent of the total demand. By far the largest users of water in the United States are farmers who irrigate their crops. It takes 652,000 gallons of water to produce just one acre of wheat. Cotton and other crops require even more water. Industry accounts for much of the rest of the nation's water use.

If water is a recyclable resource, why does it matter how much we use? For one thing, many Americans are using water more quickly than it can be replaced. Another cause for concern is pollution. Thousands of factories and communities dump waste material into oceans, rivers, and lakes. Farmers add to the problem by using chemicals to fertilize the soil and to keep away insects and other pests. Such chemicals pollute the water. Scientists have found evidence of fertilizers, pesticides, industrial chemicals, and sewage throughout the water cycle. They pollute the water not only in the community where it is originally contaminated but also in communities thousands of miles away.

Exercise 4

> **Directions:** Choose the <u>one best answer</u> for each item.

1. Which of the following conclusions does the text support?

   (1) A change in one part of an environment affects all the other parts.
   (2) There are no limits to what technology can accomplish.
   (3) Farmers cannot protect themselves from drought.
   (4) Human activity always makes environments more productive.
   (5) It was a mistake to settle on the Great Plains.

2. The text suggests that the most important long-term effect of the dust storms of the 1930s was

   (1) a reduction in the number of farmers on the plains.
   (2) an increased interest in conservation.
   (3) the destruction of livestock.
   (4) the destruction of water supplies.
   (5) the destruction of crops.

3. Which of the following statements is correct?

   (1) Condensation causes transpiration.
   (2) Surface runoff is groundwater.
   (3) Precipitation includes rain and snow.
   (4) Evaporation comes from groundwater.
   (5) Transpiration leads to evaporation.

4. Each step in the water cycle works to

   (1) increase the amount of water on Earth.
   (2) decrease the amount of water on Earth.
   (3) balance the amount of water that evaporates.
   (4) balance the amount of water plants give off.
   (5) balance other steps of the cycle.

5. The passage suggests that people affect the water cycle, not the water supply, by

   (1) using too little water.
   (2) using too much water.
   (3) contaminating water supplies.
   (4) building factories.
   (5) irrigating their land.

Check your answers on page 180.

Unit 3

CIVICS AND GOVERNMENT

Democracy

Since its founding in 1776, the United States of America has been a **representative democracy**. That is, its citizens elect people to represent them and their wishes in governmental decisions. America's democratic system has attracted many immigrants from countries with more restrictive political systems.

Before the United States became a nation, the original thirteen states were **colonies** that belonged to England. King George III of England and his parliament believed that the colonies existed only to benefit England. Between 1763 and 1775, they instituted laws and taxes that helped England's economy at the expense of the American colonies. The colonists complained bitterly about the injustices of the following policies:

- Control over colonial settlement and government

- The large army England maintained in the colonies in peacetime

- Taxes imposed on the colonies to raise money for England

- The King's refusal of colonists' requests for more economic and political freedom

During these years, the colonists engaged in increasingly rebellious acts. In 1775, the colonies sent representatives to a meeting in Philadelphia, the Second Continental Congress. In June 1776, Thomas Jefferson, a Virginia delegate who later served as the third president, was chosen to write a statement of rights and grievances. In elegant and carefully reasoned language, Jefferson's Declaration of Independence explained why the colonies should separate from England.

Jefferson began with a statement of the rights of citizens, following closely the principles of the great philosopher John Locke. He wrote that "all men are created equal" and possess "certain unalienable Rights . . . Life, Liberty and the pursuit of Happiness." To secure these rights, "Governments are instituted . . . deriving their just powers from the consent of the governed." The Declaration ends by saying that the colonies owe no allegiance to England and are free and independent in every way.

Exercise 1

Directions: Choose the one best answer for each item.

1. The fundamental idea behind democracy is
   (1) rule by the people.
   (2) representative government.
   (3) independence.
   (4) rule by the few.
   (5) unalienable rights.

2. Which two roles were performed by Thomas Jefferson?
   (1) President of the United States and author of the Constitution
   (2) Author of the Declaration of Independence and the Constitution
   (3) President of the United States and chief justice of the Supreme Court
   (4) Author of the Declaration of Independence and President of the United States
   (5) Chief justice of the Supreme Court and speaker of the House of Representatives

3. Although Thomas Jefferson wrote the Declaration of Independence, other delegates helped him, and the Second Continental Congress as a body made numerous changes. What does this process say about democracy?
   (1) Democratic decisions are usually a process of compromise, or give and take.
   (2) Most decisions are made by the few individuals who have the most knowledge.
   (3) Most democratic decisions are made in secret.
   (4) The most powerful people usually get their way.
   (5) Democracy is an inefficient way to govern.

4. Every citizen has a say in a New England town meeting, a tradition dating from the 1620s. Thomas Jefferson called town meetings "schools of political liberty." What did he mean?

   (1) The town meeting is a textbook example of direct democracy.

   (2) Town meetings are of questionable value politically.

   (3) A town meeting allows every participant to learn firsthand about self-government.

   (4) The town meeting is a free-for-all and thus teaches citizens about the dog-eat-dog world of politics.

   (5) Each participant in a town meeting must learn to fight for his or her freedom to speak.

5. Jefferson wrote that "all men are created equal" and possess "certain unalienable Rights. . . ." Although he was a great thinker, which statement below is a logical inconsistency in Jefferson's reasoning?

   (1) England taxed the colonies without representation.

   (2) Government officials were appointed, not elected.

   (3) Plantations continued to exist in the South.

   (4) Slavery continued to exist in the colonies.

   (5) The colonies suffered economically when ties with England were severed.

Check your answers on page 180.

The Federal Government

The **Constitution** of the United States, adopted in 1787, provides for a **federal system** of government, with powers divided between the national government and the states. The federal government is divided into three branches, each with specific roles and responsibilities.

The **legislative branch**—the U.S. Congress—is made up of two houses (bicameral). The House of Representatives now has 435 members. Each represents a particular geographic area of one of the fifty states. All members of the House stand for reelection every two years. Exactly how many representatives each state is allowed is determined by the population of that state. The Senate, the second house of Congress, has 100 members, two from each state, elected for terms of six years.

A suggested law, called a **bill**, can be introduced into either the House or the Senate. Majorities of both houses must vote in favor of a bill for it to pass. The bill then is sent to the White House for the president's signature. If the president signs the bill, it becomes a law. If not, the House and the Senate can still make it a law if two thirds of the members of each house vote again in favor of it.

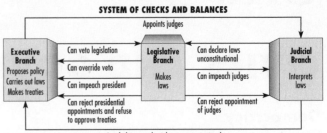

SYSTEM OF CHECKS AND BALANCES

The **executive branch** includes the offices of the president and vice president of the United States. The president is commander in chief of the U.S. armed forces (army, navy, marines, air force) and political leader of the world's largest economy. With the "advice and consent" of the Senate, the president makes treaties and appoints ambassadors, many judges, and members of the cabinet (group of advisers).

Abroad, the president is the voice of the nation, carrying out foreign policy and making treaties. At home, the president is the nation's leader as well as the head of his or her political party, either Republican or Democratic. As party leader, the president often speaks out in favor of a bill (legislation), while members of Congress from the opposite party may take an opposing view.

The **judicial branch**—the Supreme Court of the United States, the nation's highest court—consists of nine justices who, once appointed, hold their jobs for life. There are now two women justices on the Court, and there has been an African American on the Court continuously for almost three decades. The Chief Justice acts as head of the Supreme Court. The job of the Supreme Court is to interpret the Constitution, which is now two centuries old. The United States has changed greatly in ways the authors of the Constitution could never have envisioned. Today the court must find ways to apply the Constitution to the problems of modern life.

The Supreme Court plays a very important part in the system of checks and balances. Through a process called **judicial review**, the Supreme Court can determine that laws passed by Congress and signed by the president are unconstitutional and therefore invalid.

Exercise 2

Directions: Choose the one best answer for each item.

1. Which state—Arkansas or Wyoming—has more representatives in the House of Representatives, and why?

	Arkansas	**Wyoming**
Size	52,078 sq. mi.	96,989 sq. mi.
Population	2.4 million	454,000
Votes cast in 1992	925,000	199,000
Date admitted to Union	1836	1890

   (1) Wyoming, because its geographic size is larger
   (2) Arkansas, because it was admitted to the union fifty-four years before Wyoming
   (3) Arkansas, because its population is larger
   (4) Wyoming, because it sends two senators to Congress
   (5) Arkansas, because former President Bill Clinton is from that state

2. How many senators represent each state?

   (1) 50
   (2) 2
   (3) 100
   (4) 435
   (5) 6

3. Which statement best describes the duties of the President of the United States?

   (1) The president represents the United States abroad and leads either the Democrats or the Republicans, as well as the armed forces and the nation as a whole, at home.
   (2) The president leads the judicial branch.
   (3) The president speaks as a military leader for the United States abroad.
   (4) The president enforces the laws of the nation.
   (5) The president serves as Secretary of State.

4. The three branches of the federal government are

   (1) the judicial branch, the executive branch, and the system of checks and balances.
   (2) the legislative branch, the executive branch, and the judicial branch.
   (3) the legislative branch, the House of Representatives, and the Senate.
   (4) the executive branch, the judicial branch, and the House of Representatives.
   (5) the House of Representatives, the Senate, and the system of checks and balances.

Check your answers on page 180.

Federal Programs and Agencies

Ideas about the role of national government have changed greatly during the past sixty years. Before the 1930s, the U.S. government played a relatively small role in the lives of individual citizens. There were no federal programs to provide financial help to people who were unemployed, housing for poor people, or medical care for elderly people. The government did little to aid people after disasters or to support major arts groups.

The Great Depression of the 1930s was caused by many factors, including the extremely uneven distribution of the country's wealth after World War I; wild speculation in the stock market, which crashed in 1929; and the faulty belief of many Americans that the economy was self-regulating and that the government would cut back expenditures in difficult economic times. The Depression drastically changed the role of the federal government. In 1932, Franklin D. Roosevelt was elected president because of his promises to address the problems of the Depression through the creation of government programs. Roosevelt's "New Deal" covered a wide variety of needs. For example:

- The Federal Emergency Relief Act sent money to the states to supply food and clothing to aged, ill, or unemployed citizens.

- The Banking Act of 1933 created the Federal Deposit Insurance Corporation (FDIC), which established a system for protecting people's bank accounts if the banks failed.

- The Social Security Act, passed in 1935, provided pensions for retired workers and their spouses if they and their employers participated in the program. The act also included death benefits and support for surviving children up to the age of 18.

These programs and others often are referred to as **entitlements**, government programs that offer assistance to specific categories of citizens in need.

Agencies of the U.S. government deal with a wide range of issues of national concern—for example, highway safety, environmental protection, use of federal lands, and working conditions. The heads of these agencies, called secretaries, form the president's **cabinet**, a group of advisers who play an important role in running the government. Fourteen agencies make up the president's cabinet: the Departments of Defense, the Treasury, State, Justice, Labor, Agriculture, Commerce, Health and Human Services, Education, Transportation, Energy, Housing and Urban Development, Interior, and Veterans' Affairs.

The U.S. Postal Service is an independent government agency. Another independent agency is the National Aeronautics and Space Administration (NASA), which was created in 1958 and put the first men on the moon in 1969. The Selective Service System, created in 1940, registers all American men at age 18 for possible service in the U.S. military in case of war.

The Bureaucracy, Lobbyists, and PACs

Three entities or groups that affect the lives and futures of Americans are U.S. government **bureaucracy**, lobbyists, and PACs. The bureaucracy, or the organization of the government, is characterized by a formal structure of authority and specialization of tasks. More than three million civilians work in the federal bureaucracy today. Many of them are part of the **civil service**, where jobs are awarded to qualified workers who must first pass an official, task-related exam. These jobs are not awarded based on people's political views or someone else's recommendation. Civil service employees implement the laws and policies established by the government.

Although the bureaucracy is supposed to be regulated by elected officials, its sheer scope and size make regulation difficult. In addition, bureaucrats sometimes are caught between two sets of conflicting demands—for example, to lower the cost of a department's overall work and increase the number and range of tasks to be done.

Many private groups try to influence lawmakers about which bills to pass and which policies to establish. Although such groups sometimes are viewed negatively, they have legitimate interests and can sometimes influence governmental decisions toward a positive outcome for all Americans. These groups range from the well-known and powerful American Medical Association and National Rifle Association to lesser-known groups such as the Association of American Publishers and the American Agriculture Movement.

Most organizations employ **lobbyists**, people who represent an organization's interests to the appropriate elected officials and government agencies. Many lobbyists are former members of Congress or the executive branch.

Such experiences help them understand the complexities of government and gain entry into administrative agencies.

Political action committees, or **PACs**, are groups of individuals, associations, or businesses that work together to raise election money for candidates they feel will support their points of view in future governmental actions.

Exercise 3

Directions: Choose the one best answer for each item.

1. What is the general purpose of federal agencies?
   - (1) To fill the president's cabinet
   - (2) To run the public schools
   - (3) To deal with issues of safety, regulation, and welfare on the national level
   - (4) To make scientific advancements
   - (5) To nominate candidates for judgeships, Congress, and law enforcement

2. The phenomenal growth of America's urban population—people living in cities of one million or more—has led to the creation of several new cabinet departments over the years. Which of the following pairs would be most likely to deal with urban issues?
   - (1) Department of State and Department of Justice
   - (2) Department of Housing and Urban Development and Department of Transportation
   - (3) Department of Agriculture and Department of Energy
   - (4) Department of the Treasury and Department of Defense
   - (5) Department of Agriculture and Department of Justice

3. An underlying value in government entitlement programs is the belief that all people
   - (1) are created equal.
   - (2) have a right to certain basics in life such as a job, shelter, and food.
   - (3) are entitled to the same level of income and quality of life.
   - (4) should work if they are able.
   - (5) must contribute to the well-being of society.

4. In the early years of the United States, jobs in government were awarded to supporters of the elected representatives through what was called the "spoils system." How does today's civil service system differ from the spoils system?

(1) Employees are appointed by political action committees.

(2) Employees work at highly specialized tasks.

(3) Employees earn their jobs through their skill rather than by political appointment.

(4) Employees are hired by political appointment rather than skill.

(5) Employees work their way up through a hierarchy of authority.

Items 5 and 6 refer to the following cartoon.

5. Which statement best describes the cartoon?

(1) The bureaucracy is operating in the dark.

(2) The bureaucracy is an essential part of government.

(3) The bureaucracy is too politicized to be effective.

(4) The bureaucracy seems to be taking over the whole government.

(5) The bureaucracy is not efficient at the national level.

6. With which of the following statements would the cartoon's creator be most likely to agree?

(1) Getting a job in the bureaucracy is easy to do.

(2) The executive branch has gained too much power.

(3) The bureaucracy should try to hire people with more experience.

(4) Reducing the overall size of the bureaucracy would be good for the nation.

(5) Most bureaucrats are poor workers.

7. Many lobbyists are experts in their fields, and their views are often sought by bureaucrats when new policies are being planned. Officials writing new federal guidelines for the inclusion of students with special needs in regular elementary classrooms would probably want to hear the views of lobbyists for which group?

(1) American Association of Retired Persons

(2) National Association of Realtors

(3) National Education Association

(4) National Rifle Association

(5) American Agriculture Movement

Items 8 and 9 refer to the following cartoon.

8. The woman in the cartoon represents

(1) the American people.

(2) consumers.

(3) food processors.

(4) farmers.

(5) the government.

161

9. Which of the following statements best reflects the cartoonist's opinion?

   (1) There ought to be more government regulation of the food industry.
   (2) Government regulations have made canned goods safer to eat.
   (3) There is too much government regulation of the food industry.
   (4) Government regulations have made food more expensive.
   (5) Government regulations cost more than they are worth.

Check your answers on page 180.

State and Local Governments

Like the national government, all fifty states have governments divided into executive, legislative, and judicial branches. State governments levy taxes to raise money for necessary services. Some states have sales taxes, other states have income taxes, and still other states have both. States also collect fees for various kinds of licenses—marriage licenses and drivers' licenses; fishing and hunting permits; and licenses for professionals such as lawyers, doctors, and dentists.

States use the tax money they collect to provide services and meet citizens' needs. States have primary responsibility for building and maintaining roads and highways within their borders. States set licensing and operating standards for beauty parlors, restaurants, and many other types of businesses and employ inspectors to check that the standards are maintained. States also pass laws to safeguard the health and welfare of their citizens.

Local governments are almost as varied as the communities they serve. Big cities such as Chicago, Denver, and Houston have very large local governments that provide a huge number of services for their residents—police departments, fire protection, street maintenance, social services, public libraries, and so on. Small towns often have part-time officials such as mayors who serve without pay. Many cities and towns have elected mayors as well as city councils. Others are run by city managers who are hired by the elected city councils.

One form of local government is the **special district**, which usually provides a single service such as flood control, fire protection, recreation, or, most commonly, education. Special districts may or may not have the same boundaries as other local government units such as cities.

Perhaps the most confusing unit of local government is the **county**, the major local division in most states. Counties vary considerably in their types of government and in their relationships to citizens, cities, and states. Typical county responsibilities include law enforcement, highway construction, courts, schools, and libraries.

Exercise 4

Directions: Choose the one best answer for each item.

1. Both state and national governments

   (1) have three main branches.
   (2) make treaties with foreign nations.
   (3) issue passports.
   (4) have a legislature with one or more houses.
   (5) establish qualifications for citizenship.

2. Why do states require doctors and dentists to be licensed?

   (1) To generate revenue through the sale of the licenses
   (2) To maintain an acceptable level of quality of medical services for their citizens
   (3) To limit the number of doctors or dentists in the state
   (4) To regulate the prices that doctors and dentists charge their patients
   (5) To prevent doctors and dentists from other states from moving into the area

3. School systems are one type of

   (1) state agency.
   (2) special district.
   (3) federal agency.
   (4) lobbying group.
   (5) legislature.

4. Which of the following would *not* be a reason to establish a special district?

   (1) To provide a service in an area larger than a city or town
   (2) To provide a service in an area smaller than a county
   (3) To provide a service such as fire protection in an isolated rural area
   (4) To streamline government by combining city governments within a district
   (5) To solve a problem such as pollution in an area that crosses city, county, or state boundaries

Check your answers on page 181.

The United States in the World

For most of the last half-century, the United States was one of the world's two superpowers. Our major foreign policy goal was to resist the other superpower, the Soviet Union, and the communist system it promoted.

In the early 1990s, the Soviet Union and its communist system collapsed. At first, Americans cheered because the cold war between the superpowers was over. Soon, however, Americans realized that changes abroad meant changes at home. One of these changes involved spending newly available tax dollars. For decades, the national government had maintained a huge military presence at home and in Germany, Japan, the Philippines, Spain, Turkey, England, and elsewhere. It was generally agreed that this force level could be cut back, but disagreements arose about how much and what type of reduction there should be.

Cutbacks involved not just soldiers but also the businesses that supplied food, uniforms, shoes, weapons, ships, airplanes, and tanks to the U.S. military. Cities and towns that depended on these businesses for tax dollars and employment had to look for new businesses to attract to their areas.

Then came other questions:

- How should the saved military tax dollars be spent?

- What help, if any, should be given to people who lost their jobs in the cutbacks?

- What is the proper speed for cutbacks to maximize savings but minimize the problems for American workers and communities?

The answers to these questions will be determined by new leaders, new world events, and the American people.

Exercise 5

> **Directions:** Choose the one best answer for each item.

1. What was the major foreign policy goal of the United States for most of the last half-century?

   (1) To maintain military bases around the world
   (2) To contain communism
   (3) To reduce government spending
   (4) To elect new government leaders
   (5) To be the leader of nations such as Germany and the Philippines

2. After the Soviet Union broke up into fifteen separate nations, the United States began sending economic aid to the new republics. What good do American policy makers hope will come from this practice?

   (1) It will reduce inflation in the United States.
   (2) It will ensure that the new noncommunist nations become friendly to the United States and not slide back into communism.
   (3) It will prevent other nations from sending aid there.
   (4) It will create an easy way for the government to spend the money it saves on military cutbacks at home.
   (5) It will show the world that the United States is the only remaining superpower.

3. Now that communism has apparently lost its grip on Eastern Europe, some people say the United States should retreat from world affairs. What is the best argument against such a policy?

   (1) The United States should stay prepared for another wave of communism.
   (2) A superpower should never back down.
   (3) The United States should maintain a mighty military presence among nations.
   (4) Isolation is not possible in today's world, where Americans are affected by events in every corner of the earth.
   (5) The U.S. budget was committed to foreign intervention until the year 2000.

4. The secretary of state has been called the president's "right arm" in dealing with other nations. Which of the following is not a function of the State Department?

   (1) Diplomacy
   (2) Occupational health and safety
   (3) Foreign policy
   (4) Issue of passports
   (5) Management of overseas bureaus

Check your answers on page 181.

Unit 4

ECONOMICS

Consumption and Production

Think about the many economic choices you have made during the past week. How did you spend your money amid a vast array of goods and services? How much, if any, did you put away in savings? On a much broader scale, economics has to do with the production, exchange, and consumption of goods and services in a whole society.

In a modern economy, satisfying people's wants is a very complex process. Here is a model to help you picture how all kinds of goods and services are produced and distributed by the millions of people in our economy.

THE WANT-SATISFACTION CHAIN

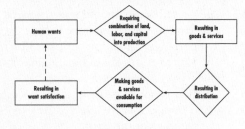

Consumption and Demand

One of the basic concepts in economics is demand. **Demand** is the amount of a product that consumers are both willing and able to buy at each price among a set of possible prices over a given time period. Look at the table and graph below.

DEMAND FOR MOVIES

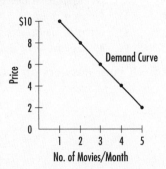

PRICE/ MOVIE	NO. OF MOVIES PER MONTH
$10	1
8	2
6	3
4	4
2	5

The table shows how many movies consumers attend per month at certain prices. The information in the table has been put on a graph to show what economists call a demand curve. The law of demand tells us that the higher the price of a movie, the lower the number of movies people will attend. For example, at $10 per movie, people will see only one movie per month.

Exercise 1

Directions: Choose the one best answer for each item.

1. Ed and Linda have just eaten delicious platters of spaghetti at their favorite Italian restaurant. They have reached which stage in the want-satisfaction chain?

   (1) Distribution
   (2) Production
   (3) Self-fulfillment
   (4) Want satisfaction
   (5) Choice making

2. What would be the result if distribution did not occur in the want-satisfaction process?

   (1) Goods and services produced could not be consumed.
   (2) Consumers would not be able to produce goods and services.
   (3) The process would go from production directly to consumption.
   (4) The process would be disrupted at the want-satisfaction stage.
   (5) The production resources of land, labor, and capital would not be needed.

3. Which of the following statements summarizes the want-satisfaction chain?

   (1) Land, labor, and capital all go into want satisfaction.
   (2) Wants recur, no matter how well or how often they are satisfied.
   (3) People are never satisfied.
   (4) Want satisfaction is a complex process involving production, distribution, and consumption of goods and services.
   (5) Want satisfaction is a complex process involving the consumption of goods and services.

4. According to the demand curve presented in the text, how many movies will the consumer attend at a price of $8?

(1) One
(2) Two
(3) Three
(4) Four
(5) Five

5. Which price policy of a movie theater is likely to result in the highest attendance at movies? (Assume the demand curve shown in the text.)

(1) Charging $3 for the first movie on weekdays
(2) Charging $10 for first-run movies
(3) Charging $6 for the first movie on weekdays
(4) Charging $8 for first-run movies
(5) Charging $2 for the first movie on weekends

6. Researchers know that people will spend more for entertainment if their incomes increase. Which statement below supports this conclusion?

(1) When moviegoers' incomes increase, the supply of movies increases.
(2) When moviegoers' incomes increase, the supply of movies decreases.
(3) When moviegoers' incomes increase, the price of a movie increases.
(4) When moviegoers' incomes increase, the demand for movies decreases.
(5) When moviegoers' incomes increase, the demand for movies increases.

Check your answers on page 181.

Productivity

The **law of diminishing returns** states that at a certain point the addition of one resource (such as labor, for example, workers who pick apples) to a fixed resource (such as land, for example, an apple orchard) will result in less product being contributed by each individual worker. For example, 50 workers picking apples in a 20-acre orchard will result in a higher level of productivity *per worker* than 100 workers picking apples in the same orchard.

Fortunately, modern producers of goods and services have figured out ways to combine scarce resources to increase productivity. In addition, the resources have improved. Education has improved human resources (labor), technology and new inventions have improved capital (money available for business development or business transactions), and modern farming methods have improved.

Supply

Supply is the amount of a product that sellers (producers) are both willing and able to sell at each price among a set of possible prices over a given time period. Look at the table and graph below.

SUPPLY OF MOVIES

PRICE/ MOVIE	NO. OF MOVIES PER MONTH
$10	1
8	2
6	3
4	4
2	5

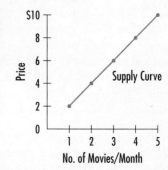

The table shows the numbers of movies that sellers (theater owners) are willing and able to offer at certain prices. The information in the table has been put on a graph to show what economists call a supply curve.

The Law of Supply and Demand

The law of supply and demand states that in a market economy, the interaction of supply and demand determines the prices and quantities of all kinds of goods and services—haircuts, auto repairs, bananas, computers, and movies. Look at the table and the graph below. The demand data and graph from page 164 and the supply data and graph from this lesson have been combined.

SUPPLY AND DEMAND FOR MOVIES

PRICE/ MOVIE	NO. OF MOVIES DEMANDED	NO. OF MOVIES SUPPLIED
$10	1	5
8	2	4
6	3	3
4	4	2
2	5	1

Price affects the quantity demanded and the quantity supplied in opposite ways. At higher prices, more of a

LOCAL GOVERNMENT

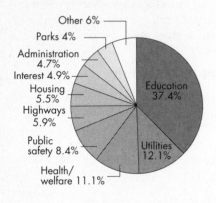

Other 6%
Parks 4%
Administration 4.7%
Interest 4.9%
Housing 5.5%
Highways 5.9%
Public safety 8.4%
Health/welfare 11.1%
Education 37.4%
Utilities 12.1%

STATE GOVERNMENT

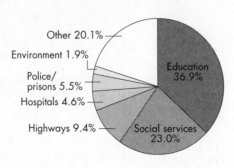

Other 20.1%
Environment 1.9%
Police/prisons 5.5%
Hospitals 4.6%
Highways 9.4%
Education 36.9%
Social services 23.0%

FEDERAL GOVERNMENT

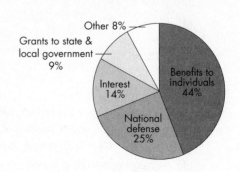

Other 8%
Grants to state & local government 9%
Interest 14%
National defense 25%
Benefits to individuals 44%

product will be supplied, but less will be demanded. At lower prices, more of a product will be demanded, but less will be supplied. This is because buyers and sellers have different goals; buyers want the lowest possible prices and sellers want the highest possible prices. Through a process of bargaining, buyers and sellers reach a market price, the price at which they agree to trade. In the movie example, at a market price of $6 per movie, suppliers will offer three movies and buyers will attend three movies. At this price, the movie market is in balance. Unless some factor affects either supply or demand, the price is not likely to change.

Exercise 2

Directions: Choose the one best answer for each item.

1. Which of the following statements best describes the law of diminishing returns?

(1) As workers are added, total output increases.
(2) As workers are added, total output decreases.
(3) As additional workers are added, additions to output decrease.
(4) As additional workers are added, additions to output increase.
(5) As additional workers are added, additions to output stay the same.

2. Which policy is likely to result in movie suppliers being willing to show more movies at all possible prices?

(1) A theater tax of $100 per movie shown
(2) An advertising campaign for movies
(3) A subsidy of $1 per customer paid to movie theaters
(4) A city council ban on movies shown after midnight
(5) A decrease in the price of popcorn

3. In the table presented in the text, what is the difference between the quantity supplied and the quantity demanded at a price of $2.00?

(1) One
(2) Two
(3) Three
(4) Four
(5) Five

Check your answers on page 181.

Government Taxation and Spending

Americans have to pay taxes for the government services they want. Government at all levels has the power to levy a wide range of taxes—on income, on sales, and on property—and to charge fees for a variety of things, such as building permits and marriage licenses.

In the United States today, there are three major types of taxes: regressive, progressive, and proportional. A **regressive tax** takes a larger percentage of income from people with lower incomes than from those with higher incomes. For example, a sales tax, especially on food, takes a larger percentage of lower-income earners' budgets because these people spend a greater share of their incomes on food than do people who earn more. A **progressive tax** is based on a person's ability to pay. Taxpayers at higher income levels pay larger portions of their incomes in taxes than people at lower income levels. Ideally, federal income taxes on both businesses and households are progressive. A **proportional tax** takes the same percentage of everyone's income. Some school taxes and many real estate taxes are proportional.

To understand the role of government in the U.S. economy, we need to know an important economic measure, the **gross domestic product (GDP)**. The GDP is the total annual value of goods and services produced by individuals, government, and business firms in the United States. In 1994, the GDP of the United States was about $6.7 trillion. Local, state, and federal expenditures combined amounted to about $2 trillion. With government involved in about one third of all economic activity, it is reasonable to ask what the government does and whether its involvement is too much or too little.

Historically, Americans have looked to the government for help with the following kinds of economic problems:

1. Price-fixing among businesses

2. Unsafe/inhumane working conditions

3. Unsafe products and medications

4. Unemployment and disability

5. Unstable economic conditions, and

6. Environmental pollution.

The circle graphs on page 166 show the percentages of their total budgets that the three levels of government spent in 1990 on activities such as national defense (federal government only), education, highways, and social services.

The federal government uses two kinds of policy to manage the economy: fiscal and monetary. **Fiscal policy** involves decisions related to government spending and taxation. **Inflation** and unemployment are two economic events the government watches. Inflation, defined as a general rise in prices, causes people to lose buying power. To correct inflation, the federal government may cut back on its own spending or try to raise taxes to control consumer spending.

Monetary policy involves decisions by the Federal Reserve Bank, the nation's central bank, to control the supply of money in the economy. The supply of money is directly related to interest rates. At higher rates of interest, people and businesses tend to borrow less money; at lower interest rates, people and businesses tend to borrow more money. The Federal Reserve controls the money supply by changing the interest rate. In inflationary times, the Federal Reserve may raise the interest rate to slow down economic activity. If the Federal Reserve wants to stimulate the economy, it will lower interest rates.

Exercise 3

Directions: Choose the <u>one best answer</u> for each item.

1. The federal withholding tax taken from your paycheck is an example of a(n)

    (1) regressive tax.
    (2) sales tax.
    (3) income tax.
    (4) property tax.
    (5) license fee.

2. Suppose that in a given year, the value of goods and services produced in the United States is divided as follows: $4.2 trillion produced by individuals; $2.1 trillion produced by government; $1.7 trillion produced by business firms. For the year, what will be the gross domestic product (GDP)?

    (1) $7.8 trillion
    (2) $7.9 trillion
    (3) $8.0 billion
    (4) $8.0 trillion
    (5) $8.1 trillion

Items 3 and 4 refer to the following graphs.

LOCAL GOVERNMENT **STATE GOVERNMENT** **FEDERAL GOVERNMENT**

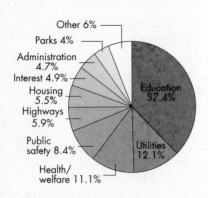
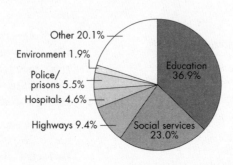
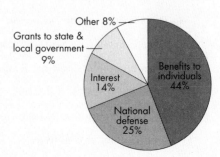

3. The greatest percentage of federal government expenditures is for

   (1) interest payments.
   (2) public safety.
   (3) benefits to individuals.
   (4) grants to states and localities.
   (5) education.

4. Which of the following conclusions is best supported by the graphs?

   (1) State and local governments bear most of the cost of education.
   (2) The amount of interest paid by the federal government is too high.
   (3) National defense accounts for 25 percent of federal expenditures.
   (4) States are responsible for most highway expenditures.
   (5) Government spending accounts for 30 percent of GDP.

Items 5 and 6 refer to the following graph.

THE NATIONAL DEBT 1981–1991
(Rounded)

Source: *Economic Report of the President, 1991*

5. Between 1981 and 1985, the national debt

   (1) stayed the same.
   (2) doubled.
   (3) tripled.
   (4) increased fourfold.
   (5) decreased.

6. Which statement best summarizes the graph?

   (1) The national debt can be controlled by wise monetary policy.
   (2) The national debt is an accumulation of annual deficits.
   (3) The national debt doubled between 1985 and 1991.
   (4) The national debt increased fourfold between 1981 and 1991.
   (5) The national debt is a serious problem for future generations.

7. What would be the most effective monetary policy in a time of severe inflation?

   (1) Encouraging banks to lend money
   (2) Raising interest rates and encouraging banks to stop lending
   (3) Encouraging banks to stop lending
   (4) Lowering interest rates
   (5) Raising interest rates

Check your answers on page 181.

Unit 5

PEOPLE AND CULTURES

Culture

Culture refers to the behavior, beliefs, and traditions of groups of people. Culture is influenced by physical environment (climate, terrain, and plant and animal life), social environment (groups of people with whom you come in contact), and technological environment (the tools that a society invents or uses).

Every society has two types of culture: material and nonmaterial. Material culture consists of those things that a society makes from its resources. Disneyland, movies, and denim jeans are part of the American material culture. Nonmaterial culture includes the beliefs and values that a society thinks are important. America's nonmaterial culture includes freedom of religion, equal rights, and democracy.

How Culture Is Learned

Through **socialization**, mostly through the influence of family members, friends, and schooling, people learn their religious beliefs, political attitudes, and outlook on the world. Two types of learning may occur during socialization. Trial-and-error learning takes place when a person tries out one kind of behavior after another in a new situation until he or she succeeds. In contrast, social learning occurs when a person imitates other people or communicates with them to gain knowledge. A toddler who is learning to talk is engaged in social learning.

Whenever information about what works in a certain situation is shared between humans, a form of cultural transmission takes place. Socially transmitted knowledge can and must be passed on to new generations if a culture is to be maintained. Through this process, called **enculturation,** the young people in a society learn about and share the culture of the older people.

Enculturation transmits negative as well as positive elements of a culture. For example, **prejudices** are judgments made about other people before all the facts are known, such as being afraid of a person of another race; **stereotypes** are assumptions that nearly everyone in a group of people has a certain characteristic—for example, that all women are bad drivers.

How Culture Changes

As individuals change, their culture changes, too. How do these changes happen? A cultural change may come from many sources, some originating within the society. The source of a change that comes from inside the society is called an **endogenous source**. The endogenous sources of the U.S. Civil Rights Act were the activists who demonstrated in America against open and deliberate racial and sexual discrimination.

The source of a change that originates outside the society is called an **exogenous source**. The exogenous sources that destroyed the hunting-and-gathering lifestyle of some Native Americans were the groups of European settlers who came to the Americas.

The following sources of cultural change can be endogenous or exogenous; sometimes the origin of a change is not clear.

1. An **innovation**—a new tool, technology, idea, or method—may be developed. *Example:* The invention of the microwave oven was an American innovation because it happened in the United States.

2. A custom, belief, or invention may spread from one culture to another through **diffusion**, or contact between societies. *Example:* Early Native Americans believed that bragging about a future accomplishment or event brought bad luck that could be neutralized by knocking on the base of an oak tree. This belief is evident when people knock on wood to keep a boast from backfiring.

3. Changes in the physical environment can cause a group of people to adjust accordingly. *Example:* As land is cleared and water is polluted in the Amazon rain forest, the native peoples of the rain forest must either move away or adapt their ways of living, hunting, and fishing.

4. An **internal conflict**, or struggle within a society because of opposing ideas, needs, wishes, or basic instincts, may cause change. *Example:* The Civil War in the United States led to freedom and new legal rights for African Americans.

5. A **revolution** may change the form of government and the structure of an entire society. *Example:* In 1979, a revolution in Iran led to the creation of an Islamic state based on strict enforcement of Shi'ite Islamic law.

Exercise 1

Directions: Choose the one best answer for each item.

1. Which one of the following statements does not describe trial-and-error learning?

   (1) Solutions to problems are discovered.
   (2) Behaviors are tried until a successful one is found.
   (3) The sharing of solutions does not occur.
   (4) Technological and social progress occurs.
   (5) The knowledge others have learned is unimportant.

2. When Jiang first began to learn English on her own, she made many mistakes. Later, she became less self-conscious and asked for help with her grammar and sentences. Jiang's language learning involved which two processes?

   (1) Enculturation and cultural transmission
   (2) Trial-and-error learning and enculturation
   (3) Social learning and enculturation
   (4) Trial-and-error learning and social learning
   (5) Prejudices and stereotypes

3. The changes in most Americans' views on the rights of racial and ethnic groups resulted from endogenous sources and

   (1) innovation.
   (2) revolution.
   (3) enculturation.
   (4) the physical environment.
   (5) internal conflict.

Items 4 and 5 refer to the following information.

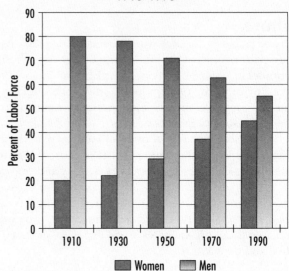

U.S. LABOR FORCE
1910–1990

Before the Industrial Revolution began in England around the year 1760, women played a major role alongside men in economic production. Because most goods were made in and sold from the home, women were not isolated from economic production. Technology from the Industrial Revolution eventually spread to the United States, and both women's and men's roles began to change. Men went to work outside the home, and women took on primary responsibility for raising children and keeping house.

4. According to the passage, what sources caused American women to withdraw from economic production?

   (1) Innovation and diffusion
   (2) Diffusion and the physical environment
   (3) Physical environment and internal conflict
   (4) Internal conflict and revolution
   (5) Revolution and innovation

5. According to the graph, the proportions of men and women in the labor force since 1910 have

   (1) remained at about the same levels.
   (2) both increased.
   (3) both decreased.
   (4) almost equalized.
   (5) shown no change.

Check your answers on page 182.

Influences on Human Behavior

Psychologists have found that the following factors influence human behavior:

- **Heredity**—The genes you inherited from your parents control the development of your brain and other body structures that affect traits or behaviors such as intelligence, anxiety, and sociability.

- **Experiences**—Experiences reflect the opportunities you have had to explore and learn about your world. You do not have exactly the same experiences as anyone else—even an identical twin.

- **Motives**—Most of the things you do are motivated by your basic needs for food, warmth, and companionship. Other motives are based on goals valued by your culture, such as being rich, important, famous, or well educated.

- **Social relationships**—Other individuals and groups influence your behavior. Your family, your religion, and the people with whom you work and play dictate your behavior in many different situations.

Personality

Your **personality** consists of the combination of ways you act, think, and feel that make you different from any other person. When a friend describes you as generous or shy, she or he is describing a personality trait that is typical of you. Why do you have your particular personality? Behavioral scientists rely primarily on three theories to explain this aspect of human behavior.

Psychoanalytic theory was developed by Sigmund Freud, a physician in Vienna who treated patients with emotional problems. Freud believed that much of human personality is controlled by forces in the unconscious mind and that those forces may be linked to childhood experiences and sexual motives.

Ivan Pavlov, who originated the **behaviorist theory**, believed that personality is learned through reward and punishment—that is, through the pleasant or unpleasant results of one's own behavior. In studies that he conducted on digestion, Pavlov started the stimulus of a clicking metronome every time he gave dogs powdered meat to eat. The dogs eventually learned to salivate when they heard the metronome alone. This simple form of learning is called **conditioning**.

Abraham Maslow was one of several psychologists who developed the **humanistic theory**, the idea that people determine their own destiny through an inner force that pushes them to grow, improve, and make decisions. According to Maslow, a person who reaches the highest level of personal development and fully realizes his or her potential has achieved self-actualization. Although very few people achieve full self-actualization, most people are partially actualized.

Exercise 2

Directions: Choose the one best answer for each item.

1. No one is around when Carlos notices that the door of the snack machine is open. Carlos still deposits his money in the machine and selects his snack. According to the
   - (1) psychoanalytic theory, Carlos' selfish and aggressive tendencies prevented him from stealing the snack.
   - (2) psychoanalytic and behaviorist theories, the positive influence of society prevented Carlos from stealing the snack.
   - (3) behaviorist theory, Carlos' exposure to inappropriate behaviors in society prevented him from stealing the snack.
   - (4) humanistic theory, the destructive forces of society prevented Carlos from stealing the snack.
   - (5) humanistic theory, Carlos' low self-concept prevented him from stealing the snack.

Items 2 and 3 refer to the following passage.

Studies of twins have shown that identical twins have almost identical IQ (intelligence quotient) test scores. The IQ scores of fraternal twins who grow up in a similar environment are just a little more similar than those of other pairs of siblings who are not twins. Similarly, studies of adopted children show that their IQs are more similar to those of their biological parents than to those of their adoptive parents.

2. The studies of twins and adopted children focused on
   - (1) motivation.
   - (2) reactions to family members.
   - (3) similarity of twins.
   - (4) heredity.
   - (5) intelligence.

3. Because identical twins have the same genes but fraternal twins share only about 50 percent of their genes, what conclusion can be drawn from the study of twins?
   - (1) Identical twins look exactly alike, but fraternal twins only resemble each other.
   - (2) A stimulating intellectual environment makes children bright like their parents.
   - (3) Twins share the same experiences.
   - (4) Intelligence is determined in part by heredity.
   - (5) Both types of twins are equally intelligent.

Check your answers on page 182.

Culture and Personality

When was the last time you and someone who was angry with you picked up rocks and took turns beating each other across the chest? This behavior may seem strange to you, but it is quite normal for the Yanomamo people of the Amazon. The culture in which people are raised plays an important role in shaping behavior and personality.

The child-rearing practices of a culture are especially important in the development of a culture's typical personality. How you were nursed, weaned, toilet trained, and nurtured; which aspects of your behavior were rewarded and which were punished; and how you were given attention and the amount of attention you were given as a child are some of the experiences that influence your personality as an adult.

Some cultures believe that physical punishment is an important and necessary part of the discipline of children. Many other cultures disagree and have found other ways to correct children's behavior. The Hopi of the American Southwest discipline children who seriously misbehave by threatening them with *kachinas*. These masked dancers, who represent spiritual beings, pretend to steal the children, only to have the attempts thwarted by the parents. The children, of course, are so thankful to their parents for saving them that they behave—at least for a while.

How much emotion you show, how you display it, and even what emotions you feel (and when) also depend on your upbringing. Some cultures, such as the Zuni villagers of the North American Southwest, teach their members to control their emotions; other cultures encourage the free expression of emotions.

Even though you have close relationships with people outside your family, people who give you emotional support, you probably feel a stronger bond with family members and turn to them when you are sad, happy, or upset. You probably express those emotions in a manner similar to the way they were modeled in your family. The diagram below shows the various factors that influence an individual's personality as an adult.

Exercise 3

> **Directions:** Choose the one best answer for each item.

1. Which of the following is *not* a factor that may influence behavior and personality?

   (1) Being raised in the Catholic faith
   (2) Growing up in a wealthy family
   (3) Crying easily
   (4) Attending military school for grades 6 through 12
   (5) Being the youngest in a family of ten

2. Children within a single culture develop different personalities because

   (1) the parents have different personalities.
   (2) the child-rearing practices were the same.
   (3) parents and other adults teach and treat their children differently.
   (4) the forms of discipline were different.
   (5) the children have different ways of showing emotion.

> Items 3 and 4 refer to the diagram below.

3. What would be the best title for the diagram?

   (1) The Organization of Society
   (2) How Children Learn
   (3) The Survival of Society
   (4) Influences on Adult Personality
   (5) Technology in the Modern World

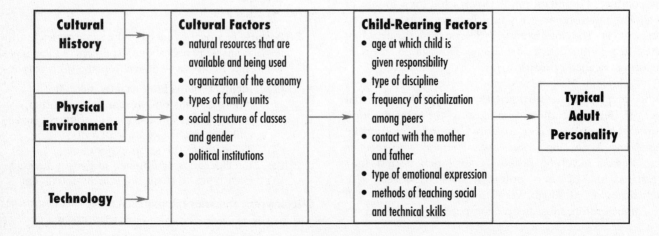

Cultural History	Cultural Factors	Child-Rearing Factors	Typical Adult Personality
Physical Environment	• natural resources that are available and being used • organization of the economy • types of family units • social structure of classes and gender • political institutions	• age at which child is given responsibility • type of discipline • frequency of socialization among peers • contact with the mother and father • type of emotional expression • methods of teaching social and technical skills	
Technology			

SOME COMMON PSYCHOLOGICAL CONCEPTS

defense mechanism: any behavior or thought process a person uses to protect himself against painful or anxious feelings (see examples below)

repression: a defense mechanism of unconsciously holding back feelings or memories about unpleasant or painful experiences

projection: a defense mechanism in which a person unconsciously "projects" one's own ideas, impulses, or emotions onto another person, as if projecting film onto a screen; for example, saying someone else looks or feels sad when you really feel sad yourself

displacement: a defense mechanism in which a person transfers an emotion to another, more acceptable object

depression: an emotional condition characterized by feelings of hopelessness or inadequacy

subconscious: part of a person's mind in which thoughts or feelings occur while the person is not fully aware of them

4. According to the diagram on the previous page, which of the following does *not* affect adult personality?

   (1) How the children are cared for when both parents work outside the home

   (2) How the adult personality affects the culture

   (3) How old the child is when he or she starts doing chores around the house

   (4) How the people gather and use the resources from the environment

   (5) How the child is encouraged in or discouraged from showing emotions

Item 5 refers to the following passage.

Conditioning shapes your behavior through three types of consequences. Positive reinforcement is any consequence you enjoy, so that you increase the frequency of your behavior. In negative reinforcement, your behavior is encouraged, or reinforced, because an unpleasant experience stops or is prevented when you behave that way. Punishment causes you to decrease the frequency of your behavior.

5. Learning occurs with conditioning because of

   (1) your understanding of the stimulus.

   (2) positive reinforcement, negative reinforcement, and punishment.

   (3) your determination to learn from every encounter.

   (4) the way you were trained to deal with stress.

   (5) the bell or metronome that operates with another stimulus.

Check your answers on page 182.

People as Members of Groups

A group is two or more people who interact regularly for a specific purpose. You probably have a closer relationship with some groups than you do with others. Your relationships with your family and close friends are probably very important to you. In fact, the main reason you spend time with these people is most likely because you value the relationships you have with them. A group whose members interact because they value one another is called a primary group. Such groups tend to be small because people typically do not develop close personal relationships with the many members of a large group.

A secondary group is one whose main purpose is something other than the development of personal relationships. The main purpose of your work group, for example, is to get a job done—although you may develop a primary group of friends within the work group. Our society today develops more secondary groups than primary groups, possibly because many families are geographically separated.

Behavioral scientists have found that groups influence behavior. For instance, you are more likely to voice your opinion among friends who hold the same values than with members of a group whose views differ from yours. In a group you are more likely to **conform**, or to go along with what the majority wants, even if they have not tried to pressure you. Another way people are influenced by groups is through **modeling**, or by observing the behavior of other group members.

Norms, Values, and Roles

The norms and values of your culture are your code for behavior. You have learned the **norms** of your culture, or how people expect you to act in certain situations. Some norms are expressed as laws with severe penalties for people who break them. For example, a person who is caught robbing a store is sent to jail. When we disregard other norms, however, the punishments are less severe—possibly just looks of disapproval.

A **value** is an idea or standard that the people of a culture think is important. Americans, for example, share a common value that all people should have equal opportunity. Racism, sexism, and poverty may work against it, but equal opportunity is an ideal that most Americans think is important.

Each **role** that you have in society also includes certain expected behaviors. A person's gender, marital status, job, economic status, and ethnic background are all linked to certain expectations. Your role at work might be to act courteously, dress neatly, and perform specific tasks. Sex or gender roles are those that our society expects you to assume because you are a male or a female.

Exercise 4

> **Directions:** Choose the one best answer for each item.

1. Which of the following is *not* a group?

   (1) Players in a softball game
   (2) People standing in line for movie tickets
   (3) Workers brainstorming solutions to a problem
   (4) People picketing outside a factory
   (5) A family eating dinner

2. Many years ago a woman was beaten and stabbed to death in her New York City neighborhood while thirty-eight of her neighbors watched from their windows. No one came to her assistance or called the police. According to the rules of group behavior, one person coming forward to help probably would have caused other neighbors to

   (1) fear becoming involved.
   (2) feel relief that someone did something.
   (3) dislike the person who helped.
   (4) offer their help as well.
   (5) pretend nothing was happening.

3. At the 1991 Tailhook Association convention in Las Vegas, a group of male Navy aviators reportedly fondled eighty-three female aviators, whom they forced to run between two lines of groping men in a hallway. Some of the men probably attacked the women because

   (1) the men had bad attitudes toward women.
   (2) everyone else was doing the same thing.
   (3) the men were prejudiced against the women.
   (4) the women asked for it.
   (5) the men and women evaluated the situation differently.

4. Gender roles are shaped by group values. What value (belief) is behind the idea that women should be teachers, not presidents?

   (1) Men are the natural leaders of the human race.
   (2) A majority of teachers are women.
   (3) Women fill many clerical positions.
   (4) Sports provides men with leadership positions.
   (5) Men and women are equal in all respects.

Check your answers on page 182.

Ethnicity and Multiculturalism

Almost every citizen or resident of the United States also belongs to one or more socially recognized ethnic and racial groups. Your ethnicity may include cultural traditions, religion, and history based on your ancestry. Your race, however, is based on physical characteristics such as skin color and facial features that may categorize you as a white American, a Native American, an African American, or an Asian American. You share your racial and national ancestry with other people, who may come from all classes of society. Your ethnic identity joins you with members of your ethnic group (or groups) and also separates you from other ethnic groups.

Many countries have homogeneous populations, that is, people with a single culture. The United States, by contrast, has a multicultural population; American citizens claim ancestry of more than 100 nationalities, making this country one of the most culturally diverse nations of the world. The graph above indicates the racial origins of Americans.

By a different measurement, 9 percent of Americans are of Hispanic origin; that is, their families come from Mexico, Cuba, Puerto Rico, or South America.

In spite of the United States' great diversity, many of its citizens suffer from racial and ethnic inequality. Most white Americans are descendants of immigrants from Northern and Western Europe who entered the United States voluntarily. Whites have always occupied an advantaged position in American society. The ancestors of other groups, such as African Americans, some Hispanics, and Native

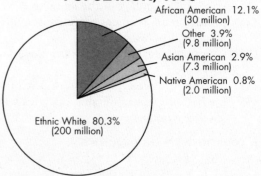

RACIAL COMPOSITION OF THE U.S. POPULATION, 1990

African American 12.1% (30 million)
Other 3.9% (9.8 million)
Asian American 2.9% (7.3 million)
Native American 0.8% (2.0 million)
Ethnic White 80.3% (200 million)

Americans, were either forcibly brought to this country or forced from their lands through conquest and colonization. These groups have experienced exploitation, social inequality, prejudice, discrimination, and poverty. Although most Asian Americans came to this country voluntarily, they too have suffered from prejudice and discrimination by other ethnic groups who view them as competitors for jobs and other resources.

Exercise 5

Directions: Choose the one best answer for each item.

Items 1 and 2 refer to the following graphs.

U.S. HOUSEHOLDS, 1990

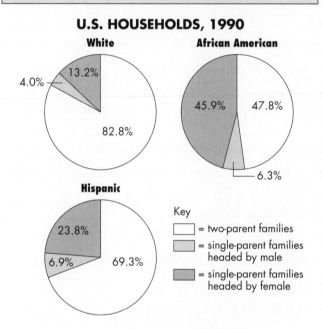

White

African American

4.0% 13.2%

82.8%

45.9% 47.8%

6.3%

Hispanic

23.8%

6.9% 69.3%

Key
☐ = two-parent families
▦ = single-parent families headed by male
▩ = single-parent families headed by female

1. In 1991, the average median incomes were $30,143 for white households, $22,586 for African-American households, and $20,885 for Hispanic households. From this information and the graphs, you can infer that

   (1) two-parent households are likely to be poor.
   (2) single-parent, male-headed African-American families make up the largest group of poor households.
   (3) single-parent, male-headed Hispanic families make up the smallest group of poor households.
   (4) the proportion of single-parent, female-headed households is lowest among the poor.
   (5) a high proportion of poor households is likely to be headed by single females.

2. Behavioral scientists might use the information in the graphs to make a case for

   (1) decreased social services for single-parent white families.
   (2) increased health services for single-parent families.
   (3) increased social services for single-parent African-American families.
   (4) increased bilingual programs for Hispanic households.
   (5) increased multicultural training for minority households.

3. What does the circle graph on the preceding page indicate about racial and ethnic diversity in the United States?

   (1) Native Americans suffer more discrimination than any other group.
   (2) The proportions of Asian Americans and African Americans in the total population are growing.
   (3) Nonwhite groups make up about one fifth of the population.
   (4) Ethnic whites include people from many different cultural backgrounds.
   (5) Asian Americans are the smallest racial group in the country.

4. Which phrase best defines the term *multicultural nation*?

   (1) A nation of many cultures, each of which claims its own nationality
   (2) A country of many nationalities, all claiming the same geographic region
   (3) A culture of many ethnic groups, each of which strictly maintains its ancestral nationality
   (4) A country of many ethnic groups, each of which claims the same nationality
   (5) A country of many ethnic groups, each of which seeks political independence

Check your answers on page 182.

Glossary

abolitionists: people wishing to abolish, or end, slavery

amendment: a change or correction

behaviorist theory: a theory of personality developed by Ivan Pavlov that is based on the belief that human behavior is learned through experience

bill: a proposed law introduced to or in a legislature; when a bill is passed by the legislature, it becomes a law

boycott: a refusal to buy a product or service

bureaucracy: a large, complex administrative structure characterized by specialization of tasks and hierarchy of authority

cabinet: presidential advisory body

civil service: body of employees who have passed specialized exams and are now employed in government service jobs

climate: the weather pattern, including temperature, rain, snow, and wind conditions, that prevails in a region

colony: a territory settled by people who remain governed by their native country

communism: an economic and political system characterized by a classless society, equal distribution of economic goods, state control of the economy, and an emphasis on the state's needs rather than on individual liberties

conditioning: a simple form of learning that can be used to change human behavior as well as to shape it

conform: to give in to or follow what the majority of the people want, even if they have not tried to pressure you

conservation: using resources in the environment carefully and wisely

constitution: a written or unwritten structure setting out the principles, duties, and limits of government

containment: the policy of attempting to prevent the spread of a political system, such as communism

county: the major unit of local government in most states

culture: the behavior, patterns, and artifacts that are made and shared by a group of people

demand: the amount of product consumers buy

diffusion: the process through which a custom, belief, or object spreads from one culture to another

endogenous source: a source of cultural change in a society that originates from within the society

entitlements: government programs that help specified groups of people

equator: an imaginary line that circles Earth exactly halfway between the North Pole and the South Pole

executive branch: the segment of government responsible for executing, or carrying out, laws passed by the legislative branch

exogenous source: a source of cultural change in a society that originates from outside the society

federal system: a type of government in which power is shared between a central government and state governments

fiscal policy: actions of the federal government related to taxing and spending

"gag rule": a rule passed in the U.S. House of Representatives to forbid any discussion of slavery

gross domestic product (GDP): the total annual value of goods and services produced in the United States

humanistic theory: a theory of personality based on the belief that people strive to achieve their fullest potential

humanitarianism: concern for the well-being of all humanity

imperialism: the policy of one country to extend its influence to other countries, seeking to gain economic and political control

inflation: a general rise in prices

innovation: a new tool, technology, idea, or method that is developed within a society

internal conflict: a struggle within a society resulting from opposing ideas, needs, or basic instincts

intervention: interference; an active role in someone else's affairs

judicial branch: the court system of the U.S. government

judicial review: the power of the courts to determine the constitutionality of laws and government actions

latitude: the position of a point on the earth's surface expressed as its distance (up to 90°) north or south of the equator

law of diminishing returns: the idea that at a certain point, additional resources fail to increase output (results) or profit (money above and beyond the cost of production)

legislative branch: the part of government responsible for making laws

lobbyists: people attempting to influence government officials on behalf of interest groups

longitude: the position of a point on Earth's surface expressed as its distance (up to 180°) east or west of the prime meridian

"Manifest Destiny": the belief of Americans in the mid-nineteenth century that they had a special mission to explore the West

migration: movement of great numbers of people from one place to another with the intention of settling in the new area

modeling: shaping behavior based on observed behavior of others

monetary policy: actions of the Federal Reserve Bank that affect interest rates and the supply of money

nonrenewable resource: a natural resource that cannot be recycled or recreated

norms: how a culture expects people to act in a certain situation

PACs: political action committees—special interest groups that attempt to influence public policy

personality: the ways you act, think, and feel that make you different from others

polar regions: high-latitude regions, near the North Pole or South Pole, with the coldest temperatures

prejudice: judgment made before all the facts are known

prime meridian: the standard (0°) meridian of Earth, passing through Greenwich, England, from which longitude is measured

progressive tax: a tax rate that increases as income increases

proportional tax: a tax rate that stays the same regardless of income

psychoanalytic theory: Sigmund Freud's theory that much of human behavior is controlled by forces in the unconscious mind that may be linked to childhood experiences and sexual motives

ratification: formal approval, usually by the states

raw material: a natural resource in a state close to its original form in nature

recyclable resource: a resource that is continually reused instead of being thrown away

regressive tax: a tax rate that is higher for lower incomes than for higher incomes

renewable resource: any resource that can be regrown or remade in its original form

representative democracy: a type of democracy in which citizens elect a few people to represent them in government

representative government: a government in which an elected or chosen few act for (or represent) the many

resource: anything that people value and use

revolution: an attempt to change the form of government and restructure society

role: a person's expected behavior based on social position, gender, and race

segregation: formal separation of races, such as in schools, churches, and restaurants

socialization: the process during which members of a society learn to participate in that society, are taught their roles, and develop a self-image

sovereignty: a government's freedom from external control by another country

special district: a local government unit set up to address a problem or provide a service in a specified area

stereotype: an exaggerated belief that assumes nearly everyone in a group of people has a certain characteristic

supply: the amount of product sellers make available

temperate zones: middle-latitude regions that are cooler than the tropics and warmer than the polar regions

tropics: low-latitude areas that generally have warm climates year-round

value: an idea or standard that the people of a culture think is important

ANSWERS AND EXPLANATIONS

Unit 1: History

Exercise 1 (page 140)

1. **The correct answer is (3). (Comprehension)** Only Connecticut and Delaware are identified on the map as colonies founded for both economic and religious reasons.

2. **The correct answer is (5). (Evaluation)** The only conclusion that could be drawn from the map is choice (5). The map itself indicates no relationship between size or location and reason for founding as suggested by choices (3) and (4). The map does not explain colonists' preferences for a particular location or indicate which colonies were successful, so choices (1) and (2) are incorrect.

3. **The correct answer is (3). (Analysis)** The passage indicates that since the land does not show the usual signs of ownership—fences, dwellings, and cattle—the "natives" have no right to the land. The passage does not mention government as in choice (1). Choice (2) misses the point of the passage. Choices (4) and (5) are contradicted by the passage.

Exercise 2 (page 142)

1. **The correct answer is (2). (Analysis)** The importance of self-government is indicated in the previous section and in the idea that the colonists were very "independent minded."

2. **The correct answer is (3). (Analysis)** The text gives some clues (e.g., Britain's "restrictive measures") that, together with the king's statement, lead to the conclusion that Britain wanted complete authority. The issue of taxes was over British, not American, taxes; the Stamp Act was not an immediate memory in a long series of events; the Revolutionary War had not yet started; and the Declaration of Independence had not yet been written, so the other choices can be eliminated.

3. **The correct answer is (3). (Application)** A strong central government may limit individual rights. Such a government would not be likely to give too many rights to states, as suggested by choice (1), or to individuals, as in choice (2). There is no reason to suppose that representative assemblies would be prevented or that the Constitution's power would be limited by a strong central government, so choices (4) and (5) are incorrect.

4. **The correct answer is (4). (Application)** A senator's qualifications are not a matter of individual rights and freedoms. Choice (1) is protected by Amendment 1, the right of free speech and assembly; choice (2) by Amendment 2, the right to keep and bear arms; choice (3) by Amendment 4, freedom from unreasonable searches and seizures; and choice (5) by Amendment 1, freedom of religion.

Exercise 3 (page 143)

1. **The correct answer is (3). (Evaluation)** Choice (3) is the only choice that can be supported by the map. Choices (1) and (2) are not factually correct, and choices (4) and (5) are not indicated by information on the map.

2. **The correct answer is (1). (Application)** Missouri and Texas, choices (2) and (4), were already slave states, and the territories in choices (3) and (5) were opened to slavery by the Dred Scott decision. California entered the Union as a free, or nonslavery, state, and the Dred Scott decision affected only territories, which were under federal control.

3. **The correct answer is (2). (Analysis)** The right of petition is one of the rights guaranteed in the First Amendment, by the free speech clause. Forbidding discussion, choice (3), and blocking petitions, choice (4), are specific actions that deny free speech, but choice (2) is a better answer because it encompasses the concept that Adams was communicating.

4. **The correct answer is (4). (Comprehension)** The only answer that can be supported by the text is choice (4).

Exercise 4 (page 144)

1. **The correct answer is (2). (Evaluation)** Choices (1), (3), (4), and (5) are statements of fact, not conclusions.

2. **The correct answer is (3). (Evaluation)** People who believed in Manifest Destiny believed the United States had a right and duty to settle the North American continent. They did not care if this destroyed the environment, choice (1), or infringed on the rights of the Native Americans who already occupied the territory, choice (2). Manifest Destiny did not extend to territory off the continent, choice (4). People who believed in the doctrine did not value peace because they were willing to fight the Native Americans for their territory.

3. **The correct answer is (3). (Analysis)** Differences in railroad width (or gauge) caused problems later in the building of nationwide rail networks, but they cannot be blamed for the difficulties caused by the inadequate rail system in the South. The rest of the choices describe real disadvantages.

4. **The correct answer is (4). (Comprehension)** Choice (4) is the only one supported by the text.

Exercise 5 (page 146)

1. **The correct answer is (5). (Analysis)** Labor unions had and have broad concerns about workplace safety, choices (1) and (4), workers' well-being, choice (2), and workers' benefits, choice (3), but getting to and from work is up to the workers.

2. **The correct answer is (2). (Application)** Factory workers were part of the manufacturing segment.

3. **The correct answer is (2). (Comprehension)** The only change represented in the graphs is the decrease in the actual proportion of agricultural workers. The graphs do not show the effect of urbanization, choice (1), changes in numbers of workers, choice (3), workers' preferences, choice (4), or changes in demand for workers, choice (5).

Exercise 6 (page 147)

1. **The correct answer is (2). (Evaluation)** The fact that American forces attacked one of Spain's Pacific colonies indicates that Cuban liberation was not the only reason for engaging in the war. None of the other choices supports or suggests an American motive for the war.

2. **The correct answer is (3). (Analysis)** The definition of imperialism in the question strongly hints that imperialism would interfere with a nation's self-determination.

3. **The correct answer is (1). (Comprehension)** The cartoon depicts the hens as all Latin-American countries, not necessarily countries protected, choice (2), or by choice not protected, choice (5), by the United States or colonized by Europe, choice (4).

4. **The correct answer is (4). (Application)** European nations are locked in the coop (that is, away from Latin America) by the Monroe Doctrine, which restricts their activities.

Exercise 7 (page 148)

1. **The correct answer is (4). (Application)** Choices (1), (3), and (5) all contain some risk but not on the scale of investing in an uncertain business venture with borrowed money. Choice (2) does not contain a risk.

2. **The correct answer is (3). (Evaluation)** Camp conditions, choice (4), loss of property, choice (5), and suspicion, choice (2), were all part of the main violation, civil rights. Japanese citizenship, choice (1), was not an issue.

3. **The correct answer is (4). (Evaluation)** The Cuban Missile Crisis went down in history as the closest the world ever came to nuclear war. The passage hints in several places at the gravity of the situation ("the nation held its breath," "war had been narrowly avoided").

Exercise 8 *(page 149)*

1. **The correct answer is (4). (Evaluation)** Only choice (4) can be supported by the map. The map does not show beliefs, choice (1), intentions, choice (3), or agreement, choice (5), and does not indicate whether schools were closed, choice (2).

2. **The correct answer is (3). (Analysis)** The immigration policy from 1924 to 1965 specifically welcomed immigrants from northern Europe.

3. **The correct answer is (3). (Application)** Humanitarianism is the main justification for intervention in a nation's affairs.

Unit 2: Geography

Exercise 1 *(page 151)*

1. **The correct answer is (Comprehension)** (a) P, (b) M, (c) P, (d) M, (e) P, (f) P, (g) P.

2. **The correct answer is (5). (Application)** Europe, choice (1), and the Arctic Ocean, choice (2), are north of the equator. Antarctica, choice (3), is south of it. Although both lines pass through Africa, choice (4), they meet just west of the continent.

3. **The correct answer is (2). (Comprehension)** The prime meridian is the starting point for measuring longitude. Choice (5) is a parallel of latitude. All other choices are various degrees of longitude.

4. **The correct answer is (2). (Application)** North America lies west of the prime meridian.

5. **The correct answer is (3). (Comprehension)** Choices (1) and (2) are incomplete. Choices (4) and (5) refer to the seat's relative location.

Exercise 2 *(page 153)*

1. **The correct answer is (1). (Analysis)** The passage suggests that summer begins south of the equator on December 21 or 22, when the sun shines directly on the Tropic of Capricorn. Therefore, winter begins a half-year later.

2. **The correct answer is (4). (Evaluation)** Since temperatures in the United States fluctuate dramatically, it cannot lie within the tropics or a polar zone. The passage states that there are two temperate zones, north and south of the equator. Since the forty-eight contiguous states (states that share their borders with other states) lie north of the equator, this is the only choice that passage supports.

3. **The correct answer is (2). (Comprehension)** The map on page 152 shows the equator at 0° latitude, dividing the earth into northern and southern hemispheres. This region would not be cold, choice (1), and longitude divides the earth into eastern and western hemispheres, choice (3). The temperate zones meet the tropics at the Tropic of Cancer and the Tropic of Capricorn, choice (4). The passage states that the sun is directly overhead at the Tropic of Cancer in June and the Tropic of Capricorn in December, eliminating choice (5).

4. **The correct answer is (3). (Application)** The graph shows a place with hot temperatures all year long and a rainy season in the summer and dry for the remainder of the year. This is typical of wet-and-dry tropical weather, found only in the tropics.

Exercise 3 *(page 154)*

1. **The correct answer is (Application)** (a) N, (b) N, (c) R, (d) R, (e) N, (f) R.

2. **The correct answer is (5). (Evaluation)** The passage shows how people have placed value on different resources throughout history depending on what their needs were. Examples are given to show that at any given time, the most valued resources were those that had the most varied or most important uses.

3. **The correct answer is (1). (Analysis)** Any action that conserves a nonrenewable resource is important. By its very nature, a renewable resource does not need to be conserved, choice (2). Using a renewable resource does not specifically affect recycling, choice (3), or pollution, choice (5). It does protect the environment, but choice (1) is more specific and therefore a better answer.

4. **The correct answer is (4). (Analysis)** Because corn can be replanted, it is a renewable resource and therefore a better one to use than nonrenewable petroleum. Choices (2), (3), and (5) are not true. Choice (1) is not relevant.

5. **The correct answer is (2). (Analysis)** Although choices (1), (4), and (5) are true, they do not explain the spread of corn throughout the world. Choice (3) is not true.

Exercise 4 *(page 156)*

1. **The correct answer is (1). (Evaluation)** The other choices are not supported by the text.

2. **The correct answer is (2). (Analysis)** Choices (1), (3), (4), and (5) were all effects of the dust storms, but they were not as important in the long run as the increased interest in conservation.

3. **The correct answer is (3). (Application)** Rain and snow are precipitation; all other statements are incorrect.

4. **The correct answer is (5). (Analysis)** Choices (1) and (2) are incorrect because the supply of water is fixed. Choices (3) and (4) focus on one aspect of the cycle rather than the cycle as a whole.

5. **The correct answer is (3). (Comprehension)** The only way that people can affect the cycle is by contaminating it. Other activities may result in shortages in some areas or flooding in others but will not affect the overall supply.

Unit 3: Civics and Government

Exercise 1 *(page 157)*

1. **The correct answer is (1). (Comprehension)** The word *democracy means* "rule by the people."

2. **The correct answer is (4). (Application)** Jefferson is said to be the main author of the Declaration of Independence and was President of the United States from 1801 to 1809.

3. **The correct answer is (1). (Analysis)** Because all people participate in democratic decisions, compromises often must be made.

4. **The correct answer is (3). (Analysis)** Jefferson was remarking that the best way to learn about political freedom is to participate directly in a self-governing political unit, such as the town meeting.

5. **The correct answer is (4). (Evaluation)** Slaves and women were not included in the dictum that "all men are created equal," even though, of course, they are people. The other choices are true but are not logically inconsistent with Jefferson's premise.

Exercise 2 *(page 159)*

1. **The correct answer is (3). (Application)** The number of representatives that a state sends to the House is determined by its population.

2. **The correct answer is (2). (Comprehension)** Each state, regardless of its size, has only two U.S. senators.

3. **The correct answer is (1). (Analysis)** Choice (3) is true, but choice (1) is the best summary of the president's overall and most important duties while in office. The other choices are untrue.

4. **The correct answer is (2). (Comprehension)** The three main branches of government are legislative, executive, and judicial.

Exercise 3 *(page 160)*

1. **The correct answer is (3). (Comprehension)** Federal agencies deal with issues of national concern.

2. The correct answer is (2). (Analysis) The increasing urbanization of America has meant that the government must devote more and more energy to dealing with transportation, housing, and other issues common to urban growth.

3. The correct answer is (2). (Evaluation) Entitlement programs are designed to provide basic assistance to people in need so that no one will be destitute. Choices (1) and (4) are not underlying values in entitlement programs. Choice (3) is untrue. Choice (5) is a tenet of a communist society more than of a democratic one.

4. The correct answer is (3). (Analysis) Civil service replaced the spoils system as a fairer method for choosing government employees. Today, civil service workers must have skills that qualify them for their jobs.

5. The correct answer is (4). (Analysis) The power and size of the bureaucracy are portrayed as being out of control and not capable of being administered by the elected leaders of government.

6. The correct answer is (4). (Evaluation) The cartoonist clearly feels that the bureaucracy is too large, so it can be assumed that reducing the size of the bureaucracy would meet with the cartoonist's approval.

7. The correct answer is (3). (Application) Because the National Education Association is made up of classroom teachers, this group could provide the guideline writers with firsthand information about dealing with students who have special needs.

8. The correct answer is (2). The purse and the grocery cart suggest a shopper. There is no indication that she represents all Americans, choice (1). The cartoon criticizes government regulations, so she is unlikely to represent the government, choice (5). There is also no hint in her appearance that she is a food processor or a farmer, choices (3) and (4).

9. The correct answer is (3). Choices (1) and (2) are not supported by the cartoon. Choices (4) and (5) are hinted at but not directly addressed in the cartoon.

Exercise 4 *(page 162)*

1. The correct answer is (1). (Application) Both federal and state governments are divided into three main branches—legislative, executive, and judicial. Choices (2), (3), and (5) refer to rights and responsibilities given to the federal government alone. Choice (4) is incorrect because one state, Nebraska, has a legislative branch with only one house.

2. The correct answer is (2). (Comprehension) Through licensing, states maintain the quality of services supplied to their citizens.

3. The correct answer is (2). (Comprehension) Schools make up the majority of all special districts in the nation.

4. The correct answer is (4). (Analysis) Special districts are set up to deal with particular problems or provide services within specified areas, regardless of other governmental boundaries. They do not replace other governments.

Exercise 5 *(page 163)*

1. The correct answer is (2). (Comprehension) After the end of World War II in 1945, the main goal of American foreign policy became the containment of communism around the globe.

2. The correct answer is (2). (Analysis) Having nations friendly to the United States in other parts of the world means America can spend less time, energy, and money on defense against possible enemies. Such an outcome in the former Soviet Union will allow the United States to spend available resources on domestic needs rather than on military superiority.

3. The correct answer is (4). (Evaluation) The United States, a world leader, cannot suddenly isolate itself from the rest of the world, particularly when events elsewhere can have a tremendous impact on the American economy and foreign policy. Foreign policy should not be decided on the basis of possible future events, choice (1), or pride, choice (2). Today, the ideal is cooperation among nations, not aggression, choice (3). No evidence exists of budget commitment to intervention, choice (5).

4. The correct answer is (2). (Application) Occupational health and safety is the responsibility of the Labor Department. All other duties listed deal with foreign relations and therefore are part of the State Department.

Unit 4: Economics

Exercise 1 *(page 164)*

1. The correct answer is (4). (Application) Ed and Linda are temporarily satisfied in their desire to eat dinner, so they have reached the stage of want satisfaction.

2. The correct answer is (1). (Analysis) Without distribution, which is required between the production and consumption stages of the want-satisfaction process, any goods and services produced would not reach consumers.

3. The correct answer is (4). (Analysis) Choices (1), (2), (3), and (5) are true but tell only part of the story, so they are not adequate as conclusions drawn from the entire process.

4. The correct answer is (2). (Comprehension) Both the table and the graph indicate that at a price of $8.00, consumers will attend two movies per month.

5. The correct answer is (5). (Analysis) Choices (2), (3), and (4) won't result in any additional movie attendance. A $3 price, choice (1), may increase weekday attendance, but the $2 price, choice (5), is likely to yield the greatest attendance, because more people attend movies on weekends than on weekdays.

6. The correct answer is (5). (Evaluation) If people spend more on entertainment when they have more money, it makes sense that the demand for movies will increase when incomes increase. The number of movies made is not directly tied to moviegoers' incomes, choices (1) and (2), nor is the price of a movie, choice (3). Choice (4) would support the opposite conclusion from the one in the question.

Exercise 2 *(page 166)*

1. The correct answer is (3). (Comprehension) The key to understanding diminishing returns is to examine additional contributions of additional workers. Although total output can increase, it does so at a decreasing rate once the law of diminishing returns sets in.

2. The correct answer is (3). (Analysis) A subsidy lowers costs and is likely to increase supply. Taxes, choice (1), raise costs. Advertising, choice (2), is designed to affect demand. A ban on late movies, choice (4), or a decrease in the price of popcorn, choice (5), affects demand.

3. The correct answer is (4). (Application) Reading both the table and graph across from a $2 price shows that five movies will be demanded and one will be supplied, for a difference of four movies.

Exercise 3 *(page 167)*

1. The correct answer is (3). (Application) Federal withholding taxes are income taxes by definition.

2. The correct answer is (4). (Comprehension) The sum of 4.2, 2.1, and 1.7 trillions of dollars is $8 trillion.

3. The correct answer is (3). (Comprehension) Benefits to individuals, such as social security, unemployment compensation, and Medicare, make up 44 percent of the federal government budget.

4. **The correct answer is (1). (Analysis)** By far, education takes the greatest percentages of both state and local government expenditures; it is not included as a major category under federal expenditures. The graphs contain no information to support choices (2), (4), and (5). Choice (3) is true, but choice (1) is better supported by all three graphs.

5. **The correct answer is (2). (Application)** Between 1981 and 1985, the national debt doubled, from $1 trillion to $2 trillion.

6. **The correct answer is (4). (Analysis)** Choice (4) is the only statement that accurately sums up the information on the graph. Choice (3) is incomplete because it includes only the years 1985–1991. Choice (2) is a definition of the term national debt and says nothing about the graph. Choices (1) and (5) are opinions that cannot be supported by the graph.

7. **The correct answer is (2). (Evaluation)** Inflation is a general rise in the price level, which erodes the spending power of money. A way to slow inflation, especially if it is severe, is to discourage people from spending by raising interest rates and encouraging banks to stop lending.

Unit 5: People and Cultures

Exercise 1 *(page 170)*

1. **The correct answer is (4). (Analysis)** Although an individual may achieve a certain amount of technological success through trial-and-error learning, there can be no social progress unless social learning and cultural transmission also occur.

2. **The correct answer is (4). (Application)** Jiang first tried out the language on her own and made many errors; later, she relied on others to help her. Choices (1), (2), and (3) are only partially correct; prejudices and stereotypes, choice (5), did not enter into Jiang's learning at all.

3. **The correct answer is (5). (Comprehension)** Americans' beliefs about the rights of racial and ethnic groups changed after some groups within our society created internal conflict to bring social injustices to the attention of the majority.

4. **The correct answer is (1). (Application)** New technology applied to manufacturing outside the home forced the many women who remained at home to be separated from economic development. The technology was an English innovation that diffused from England to the United States.

5. **The correct answer is (4). (Comprehension)** The numbers have almost equalized. In 1990, there were only 10.2 percent more men in the labor force than women, compared with a 60.2 percent difference in 1910.

Exercise 2 *(page 171)*

1. **The correct answer is (2). (Analysis)** Carlos was able to resist the temptation to steal the snack because of society's positive influence. Choice (1) is not the best answer because Carlos' selfish tendencies would have encouraged him to steal the snack. According to the behaviorist theory, Carlos' exposure to inappropriate behaviors would have encouraged him to steal the snack, choice (3). The destructive forces of society in the humanistic theory would have led to Carlos' stealing the snack, choice (4). Choice (5) is not the best answer because Carlos' low self-concept probably would have led to his stealing the snack.

2. **The correct answer is (5). (Comprehension)** Choices (3) and (4) are partly true, but the studies also examined children who were not twins and were concerned with only one trait, intelligence—not with inherited traits like height or eye color. There is no evidence for choices (1) and (2).

3. **The correct answer is (4). (Analysis)** Choice (4) is the only one that explains the focus of the passage.

Exercise 3 *(page 172)*

1. **The correct answer is (3). (Application)** Choice (3) is a behavior, not an influence.

2. **The correct answer is (3). (Analysis)** Even within one culture, parents raise their children differently enough for the children to develop different personalities.

3. **The correct answer is (4). (Analysis)** Choice (4) is the best title. Each of the other titles describes only part of the diagram.

4. **The correct answer is (2). (Comprehension)** The diagram does not show how the adult personality affects the culture, although there is a connection between the two.

5. **The correct answer is (2). (Comprehension)** Conditioning relies on reinforcers and punishment to shape behavior.

Exercise 4 *(page 174)*

1. **The correct answer is (2). (Application)** Members of a group interact with one another on a fairly regular basis.

2. **The correct answer is (4). (Analysis)** Groups can influence individual behavior through modeling. Seeing one person help, some of the other neighbors most likely would have helped, too.

3. **The correct answer is (2). (Analysis)** Some of the aviators may have been influenced by the behavior they saw modeled.

4. **The correct answer is (1). (Evaluation)** Choices (2), (3), and (4) are facts, not values. Choice (5) is a value but is contradicted by the message of the role.

Exercise 5 *(page 175)*

1. **The correct answer is (5). (Comprehension)** Most single-parent households are headed by poor African-American and Hispanic women.

2. **The correct answer is (3). (Evaluation)** The graphs show that African-American single-parent families outnumber two-parent African-American families. Assuming that many single parents, especially those who are poor, have trouble managing their households, the information indicates a pressing need for social services in that group.

3. **The correct answer is (3). (Evaluation)** The graph indicates nothing more than the proportions of racial groups at a given time. It does not show discrimination, choice (1); growth, choice (2); or cultural backgrounds, choice (4). Choice (5) is incorrect because the graph shows Native Americans to be the smallest minority group.

4. **The correct answer is (4). (Analysis)** A multicultural nation, such as the United States, is a nation of many ethnic groups that retain some of their ancestors' cultures but all claim the same nationality (American).

PART III
SCIENCE

What Will I Find on the Science Test?

The GED Science Test is a measurement of your understanding of science concepts as well as your ability to solve science problems. Many of the items on the test will focus on applications of science to daily living, such as environmental science, technology, research, and workplace skills.

CONTENT AREAS

Science is Test 3 of the GED Tests. It consists of the following three content areas. The percent of questions in each area is given in parentheses:

Life science (45%): The study of life processes and patterns and the study of humans and the environment.

Earth science (20%): The study of Earth's structure, atmosphere, weather, and resources, as well as space science.

Physical science (35%): The study of matter (chemistry) and energy (physics).

TYPES OF QUESTIONS

When you take the GED Science Test, you will have 80 minutes to answer 50 multiple-choice questions. Approximately one half of these will be stand-alone questions that will test your understanding of basic scientific concepts, processes, and methods of inquiry. The other half will be questions based on graphs, charts, diagrams, or paragraphs of information. Each question will be based on one of the six science standards developed by the National Science Education Council: fundamental understandings, unifying concepts and processes, science as inquiry, science and technology, science in personal and social perspectives, and history and nature of science. Of these, the largest percentage (60%) will represent fundamental understandings, 17% will test science in personal and social perspectives, 8% will test science as inquiry, 8% will test science as history and nature of science, 3.5% will test science as technology, and 3.5% will test science as unifying concepts and processes.

FUNDAMENTAL UNDERSTANDINGS

This strand tests your knowledge of basic scientific concepts and principles—your science literacy. Questions may cover your understanding of basic laws of motion (physical science), the theory of evolution (life science), or Earth's place in the solar system (earth and space science).

Read the passage and answer the question that follows.

Black holes are regions of space with such dense gravity that not even light can escape. Therefore, black holes cannot be observed directly by astronomers. In order to study this mysterious phenomenon, scientists will use the next generation of particle accelerator, such as the Large Hadron Collider. This massive device, now under construction in Switzerland, may allow scientists to create miniature black holes and to detect their existence by tracking the energy they release when they disappear. This in turn may allow physicists to determine if black holes really exist.

1. Scientists cannot see black holes because

   (1) they are very far away.
   (2) they trap light.
   (3) they do not really exist.
   (4) larger telescopes are needed.
   (5) they cannot track the energy the black holes release.

The correct answer is (2). To answer this question correctly, you must not only understand the passage but also understand several fundamental facts about science, including the fact that objects must give off light in order to be seen through a telescope. The other choices are incorrect statements that are not based on a fundamental understanding of scientific knowledge.

UNIFYING CONCEPTS AND PRINCIPLES

Unifying concepts and principles require you to understand how information is organized, how basic principles are interrelated, how scientists use measurement, and how form is related to function. The following question, also based on the passage above, is an example:

2. Which statement about the nature of light is suggested by this passage?

   (1) Light cannot travel through a vacuum.
   (2) Light is a form of electromagnetic radiation.
   (3) White light can be broken down into the colors of the spectrum.
   (4) Light is made of particles of matter.
   (5) Light waves and sound waves behave in similar ways.

The correct answer is (4). To answer this question correctly, you must understand not only that scientists think of light as a stream of particle but also that gravity acts on all matter. Choices (1) and (5) are incorrect, and choices (2) and (3) are correct but not suggested by the passage.

SCIENCE AS INQUIRY

Items on the GED that test this strand will require you to think like a scientist: to weigh evidence, think critically, and understand the scientific process. Here is an example:

3. A scientist suspects that the large-size particles of soot emitted by a steel mill are dangerous to people's lungs. How can she test this hypothesis?

   (1) Compare the lung function of people who live near the mill with that of people who live in a different place
   (2) Remove and biopsy one lung from a sample of people who live near the mill
   (3) Ask people to relocate closer to the mill, and test their lung function before and after the move
   (4) Compare the lung function of children and adults who live near the mill
   (5) After people die, perform autopsies to determine the degree of lung damage caused by living near the mill

The correct answer is (1). If the scientist conducted this experiment, she would be comparing two groups: an experimental group who are exposed to the condition of interest and a control group who are not. The results would be a valid test of her hypothesis. The other choices either present ethical problems, choices (2) and (3), or do not represent valid tests of the hypothesis, choices (4) and (5).

SCIENCE AS TECHNOLOGY

4. The wings on a plane provide lift because air moves faster across the curved top of the wing than across the flat bottom, and faster-moving air has lower pressure. Based on this principle, an engineer might design a plane with greater life by

   (1) increasing the size of the engine.
   (2) increasing the weight of the plane.
   (3) modifying the shape of the wing.
   (4) increasing the size of the wheels.
   (5) making the plane more aerodynamic.

The correct answer is (3). The principle stated in the item is Bernouilli's principle, which leads to the shape of an airplane wing: curved on top and flat on the bottom. Therefore, modifying that shape might provide more lift. Choices (1) and (2) would be more likely to decrease lift than to increase it, and choices (4) and (5) are incorrect.

SCIENCE IN PERSONAL AND SOCIAL PERSPECTIVE

This strand includes the knowledge you need to understand scientific information about health and the environment, as well as to develop decision-making skills. Read the following passage and answer example 5:

The great increases in human lifespan that developed countries have enjoyed over the past 100 years result from two factors: improved living standards, which include both nutrition and sanitation; and medical advances, such as the discovery of antibiotics. Both advances result from fundamental research into human nutritional needs and the nature of health and of illness. Scientists could not look for drugs that would kill microbes until they knew that microbes caused disease; they could not find ways to clean up water supplies until they knew that drinking water could harbor disease-causing organisms; and they could not develop vaccines until they understood the nature of the immune system. Similarly, current information about nutrition, exercise, and the risks of smoking and drinking is based on our current state of knowledge of basic biology and is subject to change as that knowledge evolves.

5. According to the passage, which of the following would be considered a medical advance that has improved human health?

   (1) Widespread use of polio vaccine
   (2) Use of sunscreen to prevent skin cancer
   (3) Widespread testing of drinking water
   (4) Discoveries about the dangers of high-fat diets
   (5) Improved safety of food supplies

The correct answer is (1). According to the passage, the other choices all relate to improved knowledge about human health.

HISTORY AND NATURE OF SCIENCE

This strand will test your knowledge of scientific advances and the way in which scientific discoveries build on the work of earlier scientists. The following example is also based on the passage above:

6. According to the passage, scientific information about human health is based on

   (1) knowledge of antibiotics and the nature of disease.
   (2) information about water supplies.
   (3) improved living standards.
   (4) knowledge of common health risks.
   (5) a history of scientific discoveries.

The correct answer is (5). The passage implies that the nature of scientific knowledge is subject to change as more discoveries are made. Choices (1), (2), (3), and (4) are all partially correct, but only choice (5) is universally correct, so it is the best answer.

Unit 1

LIFE SCIENCE

The Nature of Science

All of us need a basic knowledge of science, for several reasons. First, we need to use scientific information to understand news reports about scientific topics such as DNA, genetically modified food, AIDS, global warming, alternative energy sources, and the momentous scientific advance that occurred in the year 2000—the identification of a human genome sequence. Second, we need to know how science works so we can use the scientific method in our daily lives. Not only is scientific literacy important for you as an individual, but also it is important for you as a citizen of this country and the biosphere.

Science is the study of the natural world. The term **science** is used to mean either a body of knowledge determined through scientific investigation or a special way of finding things out.

Science is an ongoing process. Scientific results that are reported in scientific journals are tentative and subject to review and verification by other scientists.

Most scientific research arises from questions raised by previous research. A scientific question is stated in such a way that it can be answered by rigorous testing. A scientific study must be unbiased, which means that it must be free from all prejudice and favoritism. A scientific study must be fair.

A scientist must always report the method he or she used as well as the results of the study. For a scientific report to be accepted by the scientific community, other scientists must be able to reproduce the results. Reproducibility is a way to confirm, renounce, or use the study to further scientific knowledge. A scientific study is never accepted without replication of the method and results. Scientists must analyze, question, and try to duplicate the latest study before it can advance their understanding of the science of nutrition. Science is always a work in progress.

Scientists carry out that work by using the **scientific method**. Scientists first make observations that lead to a problem or a question. Then they come up with a possible answer to the question, called the **hypothesis**. Next, scientists design **experiments** that yield mathematical measures (data) to test their possible answers. Experimental designs usually compare an experimental group or groups with a control group. The data obtained are then analyzed statistically and a conclusion is drawn. Analysis either supports the hypothesis or does not support the hypothesis. Analysis usually leads to further questions to be studied.

Exercise 1

> **Directions:** Choose the one best answer for each item.

1. A hypothesis is
    - (1) a statement that leads to further questions.
    - (2) another name for an observation.
    - (3) the statistical method used to collect and analyze data.
    - (4) a measurable explanation of an observation.
    - (5) another name for a conclusion.

2. A scientist hypothesized that certain kinds of foods would help travelers avoid jet lag. She fed Group A a high-protein diet and Group B a high-carbohydrate diet before a flight to Europe. She tested both groups 24 hours later for signs of jet lag. What is the most important element missing from this experimental design?
    - (1) The scientist's observations are not included.
    - (2) The scientist did not consider the age of the subjects.
    - (3) The scientist did not include a control group.
    - (4) There was no mention of the number of time zones involved.
    - (5) The scientist did not include a high-fat diet.

Check your answers on page 244.

The Cell

All life is based on atoms and molecules. The basic life processes are chemical reactions. Therefore, all science is interrelated, and a knowledge of physical science, the subject of Unit 2 of this chapter, helps in the study of life science.

Cell Structure

The basic unit of life in plants and animals is the **cell**. Cells are composed of a **cell membrane,** which encloses the **cytoplasm,** and a **nucleus** that contains genetic material.

Two major classifications of cells are prokaryotes and eukaryotes. **Prokaryotes** are an ancient group of cells that developed early in the history of life and lack a true nucleus. Prokaryotic cells are primitive cells whose ancestors have been on the earth for at least 3.5 billion years. Prokaryotes are one-celled and mostly microscopic. They include bacteria and Archaea, microscopic, single-celled organisms that live in extreme environments.

Eukaryotes are cells that have a true nucleus and well-defined **organelles,** or subcellular chemical structures. Eukaryotic cells appeared on the earth about 1.8 billion years ago. Eukaryotes may exist as single cells or as multicellular organisms and are the types of cells that make up plants and animals.

All eukaryotic cells have a cell membrane that separates the cell from the outside world. Membranes are composed of tightly packed fat, protein, and carbohydrate molecules and have some openings to the outside called pores. Contained in the membrane but outside the nucleus is a jellylike fluid called cytoplasm, which contains the organelles.

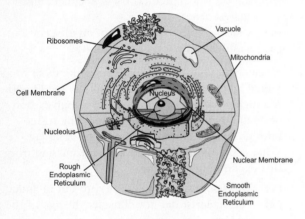

Eukaryotic Cell

The nucleus is the organelle that contains the chromosomes. The nucleus controls the cell's growth and reproduction as well as the cell's metabolism. **Metabolism** refers to the total of all physical and chemical reactions that occur in a cell.

In the cytoplasm is the **endoplasmic reticulum** (ER), an intricate, membranous canal system that assists in producing, manufacturing, or digesting large chemical molecules. The ER may contain other organelles called **ribosomes,** structures that make proteins. **Proteins** are chemicals that are vital to life and exist in many forms in plants and animals.

Chloroplasts (in plant cells) convert light energy into chemical energy in the process called photosynthesis. Only plant cells contain chloroplasts, so only plant cells can perform this basic process on which all life depends. **Mitochondria** (in both plants and animals) take the sugar molecules made in photosynthesis and transfer the chemical energy to a high-energy molecule called ATP, which the cells can use readily. The process mitochondria use is called respiration.

The cytoskeleton gives the cell its shape. It functions along with the centrioles, which are found in

animal cells and work in conjunction with cilia and flagella, tiny hairlike growths, to allow the cell to move. Also found in the cytoplasm are membranous sacs that transport materials in, within, and out of the cell.

Exercise 2

> **Directions:** Choose the one best answer for each item.

1. Which of the following lists is organized correctly from smallest to largest structure?

    (1) Atoms, molecules, organelles, cells

    (2) Skin, nucleus, nucleolus, cell

    (3) Endoplasmic reticulum, molecules, vacuoles, atoms

    (4) Cell, mitochondria, chromosome, atoms

    (5) Ribosomes, molecules, atoms, ER

2. Which organelle is found only in plant cells?

    (1) Endoplasmic reticulum

    (2) Mitochondria

    (3) Ribosomes

    (4) Nucleoli

    (5) Chloroplasts

Check your answers on page 244.

The Cell Membrane

The cell membrane contains the material inside the cell and controls what enters and leaves the cell. It is composed of phosphate/lipid (fat/oil) molecules packed together in a sandwich-like structure. Studded throughout are large protein molecules and carbohydrate chains, which are used as markers or identifiers by the cell and external molecules. Some proteins act as pores in the membrane so that some materials may pass directly into the cell. Molecules may enter and leave the cells by chemical diffusion, osmosis, or active transport (which requires energy).

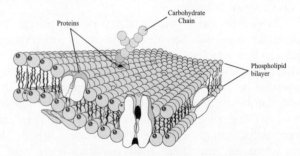

Cross-section of Cell Membrane

Cell Functions

Cell functions are chemical reactions that use the food we eat to provide energy and raw materials for the cell's use. Since food is composed of chemicals, cells break down the food and use the food molecules to make other molecules needed by the cell. All metabolic activity (cellular metabolic reactions) is made possible by the action of **enzymes,** protein molecules needed in very small amounts to bring about a chemical reaction.

The cell stores information about how to make the proteins it is composed of in DNA (deoxyribose nucleic acid) housed in the cell nucleus. Segments of DNA, called **genes**, direct the making of numerous specific proteins needed by the cell. DNA also regulates which genes are active and which proteins are made. DNA regulation allows cells to relate to their environments. DNA also governs the growth of cells and their division.

Mitosis

Plants and animals grow from one original cell that divides by a highly regulated process called **mitosis.** Mitosis is a type of cell division that is necessary for growth of an organism and for repair of damaged tissues and organs. The process of mitosis begins with one cell and produces two cells with the same number and kind of chromosomes as the original cell. Mitosis is a continuous process, but scientists have divided it into four phases to make it easier to study.

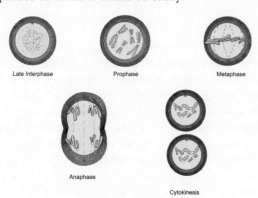

Mitosis

1. *Prophase:* The nuclear membrane disappears; the chromosomes become distinct; a spindle appears.
2. *Metaphase:* The duplicated chromosomes are lined up on the equator of the cell.
3. *Anaphase:* The duplicated chromosomes split apart and travel to opposite poles of the cell.
4. *Telophase:* A nuclear membrane develops around the chromosomes at each pole; chromosomes become indistinct. During this phase, the division of the cytoplasm, called cytokinesis, is completed. There are now two smaller cells in the space of the original cell.

Cell Cycle

Mitosis is part of a cell cycle that includes interphase, the period of time between mitotic events. Interphase begins with the growth of the newly divided cell (G_1). It includes the S phase, which is the reproduction of DNA material, and the G_2 phase, in which the cell prepares for the next mitotic division.

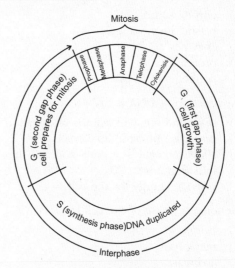

The Cell Cycle

The stained nuclear material that can be seen under a microscope during mitosis consists of **chromosomes.** Chromosomes are long, thin, coiled packages of a DNA molecule plus some proteins. Chromosomes carry the genes. A gene is the unit of heredity and is composed of a fragment of DNA (a sequence of DNA nucleotides.) A gene carries the code for a single protein.

Through mitosis, a single cell divides into a multicellular organism. Each cell in an organism, except the reproductive cells, has the same number and kind of chromosomes as the **zygote,** or fertilized egg. In spite of having the same genetic composition, the developing cells, called **stem cells** in animals, multiply and differentiate to form specialized cells such as bone cells, blood, nerves, skin, muscle cells, and others in animals. Specialized cells further develop into tissues and organs that comprise a multicellular organism, whether it is a plant or animal. DNA controls the differentiation of cells.

Exercise 3

> **Directions:** Choose the <u>one best answer</u> for each item.

1. Genes are composed of

   (1) chromosomes.
   (2) plasma membranes.
   (3) enzymes.
   (4) proteins.
   (5) segments of DNA.

2. The function of DNA is to

   (1) store and regulate cellular information.
   (2) provide a phospholipid coat.
   (3) allow molecules to enter and exit the cell.
   (4) initiate mitosis.
   (5) provide energy for the cell.

3. The longest phase of the cell cycle is

   (1) prophase.
   (2) metaphase.
   (3) anaphase.
   (4) telophase.
   (5) interphase.

Check your answers on page 244.

The Molecular Basis of Heredity

The instructions for growth and repair of the cells of all organisms—protists, fungi, plants, and animals—are carried in their DNA. DNA is composed of four smaller units called **nucleotides**. Each nucleotide is composed of a sugar molecule, a phosphate group, and one of four nitrogen bases: adenine (A), thymine (T), cytosine (C), and guanine (G).

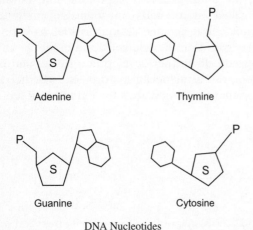

DNA Nucleotides

Because DNA is a double-stranded molecule, with a constant distance between the two strands, the nitrogen rings can only bind in certain ways. Thymine can only bond with adenine, and cytosine can only bond with guanine. A-T and C-G are called complementary nitrogen bases. While those are the only pairings possible, the order of the nitrogen bases along a DNA strand can be varied.

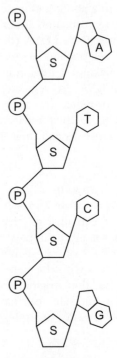

DNA Strand

The DNA molecule has two parallel strands of nucleotides united by hydrogen bonds at their complementary nitrogen bases. The molecule is coiled into a double helix shape. A single DNA molecule may contain more than 130 million base pairs, which may be arranged in any order. So the number of potential variations in nitrogen base sequences is enormous.

Hydrogen
Bonds

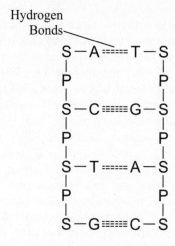

Uncoiled DN Moleule

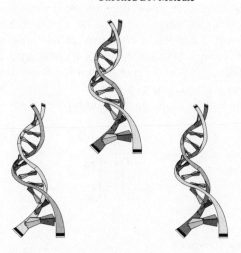

DNA Replication

The DNA in all organisms is composed of the same sugar, phosphate, and nitrogen base molecules. Different organisms differ in the amount of DNA their cells contain and in the sequence of nitrogen bases. But all living organisms have the same basic chemical structure in DNA.

Exercise 4

Directions: Choose the <u>one best answer</u> for each item.

1. Which of the following complementary base pairings is incorrect?
   - **(1)** Adenine—guanine
   - **(2)** Guanine—cytosine
   - **(3)** Cytosine—guanine
   - **(4)** Thymine—adenine
   - **(5)** Adenine—thymine

2. DNA is composed of subunits called
   - **(1)** amino acids.
   - **(2)** purines.
   - **(3)** pyrimidines.
   - **(4)** deoxyribose sugar.
   - **(5)** nucleotides.

Check your answers on page 244.

Protein Synthesis

The sequence of nitrogen bases on DNA is all-important in making, or synthesizing, proteins. The importance of proteins to life cannot be exaggerated. Proteins act as enzymes, chemical messengers, and as muscle fibers, to name just a few of their critical functions. Proteins are large molecules composed of smaller chemical molecules called **amino acids**.

In the human body, 20 different amino acids combine to form an infinite number of proteins. The sequence of nitrogen bases on the DNA molecule is the code that determines the sequence of amino acids in a protein. A sequence of three nucleotides encodes one amino acid or a regulatory function, such as "Stop." The unit of three nucleotides that encodes an amino acid is referred to as a **codon**. DNA in the cell nucleus regulates which protein will be made at a given time.

Actual protein synthesis, however, occurs on the ribosomes in the cytoplasm. Since DNA does not leave the nucleus, an intermediary molecule, RNA, is made from DNA. RNA (or ribonucleic acid) carries the code from the DNA to the cytoplasm. **Transcription** is the process of making RNA from DNA.

While RNA has the same nitrogen base sequence of DNA, it differs from DNA in three important ways: RNA is single-stranded, not double-stranded; RNA has a different sugar molecule from DNA; and RNA has a uracil (U) nitrogen base instead of the thymine (T) nitrogen base in DNA. Uracil is complementary to adenine, as is thymine in the DNA molecule.

191

There are three types of RNA with three different functions: rRNA makes up the ribosome, tRNA carries amino acids found in the cytoplasm to the ribosome, and mRNA carries the code from the nucleus to the ribosomes.

The entire process of protein synthesis consists of the following steps:

1. RNA molecules are made from DNA.
2. RNA molecules leave the nucleus and travel to the cytoplasm.
3. rRNA forms ribosomes, either on the endoplasmic reticululum or free in the cytoplasm.
4. mRNA carries the nitrogen base code signifying the amino acid sequence for a specific protein to the ribosome.
5. tRNA in the cytoplasm carries one amino acid to the mRNA-ribosome complex. tRNA carries a complementary codon to a codon on mRNA and can only bond at that point. This ensures that the "tag along" amino acid carried on tRNA will be joined in the proper sequence for that particular protein.
6. As different tRNAs reach the mRNA and bond with their complements, the various amino acids are positioned properly and bond together to form the designated protein.
7. The completed protein is released into the cytoplasm or packaged for secretion from the cell. Another similar protein may be made or the MRNA-ribosome complex may be recycled.

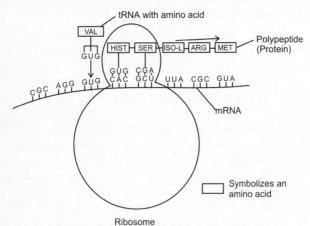

Protein Synthesis

Meiosis

The key to understanding the molecular basis of heredity is understanding how the DNA molecule is passed on to the next generation. This involves meiosis, a special type of cell division that occurs only in the formation of reproductive cells, such as the sperm and egg in humans. All human somatic cells (nonreproductive cells) contain 22 pairs of chromosomes plus a 23rd pair (XY) that determines sex. Reproductive cells, called **gametes,** or sperm and egg, contain one half the number of chromosomes. In the case of humans, this is 22 individual chromosomes, plus one sex chromosome.

In order to produce sex cells with one half the normal number of chromosomes, several additional steps in cell division are necessary. Recall that in mitosis, during interphase, DNA replicates itself (makes an exact copy of itself). It does this by unzipping along the hydrogen bonds. Each half of the DNA molecule makes a new strand using free nucleotides in the nucleus. This provides enough DNA for the daughter cells after meiosis.

Meiosis consists of two divisions, one right after the other. As a result, one cell gives rise to four cells, each with one half the number of chromosomes as the original cell.

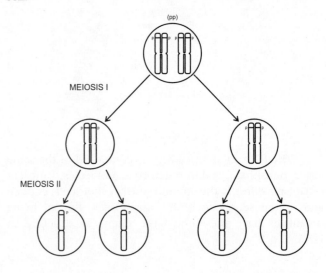

Meiosis

Meiosis results in the formation of sperm cells and egg cells. When egg and sperm unite, a zygote with a new combination of chromosomes is formed as a result of sexual reproduction. This explains why offspring may have some characteristics of each parent. Sexual reproduction is the basis of evolution, because it provides the necessary variability of genes in the offspring of a species.

Mutations are sudden unpredictable changes in a gene that occur frequently but are usually corrected. Only mutations that occur in egg and sperm cells can be passed on to the next generation.

Exercise 5

Directions: Choose the one best answer for each item.

1. The nitrogen base uracil, found in RNA, is complementary to

   (1) thymine.
   (2) adenine.
   (3) cytosine.
   (4) guanine.
   (5) the phosphate group.

2. The unit of three nitrogen bases that carries the code for a specific amino acid is the

   (1) nucleotide.
   (2) chromosome.
   (3) codon.
   (4) tRNA.
   (5) DNA.

3. Where does meiosis occur?

   (1) In the nucleus of future egg or sperm cells
   (2) In the cytoplasm of future egg or sperm cells
   (3) In the nucleus of any dividing cell
   (4) In the cytoplasm of any dividing cell
   (5) In both the nucleus and cytoplasm of any dividing cell

Check your answers on page 244.

Biological Evolution

Evolution is defined as changes in gene frequencies in a population over time. Evolution is a basic concept in biology. It is important to understand that individuals do not evolve; species evolve. The basic principal underlying evolution is survival of the fittest: some individuals in a species have the right combination of genes to survive and reproduce in their environment. Their genes are, therefore, passed on to future generations, and those genes determine the future genetic composition of the species.

Natural selection provides a scientific explanation for evolution. Natural selection is the general tendency for members of a species that are genetically better suited to their environment to survive and reproduce. This leads to changes in the genetic makeup of the species and eventually to the formation of new species over time. Natural selection involves three basic principles: First, a species can increase its population numbers greatly. Second, members of a species have great genetic variation due to sexual reproduction and mutations. Third, all members of a population compete for natural resources. Those individuals that are successful in obtaining natural resources live. Those that are not successful do not live.

The study of how organisms are related in an evolutionary sense is called **phylogeny**. A study of phylogeny shows that humans, gorillas, and chimpanzees are closely related. A related branch of biology, **taxonomy**, groups organisms into a classification scheme. Using taxonomy, biologists give each species a two-part name that designates its genus and its species. Under this system of **binomial nomenclature**, humans are classified as *Homo sapiens*, because we belong to the genus *Homo*, a group we share with several extinct but very closely related species, and the species *sapiens*, a name unique to our species.

Seven basic categories are used for naming organisms. Ranging from the smallest, most precise groupings to the largest, most inclusive, they are species, genus, family, order, class, phylum (or division), and kingdom. Humans and chimpanzees belong to the same kingdom, phylum, class, and order. Our classification splits apart only at the family level.

Exercise 6

Directions: Choose the one best answer for each item.

1. Which of the following conditions is necessary for evolution to occur?

   (1) A stable environment
   (2) A population with a stable genetic composition
   (3) A lack of genetic mutations
   (4) A population with genetic variability
   (5) An unlimited amount of resources

2. The classification category below the level of phylum is the

   (1) genus.
   (2) family.
   (3) order.
   (4) class.
   (5) kingdom.

3. What is the relationship between evolution and natural selection?

   (1) Natural selection prevents evolution.
   (2) Evolution causes natural selection.
   (3) Natural selection is one cause of evolution.
   (4) They are the same thing.
   (5) They are unrelated.

Check your answers on page 244.

Interdependence of Organisms

Atoms and molecules are continually recycled from the nonliving parts of the environment, such as soil minerals, air, and water, to living organisms. Numerous cycles go on continuously, such as the water cycle, the nitrogen cycle, and the carbon cycle.

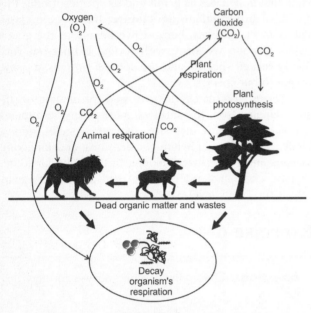

Carbon Cycle

Plants take up nonliving atoms and molecules such as water, minerals, and carbon dioxide from the soil, water, and air and convert them into biologically important compounds such as sugar. Plants use sugars for their growth and reproduction. Animals cannot convert nonliving atoms into food themselves, so they eat plants and use the plant sugars for growth and reproduction. Some animals, called **herbivores**, eat only plants. Others, called **omnivores**, eat both plants and animals. Even **carnivores**, animals that eat only other animals, depend on green plants for their food, because the animals that they eat themselves eat green plants.

An indication of the interdependence of organisms can be seen in a sketch of an ecosystem. An ecosystem consists of the nonliving parts (water, air, soil, rock), the **producers** (plants), the **consumers** (herbivores, omnivores, and carnivores), and the **decomposers** (bacteria and fungi) that live off dead plants and animals. Examples of an ecosystem include a redwood forest, a desert, a rain forest, a prairie, or even a city park or backyard.

Just as life requires atoms and molecules, it also requires energy to survive. But while atoms and molecules recycle, energy does not. Energy flows from higher energy levels to lower energy levels in one direction only. In an ecosystem, the source of energy is the sunlight that is trapped by the plants. The plants use some of the energy to produce food and to carry out other activities, such as seed production. So a smaller amount remains to be passed on to the herbivores, who also use some energy. A still smaller amount remains to be passed on to the carnivores, and an even smaller amount to the decomposers. Energy is eventually lost from an ecosystem in the form of heat.

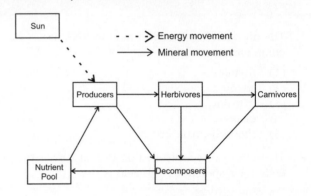

Energy and Mineral Movement
in Ecosystem

All the energy available to an ecosystem comes from the sun. Light energy, which animals cannot use for sustaining life, is converted by plants into chemical energy, which animals can use. Plants accomplish the transformation of energy by a chemical process called **photosynthesis**.

Organisms both cooperate and compete in ecosystems. An example of cooperation is insects that pollinate plants. Many of these insects have body shapes that complement flower shapes. By taking the nectar of flowers, insects pollinate the flowers, thus assisting in the sexual reproduction of plants for the next generation. An example of competition is birds that defend their territory against invasion by members of their own species. Such interactions are vital, stabilizing forces in an ecosystem.

Another major factor that brings about balance in an ecosystem is the interaction between population size and resources. Populations have the ability to increase continuously, but the environment and resource base cannot increase continuously. If population increases beyond the amount of food necessary to support it, the population size decreases until the population is in equilibrium with the food supply. The search for resources, such as food, hiding places, nesting sites, or water, is a critical factor in the interaction of organisms.

Exercise 7

Directions: Choose the one best answer for each item.

1. Which organisms incorporate nonliving atoms and molecules into sugars and other organic molecules?

   (1) Decomposers
   (2) Carnivores
   (3) Plants
   (4) Herbivores
   (5) Omnivores

2. An ecosystem consists of producers, herbivores, carnivores, decomposers, and

   (1) populations.
   (2) the biosphere.
   (3) communities.
   (4) a social system.
   (5) nonliving atoms and molecules.

3. The flow of energy in an ecosystem can best be described as a(n)

   (1) cycle assisted by bacteria.
   (2) atmospheric cycle.
   (3) solar cycle.
   (4) one-way downhill flow.
   (5) back-and-forth flow through major components.

Check your answers on page 245.

Matter, Energy, and Organization in Living Systems

Six elements are found in all living things: carbon (C), hydrogen (H), oxygen (O), nitrogen (N), phosphorus (P), and sulfur (S). In order for these elements to function in living organisms, energy is required. Without energy, animals cannot move or digest their food and plants cannot grow and reproduce. Without energy, life cannot exist.

Plants use the chemical process of photosynthesis to trap the sun's energy and build energy-containing organic molecules. In photosynthesis, plants absorb carbon dioxide (CO_2) from the air and water (H_2O) from the soil to form an energy-rich glucose molecule, $C_6H_{12}O_6$, a simple sugar, and give off oxygen to the atmosphere. Sunlight powers this reaction. The green pigment **chlorophyll**, found in plant organelles called **chloroplasts,** captures the light energy.

$$6CO_2 + 12H_2O \xrightarrow[\text{chlorophyll}]{\text{enzymes}} C_6H_{12}O_6 + 6O_2 + 6H_2O$$

Photosynthesis

The carbohydrate molecules that plants produce are then used to make the other molecules necessary for life. These are proteins, DNA, fats, and other sugars. Energy-storing chemical reactions that build molecules are called **anabolic** reactions.

Cellular respiration is the process that releases the chemical energy in molecules. The process is an energy-yielding, or **catabolic**, reaction that results in a breakdown of molecules. In aerobic respiration, oxygen is required to break down the glucose molecule into CO_2 and H_2O and a high-energy molecule called ATP. Cellular respiration occurs in organelles called mitochondria. **ATP** (adenosine triphosphate) is the molecule that supplies immediate energy for many cellular chemical reactions, such as the contraction of muscles, the transmission of nerve impulses, and the digestion of food.

$$C_6H_{12}O_6 + 6O_2 \xrightarrow[\text{cytochromes}]{\text{enzymes}} 6CO_2 + 6H_2O + ATP$$

Aerobic Respiration

All living organisms have evolved strategies to obtain the energy necessary to support life, to transport food internally, and to release it to the cell. Organisms evolved strategies to eliminate ingested matter also. Animals have various means of obtaining food and energy. Amoebae (one-celled animals) use pseudopods ("false feet") that engulf the food. A sea star inverts its stomach through its mouth and begins digesting food outside the body. Chordates (like humans) have complicated digestive systems with a mouth, esophagus, stomach, intestines, and anus.

Once the food is digested and absorbed, it is transported to the cells in the body. In chordates, the circulatory system carries the digested food in the blood to each cell in the body, where it undergoes cellular respiration.

All living organisms are dependent on energy for life. Therefore, matter and energy are key factors in an ecosystem that limit the distribution and size of populations. The flow of energy in an ecosystem must be consistent with the laws of physics. The First Law of Thermodynamics (also called the Law of Conservation of Energy) says that energy cannot be created or destroyed; it can only be transformed. As energy moves through an ecosystem, it is ultimately transformed into heat, which is a nonusable energy form. (As an example, think about how you get warm when you exercise.)

Exercise 8

> **Directions:** Choose the one best answer for each item.

1. Which of the following statements about energy is correct?

    (1) High levels of energy result from the ability of ecosystems to recycle energy.
    (2) Plants create energy in the process of photosynthesis.
    (3) Animals do not derive energy from the sun.
    (4) Cellular respiration results in formation of the energy-rich molecule ATP.
    (5) Green plants use ATP to capture energy from the sun to produce sugar.

2. The raw materials used by plants in photosynthesis are

    (1) oxygen and water.
    (2) carbohydrates and carbon dioxide.
    (3) oxygen and carbon dioxide.
    (4) carbon dioxide and water.
    (5) carbohydrates and oxygen.

Check your answers on page 245.

Behavior of Organisms

Study of the behavior of complex, multicellular organisms reveals that behavior is under genetic, hormonal, and nervous system control. Some aspects of behavior interact with the environment and have evolved over time. The study of these behaviors, called **behavioral ecology,** includes both innate and learned behaviors.

Innate Behaviors. Many behaviors, such as courtship rituals and nest building, are shared by all members of a species. Such behaviors are said to be **innate** or genetically determined. Specific genes of the fruit fly have been linked to normal fly behaviors, such as sleeping, waking, mating, learning, and memory. The genetic basis of behavior is seen in many other animals: in tongue flicks of garter snakes, in species-specific bird songs, and in the hunting or herding behaviors of certain breeds of dogs.

Being able to identify genes responsible for behavior is very important in understanding some behaviors. In addition, identification of genes and enzymes that influence learning and memory may lead to treatments for Alzheimer's disease and other diseases of the brain.

Hormonal Control of Behavior

The influence of **hormones** on behavior is well documented. Hormones travel through the body in the bloodstream and influence only certain specific cells, called target cells. Hormone secretion is influenced by the nervous system, by chemical changes in the blood, and by other hormones. Hormones control growth, sexual reproduction, and the well-known fight-or-flight response.

Pheromones are chemical signals exchanged between individuals of the same species that cause a specific behavioral response in the receiving animal. They are considered to be hormones, although they are secreted to the outside of the animal rather than into the bloodstream. Dogs use pheromones to mark their territory. Ants use them to mark trails for other ants to follow. Pheromones are also important sexual attractants.

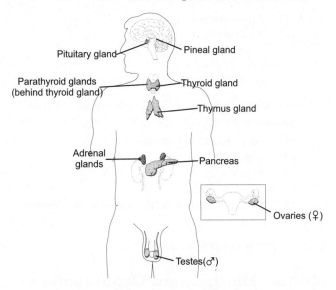

Endocrine System Showing
Major Glands

The Nervous System and the Senses

The nervous system is composed of the brain, spinal cord, nerve cells, and neuroglia cells, which protect and support nerve cells. The nervous system controls all systems of the body, including the heartbeat, breathing, food digestion, and even the endocrine system, which produces hormones.

Nerve cells (or **neurons**) are the functional parts of the nervous system. Nerves communicate with one another or with other organs, such as muscles. Nerves conduct impulses rapidly along dendrites and long cell extensions called **axons**. Bundles of axons from many nerve cells make up the nerves. **Dendrites**, the tiny extensions of the nerve cell body, receive the impulses and transmit them to the cell body. The cell body sends impulses along the axon to an organ or to another neuron. Neurons communicate with one another indirectly, by sending impulses across a minute space called a **synapse**. Neurons communicate by means of chemicals called neurotransmitters, which are able to flow across the gap and excite or inhibit adjoining neurons or organs.

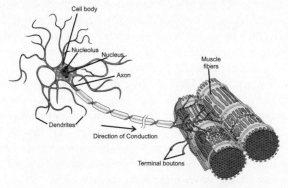

A Neuron Connecting to Muscle Fibers

The senses are an important part of the nervous system. The general senses include pain, touch, pressure, and temperature, which are sensed by neurons in the skin, organs, joints, and muscles. The special senses are taste, smell, hearing, balance, and vision. Taste and smell are the senses found in almost all animals. They are important for most basic animal activities, such as finding food and mates and avoiding predators. Many animals have additional senses. For example, some snakes can sense infrared radiation (heat) given off by animals. Bats have a form of sensory perception called echolocation that allows them to detect echoes of sounds they transmit.

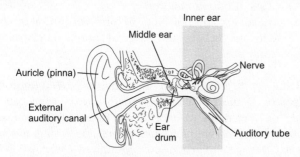

Cross-section of Ear

Vision differs greatly among animals. The octopus has an eye similar to that of humans, although it evolved along a different pathway. Insect eyes are compound eyes that detect the slightest movement even in dim light.

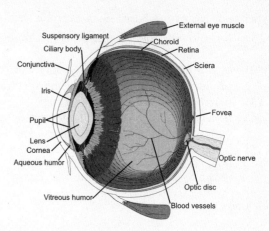

Cross-section of Eye

Evolution of Behavior

Animals use different behaviors at different times of day or at different seasons to help apportion resources. All behaviors are the product of evolution: behaviors, like physical traits, evolve to ensure reproduction and survival of the species. The members of a species must be flexible enough to adapt and change in response to a changing environment. If members of the species cannot do that, they do not survive and reproduce.

Behavioral evolution occurs in plants also. Plants can change the color of their flowers over the growing season to attract seasonal pollinating insects. Plants have evolved chemical defenses against different predators. And, of course, the exquisite match of flower shape to the shape of specific pollinating insects and birds is well known.

Exercise 9

Directions: Choose the one best answer for each item.

1. An organism's behavior is governed by
   (1) environmental stresses.
   (2) interspecific competition.
   (3) genes, hormones, and the nervous system.
   (4) behavior learned from the mother.
   (5) intraspecific dominance.

2. Behavior has evolutionary significance in that

   (1) it is the only trait of organisms that undergoes natural selection.

   (2) organisms that behave successfully will produce future generations of the species.

   (3) behavior stabilizes the gene pool.

   (4) behavioral change can be demonstrated within one generation in an animal species.

   (5) behavioral change permits the dominant member of a group to continue to be a leader over time.

Check your answers on page 245.

Science and Technology

Science is the study of the natural world. Science tries to answer such questions as "How does the immune system work?", "How are continents formed?", and "Is the universe finite or infinite?" Technology is usually considered to be applied science. It involves taking scientific findings and applying them to solve human problems. However, technology can have an impact on scientific research as well. As a result of technology, scientists put tracking collars on bears and turtles and trace animal migrations, perform arthroscopic surgery on an athlete's damaged knee, and view the brain in action. Technology may create new problems, especially in the environment.

Science and technology have tremendously changed most parts of the world over the past 250 years. Both disciplines are an essential part of the world society today. Society can and must affect the direction of scientific and technological progress. These decisions must be based on the study of alternatives, risks, costs, and benefits. Therefore, all people in a democratic society should understand basic concepts of science and technology.

Population Growth

Populations grow as a result of four major factors:

1. *The birth rate:* The birth rate, or **natality,** is the number of births per 1,000 individuals per year.
2. *The death rate:* The death rate, or **mortality,** is the number of deaths per 1,000 individuals per year.
3. *Emigration:* Emigration is movement out of a given area.
4. *Immigration:* Immigration is movement into a given area.

Population growth involves all organisms in any ecosystem, including plants, animals, fungi, and microorganisms. Of course, humans are part of the animal component.

One female housefly lays 120 eggs at a time, and there are seven generations a year. Each generation is half male and half female. One female would give rise to five trillion flies by the seventh generation. Because this does not occur in nature, something must be restraining the growth of the housefly population.

All organisms have a biotic potential for growth at a given rate. Opposing this rate of growth is environmental resistance. Environmental resistance involves factors such as food supply and other resources necessary for maintenance of a particular population size. A population that has an explosive growth rate may grow beyond the capacity of the environment to it, in which case it will undergo a rapid population die-off. The **carrying capacity** is the maximum number of individuals that can be supported in a given environment. A natural ecosystem has a balance between the biotic potential of a population and environmental resistance.

Human populations have additional factors that influence population size. These are:

1. Affluence and education, which lower the birth rate
2. Importance of children in the labor force, which raises the birth rate
3. Education and employment of women, which lowers the birth rate
4. Infant mortality rates
5. Costs of raising children
6. Availability and reliability of birth control methods
7. Religious beliefs and cultural norms concerning family size

Scientists who study human population are called **demographers**. Demographers use growth rates, fertility rates, and doubling times to explain the future of the human population. Demographers use population histograms to display the age and gender composition of a population.

From an ecological standpoint there are three main population subgroups: the prereproductive, reproductive, and postreproductive age groups. These groups give a very good idea of the future of the population. When the birth rate is high and the rate of population growth is exponential, then a population histogram is in the shape of a pyramid (shown on the lower left). A histogram with a tapering base shows a lower future growth due to the smaller prereproductive segment of the population (middle). A histogram that shows no constriction or expansion of the base shows a stationary population (right).

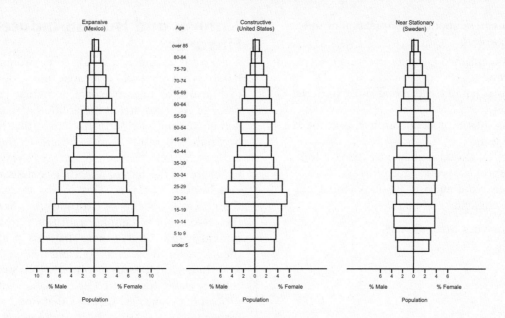

Population Histograms

Human population is increasing at an extremely rapid rate. Technology may be a big factor in enabling larger populations to live on the earth, or conversely technology may lessen the carrying capacity of the earth.

Natural Resources

Human populations use natural resources to live in and to improve their standard of living. Natural resources include air, water, soil, forests, grasslands, wetlands, oceans, streams, lakes, wildlife, minerals, and element recycling systems. Nonrenewable mineral resources include copper, iron, and uranium. Energy resources include both nonrenewable resources, such as oil, coal, and natural gas, and the renewable resources, such as sun, wind, flowing water, geothermal heat, plant matter, biomass, and hydrogen. Included as a natural resource is biodiversity and the gene pool of all living things.

A **resource** is anything we obtain from the environment to meet our needs. Many natural resources, such as minerals and nonrenewable energy resources, are finite: when the supply is depleted, it will be gone forever. Overconsumption by humans places stress on some renewable natural resources such as air and water and the natural cycles that cleanse and recycle the components of the ecosystem. Too large a human population reduces habitats for other members of the planetary ecosystem.

Some natural ecosystems, such as estuaries, can purify waste products. However, the purifying capacity is limited. Because modern life, with its pollution and overconsumption, inflicts major problems on the planet's natural resources, it is necessary for humans to gain much more knowledge about how nature works.

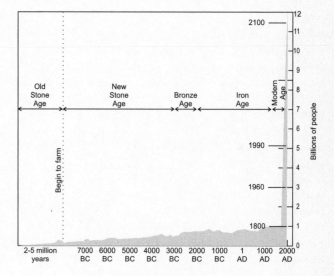

Human Population Growth

Exercise 10

Directions: Choose the one best answer for each item.

1. Environmental resistance to a growing population is best defined as
   (1) the collective limiting factors in the environment.
   (2) catastrophic environmental change.
   (3) a large postreproductive population.
   (4) exceptionally large emigration from the area.
   (5) decrease in biodiversity in the ecosystem.

2. Which statement about the population of the world is correct?

   (1) It has remained constant over the last two centuries.

   (2) It has reached the carrying capacity of the planet.

   (3) It has shown moderate growth over the last 300 years.

   (4) It has increased rapidly over the last 300 years.

   (5) It shows the effect of biotic potential and environmental resistance.

Check your answers on page 245.

Natural and Human-Induced Hazards

A hazard is a danger or a risk. In environmental terms, a hazard is anything that can cause injury, disease, or death to humans, to their personal or public property, or to parts of an ecosystem. Each different hazard carries a certain amount of risk, or likelihood that injury, disease, or death will result from exposure to the hazard. Risk analysis means evaluating the risks involved before exposure to the hazard. Another analysis that is used is **risk-benefit analysis**. This means evaluating whether the potential benefits of exposure to a hazard outweigh the risks. For example, radiation treatment carries potential risks, but cancer patients willingly subject themselves to those risks to avoid dying of cancer.

Biological hazards involve diseases such as AIDS and other sexually transmitted diseases, as well as malaria in developing countries. Diseases that once were restricted by geography to certain areas of the world are no longer so restricted. Due to ease of air travel, worldwide epidemics are a real possibility. Illegal import of animals such as bees and poisonous snakes are other sources of biological hazards.

Human-induced hazards are found in many places. One example is disposal of tons of waste produced in city and towns. In addition to biological wastes, these materials may include radioactive waste and poisonous metals. Other examples are sedimentation of rivers, lakes, and harbors; coastal erosion; degradation of soil; and loss of habitat.

Unit 2

PHYSICAL SCIENCE

Physical science is simply the study of the physical world around us. It encompasses both **chemistry**, the study of matter, and **physics**, the study of energy. But more than just these individual subjects, physical science studies the interrelated nature of these two seemingly different fields.

Motion: Speed, Velocity, and Acceleration

We will begin our study of physics with motion, because the universe is filled with objects in motion. Look around you, and you will find that almost everything is in motion: flying birds, running people, falling leaves, and even the earth, sun, stars, and galaxies. Motion can be described using terms such as speed, velocity, and acceleration.

Average speed is obtained by dividing travel distance, D, by travel time, t.

$$V = \frac{D}{t}$$

Instantaneous speed is the speed at any one instant. The speedometer of a car gives instantaneous speed. When you drive above the speed limit and are caught speeding, the police use instantaneous speed to issue a speeding ticket. You may be familiar with the unit *mph*, miles per hour, for speed. MPH can also be written as m/h. The unit for speed is obtained by dividing the unit for distance (m) by the unit for time (t). Other units for speed are km/h (kilometers per hour), cm/s (centimeters per sec), ft/s (feet per sec), and m/s (meters per sec).

When you assign direction to speed, it is called velocity. **Velocity** changes if either speed or direction changes. Velocity is expressed in the same units as speed. **Acceleration**, a, is the time rate at which the velocity changes. It is obtained by dividing the change in velocity by the time it took for that change:

$$a = \frac{\Delta V}{\Delta t}$$

The units for acceleration are mph/s, cm/s^2, ft/s^2, and m/s^2.

Exercise 1

Directions: Choose the one best answer for each item.

1. What does a car speedometer measure?
    - (1) Average velocity
    - (2) Average speed
    - (3) Instantaneous velocity
    - (4) Instantaneous speed
    - (5) Distance

2. During a summer vacation trip, a family leaves home at 7:00 a.m. and arrives at the beach at 11:30 a.m. During the trip, they took a 30-minute break for breakfast. The beach is 240 miles from their home. What is their average driving speed in mph?
    - (1) 53
    - (2) 60
    - (3) 70
    - (4) 80
    - (5) 65

3. Acceleration is the rate of change of
    - (1) time.
    - (2) speed.
    - (3) velocity.
    - (4) distance.
    - (5) displacement.

4. A sports car accelerates from 0 to 56 mph in 8 seconds. What is the acceleration?
    - (1) 56 mph
    - (2) 7 mph
    - (3) 7 mph/s
    - (4) 8 mph/s
    - (5) 448 mph/s

Check your answers on page 245.

Force and the Laws of Motion

We have seen how motion is described in terms of speed, velocity, and acceleration. Now we will look at how motion is created. **Force**, actually net force, is necessary for motion. For example, in a tug of war, if both teams pull with the exact same force in opposite directions, the net force is zero, the tug is in equilibrium, and no one moves. Motion will result only when there is a net force, which will be present only when one team exerts a greater force than the other.

Scientists use three basic laws of motion, named after Sir Isaac Newton, the seventeenth-century English physicist, to explain the movement of objects.

Newton's First Law of Motion states that **every body (object) will remain in a state of rest or of uniform motion in a straight line unless acted on by an outside net force.**

Inertia is the tendency of an object to remain either at rest or in motion. Newton's First Law of Motion is also known as the Law of Inertia. **Mass** is a measure of the inertia of an object.

Newton's Second Law of Motion states that **the net force acting on an object is equal to the product of the mass of the object and the acceleration of the object (F = ma).** This law is also known as the Law of Force. It can be used to calculate the force when the mass and acceleration are known. Boldface is used for **F** and **a** because they are vectors, or quantities that have direction as well as magnitude (size). Mass, m, is a scalar quantity: it has magnitude only. Weight (**W**) is different from mass. Weight is the force of gravity acting on the mass. **W = mg**, where **g** is the acceleration due to gravity. Weight is also a vector quantity. The unit for force is the newton, N. One N = 1 kg m/s^2.

Newton's Third Law of Motion states that **when one object exerts a force on a second object, the second object exerts a force on the first that has an equal magnitude but opposite direction.** A good example of Newton's Third Law is rocket propulsion, where the force is provided by the expelling gases that push against the earth's surface. Newton's Third Law of Motion is also known as the Law of Action and Reaction, where the action and reaction forces act on different objects. For example, when an ice skater pushes against a wall, the wall pushes the ice skater back, and this force makes the ice skater move away from the wall.

A skater moves rapidly over the ice because friction is minimized by the ice. **Friction** is the resistance to motion due to surface rubbing. Frictional forces always work in the opposite direction of motion. For example, friction produces heat in automobile engines, and oil is used to disperse this heat. We slip when we attempt to walk on ice because of the lack of friction between our feet and ice.

Exercise 2

Directions: Choose the one best answer for each item.

1. Newton's First Law is known as the law of
   (1) Inertia.
   (2) Force.
   (3) Action and Reaction.
   (4) Gravitation.
   (5) Mass.

2. During the launching of a rocket, the exploding fuel leaves the rocket and exerts a force on the earth that sends the rocket skyward. Which of the following statements best explains this phenomenon?
   (1) An object tends to remain at rest or in motion.
   (2) Force equals mass times acceleration.
   (3) For every action, there is an equal and opposite reaction.
   (4) The gravity of the earth will slow down the motion of the rocket.
   (5) You can use the position and velocity of an object to calculate its future position and velocity.

3. A net force of 3270 N accelerates a car with a mass of 1635 kg. What is the acceleration of the car?
   (1) 0.5m/s^2
   (2) 0.2m/s^2
   (3) 0.3m/s^2
   (4) 2m/s^2
   (5) 3 m/s^2

4. In item 3 above, if the engine exerts 4250 N force, what are the total frictional forces acting on the car?
   (1) 0
   (2) 980 N
   (3) 3270 N
   (4) 4250 N
   (5) 7520 N

Check your answers on page 245.

Work and Energy

So far we have analyzed motion using Newton's laws of motion. In this section, we will study motion using work and energy. A roller coaster is a good model of how energy, work, and motion interact. A roller coaster can never go as high or travel as fast later in the ride as it does on that first hill. At the start of a roller-coaster ride, you are sitting still in a car. We have seen that inertia will keep you there all day unless an outside force intervenes. The motor that drags the cars up the hill provides the work you need to get started. **Work** is the use of force to move something over a distance. Work is defined as the product of the magnitude of the force and distance. Work is a scalar quantity.

Work = Force × Distance

In order for a force to qualify as having done work on an object, the object must move and the force must cause that movement. Some examples of work that can be observed in everyday life are a mother pushing a baby in a stroller, a girl pushing a lawn mower across a lawn, a man pushing a grocery cart down the aisle of a grocery store, a student lifting a backpack full of books onto her shoulder, a weightlifter lifting a barbell above her head, and a person walking up the steps. There are cases where you may exert a force but no work is done on the object. For example, if you push on a stationary wall, no work is done because the wall does not move.

The unit scientists use for work is the joule, J. One joule is defined as equal to 1 N/m. The rate at which work is done is called **power**. Power is a scalar quantity. The unit for power is the watt, W. One watt = 1 J/s.

$$Power = \frac{Work}{Time}$$

Energy

Energy is the ability to do work. Energy comes in various forms and can be transformed from one form to another. However, the total energy will always stay the same, because energy cannot be either created or destroyed. This principle is known as the Law of Conservation of Energy. For example, the electric motor in a roller coaster uses electrical energy to drag the coaster up the hill. At the top of the hill, the electrical energy is converted into gravitational potential energy. This **potential energy**, PE, is the energy stored in an object as the result of the height it has been raised from the ground. It can be calculated using weight, which is mass times gravity, and height. Energy is a scalar quantity.

$$PE = mgh$$

As the roller coaster careens downhill, the potential energy changes into kinetic energy. **Kinetic energy**, KE, is the energy of motion. It can be calculated using mass and velocity.

$$KE = \frac{1}{2}mV^2$$

The exchange between potential energy and kinetic energy keeps the roller coaster moving up and down over the tracks.

Exercise 3

Directions: Choose the one best answer for each item.

1. According to the above definition of work, which person is doing the most work?
   (1) A stranded motorist trying to push a truck that will not move
   (2) A construction worker moving a load of bricks
   (3) A doctor listening to a patient's heartbeat
   (4) An artist making an illustration
   (5) A cashier making change

2. Two men, Joe and John, push against a stationary wall. John stops after 10 minutes, while Joe is able to push for 5 minutes longer. Compare the work they each do.
   (1) Joe does 50% more work than John.
   (2) John does 50% more work than Joe.
   (3) Joe does 75% more work than John.
   (4) John does 75% more work than Joe.
   (5) Neither of them does any work.

3. Which of the following is a newton (N)?
   (1) kg m^2/s^2
   (2) kg/(ms^2)
   (3) kg m/s^2
   (4) kg m^2/s^3
   (5) kg m/s^3

4. Which of the following is a joule (J)?
   (1) kg m^2/s^2
   (2) kg/(ms^2)
   (3) kg m/s^2
   (4) kg m^2/s^3
   (5) kg m/s^3

Check your answers on page 245.

Temperature and Heat

Temperature is a measure of how hot or cold an object is. Temperature is measured with thermometers. There are different types of thermometers: alcohol-in-glass thermometer, mercury thermometer, radiation thermometer, and resistance thermometer, to name a few. All thermometers are constructed using a measurable property of matter that changes in some way as temperature changes.

The Fahrenheit (0°F) and Celsius (0°C) temperature scales are familiar ones. The scientific community uses the Kelvin (K) scale to measure temperature. Absolute zero, 0K, is the theoretical low limit of temperature. There is no theoretical high limit for temperature. The surface temperature of the sun is about 6,000K, and the interior can reach as high as 15,000,000K.

Temperatures can be converted using the following equations, where T_f stands for Fahrenheit, T_c stands for Celsius, and T_k stands for Kelvin:

$$T_f = \frac{9}{5}T_c + 32$$

$$T_c = \frac{5}{9}(T_f - 32)$$

$$T_k = T_c + 273$$

Heat can be used to do work. It is a type of energy that comes from the vibration or movement of molecules. More vibration creates more heat. Heat is defined as energy transfer due to a temperature difference. To raise the temperature of an object, we heat it. The unit of heat, the calorie, is defined as the amount of heat required to increase the temperature of 1 gram of water by 1° Celsius (for example, from 14.5°C to 15.5°C). The food calorie, C, is defined as 1,000 calories. The unit for heat is the joule, or J. One calorie equals 4.186J. Another common unit for heat is the British thermal unit, or Btu. One Btu equals 1055J.

Heat may be transferred from one object to another by **conduction, convection**, or **radiation**. When the objects are connected by a solid material, the mechanism is called conduction. In convection, material moves and carries heat from a hot region to a cold region. Objects also exchange heat energy via electromagnetic waves. This mechanism is called radiation, which can take place through a vacuum. We receive the warmth of the sun via heat transfer by radiation.

Thermodynamics is the study of the movement of heat. The First Law of Thermodynamics states that **heat energy cannot be created or destroyed**. Instead, the energy changes form. For example, in a steam turbine, or jet engine, heat energy is changed to mechanical energy.

The Second Law of Thermodynamics states that **heat naturally flows from a hot place to a cold place.** The temperature difference between the hot place and the cold place represents the energy available to power an engine. Engine designers would love it if all this heat energy could be turned into work. This never happens, however, because some heat is lost through the friction of engine parts rubbing against one another, and some heat escapes to the outside.

Exercise 4

Directions: Choose the one best answer for each item.

1. To the nearest degree, if room temperature is 22°C, what is it in °F?

    (1) 162
    (2) 22
    (3) 72
    (4) 161.6
    (5) 0

2. The boiling point of liquid nitrogen is about 77K. Express this temperature in °F.

    (1) −320.8
    (2) 320.8
    (3) −196
    (4) 196
    (5) 77

3. A 72-kg person drinks a 140-calorie soft drink. How many stairs, height of 18cm, must this person climb to work off the drink? (1 calorie = 4186 J, g = 9.8 m/s^2)

    (1) 45,219
    (2) 4614
    (3) 1102
    (4) 830
    (5) 45

4. The Thermos bottle is used to keep a liquid cold or hot. It is constructed with a double-walled container with a vacuum in between. The purpose of this construction is to minimize heat transfer by

    (1) conduction.
    (2) convection.
    (3) radiation.
    (4) conduction and convection.
    (5) conduction, convection, and radiation.

5. According to the Second Law of Thermodynamics, heat moves from a hot place to a cold place. Given this law, which of the following is most likely to occur as you make a snowball?

(1) The snowball gets colder as it is compacted.
(2) The warmth from your hands transfers to the snow.
(3) The movement of your hands causes vibration of the frozen water molecules.
(4) The temperature of the snow limits the amount of work your body can do.
(5) Heat is lost through friction.

Check your answers on page 246.

Waves, Magnetism, and Electricity

A wave is a disturbance in a liquid or a gas. Wave behavior is most noticeable on the surface of a liquid. Sound and light also travel in waves.

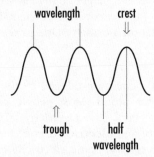

When children toss pebbles into a lake, the resulting pattern in the water is a wave. Although the wave spreads outward, the water moves only up and down when a wave passes. It does not move horizontally. The *crest* of a wave is the point at the top, and the *trough* of a wave is the point at the bottom. *Wavelength* is the distance between the crest of one wave and the crest of the next one. The distance between a crest and the next trough is a half wavelength.

Waves and sound. The number of crests passing a point in one second is called the *frequency* of the wave. Sound waves have high and low frequencies. A high-frequency sound has more waves per second and creates a high sound (like a dog whistle). A low-frequency sound has fewer waves per second and makes a low sound (like a bass drum). The frequency of a wave is measured in hertz. One *hertz* equals one wave per second. The human ear can hear sounds with frequencies ranging from 20 to 20,000 hertz. The range of sounds that a stereo system can reproduce is measured in hertz.

Waves and light. Light also travels in waves. The varying frequency of light waves causes varying colors. Human eyes can detect colors only within a certain frequency range. This range is called the *visible spectrum*, and it includes colors from low-frequency waves (red) to high-frequency waves (violet).

REFLECTION

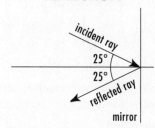

Light normally travels in straight lines or *rays*. When a beam of light hits a flat surface such as a mirror, the light is reflected back. The light ray moving toward the mirror is called the *incident ray*. The ray of light that bounces back is called the *reflected ray*. The angle of the incident ray equals the angle of the reflected ray. The *law of reflection* states that the angle of incidence equals the angle of reflection, as shown in the diagram above.

Exercise 5

Directions: Choose the one best answer for each item.

1. Which is a true statement?
(1) The trough is the highest point of the wave.
(2) Wavelength is the number of crests passing a point in one second.
(3) The human ear can detect a sound with a frequency of 200 hertz.
(4) The distance between a crest and the next trough is a wavelength.
(5) A high-frequency sound has few waves per second.

205

Item 2 refers to the diagram below.

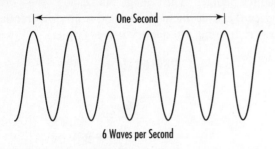

One Second

6 Waves per Second

2. Which of the following terms best describes the wave property illustrated in this diagram?

(1) Compression
(2) Frequency
(3) Visible spectrum
(4) Kinetic energy
(5) Hertz

3. Which of the following statements best explains what happens as the frequency of a wave increases?

(1) Wave crests and troughs cancel each other.
(2) Wavelengths become longer.
(3) Wavelengths become shorter.
(4) Crest and trough are 0 wavelengths apart.
(5) Frequency cannot be measured in hertz.

4. Which statement best explains why you look taller or thinner in a fun house mirror?

(1) The mirror reflects the light.
(2) The curves in the mirror distort the light rays returning to you.
(3) Light does not travel in a straight line.
(4) Air is a different medium than glass.
(5) Light echoes back and forth between the mirror and the walls.

Check your answers on page 246.

Magnetism

Magnetism is the ability of a substance to attract iron and other iron-based metals. The earth is a giant magnet. Like all magnets, it has two *magnetic poles*—north and south ends where the magnetic force is very strong.

The behavior of magnets can be described by the phrase "Opposites attract; likes repel," as shown in the diagram below. The north pole of one magnet attracts the south pole of another magnet. Two north poles move away from or repel each other.

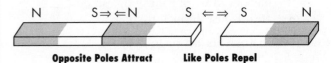

N   S⇒ ⇐N   S ⇐⇒ S   N

Opposite Poles Attract   **Like Poles Repel**

The poles of a magnet exert magnetic force in a *magnetic field*, the area subject to the influence of magnetism. If you sprinkle iron filings around a magnet, the filings line up in the area of the magnetic field. A common example of a magnetic field at work is in a tape recorder. In a tape recorder, a magnetic field aligns particles of metal on a cassette tape to record sound.

Electricity

Electricity is the energy produced by the movement of electrons between atoms. Most people use and experience electricity every day. Electricity takes two forms: **static electricity** and **electric current.**

Static electricity. Static electricity exists when an electric charge rests on an object. You're probably familiar with the small shock caused by static electricity when you shuffle across a carpet or pull off a wool sweater.

Electric current. When electrons flow, they produce an electric current. Electrons can move through solids (especially metals), gases, and liquids such as water. Substances (such as water) that allow an electric charge to flow easily are called *conductors*. Substances that do not conduct electricity, such as glass, porcelain, and plastic, are called *insulators*.

Electricity moves through wires much as water moves through pipes. You can measure the flow of a river by measuring how much water moves past a particular point. The strength of an electric current is measured in *amperes* (amps). An ampere measures how much electric charge moves past a point in one second.

Electric Circuits

An *electric circuit* is a path for electricity. A circuit begins at a power supply, goes through wires and/or electronic devices, and then returns to the power supply. You can think of an electric circuit as a complete circle. If current doesn't pass through the entire circle, the electricity doesn't flow.

SERIES CIRCUIT

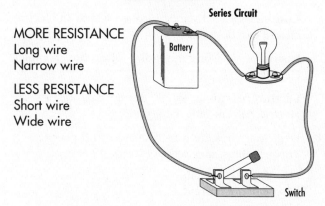

Series Circuit

MORE RESISTANCE
Long wire
Narrow wire

LESS RESISTANCE
Short wire
Wide wire

As electricity moves along a wire, it meets electrical resistance, which slows down the flow. Electrical resistance is measured in *ohms*. A metal that is a good conductor has low electrical resistance. Some substances, however, have insulating qualities that offer a lot of resistance to electricity. In some cases, a particular electrical component requires a reduced flow of current, and the manufacturer intentionally puts a resistor in the circuit to control the flow. Resistance differs according to the length and width of the wire.

PARALLEL CIRCUIT

Parallel Circuit

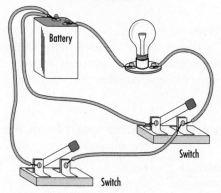

Switch

Switch

A circuit usually consists of a power source, wires, a switch, and the item you want to power. In a *series circuit*, current must flow through every part of the electrical pathway in order to return to power.

In a *parallel circuit*, the main current is divided into two or more individual pathways, and part of the current goes through each pathway. If any part of a parallel circuit is disconnected, the design of the circuit permits the current to flow through other paths. After following independent pathways, the separate parts of the current are rejoined to complete the circuit.

Exercise 6

Directions: Choose the one best answer for each item.

1. You run a comb through your hair on a dry autumn day and hear a crackling sound. Which of the following terms best applies to this phenomenon?

   (1) Magnetism
   (2) Low humidity
   (3) Static electricity
   (4) Conductor
   (5) Chemical energy

2. The strength of a current is calculated by the following formula:

$$\text{amps} = \frac{\text{quantity of charge (coulombs)}}{\text{time (seconds)}}$$

   Which of the following situations would produce a charge of 100 amps?

   (1) 10 coulombs pass in 1,000 seconds.
   (2) 100 coulombs pass in 10 seconds.
   (3) 1,000 coulombs pass in 5 seconds.
   (4) 1,000 coulombs pass in 10 seconds.
   (5) 10,000 coulombs pass in 1,000 seconds.

3. While standing at the most northern place on the earth, an explorer takes out her compass and notices that the needle points northeast. She asks her companion to check this by looking at his compass. It also points northeast. Which explanation best accounts for this?

   (1) The temperature is too cold for a compass to work.
   (2) The magnetic north pole is at a different location from the geographic North Pole.
   (3) The compass is too far away from the South Pole for it to detect Earth's magnetic field.
   (4) A compass lines up correctly only at the Equator.
   (5) Earth's magnetic field cannot be detected.

4. A few nails hang in a chain from a magnet. If you pull the magnet away, the nails fall to the ground. Which of the following statements best accounts for this?

    (1) Each nail has become a permanent magnet.
    (2) The magnetic field of the earth is stronger than the field around the magnet.
    (3) Nails tend to repel one another.
    (4) As the magnet moves farther away, its magnetic field becomes stronger.
    (5) As the magnet moves farther away, its magnetic field becomes weaker.

5. Resistance is measured in ohms. You can calculate the resistance in a circuit using the following formula.

$$\text{Ohms} = \frac{\text{volts}}{\text{amps}}$$

    Which of the following circuits has a resistance of 11 ohms?

    (1) A current of 10 amps on a 220-volt line
    (2) A current of 10 amps on a 110-volt line
    (3) A current of 10 amps on a 2,200-volt line
    (4) A current of 8 amps on a 12-volt line
    (5) A current of 16 amps on a 24-volt line

6. Which of the following terms is best defined as opposition to the flow of electric current?

    (1) Ampere
    (2) Volt
    (3) Resistance
    (4) Circuit
    (5) Current

7. Which of the following conditions would decrease the resistance of a circuit?

    (1) Lengthening the wire
    (2) Replacing a thin wire with a thicker one
    (3) Replacing a conductor with an insulator
    (4) Adding a resistor to the circuit
    (5) Breaking the circuit

Items 8 and 9 refer to the following information.

Five concepts important to electricity are defined below.

Static electricity: an electric charge resting on an object

Electric current: an electric charge in motion

Conductor: a substance through which an electric charge can flow freely

Insulator: a substance that does not conduct electricity

Earth ground: a safety device that diverts an electric current into the ground

8. Electrical wires are usually coated with plastic. This best illustrates which electrical concept?

    (1) Static electricity
    (2) Electric current
    (3) Conductor
    (4) Insulator
    (5) Earth ground

9. You start your car and the needle on the gauge marked amps moves to the + sign. This best illustrates which electrical concept?

    (1) Static electricity
    (2) Electric current
    (3) Conductor
    (4) Insulator
    (5) Earth ground

Check your answers on page 246.

Chemistry

Chemistry is the study of **matter**. This definition is meaningless unless we know what matter is. By definition, matter is anything that has mass and occupies **volume**.

A Few Examples of Matter and Nonmatter

Matter	Nonmatter
Electronic devices	Light
Food and beverages	Concepts
Air	Feelings
Furniture	Vacuum
Our bodies	Heat

The list of matter can be extended almost indefinitely, to incorporate entire celestial bodies or things smaller than a cell; the list of "not matter" is much shorter.

Mass is a measure of how much matter there is; the more matter, the more mass, and therefore, the heavier the object will be. Volume is simply a product of three-dimensional space. Length times width times height is volume. It's the amount of space an object occupies; the larger the volume, the bigger the object will be.

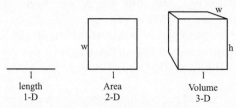

length
1-D

Area
2-D

Volume
3-D

Each dimension has characteristic properties; volume is a property of the third dimension. Although the figure above represents volume as a cube, volumes are not always such simple shapes.

Exercise 7

Directions: Choose the one best answer for each item.

1. Which of the following is not matter?

   (1) Light
   (2) Water
   (3) Sand
   (4) Air
   (5) Food

2. Based on the figure below, what can we deduce about the relationship between pressure and volume of a gas?

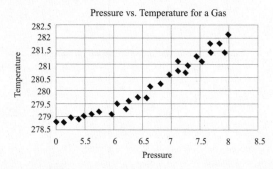

Pressure vs. Temperature for a Gas

   (1) There is a relationship between pressure and volume.
   (2) Volume decreases linearly as pressure increases.
   (3) Volume increases linearly as pressure increases.
   (4) There is no relationship between pressure and volume.
   (5) The relationship between pressure and volume is not linear.

Check your answers on page 246.

Matter and Energy

Matter is anything that has mass and occupies a volume. Mass is a measure of the quantity of matter; the greater the mass, the more matter there is.

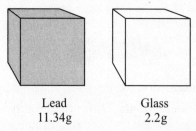

Lead
11.34g

Glass
2.2g

Equal volumes of glass and lead have different weight. Because the mass of lead is greater, there must be more matter in lead than in the same volume of glass. We say that lead has a greater density.

Volume is a property of the third dimension. *Length* is one-dimensional. The shortest distance, say, between you and the nearest tree (neglecting obstacles such as walls) is a straight line and could, in principle, be measured, but that straight line has only one direction; therefore, it is one-dimensional. *Area* is two-dimensional, defined as length times width. The plot of land that that tree is in, for example, is a two-dimensional area. Volume is area times height, or height times length times width.

Momentum. You might be wondering why we tend to refer to "mass" rather than "weight." Weight is actually a force, defined as mass times the acceleration due to gravity. A force can be thought of as a motivation to move or change motion (such as changing direction). If we hold a mass, like a ball, above the ground, it will have a tendency to fall to the ground (begin to move toward the earth). You may have heard of momentum, usually stated as the principle that an object in motion tends to stay in motion, while an object at rest tends to remain at rest, unless acted upon by an outside force (recall the discussion of the laws of motion). Momentum depends upon position, mass, and the direction the object is moving.

Consider a dump truck colliding head-on with a compact car. If they are moving at the same velocity, we all know that at the collision, the car will be pushed backward, because the truck is much heavier. Thus, the truck has greater momentum: it is more difficult to change the velocity of the truck than the car. It is possible for the car to have more momentum than the truck, but in that case, the car would have to be traveling at a much greater velocity than the truck. That is, the speed of the car would have to be far greater than the speed of the truck for the truck to be pushed backward.

It's not always so easy to determine the nature of forces. If you roll a toy car along a flat surface, you know that eventually it will stop. Does this make sense? After all, momentum should keep it rolling indefinitely until a force acts to stop it, yet you don't see any force that can stop it. Actually, there is at least one force acting on it: friction. Friction is a form of force, because it can stop motion.

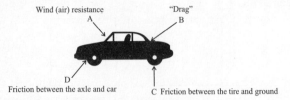

Wind (air) resistance A   "Drag" B

D Friction between the axle and car   C Friction between the tire and ground

Mass and Weight. Now that we have a better understanding of forces, we can examine the subtle difference between mass and weight. They are closely related to one another: as mass increases, weight increases as well. However, you can change the weight of a substance without changing its mass. For example, you can travel to another planet, where the gravitational force is not so great. Also, because at the equator, centrifugal force caused by the Earth's rotation creates a very small force acting in opposite to gravitational force, objects at the equator actually have slightly less weight than at the poles; however, the mass is the same because the amount of material is the same in both places.

Conservation of Energy. We've spoken a lot about forces, but we've barely mentioned energy. As we saw in Unit 2, we can classify energy into two categories: kinetic energy, or energy of motion, and potential energy, or stored energy. If you hold a mass above the ground, it has potential energy; it is not moving, because we are holding it steady, but you know that if you let it go, it will begin moving. Once you let it go, it begins accelerating, and the potential energy becomes kinetic energy, the energy of motion.

This example illustrates the Law of Conservation of Energy. The kinetic energy does not just happen; it comes from the potential energy.

Kinetic energy is the energy of motion. Because airplanes are so heavy, a rolling aircraft would be very difficult to stop (large mass means large momentum even for very small velocity). To prevent an aircraft from rolling, blocks are placed behind the wheels; these blocks prevent the conversion of potential energy (the fact that the plane is on an incline means it has the potential to roll; if it does not roll, this is "stored energy") to kinetic energy.

The Law of Conservation of Energy states that energy cannot be created or destroyed, but it can change form. That is, we can convert energy from kinetic to potential energy, or potential to kinetic energy, but the total energy cannot change. So if we were to lift a ball into the air, where does the energy come from? This is potential energy, too, but it's in the form of stored chemical energy. When we eat, we obtain energy, primarily in the form of sugar; in lifting an object, your muscles utilize stored chemical energy and convert it into mechanical energy that allows you to grasp and lift the object.

Kinetic and potential energy play an important part in chemistry. The atoms and molecules in matter move faster if they have more energy. Energy is usually seen in chemistry as heat, which can be measured in terms of temperature. The more heat there is, the more energy in the substance, and the faster the molecules and atoms in the material are moving.

The higher the temperature, the faster (represented by the size of the arrows) the molecules move. Thus, heat energy is a form of kinetic energy. In a solid or liquid, the force that binds the atoms and molecules together is potential energy.

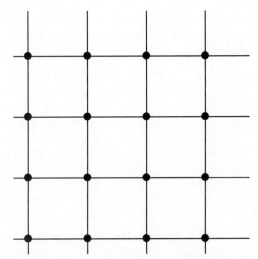

In a solid, strong intermolecular forces (potential energy, represented as lines) hold the atoms or molecules (represented by dots above) in place, allowing only simple vibrations. If you boil water, you must supply enough kinetic energy (heat) to overcome the potential energy holding the water molecules together, allowing them to escape the liquid and become a gas.

Exercise 8

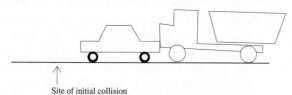

Directions: Choose the one best answer for each item.

1. Based on the figure below, what can we deduce about the mass and velocity of the car and truck?

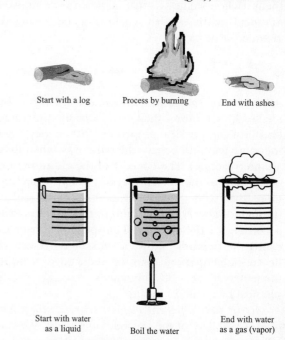

↑
Site of initial collision

   (1)   The truck has more mass than the car.
   (2)   The truck was moving faster than the car.
   (3)   The car has more mass than the truck.
   (4)   The truck was moving slower than the car.
   (5)   The car either has more mass or was moving faster than the truck.

2. If your dance partner steps on your foot with his or her heel, it will hurt more than with his or her toe. Why?

   (1)   Greater area
   (2)   Greater mass
   (3)   Same weight but smaller area
   (4)   Same mass but smaller area
   (5)   Greater weight

Check your answers on page 246.

Properties of Matter

We tend to think of properties of matter in terms of physical or chemical properties. Let's start with the easy one first: **chemical properties** are properties that, if changed, result in the formation of a different kind of matter. For example, flammability is a chemical property, because if a material burns, we know we'll get something different from it. Corrosiveness is another one, because it will result in the corrosion of whatever it is we are speaking of (as in corrosion of metals like rust in a car, or corrosion of your hand if you spill acid on it).

Physical properties are qualities that, if changed, do not fundamentally change the type of matter. For example, density is the mass of the substance per unit volume. If we have pieces of two different materials, say Styrofoam and lead, and these pieces have exactly the same volume, we know that the lead will be heavier. The heavier a material is, for some given fixed volume, the greater its density. Viscosity, or resistance to flow, is another physical property. We know that honey flows more slowly than gasoline, so honey has a higher viscosity. But if you heat the honey so that its viscosity

decreases, it's still honey. Other physical properties are size, shape, and color.

Physical properties can correspond to changes as well, provided that the material does not change chemically. For instance, ice melts at 0°C; melting point, the temperature at which solid turns to liquid, is a physical property. We change the state of ice, as it goes from solid to liquid, but it is still water. The boiling point of water is 100°C, the temperature at which liquid becomes gas. This is a physical property as well, because, after it boils, we have a new state (gas), but it's still water.

Start with a log   Process by burning   End with ashes

Start with water as a liquid   Boil the water   End with water as a gas (vapor)

In a chemical change, we end up with something fundamentally different than what we started with. In a physical change, we can have a change in state, but we still fundamentally have not changed the material we have.

This gives rise to the concept of chemical and physical changes. In a **chemical change**, you start with one material and end up with something entirely different. You put gasoline in your car's engine; after it burns, you end up with carbon dioxide and water (as well as a variety of additional trace gases). This is a chemical change, because you started with one substance but ended up with another. In a **physical change**, you do not fundamentally change what you have. For example, if you dissolve sugar in water, you now have a solution; you've caused a change (by dissolving the sugar), but you still fundamentally have water and sugar, the same things that you started with, only now they are mixed together.

211

Development of Atomic Theory

DALTON'S ATOMIC THEORY

Dalton's Atomic Theory, introduced around 1805, shifted the focus of chemistry to what was occurring on the atomic level. His theory had four primary components, which have not changed significantly since they were introduced:

1. *All matter is comprised of tiny, indestructible particles called "atoms."* Although he could not see them, Dalton suggested that matter was comprised of small particles that could not be changed, created, or destroyed.

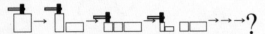

2. *All atoms of the same element are identical.* By identical, we mean they have exactly the same chemical and physical properties (that is, they react the same way and behave the same way when they are not reacting). The concept of the **element** also dates back to the ancient Greeks. Today, there are more than 100 different elements known (either through discovery or fabrication); they are arranged according to their chemical properties in a chart called the **periodic table**. A substance is taken to be an element if it cannot be reduced to a more fundamental set of substances through either physical or chemical means.

3. *Atoms of two different elements are distinguishable,* a corollary of the second component. We can tell them apart if they are different elements, but not if they are atoms of the same element.

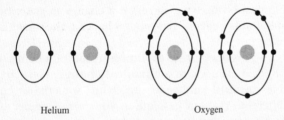

Helium   Oxygen

Dalton's Atomic Theory tells us that we should not be able to distinguish between two atoms of helium or two atoms of oxygen, but we should be able to distinguish helium atoms from oxygen atoms. Note that the atoms in the above figure are cartoon pictures of atoms and do not represent what the atoms actually look like.

4. *Atoms of two or more different elements will combine in fixed whole-number ratios to form compounds.* Probably the most important part of Dalton's Atomic Theory, this has two key components. First, we require at least two different elements to form a compound. Thus, oxygen, O_2, and ozone, O_3, are not compounds, because they contain only one type of element: oxygen. Second, the ratio of the elements forming a compound is fixed. If we vary this ratio, we change the compound. For example, in water, we always have two parts hydrogen to one part oxygen, written as H_2O. The ratio of hydrogen to oxygen is 2:1. If we change this ratio, say, to 1:1 (or, as it turns out, 2:2), as in H_2O_2, we no longer have water—we have hydrogen peroxide.

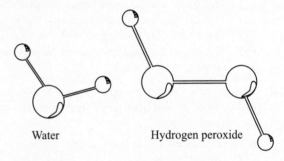

Water   Hydrogen peroxide

THE STRUCTURE OF ATOMS

Researchers were astounded to discover three particles more fundamental than the atom. One, which was exceedingly light and had a negative charge, they called the **electron**. Another, which was very heavy (relative to the electron) and had a positive charge, they called the **proton**. The mass of the electron was assigned a value of 0 (because it was so light that its mass didn't make a significant contribution to the total mass of the atom), and its charge was assigned a value of -1. The mass of the proton was assigned a value of 1 and its charge was assigned a value of $+1$. But, there was another particle, a very peculiar particle.

This new particle was not deflected in a magnetic field; its charge was 0. Scientists didn't know what to make of this new ray, so they dubbed it the mysterious *X-ray*. As it turns out, they had discovered **neutrons**, with a charge of 0 but a mass equal to that of a proton (mass 1).

ELEMENTARY PARTICLES

Particle	Symbol	Charge	Mass	Location
Proton	$_1p^+$	$+1$	1	Nucleus
Neutron	$_1n^0$	0	1	Nucleus
Electron	$_0e^-$	-1	0	Around nucleus

Now they had discovered the three elementary particles of which all atoms are composed, but to know what particles exist is a far cry from understanding how they are put together.

It was Earnest Rutherford who, in 1910, finally discovered the true structure of the atom in an experiment that he thought was a failure. Rutherford directed a beam of radioactive particles through a thin sheet of gold foil, which was a fairly typical experiment at that time. What was different this time was that instead of having a single small phosphorous screen target, he had wrapped the phosphorous screen around the entire apparatus.

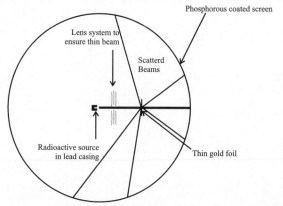

What he discovered was that there was glowing all round the screen, including almost in the exact opposite direction from the gold foil. He was so astonished by this that he wrote, "It was as if I had shot a cannonball at a piece of tissue paper and it bounced straight back toward me."

There was only one explanation for this phenomenon he could think of: somewhere, within the atom, there was a region that had matter so compact, so dense, that radiation could not penetrate it, and was actually deflected away from it. We now call that region of space the **nucleus,** the dense core of the atom that is home to the atom's protons and neutrons. The electrons are usually envisioned as being in orbit around this nucleus, although their exact behavior is, even today, not well understood. They seem to form what can best be described as clouds, but their exact path or behavior is not known.

The electrons are in shells, like the layers of an onion. We know that the outermost shell of electrons contains the only electrons that participate in the chemical and physical properties of atoms; we call this the *valence shell* electrons. The remaining electrons are all between the valence shell and the nucleus; they do not really participate in the chemistry of the element, aside from giving structure on which the valence shell electrons are built. We call these the *inner shell* electrons.

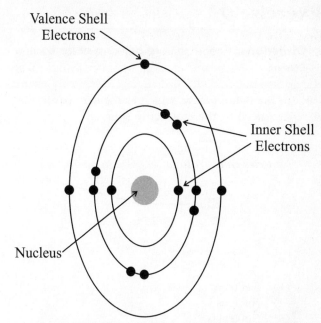

This is a cartoon diagram only; the actual structure of an aluminum atom is actually far more complicated.

When atoms collide, it is only the valence shell electrons that interact; therefore, it must be these electrons that give the elements their overall chemical and physical properties. It stands to reason then that if elements have similar electronic configurations, they must have similar chemical and physical properties. We find that this is indeed true, and it is reflected in the periodic chart.

The number of electrons can fluctuate as the element participates in bonding to form compounds. If an atom loses electrons, which are negatively charged, it will have a net positive charge. Positively charged atoms are called **cations**. If an atom gains electrons, it will have a net negative charge. Negatively charged atoms are called **anions**. Collectively, cations or anions are referred to as simply **ions**. We'll discuss this a little later.

Exercise 9

Directions: Choose the one best answer for each item.

1. In the figure below, which elementary particle is produced by the radioactive source?

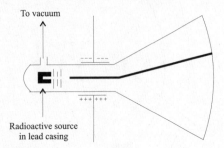

To vacuum

Radioactive source
in lead casing

(1) Electron
(2) Nucleus
(3) Neutron
(4) Proton
(5) Atom

2. Before Rutherford's experiment, a model for the atom, called the "Plum Pudding" model, was hypothesized in which the electrons, protons, and neutrons were uniformly distributed in space throughout the region occupied by the atom. What feature is lacking in this model that Rutherford's experiment found?

(1) Neutrons
(2) A dense region with high mass
(3) Protons
(4) A spherical shape
(5) Electrons

Check your answers on page 246.

The Periodic Table

The periodic table shows all known elements today.

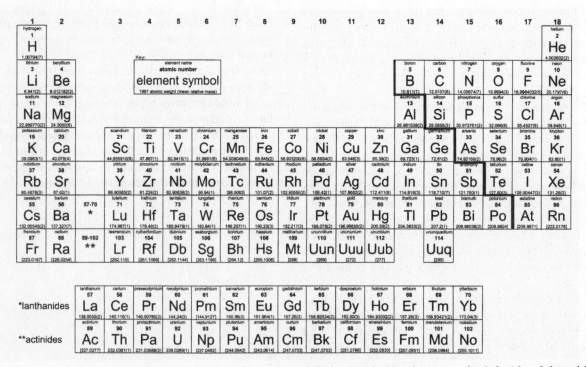

All elements in a column are *families* or *groups*, and rows are called *periods*. Metals are on the left side of the table, and nonmetals are on the right. The bold line toward the right-hand side of the periodic table separates the metals from the nonmetals. Elements on this line, called *metalloids*, have properties in between those of metals and nonmetals. The elements in the square block in the middle where the main table gets thinnest are called the *transition metals*, while the two rows on the bottom are called the *Lanthanides* (top) and the *Actinides* (bottom).

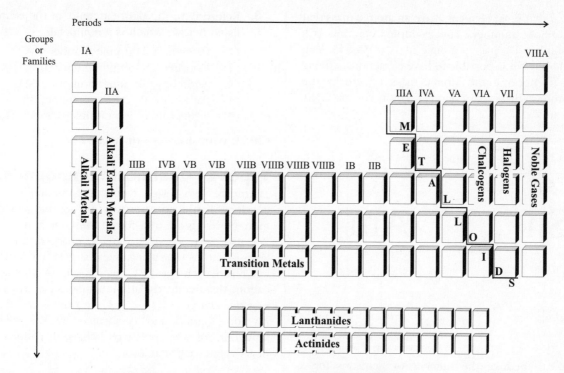

Metals tend to have all of the typical characteristics you'd expect from metals (with some exceptions): they conduct electricity and heat well, they are malleable (can be bent), they tend to be shiny, and in compounds they tend to lose electrons. **Nonmetals** are the opposite: they usually do not conduct electricity or heat, are often brittle and dull, and gain electrons in compounds.

Metalloids tend to be semiconductors (like silicon). They can be malleable or brittle, shiny or dull, and can either lose or gain electrons. They're somewhere in between metals and nonmetals.

Several columns in the periodic table have common names. For example, group IA are called the *alkali metals* (because in water they form alkaline, or basic, solutions). Group IIA, the *alkali earth metals*, include ones common in ores, like calcium and magnesium. They also form alkaline solutions when in water. Group VIIA, the *halogens,* are mostly gases that are highly corrosive and toxic; iodine, from this group, is used to clean wounds, because it kills germs. Group VIIIA are called *noble gases* because they are nonreactive, or inert.

You'll notice that each element has several things associated with it. First, each element has a one- or two-letter designation, or **atomic symbol**. Each element has an **atomic number** as well, starting with hydrogen as 1, helium as 2, and so on. These numbers are not merely arbitrary. Rather, it is equal to the number of protons in an atom of the element.

Atomic Mass

As you'll recall, of the elementary particles, only protons and neutrons have mass, and their masses are very close to each other. Each had been assigned a mass of 1, while electrons were assigned a mass of 0 (compared to the mass of the proton and the neutron, the mass of the electron is not significant). Thus, an element's **atomic mass** number is equal to the number of protons plus the number of neutrons.

Recall that the number of protons is equal to the atomic number; thus, we are not allowed to change this number without changing the identity of the element we are discussing. However, the number of neutrons is allowed to change. Two atoms with the same atomic number (same number of protons) but different number of neutrons will differ only in their atomic mass number, not their identity. We call these atoms **isotopes**.

You may notice that some elements in the periodic table, like neptunium (Np, element number 93), have an integral number (a whole number) associated with them (for Np, this number is 237). This is the atomic mass number of the most stable isotope. Any element with this kind of number is unstable and undergoes radioactive decay. These **radioisotopes** decay to become different elements, and they release radiation when they do.

Notice that most elements have an atomic mass that is not a whole number. For example, chlorine (Cl, element number 17) has an atomic mass of 35.543. You may wonder how it is possible to have a fractional atomic mass; this is because the atomic mass is actually the average atomic mass of a large quantity of naturally occurring atoms.

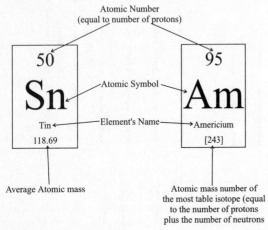

You can deduce the number of neutrons for a specific isotope in any given element by subtracting the atomic number from the atomic mass number.

Exercise 10

Directions: Choose the one best answer for each item.

1. Referring to the periodic table, which element has 32 protons?

    (1) Germanium, Ge
    (2) Gold, Au
    (3) Sulfur, S
    (4) Nickel, Ni
    (5) Polonium, Po

2. Referring to the periodic table, how many neutrons are in the most stable isotope of americium?

    (1) 95
    (2) 148
    (3) 243
    (4) 338
    (5) More information is needed before this question can be answered.

3. Referring to the periodic table, of the elements listed below, which is a nonmetal?

    (1) Calcium, Ca (atomic number 20)
    (2) Fluorine, F (atomic number 9)
    (3) Antimony, Sb (atomic number 51)
    (4) Palladium, Pd (atomic number 46)
    (5) Promethium, Pm (atomic number 61)

Check your answers on page 247.

Types of Chemical Compounds

There are two major types of compounds: ionic and covalent. **Ionic compounds** are formed when one or more electrons are transferred from one atom to another. Because electrons are negatively charged, the atom that loses electrons (loses negative charges) will be left with a net positive charge ($+1$, $+2$, $+3$, etc.); this is called a cation. Meanwhile, the atom that gains electrons has a net negative charge (-1, -2, -3, etc.) and is called an anion. An ionic compound is formed by the electrostatic attraction of the positively charged cations for the negatively charged anions.

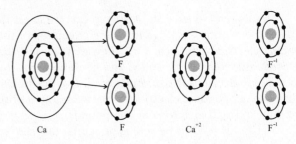

Before   After

Ionic compounds are always accompanied by a physical transference of one or more electrons. In the case above, the calcium atom loses two electrons, which are transferred to two fluorine atoms, which in turn each picks up one electron. The ionic bond is really nothing more than the attraction of these charged ions for one another.

For an ionic compound to form, one of the atoms must have a pull for electrons that is strong enough that it can literally take the electrons away; this leads to the question of what happens when one atom is not strong enough to remove electrons completely from the other. In this case, electrons must be shared. A compound in which the elements share electrons is called a **covalent compound**, and the bonds are called covalent bonds. In any covalent bond, two, and only two, electrons are shared. However, a compound can form single, double, or triple bonds (but no higher order than triple). Thus, there are two electrons shared in a single bond (one from each element involved in the bond), four electrons shared in a double bond (two in each of the two bonds), and six electrons shared in a triple bond (two in each of the three bonds).

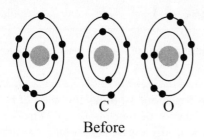

Before

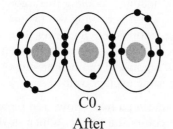

CO_2

After

For example, carbon dioxide (shown above) actually forms two double bonds (requiring that four electrons be shared on each side, two for each in the double bond).

PROPERTIES OF COVALENT AND IONIC COMPOUNDS

Covalent and ionic compounds differ in behavior. For instance, covalent compounds tend to have lower melting points and to be more malleable, while ionic compounds tend to have higher melting points and be more brittle.

PROPERTIES OF IONIC AND COVALENT COMPOUNDS

Property	Ionic Compounds	Covalent Compounds
Melting points	Typically very high	Ranges from low to moderately high
Malleability	Typically brittle (not malleable)	Ranges from brittle to malleable
Dissociates in water	Yes (if soluble)	No (even if soluble)

However, one of the greatest differences between these types of compounds is their behavior in water. Some compounds, called **electrolytes**, cause water to conduct electricity, while other compounds, called **nonelectrolytes**, do not.

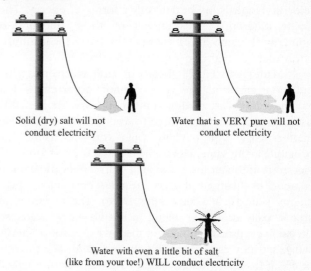

Solid (dry) salt will not conduct electricity

Water that is VERY pure will not conduct electricity

Water with even a little bit of salt (like from your toe!) WILL conduct electricity

Interactions of Matter and Energy

HEAT

The interaction of matter and energy is dependent on the form of the energy. Energy can be absorbed or released by matter, but remember that the total energy is conserved; we cannot create or destroy energy. Consider, for example, heat. Heat was originally defined as that which flows from a region of high temperature to low temperature. This definition tells us little else, because, when this standard definition of heat was formulated, little was known of the effects of heat on matter.

As it turns out, heat is directly related to the kinetic energy of the molecules and atoms in matter. Thus, the higher the temperature, the faster molecules and atoms move, and the higher their kinetic energy. When a cooler body is in contact with a warmer body, heat is transferred from one body to another because of the collisions between the molecules and atoms.

Just like their macroscopic counterparts, atoms and molecules display momentum. They move in a straight line until they collide with some object, forcing them to change direction. If that other object is another atom or molecule, then an energy transfer can be expected to occur. The atom or molecule with less kinetic energy (lower temperature) will pick up some of the kinetic energy from the atom or molecule with greater kinetic energy (higher temperature). Because the molecule with less kinetic energy now has more kinetic energy, its temperature has increased.

217

ELECTROMAGNETIC RADIATION

Another form of energy is *electromagnetic radiation*. Light falls into the category of electromagnetic radiation, but so do many other things, such as microwave radiation, infrared and ultraviolet radiation, radio and television signals, and many other forms of energy. The major difference between all of these energies is primarily the amount of energy they have; for example, ultraviolet has higher energy than infrared.

Matter can either absorb or emit electromagnetic radiation, and both are very common occurrences. For example, if you are reading this at night, you are probably using an artificial light source to read it (a light bulb). No matter what type of light bulb you are using, the principle is the same: electricity is being used to force the electrons in the atoms in the light bulb (either the gas if it is neon or filament if it is incandescent) into a high energy state (called an *excited state*). The electrons in atoms really don't like being in a high-energy state, so they will eventually go back to the lowest possible energy state that they can, called the *ground state*. The process of going from an excited state to a ground state is called *relaxation*.

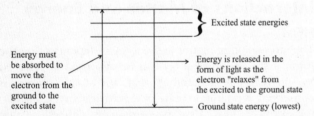

It always requires the input of energy to get the electrons into a higher energy state than their ground state, but that energy is released, often in the form of light, as the electron "relaxes" back to the ground state. Because energy cannot be destroyed, we reach that excited state when energy in the form of electrical energy is absorbed. When the atom relaxes back to the ground state, all that excess energy is again released, only this time in the form of light, but exactly equal in energy to the energy absorbed to excite the electrons in the first place.

Exercise 11

Directions: Choose the one best answer for each item.

1. Argon has about 10 times the mass of helium. What can we deduce about the behavior of a mixture of these gases (assuming the temperatures of the gases are the same)?

   (1) The helium is cooling the argon.
   (2) The argon is cooling the helium.
   (3) The argon is moving faster than the helium.
   (4) The helium is moving faster then the argon.
   (5) The argon and the helium must be moving at the same average velocity.

2. A can found on a hike shows red pigments faded but blue colors still bright. Which of the following statements explains this observation?

   (1) Red absorbs red light, and the energy associated with red light is higher energy than blue light.
   (2) Red absorbs blue light, and the energy associated with red light is higher energy than blue light.
   (3) Red absorbs red light, and the energy associated with blue light is higher energy than red light.
   (4) Red must be absorbing light, while blue is emitting light.
   (5) Red absorbs blue light, and the energy associated with blue light is higher energy than red light.

Check your answers on page 247.

States of Matter

We all know the three major states of matter: gas, solid, and liquid. If you were shown a particular material (tricks aside), you would be able to identify its state. Gases have very low density, expand to fill the volume of their container, and assume the shape of their container. Liquids have intermediate density and a fixed volume but will assume the shape of their container. Solids have the highest density, fixed volumes, and fixed shapes.

CHARACTERISTICS OF THE THREE MAJOR STATES OF MATTER

Property	Gas	Liquid	Solid
Viscosity (resistance to flow)	Low	Low to high	High
Volume	Container-dependent	Fixed	Fixed
Shape	Container-dependent	Container-dependent	Fixed
Relative temperature	Highest	Intermediate	Lowest
Relative density	Lowest	Intermediate (with rare exceptions)	Highest (with rare exceptions)

DENSITY

Not all solids have higher densities than liquids; solid iron has lower density than liquid mercury, which is easy to prove because iron will float on a pool of mercury. This is because we are comparing different elements; with very few exceptions, for any given element or compound, the solid will have a higher density than the corresponding liquid. So mercury in the solid state has a higher density than mercury in the liquid state, and iron in the solid state has a higher density than iron in the liquid state. Unfortunately, one of the extremely rare exceptions to this rule is water, the only known compound (and there is only one known element) for which the solid state is less dense than the liquid.

Exercise 12

Directions: Choose the <u>one best answer</u> for each item.

1. Vapor pressure is the pressure created in a closed container above a liquid. If a liquid has a high vapor pressure (the higher the vapor pressure, the more liquid will evaporate at a given temperature), what can we infer about the molecules in the liquid?

   (1) The kinetic energy must be great.
   (2) The intermolecular forces between the molecules must be weak.
   (3) The kinetic energy must be weak.
   (4) Nothing can be inferred from this observation.
   (5) The intermolecular forces between the molecules must be strong.

2. The substance shown in the figure below is most likely to be a(n)

   (1) solid.
   (2) compound.
   (3) element.
   (4) liquid.
   (5) gas.

Check your answers on page 247.

Solutions and Mixtures

Much like compounds, mixtures require at least two different components. However, in mixtures, these components may themselves be compounds (and often are). In addition, unlike compounds, the ratio of these components is free to vary. You'll also notice that we are discussing mixtures at this point rather than solutions; all solutions are mixtures, but not all mixtures are solutions.

PROPERTIES OF SOLUTIONS AND COMPOUNDS

Property	Solutions	Compounds
Comprised of two or more things	Yes (solute and solvent)	Yes (at least two different elements)
Fixed ratios	Yes	No

A **mixture** is a combination of two or more components. We refer to mixtures as either heterogeneous or homogeneous. A *homogeneous* mixture is the same throughout; if we were to sample a homogeneous mixture at any point, it would be identical in every way to any other portion. In a *heterogeneous* mixture, however, we have different properties depending on where we are in the mixture.

Often, heterogeneous mixtures are easy to spot; you'll see something floating in the solution, such as an impurity or even ice in a glass of water, or perhaps you'll see regions of different colors, like carpet with multicolored threads. Other times, it might be more difficult to spot a heterogeneous mixture, such as milk. However, as it turns out, if a solution is very cloudy or opaque, it must be a heterogeneous mixture. This is because the cloudiness or opaqueness is caused by light bouncing off very fine particles that are too small for the human eye to catch.

SOLUTES AND SOLVENTS

You might wonder what the difference is between a mixture and a solution. A **solution** is a homogenous mixture. To be a true solution, you must have a clear (but, again, not necessarily colorless) mixture of two or more components. Some common terms we use when discussing solutions are solvent and solute. The **solute** is the active ingredient; it is what is important in the solution, or the reason we create or choose to use it. The **solvent**, then, is what the solute is dissolved in; it is the delivery medium for the solute. Thus, in children's aspirin, the solute, the active ingredient or most important component, is the acetyl salicylic acid (aspirin); the flavorful syrup is the solvent.

In addition to these, there are several key terms relating to how much solute we have relative to the amount of solvent. If a solution is *unsaturated*, we have dissolved some solute but could dissolve more. If it is *saturated*, we have dissolved as much solute as possible at the given temperature. If it is *supersaturated*, we have dissolved more solute in the solution than possible. This last term seems very odd, but as it turns out, for solids to form from a solution (a process called *precipitation*), the crystals need something to form on. This so-called seed can be either a crystal of the same compound, or a scratch in the container, or some other imperfection. Without such a seed, a solution can actually be made that is supersaturated.

To make a supersaturated solution, we begin with a heterogeneous mixture consisting of a saturated solution and excess solute in the same very smooth (scratch-free) container. We heat up the solution, so that the excess solute dissolves. Once the solute has dissolved completely, we allow the solution to cool slowly back down. If we are careful to choose a container free of scratches, we can form a solution that has more solute dissolved than should be possible at the lower temperature.

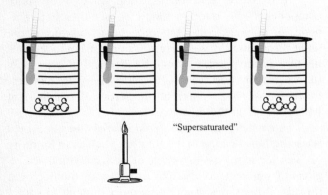

"Supersaturated"

We can also speak of a solution as concentrated or dilute. A solution is *concentrated* if it contains a lot of solute relative to the amount of solvent. It is *dilute* if it contains relatively little solute. How much solute we have relative to the amount of solvent is usually expressed in some given concentration. There are many concentration expressions, but they are basically all the same—typically, the quantity of solute per given amount of solution or solvent.

SOLUBILITY

If a substance dissolves to an appreciable extent in a solvent, we say it is *soluble*, as salt is soluble in water. However, if very little will dissolve, we say it is *insoluble*, such as pepper in water. In the special case of liquid solvent/liquid solute, we use the terms *miscible* or *immiscible* instead. Two liquids are said to be miscible if they can be mixed in any ratio without their separating out on standing. Gasoline and oil, for example, are miscible. However, if the liquids cannot be mixed without their separating on standing, they are immiscible, as in oil and vinegar.

Exercise 13

Directions: Choose the one best answer for each item.

1. A cloudy liquid is an example of a(n)
   - (1) compound.
   - (2) solution.
   - (3) element.
   - (4) solute.
   - (5) heterogeneous mixture.

2. A clear liquid is known to contain a solid solute. A sample of the liquid is tested by adding an additional amount of that particular solute, which readily dissolves. Which of the following terms best describes the original liquid?
   - (1) Unsaturated solution
   - (2) Saturated solution
   - (3) Supersaturated solution
   - (4) Solvent
   - (5) Solute

Check your answers on page 247.

Chemical Reactions

When material is changed into something new, then we have caused a **chemical reaction.** The materials we started with were the *reactants*, and what we ended up with are the *products*. For example, a rust spot on a car starts out as iron and oxygen (the most reactive component of air) that combine to form rust. Rust is fundamentally different from iron and oxygen, so this is a chemical change.

$$\text{Reactants} \qquad\qquad \text{Products}$$
$$4Fe + 3O_2 \longrightarrow 2Fe_2O_2$$

Chemical reactions are represented by formulas. Reactants, what we are starting with, are always on the left, with products always on the right. Notice that if you count the number of atoms of each element, they are the same on both sides (we have 4 iron, Fe, on the left, and 2 $\times$ 2 = 4 on the right). This is necessary because of the Law of Conservation of Matter (discussed below).

Conservation of Matter. Just as in the Law of Conservation of Energy, there is a similar law governing chemical reactions, the Law of Conservation of Matter. This law states that matter cannot be created or destroyed, but it can change form. Thus, if we burn, say, 300 tons of coal, resulting in a pile of ashes with significantly less weight, any missing mass must be present in the form of gaseous emissions. This law brings increased significance to the concept of recycling: Earth's resources are limited; if we run out of any given resource, such as aluminum, this material cannot be replaced. If we begin recycling now, we can extend the life of the resources we have, leaving more resources in reserve for future generations.

Chemical reactions are almost always accompanied by changes in energy. For example, if we burn a log, energy is released in the form of heat and light. Chemical reactions that release energy are called **exothermic.** On the other hand, if you apply a chemical cold pack to a sprained ankle, the cooling is the result of a chemical change that is occurring within the cold pack. A chemical reaction that absorbs energy (gets cold) is called **endothermic.**

The source of most of these energy changes lies within the chemical bonds. Energy is always released when a bond is formed; conversely, energy is always absorbed when a bond is broken. When we form new compounds, we are forming new bonds, but the old bonds (the bonds in the reactants) must be broken first. If we release more energy in forming the bonds in the products than is required to break the bonds of the reactants, then the reaction is exothermic. However, if it costs more energy to break the bonds in the reactants than is released in the bonds formed in the products, then the reaction will be endothermic. The heat of the reaction, called **enthalpy,** can be used to tell us the relative energies of the bonds in the products and the reactants.

$$2H_2 + O_2 \longrightarrow 2H_2O$$

In the figure above, we see two ways of writing the reaction of hydrogen with oxygen: The traditional way on top, and a more graphical way beneath. Again, notice that the Law of Conservation of Matter is conserved in both depictions. The reaction of hydrogen in oxygen is notoriously exothermic, releasing great amounts of heat; all of this energy comes from the formation of new bonds in the water (product). However, some energy first had to be absorbed to break the preexisting bonds of the hydrogen and oxygen (reactants).

Keep in mind the Law of Conservation of Energy. If energy is released, it must have been stored somewhere within the reactants to begin with. Thus, the potential energy stored within reactants is being released during an exothermic reaction. Similarly, energy can only be absorbed in an endothermic reaction if that energy is being stored in the form of potential energy in the products.

Reversible Reactions. We have a tendency to think of reactions as being one shot only: that is, once the reaction happens, it is over. This is not always true: in fact, many reactions can proceed either forward or backward (that is, either from reactants to products or from products to reactants).

$$H_2O(l) + CO_2(g) \rightleftharpoons H_2CO_3(aq)$$

Above we have a famous reversible reaction: carbon dioxide dissolves in water to form carbonic acid, but carbonic acid can also break down to form carbon dioxide in water. Soft drink manufacturers use the forward reaction by adding a lot of carbon dioxide to form carbonated beverages. The letters in parentheses provide additional information by telling us the state of each reactant and product ("l" for liquid, "g" for gas, and "aq" for aqueous, meaning "dissolved in water").

221

Exercise 14

> **Directions:** Choose the one best answer for each item.

1. What can we deduce about the reaction H_2CO_3 (aq) $\rightarrow$ H_2O (l) + CO_2 (g)?

   (1) Nothing more can be deduced.
   (2) It is endothermic.
   (3) Its entropy is decreasing.
   (4) It is exothermic.
   (5) Its entropy is increasing.

2. What is wrong with the reaction H_2SO_4 (aq) + NaOH (s) $\rightarrow$ Na_2SO_4 (aq) + H_2O (l)?

   (1) It violates the Law of Conservation of Energy.
   (2) The compounds are written incorrectly.
   (3) These reactants will not react.
   (4) It violates the Law of Conservation of Matter.
   (5) The reaction is written using the wrong notation.

3. Of the following processes, which is not a chemical reaction?

   (1) A car catches on fire after a collision.
   (2) A piece of bread begins to grow mold.
   (3) Water is driven off of a solution, leaving behind salt.
   (4) A drug combats high cholesterol.
   (5) An athlete eats food that will later supply the energy necessary to win the competition.

Check your answers on page 247.

Kinetics

PARTICLE SIZE

The study of how quickly a chemical reaction occurs is called **kinetics**. As it turns out, we have quite a bit of control over how quickly chemical reactions can occur. Among the factors that can influence reaction rate is particle size. For reactions to occur, the reactants must be in contact; the smaller the particles, the greater the surface area, and therefore the more area that is in contact and that can react.

TEMPERATURE

Another factor that can influence reaction rate is temperature. Chemical reactions occur faster at higher temperatures, because the molecules and atoms are moving faster to begin with.

CONCENTRATION

If the reaction involves a solution, we generally find that the higher the concentration of the reactants, the faster the reaction will occur. This is because the higher the concentration, the more reactants that are present and available to react.

CATALYSTS

Finally, chemical reactions can be increased by the addition of a catalyst. Catalysts are chemicals that speed up reactions but are not consumed in the reaction themselves; thus, when the reaction is complete, we will have just as much catalyst as we added in the first place. Catalysts occur both naturally and artificially. Within our bodies, enzymes are catalysts; they speed up the metabolic reactions.

EQUILIBRIUM

If we combine the concept of kinetics and reversible reactions, we come across a concept called **equilibrium**. It is always a mistake to think of chemistry as static; there is always something going on—vibration, rotation, or, in the case of a reversible reaction, the reaction continuing to occur in both the forward and reverse direction.

If we have a mixture of reactants and products together in an enclosed container for a reversible reaction, the reaction is continuously occurring in both the forward and the reverse direction. However, if the mixture is at equilibrium, then the reaction is occurring in both directions at exactly the same rate. Thus, the forward reaction is creating products just as quickly as the reverse direction is consuming these products. The end result of this is that there is no way to detect any kind of change in the system over time.

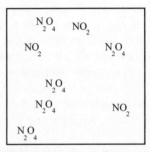

There are several ways to disturb equilibrium. If a gas is present, either as a product or a reactant, then a change in pressure will influence equilibrium; increasing pressure always favors the side with less gas.

Increasing temperature always favors the endothermic side of equilibrium. As with any reversible reaction, one direction will absorb heat, while the other will release heat.

You may think that adding a catalyst will influence equilibrium. In fact, it will not. It is true that a catalyst will speed up a chemical reaction, but it always increases both directions of an equilibrium equally. Thus, adding a catalyst will not change the equilibrium at all.

Exercise 15

Directions: Choose the <u>one best answer</u> for each item.

1. An industrial process that relies on the reversible chemical reaction (equilibrium), REACTANTS ↔ PRODUCTS, produces a better yield at high temperatures. What can we deduce about this reaction?

   (1) The reaction increases in entropy in the forward direction.
   (2) Nothing more can be deduced.
   (3) The reaction is exothermic in the forward direction.
   (4) The reaction decreases in entropy in the forward direction.
   (5) The reaction is endothermic in the forward direction.

2. When will an equilibrium stop?

   (1) When we have more reactant than product
   (2) When we have more product than reactant
   (3) Never
   (4) When the concentrations of the reactant and product reach their equilibrium values
   (5) When the concentrations of the product and reactant are equal

Check your answers on page 247.

Water Chemistry: Acids and Bases

Chemistry that occurs within water is of great interest to us as human beings because of the critical role water plays in both our ecology and our anatomy. On Earth, it is the great abundance of water that sustains life, while our bodies themselves are primarily comprised of water. If we are discussing water chemistry, we are usually describing acid/base reactions.

An **acid** is any ionic compound that has the hydronium ion, H^+, as its cation. A **base** is any ionic compound with a hydroxide, OH^-, as its anion. Thus, an acidic solution will have more hydronium ions than hydroxide ions, while a basic (or alkaline) solution will have more hydroxide ions than hydronium ions. As you might imagine, if you react an acid with a base, or H^+ with OH^-, the result is simply water, H_2O. This is referred to as a **neutralization reaction.** A neutralization reaction is a reaction between an acid and a base, and it results in the formation of water and a salt, as shown by the two examples below.

$$2HBr \ (aq) + Ca(OH)_2 \ (aq) \rightarrow CaBr_2 \ (aq) + 2H_2O \ (l)$$

$$3H_2SO_4 \ (aq) + Al(OH)_3 \ (aq) \rightarrow Al_2(SO_4)_3 \ (aq) + 3H_2O \ (l)$$

We have a very convenient and simple way of measuring and expressing the acidity of a solution, the pH scale. **pH** is an inverse measure of the concentration of hydronium ions; thus, the lower the pH, the greater the number of hydronium ions, and the more acidic the solution. On the other hand, the greater the pH, the greater the concentration of hydroxide ions, and the more basic, or alkaline, the solution will be. A pH of 7 has as many hydronium as hydroxide ions, and the solution is exactly neutral. A pH less than 7 is acidic, while a pH greater than 7 is basic.

Exercise 16

Directions: Choose the <u>one best answer</u> for each item.

1. A solution with pH 3.99 is

   (1) a base.
   (2) an acid.
   (3) a salt.
   (4) an ion.
   (5) neutral.

2. Lemon juice, which contains citric acid, is added to fish to cut the fishy smell, which is attributed to an amine compound, a base. Why does lemon juice cut the fishy smell?

   (1) Lemon is a natural cleaning solvent.
   (2) An acid and a base form a salt.
   (3) This is a fallacy with no foundation in science.
   (4) An acid and a base form water.
   (5) The smell of lemon masks the fishy smell.

Check your answers on page 247.

Unit 3

EARTH SCIENCE

Earth science encompasses all of the scientific disciplines that seek to understand the earth and the surrounding space. Earth science is usually broken down into geology, oceanography, meteorology, hydrology, and astronomy. **Geology** is the study of the solid Earth and the dynamic processes that occur on and under the surface. **Oceanography** is the integrated use of scientific inquiry in the study of the oceans. Oceanography applies physics, chemistry, geology, and biology to ocean processes. **Meteorology** is the study of atmospheric processes, weather, and climate. **Hydrology** is the study of water on Earth's surface and underground. **Astronomy** is the study of the universe and Earth's relationship to it.

Geology

Most scientists today believe that the earth, like all bodies in the solar system, originally formed from a **nebula**—a cloud of space gas and dust. Over a period of more than a billion years, gravity caused the earth's materials to contract and settle. In a process called differentiation, the materials that made up the forming planet sorted themselves out by density. Heavier (denser) materials sank to the center, and lighter materials rose to or near the surface of the proto-planet. The outer layer then cooled, creating the crust.

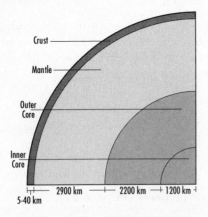

Earth is a rocky planet with an overall diameter of approximately 12,750km (7,900 miles) and an average density about 5.5 times that of water. The outermost layer, the crust, is the thinnest layer, with a thickness of 5 to 45km (3 to 25 miles). It is composed of rocks made predominantly of silicate (silicon and oxygen) minerals. The crust is also the least dense layer, with a density of 2.5 to 3.0g/cm³. There are two types of crust, continental and oceanic. Continental crust is less dense (about 2.7g/cm³) than oceanic crust (3.0g/cm³).

Below the crust is the mantle, which extends about halfway to the center of the earth (approximately 2,850 km, or 1,800 miles). It is also composed of silicate minerals rich in magnesium and iron. The mantle is denser than the crust, with a density of 3.3 to 5.5g/cm³. Due to high temperatures and pressure, this layer of rock tends to flow like thick plastic.

The third layer is the outer core, which is molten and is composed mostly of iron and nickel. This layer of Earth is denser yet. The outer core is approximately 2,270 km thick (1,400 miles). The inner core is also mostly iron, but unlike the outer core, it is solid, with a density of 12.6 to 13.0g/cm³ and a radius of approximately 1,216km (750 miles).

Exercise 1

Directions: Choose the one best answer for each item.

1. Which statement supports the conclusion that the temperature of the earth's crust rises as you get deeper?

   A. Oil pumped from deep wells is often very warm.

   B. Air is hot at the bottom of deep mines.

   C. Wells draw water from rock layers in the crust.

   (1) A only
   (2) B only
   (3) C only
   (4) A and B
   (5) B and C

2. Which layer of the earth contains material of the lowest density?

   (1) Inner core
   (2) Outer core
   (3) Crust
   (4) Mantle
   (5) Asthenosphere

Check your answers on page 247.

Minerals

Minerals are the building blocks of Earth. A **mineral** is a naturally occurring inorganic solid with a definite chemical structure. Minerals originally formed through natural processes in Earth's crust. Minerals are classified based on their chemical composition. Groups commonly used to classify minerals include oxides, sulfides, sulfates, native elements, halides, and carbonates. **Oxides** contain oxygen, the most common element in the crust. Sulfides and sulfites are minerals with sulfur complexes. **Halides** are salt compounds of various types, and **carbonates** contain carbon. Native elements are pure samples of inorganic elements, usually metals.

More than 4,000 unique minerals have been identified. Useful characteristics for identifying minerals include crystal structure, hardness, luster or shine, color, streak, cleavage/fracture, and specific gravity. Using these characteristics collectively, geologists can differentiate between mineral samples. All characteristics need to be considered, because many minerals share several of the basic characteristics.

Rocks are aggregates of different minerals. Rocks can be classified into three basic types: igneous, sedimentary, and metamorphic. All rocks form from the basic minerals of Earth. Except for the occasional meteor landing on Earth, all the building blocks for rocks have been here since Earth formed. The rock cycle describes how one rock can be transformed into other rock types and how physical processes of Earth, including erosion, weathering, heat, and pressure, interact to form and reform rocks.

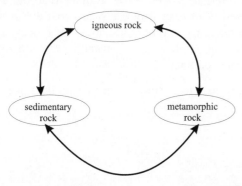

Igneous rock forms as a result of the cooling and crystallization of lava or magma. **Magma** is made of molten minerals located under Earth's surface, while **lava** is the same material once it is on Earth's surface. Igneous rocks formed from magma typically cool slowly within Earth, producing intrusive igneous rock, which has a coarser texture and larger crystal size than volcanic rocks. Granite is the most common type of intrusive rock. Volcanic rock, which cools quickly on Earth's surface, has a fine-grained texture. Basalt is an example of volcanic rock.

Sedimentary rock forms when rocks exposed at the surface undergo weathering and erosion, producing small rock fragments called sediments. Rain and wind carry these sediments away to a nearby body of water, where they fall to the bottom and are deposited in layers. The processes of compaction and cementation fuse the sediments into rocks. *Clastic* sedimentary rocks are formed from the sediments carried by water that settle on the bottom. These rocks are further classified by sediment size. An example of clastic sedimentary rock is sandstone. *Chemical* sedimentary rocks are formed from dissolved minerals when water evaporates. Limestone and chalk are common examples of this type of rock.

Metamorphic rock forms from existing rock. When rocks undergo heating and pressurization, the crystalline structure of the original or parent rock changes, and metamorphic rock results. Metamorphic rocks can form from igneous, sedimentary, or other metamorphic rocks. For example, shale, a sedimentary rock, becomes slate, and sandstone becomes quartzite. A characteristic unique to metamorphic rocks is crystalline banding, or *foliation*. This occurs when minerals within a rock, in response to heat and pressure, realign within the rock and form stripes. The metamorphic rock gneiss, formed from granite, shows foliation.

Exercise 2

> **Directions:** Choose the one best answer for each item.

1. You find a rock that is later identified as petrified wood. You are told that the fossil you have is not mineral-based. What is the justification for this claim?

    (1) The exact chemical composition is unknown.
    (2) Fossils are composed of matter that was once living.
    (3) The fossil crystal structure is cubic.
    (4) The fossil is not old enough to be a mineral.
    (5) All minerals come from the ocean.

2. You find a rock layer that is identified as sandstone in a hillside. Based on this finding, which of the following statements can be made about the hillside?

    (1) A volcano must be nearby.
    (2) The region must have been underwater at some point in time.
    (3) Heat and pressure from within Earth helped to form the rock layer.
    (4) A chemical test is required to identify the rock positively as sandstone.
    (5) There is a fault nearby.

Check your answers on page 247.

Weathering, Soil Formation, and Erosion

Weathering is the process whereby rock breaks down into smaller and smaller pieces. This process occurs as a result of mechanical action, such as water freezing and thawing in the cracks of rocks, heat causing rocks to expand and crack, or by chemical changes, such as the dissolving of minerals in water or naturally occurring acids.

An important product of weathered rock is **soil**. Soil is a mixture of weathering residues (primarily sand, silt, and clay), decaying organic matter, living creatures (bacteria, fungi, worms, and insects), air, and moisture. The thickness of soil can vary from a few centimeters to several meters. Factors that affect the type of soil are the rock material from which it forms, the climate (temperature and moisture), and the terrain. Soil is very susceptible to degradation through poor management and use by human activity. Once severely damaged, soil is virtually lost to any productive use.

Erosion is the movement of rock or soil by forces of Earth. Water, wind, gravity, and glaciers are major forces that change the face of Earth. Erosion is a primary force reshaping the landscape of Earth.

Gravity is a constant force on Earth. Just as it pulls on all of us, gravity also pulls on all landforms. Rock slides are the result of gravitational erosion. Running water is a second significant cause of erosion. Moving water picks up sediments and carries them far from their place of origin.

Wind also is a significant agent of erosion. Wind carries sediments long distances, and the abrasive effects of those sediments on other surfaces can create new sediments. A less common, but no less dramatic, agent of erosion is the movement of glaciers.

Exercise 3

> **Directions:** Choose the one best answer for each item.

1. A hillside is barren of vegetation. Which of the following agents of erosion would have a dramatic effect on the contour of the hillside?

   A. Water
   B. Wind
   C. Gravity

   (1) A only
   (2) B only
   (3) C only
   (4) A and B
   (5) A, B, and C

2. A tree grows on a cliff side. Over a number of years, the roots of the tree cause sections of the cliff to break away. This is an example of which type of weathering at work?

   (1) Ice wedging
   (2) Thermal expansion
   (3) Biological agents
   (4) Chemical agents
   (5) Wind

Check your answers on page 248.

Plate Tectonics. Plate tectonics, the theory currently used to explain the interrelationship of the processes that shape Earth, states that the surface of Earth is composed of large slabs of crust and upper mantle that are constantly shifting against one another. The theory explains earthquakes and volcanic action, the formation and location of mountain ranges, and the locations of the present continents. The plate tectonic theory attempts to explain evidence of continental movement and observed pressures at known plate boundaries.

Earth's outer shell, or **lithosphere**, comprised of the crust and upper mantle, is relatively brittle and cold. The lithosphere moves in response to pressures exerted from beneath the **asthenosphere,** a plastic region of the upper mantle on which the lithosphere glides. The heat and pressure in the asthenosphere create convection currents that exert compression and tension forces on the lithosphere.

The theory of plate tectonics seeks to explain Earth's internal processes by arguing that the crust is comprised of distinct geologic plates that are in motion. Each plate is made up of continental crust, oceanic crust, or both. These plates are constantly moving over the underlying partially molten asthenosphere at speeds ranging from 1 to 12cm ($\frac{1}{2}$ inch to 5 inches) per year.

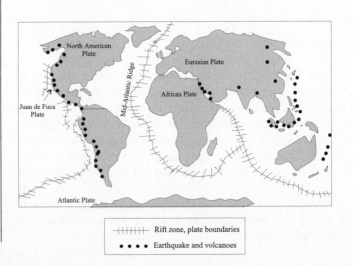

Processes within Earth cause these plates to move against one another. Most geologic activity, including earthquakes, volcanoes, and mountain building, occurs along plate boundaries. At the boundaries, plates spread apart, collide, or slide past one another. The Pacific Ring of Fire, a volcanically and seismically active region, corresponds to the boundary of the Pacific tectonic plate.

Exercise 4

Directions: Choose the one best answer for each item.

1. Plate tectonics explains which of the following geologic events?

   A. Sea floor spreading

   B. The origins of Earth

   C. The present locations of the continents

   (1) A only
   (2) B only
   (3) C only
   (4) A and B
   (5) A and C

2. Japan is located on a converging boundary between two ocean plates. In 10,000 years, what is the most likely fate for that island nation?

   (1) Nothing will happen to Japan.
   (2) Japan will most likely be underwater as the crusts form a trench.
   (3) Japan will be located 500 miles south of its present location.
   (4) Japan will most likely be on a large mountain as crust rises from the sea.
   (5) The fate of Japan cannot be predicted from the tectonic evidence.

Check your answers on page 248.

Land Forms

The topography of the surface of Earth is the result of forces within Earth and forces acting upon Earth. The internal high temperatures and pressures, as well as the forces of erosion and weathering, combine to give us Earth as we see it today. Most often, compression and tension forces from within Earth cause folding and buckling of the crust, while the forces of erosion are primarily responsible for smoothing the surface back down.

MOUNTAIN BUILDING

Mountains are as big below the surface as they are above. A foundation must exist within the crust for any landforms of significant elevation. The relative balance between the thickness of the crust above and below the surface is called **isostasy**. The average thickness of continental crust is approximately 45km (18 miles), but crust segments under mountain ranges can exceed 75km (30 miles).

Mountain building is a slow process taking tens of millions of years to accomplish. Mountain building results when forces within Earth move segments of crust so that a previously flat surface is reshaped. Mountain types fall into several major categories.

Folded mountains develop in regions where sedimentary and/or volcanic rock layers are slowly but steadily compressed. The result is a wavelike undulation in the surface, looking much like a rumpled carpet. Over time, these folds increase in size and complexity, often yielding some of the most spectacular mountains in the world. The Appalachians, Himalayas, Alps, and northern Rockies are all folded mountains.

Fault block mountains form where over time tensile forces are exerted along a crack in the crust. Fault block mountains are always bounded on at least one side by a normal fault of high-to-moderate angle. Gradual tensile forces stretch segments of crust, causing cracking and uplifting along the fault border. Two well-known mountain ranges in the United States that are comprised primarily of fault block mountains are the Tetons of Wyoming and the Sierra Nevada of California.

VOLCANOES

Erupting volcanoes are some of the most dramatic events in geology. The forces at work causing volcanic eruptions are the same as with all igneous activity: the material under the lithosphere is under a great deal of pressure at very high temperatures. Periodically, materials work to the surface and partially decrease pressure through eruptions. Volcanism is most evident in areas where the tectonic plates are weakest, such as under oceanic hot spots and along plate boundaries.

Magma, which is hot and therefore less dense than the solid lithosphere, rises and encounters areas of low resistance. The magma either follows the boundary line or melts a hole in the crust. When the magma reaches the surface and spills out onto the outer surface, an eruption occurs. Some eruptions are violent and spectacular, while others look like quiet seepage.

There are three basic types of volcanoes. Cinder cones contain thick, granitic magma, rich in both the mineral silica and water vapor. Eruptions from this type of volcano are almost always violent, throwing tons of ash, dust, and debris into the atmosphere. Shield cones contain much thinner magma with considerably less water vapor and silica. Magma during shield cone eruptions is often classified as basaltic and usually flows like a quiet river. Composite cones can experience both

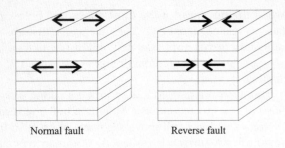

Normal fault   Reverse fault

Strike-slip fault

explosive and quiet eruptions. This happens due to moving currents within the magma below the volcano that changes the silica and water vapor content of the magma under the volcano. A general rule of thumb for violence of eruption is that the higher the water vapor and silica content of the magma, the more violent the eruption will be.

EARTHQUAKES

Just as volcanism is the result of pressures deep within Earth, so are earthquakes. Earthquakes are the vibrations caused by the shifting plates of Earth's crust. Movement of tectonic plates at their boundaries, or along smaller cracks called faults, can temporarily reduce the tension and compression forces created by the convection currents within the asthenosphere. Quakes usually occur along tectonic boundaries or existing faults, but sometimes they create new faults.

Faults are extensive cracks in rocks where crust segments slip or slide past one another. This motion is not steady but occurs in sudden jolts. The result of one of these slips causes large vibrations and tremors at the surface of Earth, producing an earthquake. Faults may or may not correspond to tectonic plate boundaries. The San Andreas Fault is an example of a fault that follows a plate boundary. **Normal faults** are cracks due to forces pulling a particular crustal plate away from another crust plate. **Reverse faults** are cracks due to forces pushing together two crust plates. **Strike-slip faults** are cracks where the particular crust plates are moving laterally against one another.

When quakes occur, three different types of seismic waves are produced. Primary waves (P waves) are compressive in nature and travel very fast. Damage from P waves tends to be moderate. Secondary waves (S waves) are transverse (side to side) and travel at an intermediate speed. Damage from S waves is slightly more extensive. Both P and S waves are body waves, meaning that they travel within the earth's crust. Surface waves travel along the surface and shake both up and down and side to side. Surface waves are the slowest, but they cause the greatest damage.

Exercise 5

Directions: Choose the one best answer for each item.

1. What type of mountains result from prolonged compressive forces on a section of lithosphere?

    (1) Volcanoes
    (2) Island chains
    (3) Fault block
    (4) Folded
    (5) Craters

2. An extinct volcano has a gradual slope and layers of fine-grained rock all around. You readily identify the fine-grained rock as basalt. The evidence you see suggests that this volcano was a(n)

    (1) cinder cone.
    (2) shield cone.
    (3) composite cone.
    (4) island volcano.
    (5) fault-block mountain.

Check your answers on page 248.

Earth's Past

The most reliable evidence places the age of Earth at approximately 4.5 billion years. This age has been established using radioactive dating methods. This type of dating, which determines the specific age of a geologic strata or sample, is called **absolute dating** and is relatively new.

Relative dating techniques, used prior to the widespread use of radioactive dating, are still used to sequence geologic events. Understanding the geologic history of a region requires an accurate means of sequencing events. Some very basic rules are used to establish the sequence of geologic events. The most important of these rules is the **Law of Superposition**. This most basic of rules states that all other factors being equal, geologic strata closer to the surface of Earth are younger than those beneath them. A second fundamental rule of relative dating is the **principle of original horizontality**. This rule states that sediments are deposited in flat horizontal sheets, all other factors being equal.

Another important concept in relative dating is the relative youth of **intrusions**. It is logical that when an igneous rock layer intrudes through another strata, it must be the younger. A fourth fundamental concept is the significance of **unconformities.** Unconformities, or breaks in the geologic record, result from a period during which erosion, rather than deposition, is the primary force molding the land.

FOSSILS

Fossils are geologic evidence of past life-forms. Fossils are found in geologic strata and can often provide clues as to the plants and animals living at the time that strata were formed. There are several types of fossils. Fossils can take the form of petrified remains, such as petrified wood, where the original organic material was replaced by minerals. They can also be the thin carbonaceous film left by the compressed body of the plant or animal. Mold and cast fossils form when sediments harden around an object, such as a shell, and later break open, leaving a mold of the original organism. Occasionally, the plant or animal dies and the entire body is preserved. An insect preserved in amber (petrified tree sap) is an example of this type of fossil. Trace fossils are the evidence of an organism's impact on the environment. These may be tracks, tooth marks, scratch marks, or evidence of nests.

Exercise 6

Directions: Use the diagram to answer items 1–3.

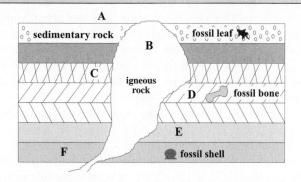

1. Which letter represents the oldest rock?

   (1) B
   (2) C
   (3) D
   (4) E
   (5) F

2. Which letter represents an intrusion?

   (1) A
   (2) B
   (3) C
   (4) D
   (5) E

3. Which statement about the area represented by the diagram is incorrect?

   (1) Many different types of fossils may be found there.
   (2) The sedimentary layers are older than the igneous rock.
   (3) The sedimentary layers have been tilted at an angle from their original position.
   (4) Layer F was underwater at one time.
   (5) Weathering is most likely taking place at the point indicated by letter A.

Check your answers on page 248.

Oceanography

The oceans cover approximately 71 percent of the surface of Earth. More than 80 percent of the Southern Hemisphere is ocean. Approximately 360,000,000km² of Earth is covered with oceans. Worldwide, the salinity of the oceans averages 3.5 percent. The primary salt in ocean water is sodium chloride (NaCl), common table salt.

Clearly defined currents circulate ocean water worldwide. These currents are primarily caused by global wind patterns and water temperature differentials. The currents help regulate temperature extremes in the oceans and within the atmosphere as well. Study the illustration to familiarize yourself with the locations of the world's oceans and continents.

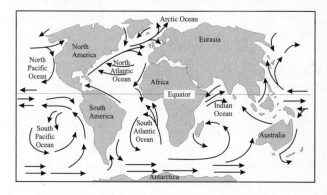

The continental margins are regions where the continents meet the oceans. The continental margins are, in turn, made up of a gently dipping continental shelf, a more steeply inclined continental slope, and (in some locations) a more gently dipping continental rise. The **continental shelf** extends outward from the coast to a depth of about 100 meters (325 feet). The continental shelf may have been dry land in the past during periods when the oceans were smaller. The continental shelf gives way to the continental slope, the true edge of the continent. The **continental slope** plunges steeply toward the ocean bottom, the **abyssal plain**, a region with a relatively constant depth of about 4 to 5km (3 miles). The abyssal plain is analogous to a desert on land, as it is a bleak and barren place. Most sea life and vegetation is clustered in the shallow water along the shores.

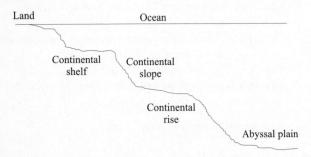

Common features of the sea floor include seamounts, ridges, and trenches. **Seamounts** are usually submarine volcanic peaks. When they reach above sea level, they form islands (the Hawaiian Islands are seamounts). **Mid-ocean ridges** form the longest linear feature on the planet's surface. Typically, mid-ocean ridges rise about 2.5km (1.5 miles) above the surrounding ocean floor and are 2km (1.2 miles) wide. They are areas of intense seismic and volcanic activity. It is here that new ocean crust is created as the sea floor spreads apart.

Ocean **trenches** are features where the depth can reach 11,000m, or 36,000 feet, although the average depth is 8,000m (26,000 feet). Trenches are long and relatively narrow (about 100km, or 60 miles). At trenches, two plates of Earth's crust are coming together, and one (always the denser oceanic crust) is descending back into the mantle, in a process called subduction.

Exercise 7

Directions: Choose the one best answer for each item.

1. The deepest part of the seafloor is called
    (1) a plain.
    (2) the continental slope.
    (3) the continental shelf.
    (4) a mid-ocean ridge.
    (5) a trench.

2. Of the following features of the sea floor, which are most directly caused by plate tectonics?
    A. Mid-ocean ridge
    B. Trench
    C. Abyssal plain
    (1) A only
    (2) B only
    (3) A and B only
    (4) A and C only
    (5) B and C only

3. The most likely reason that most ocean life is found in shallow water is
    (1) lack of predators.
    (2) presence of warm currents.
    (3) absence of human activity.
    (4) presence of sunlight.
    (5) pollution in deep waters.

Check your answers on page 248.

Meteorology

All life on Earth is dependent on the atmosphere. The atmosphere is composed primarily of three gases. Nitrogen gas (N_2) comprises about 78 percent, oxygen (O_2) makes up about 21 percent, and argon (Ar) about 0.93 percent of the atmosphere. Various other gases, including water vapor, comprise the rest.

One gas that forms a very small component in terms of abundance (only 0.035 percent) but has a big impact on weather and climate is carbon dioxide (CO_2). Carbon dioxide absorbs infrared radiation that leaves Earth's surface, resulting in the trapping of heat in the atmosphere. This process is known as the **greenhouse effect**. This is a natural process and is an important aspect of our atmosphere. Without it, our atmosphere would not be warm enough to sustain life as we know it, and our planet would probably be too cold for liquid water to exist.

However, human activity over the past century has increased and is continuing to increase the amount of carbon dioxide in the atmosphere. Extensive use of fossil fuels in cars, factories, and homes and the burning of rain forests have increased the level of carbon dioxide in the atmosphere. Many scientists now believe that this increase will cause the atmosphere to become warmer, perhaps too warm. This effect is termed **global warming**. If global warming is occurring, the changes could have significant consequences to human culture. Currently, it appears that the temperature of the atmosphere is rising. Increasing carbon dioxide levels are not exclusively responsible for this rise in temperature. Industrialization is thought to play a role in the amount of solar energy reflected back into the atmosphere as well.

Industrialization results in less forest areas and in more carbon dioxide in exhausts. Forests are important because the trees and other plants absorb CO_2 during photosynthesis and produce oxygen.

Another way human activities have an impact on the atmosphere concerns the ozone (O_3) layer. Ozone is a gas found in the upper atmosphere, where it filters harmful ultraviolet radiation from the sun. Without ozone, life could not exist on the surface of our planet. Human use of several chemicals has had a detrimental effect on the ozone layer. The best-known group of chemicals affecting the ozone layer are chlorofluorocarbons (CFCs), which are used as refrigerants and as propellants for aerosol sprays.

Layers of the Atmosphere

Earth's atmosphere is divided into four layers based on temperature gradient. The bottom layer, the **troposphere**, extends to an altitude of approximately 8 to 18 km (5 to 12 miles) and is characterized by an average decrease in temperature of 6.5°C per kilometer increase in altitude (3.5°F per 1,000 feet). It contains approximately 80 percent of the mass of the atmosphere. Virtually all clouds and precipitation form in and are restricted to this layer. Vertical mixing in this layer is extensive.

Above the troposphere and extending to about 50 km (30 miles) is the **stratosphere**. Here, the temperature remains constant to about 20km, then begins to increase with altitude. The stratosphere is important because it contains ozone (O_3), the gas that absorbs most ultraviolet light, keeping it from reaching Earth's surface and damaging life on the surface. The **mesosphere** lies above the stratosphere, and, here, as in the troposphere, temperatures decrease with increasing altitude. At about 80km (50 miles), the temperature is approximately −90°C (−130°F).

The layer above, with no well-defined upper limit, is the **thermosphere**. Here, temperatures rise again, due to the absorption of short-wave radiation by air molecules. Temperatures rise to 1,000°C (1,800°F).

Energy from the sun is the most important control over the weather and climate of Earth. Solar radiation accounts for virtually all the energy that heats the surface of Earth, drives the ocean currents, and creates winds.

Exercise 8

1. Which of the following gases is most common in Earth's atmosphere?
   - **(1)** Nitrogen
   - **(2)** Oxygen
   - **(3)** Argon
   - **(4)** Carbon dioxide
   - **(5)** Methane

2. Scientists believe that the greenhouse effect is responsible for a gradual increase in the average temperature of the atmosphere. The clearing of the rainforests worldwide is greatly contributing to this problem because

   A. burning of the forest increases carbon dioxide levels in the air.

   B. trees are primary consumers of carbon dioxide and producers of oxygen.

   C. animals in the rainforest are primary users of carbon dioxide.

   - **(1)** A only
   - **(2)** B only
   - **(3)** C only
   - **(4)** A and B only
   - **(5)** A and C only

Check your answers on page 248.

Weather

Weather results from the unequal heating of Earth's surface. The equator receives the strongest radiation from the sun, and the poles receive the least. Areas with more solar energy tend to be warmer than areas with less, and therefore the air at the equator is hottest and air at the poles is the coldest. Temperature differences also arise because the oceans and continents do not heat up equally. The movement of air, locally and worldwide, in an effort to equalize temperature, is the primary trigger for weather. The atmosphere is continually acting to redistribute solar energy from the equator toward the poles, and when air masses move, and air masses of different temperatures and water vapor content collide, weather happens.

An **air mass** is a large body of air with relatively uniform temperature and humidity. Air masses develop because of local conditions in their place of origin. The movement of air masses accounts for regional weather patterns. When two air masses of different characteristics collide, unstable weather conditions result as the two air masses mix. Rain, thunder, or violent winds can result when air masses mix. The boundary between the two air masses, where they interact, is called a **front**. When air masses collide, the warmer, less dense air mass always rises above the cooler, denser air mass, regardless of which of the masses was moving.

All air contains at least some water vapor. **Humidity** is a measure of the amount of water vapor in the air. The higher the air temperature, the more water vapor the air can hold. **Relative humidity** is a measure of the amount of water in the air in comparison with the amount it can hold. Relative humidity is expressed as the ratio of the current water vapor volume compared to the total water vapor capacity at a specific temperature. Water vapor condenses at the **dew point**, the temperature at which a given volume of water vapor causes saturation. Warm air can hold more water vapor than cold air can.

When air becomes saturated, clouds may form. Clouds are classified based on form and elevation. **Cirrus clouds** are high, thin, and usually made of ice crystals. **Cumulus clouds** are fluffy, often with a flat base. **Stratus clouds** appear as sheets that cover most of the sky. In addition, any storm cloud will carry the suffix "nimbus" in its name: thunderclouds are cumulonimbus clouds. Fog is generally classified as a cloud very near or at ground level.

Precipitation occurs when the atmosphere reaches saturation level for water vapor and attempts to reach equilibrium. Whenever the relative humidity exceeds 100 percent, precipitation is likely. While rain and snow are the most common forms of precipitation, there are others, such as hail and sleet.

Winds result from the unequal heating of the surface, moving from areas of higher atmospheric pressure (and lower temperature) to areas of lower atmospheric pressure (and higher temperature). Both localized winds and global winds follow this basic pattern. High-pressure centers occur when cool air sinks toward the surface and spreads out laterally. In low-pressure centers, air is warmer and rises upward in the troposphere. Fronts form at the boundaries of air masses that have different temperature and moisture characteristics; fronts are generally sites of active weather, such as storms and precipitation.

Exercise 9

> **Directions:** Choose the one best answer for each item.

1. The weather forecast calls for a cold front to move into your area overnight. If it is summer, what is the likely result?
   - **(1)** Humid weather for the next several days
   - **(2)** Rain as the front arrives
   - **(3)** Warmer weather as the front arrives
   - **(4)** Weather will be unchanged
   - **(5)** Hurricanes are likely

2. Thunderstorms occur on hot, humid days as a result of hot air rapidly rising and cooling. Thunderstorms often deposit heavy rains because
   - **(1)** storm clouds have high capacity for water vapor.
   - **(2)** rapidly cooling air loses much of its ability to retain water vapor.
   - **(3)** lightning is always accompanied by heavy rain.
   - **(4)** hail is much more common than rain with thunderstorms.
   - **(5)** thunderstorms are always short-lived.

Check your answers on page 248.

Hydrology

Hydrology is the study of water on the surface of Earth and in the ground. The amount of water on Earth is finite, although it takes many forms. Water may be in the ocean; the polar ice caps; or rivers, streams, and lakes on the surface of the continents. Water may also exist as vapor in the atmosphere or in the clouds.

The **hydrologic cycle** describes the movement of water on and within Earth. Ninety-eight percent of the water on Earth is found in the oceans. Most water that falls as precipitation comes originally from oceans. Water is taken into the atmosphere through evaporation in the form of water vapor. Some water vapor also reaches the atmosphere through transpiration, which occurs when green plants produce water vapor during photosynthesis. Condensation occurs when the air is saturated, causing the vapor to condense into water droplets or freeze into ice crystals. Precipitation occurs when the droplets or ice crystals become too heavy to stay suspended in the atmosphere and fall toward the surface.

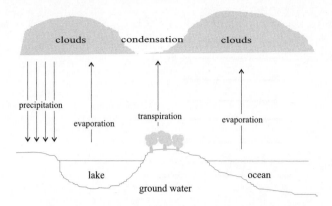

When precipitation falls on land, some water will stay above ground, where it forms runoff. Runoff water follows gravitational forces to feed river systems or collect in low areas. Standing water most often evaporates into the atmosphere. Other runoff collects to form streams, and these in turn feed rivers. Some runoff may go into lakes.

Water can also soak into the ground by infiltration and become groundwater. The level below which water in the ground is saturated is termed the **water table**. The depth of the water table depends on the climate of the area as well as the terrain and the nature of the rocks. In general, groundwater flows from areas of higher topography to areas of lower topography and flows toward the oceans, just as rivers do. The movement of groundwater is much slower than that of surface water.

Aquifers are layers of rock and sediment that contain water. Water can be pumped out of aquifers and used by people. A common aquifer material is poorly cemented sandstone. An **aquiclude** is a rock through which water is unable to flow. Examples of aquicludes are shale and granite. Aquicludes form the bottom of a water table.

WATERSHEDS

Rivers and streams are one of the means by which groundwater and precipitation eventually return to the sea. The network of streams and rivers that drains a particular portion of land is called a **watershed**. Some watersheds cover small areas, while others cover hundreds or thousands of square miles.

The primary force driving the movement of water on land is gravity. The origin of a stream or river is always at a higher elevation than the mouth of the river. The slope of the elevation a river moves through largely controls the velocity of its current. The steeper the slope, the faster the current of a river typically is. Over the course of time, rivers widen as erosion removes more and more material from the riverbank and geologic forces reduce the topographic slope.

Exercise 10

> **Directions:** Choose the one best answer for each item.

1. Water returns from Earth's surface to the atmosphere through

    A. transpiration.
    B. evaporation.
    C. precipitation.

    (1) A only
    (2) B only
    (3) C only
    (4) Both A and B
    (5) Both B and C

2. The force that drives the movement of water across and within the land is

    (1) inertia.
    (2) friction.
    (3) kinetic energy.
    (4) magnetism.
    (5) gravity.

Check your answers on page 248.

Astronomy

More has been learned about the solar system in the last thirty years than in all of our previous history. The ancient Greeks called Mercury, Venus, Mars, Jupiter, and Saturn "planets" or wanderers, because these heavenly bodies appeared to move across the sky in relation to the stars, which appeared fixed in their positions. The Greeks believed that Earth was at the center of the universe, and that the sun, the stars, and the other planets moved around it.

Over time, however, the Greeks' model was proved faulty. In 1543, the Polish astronomer Nicolaus Copernicus argued that all the planets, Earth included, traveled in regular circular paths, called **orbits**, around the sun. Copernicus argued that planetary motions were best explained with a sun-centered, or heliocentric, model. In the early 1600s, the German astronomer Johannes Kepler modified the Copernican heliocentric model to place the planets in oval-shaped, or elliptical, orbits.

At about the same time, the Italian inventor and astronomer Galileo Galilei discovered the existence of moons around Jupiter and rings around Saturn using a new invention called the telescope. This was the first direct proof that not all heavenly bodies directly orbit Earth. Galileo also discovered that Venus has phases and therefore must orbit a source of light (the sun), and planets, moon, and sun have surfaces that are imperfect and blemished. Galileo strongly supported the Copernican heliocentric model.

233

EARTH IN SPACE

Earth has two principal motions: rotation and revolution. **Rotation** is the spinning of Earth about its axis, the imaginary line running through the poles. Earth rotates once every 24 hours, producing the daily cycle of daylight and darkness. At any given time, half of Earth is experiencing daylight while the other half is experiencing darkness.

   Revolution is the motion of Earth around the sun. The distance between Earth and the sun averages about 150 million km (93 million miles). Earth's orbit is not circular but slightly elliptical. Each year on about January 3, Earth is 147km (91 million miles) from the sun, closer than any other time of the year (perihelion). On about July 4, Earth is 152km (94.5 million miles) from the sun, farther away than any other time of the year (aphelion). Even though the distance from the sun varies during the course of the year, this accounts for only slight variation in the amount of energy Earth receives from the sun and has little consequence on seasonal temperature variations.

Term	Definition	Diagram
rotation	the spinning of a body on its axis, like a top	axis
revolution	the movement of a body around another body	earth / sun

SEASONS

Probably the most noticeable aspect of seasonal variation is the difference in the length of daylight. Days are longest during the summer and shortest during the winter. However, this fact does not account fully for the seasons. Another factor that may not be as noticeable is the height of the sun above the horizon at noon. On the summer solstice, the longest day of the year, the sun is highest overhead at noon.

   The altitude of the sun affects the angle at which the sun's rays strike the surface of Earth, resulting in a difference in the intensity of solar radiation received from the sun. The more direct rays of summer result in more energy reaching Earth's surface. Also, the oblique rays must travel through more atmosphere before reaching Earth's surface, which means that they have more chance of being filtered, scattered, or reflected before reaching Earth's surface.

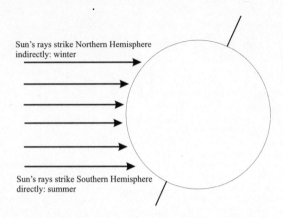

Sun's rays strike Northern Hemisphere indirectly: winter

Sun's rays strike Southern Hemisphere directly: summer

The revolution of Earth in its orbit around the sun causes this yearly fluctuation in the angle of the sun. Earth's axis is not perpendicular to the ecliptic (the plane of orbit around the sun) but is inclined at an angle of about 23° from the perpendicular. As Earth orbits around the sun, its axis remains pointed in the same direction (toward the North Star). As a result, the angle at which the sun's rays strike a given location on Earth changes continually. The more direct the solar rays, the warmer the weather.

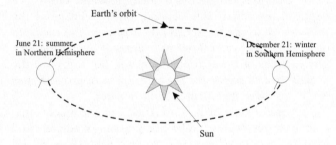

Earth's orbit

June 21: summer in Northern Hemisphere

December 21: winter in Southern Hemisphere

Sun

THE MOON

Earth has one natural satellite, the moon. Located about 384,400km (238,300 miles) from Earth, the moon orbits once every twenty-eight days. The moon is approximately one quarter the diameter of Earth, about 3,475km (2,150 miles). The moon has an average density of approximately 3.3g/cm³, roughly the same density as Earth's crust. The gravitational force on the moon is about ⅙ that of Earth. The moon completes one rotation as it revolves once around Earth. This is important, because it means that we always see the same side of the moon.

   Phases of the moon occur because the moon, as it orbits Earth, passes in and out of Earth's shadow. On nights when the moon is completely in Earth's shadow, the moon is said to be "new." As the moon passes out of Earth's shadow over successive nights, a larger and larger crescent is seen. This process is referred to as waxing. Eventually, all of the moon is visible and there is a full moon. During the second half of the month, the visible portion of the moon decreases in size, or wanes.

   Galileo observed the moon with his telescope in the early 1600s and noted that there seemed to be two distinct types of landforms. Galileo saw dark lowlands and bright, cratered highlands. Most of the lunar surface consists of densely cratered highlands. Because the moon has no atmosphere, and therefore no wind erosion, thousands of craters decorate the lunar surface. The smooth-appearing lowlands are much rarer and were later named *maria* ("seas" in Latin). The seas on the moon are actually large flats of basaltic lava that resulted from asteroid strikes millions of years ago.

Exercise 11

Directions: Choose the one best answer for each item.

1. Which of the following is a result of the rotation of Earth?
   (1) Day and night
   (2) Winter and summer
   (3) Spring and fall
   (4) The movement of continents
   (5) Different stars are visible in the Northern and Southern Hemispheres

2. What evidence did Galileo present against the geocentric model of the solar system?
   (1) Rings around Saturn
   (2) Phases of Venus
   (3) Moons of Jupiter
   (4) Irregular surfaces of the sun and moon
   (5) All of the above

3. During July, North America is farther from the sun than at any other time during the year, yet the average temperature is high throughout the continent. The best explanation is that
   (1) solar energy travels with the same concentration regardless of distance.
   (2) North America is receiving more direct sunlight due to Earth's axial tilt.
   (3) July is the Antarctic winter.
   (4) Northern Hemisphere oceans are better able to absorb energy in July.
   (5) all of the above are correct.

Check your answers on page 248.

The Sun

At the center of our solar system is the sun. Like all stars, the sun is made of glowing, burning hot gases. Although on the small side of average for a star, the sun appears large in our sky due to its relative proximity, only about 93 million miles. The sun is the largest body of the solar system. Its diameter is 109 Earth diameters, or 1,390,000 km (864,000 miles). Yet, because of the gaseous nature of the sun, its density is less than the solid Earth's, very closely approximating the density of water. The sun's composition is 90 percent hydrogen, almost 10 percent helium, and minor amounts of other heavier elements. The sun has a surface temperature of 6,000°C and an interior temperature estimated at 1,500,000°C. The source of the sun's energy is nuclear fusion. In the interior of the sun, a nuclear reaction occurs, converting four hydrogen nuclei (protons) into a single nucleus of helium. In this nuclear reaction, some of the mass of the hydrogen nuclei is converted into energy. This results in the release of a tremendous amount of energy.

The Solar System

The solar system was formed approximately five billion years ago. The accepted theory of the origin of the sun and planets is the **nebular hypothesis**. This hypothesis holds that a nebula, or cloud, of gas existed, consisting of approximately 80 percent hydrogen, 15 percent helium, and a small percentage of heavier elements. This cloud began to collapse or condense together under the influence of its own gravity. At the same time, the cloud had a rotational component to it, and, as its collapse continued, the rotational velocity increased. This rotation caused the nebula to form a disklike structure, and, within the disk, small nuclei developed from which the planets would eventually form. Most of the matter, however, became concentrated in the center, where the sun eventually formed.

As more and more matter collapsed inward, the temperature of this central mass began to rise due to compression. As the collapse continued, gravitational attraction increased, resulting in the increased compression and heating of the hydrogen gas. Eventually, the temperature became hot enough to begin nuclear fusion. The sun contains 99.85 percent of the mass of the solar system. The rest is found within the planets, moons, asteroids, and comets.

There are nine planets in the solar system. They are, in order of increasing distance from the sun, Mercury, Venus, Earth, Mars, Jupiter, Saturn, Uranus, Neptune, and Pluto (remember the mnemonic, "My Very Excellent Mother Just Served Us Nine Pies"). Based upon their gross physical characteristics, the planets fall within two groups: the terrestrial planets (Mercury, Venus, Earth, and Mars) and the Jovian (Jupiterlike) planets (Jupiter, Saturn, Uranus, and Neptune). Pluto is not included in either category, because its position at the far edge of the solar system and its small size make its true nature a mystery. The terrestrial planets are so called because of their Earthlike characteristics; all four are composed primarily of solid, rocky material. Size is the most obvious difference between the two groups.

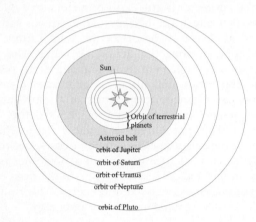

Exercise 12

> **Directions:** Choose the one best answer for each item.

1. The farther a planet is from the sun, the longer it takes to complete a revolution. The farthest planet, Pluto, takes 248 years to complete a revolution around the sun. Earth takes one year. Based on this information, how long would it take for Jupiter, located between Earth and Pluto, to revolve around the sun?

    (1) One day
    (2) Six months
    (3) One year
    (4) Twelve years
    (5) 250 years

2. The Jovian planets are much more massive than the terrestrial planets. Given this fact, what would be the effect on your weight upon landing on Saturn?

    (1) You would weigh the same on Saturn as on Earth.
    (2) You would weigh more on Saturn than on Earth.
    (3) You would weigh less on Saturn than on Earth.
    (4) You would become more massive, since Saturn is more massive.
    (5) Because Saturn is gaseous, you cannot land there.

Check your answers on page 249.

Stars

Our sun is the closest star to Earth. The next closest star is Proxima Centauri, approximately 4.3 light years away (about 25 trillion miles). The universe is very large, and stars, even close ones, are incredibly distant. Scientists believe that all stars have similar properties to our sun. They use a variety of criteria to classify and differentiate one star type from another. These criteria include stellar brightness (magnitude), color, mass, temperature, and size.

The magnitude of a star refers to its brightness. There are several reasons to explain a star's apparent dimness. **Apparent magnitude** is the observed brightness of a star as seen from Earth. **Absolute magnitude** is the true brightness of a star. With both scales, the lower the number (including negative numbers), the brighter the star. In general, a magnitude difference of 1 refers to a difference in brightness of 2.5. In other words, a star with a magnitude of 3 is 2.5 times brighter than a star with a magnitude of 4.

Temperature differences in stars are reflected in their colors. Very hot stars, with average surface temperatures of about 30,000°K, primarily emit short-wave radiation, which appears blue to the observer. Cooler stars, especially those with surface temperatures below 3000°K, emit longer wave radiation that is observed as red light.

The relationship of temperature, color, and magnitude is summarized in the Hertzsprung-Russell (H-R) diagram. Stars are plotted by luminosity and temperature. Generally speaking, the brightest stars are also the hottest, while the least luminous are the coolest. About 90 percent of all stars follow this relationship and fall into the so-called main sequence. In the H-R diagram below, the main-sequence stars appear from the upper left to the lower right. Our sun is a yellow main-sequence star, and its approximate location on the diagram is marked with the X. The stars in the upper left corner are blue giants, and those in the lower right are red dwarves.

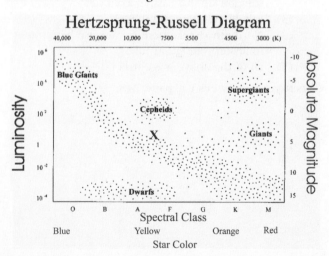

Exercise 13

Directions: Choose the <u>one best answer</u> for each item.

1. Star X has an absolute magnitude of 2. Star Y has an absolute magnitude of 4. Which statement is correct?

   (1) Star X is approximately five times brighter than Star Y.

   (2) Star Y is five times brighter than Star X.

   (3) Star X appears brighter than Star Y.

   (4) Star Y appears brighter than Star X.

   (5) Star X is a yellow main-sequence star.

2. Arrange the three types of main-sequence stars in order, from highest to lowest mass.

   A.   Yellow main-sequence stars

   B.   Blue main-sequence stars

   C.   Red main-sequence stars

   (1) A, B, C

   (2) B, C, A

   (3) C, B, A

   (4) B, A, C

   (5) A, C, B

Check your answers on page 249.

Glossary

absolute dating: dating method that establishes the actual age of a strata or sample

absolute magnitude: the true brightness of a star

abyssal plain: region of sea floor with a relatively constant depth of about 4 to 5 km (3 miles)

acceleration: the time rate at which velocity changes

acid: any ionic compound that has the hydronium ion, H^+, as its cation

air mass: a large body of air with similar temperature and humidity

amino acid: one of twenty different chemicals that proteins are made of

anabolic: a type of chemical reaction that builds molecules

anions: negatively charged atoms

apparent magnitude: the observed brightness of a star, as seen from Earth

aquiclude: rock through which water can flow

aquifer: layers of rock and sediment that contain water

asthenosphere: a plastic region of the upper mantle on which the lithosphere glides

astronomy: the study of the universe and Earth's relationship with it

atomic mass: the number of protons plus the number of neutrons in an atom of an element

atomic number: the number of protons in one atom of an element

atomic symbol: an element's one- or two-letter designation

ATP: adenosine triphosphate, the molecule that supplies immediate energy for many cellular chemical reactions

axon: long extension of neurons that transmit nerve impulses

base: any ionic compound with a hydroxide, OH^-, as its anion

behavioral ecology: study of the interaction between behavior and environment

binomial nomenclature: a system of two-part taxonomic names that designate genus and species

carbonate: a mineral that contains carbon

carnivore: an animal that eats only other animals

carrying capacity: maximum number of individuals of a species that a given environment can support

catabolic: a type of chemical reaction that breaks down molecules

cations: positively charged atoms

cell: basic unit of which all living things are composed

cell membrane: a cell's outer covering, made of protein, fat, and carbohydrate molecules

chemical change: change that results in a different type of matter

chemical properties: properties that, if changed, result in the formation of a different kind of matter

chemical reaction: combining different materials to create a new material

chemistry: the scientific study of matter

chlorophyll: the green pigment in plants that captures light energy

chloroplasts: organelles in plant cells that convert light energy into chemical energy in a process called photosynthesis

chromosome: long, thin, coiled packages of a DNA molecule and some proteins

cirrus clouds: high, thin clouds usually made of ice crystals

codon: the unit of three nucleotides that encodes an amino acid

conduction: transfer of heat between objects that are connected by a solid

consumer: the parts of an ecosystem that consume food produced by green plants

continental shelf: gently falling region of sea floor that extends outward from the coast to a depth of about 100 meters (325 feet)

continental slope: part of sea floor that plunges steeply toward the ocean bottom

convection: transfer of heat by movement of material from a hot region to a cold region

covalent compound: compound in which atoms share electrons

cumulus clouds: low, fluffy, fair-weather clouds

cytoplasm: material inside the cell membrane that contains the organelles

decomposer: living things, such as bacteria, fungi, and some insects, that break down and recycle dead organisms

demographer: a scientist who studies human population growth patterns

dendrite: short extension of nerve cell body that receives impulses

dew point: the temperature at which a given volume of water vapor causes saturation

earth and space science: the scientific disciplines that seek to understand Earth and space

electrolyte: compound that causes water to conduct electricity

electron: fundamental particle with a negative charge

element: a material that cannot be broken down into simpler materials

endoplasmic reticulum: canal system within the cell that helps produce, manufacture, and digest large chemical molecules

endothermic: chemical reaction that absorbs energy

energy: the ability to do work

enthalpy: the heat of a reaction

enzyme: protein molecule needed in very small amounts to bring about a chemical reaction

equilibrium: the condition when a reaction occurs in a mixture in both forward and reverse directions at the same time, resulting in no detectable change

erosion: the movement of rock or soil by forces of wind, water, and gravity

eukaryotes: cells that have a true nucleus and organelles

evolution: the gradual change in gene frequencies in a population over time

exothermic: chemical reaction that releases energy

experiment: method used to test a hypothesis by controlling all factors except the one under study

fault: extensive crack in rock caused by tectonic forces

fault block mountains: mountains formed by movements of Earth's crust

folded mountains: mountains formed by sidewise compression of rock layers

force: a motivation to move or to change motion

friction: the resistance to motion caused by the rubbing of surfaces against one another

front: the boundary between two air masses

gametes: reproductive cells, also called sperm and egg, each containing one half the number of chromosomes of nonreproductive cells

gene: segment of a DNA molecule that directs the cell to produce a specific protein

geology: the study of the solid Earth and the dynamic process that shapes its features

global warming: warming of the atmosphere caused by rising levels of atmospheric carbon dioxide released by human activities

greenhouse effect: trapping of heat in the atmosphere by carbon dioxide

halide: a mineral salt compound

heat: energy transfer due to a temperature difference

herbivore: an animal that eats only plants

hormones: chemicals produced by the body that act as messengers

humidity: a measure of the amount of water vapor in the air

hydrologic cycle: movement of water on and within Earth's surface

hydrology: the study of water on Earth's surface and underground

hypothesis: possible answer to a question posed by a scientist

igneous rock: rock formed as a result of the cooling and crystallization of lava or magma

inertia: the tendency of an object to remain either at rest or in motion

innate: inborn, or genetically determined

intrusion: an igneous rock layer that breaks through another strata

ionic compound: compound formed when one or more electrons are transferred from one atom to another

ions: all charged atoms, including cations and anions

isostasy: balance between the thickness of crust above and below Earth's surface

isotopes: atoms with the same atomic numbers but different atomic mass

kinetic energy: energy of motion

kinetics: the study of how quickly chemical reactions occur

lava: molten material located on Earth's surface

Law of Superposition: rule that states that geologic strata closer to the surface are younger than those beneath them

lithosphere: Earth's rocky shell, composed of the crust and upper mantle

magma: molten material located under Earth's surface

magnetism: a force that attracts metals and other magnets

mass: the amount of matter an object contains

matter: anything that has mass and occupies volume

mesosphere: layer of the atmosphere above the stratosphere

metabolism: the total of all physical and chemical reactions that occur in a cell

metals: elements that conduct electricity and heat well, are malleable, tend to be shiny, and tend to lose electrons in compounds

metamorphic rock: rock formed from heating and pressurization of existing rock

meteorology: the study of atmospheric processes, weather, and climate

mid-ocean ridge: area of ocean floor of intense seismic activity and sea-floor spreading

mineral: a naturally occurring inorganic solid with a definite chemical structure

mitochondria: organelles in plant and animal cells that carry out cellular respiration

mitosis: cell division that produces two cells identical to the original cell

mixture: a combination of two or more components

momentum: the principle that an object in motion tends to stay in motion, while an object at rest tends to remain at rest, unless acted upon by an outside force

mortality: death rate, or the number of deaths per 1,000 individuals per year

mutation: a sudden, unpredictable change in a gene

natality: birth rate, or the number of births per 1,000 individuals per year

natural selection: the tendency for members of a species that are genetically best suited to their environment to survive and reproduce

nebula: a cloud of space gas and dust

nebular hypothesis: theory that the solar system formed from a vast cloud of gas

neurons: nerve cells; cells in the nervous system that send and receive signals throughout the body

neutralization reaction: a reaction between an acid and a base, resulting in the formation of water and a salt

neutron: fundamental particle with a charge of 0 and a mass of 1

neutron star: dense object resulting from the collapse of the core of a supernova

nonelectrolyte: compound that does not cause water to conduct electricity

nonmetals: elements that do not conduct electricity or heat, are brittle and dull, and gain electrons in compounds

normal fault: fault resulting from crustal plates moving away from each other

nucleotide: one of four phosphate-sugar bases (adenine, thymine, cytosine, and guanine) that make up the "rungs" of the DNA ladder.

nucleus: dense core of an atom where neutrons and protons are found; part of a cell that contains the genetic material

oceanography: the scientific study of the oceans

omnivore: an animal that eats both plants and animals

orbit: an object's path around another object, such as a planet's path around the sun

organelles: highly specialized chemical structures within the cell

oxide: a mineral that contains oxygen

periodic table: a table that arranges elements according to the chemical properties

pH: an inverse measure of the concentration of hydronium ions; the lower the pH, the greater the number of hydronium ions and the more acidic the solution

pheromones: chemical signals exchanged between members of the same species

photosynthesis: the process by which green plants convert energy from the sun into sugar, water, and oxygen

phylogeny: branch of biology that studies how species are related

physical change: change that results in a change of state or of some other physical property

physical properties: properties that, if changed, do not fundamentally change the type of matter

physics: the scientific study of energy

plate tectonics: the theory that the surface of Earth is composed of large slabs of crust and upper mantle that are constantly shifting against each other.

potential energy: the energy stored in an object as the result of the height it has been raised above the ground

power: the rate at which work is done

principle of original horizontality: rule that states that sediments are deposited in flat horizontal sheets

producer: the parts of an ecosystem that produce food (green plants)

prokaryotes: ancient group of living things, composed of single cells and lacking a true nucleus

proteins: chemicals that are vital to life and exist in many forms in plants and animals

proton: fundamental particle with a positive charge and a mass of 1

pulsar: neutron star that sends out radio signals at regular intervals

radiation: transfer of heat by means of electromagnetic waves

radioisotopes: atoms that decay to become different elements, releasing radiation as they do so

relative dating: dating method that establishes the date of a sample in relation to that of another sample

relative humidity: a measure of the amount of water in the air in comparison with the amount the air can hold

resource: anything humans obtain from the environment to meet our needs

reverse fault: fault resulting from crustal plates moving toward one another

revolution: Earth's movement around the sun

ribosomes: structures within the cell that make proteins

risk-benefit analysis: an evaluation as to whether potential benefits outweigh potential hazards

rock: material composed of aggregates of different minerals

rotation: Earth's movement around its imaginary axis

science: a body of knowledge obtained through research, or a way of finding things out through research

scientific method: method of testing hypotheses

seamount: submarine volcanic peak

sedimentary rock: rock formed from sediments created by weathering and erosion

soil: a mixture of sand, silt, or clay; decaying organic matter; living organisms; air; and water

solute: the active ingredient in a solution

solution: a homogenous mixture

solvent: what the solute is dissolved in; the delivery medium for the solute

stem cell: cells in an embryo that have not yet become differentiated

stratosphere: layer of the atmosphere that contains ozone

stratus clouds: layered clouds that blanket the sky

strike-slip fault: fault resulting from crustal plates moving past one another

synapse: space between neurons across which impulses are conducted

taxonomy: branch of biology that groups species into a classification scheme

temperature: a measure of how hot or cold an object is

thermodynamics: the study of the movement of heat

thermosphere: top layer of the atmosphere

transcription: the process of copying the nitrogen base sequence in a strand of DNA to produce a strand of RNA

trench: long, narrow chasm in the ocean floor where two plates meet

troposphere: bottom layer of the atmosphere in which weather occurs

unconformity: a break in the geologic record

velocity: speed and direction

volume: the amount of space something takes up

water table: level below which water in the ground is saturated

watershed: network of rivers and streams that drains a particular area

weathering: the process whereby rock breaks down into small particles

weight: a force defined as mass times the acceleration caused by gravity

work: the use of force to move something over a distance

zygote: a fertilized egg

ANSWERS AND EXPLANATIONS

Unit 1: Life Science

Exercise 1 (page 187)

1. **The correct answer is (4). (Fundamental understandings)** A hypothesis is a possible answer to the problem or observation. Choice (1) is incorrect, because the conclusion usually leads to further questions. Choice (2) is incorrect, because a hypothesis is the result of observations (and the motivation for making future observations). Choice (3) is incorrect because the data are collected first and then a statistical analysis is done. Choice (5) is incorrect because a conclusion is drawn from the data collected.

2. **The correct answer is (3). (Science as inquiry)** A control group is always necessary in any experiment. The groups must be tested against a control, in this case a group of passengers who did not receive any special diet. Choice (1) is incorrect because the scientist's observations would have preceded the hypothesis. Choice (2) is incorrect because the age of the subjects in the experiment was not being tested (but the scientist should have considered age as a potential confounding variable). Choice (4) is incorrect because the time zones are not important as long as they remain constant between the groups. However, this would be important information to report so that future work can investigate any interaction between diet and number of time zones. Choice (5) is incorrect because the scientist could have included a high-fat diet, but it was not necessary and does not bias her results.

Exercise 2 (page 188)

1. **The correct answer is (1). (Fundamental understandings)** Atoms make up molecules, which make up organelles, which make up cells. Choice (2) is incorrect because skin is a complex organ composed of cells. Choice (3) is incorrect because the ER is composed of atoms and molecules. Choice (4) is incorrect because cells are composed of atoms and molecules, mitochondria, and chromosomes. Choice (5) is incorrect because ribosomes are composed of atoms and molecules.

2. **The correct answer is (5). (Fundamental understandings)** Chloroplasts are found only in plant cells and are responsible for photosynthesis. Choice (1) is incorrect because the ER is found in both plant and animal cells. Choice (2) is incorrect because mitochondria are found in both plant and animal cells. Choice (3) is incorrect because ribosomes are found in both plant and animal cells. Choice (4) is incorrect because nucleoli are found in both plant and animal cells.

Exercise 3 (page 190)

1. **The correct answer is (5). (Fundamental understandings)** Genes are segments of the DNA molecule. Choice (1) is incorrect because genes are located on chromosomes. Choice (2) is incorrect because genes are located in the nucleus, which is part of the cell that the plasma membrane encloses. Choice (3) is incorrect because genes regulate production of enzymes. Choice (4) is incorrect because genes regulate production of proteins.

2. **The correct answer is (1). (Fundamental understandings)** DNA is the molecule that regulates the cell and stores cellular information. Choice (2) is incorrect because the phospholipid layer is found in the plasma membrane. Choice (3) is incorrect because DNA is a molecule, not a chemical process. Choice (4) is incorrect because DNA is a molecule that initiates protein synthesis. Choice (5) is incorrect because ATP is the energy molecule, not DNA.

3. **The correct answer is (5). (Fundamental understandings)** In interphase, the cells grow to adult size, synthesize DNA, and store energy and materials for a new mitotic division. Choice (1) is incorrect because, while prophase may be a long phase, it is not the longest. Choices (2) and (3) are incorrect because metaphase and anaphase are both short. Choice 4 is incorrect because telophase, while longer than metaphase and anaphase, is not the longest.

Exercise 4 (page 191)

1. **The correct answer is (1). (Fundamental understandings)** Complementary base pairs are adenine—thymine and cytosine—guanine. Adenine and guanine cannot form a pair bond.

2. **The correct answer is (5). (Fundamental understandings)** Nucleotides consist of a sugar, a phosphate, and a nitrogen base. Choice (1) is incorrect because amino acids are components of proteins. Choices (2) and (3) are incorrect because purines and pyrimidines are both groups of nitrogen bases. Choice (4) is incorrect because deoxyribose sugar is the sugar molecule in DNA.

Exercise 5 (page 193)

1. **The correct answer is (2). (Fundamental understandings)** Uracil replaces thymine and so is complementary with adenine. Choice (1) is incorrect because uracil replaces thymine in RNA. Choices (3) and (4) are incorrect because cytosine and guanine are complementary. Choice (5) is incorrect because the phosphate group is not a nitrogen base.

2. **The correct answer is (3). (Fundamental understandings)** A codon is a group of three bases that encode an amino acid. Choice (1) is incorrect because a nucleotide is a unit of DNA. Choice (2) is incorrect because a chromosome is a molecule of DNA. Choice (4) is incorrect because tRNA is found in the cytoplasm. Choice (5) is incorrect because DNA is a polynucleotide.

3. **The correct answer is (1). (Fundamental understandings)** Meiosis occurs in the nucleus of the future gamete. Choices (2) and (4) are incorrect because meiosis occurs only in the nucleus of sex cells. Choice (3) is incorrect because meiosis is a special division found only in sex cells. Choice (5) is incorrect because chromosome division only occurs in the nucleus.

Exercise 6 (page 193)

1. **The correct answer is (4). (Unifying concepts and processes)** Gene frequencies cannot change if there is no genetic variability. Choices (1) and (2) are incorrect because evolution is more likely to occur in an unstable environment and requires genetic variability. Choice (3) is incorrect because mutations can enhance evolution. Choice (5) is incorrect because, as population increases, resources become limited. At this point, natural selection can lead to evolutionary change.

2. **The correct answer is (4). (Fundamental understandings)** A phylum is a group of related classes of organisms. Choice (1) is incorrect because a genus is a group of related species. Choice (2) is incorrect because a family is a group of related genera. Choice (3) is incorrect because an order is a group of related families. Choice (5) is incorrect because a kingdom is the largest group of organisms, such as plants, animals, or fungi.

3. **The correct answer is (3). (Fundamental understandings)** Natural selection is one force that can lead to evolution. Choice (1) is incorrect because natural selection is a force that is responsible for evolution. Choice (2) is incorrect because the relationship works the other way. Choice (4) is incorrect because, although they are related, they are not the same thing. Choice (5) is incorrect; they are related.

Exercise 7 *(page 195)*

1. **The correct answer is (3). (Fundamental understandings)** Only green plants carry out photosynthesis, the process that uses energy and nonliving materials to create nutrients. Decomposers, choice (1), release nonliving atoms and molecules into the environment. Carnivores, choice (2), use plant-made organic molecules to live. Choices (4) and (5) are types of animals that eat plants to obtain their organic molecules.

2. **The correct answer is (5). (Fundamental understandings)** The nonliving elements are vital parts of an ecosystem. Choices (1) and (3) are incorrect because it is the individual organisms that make up populations and communities that are parts of an ecosystem. The biosphere, choice (2), is not part of an ecosystem. It is the largest ecosystem, Earth. Choice (4) is incorrect because a social system refers to the interaction of animals in an ecosystem.

3. **The correct answer is (4). (Fundamental understandings)** Energy flows in only one direction through an ecosystem. Life depends on continual input of energy from the sun. Choices (1), (2), (3), and (5) are incorrect because energy does not cycle; it is used only once.

Exercise 8 *(page 196)*

1. **The correct answer is (4). (Unifying concepts and processes)** ATP is a quick-energy molecule formed in the mitochondria of all cells. Choice (1) is incorrect because energy does not recycle, and choice (2) is incorrect because energy can be neither created nor destroyed. Choice (3) is incorrect because animals do not receive energy directly from the sun but indirectly from plants. Choice (5) is incorrect because energy is required for all levels of organization.

2. **The correct answer is (4). (Fundamental understandings)** The products of photosynthesis are glucose (a carbohydrate), oxygen, and water. The raw materials of photosynthesis are carbon dioxide and water.

Exercise 9 *(page 197)*

1. **The correct answer is (3). (Unifying concepts and processes)** Behavior is controlled by the interaction of genes, hormones, and the nervous system. Choices (1), (2), (4), and (5) are incorrect because, although an organism does respond to the environment and to competition, its behavior is governed internally.

2. **The correct answer is (2). (Unifying concepts and processes)** Organisms that survive to reproduce will pass on their genes and their behaviors. Choice (1) is incorrect because natural selection works on all traits. Choices (3), (4), and (5) are incorrect because natural selection does not work within a single generation.

Exercise 10 *(page 199)*

1. **The correct answer is (1). (Science in personal and social perspectives)** Environmental resistance refers to the factors in the environment that limit populations. Choice (2) is incorrect, because catastrophic environmental changes may play a part in environmental resistance but are not the entire factor. Choices (3), (4), and (5) are incorrect because they do not refer to environmental resistance.

2. **The correct answer is (4). (Science in personal and social perspectives)** Human population has shown extremely rapid growth over the past 300 years.

Unit 2: Physical Science

Exercise 1 *(page 201)*

1. **The correct answer is (4). (Fundamental understandings)** The speedometer cannot measure direction, and hence it cannot measure velocity. It basically measures the speed at any one time, hence it cannot measure the average speed. The odometer measures the distance.

2. **The correct answer is (2). (Fundamental understandings)** Average driving speed is obtained by dividing travel distance, D, by travel time, t, expressed as $V = \dfrac{D}{t}$. In this problem, the travel distance is given as 240 miles. Total trip time is obtained by finding the time from 7 a.m. to 11:30 a.m., which is 4.5 hours. From this 4.5 hours, we need to deduct the 30-minute (0.5 hour) breakfast time, to find the travel time, which is therefore 4 hours. Dividing 240 miles by 4 hours will give 60 mph.

3. **The correct answer is (3). (Fundamental understandings)** Acceleration is the time rate at which the velocity changes. Hence, the answer is choice (3).

4. **The correct answer is (3). (Fundamental understandings)** Acceleration, a, is obtained by dividing the change in velocity by the time it took for that change, $a = \dfrac{\Delta V}{\Delta t}$. The change in velocity is 56 mph -0, or 56 mph. The time is 8 seconds. Hence, dividing 56 mph by 8 s gives 7 mph/s.

Exercise 2 *(page 202)*

1. **The correct answer is (1). (Fundamental understandings)** Inertia is the tendency of an object to remain either at rest or in motion. Newton's First Law of Motion is also known as the Law of Inertia.

2. **The correct answer is (3). (Unifying concepts and processes)** The downward force of the exploding fuel produces an equal and opposite reaction: the skyward movement of the rocket. Although the other statements are true explanations of situations in physics, they do not apply to this example.

3. **The correct answer is (4). (Unifying concepts and processes)** Newton's Second Law of Motion can be used to calculate the acceleration when the net force and mass are given. Acceleration is obtained by dividing the net force, 3270N, by mass, 1635kg. The answer is 2N/kg. Since N = kg m/s^2, N/kg is the same as m/s^2.

4. **The correct answer is (2). (Fundamental understandings)** The net force is the difference between the force exerted by the engine and the total frictional force. In other words, the total frictional force is equal to the difference between the force exerted by the engine and the net force. Hence, the total frictional force equals 4250N $-$ 3270N, or 980N.

Exercise 3 *(page 203)*

1. **The correct answer is (2). (Fundamental understandings)** The construction worker is moving the heaviest load and, according to the laws of physics, is doing the most work. None of the others is moving as heavy a load. The stranded motorist is not moving anything and thus is doing no work.

2. **The correct answer is (5). (Fundamental understandings)** The key point here is the stationary wall. Since the wall is not moving, no work is done on the wall, although Joe and John may have had a workout.

3. **The correct answer is (3). (Unifying concepts and processes)** Newton's Second Law gives us a relationship among force, mass, and acceleration: force = mass $\times$ acceleration. Inserting the units will give, N = kg m/s^2.

4. **The correct answer is (1). (Fundamental understandings)** The joule, J, is the unit for energy. Gravitational potential energy (PE) equals mass times gravity times height. Inserting the units will give, J = kg m/s^2 m = kg m^2/s^2.

245

Exercise 4 *(page 204)*

1. **The correct answer is (3). (Fundamental understandings)** The temperature is given in Celsius units, and we need to convert it to the Fahrenheit scale. The temperature conversion equation to use here is $T_f = \frac{9}{5}T_c + 32$. Evaluating this will yield 71.6, and rounding that answer will yield 72.

2. **The correct answer is (1). (Fundamental understandings)** First we need to convert the temperature to the Celsius scale, then to the Fahrenheit scale. Using $T_k = T_c + 273$ will yield a temperature of $-196°C$. Now using $T_f = \frac{9}{5}T_c + 32$ will yield $-320.8°F$.

3. **The correct answer is (2). (Unifying concepts and processes)** The person needs to convert all the energy from the drink to gravitational potential energy, E = mgh. The total height is given by E/mg = (140 × 4186)/(72 × 9.8) = 830.5m. The number of stairs is obtained by dividing the total height by the height of one stair, 18cm = 0.18m, 830.5/0.18 = 4614.

4. **The correct answer is (4). (Fundamental understandings)** Conduction and convection require a medium to transfer heat. Radiation is not affected by vacuum.

5. **The correct answer is (2). (Fundamental understandings)** Heat flows from a warm place to a cold place. None of the other choices reflects the Second Law of Thermodynamics.

Exercise 5 *(page 205)*

1. **The correct answer is (3). (Comprehension)** The human ear can detect sounds with frequencies from 20 to 20,000 hertz.

2. **The correct answer is (2). (Application)** The diagram illustrates frequency. Hertz is the unit used to measure frequency. The other terms are concepts in physics but are not related to the diagram in any way.

3. **The correct answer is (3). (Analysis)** High-frequency waves have shorter wavelengths. None of the other statements is accurate.

4. **The correct answer is (2). (Evaluation)** Curves in a mirror distort the reflected light rays. None of the other answers provides an explanation of the distortion.

Exercise 6 *(page 207)*

1. **The correct answer is (3). (Application)** Static electricity causes the crackling sound you hear when you comb your hair on a dry day. Choices (1), (4), and (5) have nothing to do with this phenomenon. There is low humidity in the air on a dry day, but low humidity does not make the crackling sound as suggested in choice (2).

2. **The correct answer is (4). (Evaluation)** A charge of 1,000 coulombs divided by 10 seconds equals 100 amps. None of the other situations would produce this answer.

3. **The correct answer is (2). (Analysis)** The magnetic north pole is at a slightly different location from the geographic North Pole, so even when standing at the most northern place on the earth, you would not see the magnet pointing straight down. Neither temperature nor distance from the pole would affect this. Choices (4) and (5) are not true.

4. **The correct answer is (5). (Analysis)** The nails fall to the ground because the magnetic field of the magnet becomes weaker as it is pulled away from the nails. There is no evidence to support choice (1). The force of gravity pulls the nails to the floor—not the magnetic field of the earth, as described in choice (2). Choices (3) and (4) are not true.

5. **The correct answer is (2). (Evaluation)** A potential difference of 110 volts divided by 10 amps = 11 ohms. All of the other circuits have different resistance values.

6. **The correct answer is (3). (Comprehension)** Resistance is the term that means opposition to the flow of electric current. The other terms, although relevant to the subject of electricity, have different meanings.

7. **The correct answer is (2). (Comprehension)** Thick wire offers less resistance than thin wire. When you replace a thin wire with a thicker one, the resistance in the circuit goes down. Choices (1), (3), and (4) would increase the resistance. Choice (5) would stop the flow of electricity.

8. **The correct answer is (4). (Application)** The plastic coatings insulate the wires so that electricity is confined to the wires. In preventing the electric current from passing through alternate paths, the plastic covering acts as an insulator.

9. **The correct answer is (2). (Application)** The amp gauge measures electric current. Starting your car initiates the flow of electricity from the battery to the starter, which is a drain on electric current from the battery. Once the alternator begins working, it feeds electric current back to the battery, and you see the amp gauge move to "+."

Exercise 7 *(page 209)*

1. **The correct answer is (1). (Fundamental understandings)** Sand, water, and food all have mass and volume. Air might seem like the correct answer, because, even though it has volume, it seems as though it does not have mass. In fact, air does have mass (which gives rise to air pressure); it is just difficult to measure. Light, on the other hand, does not have volume or mass. Therefore, light cannot be matter.

2. **The correct answer is (2). (Fundamental understandings)** There is some fluctuation in the graph, but the points seem to line up well. These minor fluctuations are caused by random error; we could still draw a pretty good line through all of them. Choice (1) is incorrect because it is not precise enough.

Exercise 8 *(page 211)*

1. **The correct answer is (5). (Unifying concepts and processes)** The car either has more mass or was moving faster than the truck. Typically, cars are lighter than trucks, but we cannot discount the possibility that, despite its size, the truck is lighter and the car is heavier. Either way, the car must have greater momentum, which can be achieved either by having greater velocity and less mass or by having greater mass and equal or less velocity.

2. **The correct answer is (4). (Fundamental understandings)** Your dance partner does not change in mass (or weight), so it cannot be more or less mass or weight. What's more, although the mass is related, it's your partner's weight (the force pressing on your foot) that will cause the pain. If we divide the force (in this case the weight) by the area (smaller for the heel), we have pressure (weight per unit volume). The smaller the area, the greater the pressure.

Exercise 9 *(page 214)*

1. **The correct answer is (4). (Fundamental understandings)** It is attracted to the negative plate, but only slightly, implying it has a negative charge and is heavy.

2. **The correct answer is (2). (Fundamental understandings)** If the particles are spread out as in a cloud, the beam should have passed through them without hindrance. What's more, Rutherford's experiment did not address what particles were present; it merely addressed the structure of these particles.

Exercise 10 *(page 216)*

1. **The correct answer is (1). (Fundamental understandings)** Recall that the number of protons is the atomic number of the element, and the element with atomic number 32 is Germanium.

2. **The correct answer is (2). (Fundamental understandings)** For unstable elements like Americium, the integer represents the atomic mass number of the most stable isotope, in this case 243, but the atomic mass number is equal to the number of protons plus the number of neutrons. Thus, we have $243 - 95 = 148$ neutrons.

3. **The correct answer is (2). (Fundamental understandings)** Antimony is actually a metalloid.

Exercise 11 *(page 218)*

1. **The correct answer is (4). (Unifying concepts and processes)** The helium is moving faster than the argon. The gases are at the same temperature, so one cannot be cooling the other. However, we know that they must have the same kinetic energy if they are at the same temperature (not the same velocity). Because kinetic energy is related to mass, the lighter gas (helium) would have to be moving much faster than the heavier gas (argon). One should note, by the way, that the helium atoms would not be moving ten times faster just because argon is ten times heavier; the relationship between velocity and kinetic energy is not linear. (In fact, the helium would have to be moving only about three times faster to have the same kinetic energy.)

2. **The correct answer is (5). (Unifying concepts and processes)** Red absorbs blue light, and blue is higher energy than red. We know the paint is not emitting light, because we require light to be able to see it. Thus, the light is being absorbed. The only color we see is that which is reflected; therefore, the color absorbed is the color we do not see, which is blue, and as stated previously, blue light has more energy than red light. Because the color red is absorbing the higher energy light, it fades before the color blue.

Exercise 12 *(page 219)*

1. **The correct answer is (2). (Fundamental understandings)** We cannot speak of the kinetic energy; this is a function of temperature alone, and temperature is not given. However, the weaker the intermolecular forces, the weaker the molecules must be held in the liquid, and therefore, the more molecules that will "escape" the liquid into the gaseous state.

2. **The correct answer is (4). (Fundamental understandings)** We can see that the material assumes the shape of the container but does not occupy its entire volume. We cannot infer if this is a compound or an element since there are examples in all three states for both.

Exercise 13 *(page 220)*

1. **The correct answer is (5). (Fundamental understandings)** Because it is cloudy, more than one component must be present. This is not a solution, though, because the cloudiness is created by undissolved solute particles.

2. **The correct answer is (1). (Fundamental understandings)** If we know there is already solute present, and if it is clear, then it must be a solution. Because additional solute will dissolve, it cannot be saturated; it must be unsaturated.

Exercise 14 *(page 222)*

1. **The correct answer is (5). (Unifying concepts and processes)** We cannot say whether it is giving off heat, but notice that we start with an aqueous substance (remember that aqueous means "dissolved in water"; it is a condensed state) and end up with a liquid and a gas. Conversion from a condensed state to a gas alone would lead us to suspect an increase in entropy (greater disorder), and the breakdown of one substance into two is an increase in entropy as well.

2. **The correct answer is (4). (Fundamental understandings)** Notice that there are two sodium atoms on the product side, but only one as a reactant. Other elements are off-balance as well, but sodium is the easiest to spot.

3. **The correct answer is (3). (Fundamental understandings)** In all other processes, a chemical reaction will occur, but in the solution, we had salt and water already, only dissolved. After the process, we still have salt and water, only as a solid and a vapor.

Exercise 15 *(page 223)*

1. **The correct answer is (5). (Fundamental understandings)** The reaction is endothermic in the forward direction. If we increase temperature, the equilibrium will shift to try to absorb that excess heat; this means we will favor the endothermic direction, or the products.

2. **The correct answer is (3). (Fundamental understandings)** Remember that at equilibrium, the forward and reverse reactions do not stop; however, the rate of the forward reaction is equal to the rate of the reverse reaction. Also, one cannot assume anything about the equilibrium concentrations: some equilibrium reactions have a large amount of product compared to reactant, but some have a large amount of reactant compared to product, and some have similar concentrations of both. Choice (4) is incorrect because this statement does not assume anything about the concentrations. However, even in this case, when no observable change is occurring, the reaction still does not stop.

Exercise 16 *(page 223)*

1. **The correct answer is (3). (Fundamental understandings)** A pH of less than 7 is acidic, greater than 7 is basic, and about 7 is neutral.

2. **The correct answer is (2). (Unifying concepts and processes)** An acid and a base forms a salt. The base that causes the fishy smell becomes part of a salt (a citrate salt, named for the citric acid). Because salts are not as volatile as bases (they do not evaporate as readily), the fishy smell is reduced.

Unit 3: Earth Science

Exercise 1 *(page 224)*

1. **The correct answer is (4). (Unifying concepts and processes)** Of the reasons supplied, only A and B involve heat. Warm oil and hot air are both evidence of heating.

2. **The correct answer is (3). (Fundamental understandings)** According to the text, the lightest layer of materials formed on the outside and the denser minerals sank into Earth. The outer layer of Earth is the crust.

Exercise 2 *(page 225)*

1. **The correct answer is (2). (Fundamental understandings)** The definition of a mineral states that the substances forming a mineral must have a nonliving source. Petrified wood certainly has a living origin, choice (2). Crystal structure, choice (3), and chemical composition, choice (1), are useful to identify types of minerals. Choices (4) and (5) are also incorrect.

2. **The correct answer is (2). (Fundamental understandings)** Sedimentary rocks form under water or when water evaporates; therefore for sandstone to be present, water must have been present in the past. Volcanism, choice (1), is related to igneous rocks and heat and pressure. Choice (3) is associated with metamorphic rocks. Choice (4) ignores that sandstone was identified in the question. Choice (5) is the result of crustal movements.

Exercise 3 *(page 226)*

1. **The correct answer is (5). (Fundamental understandings)** Wind, water, and gravity are all significant agents of erosion. On a barren slope with no vegetation to assist in stabilizing the soil, all three would have dramatic effects.

2. **The correct answer is (3). (Fundamental understandings)** By definition, weathering caused by tree growth would be classified as biological in origin.

Exercise 4 *(page 227)*

1. **The correct answer is (5). (Science as inquiry)** The theory of plate tectonics was developed to explain the reasons for evidence suggesting the surface of Earth was constantly moving. Geologic evidence shows continental shift over millions of years and changing dimensions for the sea floor, statements A and C. Plate tectonics does not address the origin of Earth, statement B.

2. **The correct answer is (2). (Science in personal and social perspective)** Converging plates either cause mountains or trenches. Mountain building, choice (4), typically occurs when continental crusts are involved. Japan is on oceanic crust, and compression at oceanic plates usually results in trenches. Japan does actually sit on a plate boundary where trenching is taking place. Choice (2) is the result of trenching over some years. No evidence suggests lateral movement, choice (3), is expected; and choices (1) and (5) are incorrect.

Exercise 5 *(page 228)*

1. **The correct answer is (4). (Fundamental understandings)** Folded mountains are the result of compressive forces. Fault block mountains, choice (3), are the result of pulling forces, and volcanoes, choice (1), are the result of Earth's internal heat.

2. **The correct answer is (2). (Fundamental understandings)** Shield cones are characterized by large-diameter cones with gradual slopes that produce basaltic lava. Cinder cones, choice (1), typically produce granitic lava and have a much steeper slope profile. Composite cones, choice (3), can have basaltic lava for periods but will often have evidence of granitic lava as well.

Exercise 6 *(page 229)*

1. **The correct answer is (5). (Fundamental understandings)** The principle of superposition states that the lowest strata were laid down first. Therefore, letter F, the bottom layer, represents the oldest rock.

2. **The correct answer is (2). (Fundamental understandings)** Letter B represents an igneous intrusion. Intrusions that break through rock layers, as shown, are younger than the rock in which they are found.

3. **The correct answer is (3). (Science as inquiry)** This question brings together all of the information on Earth history and fossils in the text. Choice (1) is correct, because the diagram shows at least three different types of fossils. Choice (2) is correct, because we know that intrusions are younger than the surrounding sedimentary layers. Choice (3) is incorrect, because the sedimentary layers are horizontal, as they were when they were laid down. Choice (4) is correct, because the fossil shell suggests that the area was once underwater. Choice (5) is correct, because weathering has revealed the top of the igneous intrusion at the surface.

Exercise 7 *(page 230)*

1. **The correct answer is (5). (Fundamental understandings)** The text states that trenches are the deepest feature on the ocean floor. The abyssal plain, choice (1), is also deep, though not as deep as the average depth of a trench.

2. **The correct answer is (3). (Fundamental understandings)** Trenches are areas where one plate is moving under another, and mid-ocean ridges are areas where plates are moving apart. Therefore, both are examples of tectonic features.

3. **The correct answer is (4). (Unifying concepts and processes)** Life is abundant in shallow seas because the penetration of sunlight allows plants to grow, and all animal life is dependent on plant life. Choice (1) is incorrect because the absence of predators is the result, not the cause, of lack of living things. Choice (2) is incorrect because both warm and cold currents can support life. Choice (3) is incorrect because most human activity actually takes place in shallow coastal waters. Choice (5) is incorrect because both deep and shallow ocean waters are now polluted.

Exercise 8 *(page 231)*

1. **The correct answer is (1). (Fundamental understandings)** Choice (1), nitrogen is approximately 78 percent of the atmosphere. Choice (2), oxygen, is about 21 percent of the atmosphere. Argon, choice (3), comprises about 0.93 percent of the atmosphere. All other gases, (choices (4) and (5) make up the remaining 0.7 percent.

2. **The correct answer is (4). (Fundamental understandings)** Trees are important because photosynthesis uses carbon dioxide and produces oxygen, statement A. In addition, burning of trees releases carbon dioxide into the atmosphere, statement B. Animals are producers of carbon dioxide, not consumers, statement C. Statements A and B are true, so the correct answer is choice (4).

Exercise 9 *(page 232)*

1. **The correct answer is (2). (Fundamental understandings)** Fronts are most commonly accompanied by rain, due to the instability caused by mixing of air masses of different temperatures and water vapor contents. Choice (3) might be an option except during summer air temperature is fairly high, with associated high water vapor content in the air. When that warm air meets the colder air at the front, the temperature drop releases large amounts of water into the air.

2. **The correct answer is (2). (Fundamental understandings)** Rapidly cooling air has a suddenly decreased capacity to retain water vapor. The resulting condensation within the clouds releases large quantities of rain.

Exercise 10 *(page 233)*

1. **The correct answer is (4). (Fundamental understandings)** According to the text, water reaches the atmosphere from Earth's surface through evaporation and transpiration. Therefore, choice (4), A and B, is correct. Precipitation is the term for water that reaches the surface of Earth from the atmosphere.

2. **The correct answer is (5). (Unifying concepts and processes)** Gravity, which makes objects move toward the center of Earth, causes water to move downward. This is ultimately responsible for the flow of rivers and for the movement of water toward the oceans.

Exercise 11 *(page 235)*

1. **The correct answer is (1). (Fundamental understandings)** As Earth rotates, it is day on the side that faces the sun. Choices (2) and (3) are incorrect because the seasons do not depend on daily rotation of Earth. Choice (4) is unrelated to rotation. Choice (5) is a function of what part of the galaxy the hemisphere is facing.

2. **The correct answer is (5). (History and nature of science)** Each of the four listed statements is a piece of evidence that Galileo presented in support of heliocentrism and against the older theory of geocentrism.

3. **The correct answer is (2). (Unifying concepts and processes)** The angle of sunlight is the most significant factor in the warming of the atmosphere. Higher concentrations of solar energy are obtained when the light is most direct and the least amount of atmosphere is penetrated. During July in North America, the sun is most direct. Choice (1) is correct in that the energy is unchanged by space travel, but it does not account for the important fact that it must disperse over a wider region with longer distance. In addition, the more atmosphere that is penetrated, the more energy that is reflected prior to reaching the ground. Choice (3) is correct but irrelevant to the question, and choice (4) is inaccurate.

Exercise 12 *(page 236)*

1. **The correct answer is (4). (Fundamental understandings)** According to the information supplied, the time it takes for Jupiter to revolve around the sun should be between that of Earth (1 year) and that of Pluto (248 years). Only choice (4) fits this information.

2. **The correct answer is (2). (Unifying concepts and properties)** Weight is a measure of the force of gravity. More massive objects exert more gravitational force. Given that Saturn is much more massive than Earth, a person would weigh much more on Saturn than on Earth. Choice (4) is incorrect because although weight changes on different planets, mass does not.

Exercise 13 *(page 237)*

1. **The correct answer is (1). (Unifying concepts and processes)** The brighter the star, the lower the magnitude. Because every increase in absolute magnitude of 1 means that a star is 2.5 times dimmer, a star of magnitude 4 is five times dimmer than a star with a magnitude of 3. Choice (2) is the opposite of the correct answer. Choices (3) and (4) are incorrect because a star's absolute magnitude tells you nothing about its apparent magnitude. Choice (5) is unsupported by the text.

2. **The correct answer is (4). (Fundamental understandings)** Highest in mass are blue main-sequence stars, next most massive are yellow main-sequence stars, and least massive are red main-sequence stars.

PART IV
LANGUAGE ARTS, READING

What Will I Find on the Language Arts, Reading Test?

The GED Language Arts, Reading Test—Test 4 on the GED—measures your ability to understand, analyze, and respond to ideas found in works of literature and in business and how-to documents. In other words, you will interpret thoughts, feelings, and ideas expressed in writing by other people. The following information will help you understand what you will find on the Language Arts, Reading Test.

The GED Language Arts, Reading Test is *not* a measure of how much you know about literary history, techniques, or writers. It does *not* ask you to identify writers or to remember when a work of literature was written. The Visual component passages do *not* test your knowledge of art history. Finally, the test does *not* include trick questions designed to make you doubt your impressions and opinions about a literature passage. Most questions on the test ask you to think logically and carefully about what a written passage is communicating to you.

The Language Arts, Reading Test includes two major content areas, Literature and Nonfiction. These are further broken down into the following categories:

- **Literature** includes fiction, poetry, and plays. Literature, which makes up 75 percent of the test, is broken down into three time periods:

  - *Pre-1920*

  - *1920 to 1960*

  - *1960 to the Present*

All time periods will be included on the test.

- **Nonfiction** makes up 25 percent of the test and includes two major types of passages:

  - *Viewing component,* which consists of detailed descriptive prose. Questions will test your understanding of the descriptions in the passage.

  - *Business-related document,* such as an employee handbook or instructions for using hardware or software. Questions will test your ability to understand and follow directions.

The test will include both types of documents, viewing and business-related.

The test you take will consist of forty multiple-choice questions. Each set of questions relates to a literature passage that is 300–400 words long or a poem that is eight to twenty-five lines long. To give you an idea of what each passage is about, each passage begins with *a purpose question.* For example, a passage about applying for a job might have the question, How Do You Submit Your Application? This question helps you to focus on the central idea of the passage even before you begin to read it.

Each of the forty questions on the test is multiple choice and has five answer choices. These questions are based on four different learning objectives: *Comprehension,* or understanding; *Application,* or using information learned from the passage; *Analysis,* or understanding literary language; and *Synthesis,* or grasping overall or underlying meanings. You may be asked to identify the passage's main idea, to determine a character's motives or feelings, or to define a term.

Comprehension questions comprise approximately 20 percent of the test. Application questions account for approximately 15 percent. Analysis and Synthesis questions each comprise 30 to 35 percent of the test. Therefore, more than half the test is designed to measure these higher-order thinking skills.

Read the following passage, an excerpt from a novel. Then take a look at the questions that follow. One question of each type is given here, along with the right answers and detailed explanations.

WHAT IS THE KEY TO THE MYSTERY?

Line Although it was midafternoon, it was nearly as
dark as a summer night. The ship swayed uneasily
at her anchor as the wind howled around her, the
rigging giving out musical tones, from the deep
5   bass of the shrouds to the high treble of the
running rigging. Already the snow was thick
enough to blur the outlines of the objects on
deck. . . . The officer of the watch stood shivering
in the little shelter offered by the mizzenmast
10   bitts, and forward across the snow-covered deck a

few unhappy hands crouched vainly seeking shelter under the high bulwarks.

15 The two officers who emerged upon the quarter-deck held their hats onto their heads against the shrieking wind. The shorter, slighter one turned up the collar of his heavy coat and attempted instinctively to pull the front of it tighter across his chest to keep out the penetrating air. As he spoke in the grey darkness he had to 20 raise his voice to make himself heard, despite the confidential nature of what he was saying.

"It's your best chance, Peabody."

The other turned about and stood to windward with the snow driving into his face 25 before he answered with a single word.

"Aye," he said.

—From *The Captain from Connecticut,*
by C. S. Forester

1. Based on the information in this passage, when and where does this scene take place?

    (1) On a ship on a summer night
    (2) On a ship on a winter afternoon
    (3) On a ship on a winter night
    (4) On a ship on a summer afternoon
    (5) In an inn on a winter afternoon

The correct answer is (2). The first paragraph reveals the answer to this *Comprehension* question. The passage states that "although it was midafternoon, it was nearly as dark as a summer night," so we know it is afternoon. Later we learn that snow is falling, so we know it is winter. In the second sentence, we learn that "the ship swayed uneasily," and many other nautical details are given as well. Careful attention to these details reveals that the correct answer is choice (2).

2. Based on what we learn about Peabody at the end of the passage, we can tell that, in a dangerous situation, he would be likely to

    (1) run away.
    (2) try to talk his way out.
    (3) act decisively.
    (4) ask for help.
    (5) pray for guidance.

The correct answer is (3). This *Application* question directs your attention to the end of the passage, lines

14-16. Note that when his companion hints at danger, Peabody faces directly into the storm and answers with a single word, "Aye." These are not the actions of a man who is likely to run away, to use his verbal abilities, or to rely on others for assistance. The best choice is (3)—Peabody would be likely to act decisively to face the danger directly.

3. Which phrase from the passage is an example of personification?

    (1) "It was nearly as dark as a summer night."
    (2) "The deep bass of the shrouds . . ."
    (3) "The shrieking wind . . ."
    (4) "Stood shivering in the little shelter . . ."
    (5) "The ship swayed uneasily . . ."

The correct answer is (5). Later in this section, we will discuss various figures of speech in detail. Personification means describing something that is not human in human terms. In this case, choice (5) describes the ship as swaying "uneasily," a feeling that applies only to humans, so it is the correct choice.

4. What is likely to happen next in this novel?

    (1) Peabody will attempt a daring and reckless exploit.
    (2) Peabody will report his friend for spying.
    (3) The two officers will seek shelter from the storm.
    (4) The two officers will tell the sailors to go inside.
    (5) The sailors will turn against the officers.

The correct answer is (1). This Synthesis question asks you to consider the overall feeling of the passage, as well as details of character and plot. To *synthesize* means to mix things together to create something new, and synthesis questions ask you to create a new understanding of a reading passage by bringing together all the clues at your disposal. In this case, details of the setting—the ship is "swaying uneasily"—and of the characters' actions point to a daring and reckless exploit, so choice (1) is the correct answer. The first speaker's words, "It's your best chance," hint that it isn't much of a chance, so something dangerous is afoot. Peabody's stance, with the snow driving into his face, indicates that he will face danger. The other choices are not indicated by the details of the passage.

Unit 1

FICTION

In this unit, you will practice reading and interpreting **fiction**, or made-up stories about imaginary people and events. The examples of fiction you read may be contemporary or classic, old or new, but all are works of imagination. In fiction writing, writers use imaginative language, choosing words carefully to create atmospheric and meaningful effects, as we saw in the passage in the previous section.

Finding a Topic and Main Idea

No matter what you are reading—a story, a memo from your boss, a letter from a friend, or a passage on the GED test—the first thing you'll want to know is "What is this about?" In other words, what is the topic? The topic of a story is simply its subject. Identifying the topic will lead you to the writer's main idea. The **main idea** is the central point or idea that the writer wants to communicate. A main idea may be stated directly, or it may be unstated but strongly suggested.

Like a stated main idea, an unstated or implied main idea also conveys the writer's most important point. To identify an unstated main idea on the GED test, ask yourself these questions:

- What is the topic? How can I tell?
- What do the supporting details say about that topic?
- What central idea or point do the details make clear?

If a main idea is stated directly, it often appears in the first or last sentence of a passage. The rest of the sentences in the passage contain **supporting details** that give more information about the main idea.

Exercise 1

Directions: Items 1 and 2 refer to the following passage from a novel. As you read the passage, ask yourself, "What is the author's topic?" Then answer the questions.

HOW ARE GUIDO AND VINCENT RELATED?

Line   Guido Morris and Vincent Cardworthy were third cousins. No one remembered which Morris had married which Cardworthy, and no one cared except at large family gatherings when this topic
5   was introduced and subject to the benign opinions of all. Vincent and Guido had been friends since babyhood. They had been strolled together in the same pram and as boys were often brought together, either at the Cardworthy house in Petrie,
10   Connecticut, or at the Morris's in Boston, to play marbles, climb trees, and set off cherry bombs in trash cans and mailboxes. As teenagers, they drank beer in hiding and practiced smoking Guido's father's cigars, which did not make them sick, but
15   happy. As adults, they both loved a good cigar.
        At college they fooled around, spent money, and wondered what would become of them when they grew up. Guido intended to write poetry in heroic couplets, and Vincent thought he might
20   eventually win the Nobel Prize for physics. In their late twenties they found themselves together again in Cambridge . . .

—From *Happy All the Time,* by Laurie Colwin

1. What is this passage mostly about?
    (1) The Cardworthy house in Petrie, Connecticut
    (2) The Cardworthy and Morris families
    (3) The friendship between Guido and Vincent
    (4) Guido and Vincent's childhood mischief
    (5) Guido and Vincent's college life

2. Based on this passage, this entire novel is going to be about Guido and Vincent's

- **(1)** childhood.
- **(2)** quarrels.
- **(3)** families.
- **(4)** adult lives.
- **(5)** wives.

Check your answers on page 277.

Identifying Diction and Tone

The term **diction** refers to word choice. Just as you change your spoken words to make them appropriate for different situations, writers change their words to clarify and strengthen their ideas. Diction can be casual, formal, informal, conversational, or even full of slang.

As writers make decisions about their diction, they are developing the tone of their writing. **Tone** means the attitude, or feeling, that a passage conveys. The tone of a passage can be funny, scary, impersonal, passionate—anything the writer wants it to be.

The following two sentences show how different word choices can change the tone of a passage:

Sentence 1: Chandra listened with quiet surprise to her supervisor's words; then she put down the phone and walked into the hall.

Sentence 2: Chandra listened with astonishment to her supervisor's lecture; then she slammed down the phone and stormed into the hall.

Another tone that you will find in literature is irony. **Irony** in literature—and in life—happens when there is a startling difference between what you expect to happen and what actually happens.

Exercise 2

Directions: Read the following passage and answer items 1–4. As you read, consider the author's main idea, choice of diction, and tone.

WHAT ARE THE CHARACTERS WAITING FOR?

Line General Sash was a hundred and four years old. He lived with his granddaughter, Sally Poker Sash, who was sixty-two years old and who prayed every night on her knees that he would live until
5 her graduation from college. The General didn't give two slaps for her graduation but he never doubted he would live for it. Living had got to be such a habit with him that he couldn't conceive of any other condition. A graduation exercise was
10 not exactly his idea of a good time, even if, as she said, he would be expected to sit on the stage in his uniform. She said there would be a long procession of teachers and students in their robes but that there wouldn't be anything to equal him
15 in his uniform. He knew this well enough without her telling him, and as for the damn procession, it could march to hell and back and not cause him a quiver. He liked parades and floats full of Miss Americas and Miss Daytona Beaches and Miss
20 Queen Cotton Products. He didn't have any use for processions and a procession full of school-teachers was about as deadly as the River Styx to his way of thinking. However, he was willing to sit on the stage in his uniform so that they could
25 see him.

Sally Poker was not as sure as he was that he would live until her graduation. There had not been any perceptible change in him for the last five years, but she had the sense that she might be
30 cheated out of her triumph because she so often was.

—From "A Late Encounter with the Enemy,"
by Flannery O'Connor

1. The diction in this passage could best be described as

- **(1)** informal.
- **(2)** literary.
- **(3)** formal.
- **(4)** archaic.
- **(5)** comical.

2. Which statement best describes the tone of this passage?

    (1) The tone is extremely melodramatic.

    (2) The author obviously strives to create a tone of suspense.

    (3) The tone is highly ironic.

    (4) The tone is droll and deliberately flat.

    (5) No particular tone comes across from this passage.

3. What is the source of the irony in this passage?

    (1) Sally Poker's desire to triumph at her graduation

    (2) The General's desire to sit on the stage at the graduation

    (3) The hints that the General will die before the graduation

    (4) Sally Poker and the General's agreement about the importance of the graduation

    (5) Sally Poker and the General's different feelings about the graduation

4. Based on the passage, the General can best be described as

    (1) kind and generous.

    (2) angry and mean.

    (3) selfish and vain.

    (4) good-hearted but silly.

    (5) well-meaning but awkward.

Check your answers on page 277.

Drawing Conclusions

When you draw a **conclusion** about something, you use analysis or synthesis skills to make a judgment. When you read, you use information about people, places, and events to arrive at ideas not directly stated in the passage. For example, in the last passage, the author never states that the General is vain and selfish; you draw this conclusion based on what you know of his thoughts.

Considering New Situations

On the GED Test, you will be asked to apply information and ideas from a fiction or other passage to new situations. Remember: application means using knowledge, skills, or information in new ways. One of the best ways to practice for questions like this is to consider how you might apply an author's ideas, experiences, or characters to your own life. For example, have you ever thought or acted like General Sash?

Recognizing Setting and Mood

When you begin to read a passage of fiction, you're entering a new world that an author has imagined. You'll want to discover the place you're reading about . . . what it looks like . . . how it makes you feel.

Often the first thing you learn about is the **setting**, the place and time of the story. Knowing the setting helps you analyze the characters' words and actions and understand what's happening.

The setting also helps you recognize the **mood**, or atmosphere, the author creates. Atmosphere is the way a place *feels*. It is the emotional effect created by the setting. For example, think about the feeling each of these settings creates:

- A sunrise in the mountains (hope; expectation)

- A bleak, crumbling castle during a thunderstorm (myster; horror)

- A cozy fireside in a cabin in the woods (relaxation; romance)

Setting is important to what characters do and say. When you identify a setting, think about how it might influence the events of the story. For example, if the setting is a funeral, the action and events may reflect people's feelings about the person who died and how that death will affect them. Whatever the setting, you can be sure that the writer chose it for a reason.

Understanding Characterization

Sometimes you may hear a comment like, "Oh, my Uncle Frank is such a character!" By this, the person speaking probably means that Uncle Frank is a particularly interesting person with many memorable qualities and habits. In much the same way, **characters** in fiction writing are distinct people with specific qualities of personality and physical appearance. The characters' appearance or basic traits may be based on those of real people, but the characters never actually existed. They come to life through the written word.

Writers describe characters in two ways: by telling us *what the person looks like* and by *showing how the person behaves, or acts*. Both kinds of description help to create a picture of the character in the reader's mind.

Identifying Narrator and Point of View

Perspective is a way of looking at people, events, or issues. In nonfiction, the perspective is usually that of the writer. In fiction, however, the person who tells the story is called the **narrator**. The narrator's perspective is called **point of view**.

For example, if a character named Lee is telling his own story, he might say "I went on a date last Friday" or

"I felt lost and worried." In this story, Lee is the narrator, and the story is told from his point of view. We say the story is told in the *first person*. If someone else (an outside observer) is telling the story, however, that person might say "*Lee* went on a date last Friday." or "*He* felt lost and worried." Then the author is telling the story in the *third person*. First person and third person are the two main narrative *voices* in fiction.

Recognizing Time Periods

The fiction passages on the GED are divided into three time periods: before 1920, 1920-1960, and 1960 to the present. Some questions will ask you to identify the time period in which a story takes places. You can do this based on details about the characters' dress, about means of transportation and other technology mentioned in the passage, and about manners and modes of speech. For example, if characters speak in very formal language and mention riding in a stagecoach, the passage probably comes from a novel set in the time period before 1920.

Making Comparisons between Texts

Some synthesis questions on the GED Test will ask you to make comparisons between a given passage and a brief excerpt from another work of literature. You can do this by looking for clues about the main passage's overall meaning or tone, and contrasting features of the brief excerpt. For example, is the tone of the two passages similar or different? Do they appear to be set in the same or different time periods? Do they express the same or a different central idea?

Exercise 3

> **Directions:** Read the following passage and answer items 1–4.

WHAT IS THIS MAN FEELING?

Line Noise fills Andras Melish's house. Andras's
daughter, Renee, is practicing piano, banging
away. His son, Alex, clatters up and down the
stairs with an old fish tank he's converted into a
5   terrarium. Outside, the Curtis boy is mowing the
lawn. Andras hides upstairs in the bedroom,
reading about the Syrian invasion of Lebanon in
the *Economist*, and hoping Nina won't call him.
        Often he avoids her. It makes him feel guilty,
10   but he can't help it. She is beautiful, his young
wife. Her red hair, her Spanish accent—even her
sharp temper—seem to him exotic, a remnant of
her childhood in Buenos Aires. Andras still carries

with him his first seventeen years in Budapest and
15   the corresponding mystique of the tropical, the
sun, the flaming colors, on the other side of the
world. Nina is all that to his cool grey eyes.

—From *Kaaterskill Falls*, by Allegra Goodman

1. Andras's feelings about his wife and family can best be described as

    (1) angry.
    (2) distant.
    (3) adoring.
    (4) ambivalent.
    (5) passionate.

2. "All this light was pouring in on me, and I started to open my eyes. I didn't know where in the world I was, and I reached over, but no one was there." In what way does this excerpt contrast strongly with the passage above?

    (1) The central character of this excerpt is a woman, whereas Andras is a man.
    (2) The central character of this excerpt is alone, while Andras is at home with his family.
    (3) The central character of this excerpt tells us her thoughts, while Andras does not.
    (4) The excerpt mainly concerns the sense of hearing, while the passage concerns the sense of sight.
    (5) The central character of the excerpt is described vividly, while Andras is not.

3. What is the main idea of the first paragraph?

    (1) Noise fills Andras Melish's house.
    (2) Andras is reading the *Economist*.
    (3) Lebanon has been invaded.
    (4) Renee is banging on the piano.
    (5) Alex clatters up the stairs.

4. When does this story take place?

    (1) In ancient times
    (2) Between 1600 and 1700
    (3) Between 1700 and 1800
    (4) Between 1800 and 1900
    (5) In the present

Check your answers on page 277.

Exercise 4

HOW MIGHT THIS PLACE AFFECT THIS COUPLE'S LIFE?

Line   Although it was only four o'clock, the winter day
        was fading. The road led southwest, toward the
        streak of pale, watery light that glimmered in the
        leaden sky. The light fell upon the two sad young
5   faces that were turned mutely toward it: upon the
        eyes of the girl, who seemed to be looking with
        such anguished perplexity into the future; upon
        the sombre eyes of the boy, who seemed already
        to be looking into the past.
10   The little town behind them had vanished as
        if it had never been, had fallen behind the swell of
        the prairie, and the stern frozen country received
        them into its bosom. The homesteads were few
        and far apart; here and there a windmill gaunt
15   against the sky, a sod house crouching in a
        hollow. But the great fact was the land itself,
        which seemed to overwhelm the little beginnings
        of human society that struggled in its sombre
        wastes. It was from facing this vast hardness that
20   the boy's mouth had become so bitter; because he
        felt that men were too weak to make any mark
        here, that the land wanted to be let alone, to
        preserve its own fierce strength, its peculiar,
        savage kind of beauty, its uninterrupted mournful-
25   ness.

—From *O Pioneers!* by Willa Cather

1. Which of the following best describes this landscape?

    (1) Wealthy and luxurious
    (2) Sunny and bright
    (3) Barren and powerful
    (4) Green and flowering
    (5) Warm and nurturing

2. Based on this description, which of the following would be most likely to happen?

    (1) The pioneers will be able to cultivate this land easily.
    (2) A tornado will destroy everything the pioneers have worked for.
    (3) The pioneers will nearly starve during a fierce winter storm.
    (4) The land will challenge the pioneers as they try to build their town.
    (5) The young couple will die before completing their prairie home.

WHAT DOES IGNATIUS LOOK LIKE?

Line   A green hunting cap squeezed the top of the
        fleshy balloon of a head. The green earflaps, full of
        large ears and uncut hair . . . stuck out on either
        side like turn signals indicating two directions at
5   once. Full, pursed lips protruded beneath the
        bushy black moustache and, at their corners, sank
        into little folds filled with disapproval and potato
        chip crumbs. In the shadow under the green visor
        of the cap Ignatius J. Reilly's blue and yellow eyes
10   looked down upon the other people waiting
        under the clock at the Holmes department store.

—From *A Confederacy of Dunces*
by John Kennedy Toole

3. Comparing the green earflaps to turn signals effectively creates a vivid image of

    (1) ears that lie flat to the head.
    (2) a handsome man.
    (3) ears that stick straight out.
    (4) Ignatius's good driving skills.
    (5) Ignatius's warm personality.

4. In this description, Ignatius seems to be

    (1) part of the crowd around him.
    (2) hiding under his cap while observing people.
    (3) dressed to go somewhere formal.
    (4) aware that he looks somewhat out of place.
    (5) angry at the shoppers in the store.

5. Which of the following best describes the narrator's tone?

    (1) Humble
    (2) Suspenseful
    (3) Uncertain
    (4) Comical
    (5) Angry

Check your answers on page 277.

Studying Plot

Every work of fiction has a **plot**. The plot is simply the sequence of events in the story—the answer to the question, *What happened?*

    Usually, the plot follows a simple pattern of rising action, crisis, and falling action. The meaning of these terms is explained in Figure 1.

FIGURE 1

A plot usually follows the sequence of rising action, crisis, and falling action

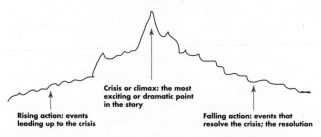

Crisis or climax: the most exciting or dramatic point in the story

Rising action: events leading up to the crisis

Falling action: events that resolve the crisis; the resolution

Recognizing Figurative Language

In the description of Ignatius J. Reilly on page 258, the author describes Ignatius's head as a "fleshy balloon." Of course, the author doesn't mean that Ignatius's head is actually a balloon. Instead, he uses **figurative language** to create a humorous, vivid **image**, or mental picture, of the size and shape of Ignatius's head.

    When you read figurative language, remember that the words aren't supposed to be taken literally. They're meant to capture your imagination and help you see new relationships between things. Compare these types of figurative language:

    Sentence 1: Juanita's sparkling eyes are like gemstones. (simile)
    Sentence 2: Juanita's smile is dynamite. (metaphor)

A **simile** is a comparison. You can always recognize a simile because it contains the words *like* or *as*. A **metaphor** takes a comparison one step further: two things are described as if they are one and the same. The words *like* or *as* do not appear. For example, to make a stronger point about Juanita's powerful smile, the writer of sentence 2 says that her smile actually *is* dynamite.

Another type of figurative language is the symbol. A **symbol** is something that is used to *represent* another thing. For example, a flag is a symbol of a country. The dove symbolizes peace.

Exercise 5

> **Directions:** Item 1 refers to the following passage. Read the passage and answer the question.

WHAT HAPPENS TO DEERSLAYER?

Line   When about a hundred yards from the shore, Deerslayer rose in the canoe . . . then quickly laying aside the instrument of labor, he seized that of war. He was in the very act of raising the rifle,
5   when a sharp report was followed by the buzz of a bullet that passed so near his body, as to cause him involuntarily to start.

    The next instant Deerslayer staggered, and fell his whole length of the bottom of the canoe.
10 A yell—it came from a single voice—followed, and an Indian leaped from the bushes upon the open area of the point, bounding towards the canoe. This was the moment the young man desired. He rose on the instant, and leveled his own rifle at his
15 uncovered foe; but his finger hesitated about pulling the trigger on one whom he held at such a disadvantage. This little delay, probably, saved the life of the Indian, who bounded back into the cover as swiftly as he had broken out of it.
20   In the meantime Deerslayer had been swiftly approaching the land, and his own canoe reached the point just as his enemy disappeared. . . . [He] did not pause an instant, but dashed into the woods and sought cover.

                —From *The Deerslayer*
                by James Fenimore Cooper

1. The climax, or most dramatic point, of this passage is when

    (1) Deerslayer paddles toward land.
    (2) the Indian takes cover in the woods.
    (3) Deerslayer takes cover in the woods.
    (4) Deerslayer's canoe touches ground.
    (5) Deerslayer raises his rifle and takes aim.

Item 2 refers to the following passage. Read the passage and answer the question.

HOW DOES THE BOY INTERPRET HIS SURROUNDINGS?

Line The mist was heavier yet when I got out upon the
marshes, so that instead of my running at everything, everything seemed to run at me. This was
very disagreeable to a guilty mind. The gates and
5   dykes and banks came bursting at me through the
mist, as if they cried as plainly as could be, 'A boy
with Somebody-else's pork pie! Stop him!' The
cattle came upon me with like suddenness, staring
out of their eyes, and steaming out of their
10   nostrils, 'Holloa, young thief!' One black ox, with
a white cravat on—who even had to my awak-
ened conscience something of a clerical air—fixed
me so obstinately with his eyes, and moved his
blunt head round in such an accusatory manner as
15   I moved round, that I blubbered out to him, 'I
couldn't help it, sir! It wasn't for myself I took it!'

—From *Great Expectations*
by Charles Dickens

2. In this excerpt, what do the cattle, the mist, the
gates, and banks all symbolize to the boy as they
"seemed to run at [him]"? (line 3)

(1) His fear of being lost in the mist
(2) The boy's guilty conscience
(3) The boy's love of nature
(4) His fear of the outdoor world
(5) His joy at having something to eat

Check your answers on page 277.

Exercise 6

Directions: Choose the <u>one best answer</u> for each item.

Items 1–4 refer to the following excerpt from a novel.

WHAT IS MRS. BENNET HOPING?

Line It is a truth universally acknowledged, that a single
man in possession of a good fortune, must be in
want of a wife.

However little known the feelings or views
5   of such a man may be on his first entering a
neighbourhood, this truth is so well fixed in the
minds of the surrounding families, that he is
considered as the rightful property of some one or
other of their daughters.
10   "My dear Mr. Bennet," said his lady to him
one day, "have you heard that Netherfield Park is
let at last?"
Mr. Bennet replied that he had not.
"But it is," returned she, "for Mrs. Long has
15   just been here, and she told me all about it."
Mr. Bennet made no answer.
"Do you not want to know who has taken
it?" cried his wife impatiently.
"You want to tell me, and I have no objec-
20   tion to hearing it."
This was invitation enough.
"Why, my dear, you must know, Mrs. Long
says that Netherfield is taken by a young man of
large fortune from the north of England; that he
25   came down on Monday in a chaise and four to see
the place, and was so much delighted with it that
he agreed with Mr. Morris immediately; that he is
to take possession before Michaelmas, and some
of his servants are to be in the house by the end
30   of next week."
"What is his name?"
"Bingley."
"Is he married or single."
"Oh! Single, my dear, to be sure! A single
35   man of large fortune; four or five thousand a year.
What a fine thing for our girls!"

—From *Pride and Prejudice* by Jane Austen

1. Where is the main idea of this passage stated?

   (1) In the middle of the excerpt
   (2) In the first sentence
   (3) Nowhere, except indirectly
   (4) In the last sentence
   (5) Nowhere, because there is none

2. In this conversation, Mrs. Bennet assumes that

   (1) Netherfield Park has been rented.
   (2) her husband is interested in her story.
   (3) her oldest daughter will fall in love with Bingley.
   (4) Mr. Bingley is looking for a wife.
   (5) her husband is an interfering man.

3. Based on this passage, if Mrs. Bennet worked in an office instead of keeping a home, she could be expected to

   (1) fight for employees' rights.
   (2) quickly become the office manager.
   (3) be the most industrious worker in the office.
   (4) consistently arrive late for work, without an excuse.
   (5) pry into the personal lives of her coworkers.

4. Why is Mrs. Bennet interested in Mr. Bingley?

   (1) He is a wealthy man.
   (2) His goal is to get married.
   (3) He is the son of a politician.
   (4) He is a poor man.
   (5) He has a promising career.

Check your answers on page 278.

Unit 2

POETRY

A **poem** is a piece of writing that communicates an intense and often emotional message. In general, poems are different from other literary forms in two ways: (1) Poems are often shorter pieces of writing, and (2) they have a different structure. A poet usually divides the lines of a poem into stanzas, which are like the verses of a song.

Poets often express ideas indirectly through rhyme, rhythm, and figurative language. The rhyme and rhythm help set the mood of a poem. They stem from a time when poems were sung out loud before they were written down.

Rhyme and Rhythm

A writer of prose uses paragraphs to break up a passage, making it easier to understand. Similarly, a poet breaks a poem into **stanzas**, or sections. Stanzas can do more than make a poem simpler to read, however. With each new stanza, the poet may introduce a new setting or speaker, a plot element, or a change in mood or tone.

Think about the song you have heard on the radio most recently. In popular songs, rhyme and rhythm make the words and the message more powerful. Poets use rhyme and rhythm in much the same way.

Rhyme is the sound likeness of two words. Rhyming words are effective in poetry because their sounds complement each other. Sometimes those sounds are exactly alike (as in *cat/hat* and *alive/survive*); at other times (as in *pound/pond*), the sounds are not exactly the same but are close enough to give the effect of a rhyme.

Rhyming words are also used to link ideas. In addition, rhyme may determine the structure of a poem. For example, a stanza in which the last words in lines 1 and 2 rhyme and the last words in lines 3 and 4 rhyme has a **rhyme scheme** of *aabb*.

Rhythm is the sound patterns that words make when placed together. Think about dancing. When you dance, your body moves to the rhythm of the music. In many poems, words do the same thing. Sometimes the rhythm is so strong and regular you can clap your hands to it. At other times, the rhythm is purposely uneven. A poet may want to capture dissimilar ideas or keep the reader's attention. Instead of rhythm, a poet may use *repetition*—the repeated use of a word or phrase—to make a point.

Although stanzas, rhyme, and rhythm can be important elements in a poem, some poems do not use all these techniques. When a poem contains irregular rhythm and rhyme, or no rhyme, the structure is called **free verse**. Many modern poets write free verse.

Exercise 1

Directions: Items 1 and 2 refer to the following poem. As you read this poem, think about how free verse makes the poem effective. Then answer the questions.

WHAT THOUGHTS COME TO THE SPEAKER'S MIND?

Line Do not boast of your speed,
       O blue-green stream running by the hills:
       Once you have reached the wide ocean,
       You can return no more.
5   Why not stay here and rest,
       When moonlight stuffs the empty hills?
       Mountains are steadfast but the mountain streams
       Go by, go by,
       And yesterdays are like the rushing streams,
10   They fly, they fly,
       And the great heroes, famous for a day,
       They die, they die.
       Blue mountains speak of my desire,
       Green waters reflect my lover's love:
15   The mountains unchanging,
       The waters flowing by.
       Sometimes it seems the waters cannot forget me,
       They part in tears, regretting, running away.
       His guests are merry and joking.
20   A distant voyage is like chewing sugar cane,
       Sweetness mixed with bitterness.
       Return, soon I shall return to my home—
       Though beautiful, this is not my land.

—"Do Not Boast of Your Speed"
by Hwang Chin-i

1. This poem is primarily about

   (1) marriage.
   (2) an athletic event.
   (3) the birth of a child.
   (4) the love of nature.
   (5) the passage of time.

262

2. Lines 7-12 differ from the rest of the poem because they

- **(1)** do not contain any figurative expressions.
- **(2)** use rhyme and rhythm to describe the speaker's ancestors.
- **(3)** address the ocean directly, as if it were a person.
- **(4)** use rhyme and rhythm to describe the passage of time.
- **(5)** contain no rhyme or rhythm and quote a different speaker.

Check your answers on page 278.

Recognizing Alliteration

"Who is the bravest, boldest, and best leader that our beloved country has ever seen?" This question contains four words that begin with *b*. Read it out loud, and notice how the words beginning with *b* catch your attention. Think, too, about how the sound links the leader with the country. Poets often place words that start with the same letter near each other to create this kind of effect. This technique is called alliteration.

Understanding Figurative Language: Personification and Symbolism

Like other writers, poets sometimes depend on figurative language to communicate ideas and observations. Figurative language is not meant to be taken literally; rather, it compares things in an unusual way. It creates mental images that help readers see ideas in new ways, too.

Symbolism and personification are two more types of figurative language. **Symbolism** is figurative language in which an object, a person, or an event represents something else. For example, a country's flag usually symbolizes its pride and its people. A wedding ring symbolizes long-lasting love. Black clothing often symbolizes mourning. **Personification** takes symbolism one step further. When an object is personified, it is given human qualities. (Just remember: *person*ification = like a *person*.) For example, a building doesn't experience feelings and emotions. Still, a writer might say, "The old building stood its ground bravely against the wrecking ball."

Exercise 2

> **Directions:** Items 1-3 refer to the following poem. As you read this poem, consider what new ideas the poet suggests. Then answer the questions.

HOW IS DEATH PERSONIFIED?

Line	
	Because I could not stop for Death,
	He kindly stopped for me;
	The carriage held but just ourselves
	And Immortality.
5	We slowly drove, he knew no haste,
	And I had put away
	My labor, and my leisure too,
	For his civility.
	We passed the school where children played
10	Their lessons scarcely done;
	We passed the fields of gazing grain,
	We passed the setting sun.
	We paused before a house that seemed
	A swelling of the ground;
15	The roof was scarcely visible,
	The cornice but a mound.
	Since then 'tis centuries; but each
	Feels shorter than the day
	I first surmised the horses' heads
20	Were toward eternity.

—"Because I Could Not Stop for Death"
by Emily Dickinson

1. In this poem, death is personified in the form of a(n)

- **(1)** elderly grandfather.
- **(2)** frightening old woman.
- **(3)** courteous carriage driver.
- **(4)** energetic young man.
- **(5)** silent young boy.

2. "We slowly drove, he knew no haste,/And I had put away/My labor, and my leisure too,/For his civility." (lines 5-8)

Which of the following best restates these thoughts?

- **(1)** We drove quickly because I was eager to return home.
- **(2)** Because the driver was rude, I asked to be taken home.
- **(3)** I was impressed by his politeness but soon felt ready to get back to work.
- **(4)** We drove hastily toward the setting sun as I enjoyed my leisure.
- **(5)** I no longer required work or rest, so I was content to move slowly.

3. The house to which the speaker refers in the fourth stanza (lines 13-16) symbolizes

   (1) the earth.
   (2) a small apartment.
   (3) her birthplace.
   (4) a gravesite.
   (5) a mansion.

Check your answers on page 278.

Identifying Theme and Main Idea

As in other kinds of writing, the main idea of a poem is its central point. The theme of a poem, however, is a broader statement or belief about life, relationships, feelings, or behavior. In a poem about reapers, for example, the poet's subject might be "work." The poet's theme might be "the monotony of physical labor." The poet's main idea might be "People can be hypnotized by the routine of their work, becoming blind to the world around them."

Exercise 3

Directions: Items 1–4 refer to the following poem. As you read, think about the tone of the poem and how you would state its theme. Then answer the questions.

WHERE IS THE SPEAKER GOING?

Line Farewell, my younger brother!
From the holy places the gods come for me.
You will never see me again; but when the showers pass and the thunders peal,
5   "There," you will say, "is the voice of my elder brother."
And when the harvest comes, of the beautiful birds and grasshoppers you will say,
"There is the ordering of my elder brother!"

           —"Farewell, My Younger Brother,"
           a traditional Navajo poem

1. Based on line 2, you can assume that the speaker

   (1) is near death.
   (2) is not religious.
   (3) has a brother who is dying.
   (4) wants to leave town.
   (5) is afraid.

2. The speaker mentions being remembered in all of the following EXCEPT

   (1) grasshoppers.
   (2) rain.
   (3) springtime flowers.
   (4) thunder.
   (5) the time of harvest.

3. Which of the following best states the main idea of this poem?

   (1) Every harvest is beautiful.
   (2) Nature should be revered.
   (3) An elder brother is a good teacher.
   (4) A person's spirit carries on after death.
   (5) Brothers should be lifelong friends.

4. If the younger brother applied the theme of this poem to his life, he would most likely become a

   (1) loving parent.
   (2) nature photographer.
   (3) big-game hunter.
   (4) skilled lumberjack.
   (5) fiery preacher.

Items 5–8 refer to the following sonnet.

As you read this sonnet, think about how this classical work of literature provides a timeless record of human emotion and about the ways in which you could apply Browning's images and ideas to life today. Then answer the questions.

WHAT STRONG EMOTIONS DOES THIS SPEAKER EXPRESS?

Line How do I love thee? Let me count the ways.
I love thee to the depth and breadth and height
My soul can reach, when feeling out of sight
For the ends of Being and ideal Grace.
5   I love thee to the level of every day's
Most quiet need, by sun and candlelight.
I love thee freely, as men strive for Right;
I love thee purely, as they turn from Praise.
I love thee with the passion put to use
10 In my old griefs, and with my childhood's faith.
I love thee with a love I seemed to lose
With my lost saints,—I love thee with the breath,
    Smiles, tears, of all my life!—and, if God choose,
    I shall but love thee better after death.

      —Sonnet XLIII by Elizabeth Barrett Browning

5. The speaker connects her feelings of love with all of the following EXCEPT

(1) purity.
(2) freedom.
(3) passion.
(4) fear.
(5) faith.

6. Which of the following literary techniques is used most often in this sonnet?

(1) Repetition
(2) Falling action
(3) Stage directions
(4) Foreshadowing
(5) Personification

7. If this sonnet were reviewed in a modern-day magazine, the reviewer would most likely characterize it as

(1) emotionless.
(2) dramatic.
(3) dull.
(4) manipulative.
(5) inexpressive.

8. Which of the following song titles best summarizes the main idea of this sonnet?

(1) "Tears of a Clown"
(2) "We Are the World"
(3) "We Are Family"
(4) "Tracks of My Tears"
(5) "I Will Always Love You"

Check your answers on page 278.

Unit 3

DRAMA

A **drama** is a play that can be read or performed on stage by actors.

When you watch a play, you can see how the actors react to one another. You can see that time passes. A **playwright** has other ways to help you picture these things when you read a play.

Understanding Setting and Stage Directions

Plays are divided into acts, which are further divided into *scenes*. Each scene advances the time and/or place of the action—that is, changes the setting. The *setting* of a drama is the time and place in which the action occurs. Identifying a play's setting might help you anticipate the action, since time and place can influence what happens. For example, if the setting is a small, cold Alaskan town, the action might focus on how people in the town cope with the long winter.

A playwright provides other clues through **stage directions**, which often appear in *italics*. Stage directions describe how the stage looks and how the actors should stand, move, look, or speak.

Recognizing Foreshadowing

Foreshadowing is the technique of suggesting an event that will occur later in the play. The foreshadowing may be found in stage directions or in a character's words or actions. For example, if a character wonders out loud when another character might come home after a long absence, the playwright may be foreshadowing this character's return. Watching for foreshadowing helps you understand what is happening—and what will happen—in a drama.

Analyzing Characters, Dialogue, and Conflict

Dialogue, or conversation, is the most important element in a play. By listening closely to dialogue between characters, you can gather information.

A **monologue** is a long speech by one character when another character is on stage. A soliloquy occurs when the character is alone on stage. Monologues and soliloquies are important because characters reveal important feelings or experiences during these long and usually emotional speeches.

As you read, keep in mind that each character in a play has a different perspective to express. The different perspectives often result in a **conflict**, or problem.

The most common types of conflict in drama (and in all types of literature) are:

- Conflict between people (such as friends or family members)

- Conflict between a person and society (such as a person who opposes prejudice)

- Conflict between a person (or people) and an element of nature (such as a hurricane)

- Internal conflict—a spiritual or moral disturbance within one character

Exercise 1

Directions: Items 1 and 2 refer to the following passage. As you read this passage, use the stage directions to imagine the scene and the action. Then answer the questions.

WHAT BRINGS THESE CHARACTERS TOGETHER?

Line   *The stage is empty except for a few pale stars.*
Calorías and Julio enter. Calorías carries the
cello on his shoulder.
Guicho: (*Out of sight*) CA-LO-RIIIIAAS! CAAA-
5   LOOOO-RIIIIAAS!
Guicho appears over a dune. Calorías and Julio
stand looking at each other. Guicho takes out his
knife.
Julio: Hey Guichito.
10 Calorías: Why Guicho, you comin' with us?
Guicho: No.
Calorías: Ah yes. I see now. You have a knife.
        (*Approaching*) Perhaps you're angry. Did
        I hurt a friend of yours? (*He laughs*) Have
15   you come to kill me, little boy?
Guicho shakes his head. He is terrified.
Guicho: I want the guitarrón.
Julio: Ay Guichito. Go away.
Calorías: (*Picking up the cello*) This. Ah yes. It is
20   this you want.
Guicho: Just give it to me.
Calorías: If only it were so simple . . . eh? But I
        can't give it to you. I have to destroy it.

        —From *The Guitarrón* by Lynne Alvarez

1. The setting of this passage is

   (1) backstage at an orchestra hall.
   (2) early morning in a Latin-American city.
   (3) nighttime in a desert-like place.
   (4) a junkyard.
   (5) late afternoon at the seashore.

2. The stage directions in lines 13–19 show that Calorías is

   (1) foolish.
   (2) eager to make friends with Guicho.
   (3) afraid but hopeful.
   (4) cruel.
   (5) easily misled by Julio.

Items 3–6 refer to the following passage. Read the passage. Then answer the questions.

WHY DO THESE CHARACTERS DISAGREE?

Line Troy: Your mama tells me you got recruited by a college football team? Is that right?

Cory: Yeah. Coach Zellman say the recruiter gonna be coming by to talk to you. Get you
5   to sign the permission papers.

Troy: I thought you supposed to be working down there at the A&P. Ain't you supposed to be working down there after school?

Cory: Mr. Stawicki say he gonna hold my job for
10   me until after the football season. Say starting next week I can work weekends.

Troy: I thought we had an understanding about this football stuff. You suppose to keep up with your chores and hold that job down at
15   the A&P. Ain't been around here all day on a Saturday. Ain't none of your chores done . . . and now you telling me you done quit your job.

Cory: I'm gonna be working weekends.
20   Troy: You damn right you are! Ain't no need for nobody coming around here to talk to me about signing nothing.

Cory: Hey, Pop, you can't do that. He's coming all the way from North Carolina.
25   Troy: I don't care where he coming from. The white man ain't gonna let you get nowhere with that football no way. You go and get your book-learning where you can learn to do something besides carrying people's
30   garbage.

—From *Fences* by August Wilson

3. Which of the following best describes Cory's perspective?

   (1) He wants to own the A&P.
   (2) He wants to give up football.
   (3) He wishes that he were better at football.
   (4) He can work and still play football.
   (5) He does not like the recruiter.

4. Which of the following best describes Troy's perspective?

   (1) He thinks Cory should continue working.
   (2) He is worried about his wife's reaction.
   (3) He wishes that Cory were a better player.
   (4) He admires and respects the recruiter.
   (5) He is jealous of Cory's athletic skill.

5. As a father, Troy could best be described as

   (1) sympathetic.
   (2) wise.
   (3) cruel.
   (4) strict.
   (5) easygoing.

6. Which of the following is not clear by the end of this passage?

   (1) Coach Zellman's perspective
   (2) Cory's desire to play football
   (3) Cory's talent as a football player
   (4) Troy's perspective
   (5) Whether Cory will play college football

Check your answers on 278.

Understanding Comedy and Tragedy

Many plays are categorized as either comedies or tragedies. In a **tragedy**, a major character may suffer great misfortune or ruin, especially as a result of a choice he or she has made. Often the tragic choice involves a moral weakness. Tragedies are designed to evoke strong feelings of sadness and empathy in the audience.

A **comedy** is intended to amuse. It may be lighthearted or hilarious, and it usually has a happy ending. Humor is used for many reasons: to break up the tension and conflict in drama, to reveal a character's personality, or to make an audience more receptive to the ideas being presented. Humor is also an important part of life, and drama is usually meant to remind us of elements of our own lives.

Two kinds of comedy are farce and satire. A **farce** contains humorous characterizations and improbable plots. For example, in a farce, two women might dress as men and never be recognized as women. A **satire** makes fun of human characteristics (such as pride or jealousy) or failings (such as being unable to communicate with one's children or being a fool for love). Irony and clever language are often used in satire. In both farce and satire, the characters and their actions are exaggerated to make the drama more entertaining and as a comment on society.

Exercise 2

Directions: Items 1–4 refer to the following passage. As you read, look for universal themes and situations. Then answer the questions.

WHAT PAST PROBLEMS DO LOLA AND DOC DISCUSS?

Line Lola: You were so nice and so proper, Doc; I thought nothing we could do together could ever be wrong—or make us unhappy. Do you think we did wrong, Doc?

5 Doc: (*consoling*) No, Baby, of course I don't.

Lola: I don't think anyone knows about it except my folks, do you?

Doc: Of course not, Baby.

Lola: (*follows him in*) I wish the baby had lived,

10 Doc. . . . If we'd gone to a doctor, she would have lived, don't you think?

Doc: Perhaps. . . . We were just kids. Kids don't know how to look after things.

Lola: (*sits on couch*) If we'd had the baby she'd be

15 a young girl now; and then maybe you'd have saved your money, Doc, and she could be going to college—like Marie.

Doc: Baby, what's done is done.

Lola: It must make you feel bad at times to think

20 you had to give up being a doctor and to think you don't have any money like you used to.

Doc: No . . . no, Baby. We should never feel bad about what's past. What's in the past can't be

25 helped. You . . . you've got to forget it and live for the present. If you can't forget the past, you stay in it and never get out.

—From *Come Back, Little Sheba* by William Inge

1. Based on Doc's words in lines 23–27, with which of the following proverbs would he be most likely to agree?

   (1) Waste not, want not.
   (2) A stitch in time saves nine.
   (3) Count your pennies.
   (4) Don't cry over spilled milk.
   (5) Little wealth, little care.

2. Which of the following would be the best title for this passage?

   (1) A Happy Marriage
   (2) Secrets of the Past
   (3) Saving for College
   (4) How to be a Good Doctor
   (5) A Scary Future

3. Which of the following best describes the tone of this conversation?

   (1) Whining
   (2) Bitter
   (3) Challenging
   (4) Apologetic
   (5) Understanding

4. What does the dialogue between Lola and Doc suggest about their relationship?

   (1) It is strained and awkward.
   (2) They enjoy being silly together.
   (3) It is a close, loving relationship.
   (4) Everything they say and do seems rehearsed.
   (5) It is full of frustration.

Check your answers on page 279.

Unit 4

NONFICTION

Nonfiction is factual writing about real people, places, and events. Four types of nonfiction passages may be included on the GED: informational texts, business documents, literary nonfiction, and visual arts. This section will define each of these types and explain their key features. The Exercises will include examples of each type of nonfiction you are likely to encounter on the GED Test.

Informational Texts

Informational texts are factual materials that you read to obtain information. Examples are textbooks, training manuals, and the book you are reading right now. When you read informational texts, you are looking for facts and for ways to organize them in a logical way. Each type of informational text has a specific purpose, which may be to present information, to present information in such a way that the reader is persuaded to take some action, or to teach the reader how to do something.

Business Documents

When you are working or looking for a job, you read many different types of business documents: employee handbooks, training manuals, instructions, to name just a few. Business documents are similar to informational texts in that you read them to obtain information, but they are different in one key way. When you read a business document, you are looking for specific rules and procedures to follow. For example, a business document may tell you how to apply for a job, how to apply for college, or how to use a word-processing program. Business documents are rule oriented and organized so that you can find key information easily.

Distinguishing Fact from Opinion

When you read informational text, you should always read critically to separate the author's opinion from facts. In most cases, informational text contains a combination of facts and opinion. A **fact** is something that can be proved beyond the point of reasonable argument. For example, "John F. Kennedy was elected president of the United States in 1960" is a fact that can be verified. In contrast, "John F. Kennedy was a great president" is an **opinion**. Evidence could be produced either to support or deny this statement, and reasonable people might well disagree about whether it is true or false.

Identifying Perspective

A **perspective** is the standpoint from which a person views something. Because your life experiences are different from everyone else's, your perspective will be different as well. When you read, try to identify the perspective of the writer. For example, evaluate the language the writer uses to determine if he or she views the topic favorably. Think about how the language would be different if he or she held a different perspective.

Cause and Effect

Informational texts make frequent use of cause-and-effect relationships. This means that one event (the cause) leads to another event (the effect). Knowledge of cause-and-effect relationships is often tested by asking questions about why something happens, requiring you to state the cause.

Exercise 1

> **Directions:** Items 1–3 refer to the following informational passage. It comes from the Web site of the Carnegie Institution, a scientific organization in Washington, DC. As you read the passage, think about the kinds of information it contains and how you can organize this information in your mind so that you can use it most effectively.

WHAT IS THE CARNEGIE ORGANIZATION OF WASHINGTON?

Line   The Carnegie Institution of Washington, a private, nonprofit organization engaged in basic research and advanced education in biology, astronomy, and the earth sciences, was founded by Andrew
5   Carnegie in 1902 and incorporated by an Act of Congress in 1904. Mr. Carnegie, who provided an initial endowment of $10 million and later gave additional millions, conceived the Institution's purpose "to encourage, in the broadest and most
10   liberal manner, investigation, research, and discovery, and the application of knowledge to the improvement of mankind."

    From its earliest years, the Carnegie Institution has been a pioneering research organization,
15   devoted to fields of inquiry that its trustees and staff consider among the most significant in the development of science and scholarship. Its funds

are used primarily to support investigations at its own research departments. Recognizing that
20 fundamental research is closely related to the development of outstanding young scholars, the Institution conducts a strong program of advanced education at the predoctoral and postdoctoral levels. Carnegie also conducts distinctive programs
25 for elementary school teachers and children in Washington, DC. At First Light, a Saturday "hands-on" science school, elementary school students explore worlds within and around them. At summer sessions of the Carnegie Academy for
30 Science Education, elementary school teachers learn interactive techniques of science and mathematics teaching.

> —From the Web site of the Carnegie Institution of Washington

1. According to the passage, the Carnegie Institution's two main functions are

   (1) research and education.
   (2) fundraising and investigation.
   (3) science and scholarship.
   (4) education for teachers and students.
   (5) summer school and Saturday science school.

2. From whose perspective is this passage written?

   (1) Andrew Carnegie's
   (2) A Carnegie Institute employee's
   (3) A jobseeker's
   (4) A student's
   (5) The Carnegie Institute's

3. According to the passage, First Light is a program for

   (1) elementary school teachers.
   (2) elementary school students.
   (3) predoctoral students.
   (4) postdoctoral students.
   (5) scientists.

Check your answers on page 279.

Exercise 2

Directions: Items 1–4 are based on the following business document, an excerpt from a college admissions guide. Read the passage carefully for information on how to enroll as a student at Lee College. Then answer the questions.

HOW DO I BECOME A STUDENT AT LEE COLLEGE?

Apply for Admission

- *Submit an application and residency documentation (as needed) to Admissions and Records Office in Moler Hall.* The state requires the college to charge tuition at the out-of-state rate for students who have resided in Texas less than one year. Out-of-state students must sign an oath that their intent is to become a permanent resident of Texas. Such students will be reclassified as in-state for tuition purposes after one year has elapsed. Proof of residence is also required for in-district status.

- *Obtain New Student Information Card.* Admission & Records Office, Moler Hall.

Have Transcripts Sent to Lee College

- *Arrange for official high school transcripts or GED grade report to be sent to Lee College.*

- *Students transferring from another college must have official transcripts mailed directly to Lee College Admissions and Records Office or brought in an envelope sealed by the institution.* Students who are unable to obtain transcripts prior to submitting their application for admission will be given 2–3 weeks to compete their admissions file.

Apply for Financial Aid

- Moler Hall. Refer to page 7 for details.

See a Counselor

- *Bring New Student Information Card to Counseling Center.*

- Arrange for TASP and/or Placement testing in Counseling. (See pages 8–9.)

Attend New Student Orientation

- Rundell Hall, July 12 from 8:30 a.m. to 12:00 p.m. See page 16 or inquire in Counseling Center for alternate dates.

Register for Classes

- *Register for classes.* See **Registration Options and Payment Deadlines** on pages 5 and 6.

Pay Tuition and Fees

- If you have financial aid, go to the Financial Aid Office in Moler Hall to process payment. Otherwise pay in Rundell Hall at the cashier's window. See pages 11–14 for details.

Buy Books

- *Either online at www.leecollegebooks.com or in Moler Hall Bookstore. See page 15.*

Student Identification Cards

- *Required for all students. To obtain or update a Lee College ID card after classes start, you will need your paid receipt & a photo ID.* During on-campus registration, ID photos can be taken in Moler Hall. After on-campus registration, IDs will be made at the Library Circulation Desk. During the first week of classes, IDs will be taken during regular Library hours. After that, IDs will only be taken on Tuesdays and Wednesdays from 10:30–11:30 a.m. and from 6:30–7:30 p.m. or on Saturdays from Noon–1 p.m. IDs will be made on demand if required to check out Library material.

1. The author's purpose in writing this passage is to
   - (1) persuade students to attend Lee College.
   - (2) inform students about programs at Lee College.
   - (3) tell students how to apply for financial aid.
   - (4) explain admissions procedures at Lee College.
   - (5) give student regulations at Lee College.

2. According to the passage, where would you obtain a New Student Information Card?
   - (1) Moler Hall Bookstore
   - (2) Rundell Hall
   - (3) Counseling Center
   - (4) The Library Circulation Desk
   - (5) Admissions and Record Office

3. According to the passage, how many ways of buying books are there?
   - (1) 1
   - (2) 2
   - (3) 3
   - (4) 4
   - (5) 5

4. It is important to submit proof of residency, because students who do not live in the local area
   - (1) may not attend Lee College.
   - (2) require higher grades to be admitted.
   - (3) pay higher tuition.
   - (4) must live in on-campus housing.
   - (5) must apply for admission in person.

Check your answers on page 279.

Exercise 3

> **Directions:** Items 1–3 are based on an excerpt from an employee handbook. Read the passage carefully, and then answer the questions.

HOW IS THE PERFORMANCE OF HOURLY EMPLOYEES EVALUATED?

Line Hourly Staff Employees are asked annually to complete a self-appraisal form by April 30th of each year. At the same time the hourly employee receives the self-appraisal form, his/her supervisor

5 will receive a performance appraisal form. These forms are to be filled out by the hourly employee and the supervisor and then discussed.

     Performance evaluations and supervisory recommendations are to be discussed individually

10 and privately with each Employee. The evaluation is then forwarded to the appropriate Vice President for final decisions regarding a merit increase. Employees are to receive a copy of the evaluation and recommendations and may make written

15 comments regarding their evaluation for inclusion in their personnel files.

     Supervisors will provide additional evaluation opportunities within the first year of an Hourly Staff member's employment. The initial evaluation,

20 along with continued support and training, provides the best opportunity for successful performance on the part of new Hourly Staff members, as well as providing adequate information for informed personnel decisions.

—From *Personnel Policies and Procedures,*
Cardinal Stritch University

1. How often do employees complete a self-appraisal form?
   - (1) Each week
   - (2) Each month
   - (3) Every six months
   - (4) Each year
   - (5) Every two years

2. After the employee and the supervisor fill out their appraisal forms, what is the next step in the evaluation?

(1) The employee and supervisor discuss the two appraisal forms.

(2) The supervisor discusses the appraisals with the Vice President.

(3) The appraisals are sent to the Vice President.

(4) The employee meets with the Vice President.

(5) The Vice President decides on the employee's merit increase.

3. Suppose that an employee who has been on the job for three months is not performing as well as expected. What would the supervisor most likely do first?

(1) Contact the appropriate Vice President and ask to begin a formal evaluation

(2) Warn the employee

(3) Fire the employee

(4) Make a complaint in writing

(5) Complete an appraisal form and have the employee complete a self-appraisal

Check your answers on page 279.

Visual Information

Many nonfictional texts have a strong visual component—that is, they rely on detailed descriptions to convey information to the reader. Examples of nonfiction works that include much descriptive information are reviews about art, theater, and film; history books; art books; and works about nature. Even science books can have a strong visual component; for example, a science book or article might describe an experiment, piece of apparatus, animal, or plant in great detail. When you read descriptive text, you should attempt to visualize the scene being described in your mind's eye. This will allow you to understand how the parts relate to the whole and, in general, to understand the author's meaning.

Interpreting Comments on the Visual Arts

Visual arts include painting, photography, sculpture, and architecture. People enjoy visual arts because such works show them something new about themselves or society.

Some basic information that appears in comments, such as reviews or textbooks, about the visual arts, includes:

- The title of the work of art and the name of the artist

- Where the work can be seen

- The reviewer's opinion; whether the work is of value, and why

- How the work was created

Exercise 4

Directions: Items 1–3 refer to the following excerpt from a classic book about nature. This detailed description of a small feature of the natural world vividly conveys the writer's sense of wonder and delight.

WHAT MAKES THIS PLACE SPECIAL?

Line A dawn wind stirs on the great marsh. With almost imperceptible slowness it rolls a bank of fog across the wide morass. Like the white ghost of a glacier the mists advance, riding over pha-
5 lanxes of tamarack, sliding across bogmeadows heavy with dew. A single silence hangs from horizon to horizon.

Out of some far recess of the sky a tinkling of little bells falls soft upon the listening land.
10 Then again silence. Now comes a baying of some sweet-throated hound, soon the clamor of a responding pack. Then a far clear blast of hunting horns, out of the sky into the fog.

High horns, low horns, silence, and finally a
15 pandemonium of trumpets, rattles, croaks, and cries that almost shakes the bog with its nearness, but without yet disclosing whence it comes. At last a glint of sun reveals the approach of a great echelon of birds. On motionless wings they
20 emerge from the lifting mists, sweep a final arc of sky, and settle in clangorous descending spirals to their feeding grounds. A new day has begun on the crane marsh.

—From *A Sand County Almanac*, by Aldo Leopold

1. What is the main thing that is happening in this passage?

   (1) Hunters with dogs are killing cranes.
   (2) Dawn is breaking over the marsh.
   (3) The writer has killed a crane.
   (4) The cranes have flown away from the marsh.
   (5) The sun has set, and all is still.

2. Which sentence from the passage includes an example of alliteration?

   (1) "A dawn wind stirs on the great marsh . . ."
   (2) "A single silence hangs from horizon to horizon . . ."
   (3) "Then a far clear blast of hunting horns . . ."
   (4) "Now comes a baying of some sweet-throated hound . . ."
   (5) "A new day has begun on the crane marsh . . ."

3. What is the best way to describe the author's perspective on the scene he describes in this passage?

   (1) Fear
   (2) Distancing
   (3) Joy
   (4) Anger
   (5) Awe

Check your answers on page 279.

Exercise 5

Directions: Items 1–4 refer to this descriptive passage from a history book. Read the passage carefully and attempt to visualize the subject in your mind. Then answer the questions.

WHY DID A CITY GROW HERE?

Line Geography was destiny. From prehistoric times, Britain's grandest river ran through a broad valley, fed by streams from wooded hills now called Highgate and Hampstead and from higher ground
5   beyond Camberwell, down to the North Sea. The Thames was wider and shallower than now; marshes and mud-flats abounded, and islands appeared at low tide—names like Battersea and Bermondsey commemorate former islands. (The
10   Anglo-Saxon *ea* means island, so Battersea is Peter's Island.) The Thames valley offered hospitable terrain for pastoralists, and Neolithic sites sprang up; but though settlements have been discovered—at Runnymede, Staines, and Heath-
15   row, for instance—there is no proof that central London was permanently settled by the Celts

before the Romans. Nevertheless, geology and geography foreordained that it would, in time, become a choice place of habitation.
20   Strategic considerations and physical features marked this spot as suitable for civilization. It was the lowest point where the Thames could be forded and bridged. Here, forty miles from the sea, the river was blessed with a gravel bed. In
25   contrast to treacherous mudbanks, gravel subsoil provided safe landings for trading craft crossing the Channel and venturing up the Thames.

   —From *London, A Social History,* by Roy Porter

1. According to the passage, gravel subsoil allows

   (1) people to ford the river.
   (2) people to build bridges.
   (3) boats to land safely.
   (4) animals to drink from the river.
   (5) people to build houses.

2. Which sentence states the main idea of the passage?

   (1) Geography was destiny.
   (2) The Thames was wider and shallower than now.
   (3) Anglo-Saxon *ea* means island.
   (4) London was the lowest point where the Thames could be forded.
   (5) The river was blessed with a gravel bed.

3. Of the following place names, which probably means "island"?

   (1) Kent
   (2) Thames
   (3) Camberwell
   (4) Hammondsey
   (5) Staines

4. "London grew astonishingly in the nineteenth century, with its hordes of labourers and landlords, its pen-pushers and porters. Between 1841 and 1851 alone, some 330,000 migrants flooded into the capital . . ."

   This passage from later in the same book tells you that

   (1) the Thames valley included good farmland.
   (2) London's destiny was eventually fulfilled.
   (3) the gravel beds allowed for boat moorings.
   (4) there was plenty of water for flocks.
   (5) people traveled up the river to settle there.

Check your answers on page 280.

Exercise 6

Direction: Items 1–3 refer to the following passage from an anatomy textbook. It describes a condition that affects the eyes of many elderly people. Read the passage carefully, visualize the descriptive material, and answer the questions that follow.

WHAT CAUSES CATARACTS?

Line The transparency of the lens depends on a precise combination of structural and biochemical characteristics. When the balance becomes disturbed the lens loses its transparency, and the

5 abnormal lens is known as a cataract. Cataracts may result from drug reactions, injuries, or radiation, but senile cataracts are the most common form.

    Over time, the lens takes on a yellowish hue,

10 and eventually it begins to lose its transparency. As the lens becomes "cloudy," the individual needs brighter and brighter reading lights, and visual clarity begins to fade. If the lens becomes completely opaque, the person will be functionally

15 blind, even thought the retinal receptors are normal. Modern surgical procedures involve removing the lens, either intact or in pieces, after shattering it with high-frequency sound. The missing lens can be replaced by an artificial

20 substitute, and vision can then be fine-tuned with glasses or contact lenses.

    —From *Fundamentals of Anatomy and Physiology*, by Frederick Martini

1. In a person who has cataracts, the lens of the eye becomes

  (1) cloudy.
  (2) thick.
  (3) soft.
  (4) brittle.
  (5) dark.

2. A person who is developing cataracts would be likely to make the comment,

  (1) "It seems very warm in here."
  (2) "Please speak up."
  (3) "My soup isn't hot enough."
  (4) "My feet are cold."
  (5) "The light seems very dim."

3. According to the passage, the most common cause of cataracts is

  (1) disease.
  (2) radiation.
  (3) old age.
  (4) drug reactions.
  (5) surgery.

Check your answers on page 280.

Glossary

characters: the imaginary people portrayed in a piece of fiction

comedy: drama that is intended to amuse through its lighthearted approach and happy ending

conclusion: a judgment or opinion based on information an author provides

conflict: a clash of ideas, attitudes, or forces

dialogue: a conversation between characters

diction: word choice; the types of words a writer uses in different situations

drama: a play that can be read or performed

fact: something that can be proved to be true

farce: a comedy that contains humorous characterizations and improbable plots

fiction: writing about imaginary people and events

figurative language: imaginative words and phrases that create a vivid image

foreshadowing: a technique used to suggest what will happen later

free verse: poetry that contains little or no rhyme or rhythm

image: a mental picture created for the reader by a skillful choice of words

irony: a situation in which there is a startling difference between what is expected to happen and what actually does happen

main idea: the point or idea that the writer wants to communicate

metaphor: a comparison in which two things are described as the same—without the use of the words *like* or *as*

monologue: a long and often emotional speech by one character, often revealing important feelings or events, when another character is present

mood: the feeling or atmosphere that a piece of writing conveys

narrator: the person or character who tells the story

opinion: a belief that cannot be proved absolutely but that can be supported with evidence

personification: figurative language in which something that is not human is given human characteristics

perspective: a way of looking at people, places, and events

playwright: the author of a drama

plot: the sequence of events in a story

poem: relatively brief, often intense and emotional work of literature

point of view: the perspective of the narrator

rhyme: the use of words with endings that sound alike

rhyme scheme: a pattern of rhyming sounds that gives structure to a poem

rhythm: the pattern of sounds formed by words

satire: a comedy that makes fun of human characteristics or failings

simile: a figure of speech in which two things are compared through the use of the words *like* or *as*

stage directions: information that describes the stage setting and the movements of the characters in a drama

stanza: two or more lines of poetry grouped together

supporting idea: a fact that provides more information about a main idea

symbol: something used to represent something else

symbolism: figurative language in which an object, person, or event represents a larger, more abstract idea

tone: the attitude or feeling that a piece of writing conveys

tragedy: drama that ends in great misfortune or ruin for a major character, especially when a moral issue is involved

ANSWERS AND EXPLANATIONS

Unit 1: Fiction

Exercise 1 *(page 254)*

How Are Guido and Vincent Related?

1. **The correct answer is (3). (Analysis)** Although the main idea is never directly stated in this passage, every sentence is about the relationship between Guido and Vincent, leading to the conclusion that that is the topic of the passage. The other choices given are all details that support the main idea.

2. **The correct answer is (4). (Synthesis)** This question really asks you to speculate about the main idea of the entire work from which the passage comes. The key to this question appears in the last full paragraph, where Guido and Vincent begin to think about their future careers. Finally, we learn that they find themselves together again in their late twenties. This implies that the novel will focus on this time period and the key events that determine the characters' adult lives. The remaining choices are details from the passage.

Exercise 2 *(page 255)*

What Are the Characters Waiting For?

1. **The correct answer is (1). (Analysis)** The diction is best described as informal, conversational, or everyday. No formal or archaic, or old-fashioned, words are used, choices (2), (3), and (4). Although the passage is slyly comic, choice (5), this term applies to tone more than to diction.

2. **The correct answer is (4). (Synthesis)** The author uses very simple, undramatic language in an effort to keep the tone flat. The drollness and sly comedy comes out in the choice of language, such as "the General didn't give two slaps." Because the language used is so simple, choices (1), (2), and (3) are incorrect. Choice (5) is incorrect because the flat tone obviously results from careful choice of language rather than from lack of artistry.

3. **The correct choice is (5). (Analysis)** The passage makes it clear that the General is bored by the idea of the graduation but will consent to sitting on stage and being admired, while Sally is sure that he will die before her "triumph." To him, the graduation is a bore; to her, it is a triumph. This difference is a source of great irony. Choices (1) and (2) are incorrect because each provides only half of the right answer. Choices (3) and (4) are not supported by the passage.

4. **The correct answer is (3). (Analysis)** The General is vain because he thinks only of people admiring him in his uniform. He is selfish because he thinks only of himself and his own likes and dislikes.

Exercise 3 *(page 257)*

What Is This Man Feeling?

1. **The correct answer is (4). (Synthesis)** Andras is engaged throughout the passage in thinking deeply about his wife and family, so he is not distant, choice (2), but rather ambivalent. Ambivalent implies that his feelings are both positive and negative, a statement borne out by the passage. Although angry feelings, choice (1), are mentioned, they refer to Nina, not to Andras. And while Andras seems to love Nina, his feelings cannot be described as adoring or passionate, so choices (3) and (5) are incorrect.

2. **The correct answer is (2). (Synthesis)** This question asks you to compare two passages, one of which is a brief excerpt. The major point of contrast is that the central character in the novel is alone, while Andras, the central character in the main passage, is at home surrounded by his family. Choice (1) can be eliminated because we do not know if the central character in the excerpt is a woman or not. Choice (3) is incorrect because we hear the thoughts of both characters. Choice (4) is incorrect because the opposite is true—the excerpt uses images of light, while the passage describes sounds. Choice (5) is incorrect because neither character is described vividly.

3. **The correct answer is (1). (Analysis)** The main idea of the paragraph is stated in the first sentence. The remaining choices are details from the paragraph.

4. **The correct answer is (5). (Synthesis)** Many clues point to this: the reference to the Israeli invasion of Lebanon, the references to the movement of people across the globe, from Argentina and Budapest, the reference to the *Economist* newsmagazine. In addition, the language is quite modern.

Exercise 4 *(page 258)*

How Might This Place Affect This Couple's Life?

1. **The correct answer is (3). (Comprehension)** Lines 12 and 17-18 describe the landscape as frozen and overwhelming, respectively. It is a place of "vast hardness" (line 19) and of a "savage kind of beauty" (line 24). All of the other choices present positive descriptions.

2. **The correct answer is (4). (Synthesis)** According to lines 16-19, "the great fact was the land itself, which seemed to overwhelm the little beginnings of human society that struggled in its sombre wastes." Thus, it is likely that the pioneers will face many challenges as they try to tame this land. Choice (1) contradicts this likelihood. There is no evidence for the other choices, although such events could take place.

What Does Ignatius Look Like?

3. **The correct answer is (3). (Analysis)** Ignatius's ears stick out from his head, much like turn signals. Choice (1) suggests the opposite. Choices (2), (4), and (5) all suggest a positive impression of Ignatius's appearance or behavior, which the passage does not support.

4. **The correct answer is (2). (Synthesis)** Ignatius seems to be hiding under his cap and observing the other people from a distance. Choice (1) suggests the opposite, that he is part of the crowd. Ignatius is casually dressed, so choice (3) is incorrect. There is no evidence to support choices (4) and (5).

5. **The correct answer is (4). (Synthesis)** The best choice is comical. The author's images suggest that there may be morbid or absurd elements to the story. That is a literary genre known as *black humor*.

Exercise 5 *(page 259)*

What Happens to Deerslayer?

1. **The correct answer is (5). (Analysis)** The most exciting, dramatic moment is when Deerslayer takes aim at the Indian. This moment of tension is followed by events that result from his decision not to fire. The other choices are all events that either lead up to or follow this climax.

How Does the Boy Interpret His Surroundings?

2. **The correct answer is (2). (Analysis)** Everything that the boy sees reminds him that he has stolen something. Choices (1), (3), and (4) are incorrect because he does not state his fear of being lost, love of nature, or fear of the outside world. He probably is happy to have some food, as choice (5) states; in this passage, however, what he thinks about is his guilt.

Exercise 6 *(page 260)*

What Is Mrs. Bennet Hoping?

1. **The correct answer is (2). (Comprehension)** The main idea of this passage, that ". . . a single man in possession of a good fortune, must be in want of a wife," is stated directly in the first sentence. The rest of the conversation serves to illustrate this belief.

2. **The correct answer is (4). (Synthesis)** Mrs. Bennet is assuming that Bingley actually does want a wife. Choice (1) is incorrect because the reader knows for a fact that Netherfield Park has been rented. There is no mention of Mrs. Bennet's older daughter in particular, as choice (3) indicates. Lines 16–21 suggest that Mrs. Bennet does not care whether her husband is interested, so choice (2) can be eliminated. There is no evidence for choice (5).

3. **The correct answer is (5). (Application)** Mrs. Bennet's main characteristic in this passage is her nosiness into the lives of those around her. Choices (3) and (4) can be eliminated because the passage does not indicate how hardworking or lazy she might be. Ambition, which is suggested in choices (1) and (2), is hinted at, but it is not nearly as strong a characteristic in Mrs. Bennet as are curiosity and love for gossip.

4. **The correct answer is (1). (Synthesis)** Mrs. Bennet's references to Mr. Bingley's yearly salary and his having rented Netherfield Park indicate that she is impressed by his wealth. Choice (4) states the opposite, that he is poor. She does not know for certain who his father is or that he wants to marry, so choices (3) and (2) are incorrect. There is no discussion of his career, so choice (5) can be eliminated.

Unit 2: Poetry

Exercise 1 *(page 262)*

What Thoughts Come to the Speaker's Mind?

1. **The correct answer is (5). (Synthesis)** The reference to a voyage refers to the poet's impending death. The poet is reflecting on the passing of time.

2. **The correct answer is (4). (Analysis)** By repeating the phrases "Go by," "They fly," and "They die," the speaker uses rhyme, rhythm, and repetition to make the point that time passes. Line 10 contains a simile, so choice (1) is incorrect. Choice (2) can be eliminated because the speaker mentions great heroes, not his own ancestors. Choices (3) and (5) are incorrect because the speaker does not mention the ocean in these lines and because he does use rhyme and rhythm.

Exercise 2 *(page 263)*

How Is Death Personified?

1. **The correct answer is (3). (Comprehension)** Lines 2–5 introduce Death as a courteous carriage driver. There is no evidence of his age, as choices (1), (4), and (5) suggest. Because Death is characterized as male, choice (2) is incorrect.

2. **The correct answer is (5). (Comprehension)** The speaker has "put away" her labor and leisure (work and rest) because her life is over; Death is kind, she is content to move slowly. Choices (1), (2), and (3) are incorrect because they imply that the speaker wants to be taken home. Choice (4) can be eliminated because the speaker says that they drove slowly (line 5).

3. **The correct answer is (4). (Analysis)** The "house" is a gravesite. Choices (2) and (5) are incorrect because the speaker is using a figurative image. It is more specific than the earth as a whole, so choice (1) can be eliminated. There is no evidence to suggest she is at her place of birth, as choice (3) indicates.

Exercise 3 *(page 264)*

Where Is the Speaker Going?

1. **The correct answer is (1). (Synthesis)** From the phrase "the gods come for me" (line 2), it can be assumed that the speaker is near death. The references to "holy places" and "gods" mean the speaker is likely a religious person, so choice (2) can be eliminated. There is no evidence for the other choices.

2. **The correct answer is (3). (Comprehension)** Choice (1) is mentioned in line 8, choices (2) and (4) appear together in line 4, and choice (5) is the subject of line 7.

3. **The correct answer is (4). (Synthesis)** The speaker's point is that his spirit will live on in nature after death. The speaker might agree with the other choices, but these do not relate to the speaker's beliefs about death and spirituality.

4. **The correct answer is (2). (Application)** If the younger brother believes the speaker, he will probably have a greater respect for nature, since the speaker's spirit is a part of nature. Choices (3) and (4) can be eliminated because they suggest a disregard for nature. Choices (1) and (5) are incorrect, respectively, because nothing is suggested about the younger brother's children or about spreading the speaker's message to others.

What Strong Emotions Does This Speaker Express?

5. **The correct answer is (4). (Comprehension)** The speaker never compares her strong feelings to fear or any negative emotion. In lines 7–9, the speaker compares her love to the other choices.

6. **The correct answer is (1). (Analysis)** The speaker repeats the phrase "I love thee . . ." in lines 1, 2, 5, 7, 8, 9, 11, 12, and 14. This brief sonnet does not follow any strict narrative pattern of rising action, crisis, and falling action, so choice (2) is incorrect. Stage directions are used only in drama, so choice (3) can be eliminated. The speaker states that her love will continue after death. This statement does not stand out from the rest of the poem as a foreshadowing of her own death, so choice (4) is not the best answer. The speaker does not personify inanimate objects to describe her feelings, so choice (5) can be eliminated.

7. **The correct answer is (2). (Application)** Phrases such as "I love thee to the depth and breadth and height/My soul can reach . . ." (lines 2–3) and "I love thee with the breath,/Smiles, tears, of all my life!" (lines 12–13) are dramatic statements, full of emotion and exaggeration. Choices (1), (3), and (5) suggest the opposite and can be eliminated. The speaker's tone is one of honesty, not deceit or manipulation, so choice (4) can be eliminated.

8. **The correct answer is (5). (Application)** The speaker states her undying love, so choice (5) is the best answer. Choices (1) and (4) suggest a sad or negative theme and can be eliminated. The speaker is declaring her unity with one other person. Because choices (2) and (3) suggest connection with a larger group of people, they are incorrect.

Unit 3: Drama

Exercise 1 *(page 266)*

What Brings These Characters Together?

1. **The correct answer is (3). (Comprehension)** According to line 1, "a few pale stars" are shining, so choice (5) is incorrect. The fact that Guicho enters over a dune (line 6) suggests a desert or desert-like setting, thus eliminating the other choices.

2. **The correct answer is (4). (Synthesis)** These stage directions call for Calorías to confront Guicho, laugh at him, and then put his hands on Guicho's cello. These actions—especially when added to his words at this point—show his pleasure at causing Guicho distress. There is no evidence for the other choices.

Why Do These Characters Disagree?

3. **The correct answer is (4). (Comprehension)** Cory's perspective, or opinion, is that he will be able to play football and continue working on the weekends. The clearest statement of this is in lines 9-11. There is no evidence for the other choices.

4. **The correct answer is (1). (Comprehension)** Troy's perspective is that football is not practical and won't make Cory a success. In lines 25-27 Troy states, "The white man ain't gonna let you get nowhere with that football no way." There is no evidence for the other choices.

5. **The correct answer is (4). (Synthesis)** Statements such as, "You damn right you are! Ain't no need for nobody coming around here to talk to me about signing nothing" (lines 20-22) show that Troy is a strict parent. Choice (5) states the opposite. Cruel is too strong a word to describe Troy, so choice (3) is incorrect. Troy may be sympathetic sometimes, but not in this situation, so choice (1) can be eliminated. Troy may be trying to pass along wise advice, as choice (2) suggests, but his emotion undercuts his wisdom.

6. **The correct answer is (5). (Synthesis)** The passage does not resolve what Cory will choose to do. All the other choices describe information that is directly stated or strongly suggested in the passage.

Exercise 2 *(page 268)*

What Past Problems Do Lola and Doc Discuss?

1. **The correct answer is (4). (Application)** Doc believes that "what's in the past can't be helped" (lines 24-25)—a good restatement of the proverb about spilled milk. Choices (1), (2), and (3) apply to being frugal and efficient, not to thoughts about the past. The passage indicates that Doc and Lola do not have a lot of money, as choice (5) suggests, but that choice can be eliminated because they have seen a good bit of care in the past.

2. **The correct answer is (2). (Synthesis)** Lola and Doc are discussing secret events in their past. They seem to have a good marriage, but these memories are sad, so choice (1) is not the best answer. Doc "had to give up being a doctor . . ." (line 20), but they do not discuss this profession, so choice (4) is incorrect. References to college and the future do not suggest ways to succeed, so choices (4) and (5) are not logical.

3. **The correct answer is (5). (Analysis)** The stage direction in line 5 indicates that Doc is "consoling." Lola refers to how Doc must feel at times because he had to give up being a doctor and doesn't have the money he once had (lines 19-22). Both try to be understanding. Doc affectionately refers to Lola as "Baby." Neither whines, so choice (1) is incorrect. Although Lola has regrets (lines 9-11), there is no indication that either she or Doc is bitter, so choice (2) is incorrect. There are no challenges or apologies, so choices (3) and (4) are incorrect.

4. **The correct answer is (3). (Analysis)** Doc and Lola discuss their past problems in a loving manner. She asks him what he thinks (lines 3-4, 6-7, and 10-11). He calls her "Baby," consoles her (lines 5, 8, and 12-13), and encourages her to "live for the present" (line 26). There is no evidence for choices (1) and (4). Although Doc calls Lola "Baby," there is no indication of their acting silly together, so choice (2) is incorrect. They are discussing past problems. There is no evidence that their current relationship is full of frustration, so choice (5) is incorrect.

Unit 4: Nonfiction

Exercise 1 *(page 269)*

What Is the Carnegie Organization of Washington?

1. **The correct answer is (1). (Comprehension)** The answer is stated in the first sentence of the passage. All the other choices are phrases from the passage, but they are not the Institution's purpose. Choice (3) is close to the correct answer, but it is vague rather than precise, so choice (1) is the better choice.

2. **The correct answer is (5). (Analysis)** Because all the language used in the passage is highly favorable to the Institution, it is written from the perspective of the Institution itself.

3. **The correct answer is (2). (Comprehension)** The answer is stated directly in the next-to-last sentence of the passage. The other choices are groups mentioned in the passage as participating in other Carnegie programs.

Exercise 2 *(page 270)*

How Do I Become a Student at Lee College?

1. **The correct answer is (4). (Analysis)** Although the passage mentions where to find information about financial aid, choice (3), its main purpose is to give admissions procedures. Choices (1), (2), and (5) are not supported by the passage.

2. **The correct answer is (5). (Comprehension)** This is stated in the first section, under the heading "Apply for Admission." Although the passage also states that the bookstore is in Moler Hall, you would not apply for admission in that part of the building.

3. **The correct answer is (2). (Comprehension)** Under the heading "Buy Books," the passage states that you may either buy books on line or go to Moler Hall.

4. **The correct answer is (3). (Comprehension)** In the first paragraph of the passage, under the heading, "Apply for Admission," it states that students must submit proof of residency in order to be eligible for in-state fees.

Exercise 3 *(page 271)*

How Is the Performance of Hourly Employees Evaluated?

1. **The correct answer is (4). (Comprehension)** The passage states that employees complete a self-appraisal form by April 30 of each year.

2. **The correct answer is (1). (Comprehension)** This step is listed, in order, in the first paragraph of the passage. The other choices all list steps that occur later in the process.

3. **The correct answer is (5). (Application)** The last paragraph states that supervisors should provide additional opportunities for evaluation during the first year of employment. This implies that if a new employee is experiencing difficulties, the first step would be to begin a formal evaluation by completing the two appraisal forms.

Exercise 4 *(page 272)*

What Makes This Place Special?

1. **The correct answer is (2). (Synthesis)** The passage describes the dawn on the marsh, from the first faint signs until the cranes arrive to feed. Although hunters and hunting dogs are mentioned, there is no evidence for choices (1) or (3). Choices (4) and (5) are not supported by the passage.

2. **The correct answer is (2). (Analysis)** Alliteration refers to the repetition of sounds at the beginning of words. This sentence repeats both the "s" sound in "single silence" and the "h" sound in "horizon to horizon." None of the other choices uses this technique.

3. **The correct answer is (5). (Synthesis)** You can determine the correct answer to this question by considering the author's tone and choice of language throughout the passage; also, you can eliminate the other choices as unsupported by that language. The language is calm but elevated, deliberate and cadenced, almost poetic. The overall effect is quiet awe at the wonder of the scene.

Exercise 5 *(page 273)*

Why Did a City Grow Here?

1. **The correct answer is (3). (Comprehension)** This item is related to cause and effect, but the answer is stated in the last paragraph of the passage. Although choices (1) and (2) are mentioned in the passage, they are not the reason that gravel banks are advantageous. Choices (4) and (5) are not supported by the passage.

2. **The correct answer is (1). (Analysis)** The main idea is stated in the first sentence of the first paragraph, and the rest of the passage is mostly detail.

3. **The correct answer is (4). (Application)** The passage states that *ea* meant island, and it gives an example of a name, Bermondsey, that is parallel with the correct answer, Hammondsey. There is no support for the other choices in the passage.

4. **The correct answer is (2). (Synthesis)** The main passage describes a place that is still unsettled, yet destined for greatness by its geography. The excerpt depicts a time when vast numbers of people are pouring into the city—its destiny fulfilled. There is no support for the other choices in the main passage; choice (5) is incorrect because by the 1840s people would have arrived in London by railroad and coach, not by boat.

Exercise 6 *(page 274)*

What Causes Cataracts?

1. **The correct answer is (1). (Comprehension)** The correct answer is stated directly in the first paragraph (lines 3–5).

2. **The correct answer is (5). (Application)** The passage states that the person would need brighter and brighter light in order to see; therefore, the person would be likely to mention that the light seemed dimmer than usual. The other choices are not supported by the passage.

3. **The correct answer is (3). (Comprehension)** The passage states that senile cataracts, or cataracts related to old age, are the most common form. Choices (1), (2), and (4) are incorrect because these are all mentioned as minor causes, while the question asks for the most common cause. Choice (5), surgery, is mentioned in the passage as a cure, not a cause.

PART V
MATHEMATICS

What Will I Find on the Mathematics Test?

The GED Mathematics Test is made up of two separate but equally weighted booklets: Part I has 25 questions and allows the use of a calculator, Part II has 25 questions and needs to be completed without the use of a calculator. Both sections must be successfully completed in order to receive a score. The Casio *fx-260 Solar* (scientific) calculator will be furnished at the testing site. Several sample questions will be provided prior to the actual test so you can practice and become familiar with the calculator. Knowing how to use the calculator beforehand will significantly improve your test score. A page of formulas will be included. You will have 90 minutes to complete the exam.

Arithmetic, measurement, algebra, geometry, number relations, trigonometry, and data analysis will be tested, with an emphasis on data analysis and statistics. Most of the questions are multiple choice, each with five choices. About 25 percent of the questions are set-up questions, where you do not have to actually calculate an answer for the problem but rather identify the correct way to solve the problem. You will be required to perform multistep problems with and without the use of calculators where you have to use multiple pieces of information that may be presented to you through pie charts, bar graphs, and tables and arrive at a conclusion. Approximately 20 percent of the problems appearing in both parts of the exam are alternate-format (not multiple choice). This is similar to a free-response answer, where you will be provided with a grid or coordinate plane that you will need to fill out with the correct response.

F.Y.I.

The GED is based on the philosophy that the expectations for today's high school graduates are very different from the past. The present generation of students is exposed to calculators early in their mathematical education. In order to be able to survive in this new technological environment, more emphasis is now being put on the ability to analyze and solve problems with or without the use of calculators rather than just mechanically follow algorithms. In order to meet these requirements, the GED also includes trigonometry, the use of calculators, and alternate-format questions.

RUBRICS AND SUGGESTIONS FOR IMPROVED TEST PERFORMANCE

- Study the given information thoroughly and answer the question(s) that follow. Refer to the information as often as necessary to answer the questions.

- Manage your time wisely. Do not spend too much time on any one problem. Answer *all* of the questions. You will not be penalized for incorrect answers.

- The degree of difficulty of the problems does not depend on the progression of the test.

- The alternate-format problems will be randomly distributed throughout the two booklets in the following manner: Booklet One has 6 standard grids and 1 coordinate-plane grid. Booklet Two has 2 standard grids and 1 coordinate-plane grid. The difficulty level of these types of problems ranges from extremely easy to challenging.

- A sheet of formulas will be provided. Not all problems will require the use of a formula. Not all formulas will be used in the test.

- Some questions contain more information than is needed to solve the problem. Some problems will not have enough information given, in which case, the correct answer is "not enough information is given."

- The numeric multiple-choice answer choices will always appear in ascending or descending order. Other than percent (%), degree (°), and dollar ($), answers will not contain any units of measurement.

- Do not make marks on the test booklet. Use blank paper for your calculations. Record your answers on the separate answer sheet provided. Be sure all requested information is properly recorded on the answer sheet.

- To record your answers for the multiple-choice questions, mark the numbered space on the answer sheet beside the number that corresponds to the question in the test booklet.

- For multiple-choice answers, mark only one answer bubble for each question. Duplicate markings for the same question will be scored as incorrect.

- To record your answers to the alternate-format question that requires the standard grid, write the actual numeric answer down in the blank spaces at the top of the grid, then fill in the circles that correspond to the correct numbers of your answer. The standard grid *does not* allow you to write negative numbers with mixed numbers. There are only 5 spaces on the standard grid.

- To record your answers for the alternate-format question that requires the coordinate plane grid, identify the correct coordinate and fill in the circle that corresponds to it. The maximum range for both x and y is $(6, -6)$.

- Many problems will explicitly (or sometimes, implicitly) ask you to round off answers. Along with your knowledge of the typical rounding rule, you also need to pay close attention to the story line of the problem so you can make the rounding decision wisely. For example, monetarly amounts should be rounded to the nearest hundredths, whereas people, cars, packaged items, etc. should always be rounded to the next greater whole number.

- Do not make any stray or unnecessary marks (for example, do not doodle or rest your pencil) on the answer sheet.

- If you change your answer, erase the first mark *completely*.

- *Do not* fold or crease your answer sheet.

- Use a #2 pencil to fill in the bubbles.

- For the actual exam, carry extra pencils, a couple of good-quality erasers (that won't smear), and a pencil sharpener.

- Familiarize yourself with the Casio *fx-260 Solar* (scientific) calculator before the test.

- On the day of the exam, arrive early at the testing center so you won't feel rushed or stressed.

USING THE GRIDS

Example 1: Multiple Choice

If a grocery bill totaling $15.75 is paid with a $20 bill, how much change should be returned?

(1) $3.25
(2) $3.75
(3) $4.25
(4) $4.75
(5) $5.26

The correct answer is $4.25. Therefore, bubble number 3 is filled in on the answer sheet.

Example 2: Standard Grid

Add the following: 1.3, 0.3, and 9.

Answer this question using the standard grid on your answer sheet.

The correct answer is 10.6, which can be filled out in either one of the following ways:

Example 3: Standard Grid

Perform the operations $5\frac{1}{2} - 2\frac{1}{4} =$

Answer this question in the standard grid on your answer sheet.

Even though the correct answer is $3\frac{1}{4}$, we must rename it as its improper form for the standard grid. So, we write 13/4 and fill out the grid in either of the following ways:

1	3	/	4	
	⊘	●	⊘	
⦁	⦁	⦁	⦁	⦁
⓪	⓪	⓪	⓪	⓪
●	①	①	①	①
②	②	②	②	②
③	●	③	③	③
④	④	④	●	④
⑤	⑤	⑤	⑤	⑤
⑥	⑥	⑥	⑥	⑥
⑦	⑦	⑦	⑦	⑦
⑧	⑧	⑧	⑧	⑧
⑨	⑨	⑨	⑨	⑨

	1	3	/	4
	⊘	⊘	●	
⦁	⦁	⦁	⦁	⦁
⓪	⓪	⓪	⓪	⓪
①	●	①	①	①
②	②	②	②	②
③	③	●	③	③
④	④	④	④	●
⑤	⑤	⑤	⑤	⑤
⑥	⑥	⑥	⑥	⑥
⑦	⑦	⑦	⑦	⑦
⑧	⑧	⑧	⑧	⑧
⑨	⑨	⑨	⑨	⑨

Example 4: Coordinate Plane Grid

Mark $(-3,2)$ on the coordinate plane grid.

Answer this question using the coordinate plane grid provided on your answer sheet.

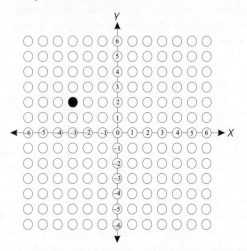

A QUICK PREVIEW

Here are some typical questions that you may encounter in your GED math exam. These represent the different areas of math covered in the GED.

ARITHMETIC

Arithmetic is the foundation of all mathematics. Your ability to perform basic operations involving whole numbers, fractions, and decimals will enhance your mathematical aptitude in other areas such as statistics, algebra, and trigonometry. Measurements, number relationships, ratios, and percents also fall under the category of arithmetic.

The following is an example of a multiple-choice question without the use of a calculator:

Example 1

Charlotte collected 200 different toys for charity. She gave the local church and orphanage 75 and 55 toys, respectively. How many toys does she have left to give away to other charities?

- **(1)** 130
- **(2)** 70
- **(3)** 125
- **(4)** 145
- **(5)** 330

The correct answer is (2). An efficient way to solve this problem is to add the toys she gives away to the church and orphanage and then subtract that amount from the total number of toys she had originally.

$$75 + 55 = 130, 200 - 130 = 70$$

Now we will look at a problem that has a similar concept but will require a calculator.

Example 2

The balance in Yuri's bank account last month was $976.16. After he deposited his paycheck of $1,204.87 from his first job and $720.96 from his second one, he wrote checks for $990 (rent), $79.93 (telephone), and $360.62 (credit card). What is the current balance in Yuri's account?

(1) $29.52
(2) $495.28
(3) $1430.55
(4) $1,471.44
(5) $2,901.99

The correct answer is (4).

New balance = old balance + both paychecks
           − all checks written

New balance = $976.16 + $1,204.87 + $720.96
           − $990 − $79.93 − $360.62

New balance = $1,471.44

STATISTICS AND DATA ANALYSIS

The next problem is an example of a set-up problem where you must use a graph to interpret your answer.

Example 3

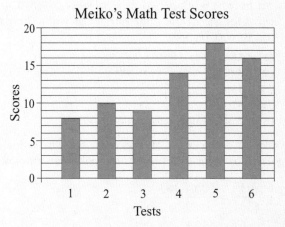

You have been given a graphical representation of Meiko's math test scores. Which of the following expressions can be used to find her mean test score?

(1) $\dfrac{1 + 2 + 3 + 4 + 5 + 6}{6}$

(2) $\dfrac{3 + 4}{2}$

(3) $\dfrac{8 + 18}{2}$

(4) $\dfrac{8 + 16}{2}$

(5) $\dfrac{8 + 10 + 9 + 14 + 18 + 16}{6}$

The correct answer is (5). By definition, *mean* implies "add up all scores and divide by the total number of scores available." Hence, the correct answer is

$$\frac{8 + 10 + 9 + 14 + 18 + 16}{6},$$

which is choice (5).

ALGEBRA

Here is an algebra problem that tests your understanding of ratios and proportions.

Example 4

Art bought 6 unopened wax packs of baseball cards for $3. At the same rate, what would he pay for 50 wax packs?

(1) $18
(2) $25
(3) $59
(4) $100
(5) Not enough information is given.

The correct answer is (2). You can solve it by writing a proportion, using x to represent the unknown amount.

$$\frac{6 \text{ packs}}{\$3} = \frac{50 \text{ packs}}{x}$$

$$6x = \$150$$

$$x = \frac{\$150}{6}$$

$$x = \$25$$

GEOMETRY

About 20 percent of the GED Math Test is about geometry. The geometry concepts tested on the GED Math Test are useful ones. In fact, you can probably already solve many of the geometry problems using your understanding of arithmetic. Try this problem.

Example 5

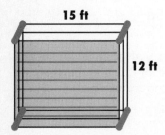

Su Ji plans to fence off an area of her yard for a vegetable garden. She stakes out a rectangular plot that is 15 feet long and 12 feet wide. How many feet of fencing will she need to enclose the garden?

(1) 24
(2) 27
(3) 30
(4) 54
(5) 180

The correct answer is (4). You can use a formula to solve the problem. When you take the GED Math Test, you will be given a page of formulas that you can refer to at any time. One of the formulas is for finding the perimeter of a rectangle.

Perimeter (P) of a Rectangle

$$P = 2l + 2w; \text{ where } l = \text{length, and } w = \text{width}$$

To use the formula, substitute the values from the problem and solve.

$$P = 2(15) + 2(12)$$
$$= 30 + 24$$
$$= 54$$

TRIGONOMETRY

Don't worry. Trigonometry is easier than you think! Trig, as it is often called for short, is the study of triangles and their properties. It is a marriage of algebra and geometry. Its uses are too many to list, but here's an example that will give you an idea. Let's do this problem using the alternate-format, which means you will not be given multiple-choice answers; rather, you will find the answer and fill out a standard grid.

Example 6

Ranger Smith is standing 47 ft from a tall tree. He uses a sextant to measure the angle of elevation from the ground to the top of the tree and makes the following diagram. What is the height of the tree rounded to the nearest tenth?

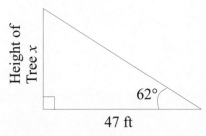

You can select the appropriate Trig formula from the formula sheet that will be given to you to solve this problem. We will use the tangent relationship to solve this problem.

$$tan\theta = \frac{opposite}{adjacent}$$

$$tan62° = \frac{x}{47}$$

$$x = (47) \cdot (tan62°)$$

$$x = 88.39 \approx 88.4$$

So, Ranger Smith now knows that the tree is approximately 88.4 ft tall.

The following is a sample of what the standard grid looks like. As you can see, there can be more than one correct way to fill out the bubbles for the same answer.

The standard grid allows you to enter numbers as small as one ten-thousandth and as large as ninety-nine thousand nine hundred ninety-nine. You can only input numbers in decimal form and fraction form as long as the fraction is proper or improper. Mixed numbers cannot be entered. Also, there is no allowance for negative numbers on these grids, so remember your answer to one of these alternate-format questions cannot ever be negative!

The next example is to show you the usage of the coordinate plane grid.

Example 7

On the coordinate plane grid on your answer sheet, mark the point $(-5,3)$.

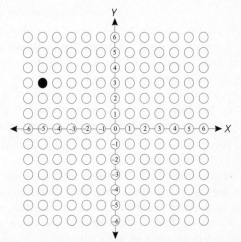

As you know $(-5,3)$ is an ordered pair of the form (x,y). Positive x and y move right and up respectively and negative x and y move left and down respectively. Therefore, from the origin $(0,0)$ we move 5 units to the left and then go up 3 units.

USING THE CALCULATOR

As we discussed earlier, you will be allowed to use a calculator to help you answer the first 25 questions on the math test. Your initial thought upon hearing this may have been, "This is great. With a calculator, any math test will be very easy!" Not so fast.

The majority of the math questions on the calculator section emphasize problem solving and the application of mathematical ideas. This means that you are not going to see any questions in this section that ask you to simply perform a mathematical calculation; that, of course, could easily be done using a calculator. The stated reason for allowing you to use a calculator on the test is "to eliminate the tedium of complex calculations in realistic settings." What this means is that, while the calculator will certainly help you to "crank out the numbers" in these problems, you are going to have to begin by thinking about how to approach and set up the problem before you can even begin to think about using the calculator. As a simple example, consider a geometry problem that gives the lengths of the two legs of a right triangle as 10 and 12 and asks you for the length of the hypotenuse.

287

Further, let us suppose that the five answer choices are:

(1) 14.9
(2) 15.1
(3) 15.5
(4) 15.6
(5) 15.9

Once you obtain the answer $\sqrt{244}$, your calculator will be extremely useful to help you quickly compute the value of this square root to the nearest tenth. But unless you understand the purpose of and how to use the Pythagorean theorem, there is no way that you will be able to get this far. Unless you understand that $a^2 + b^2 = c^2$, and that therefore, the missing length is given by the formula $\sqrt{10^2 + 12^2} = \sqrt{100 + 144} = \sqrt{244}$, your calculator will not be of much help.

That being said, the calculator will still be of tremendous use to you on the test, and therefore it is crucial that you know how to use it quickly and accurately. Everyone taking the test will be given the same type of calculator to use, the Casio *fx-260 Solar*.

Now, as you no doubt know, every calculator is set up a little bit differently. For example, the clear keys tend to be in different locations on different calculators, and perhaps they are labeled differently.

Even though you will be given time before the test begins to practice with the calculator, it may take you a little while to get used to it, especially if you are already used to a different calculator made by a different company. Therefore, a very helpful thing to do before the test date would be this: Go to a local stationery store and purchase a Casio *fx-260 Solar*. The calculator is readily available (specifically because the manufacturer knows that this is the calculator that is going to be used on the GED) and should cost between $10 and $15. If you spend a lot of time practicing with it before the test, you will know your way around it like a pro by the time you take the test. You won't have to waste time looking for a particular key or trying to figure out how to use the "shift" key.

By this time, you are probably very familiar with calculators and can easily use them to add, subtract, multiply, and divide. Still, there are a few pointers that you should remember in regard to using the calculator on your test.

1. When you are first given the calculator, turn it on by pressing the ON key, which is located in the upper right-hand corner.

2. In order to prepare for the next question after you complete a question, be certain to clear the calculator by either pressing the ON key, or the red AC key. AC stands for "All Clear." If you do not clear your calculator between problems, you run the risk of having your answer to problem 4 add into your answer to problem 5.

3. Any arithmetic operation can be entered in the order in which it is written. The calculator is already programmed to adhere to the algebraic order of operations. Therefore, if you wish to compute, say $5 + 2 \times 3$, simply key in:

5 + 2 × 3 =

The answer will be 11. Note that the calculator has performed the multiplication before the addition, as is appropriate according to the order of operations.

4. Should you ever need to multiply an expression in parentheses by another number, be certain to press the × key on the calculator when appropriate. For example, suppose that you need to compute $4(3 + 2)$. Even though, in algebra, it is not necessary to write a times sign after the 4, when you do the computation on the calculator, it will be necessary. Therefore, to compute $4(3 + 2)$, key in:

4 × (3 + 2) =

The calculator will show the correct answer of 20.

5. To enter a negative number using the calculator, enter the number without a sign, and then press the "change sign" key, which looks like this +/- Therefore, to perform the subtraction $-9 - -4$, you must key in:

9 +/- − 4 +/- =

The calculator will show the correct answer, -5.

6. One of the trickier things to do with the calculator is to use it to compute a square root. To do this, you must use the SHIFT key and the x^2. Say, for example, we need to find $\sqrt{244}$, as required in the sample problem on page 288. You would begin by entering the number 244 in the calculator, then press the "shift" key, and then the x^2 key. By shifting the x^2 key, you access its second function, which is the square root. Conclude by pressing = . To summarize, to determine $\sqrt{244}$, key in the following:

2 4 4 SHIFT x^2 =

WHAT YOU WILL FIND IN THIS BOOK . . .

In the following units, you will find pertinent material that will facilitate your preparation for the GED. There are eleven units covering arithmetic, word problems, decimals, fractions, ratios and proportions, percent, data analysis and statistics, measurement, algebra, geometry, and trigonometry. The GED exam covers all of these areas. The problems in these units are reflective of what you could see in a real GED exam.

The units are written as a review of the topics. You will find helpful hints and insights into problem solving. Also included are techniques and "tricks" that you could use for coming up with the "best answer." It is a well-known fact that a student may use various tactics to arrive at a correct answer. Sometimes working backward, using common sense or guess-and-check, and other not-so-straight-forward methods work just fine to reach your ultimate goal, which is to attain the desired response!

Through these units you will be exposed to typical GED test questions and the different question formats that you may encounter in the actual exam. All the answers and explanations are provided at the end of Part V, the mathematics section. A representative formula sheet is also included for your benefit. You will have access to a similar sheet during your actual exam. It is an excellent idea to familiarize yourself with these formulas before you take the GED. The next few units will help you learn how to effectively use these formulas to derive appropriate answers.

Unit 1

ARITHMETIC

The word **arithmetic** is derived from the Greek *arithmetike,* which is the combination of the two words, *arithmos,* translating to "number," and *techne,* meaning an art or skill. Therefore, arithmetic literally means the art of counting. The most ancient and rudimentary form of mathematics is arithmetic.

Scientists and archeologists have found evidence of advanced, organized mathematics as far back as the third millennium B.C.E. among the ancient Mesopotamians of Babylonia and the Egyptians. The mathematics of these ancient times was predominantly arithmetic with some knowledge of geometry, which is why counting, measuring, and calculating were the primary concern.

The importance of arithmetic has only increased over time as it is, after all, the building block of all mathematics.

Whole Numbers

The population of the world increases every second. At one point in 1992, the population was recorded as this:

BILLIONS		HUNDRED MILLIONS	TEN MILLIONS	MILLIONS		HUNDRED THOUSANDS	TEN THOUSANDS	THOUSANDS		HUNDREDS	TENS	ONES
5	,	7	7	8	,	9	0	7	,	5	4	3

When reading or writing whole numbers, use a comma to mark the end of each group. Read each number group from left to right as if it were a number in the hundreds. Then at the comma, read the group name of *billion, million,* or *thousand.* Do not use the word *and* when reading whole numbers.

The zero in the ten thousands column is a *placeholder.* A placeholder fills the column, but it is not read.

5,	778,	907,	543
5 billion,	778 million,	907 thousand,	543

In words, the population of the world in 1992 is written *five billion, seven hundred seventy-eight million, nine hundred seven thousand, five hundred forty-three.*

The following symbols are used to compare numbers.

> Greater than	5 > 3	Five is greater than three.
< Less than	3 < 5	Three is less than five.
= Equal to	3 = 2 + 1	Three is equal to two plus one.

Examples:

$$13 < 17 \qquad 20 > 5$$
lesser ←   → lesser

Note: When using > or < symbols, remember that the arrow points to the *lesser* number.

To compare whole numbers, first count the number of digits. The whole number with more digits is always greater.

$$60,000 > 6,000$$

If the number of digits is the same, compare the digits in both numbers working from left to right.

$$652 > 642 \text{ because } 5 > 4$$

Exercise 1

Directions: For items 1–8, write the whole number in words.

1. 504

2. 1,420

3. 7,060

4. 34,000

5. 201,900

6. 1,450,323

7. 257,005,009

8. 6,000,000,000

Directions: For items 9 and 10, solve as directed.

9. The following chart shows population figures for some cities for both 1980 and 1990. Compare the figures for the two years shown. Then complete the chart by adding > (greater than) or < (less than) symbols.

City	1990	> or <	1980
Phoenix	1,003,800		789,704
Chicago	2,852,041		3,005,072
Milwaukee	642,860		636,212
Philadelphia	1,608,942		1,688,210
Detroit	1,056,180		1,203,339
Jacksonville	649,437		540,920

10. Four businesses made donations to the Mt. Vernon Community Center this year. The amounts are shown in the table below.

Company	Amount Donated
Kids Plus Fashions	$1,060
The Toy Box	$1,580
The Playroom	$1,805
Kids First	$1,295

Which of the companies gave the greatest amount to the community center?

Check your answers on page 408.

Rounding Whole Numbers

Rounding makes it easier to work with numbers.

Whole numbers can be rounded to the nearest ten or the nearest trillion or to any place value column in between. How a number is rounded depends on your needs.

For example, suppose a problem on the GED Math Test asks you to round 338 to the nearest hundred. When you round 338 to the nearest hundred, you are actually finding out whether 338 is closer to 300 or 400.

To round whole numbers:		Example:
Step 1	Underline the digit in the place to which you are rounding.	Round 338 to the hundreds place. 338
Step 2	Circle the number to its right.	3(3)8

Now look at the circled number.

Step 3

If the circled number is:		Example:
0, 1, 2, 3, or 4	Replace the circled digit and any digits to its right with zeros.	3(3)8 rounds to 300.
5, 6, 7, 8, or 9	Add 1 to the underlined digit and replace the circled digit and any digits to its right with zeros.	But 3(5)8 rounds to 400.

Examples:

- Round 67,149 to the nearest ten thousand.

  Underline the ten thousands place 6 and circle the (7). 6(7),149

  Since 7 > 5, add 1 to the 6 and replace the digits to the right with zeros. The nearest ten thousand is 70,000.

- Round 67,149 to the nearest thousand. 67,(1)49

  Since 1 < 5, replace 1 and the digits to the right with zeros. The nearest thousand is 67,000.

- Round 67,149 to the nearest hundred thousand. _(6)7,149

There isn't a digit in the hundred thousands column because the number 67,149 is less than 100,000. The column to the right of the hundred thousands column contains a 6. Since 6 > 5, write 1 in the hundred thousands column and replace the digits to the right with zeros. The nearest hundred thousand is 100,000.

Exercise 2

Directions: Round each number.

1. Round 586 to the nearest hundred.

2. Round 5,280 to the nearest thousand.

3. Bob is filling in a purchase authorization form at his work. His boss wants him to order a bookcase for the office. Bob has to list prices on the form to the nearest $10. If the price for the bookcase he wants is $98, what amount should he write on the form?
   - (1) $10
   - (2) $90
   - (3) $98
   - (4) $100
   - (5) $110

4. A newspaper covering the beach cleanup reported the total number of volunteers rounded to the nearest ten. If there were 288 volunteers present, what number did the newspaper report?
   - (1) 200
   - (2) 250
   - (3) 280
   - (4) 290
   - (5) 300

5. Arlington Stadium, the prior home of the Texas Rangers, had a maximum seating capacity of 43,508. What was the stadium's seating capacity to the nearest thousand?
   - (1) 40,000
   - (2) 43,000
   - (3) 43,500
   - (4) 44,000
   - (5) 50,000

6. In 1991 there were about 5,641,000 cars registered in the state of Michigan. To the nearest hundred thousand, how many cars were registered in Michigan?
   - (1) 6,000,000
   - (2) 5,700,000
   - (3) 5,650,000
   - (4) 5,640,000
   - (5) 5,600,000

Check your answers on page 408.

Adding Whole Numbers

To add whole numbers, line up the numbers starting from the right so that each column has digits with the same place value.

When a column of digits has a sum equal to or greater than 10, you need to carry to the next column on the left.

Example:

Add: 14, 130, and 56.

$$\begin{array}{r} \overset{1}{}14 \\ {}_{1}14 \\ 130 \\ +86 \\ \hline 230 \end{array}$$

Aligning numbers allows you to add ones to ones, tens to tens, and so on.

The sum is 230. The answer to an addition problem is called the **sum**. You will usually use addition when a problem asks you to combine figures or to find a sum or a total.

Addition Tip: You can add more quickly if you look for numbers that go together to make 10, 100, and 1,000.

$$\begin{array}{r} 2 \\ \left.\begin{array}{r} 16 \\ 74 \end{array}\right\} 10 \\ \left.\begin{array}{r} 32 \\ +28 \end{array}\right\} 10 \\ \hline 150 \end{array}$$

You can easily see that the sum of the ones column is 20.

Exercise 3

Directions: For items 1–10, find the sums. For item 11, solve as directed.

1. 728 + 1,113

2. 15 + 408 + 2,638

3. 13 + 21 + 47 + 19

4. 1,409,275 + 54,400

5. 28,490 + 102,117 + 5,063

6. 25 + 180 + 250 + 75 + 120

7. 2,509,800 + 14,750 + 300,500

8. 22 + 54 + 40 + 38 + 16

9. 206 + 1,414 + 320 + 145 + 2,800

10. 589,752 + 605,578 + 110,915

11. The Fairfax Cinema recently added a 10 a.m. showing for all children's features. Attendance at the morning showings for the last four weekends was 228, 276, 300, and 249. How many people attended the early matinees on those weekends?

   (1) 953
   (2) 1,043
   (3) 1,053
   (4) 1,063
   (5) 1,153

Check your answers on page 408.

Subtracting Whole Numbers

To subtract whole numbers, align the numbers at the right with the greater number on top. Then subtract working from right to left.

In the example below, you need to **borrow** in order to subtract in the ones column. Borrow "ten" from the column to the left and add it to the digit you are subtracting from.

Example:

Subtract 1,395 from 5,024.

$$\begin{array}{r} 4\,9\,1\,1 \\ 5,024 \\ -1,395 \\ \hline 3,629 \end{array}$$

The answer to a subtraction problem is called the **difference**. You will usually use subtraction when a problem asks you to separate or compare two numbers.

You can easily check subtraction using addition. Add the difference (the answer) to the number you subtracted. The result should be the number you subtracted from.

Subtract: 5,024   **Check:** 3,629
        −1,395   +1,395
         3,629   5,024

Exercise 4

Directions: For items 1–10, find the differences. Check your work using addition. For item 11, solve as directed.

1. 184 − 61
2. 1,697 − 538
3. 2,359 − 1,769
4. 13,504 − 8,755
5. 200 − 112
6. 10,000 − 5,425
7. 50,914 − 49,358
8. 190,325 − 88,500
9. 3,532,500 − 1,975,250
10. 8,000,000 − 5,425,680
11. When Angela left Los Angeles to drive home to visit her brother in Nashville, the odometer of her car read 45,964 miles. When she got back to Los Angeles, the odometer read 50,066 miles. How many miles did she put on her car on the trip?

   (1) 4,002
   (2) 4,102
   (3) 5,002
   (4) 5,102
   (5) 14,102

Check your answers on page 408.

Multiplying Whole Numbers

There are several ways to indicate multiplication. All these examples are read "six times five."

$$6 \times 5 \qquad 6 \cdot 5 \qquad 6(5)$$

The GED Math Test often uses parentheses to indicate multiplication.

To multiply whole numbers, align the numbers at the right. After the multiplication is done, decide where the commas belong in the answer by counting from the right in groups of three.

Example:

Multiply 542 by 23.

$$
\begin{array}{r}
5\,4\,2 \\
\times\ \ 2\,3 \\
\hline
1\,6\,2\,6 \\
1\,0\,8\,4 \\
\hline
1\,2\,4\,6\,6 \\
\end{array}
$$

Count in three places from the right and place the comma: 12,466

The answer to a multiplication problem is called the **product**. Use multiplication whenever a problem asks you to combine, join, or add the same amount several times.

Exercise 5

Directions: For items 1–4, find the products. For items 5 and 6, solve as directed.

1. 8 × 27

2. 25(140)

3. 60 × 36

4. 29(3,016)

5. Mark put $100 down on a stereo system. He agrees to pay $55 each month for 10 months to pay the balance he owes. What is Mark's total cost for the new system?
    (1) $550
    (2) $650
    (3) $1,550
    (4) $5,500
    (5) $5,600

6. Kim's new job pays $280 per week. How much should she expect to earn in one year (52 weeks)?
    (1) $3,360
    (2) $8,900
    (3) $11,860
    (4) $14,460
    (5) $14,560

Check your answers on page 408.

Dividing Whole Numbers

Division is used to find out how many times one number divides into another number. A division problem can be written three ways. Each of these examples means "2,436 divided by 12."

$$2{,}436 \div 12 \qquad 12\overline{)2{,}436} \qquad \frac{2{,}436}{12}$$

On the GED Math Test, division is usually shown with a fraction bar, such as $\frac{198}{7}$. To divide whole numbers, we use a process called long division.

Example:

Since 12 will not divide 3, put a 0 in the answer and bring down the next digit.

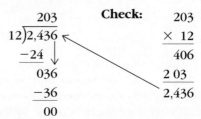

The answer to a division problem is called the **quotient**. You will usually use division when a problem asks you to separate an amount into groups or pieces of equal size. Check division by using multiplication.

Exercise 6

Directions: For items 1 and 2, find the quotients. Check your work using multiplication. For items 3 and 4, solve as directed.

1. $\dfrac{288}{9}$

2. $3,045 \div 15$

3. Cassady has a collection of 6,000 baseball cards. He plans to put his collection into albums. If each album page can hold 12 cards, how many album pages will he need?

    (1) 50
    (2) 200
    (3) 250
    (4) 400
    (5) 500

4. Laura is in charge of ordering supplies for the word processing pool at her work. The word processors use diskettes that come in boxes of 10. If Laura needs 200 diskettes, how many boxes should she buy?

    (1) 10
    (2) 20
    (3) 50
    (4) 100
    (5) 200

Check your answers on page 408.

Exercise 7

Directions: These are miscellaneous arithmetic problems. Treat these problems like an alternate-format question where you would need to fill out a standard grid. (*Calculator permitted.*)

1. Nan's truck odometer read 45,987 at the start of a trip and 47,837 miles at the end. If she gets an average of 25 miles per gallon, how many gallons of gas did she use on this trip?

2. Mrs. Ali is helping her daughter's second grade teacher in organizing the Valentine's Day party. There are 26 children in the class. They estimate each child may be allowed to have two glasses of juice. Mrs. Ali notices that the suggested serving size on the *California's Best* orange juice is 8 ounces per serving. How many one-gallon (128 ounces) containers of juice does she need to buy?

3. The graph below shows "nose-bleed section" ticket prices for entertainment events. Jessica and her three friends, being college students, are only interested in these tickets. How much will they spend over the weekend if they to go to a basketball game and a concert?

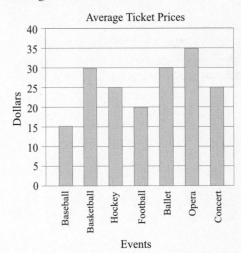

4. The Quick Copy Center takes inventory of its paper stock at the end of each day. If there are 12 reams of paper in each carton, how many more reams of green paper were in stock than the beige paper at the end of Monday, October 18?

Copier Paper Inventory
Monday, October 18

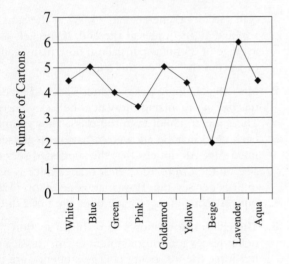

Paper Stock

5. Dollar Night at the Movie Megaplex

Admission	$9
Hot Dog	$2
Large Popcorn	$4
Soda	$2

Vickie and Bill went to the movies together. While Bill bought their tickets, Vickie got a large popcorn to share and a soda for each of them. How much money did they spend altogether?

Check your answers on page 408.

Unit 2

UNDERSTANDING WORD PROBLEMS

Word Problems

Word problems are an integral part of our existence. Even though we may not be consciously aware of it, since we learned to count, we have been solving word problems every day of our lives. As a child, if you ever had to divide and share candy fairly with your siblings, you have tackled a word problem. If you've gone to the all-night convenient store and bought bread, a couple of cans of soup, and a newspaper and tried to figure out whether the five dollar bill in your pocket was enough to pay for it all, you were solving a word problem.

Any numerical problem that relates to the real world is a word problem. As word problems come from all walks of life, so we require all types of mathematics to solve them, such as arithmetic, algebra, geometry, trigonometry, and statistics. The new GED mathematics exam tests your ability to relate what you have learned from a book to real-life situations or vice-versa. Therefore the new GED math exam presents most of its problems via a short prose, and your ability to interpret this information becomes an integral part of your test-taking skill.

As an adult, you use common sense to solve most math situations in your life. You analyze a problem, choose a strategy for solving it, and carry out your plan.

The problems on the GED Math Test are drawn from everyday life experiences, but because the situations are not happening to you, word problems can seem difficult. The following plan can help you make sense of word problems.

PROBLEM-SOLVING PLAN
- Read and Restate the Question
- Find the Facts You Need
- Choose a Problem-Solving Method
- Estimate
- Compute and Check

Read and Restate the Question: One of the critical factors in doing well on the math portion of the GED Test is reading the problem and the questions carefully. A good way to make sure you understand what you have read is to put the question in your own words.

Find the Facts You Need: Some of the problems on the GED Math Test have too many facts. Some do not have enough information. Sometimes you will have to do an extra step to find one of the facts you need. Whatever the situation, before you begin any calculations, think about what facts you need to answer the question asked in the problem. You need the *right* facts to find the *right* answer.

Choose a Problem-Solving Method: Once you understand the question and find the facts, you need to choose a method to solve the problem. You will probably use one or more of the four arithmetic operations (addition, subtraction, multiplication, and division). At times, you may want to make a sketch, table, or a list.

Estimate: Over one half of the items on the GED Math Test can be solved by estimation alone. To estimate, work with simpler numbers. For example, instead of dividing 384 by 48, think 400 divided by 50. A good estimate will often give you enough information to choose the correct answer from the choices. If it does, you have finished that item. If it doesn't, continue with the problem-solving plan.

Compute and Check: Perform the calculations you have chosen to find the answer. Then check to see if your answer makes sense. The answer should be reasonably close to your estimate. You can also use addition to check subtraction and multiplication to check division.

Many of the problems on the GED Math Test will be multiple choice with five options. If these problems have numeric answers, they will be arranged in ascending (least to greatest) or descending (greatest to least) order. Sometimes the problems will offer you choices for the correct set-up and you will be asked to select the right one. The alternate-format problems will require you to solve the problem completely and fill out a standard grid or a coordinate plane grid. (For more information on the standard grid and coordinate plane grid, read the *Introduction* and the unit on *Practice Tests*).

For all the different ways the questions can be asked, you can just about use as many unique approaches to solving the problem. Don't be afraid to use guess and check, patterns, working-backward techniques, and even a little intuition. However, remember the foremost way you can do well on any mathematics exam is to actually master the concepts. There are no short cuts. Diligence, perseverance, and a lot of practice will get you where you want to be!

Exercise 1

Directions: Choose the <u>one best answer</u> for each item.

1. The Wilkinsons' gas bill for December was $64. Their bills for January and February were $78 and $62, respectively. What was their average monthly bill for the three winter months?

   (1) $64
   (2) $68
   (3) $80
   (4) $102
   (5) $204

2. Liza supervises packing at a manufacturing company. Today her crew must pack videotapes into cartons. Each carton holds 22 videos. How many cartons must Liza have on hand to pack 5,720 videotapes?

   (1) 306
   (2) 260
   (3) 240
   (4) 214
   (5) 205

Check your answers on page 408.

Solving Problems with Extra or Missing Information

The GED Math Test writers recognize that problems in life often have too little information, too much information, or both. They write problems to test your ability to figure out which facts you need to solve a problem.

Example:

Mei wants to buy a sweater originally priced at $62. The sweater is now on sale for much less. Mei plans to use a $35 gift certificate to help pay for the sweater. How much more does she owe?

(1) $97
(2) $37
(3) $27
(4) $17
(5) Not enough information is given.

The correct answer is (5). This problem seems easy enough. You have two amounts: $62 and $35. The words "how much more" suggest subtraction.

$62 − $35 = $27. Choice (3) is correct, right? Wrong!

Read carefully. You have two facts, but they aren't the facts you need. You are trying to find the difference between the sale price of the sweater and the amount of the gift certificate. But you don't know the sale price of the sweater. The original price was $62.

Not enough information is given will be the fifth choice on several of the items you will see on the GED Math Test. Some of the time, that option will be the correct choice. Always read carefully, and think about which facts you need to solve the problem.

Example:

The Vision Center is offering a two-week special. You can buy 2 pair of eyeglasses (regularly priced at $59 each) for only $79. You can also save $20 on any pair of designer eyeglasses. How much would it cost to buy a pair of designer eyeglasses that originally cost $139?

(1) $39
(2) $98
(3) $119
(4) $158
(5) Not enough information is given.

The correct answer is (3). This problem has more than enough information. You are asked to figure out how much a pair of designer eyeglasses will cost. You need two facts: the original price of the glasses ($139) and the amount the glasses are marked down ($20).

Subtract to find the answer: $139 − $20 = $119.

You don't need to know that you can buy 2 pair of eyeglasses for $79 or that those glasses usually cost $59 per pair.

Exercise 2

Directions: Choose the <u>one best answer</u> for each item.

1. Sarom is paying his bills. His rent is $450, his electric bill is $32, and his phone bill is $42. Because he recently switched long-distance companies, he has a $25 coupon that will reduce his phone bill. How much should Sarom pay the phone company?

   (1) $10
   (2) $17
   (3) $67
   (4) $499
   (5) Not enough information is given.

2. Aida and Ralph are buying baby furniture at a sale at Baby Blocks. They buy a crib (originally priced at $229) for only $139. They also buy a changing table that usually sells for $78. How much did they save on the changing table?

(1) $151
(2) $90
(3) $61
(4) $12
(5) Not enough information is given.

3. In 1992, the Mayor of Los Angeles was paid a salary of $117,884. By contrast, the Mayor of San Diego earned only $65,300. The San Diego City Manager was paid more, earning $126,375 for the year. What was the difference in salaries for the mayors of Los Angeles and San Diego?

(1) $183,184
(2) $61,075
(3) $52,584
(4) $8,491
(5) Not enough information is given.

4. In 1990, the U.S. Government estimated that 34,719,000 people did not have any type of health insurance. Even North Dakota, which ranked first in health coverage, had 40,000 people without insurance. The state with the greatest number of uninsured was California with 5,693,000 people uninsured. How many people in California have health insurance?

(1) 5,653,000
(2) 5,733,000
(3) 29,026,000
(4) 34,679,000
(5) Not enough information is given.

Check your answers on 408.

Solving Set-Up Problems

Set-up problems measure your ability to see a way to solve a problem. Instead of solving the problem, you are asked to choose which of the given expressions would be a right way to *set up* the problem.

Example:

For three days in August, the daily high temperatures for Fayetteville, North Carolina, were 93, 96, and 108 degrees. Which expression could be used to find the average high temperature for the three-day period?

(1) $93 + 96 + 108$

(2) $3(93 + 96 + 108)$

(3) $\dfrac{93 + 96 + 108}{3}$

(4) $93 + 96 + \dfrac{108}{3}$

(5) $\dfrac{108}{3} + (93 + 96)$

The correct answer is (3). You already know how to find an average. To solve this problem, you need to add the temperatures and divide by 3 (the number of temperatures). Which of the answer choices does that?

To solve set-up problems, you must know the order of operations. These rules help you translate a problem-solving method from words into numbers and symbols.

THE ORDER OF OPERATIONS

1. Do any operations in parentheses first.
2. Working from left to right, do any multiplication or division.
3. Working from left to right, do any addition or subtraction.

Examples:

$5 + 6(4)$	Do the multiplication step first.
$5 + 24$	Then do the addition step.
29	The correct answer is 29.
$7(6 + 2) - \dfrac{4}{2}$	Do the operations in parentheses.
$7(8) \quad - \dfrac{4}{2}$	Multiply, then divide.
$56 \quad - 2$	Subtract.
54	The correct answer is 54.

Sometimes you know how to solve a set-up problem, but you can't find your answer among the answer choices. That doesn't mean that you are wrong. Many problems can be solved in more than one way. These two expressions look different, but they have the same result.

$$2(15) + 2(8) = ? \qquad 2(15 + 8) = ?$$
$$30 + 16 = 46 \qquad 2(23) = 46$$

Exercise 3

Directions: Solve the following problems using the correct order of operations.

1. $7(8 - 6)(5 + 7)$

2. $\dfrac{36}{4} - 5 + 2(10)$

3. $10(5 + 2) - \dfrac{36}{4}$

4. $10(5) + \dfrac{36}{2} - 4$

Directions: Choose the one best answer for each item.

5. Software Shack is taking inventory. Vanna counts 12 boxes of high-density diskettes on the shelf in the store. She also finds a carton containing another 30 boxes in the storeroom. If each box holds 10 disks, which expression can Vanna use to compute how many high-density disks to list on the inventory form?

   (1) 12(30)(10)
   (2) 10(12 + 30)
   (3) 30(10) + 30(12)
   (4) 12(10 + 30)
   (5) 12(10) + 12(30)

6. On the way home from work, Gerry picked up two $8 pizzas for his family. When he got home, he found out his sister and her children would be staying for dinner. He went back to the restaurant and bought a large pizza for $12. Which expression can be used to figure out how much the pizzas cost altogether?

   (1) 2($8) − $12
   (2) 2($8) + 2($12)
   (3) 2($8 + $12)
   (4) 2($8)($12)
   (5) 2($8) + $12

7. Linda used to earn $9 an hour. She recently got a new job that pays $13 an hour. Linda worked 40 hours a week at the old job, but she will work only 35 hours per week on the new job. Which expression could be used to figure out how much more Linda will earn a week on her new job than she earned at her old job?

   (1) $9(40) + $13(35)
   (2) (40 − $9) + (35 − $13)
   (3) $13(35) − ($9 + 40)
   (4) $13(40) − $9(35)
   (5) $13(35) − $9(40)

Check your answers on page 409.

Working with Item Sets

Item sets are groups of problems that use the same set of information. Sometimes the information is given in a paragraph. Because tables and graphs are often used to organize large amounts of facts, they are also used frequently to make item sets.

To avoid mistakes when solving item sets:

- Read all titles on the table, graph, or figure before you read the problems.

- On a graph, read the key and any markings along the sides.

- Read the direction line that tells you exactly which test items are based on the table, graph, or figure.

- Work the problems one at a time.

- Make sure you understand the question the item is asking.

- Make sure you find the right facts before you compute.

Exercise 4

Directions: Choose the <u>one best answer</u> for each item.

Items 1 and 2 are based on the following table.

Location	Elevation
Mount Everest	29,028 feet above sea level
Mount McKinley	20,320 feet above sea level
Mount Whitney	14,491 feet above sea level
Mount Hood	11,239 feet above sea level
Eagle Mountain	2,301 feet above sea level

1. What is the difference in elevation between Mount Hood and Mount McKinley?

    (1) 5,829 feet
    (2) 9,081 feet
    (3) 9,991 feet
    (4) 14,537 feet
    (5) Not enough information is given.

2. Which location is approximately twice the elevation of Mount Whitney?

    (1) Mount Everest
    (2) Mount McKinley
    (3) Mount Hood
    (4) Eagle Mountain
    (5) Not enough information is given.

Items 3–5 are based on the following graph.

THE ELECTRONIX TOY CO., VIDEO GAMES SOLD
First-Year Sales, 2000

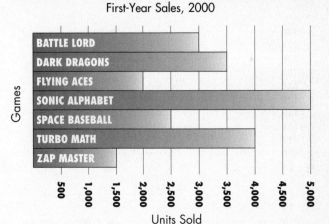

3. About how many game units were sold during the first year of sales for Battle Lord, Dark Dragons, and Flying Aces?

    (1) Between 4,000 and 5,000
    (2) Between 5,000 and 6,000
    (3) Between 6,000 and 7,000
    (4) Between 7,000 and 8,000
    (5) Between 8,000 and 9,000

4. Sonic Alphabet was the company's best-selling educational game during the year. About how many more Sonic Alphabet games did the company sell than Space Baseball games?

    (1) Between 1,000 and 2,000
    (2) Between 2,000 and 3,000
    (3) Between 3,000 and 4,000
    (4) Between 4,000 and 5,000
    (5) Not enough information is given.

5. Electronix Toys hopes to sell three times as many units of Flying Aces and Zap Master next year. Which expression can be used to find how many units of those games the company hopes to sell?

    (1) 2,000 + 1,500 + 3
    (2) 3(2,000) − 3(1,500)
    (3) 3(2,000)(1,500)
    (4) 3(2,000 + 1,500)
    (5) 3(2,000 − 1,500)

Items 6–8 are based on the following graph.

ADVENTURE PARK
Ticket Prices

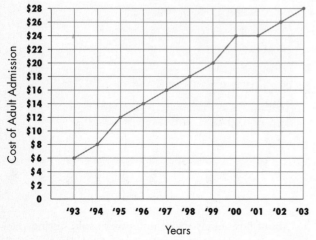

6. The price of a ticket to Adventure Park increased every year but one. In which year did ticket prices remain the same?

(1) 1998
(2) 1999
(3) 2000
(4) 2001
(5) Not enough information is given.

7. To celebrate the twenty-fifth anniversary of the park's opening, Adventure Park owners have decided to reduce the price of a ticket to $12 on weekdays only. In what year was $12 the regular price of admission to the park?

(1) 1994
(2) 1995
(3) 1996
(4) 1997
(5) Not enough information is given.

8. Which expression can be used to find out how much more it costs two adults to enter the park in 2003 than it did in 1993?

(1) $2(\$28) - 2(\$6)$
(2) $\$28(\$6 - 2)$
(3) $\$28 + \$28 + \$6 + \$6$
(4) $2(\$6)(\$28)$
(5) $\dfrac{\$28}{2} - \dfrac{\$6}{2}$

Check your answers on page 409.

Exercise 5

Directions: These are miscellaneous word problems. You will find more word problems after each unit relating to the specific concept discussed in that unit. Treat these problems like an alternate-format question where you would need to fill out a standard grid. (*Calculator permitted.*)

1. The West Beach Swim Team plans to purchase 10 Team USA suits in July and 20 solid-color suits in September. How much will they pay for these suits? The following chart gives a breakdown of the quantity discounts.

Quantity Discounts	1–9	10–19	20+
Team USA Suits	$27 each	$24 each	$20 each
SlimStripe Suits	$25 each	$22 each	$19 each
Solid-color Suits	$22 each	$21 each	$18 each

2. A factory spends $1,536 per 24-hour day for electrical power. How much does the factory spend on 2 hours of power usage?

Items 3–5 refer to the chart below.

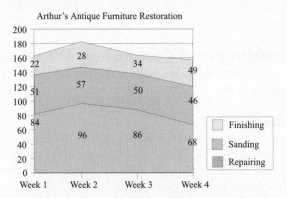

Arthur's Antique Furniture Restoration

Arthur of Arthur's Antique Furniture Restoration has made some observations regarding the performance time of the different departments of his small shop. Along with his handful of regular adult employees, he also hires high school students over the summer. The chart shows how much total time in hours was spent on the different aspects of furniture restoration (finishing, sanding, and repairing) over a four-week period during the summer, right after he hired his young employees.

3. How many total hours were spent in all aspects of restoration in the week of highest input time?

4. How many hours were spent on sanding over the four weeks?

5. In all the four weeks, compared to the finishing department, how many more hours did the repair department work?

Check your answers on page 409.

Unit 3

DECIMALS

Decimals and fractions go hand in hand in that if the number is rational, it can be represented in both decimal and fraction form. Both decimals and fractions represent part of a whole. Why, you might ask, do we have more than one form of representation? For the ease of presentation of information, under different situations one form may be preferred over the other. Also, irrational numbers like π and $\sqrt{2}$, can never be represented through a fraction; it can only be approximately represented through a decimal form.

Place Value

Decimals name parts of the whole. Decimal parts are written to the right of the whole number after a decimal point. The decimal point indicates the end of the whole number *and* the beginning of the decimal part.

A **mixed decimal** is a whole number *and* a decimal part. For this reason, when we read a mixed decimal, we say "and" at the decimal point, just as we do when we read $5.75 as five dollars *and* seventy-five cents.

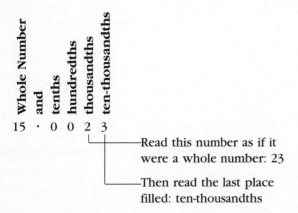

This mixed decimal would be read **15** *and* **23 ten-thousandths.**

Rounding and Comparing Decimals

Some problems ask you to round the answer to a certain decimal place.

Example:

Using a calculator, Jenna finds that the interest she will owe on her school loan this month is $23.626875. To the nearest cent, how much interest does Jenna owe?

Follow these steps to round decimals:

Step 1	Underline the digit in the place to which you are rounding.	$23.6<u>2</u>6875
Step 2	Circle the number to its right.	$23.6<u>2</u>⑥875
Step 3	If the circled number is:	

0, 1, 2, 3, or 4	Drop the circled digit and any digits to its right.
5, 6, 7, 8, or 9	Add 1 to the underlined digit, then drop the circled digit and any digits to its right.

Since $6 > 5$, add 1 to the 2 in the hundredths place, and drop the digits to the right. Jenna owes $23.63 in interest.

To compare decimals, add zeros after the last decimal place of the number with fewer decimal places so that the number of decimal places in both numbers is the same.

Example:

A special bolt manufactured for use in a communications satellite is supposed to measure 15.1 centimeters in length. Instead, each of the bolts in the last hour's production run measures 15.09 centimeters. Are these new bolts too long or too short?

You can easily see that 15.10 (or 15.1) is greater than 15.09.

$$15.1 > 15.09$$

The bolts are too short.

Exercise 1

Directions: Choose the one best answer for each item.

1. Thirteen and 5 hundredths is written as _____.
   - (1) 13.005
   - (2) 13.05
   - (3) 13.5
   - (4) 13.50
   - (5) 13.500

2. Which of the following values are arranged in descending order (greatest to least)?
   - (1) 0.2, 0.23, 0.235, 0.25, 0.255
   - (2) 0.255, 0.25, 0.235, 0.23, 0.2
   - (3) 0.2, 0.23, 0.235, 0.255, 0.25
   - (4) 0.235, 0.255, 0.23, 0.25, 0.2
   - (5) 0.2, 0.23, 0.25, 0.235, 0.255

3. Hugh Duffy of Boston holds the record for the highest season batting average in baseball. In 1894, he had 236 hits in 539 times at bat for an average of 0.43784786642. To the nearest thousandth, what is Duffy's record average?
   - (1) 0.436
   - (2) 0.437
   - (3) 0.4378
   - (4) 0.43785
   - (5) 0.438

4. The foreign currency exchange rates change daily. If the daily rate of exchange for the British pound is 1.598 U.S. dollars, what is the exchange rate rounded to the nearest hundredth?
   - (1) 1.598
   - (2) 1.58
   - (3) 1.59
   - (4) 1.60
   - (5) 2.00

5. Which of the following is greater than 23.46?
   - (1) 23.0419
   - (2) 23.358
   - (3) 23.409
   - (4) 23.460
   - (5) 23.5

6. On a calculator, sales tax on an item priced at $5.75 is displayed as 0.474375. To the nearest whole cent, what is the amount of the sales tax?
   - (1) $0.38
   - (2) $0.40
   - (3) $0.47
   - (4) $0.48
   - (5) $0.75

Check your answers on page 409.

Adding and Subtracting Decimals

When adding or subtracting decimal numbers, first line the numbers up at the decimal point. Lining up the decimal points keeps the whole number and decimal place value columns in line.

Then add zeros after the decimal part of each number so that all the numbers in the problem have the same number of decimal places.

Examples:

Add: $77.23 and $88   16.2 + 90 + 7.043

```
$  77.23              16.200
+88.00                90.000
$ 165.23             +7.043
                     113.243
```

Adding zeros is particularly important when you are subtracting. The example below shows a common mistake people make when working with decimals.

	Incorrect	**Correct**
Subtract:	$ 88.	$ 88.00
	−77.23	−77.23
	$ 11.23	$ 10.77

The zeros in the examples above fill a place value column without changing the value of the number. Add zeros only to the right of the rightmost digit after the decimal point. Inserting a zero between the decimal point and a digit changes the value of the number.

$5.2 = 5.20$ $5.2 \neq 5.02$
five and   five and   ($\neq$ means *is*
two tenths   two hundredths   *not equal to*)

Addition and subtraction are *inverse*, or *opposite*, operations. To check a subtraction problem, use the inverse operation addition.

Solve: $ 125.63   **Check:** $ 58.18
          −67.45   +67.45
          $ 58.18 $ 125.63

Exercise 2

Directions: Solve the following problems.

FIND THE SUMS.

1. 13.4 + 4.56 + 789.2
2. 134 + 1.456 + 78.92
3. $62.59 + $123.98 + $568
4. 5.00076 + 15.9 + 7.2309
5. $6,000 + $349.07
6. 0.98 + 0.89 + 0.0098

FIND THE DIFFERENCES.

7. 76.9 − 48.37
8. 76.9 − 4.083
9. 10,000 − 34.89
10. $56 − $34.75
11. $100 − $23.67
12. 23.45 − 23.045

13. Luisa stopped at several stores this afternoon. She spent $52.35 at Hardy's Hardware, $123.67 at Sheer's Market, and $16.98 on a prescription at Wen's Pharmacy. How much did she spend altogether?

    (1) $140.65
    (2) $176.02
    (3) $192.99
    (4) $193.00
    (5) $196.02

14. On Thursday, the French franc was worth 0.1865 U.S. dollar. On Friday, the rate was 0.1849 U.S. dollar. By how much did the value of the franc go down?

    (1) 0.0016
    (2) 0.0024
    (3) 0.016
    (4) 0.16
    (5) 0.3714

15. Kareem stopped at the grocery store on his way home to pick up five items for $2.59, $3.89, $1.32, $0.89, and $1.29. What was the total cost of his purchases?

    (1) $5.24
    (2) $6.84
    (3) $7.79
    (4) $9.98
    (5) $12.98

16. Joretta, a technician, has a cable that is 1.6 cm in diameter. She needs a cable that is 0.85 cm in diameter. How many centimeters too large is the diameter of the cable she has?

    (1) 0.075
    (2) 0.21
    (3) 0.75
    (4) 0.975
    (5) 2.45

Check your answers on page 409.

Multiplying Decimals

FOLLOW THESE STEPS TO MULTIPLY DECIMAL NUMBERS:

Example: (0.542)(2.3)

Step 1	Line the numbers up at the right just as you do with whole numbers.	$\begin{array}{r} 0.5\,4\,2 \\ \times\ 2.3 \\ \hline \end{array}$

Step 2	Multiply as you would with whole numbers.	$\begin{array}{r} 0.5\,4\,2 \\ \times\ 2.3 \\ \hline 1\,6\,2\,6 \\ 1\,0\,8\,4\ \ \\ \hline 1\,2\,4\,6\,6 \end{array}$

Step 3 To place the decimal point in the answer, add up the total number of decimal places in the original problem. Then count in that number of places from the right, and place the decimal point in the answer.

$\begin{array}{r} 0.5\,4\,2 \\ \times\ 2.3 \\ \hline 1.2\,4\,6\,6 \end{array}$ (3 decimal places)
(1 decimal place)
(4 total decimal places)

(0.542)(2.3) = **1.2466**

The number you get when you multiply two or more numbers together is called the **product**.

Exercise 3

Directions: Find the products in the following problems.

1. (5.24)(2.16)

2. (1.23)(23.4)

3. 21(22.2)

4. 0.004(1.2)

5. 15($3.07)

6. Bonita's weekly take-home pay is $279.25. What is her take-home pay for the year? (Use 52 weeks equals 1 year.)

   (1) $1,452.10
   (2) $3,351.00
   (3) $10,367.75
   (4) $13,962.50
   (5) $14,521.00

7. Herb bought 2.8 pounds of ground turkey at $2.95 a pound. How much will the turkey cost?

   (1) $0.826
   (2) $5.75
   (3) $8.26
   (4) $9.26
   (5) $82.60

8. Penny works as a courier for a small business. She uses her own car and is reimbursed for mileage at the rate of $0.42 a mile. Last week, she drove 37 miles each day for three days. How much money will she be reimbursed?

   (1) $1.26
   (2) $15.54
   (3) $46.62
   (4) $93.24
   (5) $139.86

Check your answers on page 409.

Dividing Decimals

The division steps for decimal numbers are the same as for whole numbers, but there are special rules for placing the decimal point in the quotient.

$$\text{divisor} \rightarrow \quad 5\overline{)125} \quad \begin{array}{l}25 \quad \leftarrow \text{quotient} \\ \leftarrow \text{dividend}\end{array}$$

Examples:

$$1.25 \div 5 \qquad 2.436 \div 0.12 \qquad 24.36 \div 0.012$$

$$5\overline{)1.25}^{\,0.25} \qquad .12\overline{)2.436}^{\,20.3} \qquad .012\overline{)24.360}^{\,2,030}$$

If there is no decimal point in the divisor, move the decimal point straight up into the quotient.

If there is a decimal point in the divisor, move it as far as you can to the right. Then move the decimal point in the dividend **an equal number of places.**

If there are not enough places in the dividend, **add zero(s) in the dividend.**

To check your division, multiply the quotient (answer) by the divisor.

Examples:

0.25	20.3	2030
× 5	× .12	× .012
1.25	406	4 060
	2 03	20 30
	2.436	24.360

Notice that the end zero in the last answer is crossed out. Because the zero isn't needed as a place holder, it is usually dropped from the answer.

Exercise 4

Directions: Find the quotients in the following problems.

1. 1.75 ÷ 7

2. 332.2 ÷ 1.1

3. JB Machine charges $0.08 for each T-4 toggle bolt. If a customer paid $64 for toggle bolts, how many did he buy?

   (1) 8
   (2) 80
   (3) 800
   (4) 8,000
   (5) Not enough information is given.

4. Kwon Manufacturing Company gives each of its 250 employees a quarterly bonus. At the end of the first quarter, the company has $9,876.47 to distribute equally among the employees. To the nearest cent, how much will each employee receive?

    (1) $39.51
    (2) $37.41
    (3) $35.34
    (4) $34.00
    (5) $30.68

Check your answers on page 409.

Estimating with Decimals

Estimating is a useful tool for solving GED math problems containing decimals. To use estimation, you round some or all of the numbers in the problem to make the numbers easier to use. The shortcuts below are useful for making estimates involving a power of ten (10, 100, 1,000, and so on).

To multiply a decimal by a power of 10:

Move the decimal point one place to the *right* for every zero.

Examples:

$$0.024 \times 10 \rightarrow 0.024 = 0.24$$

$$0.024 \times 100 \rightarrow 0.024 = 2.4$$

$$0.024 \times 1000 \rightarrow 0.024 = 24$$

To divide by a power of 10:

Move the decimal point one place to the *left* for every zero.

Examples:

$$45 \div 10 \rightarrow 45 = 4.5$$

$$45 \div 100 \rightarrow 45 = 0.45$$

$$45 \div 1000 \rightarrow 045 = 0.045$$

Exercise 5

> **Directions:** Choose the <u>one best answer</u> for each item.

1. St. John's sold 1,000 raffle tickets for a color TV at $2.50 each. How much money did they receive from ticket sales?

    (1) $2.50
    (2) $25.00
    (3) $250.00
    (4) $2,500.00
    (5) $25,000.00

2. Michelle and her nine coworkers bought an engraved pendant for $125.40 as a retirement gift for their supervisor. How much money will each person chip in as his or her share?

    (1) $1,254.00
    (2) $125.40
    (3) $12.54
    (4) $1.25
    (5) $0.13

3. Midtown Daily News estimates that one in every hundred newspapers is not delivered on time. If their daily distribution is 25,000 newspapers, how many newspapers are probably delivered late?

    (1) 2,500
    (2) 250
    (3) 25
    (4) 2.5
    (5) Not enough information is given.

4. Continental Cellular Telephone charges $0.95 per minute for calls made during the peak hours of 7 a.m. to 6 p.m. What will a caller be charged for a 5-minute call made at 3 p.m.?

    (1) $2.85
    (2) $4.75
    (3) $5.70
    (4) $6.65
    (5) $14.25

Check your answers on page 409.

Exercise 6

Directions: These are miscellaneous problems dealing with decimals. Treat these problems like an alternate-format question where you would need to fill out a standard grid. (*Calculator permitted.*)

1. Shama went to the grocery store and bought 2 jars of spaghetti sauce for $4.59 each, a jar of instant coffee for $7.89, and a jumbo pack of kitchen towels for $8.50. How much change will she receive if she uses $30 to pay for all her purchases?

2. Gerald deposited his monthly paycheck of $2,079.63 to his checking account. He then paid the following bills: $988 for rent, $256.79 for utilities, $273.65 for car payment, and $345.78 for credit cards. He already had a balance of $509.67 in his checking account when he deposited his paycheck. What is his current balance? Round answer to nearest dollar.

Items 3 and 4 refer to the chart below.

Marisol Sanchez's Pay Stub

Hours	Total Earned	Deductions	
40	$420.00	Fed. Tax	$37.80
		State Tax	21.00
		Soc. Sec.	18.90
		Health Plan	9.25
		NET PAY	XXXXXXXXXX

3. Using the information given on the pay stub, how much does Marisol earn per hour?

4. What is her net pay (after deductions)? Round answer to nearest dollar.

Check your answers on page 410.

Unit 4

FRACTIONS

Just as whole numbers are used to count whole things like people, houses, and cars, fractions are used to count *parts* of a whole thing. For example, consider the nine planets of the "whole" solar system: Mercury, Venus, Earth, Mars, Jupiter, Saturn, Uranus, Neptune, and Pluto. Among these, Jupiter, Saturn, Uranus, and Neptune are called the gas giants. So 4 out of the 9 planets are gas giants. Therefore, $\frac{4}{9}$ represents the part (fraction) of the whole system of planets that are gas giants. We use the concept of fractions in everyday life when we use phrases like "half a mile" or "quarter cup." Fractions can be added, subtracted, multiplied, and divided.

Fractions name part of the whole. The **denominator** of the fraction tells us how many equal parts there are in the whole. The **numerator** tells how many of those parts are shaded.

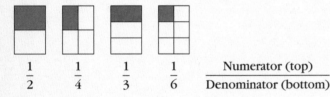

$\frac{1}{2}$	$\frac{1}{4}$	$\frac{1}{3}$	$\frac{1}{6}$	Numerator (top)
				Denominator (bottom)

Fractions can also name part of a group or set.

- Five months is $\frac{5}{12}$ of a year.

- Two feet is $\frac{2}{3}$ of a yard.

The fractions we have looked at so far have been *proper fractions*. A proper fraction represents part of a whole. In a proper fraction, the numerator is less than the denominator.

Examples:

$$\frac{1}{3} \qquad \frac{7}{8} \qquad \frac{5}{16}$$

In an **improper fraction**, the numerator is equal to or greater than the denominator.

$$\frac{3}{3} \qquad \frac{5}{4} \qquad \frac{8}{8} \qquad \frac{7}{2}$$

A **mixed number** is a whole number with a fraction. It represents one or more wholes *and* part of a whole.

$$1\frac{2}{3} \qquad 13\frac{1}{4} \qquad 2\frac{5}{6}$$

RENAMING FRACTIONS AND MIXED NUMBERS

Sometimes you need to change how a fraction is written. For example, when the answer to a problem is an improper fraction, the fraction could be renamed as a whole or mixed number.

To rename an improper fraction as a whole or mixed number, divide the numerator by the denominator. If there is a *remainder*, or amount left over, write it over the denominator.

Examples:

$$\frac{3}{3} = 3\overline{)3}^{\,1} = 1$$
$$\underline{3}$$

$$\frac{5}{3} = 3\overline{)5}^{\,1} \quad \frac{2}{3} = 1\frac{2}{3}$$
$$\underline{3}$$
$$2$$

$$\frac{15}{7} = 7\overline{)15}^{\,2} \quad \frac{1}{7} = 2\frac{1}{7}$$
$$\underline{14}$$
$$1$$

To rename a mixed number as an improper fraction, reverse the process above. Multiply the denominator by the whole number, and add the numerator.

Examples:

$$1\frac{2}{3} = \frac{?}{3} \quad \begin{array}{l} \text{Multiply } 1 \times 3. \\ \text{Then add 2.} \end{array} \quad 1\frac{2}{3} = \frac{1 \times 3 + 2}{3} = \frac{5}{3}$$

$$2\frac{1}{7} = \frac{?}{7} \quad \begin{array}{l} \text{Multiply } 2 \times 7. \\ \text{Then add 1.} \end{array} \quad 2\frac{1}{7} = \frac{2 \times 7 + 1}{7} = \frac{15}{7}$$

The fractions in the answer choices on the GED Math Test are always renamed to simplest form. To rename a fraction to simplest form, divide the numerator and the denominator by the *same* number. Renaming a fraction from greater numbers to lesser numbers is called **simplifying to simplest form.**

Examples:

$$\frac{2}{4} \quad \frac{2 \div 2}{4 \div 2} = \frac{1}{2}$$

$$\frac{4}{12} \quad \frac{4 \div 4}{12 \div 4} = \frac{1}{3}$$

$$\frac{35}{42} \quad \frac{35 \div 7}{42 \div 7} = \frac{5}{6}$$

To rename to greater terms, multiply the numerator and denominator by the same number.

Examples:

$$\frac{2}{3} = \frac{?}{6} \quad \frac{2 \times 2}{3 \times 2} = \frac{4}{6}$$

$$\frac{5}{6} = \frac{?}{42} \quad \frac{5 \times 7}{6 \times 7} = \frac{35}{42}$$

COMPARING FRACTIONS BY USING THE CROSS-MULTIPLICATION TRICK

To use the **cross-multiplication trick** means to multiply diagonally "across" the sign that links two fractions. You can use cross-multiplication to compare fractions.

If two fractions are *equal*, you will get the same answer when you cross-multiply.

$$4(2) = 8 \qquad 8(1) = 8$$
$$\frac{1}{4} \diagdown \frac{2}{8}$$

$8 = 8$ These fractions are equal.

If two fractions are *not equal*, when you cross-multiply you will get a greater number by the greater fraction.

$$8(1) = 8 \qquad 2(7) = 14$$
$$\frac{1}{2} \diagdown \frac{7}{8}$$

8 is less than (<) 14 so $\frac{1}{2} < \frac{7}{8}$

Exercise 1

Directions: Solve the following problems.

The directors of a community center invited area teenagers to help paint their building. The teens kept their own records. In order to compare their work, complete each column below.

Name	Paint Used (in quarter gallons)	Total Gallons Used
1. Nancy	$\frac{9}{4}$	
2. Tyrone		$3\frac{3}{4}$
3. Pava	$\frac{6}{4}$	
4. Carmen	$\frac{12}{4}$	
5. Hank		$4\frac{1}{4}$

Fill in each blank with $<$, $>$, or $=$.

6. $\frac{1}{3}$ _____ $\frac{7}{8}$

7. $\frac{2}{3}$ _____ $\frac{6}{9}$

8. $\frac{7}{9}$ _____ $\frac{4}{7}$

9. $\frac{6}{7}$ _____ $\frac{3}{8}$

Items 10 and 11 refer to the following number line.

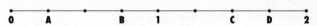

10. What is the value of Point A?

(1) $\frac{1}{3}$

(2) $\frac{1}{4}$

(3) $\frac{1}{5}$

(4) $\frac{1}{2}$

(5) $\frac{1}{8}$

11. Which point represents the mixed number $1\frac{1}{2}$?

(1) A
(2) B
(3) C
(4) D
(5) None of the above

12. Which of the following pairs of fractions are equal?

(1) $\frac{5}{10}$ and $\frac{5}{11}$

(2) $\frac{9}{11}$ and $\frac{18}{23}$

(3) $\frac{10}{20}$ and $\frac{5}{5}$

(4) $\frac{3}{15}$ and $\frac{1}{5}$

(5) $\frac{6}{8}$ and $\frac{2}{4}$

13. Which of the following is equal to $\frac{2}{3}$?

(1) 5 inches as part of a foot
(2) 15 minutes as part of an hour
(3) $300 as part of Bun's $450 pay
(4) 8 hours as part of a day
(5) 500 Democrats as part of the 1,200 registered voters

14. Which of the following is equal to $\frac{3}{4}$?

(1) $2 as part of $10
(2) 9 eggs as part of a dozen
(3) 2 weeks as part of a month
(4) 90 points out of a possible 100 points
(5) 24 inches as part of a yard

Check your answers on page 410.

Estimating with Fractions

On the GED Math Test there may be times when you are asked to find an approximate fraction. At other times, you may find it helpful to use approximation to estimate an answer. There are two useful ways to find an approximate answer.

METHOD A

Round the numerator and denominator to the nearest 10 or 100 and rename.

Example:

The theater club has 80 members. 58 members have bought tickets to see "My Favorite Husband." This is approximately what fraction of the total members?

$\frac{58}{60}$ rounds to $\frac{60}{80}$ **Rename:** $\frac{60 \div 20}{80 \div 20} = \frac{3}{4}$

METHOD B

Check to see if one value is an approximate multiple of the other.

Example:

Of the 11 members of the student council, 6 voted "no" on the proposed fund-raiser. Approximately what fraction of the council voted "no"?

In this problem, $\frac{6}{11}$ of the council members voted against the proposal. The fraction $\frac{6}{11}$ is close to $\frac{6}{12}$, which simplifies to $\frac{1}{2}$. So $\frac{6}{11}$ is approximately $\frac{1}{2}$.

Exercise 2

Directions: Choose an approximate fraction for each of the following items.

1. Eleven days is approximately what fraction of a month?

(1) $\frac{1}{8}$

(2) $\frac{1}{6}$

(3) $\frac{1}{4}$

(4) $\frac{1}{3}$

(5) $\frac{1}{2}$

2. Uma collected $52 of the $100 promised by her office staff as a donation to "Toys for Tots." Approximately what fractional part has Uma collected?

(1) $\frac{1}{8}$

(2) $\frac{1}{6}$

(3) $\frac{1}{4}$

(4) $\frac{1}{3}$

(5) $\frac{1}{2}$

3. The Belkakis Photo Club meets monthly. In June, 5 of the 42 members were absent. Approximately what fraction of the club was absent?

(1) $\frac{1}{8}$

(2) $\frac{2}{5}$

(3) $\frac{1}{2}$

(4) $\frac{5}{6}$

(5) $\frac{7}{10}$

4. George has driven 72 of the 98 miles to Youngville. Approximately what fraction of the trip has he driven?

(1) $\frac{1}{8}$

(2) $\frac{2}{5}$

(3) $\frac{1}{2}$

(4) $\frac{5}{6}$

(5) $\frac{7}{10}$

Check your answers on page 410.

Adding and Subtracting Like Fractions

Values can only be added to or subtracted from like terms. Whole numbers are added to whole numbers. Decimal parts are subtracted from other decimal parts.

Fractions have **like terms** when they have the same denominator. When fractions have the same denominator, their numerators can be added or subtracted. The answer, if necessary, is renamed in simplest form.

Examples:

$$\begin{array}{r} \frac{3}{8} \\ + \frac{1}{8} \\ \hline \frac{4}{8} = \frac{1}{2} \end{array} \qquad \begin{array}{r} \frac{2}{3} \\ + \frac{2}{3} \\ \hline \frac{4}{3} = 1\frac{1}{3} \end{array} \qquad \begin{array}{r} \frac{3}{5} \\ - \frac{2}{5} \\ \hline \frac{1}{5} \end{array} \qquad \begin{array}{r} \frac{5}{6} \\ - \frac{1}{6} \\ \hline \frac{4}{6} = \frac{2}{3} \end{array}$$

To add mixed numbers with like denominators:

Step 1 Add the fractions together. Check to see if the fractional part can be simplified or renamed as a mixed number.

$$\begin{array}{r} 7\frac{3}{5} \\ + 5\frac{4}{5} \\ \hline \frac{7}{5} = 1\frac{2}{5} \end{array}$$

Step 2 Add the whole numbers together, remembering to include any whole number from the simplified fraction.

$$\begin{array}{r} 7\frac{3}{5} \\ + 5\frac{4}{5} \\ \hline 12 \ + 1\frac{2}{5} = 13\frac{2}{5} \end{array}$$

To subtract mixed numbers with like denominators:

Step 1 Borrow, if necessary. Rename the 1 you borrowed as a fraction, using the denominator from the number you are subtracting.

$$\cancel{6}\,\frac{5}{12} = 6\,\frac{5+12}{12} = 6\,\frac{17}{12}$$
$$-\ 2\,\frac{7}{12}$$

Step 2 Subtract the fractions. Check to see if the difference can be simplified.

$$6\,\frac{17}{12}$$
$$-\ 2\,\frac{7}{12}$$
$$\overline{\frac{10}{12} = \frac{5}{6}}$$

Step 3 Subtract the whole numbers.

$$6\,\frac{7}{12}$$
$$-\ 2\,\frac{7}{12}$$
$$\overline{4\,\frac{5}{6}}$$

Exercise 3

Directions: Solve the following problems.

1. $\dfrac{1}{4} + \dfrac{3}{4}$

2. $\dfrac{7}{10} + \dfrac{5}{10}$

3. $4\dfrac{1}{3} + 2\dfrac{1}{3}$

4. $\dfrac{3}{4} - \dfrac{1}{4}$

5. $\dfrac{11}{12} - \dfrac{7}{12}$

6. $7 - \dfrac{1}{2}$

7. $12\dfrac{2}{5} - 7\dfrac{4}{5}$

8. Gabriela is happy that she has had time to jog three days this week. She ran $2\dfrac{1}{4}$ miles on Monday, $3\dfrac{1}{4}$ miles on Wednesday, and $3\dfrac{3}{4}$ miles on Friday. How many miles did she jog this week?

   (1) $8\dfrac{1}{4}$

   (2) $8\dfrac{1}{2}$

   (3) $9\dfrac{1}{4}$

   (4) $9\dfrac{1}{2}$

   (5) 9

9. Before Karen left for the skiing trip, the gasoline tank of her car was $\dfrac{3}{4}$ full. When she returned, the gauge showed she had $\dfrac{1}{4}$ tank left. How much of a tank of gasoline did she use?

   (1) $\dfrac{1}{8}$

   (2) $\dfrac{1}{4}$

   (3) $\dfrac{1}{3}$

   (4) $\dfrac{1}{2}$

   (5) $\dfrac{2}{3}$

10. The Garabedians have a wood-burning stove. They bought 2 cords of wood in November. They have used $\dfrac{2}{3}$ of a cord. How many cords of wood do they have left?

    (1) $\dfrac{1}{2}$

    (2) $\dfrac{3}{4}$

    (3) $\dfrac{2}{3}$

    (4) 1

    (5) $1\dfrac{1}{3}$

11. Jack won an award that measures $6\frac{1}{4}$ inches on each side. He plans to mount the square award on a piece of wood so that the award has a $\frac{3}{4}$ inch border on all sides. What must the piece of wood measure in inches on each side to frame the award according to Jack's plan?

   (1) $6\frac{3}{4}$

   (2) 7

   (3) $7\frac{1}{2}$

   (4) $7\frac{3}{4}$

   (5) $8\frac{1}{4}$

12. The Evergreen Landscaping Company has been hired to surround a golf course with drought-resistant plants. The company completed $\frac{1}{8}$ of the job last week and $\frac{3}{8}$ this week. What fraction of the job remains to be completed?

   (1) $\frac{5}{8}$

   (2) $\frac{1}{2}$

   (3) $\frac{1}{4}$

   (4) $\frac{1}{8}$

   (5) Not enough information is given.

Check your answers on page 410.

Adding and Subtracting Unlike Fractions

Fractions with different denominators (**unlike terms**) must be renamed before they can be added together or subtracted from one another.

What is $\frac{1}{2} + \frac{1}{3}$?

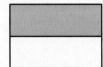

In order to add or subtract, the fractions must be renamed with the same or **common denominator**.

If we cut both rectangles into 6 pieces, we can see that $\frac{1}{2} = \frac{3}{6}$ and $\frac{1}{3} = \frac{2}{6}$.

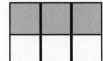

To add or subtract fractions with unlike denominators:

Step 1 Find a common denominator for the fractions.
Step 2 Rename the fractions in like terms.
Step 3 Add or subtract as you would like fractions.

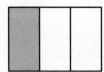

To find a common denominator, use these methods:

Check to see if one denominator is a multiple of the other.

- For $\frac{1}{2}$ and $\frac{3}{4}$, use 4 as the denominator.

- For $\frac{2}{3}$ and $\frac{7}{12}$, use 12 as the denominator.

If one denominator is not a multiple of the other, find a third number that is divisible by both denominators.

- For $\frac{2}{3}$ and $\frac{4}{5}$, use 15 as the denominator.

- For $\frac{1}{4}$ and $\frac{5}{6}$, use 12 as the denominator.

315

If all else fails, multiply one denominator by the other. This method will always give a common denominator, but the number may be greater than necessary, and it may be necessary to simplify the final answer.

- For $\frac{1}{5}$ and $\frac{3}{7}$, use 35 as the denominator.

- For $\frac{2}{3}$ and $\frac{5}{8}$, use 24 as the denominator.

Exercise 4

Directions: Solve the following problems.

1. $\frac{1}{2} + \frac{2}{3}$

2. $\frac{3}{5} + \frac{3}{4}$

3. $\frac{3}{4} - \frac{1}{3}$

4. $\frac{7}{8} - \frac{1}{2}$

5. Mike mailed two documents together, which weighed $\frac{2}{3}$ pound and $1\frac{1}{6}$ pounds, respectively. How many pounds did his package weigh?

   (1) $1\frac{1}{2}$

   (2) $1\frac{3}{4}$

   (3) $1\frac{5}{6}$

   (4) $1\frac{7}{8}$

   (5) $2\frac{1}{6}$

6. The photo of Isaiah's son is $5\frac{11}{16}$ inches, just a little too wide for the $5\frac{1}{2}$ inch frame. What fraction of an inch should Isaiah cut off of the photo?

   (1) $\frac{1}{18}$

   (2) $\frac{1}{10}$

   (3) $\frac{1}{8}$

   (4) $\frac{3}{16}$

   (5) $\frac{5}{18}$

7. Ricardo is biking $20\frac{2}{3}$ miles to Silver Lake. After he passes the $4\frac{1}{2}$ mile marker, how many more miles does he have to go?

   (1) $15\frac{1}{6}$

   (2) $16\frac{1}{6}$

   (3) $16\frac{3}{8}$

   (4) $16\frac{5}{8}$

   (5) $17\frac{1}{6}$

8. The McKiernan family is getting together for Thanksgiving dinner at Betty's house. Betty bought a $12\frac{1}{2}$ pound turkey. Her sister-in-law Ann bought a $13\frac{3}{4}$ pound turkey. How many pounds of turkey will the family have altogether?

   (1) $25\frac{1}{4}$

   (2) $26\frac{1}{4}$

   (3) $26\frac{3}{8}$

   (4) $26\frac{1}{2}$

   (5) $26\frac{3}{4}$

Items 9 and 10 refer to the following information.

Carlos told his children that he feels they watch too much television. His son Juan had watched TV for $1\frac{1}{2}$ hours that morning and $2\frac{1}{4}$ hours that afternoon. His daughter Luz had watched $\frac{1}{2}$ hour longer than Juan in the morning but only $1\frac{1}{2}$ hours total in the afternoon.

9. How many hours did Luz watch all together?

   (1) $3\frac{1}{2}$

   (2) $3\frac{3}{4}$

   (3) 4

   (4) $4\frac{1}{4}$

   (5) $4\frac{3}{4}$

10. How many hours more did Juan watch TV than Luz?

    (1) $\frac{1}{16}$

    (2) $\frac{1}{12}$

    (3) $\frac{1}{8}$

    (4) $\frac{1}{6}$

    (5) $\frac{1}{4}$

Check your answers on page 411.

Multiplying and Dividing Fractions

Ramona works as an assistant for the County Clerk. She works $7\frac{1}{2}$ hours each day. Ramona estimates that $\frac{1}{3}$ of each day is spent processing voter registration records. How many hours per day does she work on voter records?

To solve this problem, you need to answer:

What is $\frac{1}{3}$ of $7\frac{1}{2}$?

To multiply fractions or mixed numbers:

Example: $7\frac{1}{2} \times \frac{1}{3}$

Step 1   Rename mixed numbers to improper fractions. Write any whole number as a fraction. $7\frac{1}{2} \times \frac{1}{3} = \frac{15}{2} \times \frac{1}{3}$

Step 2   Divide common factors where possible by dividing any numerator and any denominator by the same number. $\frac{\overset{5}{\cancel{15}}}{2} \times \frac{1}{\underset{1}{\cancel{3}}}$

Step 3   Multiply numerator by numerator and denominator by denominator. $\frac{\overset{5}{\cancel{15}}}{2} \times \frac{1}{\underset{1}{\cancel{3}}} = \frac{5}{2}$

Step 4   Rename, if necessary, renaming improper fractions to mixed numbers or simplifying. $\frac{5}{2} = 2\frac{1}{2}$

Ramona spends 2½ hours per day on voter records.

Example:

How many $\frac{3}{8}$'s are in $4\frac{1}{2}$? The strip below is $4\frac{1}{2}$ inches long. The strip is divided into twelve pieces, each $\frac{3}{8}$ inch long. $\quad 4\frac{1}{2} \div \frac{3}{8} = 12$

To divide with fractions or mixed numbers:

Example: $\quad 4\frac{1}{2} \div \frac{3}{8}$

Step 1 Write all mixed and whole numbers as improper fractions.

$$4\frac{1}{2} \div \frac{3}{8} = \frac{9}{2} \div \frac{3}{8}$$

Step 2 Rewrite the problem by multiplying by the reciprocal.

$$\frac{9}{2} \div \frac{3}{8} = \frac{9}{2} \times \frac{8}{3}$$

Step 3 Divide common factors where possible.

$$\overset{3}{\cancel{\frac{9}{2}}} \times \overset{4}{\cancel{\frac{8}{3}}}_{1}$$

Step 4 Multiply numerator by numerator. Then multiply denominator by denominator.

$$\frac{3}{1} \times \frac{4}{1} = \frac{12}{1}$$

Step 5 Rename, if necessary, renaming improper fractions to mixed or whole numbers or simplifying.

$$\frac{12}{1} = 12$$

Exercise 5

> **Directions:** Choose the <u>one best answer</u> for each item.

1. Savita's car has a $13\frac{1}{2}$ gallon tank. It is $\frac{3}{4}$ full. How many gallons of gas are in her car's tank?

   (1) $9\frac{7}{8}$

   (2) 10

   (3) $10\frac{1}{8}$

   (4) $10\frac{1}{4}$

   (5) $10\frac{5}{8}$

2. How many feet of wood are needed to replace 5 staircase boards if each is $4\frac{2}{3}$ feet long?

   (1) 20

   (2) $20\frac{1}{3}$

   (3) $21\frac{1}{3}$

   (4) $22\frac{2}{3}$

   (5) $23\frac{1}{3}$

3. The Brownville PTA needs to cover 3 tables for the banquet. How many yards of fabric are needed if each tablecloth requires $2\frac{3}{4}$ yards?

   (1) $8\frac{1}{4}$

   (2) 8

   (3) $7\frac{3}{4}$

   (4) $7\frac{1}{2}$

   (5) $6\frac{3}{4}$

4. Richard's Farms has decided to allow the community to use $7\frac{1}{2}$ acres of their land for vegetable gardens this summer. If the town divides the area into 8 plots, how many acres will each plot be?

(1) $\dfrac{7}{16}$

(2) $\dfrac{1}{2}$

(3) $\dfrac{15}{16}$

(4) $15\dfrac{1}{2}$

(5) 60

5. Mary is cutting $\frac{3}{4}$ inch strips from a piece of cardboard that is 12 inches wide. How many strips will she get?

(1) 8
(2) 9
(3) 12
(4) 16
(5) 34

6. Jenkin's Market gives each worker a $\frac{1}{4}$ hour break every 3 hours. If only one worker takes a break at one time, how many workers can take a break during a 3-hour span?

(1) 10
(2) 11
(3) 12
(4) 13
(5) 14

Check your answers on page 411.

Exercise 6

Directions: These are miscellaneous problems dealing with fractions. Treat these problems like an alternate-format question where you would need to fill out a standard grid. (*Calculator permitted.*)

1. If a shipment of 110 similar packages weighs $78\frac{4}{7}$ pounds, how much will one package weigh?

2. At the end of October, Maggie figures out that 38 of the 180 schooldays have gone by. What fraction of the school year is left?

3. An amusement park received a shipment of 5,000 necklaces to use as prizes. Of the necklaces, $\frac{3}{10}$ were found to be defective. Of the defective necklaces, $\frac{3}{4}$ could be repaired. How many necklaces could be repaired?

4. Christina jogs $1\frac{3}{4}$ miles five days per week and $2\frac{1}{2}$ miles on Saturday. How many miles does she run weekly?

Check your answers on page 411.

Unit 5

RATIO AND PROPORTION

Ratios and proportions are an application of fractions. We often hear comments like, "In a certain college, 4 out of every 7 students are male." This means that among 7 people surveyed, 4 are male and 3 are female. Therefore, we can now say that there is a 4 to 3 ratio of male to female. In essence we are saying, "for every 4 men we encounter, we must come across 3 women." It is a comparison of like quantities and can be expressed as a fraction.

We can extend this concept to rates such as gas mileage. When we say, "My car gets a mileage of 40 miles per gallon," we are saying that for every 40 miles I travel one gallon of gas is being consumed. This is a comparison of two unlike quantities, and this, too, can be expressed as a fraction. Once we know the rate (mileage per one-gallon), we can use a proportion to find how much gas would be needed to go on a 300-mile trip.

A **proportion** is an equation that consists of two equivalent ratios that have been set equal to each other.

A **ratio** is a comparison of two numbers used to show a relationship or pattern.

A ratio can compare two similar values, such as men to women (both are people) and length to width (both are measures of length).

A ratio can also compare different units of measure: home runs per at bats, miles per hour, miles per gallon, and price per item. A ratio that compares different units of measure is called a **rate**.

A class has 5 women and 7 men. That ratio can be written three ways, each of which would be read 5 to 7.

With a Colon	Without a Colon	As a Fraction
5:7	5 to 7	$\dfrac{5}{7}$

The notation for ratios most often used on the GED Math Test is the fraction notation. The first number stated in the ratio is *always* written first or on top of the fraction bar!

Ratios communicate best when they are renamed in lowest terms. Like a fraction, you can rename a ratio. However, there is one important difference between ratios and fractions. Improper fractions are rewritten as whole or mixed numbers, but ratios are not.

Example:

Lorraine earns $400 weekly while her husband, Ron, earns $300. What is the ratio of Lorraine's earnings to her husband's earnings?

Write the ratio:

$$\frac{\$400}{\$300}$$

Rename it:

$$\frac{\$400}{\$300} \div \frac{100}{100} = \frac{4}{3}$$

The 4:3 ratio tells us that for every $4 Lorraine earns, Ron earns $3.

Sometimes you have to calculate one of the numbers in the ratio. How could you find the ratio of Lorraine's pay to their *total* weekly earnings?

Example:

First **add** their earnings to find the total.

$$\$400 + \$300 = \$700$$

Then **write** the ratio and rename it:

$$\frac{\text{Lorraine's Earnings}}{\text{Total Earnings}} = \frac{\$400}{\$700} \div \frac{100}{100} = \frac{4}{7}$$

Exercise 1

Directions: For items 1–5, write a ratio in lowest terms. For items 6–8, choose the <u>one best answer</u> for each item.

1. The directions say to mix 5 cups water with 2 cups of cleaning solution. What is the ratio of water to solution?

2. The following statistics were given for Lisa's favorite team. What is their win:loss ratio?

Wins	Losses	Average	Streak
59	30	0.663	Win 1

3. Carolyn drove 375 miles to New York City. Her car used 15 gallons of gas. What was the rate of miles to gallons that she got on this trip?

4. The auto salesperson sold 36 cars last year. What is the ratio of cars sold per month?

5. Harry put $75 in his savings account and used the rest of his paycheck to pay bills totaling $325. What is the ratio of money saved to his *total pay*?

    (1) 3:16
    (2) 3:13
    (3) 1:4
    (4) 3:8
    (5) 1:2

6. On Monday, the Bijou Theater sold 120 children's tickets and 240 adults' tickets. What is the ratio of children's tickets to total tickets sold?

    (1) 3:1
    (2) 2:1
    (3) 1:2
    (4) 1:3
    (5) Not enough information is given.

Items 7 and 8 refer to the following information.

There are 25,000 registered voters in Big City. 15,000 voted during the last election.

7. What is the ratio of registered voters who *did not* vote to the total number of registered voters?

    (1) $\dfrac{2}{7}$

    (2) $\dfrac{2}{5}$

    (3) $\dfrac{3}{5}$

    (4) $\dfrac{5}{2}$

    (5) Not enough information is given.

8. What is the ratio of registered voters who did not vote to those who did vote?

    (1) $\dfrac{2}{5}$

    (2) $\dfrac{3}{5}$

    (3) $\dfrac{2}{3}$

    (4) $\dfrac{3}{2}$

    (5) Not enough information is given.

Check your answers on page 411.

Proportion

A **proportion** represents two equal ratios. A variety of word problems can be solved by setting up a proportion.

Example:

Aida is preparing chicken diablo for the mayor's reception. She plans on using 6 pounds of chicken for every 9 guests. If the mayor has invited 150 guests, how many pounds of chicken will Aida need?

Carefully set up a proportion stating the values of both ratios. Write the known relationship as the first ratio. The second ratio must follow the pattern of the first *in the same order*.

$$\text{pounds} \quad \frac{6}{9} = \frac{n}{150} \quad \text{pounds}$$
$$\text{guests} \qquad\qquad\qquad \text{guests}$$

or

$$\text{guests} \quad \frac{9}{6} = \frac{150}{n} \quad \text{guests:}$$
$$\text{pounds} \qquad\qquad\qquad \text{pounds:}$$

Now you are ready to solve for the value of n.

To find the unknown value in a proportion (the value of n):

Step 1 Multiply the known denominator by the known numerator across from it.

$$\frac{9}{6} = \frac{150}{n} \qquad 6(150) = 900$$

Step 2 Divide that answer by the numerator or denominator that remains.

$$\frac{9}{6} = \frac{150}{n} \qquad 900 \div 9 = 100$$

$$\frac{9}{6} = \frac{150}{100}$$

Aida will need 100 pounds of chicken.

Exercise 2

Directions: Solve the following problems by setting up and solving proportions.

1. The Murray Engraving Company prints formal invitations and announcements. Their standard price is $35 per 100 invitations. A company wants to purchase 1,200 announcements to advertise the grand opening of a new store. How much will the company be charged for the announcements?

   (1) $34
   (2) $210
   (3) $420
   (4) $525
   (5) $3,500

2. If 12 cans of oil cost $16.68, how much do 3 cans cost?

   (1) $1.39
   (2) $4.17
   (3) $8.34
   (4) $16.68
   (5) $50.04

3. Two quarts of oil cost $4.50. How much will 5 quarts cost?

   (1) $9.00
   (2) $9.50
   (3) $11.25
   (4) $22.50
   (5) Not enough information is given.

Items 4 and 5 refer to the following blueprint.

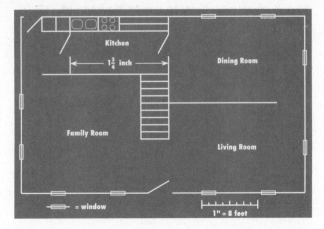

4. According to the architect's plan, how many feet wide will each living room window be?

   (1) $\frac{1}{4}$
   (2) $\frac{1}{2}$
   (3) 1
   (4) 2
   (5) 3

5. According to the architect's plan, how many feet wide will the kitchen be?

   (1) 8
   (2) 10
   (3) 12
   (4) 13
   (5) 14

6. Jerry works in the ticket office of the Community Theater. He mailed 5 tickets to the Higgins family, who sent a check for $77.50. At that rate, how many tickets should he send to MNG Offices, who sent a check for $232.50?

   (1) 15
   (2) 20
   (3) 25
   (4) 30
   (5) 35

7. Carl drove 375 miles to New York City. His car used 15 gallons of gas. If he gets the same mileage on his next trip, how many miles can he drive on 25 gallons of gas?

    (1) 225
    (2) 500
    (3) 625
    (4) 825
    (5) 9,375

Items 8–10 refer to the following information.

The Village School Committee is seeking to integrate all city schools. After gathering information about the community's ethnic distribution, the committee decides that in every group of 20 children, there should be 8 African Americans, 6 Caucasians, 4 Hispanics, and 2 Asians.

8. If Green Elementary School has 750 students, how many Hispanic students are needed?

    (1) 4
    (2) 40
    (3) 150
    (4) 200
    (5) Not enough information is given.

9. If Elm Middle School has 640 African Americans, how many Asian students are needed to achieve full integration?

    (1) 60
    (2) 80
    (3) 100
    (4) 160
    (5) Not enough information is given.

10. If South High School's enrollment of 5,000 is representative of the ethnic distribution within the community, how many of the students are Caucasian?

    (1) 150
    (2) 1,500
    (3) 2,000
    (4) 3,000
    (5) Not enough information is given.

Check your answers on page 412.

Proportions in Set-up Problems

Some of the problems on the GED Math Test are set-up problems. In a set-up problem, you are asked to choose the correct way to solve the problem from the five answer choices you are given.

To choose the proper set up for a proportion problem:

> **Step 1** Carefully set up a proportion to solve the problem.
>
> **Step 2** Write an expression for the cross products.
>
> **Step 3** Look carefully at the answer choices and choose the option that shows the correct multiplication and division set up.

Test-Taking Tip: Always write the ratios in a proportion in the same order. Before writing a proportion to solve an item in the test, quickly jot down the labels in the order you want the numbers in the ratios to appear.

Example:

$$\frac{miles}{hours}$$

Now try this GED Math Test problem.

Example:

The scale of miles on a map shows that 2 inches equals 400 miles. Which of the expressions below could be used to find how many miles are represented by 3 inches?

(1) $\dfrac{(2)(3)}{400}$

(2) $\dfrac{(3)(400)}{2}$

(3) $\dfrac{(3)(2)}{400}$

(4) $\dfrac{(3)(400)}{1}$

(5) Not enough information is given.

Step 1 Set up the proportion as you see it.

$$\frac{2}{400} = \frac{3}{x}$$

Step 2 Write an expression. $\dfrac{400(3)}{2}$

Step 3 Now compare your expression to the answer choices.

The correct answer is (2). Choice (2) shows 3 and 400 multiplied together and their product divided by 2 $\dfrac{(3)(400)}{2}$.

Exercise 3

1. An ad on television says that 4 out of every 5 doctors interviewed recommended Vestamint antacid pills. If 500 doctors were interviewed, which of the following expressions represents the number of doctors who recommended Vestamint?

   (1) $\dfrac{5(500)}{4}$

   (2) $\dfrac{(4)500}{5}$

   (3) $\dfrac{4(5)}{500}$

   (4) $4(5)(500)$

   (5) Not enough information is given.

2. Franco's car gets 23 miles per gallon. If he drove 460 miles to San Francisco, which of the following expressions represents the gallons of gas he used?

   (1) $\dfrac{1(460)}{23}$

   (2) $\dfrac{23(460)}{1}$

   (3) $460(1)(23)$

   (4) $\dfrac{460(23)}{1}$

   (5) Not enough information is given.

3. Ned drove 23 miles in ½ hour. At the same rate, how far will he drive in 2 hours?

   (1) $\dfrac{23(2)}{\frac{1}{2}}$

   (2) $\dfrac{\frac{1}{2}(23)}{2}$

   (3) $\dfrac{2(\frac{1}{2})}{23}$

   (4) $2(\frac{1}{2})(23)$

   (5) $\dfrac{23}{\frac{1}{2}(2)}$

4. The Milton schools superintendent has announced that she will hire new teachers to bring the student-teacher ratio in the Milton schools to 20 to 1. If there are 12,000 students in Milton schools, which of the following expressions represents the number of additional teachers to be hired by the school superintendent?

   (1) $\dfrac{1(12,000)}{20}$

   (2) $\dfrac{20(12,000)}{1}$

   (3) $\dfrac{1(20)}{12,000}$

   (4) $1(20)(12,000)$

   (5) Not enough information is given.

5. Carrie is making a dessert that calls for 6 ounces of chocolate chips to make 8 servings. Which of the following expressions could be used to figure out how many ounces she will need to make 12 servings?

   (1) $\dfrac{6(12)}{8}$

   (2) $\dfrac{8(12)}{6}$

   (3) $\dfrac{6(8)}{12}$

   (4) $6(8)(12)$

   (5) $\dfrac{12}{6(8)}$

6. Steve earned $325 for 25 hours of work. At the same rate, which of the following expressions represents the amount (in dollars) he would earn for 40 hours of work?

   (1) $40(325)(25)$

   (2) $\dfrac{25(40)}{325}$

   (3) $\dfrac{25(325)}{40}$

   (4) $\dfrac{40(325)(25)}{50}$

   (5) $\dfrac{40(325)}{25}$

Check your answers on page 412.

Exercise 4

Directions: These are miscellaneous problems dealing with ratio and proportion. Treat these problems like an alternate-format question where you would need to fill out a standard grid. (*Calculator permitted.*)

1. Arthur of Arthur's Antique Furniture Restoration has made some observations regarding the performance time of the different departments of his small shop. Along with his handful of regular adult employees he also hires high school students over the summer. The chart shows how much total time in hours was spent on the different aspects of furniture restoration (finishing, sanding, and repairing) over a four-week period during the summer, right after he hired his young employees.

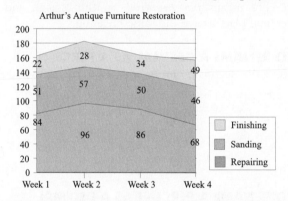

Arthur's Antique Furniture Restoration

What is the ratio of repairing to finishing in Week 3?

2. A gardener who is 6 feet tall casts a shadow 4 feet in length. At the same time, a tree casts a shadow 20 feet in length. What is the height of the tree?

3. Using satellite photography, geologists have determined that in four years, the Channel Islands off the coast of California have moved 18 millimeters along earthquake faults. If motion continues at this rate, how many millimeters will the islands move in 25 years?

4. A survey claims that 2 out of every 3 children prefer Krunchy brand potato chips. According to the survey, how many children in a school with 210 kids would prefer Krunchy chips?

Check your answers on page 412.

Unit 6

PERCENT

The concept of percent is applied every day of our lives when we are calculating things like the tip at a restaurant, sales tax, discounts, commissions, mortgage, and interest. The word **percent** is derived from the Latin phrase *per centum* meaning "per 100." For example, if we said 70% of the audience of a concert was teenagers, we are implying that for every 100 people we count, 70 of them will be teenagers. In reality there may have been 1,470 people in the concert, which would mean there were 1,029 teenagers. As you can see, percents allow us to perceive information in a more comprehensive and comparable manner.

Percent is a special rate or ratio meaning **per hundred**. 100% of something is all of it. 100% of a dollar is a dollar. 100% of a figure is the whole figure or one figure. When a percent is greater than 100, it represents more than one. For example, when profits are 200%, it means that they doubled.

Percents (per hundred) can be written as fractions or decimals. In many problems, you may find it helpful to rename percent values as decimals or fractions or vice versa.

PERCENT AND FRACTION EQUIVALENTS

TO RENAME A FRACTION AS A PERCENT

Write a proportion with the fraction as one ratio and $\frac{x}{100}$ as the other ratio. Solve for the unknown by:

Making an Equivalent Fraction

$$\frac{1}{5} \qquad \frac{1}{5} = \frac{x}{100} \qquad \frac{1}{5} \times \frac{20}{20} = \frac{20}{100} \qquad 20\%$$

$$\frac{12}{25} \qquad \frac{12}{25} = \frac{x}{100} \qquad \frac{12}{25} \times \frac{4}{4} = \frac{48}{100} \qquad 48\%$$

or

Using Properties of Proportions

$$\frac{1}{3} \qquad \frac{1}{3} = \frac{x}{100} \qquad \frac{1(100)}{3} \qquad 33\tfrac{1}{3}\%$$

$$\frac{5}{8} \qquad \frac{5}{8} = \frac{x}{100} \qquad \frac{5(100)}{8} \qquad 62\tfrac{1}{2}\%$$

TO RENAME A PERCENT AS A FRACTION

Write the percent over 100 and drop the % sign. Rename the fraction in simplest form or as a mixed number, if possible.

$$6\% \qquad \frac{6}{100} \qquad \frac{3}{50}$$

$$250\% \qquad \frac{250}{100} \qquad \frac{5}{2} = 2\frac{1}{2}$$

PERCENT AND DECIMAL EQUIVALENTS

Percent means *per hundred*, so the % sign and two decimal places have the same meaning.

TO RENAME A DECIMAL AS A PERCENT

Move the decimal point two places to the right and add a % sign.

0.02	0.02	2%
0.13	0.13	13%
3.6	3.60	360%

TO RENAME A PERCENT AS A DECIMAL

Move the decimal point two places to the left and drop the % sign.

6%	06	0.06
30%	30	0.3
250%	250	2.5

Exercise 1

Directions: Complete the tables below. Choose the one best answer for each item.

	Percent	Fraction		Decimal	Percent
1.		⅛	**8.**		7%
2.	25%		**9.**		10%
3.	40%		**10.**	0.18	
4.		½	**11.**	0.65	
5.		⅗	**12.**		125%
6.	70%		**13.**		180%
7.	75%		**14.**	2.5	

15. 25% equals $\frac{1}{4}$. Which of the following can you do to find 25% of a number quickly?

    (1) Divide the number by 10.
    (2) Divide the number by 4.
    (3) Divide the number by 2.
    (4) Multiply the number by 2.
    (5) Don't do anything; the number doesn't change.

16. Which of the following can you do to find 200% of a number quickly?

    (1) Divide it by 10.
    (2) Divide it by 2.
    (3) Multiply by 4.
    (4) Multiply by 2.
    (5) Don't do anything; you cannot find 200% of a number.

Check your answers on page 413.

Solving Percent Problems Using Proportion

One of the best ways to solve percent problems is to use your knowledge of ratio and proportion. You can write a proportion using percent as a ratio to solve percent problems.

$$\frac{\%}{100} = \frac{\text{Part}}{\text{Whole}}$$

Examples:

What is 8% of 900?

Write a proportion using the elements from the problem. Use a variable for the unknown part.

$$\frac{\%}{100} \quad \frac{8}{100} = \frac{x}{900} \quad \frac{\text{(is) Part}}{\text{(of) Whole}}$$

Solve:

$$\frac{8(900)}{100} = \frac{7,200}{100} = 72$$

72 is 8% of 900.

You can also use proportion to solve for the unknown whole.

Eighty is 50% of what number?

The question "of what number" indicates that the whole is missing.

$$\frac{\%}{100} \quad \frac{50}{100} = \frac{80}{x} \quad \frac{\text{(is) Part}}{\text{(of) Whole}}$$

Solve:

$$\frac{100(80)}{50} = 160$$

Eighty is 50% of what number? Eighty is 50% of 160.

You can also use proportion to solve for the unknown percent.

Four hundred is what percent of 500?

The question "what percent" indicates that the percent is missing.

$$\frac{\%}{100} \quad \frac{x}{100} = \frac{400}{500} \quad \frac{\text{(is) Part}}{\text{(of) Whole}}$$

Solve:

$$\frac{100(400)}{500} = 80$$

400 is 80% of 500.

Remember that to solve percent problems using proportion:

- Figure out what element in the problem is missing.
- Set up the proportion.
- Solve for the missing element.

Exercise 2

Directions: Solve the following percent problems.

1. What is 90% of 180?

$$\frac{\%}{100} \quad \underline{} = \underline{} \quad \frac{\text{(is) Part}}{\text{(of) Whole}}$$

2. What percent of 250 is 50?

$$\frac{\%}{100} \quad \underline{} = \underline{} \quad \frac{\text{(is) Part}}{\text{(of) Whole}}$$

3. 100% of what number is 20?

$$\frac{\%}{100} \quad \underline{} = \underline{} \quad \frac{\text{(is) Part}}{\text{(of) Whole}}$$

4. 70% of what number is 35?

$$\frac{\%}{100} \quad \underline{} = \underline{} \quad \frac{\text{(is) Part}}{\text{(of) Whole}}$$

5. The Suttons are planning a vacation in Cancun. Their travel agent tells them that they can purchase a travel package for seven nights' lodging for $1,950. The agent offers them a 15% discount if they make their reservations today. How much will they save if they take advantage of the discount?

   (1) $19.50
   (2) $146.25
   (3) $195.00
   (4) $292.50
   (5) Not enough information is given.

6. Last year Monica earned $54 interest on her savings account. The interest rate was 4.5%. How much money was in her account before the interest was added?

   (1) $120
   (2) $1,200
   (3) $1,500
   (4) $7,500
   (5) $12,000

Items 7 and 8 refer to the following information.

Reggie's union negotiated a 6% cost of living increase. Reggie makes $29,500 a year.

7. By how much will Reggie's pay increase?

   (1) $17.70
   (2) $177
   (3) $1,070
   (4) $1,770
   (5) $2,770

8. What will Reggie's yearly salary be after the cost of living increase?

   (1) $29,577
   (2) $29,677
   (3) $31,270
   (4) $47,200
   (5) Not enough information is given.

9. Louise went shopping and bought a blouse for $24, slacks for $31.99, and shoes for $42.49. All her purchases are subject to a 5% sales tax. What is the total cost of her purchases including tax?

   (1) $4.92
   (2) $98.48
   (3) $103.40
   (4) $147.68
   (5) $149.24

10. Marylee works on commission. This month she has earned $325 for the first week, $480 for the second week, and $275 this week. What is the rate, or percent, of commission that she earns?

    (1) 2%
    (2) 4%
    (3) 5%
    (4) 6%
    (5) Not enough information is given.

Check your answers on page 413.

Percent of Increase and Decrease

The **percent of increase or decrease** measures the change from one price or amount to another. Articles in the newspaper inform us that the value of real estate, for example, changes from time to time depending on factors in the economy. A person who buys a home one year finds its value has usually increased or decreased by the next year.

A different proportion can be used to find the percent of increase or decrease.

$$\frac{\% \text{ of Increase or Decrease}}{100} = \frac{\text{Change in Amount}}{\text{Original Amount}}$$

The change in amount is found by subtracting to find the difference between the original or earlier amount and the newer amount. This difference is compared to the original amount.

Example:

American Cinema has raised the price of admission from $6 per person to $7.50 per person. What is the percent of increase?

Step 1 Subtract to find the change between the original and the newer amount.

$$\begin{array}{r} \$7.50 \\ -6.00 \\ \hline \$1.50 \end{array}$$

Step 2 Put this amount over the original or earlier amount in a proportion.

$$\frac{\%}{100} = \frac{1.50}{6}$$

Step 3 Solve for percent.

$$\frac{100(1.50)}{6} = 25$$

The percent of increase is **25%**.

Example:

The Lunville High School had an enrollment of 1,050 students in 1994. This was less than the 1993 enrollment of 1,200. What was the percent of decrease in enrollment from 1993 to 1994?

Step 1 Subtract to find the change between the original and the newer amount.

$$\begin{array}{r} 1,200 \\ -1,050 \\ \hline 150 \end{array}$$

Step 2 Put this amount over the original or earlier amount in a proportion.

$$\frac{\%}{100} = \frac{150}{1,200}$$

Step 3 Solve for percent

$$\frac{100(150)}{1,200} = 12.5$$

The percent of decrease was **12.5%**.

Exercise 3

Directions: Choose the one best answer for each item.

1. During the 1990s, many companies have reduced their workforce. TGH Electronics employed 15,000 workers in 1992. By 1994, their workforce was cut to 7,500. By what percent did their workforce decrease?

   (1) 5%
   (2) 10%
   (3) 20%
   (4) 50%
   (5) 100%

2. Tresses and Dresses Fashion Salon posted a notice that as of February 1, its prices will increase. A wash, cut, and blow dry will be $25; a tint will be $60; and a permanent will be $95. What is the percent of increase in the price for a permanent?

   (1) 5%
   (2) 10%
   (3) 20%
   (4) 25%
   (5) Not enough information is given.

3. Fly-Us Airlines has lowered the economy fare from Chicago to Los Angeles from $264 to $212. To the nearest whole percent, what is the percent of decrease in airfare?

   (1) 16%
   (2) 18%
   (3) 20%
   (4) 25%
   (5) Not enough information is given.

4. Guiseppi's Pizza raised the price of a plain cheese pizza from $6.70 to $7.37. By what percent did the price for a plain cheese pizza increase?

   (1) 5%
   (2) 10%
   (3) 20%
   (4) 25%
   (5) Not enough information is given.

5. Jody received a notice from the manager of Windsor Apartments that all rents will be increased by 8% effective June 1. Jody's rent is $450 a month now. How much will his rent be, effective June 1?

   (1) $486
   (2) $496
   (3) $500
   (4) $550
   (5) $586

6. In order to avoid lay-offs at Niki Computers, each assembler is being asked to take a 3% cut in pay. This would mean a loss of $420 a year to Maureen. What is her present salary before the paycut?

   (1) $1,400
   (2) $12,000
   (3) $14,000
   (4) $16,000
   (5) Not enough information is given.

7. Captive breeding of the Wild California Condor has increased the population from 20 to 64 birds. What is the percent of increase in the number of condors?

   (1) 31%
   (2) 44%
   (3) 69%
   (4) 220%
   (5) 320%

8. The regular price of a camera is $199. The sale price is $171. About what percent is the camera discounted?

   (1) 14%
   (2) 25%
   (3) 30%
   (4) 86%
   (5) Not enough information is given.

Check your answers on page 413.

Solving Simple Interest Problems

When you have money in a savings account, the bank pays you interest. When you buy something on credit, you must pay interest. **Interest** is a percent paid for using someone else's money.

A formula for finding simple interest (i) is given on the GED Math Test list of formulas.

$i = prt$; where p = principal, r = rate, t = time

The **principal** is the amount of money borrowed.

The **rate** is the percent of interest charged or paid yearly. The percent must be written as a decimal or fraction in order to multiply.

The **time** is the number of years or part of a year for which the money is borrowed. When the time is in months, it should be written as a fraction with the denominator 12 (months in a year).

Example:

Find the simple interest on a new car loan of $8,000 at 9% interest for 4 years.

$i = prt$ principal is $8,000

rate 9% as a fraction $\left(\dfrac{9}{100}\right)$, or a decimal (0.09)

time is 4 years

$i = \$8,000 \times \dfrac{9}{100} \times 4$ **or** $i = \$8,000(0.09)(4)$

$$\dfrac{8,000}{1} \times \dfrac{9}{100} \times \dfrac{4}{1} = \$2,880$$

$$
\begin{array}{r}
\$8,000 \\
\times\ 0.09 \\
\hline
\$\ 720.00 \\
\times\qquad 4 \\
\hline
\$2,880.00
\end{array}
$$

PARTS OF A YEAR

Example:

Find the simple interest earned on a savings account of $250 at 3% interest for 4 months.

$i = prt$ **principal is $250**

rate 3% as a fraction $\left(\dfrac{3}{100}\right)$,

or a decimal (0.03)

time is 4 months, or $\dfrac{4}{12}$ of a year

The rate is annual. If the time includes months, the months are placed in a fraction with 12 and simplified, if possible.

$$\frac{4 \text{ months}}{12 \text{ months}} = \frac{1}{3}$$

$$i = \$250\left(\frac{3}{100}\right)$$

$\left(\dfrac{1}{3}\right)$ **or** $i = \$250\,(0.03)\left(\dfrac{1}{3}\right)$

$$\frac{\$\overset{5}{\cancel{250}}}{1} \times \frac{\overset{1}{\cancel{3}}}{\underset{2}{\cancel{100}}} \times \frac{1}{\underset{1}{\cancel{3}}} = \frac{\$5}{2} = \$2.50$$

$\begin{array}{r} \$ \ 2.50 \\ \times \ 0.03 \\ \hline \$ \ 7.50 \end{array} \times \dfrac{1}{3} = \$2.50$

AMOUNT TO REPAY

Example:

Stacy and Bob bought a new living room set for $2,400, which they agreed to pay for over 2 years at a 10% interest rate. How much money will they pay for the living room furniture?

This is a two-step problem.

Step 1 Find the amount of interest.

$i = \$2,400\left(\dfrac{10}{100}\right)(2)$ **or** $i = \$2,400\,(0.1)(2)$

$\dfrac{\$2,\cancel{400}}{1} \times \dfrac{10}{\cancel{100}} \times \dfrac{2}{1} = \$480$

$\begin{array}{r} \$ \ 2,400 \\ \times \quad 0.1 \\ \hline 240.0 \\ \times \qquad 2 \\ \hline \$480.00 \end{array}$

Step 2 Add the interest to the principal to find the final cost.

$\begin{array}{r} \$2,400 \\ + \quad 480 \\ \hline \$2,880 \end{array}$ Amount to repay

Exercise 4

1. Peter borrowed $2,000 from the Carpenter's Credit Union for 2 years at 9% interest. How much interest must he pay?

2. Carlos bought a new sofa for $599 at 10% interest with 6 months to pay. How much interest must he pay?

3. The Pepicellis want to buy a new home at a mortgage rate of 8.5%. Which expression below shows the interest that they will pay if they get a $125,000 mortgage for 25 years?

    (1) $125,000(8.5)(25)
    (2) $125,000(0.085)
    (3) $125,000(0.085)(25)
    (4) 25(0.085)
    (5) $125,000(25)

4. Voeurn financed his $8,800 car at 7% for 5 years. What is the <u>total amount</u> that Voeurn must repay?

    (1) $3,080
    (2) $8,800
    (3) $9,108
    (4) $11,880
    (5) $12,880

5. Angela put a $1,000 down payment on a used car costing $4,200. She got a simple interest loan from her bank for the remaining amount. The loan is for 3 years at an annual interest rate of 8%. What is the total amount Angela will repay the bank?

    (1) $768
    (2) $1,008
    (3) $3,968
    (4) $4,948
    (5) $5,208

Check your answers on page 413.

Exercise 5

Directions: These are miscellaneous problems dealing with the use of percents. Treat these problems like an alternate-format question where you would need to fill out a standard grid. (*Calculator permitted.*)

1. Mr. Beltran's yearly earnings are $92,565. What is his monthly car payment? Round to the nearest dollar.

Mr. Beltran's Monthly
Household Budget

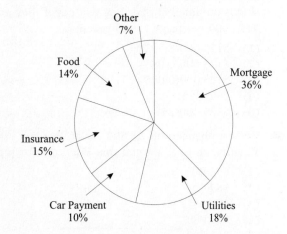

2. Wayne's computer hard drive has used only 1.4 gigabytes (gb) of space. If this is $3\frac{1}{2}$% of the total disk space, what is the hard drive capacity of Wayne's computer?

3. Julius works as an office assistant at a large real estate firm. Recently he made a graph showing his hourly wage for the years 1995–2001. What percent raise did Julius receive at the beginning of 1999?

4. A discount store takes 15% off of the ticketed price on any item it has in the store. With a coupon from its Web site, it takes an additional 20% off the discounted price of any linen. If Natasha buys a comforter that is marked $112, how much will she pay at the checkout stand?

Check your answers on page 414.

Unit 7

DATA ANALYSIS AND STATISTICS

Statistics deals with the collection, organization, and analysis of numerical data. Experiments are designed so as to make it possible to interpret the data and make inferences (decisions) and predictions. This is why it is called data analysis.

People have used statistics since the beginning of civilization when symbols and illustrations were utilized to count and document numbers of people, animals, and commodities on slabs of stone, animal skins, tree bark, and the walls of caves. We still use visual images called graphs to represent the relationship between the numbers and the items they are representing, and we try to interpret their meaning and significance.

Mean, Median, and Mode

The following is a graph representing a fictitious set of data for you to analyze.

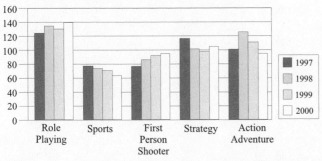

Video Game Sales (× 1,000)

Mean is simply the average. You add up all the data points and divide by the total number of available data values.

Median is the middle number when all the data values have been put in order (ranked). When there is an odd number of data values, the middle number *is* the median. When there is an even number of data values the average of the two middle numbers is the median.

Mode is the most frequently occurring data point in a given set of data values.

Examples:

Which genre had the lowest **mean** (average) sale?

You would look at each group, find the individual averages, and compare them. By inspection you can see that all the bars relating to "Sports" seem to be the lowest. The mean of this group is $\frac{78 + 74 + 72 + 68}{4} = 73$. So the lowest mean sales was "Sports" at 73,000.

What was the **median** sales for "Action Adventure" between the years of 1997 and 2000?

First arrange the sale prices in ascending order: 97, 100, 110, 125. The total number of data values is 4, which is even, so we look at the two middle numbers, 100 and 110, and find their average: $\frac{100 + 110}{2} = 105$. The median sales was 105,000.

What was the **mode** for all the genres through all the years?

We look for the most frequently occurring number in the entire data set. 78, 97, 100, and 125 are modes because they each appear twice in the entire data set.

Tables

Many important decisions depend on our ability to interpret data. Bits of information are easier to understand and use when they are well organized.

In a **table**, information is organized in columns and rows. **Columns** go up and down. To remember this, think of columns on buildings, such as the Lincoln Memorial in Washington, DC. **Rows** go across. Think about finding your seat in a row at a sporting event. Columns and rows have labels that indicate what information will be found within them.

The title of the table indicates what information is included in the table as a whole.

LIVING ARRANGEMENTS OF YOUNG ADULTS IN 2000
Shown in Percents

	Males 18–24	Females 18–24	Males 25–34	Females 25–34
Child of Householder	58.1	47.7	15.0	8.1
Family Householder	14.8	29.5	55.9	73.3
Nonfamily Householder	9.9	8.0	16.2	9.9
Other	17.3	14.8	13.0	8.7

Source: Bureau of the Census; U.S. Department of Commerce

In a table the place where a particular row and column meet is called a **cell**.

Examples:

What percent of men between the ages of 25 and 34 are family householders?

Look across the row that reads *Family Householder* to the number in the column under *Males 25-34*. You can see that the cell labeled 55.9% represents the percent of men in this age group who are family householders.

What are the living arrangements for the highest percent of females ages 18-24?

Look down the column labeled *Females 18-24;* the highest number is 47.7%. Look across the row that contains 47.7% to the heading *Child of Householder*. The greatest percent of women, ages 18-24, are children of the householder.

Some problems on the GED Math Test will ask you to work with the figures given on a table to solve problems. Carefully use the table to find the right facts. Then use the facts to calculate the answer.

MEDIAN PRICE OF EXISTING SINGLE-FAMILY HOMES

City	1998	2000	2002
Akron, OH	$ 59,900	$ 67,700	$ 75,500
Baltimore, MD	$ 88,700	$105,900	$111,500
Boston, MA	$181,200	$174,200	$168,200
Charleston, SC	$ 73,100	$ 76,200	$ 82,000
Daytona Beach, FL	$ 62,600	$ 64,100	$ 63,600
Honolulu, HI	$210,000	$352,000	$342,000
Louisville, KY	$ 54,500	$ 60,800	$ 69,700
New York, NY	$183,800	$174,900	$169,300
San Francisco, CA	$212,900	$259,300	$243,900
Spokane, WA	$ 51,100	$ 55,500	$ 71,300

Source: National Association of Realtors

When a list of prices is arranged from least to most expensive, the median price is the price in the middle of the list. In this table, the median prices represent typical prices for homes in these cities.

Example:

In 2002, the median price of a home in Daytona Beach, Florida, was about what fraction of the median price of a home in San Francisco, California?

(1) $\dfrac{1}{5}$

(2) $\dfrac{1}{4}$

(3) $\dfrac{1}{3}$

(4) $\dfrac{1}{2}$

(5) $\dfrac{2}{3}$

The question asks for a comparison of prices in 2002. Be sure to look in the proper column. In 2002, the median price of a home in Daytona Beach was $63,600 and in San Francisco it was $243,900. Because the question uses the word "about," your answer does not need to be exact. Use rounding to make the work easier.

$$\frac{\$63,600}{\$243,900} \text{ rounded to } \frac{\$6\cancel{0},\cancel{0}\cancel{0}\cancel{0}}{\$24\cancel{0},\cancel{0}\cancel{0}\cancel{0}} \text{ is about } = \frac{1}{4}$$

The correct answer is (2).

Exercise 1

> **Directions:** Choose the one best answer for each item.

> Items 1–4 refer to the following table.

NUMBER OF SICK DAYS PER YEAR
per 100 currently employed people

Illness or Injury	18–24 Years	25–44 Years	45–64 Years
Common Cold	30.3	15.5	15.8
Influenza	72.2	66.2	63.1
Acute Bronchitis	6.5	6.7	3.6
Pneumonia	3.8	1.5	4.3
Fractures/Dislocations	28.7	29.0	8.0
Sprains/Strains	43.7	39.8	17.3
Open Wounds	33.2	7.7	5.1

Source: National Center for Health Statistics

1. About how many sick days related to acute bronchitis will be taken in a year by 100 workers between the ages of 45 and 64?
   - (1) 3-4 days
   - (2) 5-6 days
   - (3) 7-8 days
   - (4) 8-9 days
   - (5) Not enough information is given.

2. About how many sick days related to fractures or dislocations will be taken in a year by 100 workers between the ages of 18 and 24?
   - (1) 1-2 days
   - (2) 3-4 days
   - (3) 6-7 days
   - (4) 17-18 days
   - (5) 28-29 days

3. Which illness or injury caused the fewest sick days for people between the ages of 25 and 44?
   - (1) Acute Bronchitis
   - (2) Open Wounds
   - (3) Pneumonia
   - (4) Common Cold
   - (5) Influenza

4. Which illness or injury caused the greatest number of sick days to be taken by all age groups?
   - (1) Common Cold
   - (2) Influenza
   - (3) Pneumonia
   - (4) Sprains/Strains
   - (5) Open Wounds

> Items 5 and 6 refer to the following table.

AIRLINE ON-TIME PERFORMANCE RATINGS

Airline	Percent of Flights
Northeast	92.7
AirGo	91.6
Aero USA	87.5
EastAir	84.1
Pegasus	74.2

5. How many flights out of 1,000 could be expected to be on time for Pegasus Airlines?
   - (1) 159
   - (2) 258
   - (3) 371
   - (4) 742
   - (5) 841

6. Of 750 WestAir flights, 94 arrived late. WestAir's on-time percent is nearest that of which of the following airlines?
   - (1) Northeast
   - (2) AirGo
   - (3) Aero USA
   - (4) EastAir
   - (5) Pegasus

335

Items 7–9 refer to the following table.

REFEREE ANNUAL SALARY SCALES

Years of Service	NHL	NBA
0–4	$50,000	$ 57,000
5–9	$60,000	$ 75,000
10–14	$80,000	$ 94,000
15–19	$90,000	$116,000
20+	$90,000	$141,000

7. After 12 years of service, how much more do NBA referees earn than NHL referees?

- **(1)** $4,000
- **(2)** $14,000
- **(3)** $26,000
- **(4)** $37,000
- **(5)** Not enough information is given.

8. If the NHL gives a 50 percent increase in salary to referees who have served from 5 to 9 years, which expression can be used to find the new annual salary for those referees?

- **(1)** $\dfrac{\$60,000}{0.5}$
- **(2)** $\dfrac{\$60,000}{0.5} + \$60,000$
- **(3)** 0.5($60,000)
- **(4)** 0.5($60,000) + $60,000
- **(5)** 50($60,000)

9. The NHL plans to increase the annual salary of referees with 20+ years of service another $75,000. How much more will an NHL referee earn with 20+ years of service than an NBA referee with the same years of service if the proposed change takes place?

- **(1)** $24,000
- **(2)** $51,000
- **(3)** $66,000
- **(4)** $75,000
- **(5)** Not enough information is given.

Items 10–12 refer to the table "Median Price of Existing Single-Family Homes" given on page 334.

10. The median price of a home in Akron in 1988 was about what fraction of the approximate median price of a house in Akron in 1992?

- **(1)** $\dfrac{1}{4}$
- **(2)** $\dfrac{1}{3}$
- **(3)** $\dfrac{1}{2}$
- **(4)** $\dfrac{2}{3}$
- **(5)** $\dfrac{4}{5}$

11. Rose and Taesung Kim bought a median-priced house in Louisville, Kentucky, in 1988. In 1992, Rose was offered a position in Baltimore, Maryland. The raise in salary enabled them to buy a median-price home in Baltimore. Approximately how many times greater in value was their home in Baltimore in 1992 than their home in Louisville in 1988?

- **(1)** Two
- **(2)** Three
- **(3)** Four
- **(4)** Five
- **(5)** Six

12. From 1988 to 1992, which cities showed a decline in value of a median-priced home?

- **(1)** San Francisco and Louisville
- **(2)** Boston and New York
- **(3)** Daytona Beach and Boston
- **(4)** Baltimore and Spokane
- **(5)** New York and Charleston

Check your answers on page 414.

Line Graphs

When a newspaper article contains a great deal of statistical information, the newspaper often uses a graph to show the data. The graph helps people reading the article more easily see the values being compared.

A **graph**, like a table, is used to organize numerical data.

MICCA MOTORS MONTHLY SALES FOR 2000 AND 2001

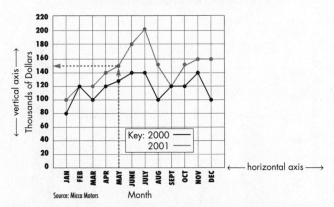

Source: Micca Motors

On a **line graph**, a point is plotted at the intersection of the horizontal and vertical axes to show a value. After many values are plotted, the points are connected with a line.

Now use the graph to answer this question.

Example:

What were the monthly sales for May 2001?

The 2001 sales figures are shown by the screened line. The point for May is halfway between the lines for 140 and 160, or $140,000 and $160,000. Its value is 150. The sales for Micca Motors in May 2001 were $150,000.

Exercise 2

Directions: Complete the line graph by plotting the points given in item 1. Then use the graph to answer items 2 and 3.

AVERAGE WEEKDAY MILEAGE FOR DUNNE'S SALES PERSONNEL

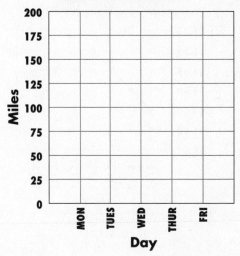

1. Plot and connect the following points on the graph above.

   - Monday   100 miles
   - Tuesday   50 miles
   - Wednesday   50 miles
   - Thursday   75 miles
   - Friday   150 miles

2. How many miles (total) does the average sales-person drive each week?

   (1) 85
   (2) 150
   (3) 425
   (4) 525
   (5) 600

3. How many more miles are driven from Wednesday through Friday than on Monday and Tuesday?

   (1) 50
   (2) 75
   (3) 100
   (4) 125
   (5) 275

337

Directions: Choose the one best answer for each item.

Items 4 and 5 refer to the following graph.

GASOLINE PRICE COMPARISON
November 24 to November 30

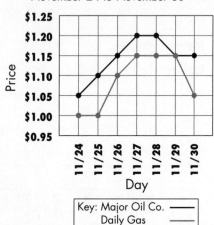

Key: Major Oil Co. ——
Daily Gas ——

4. What was Major Oil's price for 1 gallon of gasoline on November 27, the start of the Thanksgiving holiday?

   (1) $1.00
   (2) $1.05
   (3) $1.10
   (4) $1.15
   (5) $1.20

5. If each station had 200 customers on November 28, how many dollars more did Major Oil take in for gas purchases than Daily Gas?

   (1) $200
   (2) $100
   (3) $50
   (4) $10
   (5) Not enough information is given.

Check your answers on page 414.

Bar Graphs

Bar graphs are also used to make comparisons. Like line graphs, bar graphs have two axis lines. Bars instead of points are used to show numerical values. The end of each bar on the graph corresponds to a value on the scale. Note: Sometimes you will see a break, or jagged line, in a graph. This is used to save space.

JUNK MAIL
Pieces of Direct Mail Rounded to the Nearest Ten

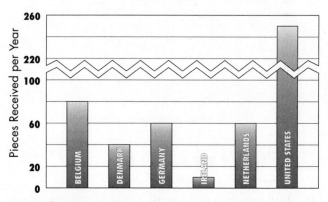

Source: Post offices in countries listed

Example:

How many pieces of junk mail does the average American receive each year? Find the bar that corresponds with the United States and follow the end of the bar to the numerical scale. The end of the bar falls halfway between 240 and 260, which is 250.

DOUBLE BAR GRAPHS

The following bar graph uses two bars. The top bar shows the percent of household work done by men. The bottom bar shows the percent of household work done by women. This is an effective way to show several comparisons on one graph.

PERCENT OF MEN AND WOMEN IN DUAL-EARNER FAMILIES WHO TAKE THE GREATER RESPONSIBILITY FOR HOUSEHOLD WORK

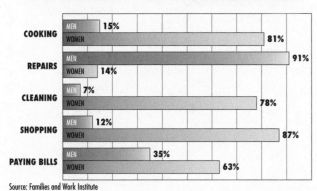

Source: Families and Work Institute

Exercise 3

Directions: Choose the one best answer for each item.

Items 1–3 refer to the double bar graph shown above.

1. If 2,500 individuals from dual-earning families participated in this study, how many were men who take the greater responsibility for shopping?

    (1) 12
    (2) 98
    (3) 256
    (4) 300
    (5) 550

2. Which of the following statements is supported by the graph?

    (1) About one fourth as many men as women do the cooking.
    (2) More than ten times as many women than men do the cleaning.
    (3) About one third as many women as men do the repair work.
    (4) More than ten times as many women than men do the shopping.
    (5) More than twice as many women than men pay the bills.

3. Based on the percents on the graph, out of 1,000 dual-earning couples, how many more women than men take a greater responsibility for doing the cleaning for the family?

    (1) 355
    (2) 425
    (3) 710
    (4) 850
    (5) Not enough information is given.

Items 4 and 5 refer to the following information.

U.S. HOMES WITH PERSONAL COMPUTERS

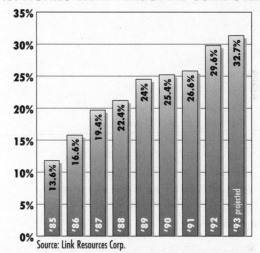

Source: Link Resources Corp.

4. By the end of 1992, 27 million homes had personal computers. At the time, about how many U.S. homes *did not* have computers?

    (1) 63 million
    (2) 105 million
    (3) 127 million
    (4) 150 million
    (5) Not enough information is given.

5. According to the chart, how many homes were projected to own computers in 1993?

    (1) 32.7 million
    (2) 63 million
    (3) 198 million
    (4) 105 million
    (5) Not enough information is given.

Check your answers on page 414.

Circle Graphs

Pie or **circle graphs** are often used to show relationships between parts of the whole. The circle represents the whole amount being considered. When the sections of a circle graph are labeled as percents, the whole circle will total 100%.

The graph below shows the U.S. population by age. Notice that it does not give the population quantities in numbers. It gives only the percents of the total population that are within each age range.

U.S. POPULATION BY AGE, 2000

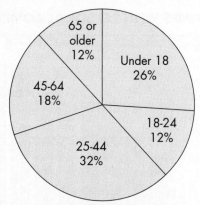

Source: Bureau of the Census, U.S. Department of Commerce, 2000 Census

Example:

What percent of the population is under 25 years of age?

(1) 12%
(2) 26%
(3) 32%
(4) 38%
(5) 50%

To answer this question, you need to add the percents for two age groups: those under 18 and those between 18 and 24.

Add: 26% + 12% = 38%

The correct answer is (4).

Some circle graphs show amounts instead of percents. The circle graph below shows how all of the Garcias' monthly income is spent. When the sections of the circle graph are added together, you have $1,700 which is the total monthly expenditures for the Garcia family.

GARCIA FAMILY MONTHLY BUDGET

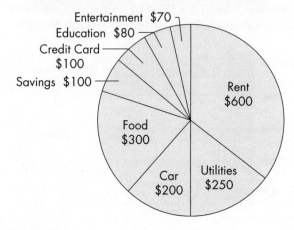

Example:

1. What <u>percent</u> of the whole budget goes to rent and utilities?

(1) 10%
(2) 20%
(3) 25%
(4) 50%
(5) 75%

Rent and utilities add up to $850 of the $1,700. To find the percent, set up a proportion.

$$\frac{x}{100} = \frac{\$850}{\$1,700} \qquad \frac{100(\$850)}{\$1,700} = 50$$

The correct answer is (4).

Exercise 4

Directions: Choose the one best answer for each item.

Items 1 and 2 refer to the graph "U.S. Population By Age" on page 340.

1. What fraction of the population is 45 years of age or older?

   (1) $\dfrac{3}{10}$

   (2) $\dfrac{1}{2}$

   (3) $\dfrac{2}{3}$

   (4) $\dfrac{3}{4}$

   (5) $\dfrac{7}{8}$

2. If the population of the United States is approximately 258 million, how many people are under 18 years of age?

   (1) 13,570,000
   (2) 26,000,000
   (3) 30,960,000
   (4) 52,098,000
   (5) 67,080,000

Items 3 and 4 refer to the graph of the "Garcia Family Monthly Budget" on page 340.

3. What is the *ratio* of entertainment to savings in the Garcias' budget?

   (1) $\dfrac{1}{17}$

   (2) $\dfrac{3}{17}$

   (3) $\dfrac{1}{2}$

   (4) $\dfrac{5}{8}$

   (5) $\dfrac{7}{10}$

4. Savings is what fraction of the total budget?

   (1) $\dfrac{1}{17}$

   (2) $\dfrac{3}{17}$

   (3) $\dfrac{1}{2}$

   (4) $\dfrac{5}{8}$

   (5) $\dfrac{7}{10}$

Items 5 and 6 refer to the following information.

During a recent beach cleanup, 800 pounds of refuse were collected. Refer to the chart for the quantity and type.

BEACH CLEANUP RESULTS

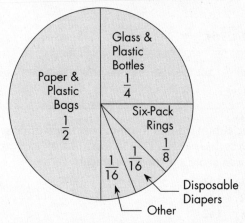

5. How many pounds of the garbage collected came from disposable diapers?

   (1) 400
   (2) 200
   (3) 100
   (4) 50
   (5) Not enough information is given.

6. What percent of refuse collected came from glass and plastic bottles?

   (1) 75%
   (2) 50%
   (3) 25%
   (4) 16%
   (5) Not enough information is given.

Check your answers on page 415.

Finding the Mean

A very useful way to summarize information is to find the **mean**, or average.

Example:

The temperatures for a 7-day period in Boston in September were as follows: 63°, 62°, 70°, 80°, 61°, 58°, and 61°. The newspaper reported that the mean temperature was 65°.

To find the mean:

Step 1 Add the values listed.

$63° + 62° + 70° + 80° + 61° + 58° + 61° = 455°$

Step 2 Divide by the number of items in the list.

$\dfrac{455°}{7 \text{ days}} = 65°$ Weekly mean

A mean is a measure of central tendency. In other words, the mean is a measurement of the *center* value of a list of numbers. When you solve for the mean, check to see if your answer is a value between the highest and lowest values in the list.

Exercise 5

Directions: Choose the one best answer for each item.

1. Delia bowled in a 5-game tournament. Her scores were 134, 131, 147, 156, and 142. What was her mean score for the tournament?

   (1) 131
   (2) 134
   (3) 142
   (4) 147
   (5) 156

2. Lillian called eight offices in her area and asked each secretary who answered what was his or her yearly salary. What is the mean salary of the following replies: $15,200, $18,000, $14,500, $11,800, $21,500, $16,300, $10,900, and $17,400?

   (1) $10,000
   (2) $13,525
   (3) $14,500
   (4) $15,700
   (5) $21,500

Check your answers on page 415.

Finding the Median

The median is another way to summarize a list of numerical data. When the values in a list are arranged in numerical order, the **median** is the middle value.

To find the median, arrange the values in order, and choose the value in the middle position.

Examples:

1. Find the median of the heights: 6 ft 2 in, 5 ft 11 in, and 6 ft.

   The median height is 6 feet.

   6 feet 2 inches ↑ 1 above

   (6 feet)

   5 feet 11 inches ↓ 1 below

2. The list of cars below has an even number of values. How can you find the median price?

Car Size	Price
Compact	$10,000
Mid-Sized	$13,400
Minivan	$18,300
Luxury	$35,000

   To find the median when there are an even number of values:

   Step 1 Identify the *two* values in the middle.

   $13,400
   $18,300

   Step 2 Find the *mean* of these two values.

   $$\begin{array}{r} \$13,400 \\ +18,300 \\ \hline \$31,700 \end{array} \qquad \begin{array}{r} \$15,850 \\ 2\overline{)\$31,700} \end{array}$$

   The median price is $15,850.

Exercise 6

Directions: Choose the one best answer for each item.

Items 1 and 2 refer to the following table.

Church's Pizza	Small (12-inch)	Large (16-inch)
Cheese	$5.00	$ 7.75
Special	$8.75	$12.25
Vegetarian	$8.00	$11.75
Pepperoni	$5.75	$ 8.75
Hawaiian	$6.50	$ 9.75

1. What is the median price for a small pizza at Church's?

   (1) $5.00
   (2) $6.50
   (3) $6.80
   (4) $8.00
   (5) $8.75

2. What is the median price for a large pizza at Church's?

   (1) $7.75
   (2) $8.75
   (3) $9.75
   (4) $10.05
   (5) $11.75

3. Arthur's phone bills for the past four months were $42.65, $58.27, $70.01, and $68.43. What was the median amount of his phone service for those months?

   (1) $63.35
   (2) $67.89
   (3) $70.01
   (4) $237.55
   (5) $307.26

Check your answers on page 415.

Simple Probability

"What chance do you have?" is another way of asking "What is the probability?" **Probability** is a ratio that compares the chances of a particular result with the total number of possibilities.

The probability that you will get heads when flipping a coin is 1 in 2. The probability ratio is often written as a fraction.

$$\frac{\text{chances of a particular result}}{\text{total possibilities}} \quad \frac{1 \text{ head}}{2 \text{ sides}} = \frac{1}{2}$$

The chances of winning a lottery might be given as 1 in 5,000,000. This is because approximately 5,000,000 tickets are sold and each ticket has one chance of winning.

$$\frac{1 \text{ chance to win}}{5,000,000 \text{ chances to win}}$$

Example:

The Flanagans made a trick-or-treat grab bag of candy. They put in 40 Milky Ways, 32 Hershey bars, and 24 Snickers. What is the probability that the first child will get a Milky Way?

Since all the candy is mixed together in the grab bag, you must add it to see the total number of possibilities.

40 Milky Ways + 32 Hershey bars + 24 Snickers = 96 candy bars

$$\frac{\text{the chance of a particular event (Milky Way)}}{\text{the total number of possibilities}} \quad \frac{40}{96}$$

Probabilities, like other ratios, are renamed in simplest form.

$$\frac{40 \div 8}{96 \div 8} = \frac{5}{12}$$

The probability is 5 in 12, or $\frac{5}{12}$.

Exercise 7

Directions: Find the probability in each of the following problems.

1. Each multiple-choice question has 5 answer choices. If you guess, what is the probability that you will be correct?

   (1) $\dfrac{3}{4}$

   (2) $\dfrac{2}{3}$

   (3) $\dfrac{1}{2}$

   (4) $\dfrac{2}{5}$

   (5) $\dfrac{1}{5}$

2. Terry bought 8 raffle tickets for a chance to win a trip to see a space shuttle launch. If 200 tickets are sold, what is the probability that Terry will hold the winning ticket?

   (1) $\dfrac{1}{8}$

   (2) $\dfrac{1}{16}$

   (3) $\dfrac{1}{25}$

   (4) $\dfrac{1}{50}$

   (5) $\dfrac{1}{200}$

3. If you choose a day of the week at random, what is the probability that it will be a Tuesday?

   (1) $\dfrac{3}{4}$

   (2) $\dfrac{2}{3}$

   (3) $\dfrac{1}{2}$

   (4) $\dfrac{1}{7}$

   (5) $\dfrac{1}{30}$

4. Betty Ann bought 12 tickets for the state lottery jackpot. One million tickets were sold. What is the probability that she will win?

   (1) $\dfrac{1}{1,000,000}$

   (2) $\dfrac{3}{250,000}$

   (3) $\dfrac{1}{62,500}$

   (4) $\dfrac{1}{100,000}$

   (5) $\dfrac{1}{1,000}$

5. With one roll of a six-sided die, what is the probability that Merilyn will roll a six?

   (1) $\dfrac{1}{6}$

   (2) $\dfrac{1}{3}$

   (3) $\dfrac{1}{2}$

   (4) $\dfrac{2}{3}$

   (5) $\dfrac{5}{6}$

6. With one roll of a six-sided die, what is the probability that Fred will *not* roll a three or four?

   (1) $\dfrac{1}{6}$

   (2) $\dfrac{1}{3}$

   (3) $\dfrac{1}{2}$

   (4) $\dfrac{2}{3}$

   (5) $\dfrac{5}{6}$

7. Sam has a fish tank that contains 40 female guppies and 40 male guppies. If Sam chooses a fish at random from the tank, what is the probability that it will be male?

(1) $\frac{1}{2}$

(2) $\frac{1}{4}$

(3) $\frac{1}{8}$

(4) $\frac{1}{10}$

(5) $\frac{1}{40}$

8. Cathy's telephone has 18 numbers stored in its memory for speed dialing. Six of the numbers are long distance. If Cathy's son David accidentally dials one of the numbers, what is the probability that David has just made a long-distance call?

(1) $\frac{1}{9}$

(2) $\frac{1}{6}$

(3) $\frac{1}{3}$

(4) $\frac{2}{3}$

(5) Not enough information is given.

9. A spinner has three sections colored red, yellow, and blue. The red section is twice the size of either the yellow or blue sections. What is the probability of the spinner landing on red?

(1) $\frac{3}{4}$

(2) $\frac{2}{3}$

(3) $\frac{1}{2}$

(4) $\frac{3}{8}$

(5) Not enough information is given.

Check your answers on page 415.

Exercise 8

Directions: Use the graphs to find necessary information and answer the following questions. Treat these problems like an alternate-format question where you would need to fill out a standard grid. (*Calculator permitted.*)

Mr. Beltran's Monthly Household Budget

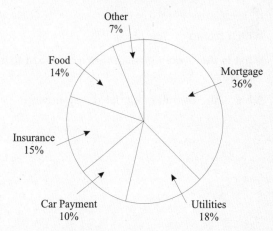

1. If Mr. Beltran makes $82,350 a year, approximately how much does he spend on insurance in a month? (Round to nearest dollar amount.)

2. What is the probability that Mr. Beltran will spend money on other things?

3. In a certain month, Mr. Beltran earned $8,632. How much did he pay for mortgage if he kept his budget the same? (Round to nearest dollar amount.)

Items 4–6 refer to the following.

The Orange County Spinners Society sponsored a competition where half of the first, second, and third prize winning amounts went toward a children's charity and the other half went toward the ASPCA (American Society for the Prevention of Cruelty to Animals). The three teams consisted of three spinners each. The ranks were decided by calculating the average yardage of yarn spun (gathered in spools).

Yarn Spun (in yards × 100)

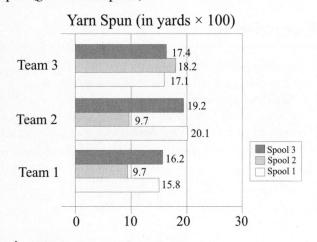

4. Which team got first place?

5. What is the overall median yardage of yarn that was spun?

6. What is the overall mode for the spun yarn?

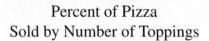

Items 7–9 refer to the following chart.

Percent of Pizza Sold by Number of Toppings

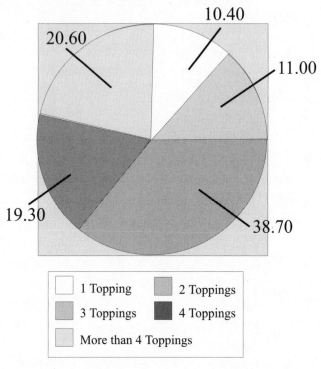

7. What percentage of people ordered pizza with at least 3 toppings?

8. What percentage of people ordered pizza with at most 4 toppings?

9. What percentage of people ordered pizza with 2 to 4 toppings?

Check your answers on page 415.

Unit 8

MEASUREMENT

Using measurements is an integral part of our lives. Without measurements, there is no way to gauge or express magnitudes and quantities. For example, when you bake a cake, you need to measure the amount of ingredients; during a surgical procedure, doctors must accurately measure the amount (volume) of anesthesia given to the patient; or you may want to record the number of miles you drive for accounting purposes.

U.S. System of Measurement

The U.S. system of measurement was brought by the colonists from England before the American Revolution. The United States still uses this system to measure length, weight, and volume. However, time is measured in the same way throughout the world.

Measurements are made using scales. Every scale is marked and labeled using some unit of measure. The diagram below is part of a one-foot ruler. Each numbered line represents one inch. The pencil measures 5 inches long.

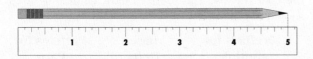

Weight (or mass) and volume are also measured using scales. Pressure-sensitive scales measure weight. Liquids are poured into calibrated containers.

The common units of the U.S. system are shown below.

Units of Length (Distance)

12 inches (in)	= 1 foot (ft)
3 feet (ft)	= 1 yard (yd)
36 inches (in)	= 1 yard (yd)
5,280 feet (ft)	= 1 mile (mi)

Units of Weight (Mass)

16 ounces (oz)	= 1 pound (lb)
2,000 pounds (lb)	= 1 ton (T)

Units of Volume

8 fluid ounces (fl oz)	= 1 cup (c)
2 cups (c)	= 1 pint (pt)
2 pints (pt)	= 1 quart (qt)
4 cups (c)	= 1 quart (qt)
4 quarts (qt)	= 1 gallon (gal)

Units of Time

1 year (yr)	= 365 days (d)
1 year (yr)	= 52 weeks (wk)
1 week (wk)	= 7 days (d)
1 day (d)	= 24 hours (hr)
1 hour (hr)	= 60 minutes (min)
1 minute (min)	= 60 seconds (sec)

Example:

How many minutes are in 5 hours? How many days are in 126 hours? These are questions that can be answered by renaming measurements. Use these steps to change to smaller or larger units of measure.

Multiply to change larger units to smaller units.	Divide to change smaller units to larger units.
5 hours = ? minutes 1 hour = 60 minutes	126 hours = ? days 24 hours = 1 day
$\begin{array}{r} 60 \\ \times\ 5 \\ \hline 300 \text{ minutes} \end{array}$	$\begin{array}{r} 5 \text{ R6} \\ 24\overline{)126} \end{array}$

126 hours = 5 days 6 hours

Exercise 1

Directions: Match the measure in Column A with an object or area in Column B that might have that measurement.

	Column A		Column B
_____	**1.** 6 inches	**a.**	one lap around a track field
_____	**2.** $\frac{1}{4}$ cup	**b.**	volume of a milk carton
_____	**3.** 1½ oz	**c.**	height of a 7-year-old girl
_____	**4.** 3 gal	**d.**	weight of a package of hamburger
_____	**5.** $\frac{1}{2}$ inch	**e.**	weight of a newborn baby
_____	**6.** $\frac{1}{4}$ mile	**f.**	weight of a jar of spices
_____	**7.** 1 pint	**g.**	amount of water in a bucket
_____	**8.** 4 feet	**h.**	thickness of a book
_____	**9.** 2 tons	**i.**	amount of vegetable oil in a cake recipe
_____	**10.** 2 qt	**j.**	height of a drinking glass
_____	**11.** 2 lb	**k.**	volume of a small container of ice cream
_____	**12.** 6 lb 12 oz	**l.**	weight of a freight car on a train

Directions: Solve the following as directed.

13. How many feet are in 36 inches?

14. 47 inches = _____ feet _____ inches

15. 20 ounces = _____ pounds _____ ounces

16. Change 34 ounces to pounds.

17. 36 hours = _____ days _____ hours

18. How many days are in 76 hours?

19. How many ounces are in 5.4 pounds?

20. Change 14 quarts to gallons.

21. 5,000 lb = _____ tons _____ pounds

22. Which of the following units would likely be used to state the weight of a baseball?

(1) fluid ounces
(2) pounds
(3) inches
(4) ounces
(5) quarts

Check your answers on page 415.

Metric System of Measurement

The metric system was developed in France in the late 1700s. Today it is the international measuring system of science throughout the world. The metric system is popular worldwide because it is a simple system to use and learn.

The metric system is a decimal system that uses prefixes to show whether a unit is *part* of the base unit or a *multiple* of the base unit.

For instance, a centimeter is part of a meter $\left(\frac{1}{100}\right)$, and a kilometer is a multiple of a meter (1,000 meters). The prefixes centi- and kilo- tell you how the unit of measure compares to a meter. Once you learn and understand the prefixes used in the metric system, it is easy to use.

The prefixes used in the metric system are shown in the chart below. The prefixes most commonly used are shown in boldface.

Prefixes for Multiples			**Base Units**	**Prefixes for Parts**		
Kilo-	Hecto-	Deka-	Meter Liter Gram	Deci-	**Centi-**	**Milli-**
1,000	100	10	1	0.1	**0.01**	**0.001**

The basic unit of length in the metric system is the **meter**. A meter is just a little longer than a yard. A kilometer (1,000 meters) is a little more than half a mile. It is about 0.6 mile.

The basic unit of weight in the metric system is the **gram**, but the kilogram is used more often. A kilogram, which equals 1,000 grams, is about 2 pounds, so kilograms are used in the metric system to measure quantities that we would measure in pounds. A gram is not very heavy. A paper clip weighs about 1 gram. Milligrams are used to measure very small quantities, for example, the amount of sodium in a potato chip.

The basic unit of liquid measure in the metric system is the **liter**. We buy soda in liter and 2-liter bottles. A liter is a little larger than a quart. Very small amounts of liquid are measured in milliliters. A teaspoon is equal to about 5 milliliters.

The common metric units are shown below.

Metric Units of Length

1 kilometer (km)   = 1,000 meters (m)
1 meter (m)   = 100 centimeters (cm)
1 centimeter (cm) = 10 millimeters (mm)
1 meter (m)   = 1,000 millimeters (mm)

Metric Units of Weight

1 metric ton (T)   = 1,000 kilograms (kg)
1 kilogram (kg)   = 1,000 grams (g)
1 gram (g)   = 100 centigrams (cg)
1 centigram (cg)   = 10 milligrams (mg)

Metric Units of Volume

1 kiloliter (kL)   = 1,000 liters (L)
1 liter (L)   = 100 centiliters (cL)
1 centiliter (cL) = 10 milliliters (mL)

Follow these steps to rename metric units:

Step 1 Set up a proportion using the measurement fact you need.

Step 2 Solve the proportion.

Example:

How many liters are in 7 kiloliters? How many grams are in 8.5 centigrams? You can use what you know about metric prefixes to rename metric units.

Rename 7 kiloliters as liters.

Rename 8.5 centigrams as grams.

Set up a proportion.

$$\frac{kL}{L} \quad \frac{1}{1,000} = \frac{7}{?} \quad \frac{kL}{L}$$

Set up a proportion.

$$\frac{g}{cg} \quad \frac{1}{100} = \frac{?}{8.5} \quad \frac{g}{cg}$$

Solve the proportion.

$$\frac{1,000(7)}{1} = 7,000L$$

$$7,000\ L = 7kL$$

Solve the proportion.

$$\frac{1(8.5)}{100} = 0.085g$$

$$0.085g = 8.5cg$$

Exercise 2

Directions: Match the measure in Column A with an object or area in Column B that might have that measurement.

Column A		Column B
_____ 1. 2mm	**a.**	width of the cutting edge of a table knife
_____ 2. 3.5kg	**b.**	amount in a bottle of vanilla extract
_____ 3. 2km	**c.**	volume of a tankful of gasoline
_____ 4. 29mL	**d.**	distance when walking 10 city blocks
_____ 5. 50L	**e.**	weight of a newborn baby

Directions: For items 6–8, rename the following metric units by proportion. For items 9 and 10, choose the <u>one best answer</u>.

6. Rename 5 meters as centimeters.

7. Rename 60 kiloliters as liters.

8. Convert 8,762 grams to kilograms.

9. The New Wave Swim Team uses a 50-meter pool during the summer to prepare for long-course events. Josh competes in the 1,500 *meter*. How many *kilometers* are in this event?

   (1) 1.5
   (2) 15
   (3) 50
   (4) 150
   (5) 1,500

10. Which of the following units would likely be used to state a child's height?

   (1) Kilometers
   (2) Grams
   (3) Centimeters
   (4) Millimeters
   (5) Milliliters

Check your answers on page 416.

Addition and Subtraction of Measurements

When adding measurements in the U.S. system, you cannot carry as you would with whole numbers because the U.S. system is not based on units of 10.

Follow these steps to add measurements.

Step 1 Add the units separately.

Step 2 Simplify the answer, if necessary, by dividing to change the smaller units to larger units.

Example:

Add 2 lb 12 oz + 5 lb 7 oz

$$
\begin{array}{ll}
2 \text{ lb } 12 \text{ oz} & \text{Simplify the answer.} \\
+ 5 \text{ lb } 7 \text{ oz} & \text{Use the fact: 16 oz = 1 lb.} \\
\hline
7 \text{ lb } 19 \text{ oz} & \text{Divide 19 oz by 16.}
\end{array}
$$

$$
\begin{array}{r}
1 \\
16\overline{)19} \\
-16 \\
\hline
3 \text{ oz}
\end{array}
$$

Add this to the pounds column.

$$
\begin{array}{r}
1 \text{ lb } 3 \text{ oz} \\
+ 7 \text{ lb} \\
\hline
8 \text{ lb } 3 \text{ oz}
\end{array}
$$

The total is 8 lb 3 oz.

To subtract measurements in the U.S. system, you need to keep the common equivalents in mind. If borrowing is necessary, you cannot automatically borrow 10 as you do when working with whole numbers.

Follow these steps to subtract measurements.

Step 1 Subtract the smaller units first. If borrowing is necessary, borrow from the larger units and rename the one you borrowed in terms of the smaller unit.

Step 2 Subtract the larger units.

Example:

Subtract 6 ft 7 in from 11 ft 6 in

$$
\begin{array}{lll}
11 \text{ ft } 6 \text{ in} & \text{Borrow 1} & \overset{10}{\cancel{11} \text{ ft}} \ 6 \text{ in} + 12 \text{ in} = 18 \text{ in} \\
- 6 \text{ ft } 7 \text{ in} & \text{foot, rename} & - 6 \text{ ft} \qquad\qquad - 7 \text{ in} \\
& \text{it as 12} & \overline{\ 4 \text{ ft}} \qquad\qquad \overline{\ 11 \text{ in}} \\
& \text{inches, and} & \\
& \text{add it to the} & \\
& \text{inches col-} & \\
& \text{umn.} &
\end{array}
$$

The difference is 4 ft 11 in.

Exercise 3

Directions: Solve as indicated. Simplify your answers if possible.

1. 11 in + 8 in

2. 3 ft 6 in − 2 ft 8 in

3. 1 hr − 24 min

4. 8 ft 7 in + 9 ft 5 in

5. 2 yd 2 ft + 3 yd 1 ft

6. 8 lb 12 oz + 10 lb 14 oz

7. 2 gal 1 qt − 1 gal 3 qt

8. 6 yd − 2 ft

9. 1 qt 3 c + 3 c

10. 4 lb 12 oz − 2 lb 2 oz

Directions: Choose the one best answer for each item.

11. Georgina wants to move her bookshelves from one room to another. One bookshelf is 42 inches wide, the other is 3 feet wide. When she puts the bookshelves end to end, how many feet and inches in length will they be?

    (1) 3 ft 6 in
    (2) 5 ft 10 in
    (3) 6 ft 6 in
    (4) 7 ft 6 in
    (5) 7 ft 0 in

12. Lael and Ryan both rented videos to watch on Friday night. Lael's is 135 minutes. Ryan's is 162 minutes. How much time would it take for them to watch both videos?

   (1)   3 hours 52 minutes
   (2)   4 hours 57 minutes
   (3)   5 hours
   (4)   5½ hours
   (5)   6 hours

13. Josie works at a fabric store. Each time she cuts fabric from a bolt, she must subtract it and write how much is left. The bolt had 12 yd 1 ft before she cut off 3 yd 2 ft. How much fabric is left on the bolt?

   (1)   7 yards 1 foot
   (2)   7 yards 2 feet
   (3)   8 yards
   (4)   8 yards 1 foot
   (5)   8 yards 2 feet

14. Luan has three suitcases for his flight to Vietnam. One weighs 24 lb 8 oz, the second weighs 12 lb 7 oz, and the third suitcase weighs 15 lb 10 oz. How many pounds over the weight allowance is Luan's luggage?

   (1)   10 lb
   (2)   12 lb 9 oz
   (3)   20 lb
   (4)   42 lb 9 oz
   (5)   Not enough information is given.

Check your answers on page 416.

Multiplication of Measurements

Multiplication can be thought of as repeated addition. Instead of adding a number or measurement 4 times, you multiply by 4. Because multiplication and addition are related, the steps are similar for working with measurements.

Follow these steps to multiply measurements in the U.S. system.

   Step 1 Multiply the units separately.

   Step 2 Simplify the answer, if necessary, using division to change the smaller units to larger ones.

Example:

   5(6 gal 3 qt) = ?

Multiply:

$$
\begin{array}{r}
6 \text{ gal} \quad 3 \text{ qt} \\
\times \qquad\quad 5 \\
\hline
30 \text{ gal } 15 \text{ qt}
\end{array}
$$

Compare the units. Use the fact: 4 qt = 1 gal. Do you have more than 4 qt? Yes.

Divide: 15 qt by 4:
$$
\begin{array}{r}
3 \text{ gal} \\
4\overline{)15} \\
-12 \\
\hline
3 \text{ qt}
\end{array}
$$

Add:
$$
\begin{array}{r}
3 \text{ gal } 3 \text{ qt} \\
+ 30 \text{ gal} \\
\hline
\end{array}
$$
Answer: **33 gal 3 qt**

Exercise 4

Directions: For items 1–6, multiply the following. Simplify your answers when necessary. For item 7, choose the <u>one best answer.</u>

1. 3(6 ft 5 in)

2. 3(4 d 15 hr)

3. 10(8 lb 12 oz)

4. 7(7 gal 3 qt)

5. 6(2 qt 3 pt)

6. 2(18 lb 10 oz)

7. Eileen is a window washer. She averages 5 minutes per window inside and out. About how many hours will it take her to complete the Finance Office Building, which has 60 windows?

   (1)   2
   (2)   3
   (3)   4
   (4)   5
   (5)   6

Check your answers on page 416.

Division of Measurements

Janet needs to cut a board into 5 equal pieces. If the board measures 6 ft 8 in, how long will each piece be? (Disregard any waste.)

Follow these steps to divide measurements.

Step 1   Divide 5 into the larger unit of measure first.

Step 2   Change the remainder. Multiply to change the remaining larger units to smaller units.

Step 3   Add these smaller units to the smaller units in the original problem and divide.

Example: 6 ft 8 in ÷ 5

$$\begin{array}{r} 1\text{ft} \\ 5\overline{)6\text{ ft 8 in}} \\ -5 \\ \hline 1\text{ ft} \end{array}$$

Change the remainder to smaller units.

1 ft(12) = 12 in

$$\begin{array}{r} 12\text{ inches} \\ +\ 8\text{ inches} \\ \hline 20\text{ inches} \end{array}$$

Add these smaller units to the smaller units in the original problem.

$$\begin{array}{r} 4\text{ in} \\ 5\overline{)20\text{ in}} \end{array}$$

6 ft 8 in ÷ 5 = **1 ft 4 in**

Exercise 5

Directions: Divide to solve the following.

1. 7 mi 4,362 ft ÷ 6

2. $\dfrac{13\text{ hr }30\text{ min}}{3}$

3. 4 gal 2 qt ÷ 3

4. 12 ft 9 in ÷ 3

5. What is the average height of the three Gonzalez children? Jose is 4 ft 7 in, Eva is 4 ft 9 in, and Rafael is 5 ft 2 in.
   - (1)   4 ft 10 in
   - (2)   4 ft 11 in
   - (3)   5 ft
   - (4)   5 ft 1 in
   - (5)   5 ft 2 in

6. Mickey has been hired to paint the exterior of a house, which would take him twelve 8-hour days to do alone. He has hired 2 workers to help him. Assuming that they all work at the same rate, how long will it take the three of them to complete the job?
   - (1)   Three days
   - (2)   Three days 5 hours
   - (3)   Four 8-hour days
   - (4)   Five 8-hour days
   - (5)   Five days 6 hours

Check your answers on page 416.

Operations with Metric Measurements

When metric measurements are expressed in the same units, they can be added and subtracted in the same way you add and subtract decimals. Meters can be added to meters. Kilograms can be subtracted from kilograms. Just line up the decimal points and carry out the operation.

Add: 4.5m + 17.6 m

$$\begin{array}{r} 4.5\text{m} \\ +17.6\text{m} \\ \hline 22.1\text{m} \end{array}$$

Carry the 1 just as in other decimal problems.

Subtract: 12.4kg − 0.6kg

$$\begin{array}{r} 12.4\text{kg} \\ -0.6\text{kg} \\ \hline 11.8\text{kg} \end{array}$$

Borrow just as in other decimal problems.

Multiplication and division of metric measures are the same as in other decimal problems.

Examples:

Multiply 17.8 liters by 5

Then place the decimal point in the answer.

$$\begin{array}{r} 17.8\text{ liters} \\ \times\ 5 \\ \hline 89.0\text{ liters} \end{array}$$

Divide 3.45 meters by 5

Place the decimal point in the quotient and divide.

$$\begin{array}{r} 0.69\text{ meter} \\ 5\overline{)3.45\text{ meters}} \\ -3\ 0 \\ \hline 45 \\ -45 \end{array}$$

Exercise 6

Directions: Solve as directed.

1. 9.9L + 99L

2. 5.8mm + 7.2mm

3. 13.4km − 500m

4. 3.45km − 1.2km

5. 4(5.6cm)

6. 9(5.450kg)

7. $\dfrac{1.6km}{4}$

8. 5.36m ÷ 4

Directions: Choose the one best answer to each item.

9. When making a tablecloth for the banquet, Laurie trimmed 64cm from a piece of fabric 220cm long. How many centimeters long was the remaining fabric?
   - **(1)** 156
   - **(2)** 325
   - **(3)** 460
   - **(4)** 465
   - **(5)** 523

10. Mary packaged her candied nuts in tins that weighed 2.5kg each. She mailed 8 of these packages as holiday gifts. How many kilograms of nuts did she mail altogether?
    - **(1)** 10.5
    - **(2)** 12.5
    - **(3)** 15
    - **(4)** 20
    - **(5)** 25.5

11. Jose and two friends are taking a 1,266-km trip that they hope to complete in two days. Which of the following expressions would be used to find the number of kilometers that they must drive each day?
    - **(1)** $\dfrac{1,266}{3}$
    - **(2)** $\dfrac{3(1,266)}{2}$
    - **(3)** $\dfrac{1,266}{2}$
    - **(4)** $\dfrac{2(1,266)}{3}$
    - **(5)** 2(3)(1,266)

12. Seong-Jin has two lengths of wire: 185 centimeters and 340 centimeters. What is the total length of the wire in meters?
    - **(1)** 1.55m
    - **(2)** 5.25m
    - **(3)** 15.5m
    - **(4)** 52.5m
    - **(5)** 525m

13. Caroline runs 5 kilometers every day. She carries a water bottle as she runs and drinks 2 ounces of water every 500 meters. If the bottle is full when she starts, how many ounces will remain when she completes her run?
    - **(1)** 4
    - **(2)** 7
    - **(3)** 10
    - **(4)** 20
    - **(5)** Not enough information is given.

Items 14 and 15 refer to the following drawing.

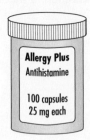

14. Baird takes two capsules of the medication shown four times a day for three days. How many milligrams of the medication does he take over the three-day period?

   (1) 100mg
   (2) 200mg
   (3) 300mg
   (4) 600mg
   (5) Not enough information is given.

15. How many grams of medication are contained in 100 capsules?

   (1) .25g
   (2) 2.5g
   (3) 25g
   (4) 250g
   (5) 2,500g

Check your answers on page 416.

Finding Perimeter

Perimeter is the linear distance around a flat figure. To put the finishing trim along the floor and ceiling edges of a room, you would need to find the perimeter of the room. The lengths of all the sides of a figure are added to find its perimeter.

The figures below show the addition used to find the perimeter of each.

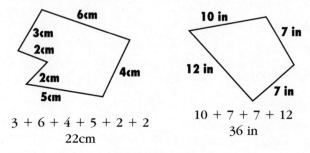

3 + 6 + 4 + 5 + 2 + 2
22cm

10 + 7 + 7 + 12
36 in

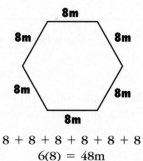

8 + 8 + 8 + 8 + 8 + 8
6(8) = 48m

You can use formulas to find the perimeters of squares and rectangles.

A **square** has four equal sides. You can find the perimeter of a square by multiplying the length of one side by 4.

Square $P = 4s$; where s = side

$P = 4s$
$P = 4(3)$
$P = 12cm$

A **rectangle** has four sides also. The sides opposite each other are equal and parallel to each other. (One pair of sides = length, the other pair of sides = width.) You can find the perimeter by multiplying the length by 2 and the width by 2 and adding the products.

Rectangle $P = 2l + 2w$; where l = length, w = width

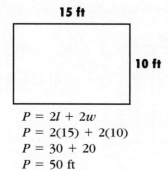

15 ft

10 ft

$P = 2l + 2w$
$P = 2(15) + 2(10)$
$P = 30 + 20$
$P = 50$ ft

Example:

What is the length of side *CD* in the figure below? To find the figure's perimeter, you need to find the missing segment length.

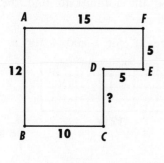

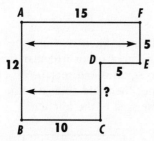

Look at the second figure. The arrows show that side *CD* is opposite side *AB*. You also see that the total of side *EF* and side *CD* must equal 12 units, the length of side *AB*. So side *CD* must equal 12 − 5, or 7 units.

On the GED Math Test, you can often find a missing length using the lengths of the sides you have been given.

Exercise 7

Directions: Find the perimeter of each of the figures below.

1.

3cm

7cm

2.

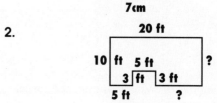

20 ft

10 ft 5 ft ?

3 ft 3 ft

5 ft ?

3.

7cm

? 7cm

6cm

3cm

?

4.

7 in

5 in

5 in

15 in 5 in

3 in

?

?

5. Libby's house is on a square lot that measures 15 meters on each side. How many meters of fence does she need to enclose her lot?

    (1) 15
    (2) 30
    (3) 45
    (4) 60
    (5) 75

6. How many inches of framing are needed for an 8-inch by 11-inch photo?

    (1) 19
    (2) 27
    (3) 38
    (4) 88
    (5) 100

Check your answers on page 417.

Finding Area

Area is the measure of the surface within a figure. Area is measured in square units. As you see in the figure below, a square that is 3 centimeters by 3 centimeters contains 9 *square* centimeters.

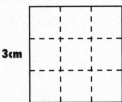

The formula for finding the area of a square uses an exponent. In the expression 4^2, the 4 is called the **base** and ^{2} is called the **exponent**. The exponent tells you how many times to multiply the base by itself.

4^1	Multiply 4 one time	4	= 4
4^2	Multiply 4 two times	4(4)	= 16
4^3	Multiply 4 three times	4(4)(4)	= 64
4^4	Multiply 4 four times	4(4)(4)(4)	= 256

To find the area of a square, take the measure of the side to the second power—or **square** it—as shown in the following formula.

Square $A = s^2$; where s = side

Example:

The area of the square in the figure below can be found by substituting 6 for s in $A = s^2$.

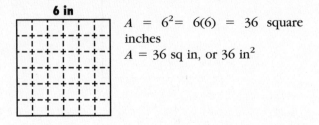

$A = 6^2 = 6(6) = 36$ square inches
$A = 36$ sq in, or 36 in^2

To find the area of a rectangle, multiply the length times the width as shown in the following formula.

Rectangle $A = lw$; where l = length, w = width

Example:

Now use the formula to find the area of this rectangle.

Substitute 12 for l and 4 for w and multiply.

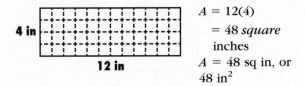

$A = 12(4)$
   $= 48$ *square* inches
$A = 48$ sq in, or 48 in^2

Example:

The Goldhamers' kitchen (shown below) is L-shaped. To find the area of an irregular figure, divide the space into squares and rectangles. Find the area of each shape; then add them to find the total area. What is the area of the kitchen?

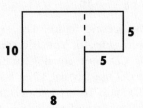

Find the area of the square.
$A = s^2$
$A = 5^2$
$A = 25$ sq ft

Find the area of the rectangle.
$A = lw$
$A = 10(8)$
$A = 80$ sq ft

Add: $25 + 80 = 105$ sq ft

Answer: The total area of the Goldhamers' kitchen is 105 sq ft.

Exercise 8

Directions: Find the area of each figure below.

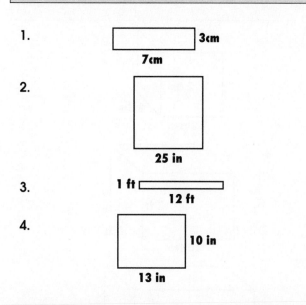

1.

   3cm

   7cm

2.

   25 in

3. **1 ft**

   12 ft

4.

   10 in

   13 in

Directions: Choose the <u>one best answer</u> for each item.

Item 5 refers to the following information.

Sue Cheng has had a brick patio laid in her backyard as shown below. The rest of the yard is to be seeded with grass.

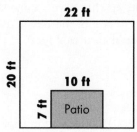

22 ft

20 ft

10 ft

7 ft Patio

5. How many square feet of lawn will Sue have?

  (1) 84
  (2) 270
  (3) 300
  (4) 370
  (5) 440

6. Andrews Asphalt received an order to resurface a parking lot that is 188 meters long and 83 meters wide. What is the area to be resurfaced?

  (1) 22,493m^2
  (2) 15,604m^2
  (3) 11,025m^2
  (4) 542m^2
  (5) 459m^2

7. Tricia planted her vegetable garden in a square corner of her yard that measured 15 feet on each side. How many square feet were in Tricia's garden?

  (1) 15
  (2) 30
  (3) 60
  (4) 100
  (5) 225

8. How many square feet of butcher block are needed to cover a countertop that is 3 feet wide and 4 feet long?

  (1) 7
  (2) 10
  (3) 12
  (4) 14
  (5) 16

Check your answers on page 417.

Finding the Volume of Solid Figures

We have dealt with volume as the measure of how much liquid a container can hold. **Volume** is also the measure of how much space there is within a three-dimensional or solid figure. This volume is measured in cubic units.

A **rectangular container** is a three-dimensional figure with all right angles (90°). Picture a cardboard box. To find the volume, you are figuring out how many cubes (smaller boxes) will fit into the large box.

To find the volume of a rectangular container, multiply the length times the width times the height as shown in the following formula.

Rectangular Container $V = lwh$,

      where l = length,

         w = width,

         h = height

Example:

Now find the volume of this rectangular container.

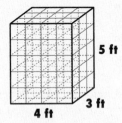

5 ft
3 ft
4 ft

Put the values from the diagram in the formula.

$V = 4(3)(5) = 60$ cubic feet
$V = 60$ cu ft, or 60 ft^3

A **cube** is a solid figure in which all sides are of equal measure. The length, width, and height are the same in a cube. The figure below shows a cube with the measure of 3 inches on each side.

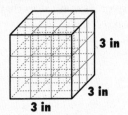

3 in
3 in
3 in

$V = 3(3)(3) = 27$ cubic inches
$V = 27$ cu in, or 27 in^3

To find the volume of a cube, take the measure of the side to the third power, or **cube** it, as shown in the following formula.

Cube $V = s^3$; where $s = $ side

Example:

The volume of this cube is found by substituting 7 for s in $V = s^3$.

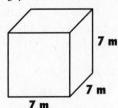

7 m
7 m
7 m

$V = 7(7)(7) = 343$ cubic meters
$V = 343$ cu m, or 343 m^3

Volume is used to solve problems in situations where you need to find the amount of space in a three-dimensional area. Some common applications in which you would need to find volume are air-conditioning a room, filling a swimming pool with water, and measuring the storage capacity of a closet or room.

Exercise 9

Directions: Find the volume of each of the following figures.

1.

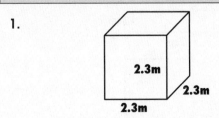

2.3m
2.3m
2.3m

2.

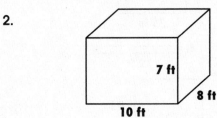

7 ft
8 ft
10 ft

3.

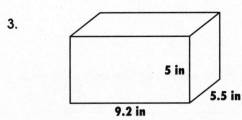

5 in
5.5 in
9.2 in

Directions: Choose the one best answer for each item.

4. Smart Moving and Storage decides to order new packing cartons that have a cube shape. What is the volume of one of the new cartons if each side of the carton measures 2 feet?

   (1)   4 cu ft
   (2)   6 cu ft
   (3)   8 cu ft
   (4)   12 cu ft
   (5)   Not enough information is given.

5. The Abisi Photography Company sells photographic equipment. They pack photo albums in boxes that measure 1 cubic yard. How many boxes can they fit in a storage closet that measures 5 yards long, 3 yards wide, and 4 yards high?

   (1) 20
   (2) 60
   (3) 180
   (4) 200
   (5) 240

6. When Tom decided to install air conditioning in his studio, the salesperson asked him how many cubic feet he wanted to cool. He measured the space and told the salesperson that it was 20 feet long, 16 feet wide, and 10 feet high. How many cubic feet does his studio measure?

   (1) 2,000
   (2) 2,500
   (3) 2,800
   (4) 3,200
   (5) 3,600

Check your answers on page 417.

Exercise 10

Directions: These are miscellaneous problems dealing with different types of measurements. Treat these problems like an alternate-format question where you would need to fill out a standard grid. (*Calculator permitted.*)

1. Ashley has a roll of Velcro that is 4 meters long. How many 10-centimeter lengths can be cut from the roll?

2. Three 10-lb. bags of potatoes were weighed on a somewhat accurate scale. The weights were 10 lbs 3 oz, 9 lbs 11 oz, and 9 lbs 10 oz. What was the average weight of the bags? For the standard grid, leave your answer in pounds and round your answer to the nearest tenths. For more practice, change that answer back to the nearest whole pounds and ounces.

3. Marla rode 75 kilometers on her bike along the beach. Jack rode 55 miles along the same bike path. What is the difference in kilometers? 1 kilometer = 0.62 miles. Round answer to nearest tenth.

Check your answers on page 417.

Unit 9

ALGEBRA

In classical algebra, we use symbols for unknown quantities instead of specific numbers and apply arithmetic operations to determine ways of managing these symbols to solve equations. Modern algebra is a subsequent evolution of classical algebra in that mathematicians study a set of objects with rules that have a relationship among them. Algebra may justifiably be called the language of mathematics. What you are studying now is classical algebra.

The ninth-century Arab mathematician al-Khwarizmi is given the honor of being the father of this discipline, which was termed "the science of restoration and balance." He wrote the first Arabic treatise on algebra. The name is derived from the Arabic word *al-jabre*, meaning restoration.

Signed Numbers

Temperatures drop below zero; unfortunately, so do checking account balances on occasion. These numbers can be shown using **signed numbers**. Signed numbers are used to show how far a number is from zero.

Most numbers that you use are positive numbers. As you see on the number line below, **positive numbers** are all numbers greater than zero. **Negative numbers** are all numbers less than zero. Zero, itself, is neither positive nor negative.

On a horizontal number line (shown below), the values *increase* or are greater as you move to the right. Values *decrease* or are less as you move to the left.

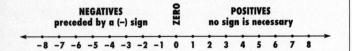

Exercise 1

Directions: Choose the one best answer for each item.

Items 1–3 refer to the following number line.

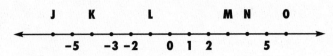

1. What is the value of point J?
   - (1) −8
   - (2) −7
   - (3) −6
   - (4) −5
   - (5) −4

2. What is the value of point M?
   - (1) −1
   - (2) 0
   - (3) 3
   - (4) 4
   - (5) 6

3. Which is a true statement?
   - (1) L < K
   - (2) K > 2
   - (3) N < 5
   - (4) 1 < −3
   - (5) −5 > L

Check your answers on page 417.

Adding and Subtracting Signed Numbers

Example:

It was 3° at noon on a cold winter day. The temperature dropped 5° by 6 p.m. What was the temperature after it had dropped?

"Dropped 5°" can be written as -5. You need to add $+3$ and -5. Look at the number line. Begin at 3, then move to the left 5 points. The temperature dropped to $-2°$.

Rules for adding signed numbers:

- To add signed numbers with the <u>same sign</u>, use these steps.

Example: $-2 + (-3)$

Step 1 Add the absolute values. $2 + 3 = 5$

Step 2 Keep the same sign for the sum. $-2 + (-3) = -5$

- To add signed numbers with <u>different signs,</u> use these steps.

Example: $4 + (-6)$

Step 1 Subtract the absolute values. $6 - 4 = 2$

Step 2 Use the sign of the number with the greater absolute value for the sum. 6 has a greater absolute value, so use a negative sign. $4 + (-6) = -2$

Now let's take a look at a situation that requires subtraction.

Example:

On a cold winter day, the temperature in Smallville is 5°. The temperature in Metropolis is even colder at $-1°$. What is the difference between the two temperatures?

To find the difference, subtract the colder temperature from the warmer one. $5 - (-1)$

You can solve this problem easily using the number line at the right. Count the places between the two points. There are 6. $5 - (-1) = 6$

Rules for subtracting signed numbers:
Examples:

		$5 - (-1)$	$-2 - (-6)$
Step 1	Change the subtraction sign to an addition sign, *and* change the sign of the number to its right.	becomes $5 + 1$	becomes $-2 + 6$
Step 2	Complete the problem using the rules for adding signed numbers.	Add and keep the sign. $5 + 1 = 6$	Subtract and use the sign of the larger value. $-2 + 6 = 4$

Remember that you can always replace double-negative signs with an addition sign.

Exercise 2

> **Directions:** Choose the <u>one best answer</u> for each item.

1. A volcano erupted 200 feet below sea level. Lava spurted 328 feet above the tip of the volcano. Which of the following expressions could be used to find the height above sea level that the lava reached?

    (1) $-200 - 328$
    (2) $-200 + 328$
    (3) $200 + 328$
    (4) $200 - 328$
    (5) $328 + 200$

2. What is the total of
$-4 + (-23) + (-67) + (-1) + 45$?

    (1) -50
    (2) -49
    (3) 0
    (4) 49
    (5) 50

3. The elevation of the Caspian Sea is 92 feet below sea level. The elevation of Lake Torrens in Australia is 92 feet above sea level. How much higher in elevation is Lake Torrens than the Caspian Sea?

  (1)   −184 feet
  (2)   0 feet
  (3)   184 feet
  (4)   368 feet
  (5)   Not enough information is given.

4. The temperature on Tuesday was 22°. On Wednesday, the temperature had dropped to 4 below zero (−4°). Which expression below would be used to show how many degrees the temperature dropped?

  (1) $22 + (-4)$
  (2) $22 - (-4)$
  (3) $(-4) + 22$
  (4) $(-4) - 22$
  (5) $22 - 4$

5. What is the sum of 9, −10, 11, and −49?

  (1)   39
  (2)   38
  (3)   −38
  (4)   −39
  (5)   −40

6. Which of the following expressions is equal to $6 - (-3) + (-2)$?

  A. $6 + 3 - 2$
  B. $6 - 3 + 2$
  C. $6 + 3 + (-2)$

  (1)   A and B
  (2)   B and C
  (3)   A and C
  (4)   A, B, and C
  (5)   None of the above

7. On Tuesday, it was 5° above zero. By Wednesday morning, the temperature had dropped 10°. Thursday's temperature was 10° above zero. Which expression below will give the difference in the temperature from Wednesday to Thursday?

  (1) $10 + (5 - 10)$
  (2) $10 - (5 + 10)$
  (3) $10 + (5 + 10)$
  (4) $10 - (5 - 10)$
  (5) $(5 - 10) - 10$

Check your answers on page 417.

Multiplying and Dividing Signed Numbers

Rules for multiplying and dividing signed numbers:

Step 1   Multiply or divide just as if the numbers were all positive.

Step 2   Figure out the sign of the answer. Two numbers of the same sign will give a positive answer. Two numbers with different signs will give a negative answer.

Study the following examples.

Problem	Operation and Rule
$4(-2) = -8$	*Multiply.* Different signs yield a negative number.
$\dfrac{-8}{-2} = 4$	*Divide.* The same signs yield a positive number.
$-6(-5) = 30$	*Multiply.* The same signs yield a positive number.
$\dfrac{-15}{3} = -5$	*Divide.* Different signs yield a negative number.

We can draw a few shortcuts from these rules.

Example:

Find the product of $(-1)(-1)(-1)(-1)$.

The answer is 1.

An **even number of negatives multiplied** together will give a **positive** answer.

Example:

Find the product of $(-1)(-1)(-1)(-1)(-1)$.

The answer is −1.

An **odd number of negatives multiplied** together will give a **negative** answer.

Exercise 3

Directions: Find the product or quotient of the following.

1. 6(10)

2. −5(12)

3. −6(−7)

4. $\frac{20}{-4}$

5. $\frac{-25}{5}$

6. $\frac{-45}{-9}$

7. What is the value of $4(-3)(-2)(1)$?
   - **(1)** −24
   - **(2)** −14
   - **(3)** −10
   - **(4)** 10
   - **(5)** 24

8. What is the value of $\frac{-7(6)}{-3}$?
   - **(1)** 14
   - **(2)** 12
   - **(3)** −10
   - **(4)** −10
   - **(5)** −14

Check your answers on page 418.

Working with Expressions

In mathematics, an **expression** is a way of writing a number relationship using symbols instead of words. You can also write a number relationship when one or more of the numbers are unknown. Letters, called **variables**, represent the unknown numbers.

Algebraic expressions use variables, numbers, and symbols to express numerical relationships.

In Words	In Symbols
Some amount	n (any variable)
Two numbers	x and y (any two variables)
An amount increased by 10	$t + 10$
An amount minus 15	$b - 15$
An amount subtracted from 15	$15 - b$
The product of an amount and 7	$7y$
The quotient of an amount divided by 11	$\frac{n}{11}$
A number times itself	m^2

Study these next examples to see how words like *quantity*, *total*, and *all* are used to indicate the part enclosed within parentheses. The word quantity is most often used to indicate an operation in parentheses.

In Words	In Symbols
The quantity of an amount minus five	$(x - 5)$
Five times the quantity of six and four	$5(6 + 4)$
Seven times the total of an amount and seven	$7(n + 7)$
The product of eight and the quantity of fifteen plus a number	$8(15 + s)$
Twice an amount minus that amount plus four, all multiplied by ten	$10(2w - w + 4)$

To solve an algebra problem, the first step is to translate the words of the problem into mathematical symbols. On the GED Math Test, there will be set-up problems that test your ability to choose the correct algebraic expression to represent the situation in a word problem.

Exercise 4

Directions: Choose the one best answer for each item.

1. If b represents the number of items bought for $2 each, which expression would be used to represent the total cost?

   (1) $b - \$2$
   (2) $b + \$2$
   (3) $\$2b$
   (4) $\dfrac{b}{\$2}$
   (5) $(b - \$2)$

2. Last week, Mary paid $35 more for groceries than she paid this week. If x is the amount she paid this week, which of the following expressions represents the amount she paid last week?

   (1) $\$35 - x$
   (2) $x - \$35$
   (3) $\$35x$
   (4) $x + \$35$
   (5) $\dfrac{x}{\$35}$

3. Mike bought 3 cassettes and paid with a $20 bill. If y represents the price of each cassette, which expression would be used to represent his change?

   (1) $\$20 - 3y$
   (2) $3y - \$20$
   (3) $\dfrac{\$20 - y}{3}$
   (4) $3(\$20 - y)$
   (5) $\$20 + 3y$

4. Which expression would be used to represent 15 subtracted from a number times itself?

   (1) $2p - 15$
   (2) $15 - 2p$
   (3) $15p^2$
   (4) $15 - p^2$
   (5) $p^2 - 15$

5. Nancy and five women from her office chipped in on a gift for their supervisor. If g represents the price of the gift, which expression would be used to represent Nancy's share of the gift?

   (1) $5g$
   (2) $6g$
   (3) $g + 6$
   (4) $\dfrac{g}{6}$
   (5) $\dfrac{6}{g}$

6. The price of each pound of lobster has risen $1 since last week. If the price of one pound of lobster last week is represented by w, which expression represents the price of a two-pound lobster *this week*?

   (1) $2w + \$1$
   (2) $w^2 + \$1$
   (3) $2(w + \$1)$
   (4) $2(w^2 + \$1)$
   (5) $2w^2 + \$1$

7. Harry runs 3 miles less each day than his brother Mike does. If m represents the number of miles that Mike runs, which of the following expressions represents the total miles that Harry runs in 6 days?

   (1) $6m - 3$
   (2) $6(m - 3)$
   (3) $m - 6$
   (4) $\dfrac{m - 3}{6}$
   (5) $6(m + 3)$

8. Which expression could be used to find 43 minus the quantity of x plus $2y$?

   (1) $(x + 2y) - 43$
   (2) $-43 + (2y - x)$
   (3) $43(x + 2y)$
   (4) $43 - 2xy$
   (5) $43 - (x + 2y)$

Check your answers on page 418.

Finding Square Roots

3

3

A value taken to the second power is said to be *squared*.

The expression 3^2 is read *three squared*.

The symbol $\sqrt{}$ means **square root**. Finding the square root is the opposite of squaring. The square of 3 is 9, so $\sqrt{9}$ is 3.

To find the square root, think, "What number times itself will give this value?"

The following square roots are those most commonly found on the GED Math Test.

$\sqrt{1} = 1$	$\sqrt{64} = 8$	$\sqrt{225} = 15$
$\sqrt{4} = 2$	$\sqrt{81} = 9$	$\sqrt{400} = 20$
$\sqrt{9} = 3$	$\sqrt{100} = 10$	$\sqrt{900} = 30$
$\sqrt{16} = 4$	$\sqrt{121} = 11$	$\sqrt{1,600} = 40$
$\sqrt{25} = 5$	$\sqrt{144} = 12$	$\sqrt{2,500} = 50$
$\sqrt{36} = 6$	$\sqrt{169} = 13$	$\sqrt{3,600} = 60$
$\sqrt{49} = 7$	$\sqrt{196} = 14$	$\sqrt{10,000} = 100$

To find the square root of a value on the table, you can approximate an answer.

Example:

Find the square root of 72.

Step 1 Find which numbers the square root value falls between.

$\sqrt{64} = 8$
$\sqrt{72} = ?$
$\sqrt{81} = 9$

Step 2 The square root of the value is between their square roots.

$\sqrt{72}$ is between 8 and 9

Exercise 5

Directions: Find the following square roots.

1. $\sqrt{100}$

2. $\sqrt{225}$

3. $\sqrt{196}$

4. $\sqrt{144}$

5. $\sqrt{49}$

6. $\sqrt{400}$

7. If the area of a square is 64 square meters, how many meters long is each side?

    (1)   4
    (2)   8
    (3) 16
    (4) 24
    (5) 32

8. $\sqrt{200}$ is

    (1)   Between 10 and 11
    (2)   Between 11 and 12
    (3)   Between 12 and 13
    (4)   Between 13 and 14
    (5)   Between 14 and 15

Check your answers on page 418.

Scientific Notation

Scientific notation is a method of writing a number that has many digits. Powers of 10 are used to rewrite the number.

Multiplying or dividing by 10, 100, or 1,000 can be done quickly by moving the decimal point to the right or left. This is what is done in scientific notation. Remember that the exponent equals the number of places to move the decimal point. The exponent indicates place value.

In scientific notation, the number 45,678,000,000 is written 4.5678×10^{10}.

365

To write a number using scientific notation:

Step 1 Place the decimal point to the right of the first digit, and count how many places to the **left** you have moved the decimal point.

4.5678000000   *10 places*

Step 2 Drop the zeros in the number, and write it multiplied by 10 to the power equal to the number of places counted.

4.5678×10^{10}

To interpret a number using scientific notation:

Step 1 Move the decimal point to the right the number of decimal places indicated by the exponent. Add zeros as needed.

$1.506 \times 10^6 = 1.506000.$

Step 2 Count from the right to put a comma after every group of three digits.

1,506,000

Exercise 6

> **Directions:** Choose the one best answer for each item.

1. Which expression is 2,345,000 in scientific notation?
   - (1) 23.45×10^2
   - (2) 2.345×10^4
   - (3) 2.345×10^6
   - (4) 2.345×10^7
   - (5) 234.5×10^2

2. The planet Pluto stays about 3.6×10^9 miles from the sun. How would that distance be written as a whole number?
   - (1) 360,000
   - (2) 3,600,000
   - (3) 36,000,000
   - (4) 360,000,000
   - (5) 3,600,000,000

3. Which of the following statements is true?
   - (1) 4×10^3 is greater than 4,500.
   - (2) 4×10^3 is equal to 40,000.
   - (3) 4×10^3 is equal to 10,000.
   - (4) 4×10^3 is equal to 4,000.
   - (5) 4×10^3 is less than 400.

4. The distance from Mars to Earth is about 56,000,000 kilometers. How would this distance be written in scientific notation?
   - (1) 5.6×10^8
   - (2) 5.6×10^7
   - (3) 5.6×10^6
   - (4) 5.6×10^5
   - (5) 5.6×10^4

Check your answers on page 418.

Simplifying Algebraic Expressions

In algebra, terms are added and subtracted. A term has a **variable**, or letter part, and a **coefficient**, or number part.

In the expression $3t + 2c$

3 is the coefficient of t 2 is the coefficient of c

Simplifying an expression means combining like terms. To add or subtract like terms, combine their coefficients using the rules for signed numbers.

When there is no coefficient in front of a variable, the coefficient is 1.

$3t + 4t + 5t$	$3 + 4 + 5$	$= 12t$
$3t - 4t + 5t$	$3 - 4 + 5$	$= 4t$
$6s + 8s + s$	$6 + 8 + 1$	$= 15s$
$10b - 8b$	$10 - 8$	$= 2b$
$15y - 5y - (-y)$	$15 - 5 + 1$	$= 11y$

A **constant** is a number that does not have a variable. In the example below, 4 and 9 are constants. Constants can be combined as like terms.

$3n + 4 - 9 = 3n - 5$

Variables with different exponents (y, y^2, or y^3) are *not* like terms. To simplify any expression, combine like terms only.

$$3x^2 + 5x + 7 + 5x^2 - 2x - 3$$

x^2 terms	x terms	constants	
$3x^2 + 5x^2$	$5x - 2x$	$7 - 3$	
$8x^2$	$3x$	4	$= 8x^2 + 3x + 4$

You may need to remove parentheses to simplify an expression.

Example:

Ellen bought 2 bouquets of flowers for $8 each and 2 vases for $4 each. You can find the total she spent in two different ways.

1. Add the amounts and multiply by 2: 2($8 + $4) = 2($12) = $24

2. Multiply each amount by 2, and then add: 2($8) + 2($4) = $16 + $8 = $24

   Both ways are equal: 2($8 + $4) = 2($8) + 2($4)

This example illustrates the **distributive law** of multiplication, which states that when a number is multiplied by a sum or difference within a set of parentheses, you may do either of these things:

1. Do the operation in parentheses and then multiply.
2. Multiply each number in the parentheses by the value outside and then do the addition or subtraction operation.

This law is used in algebra to simplify an expression when the value for the variable is not known. To multiply a value by a variable expression, multiply the coefficient by each value within the parentheses.

Examples:

Simplify:

$6(x + 4)$ $10(3n^2 - 6n - 3)$ $-2(7y - 8)$

$6(x + 4)$ $10(3n^2 - 6n - 3)$ $-2(7y - 8)$

$6(x) + 6(4)$ $10(3n^2) - 10(6n) - 10(3)$ $-2(7y) + (-2)(-8)$
$6x + 24$ $30n^2 - 60n - 30$ $-14y + 16$

Exercise 7

Directions: Choose the one best answer to each item.

1. What is $7s + 6s + s + s + 4s$ in simplified form?
   - **(1)** $19s$
   - **(2)** 19
   - **(3)** $17s$
   - **(4)** $17s^2$
   - **(5)** $19s^2$

2. What is $0.8h + 1.7h$ in simplified form?
   - **(1)** $0.25h$
   - **(2)** $0.9h$
   - **(3)** $1.36h$
   - **(4)** $2.5h$
   - **(5)** $25.0h$

3. Which of the following is equal to $4(t - 7)$?
   - **(1)** $4(t + 7)$
   - **(2)** $4(t) - 7$
   - **(3)** $4(t) - 4(7)$
   - **(4)** $4(t) + 4(7)$
   - **(5)** $4t - 11$

4. Which of the following expressions is equal to $5(3t^2 + t - 2)$?
   - **(1)** $15t^2 + t - 10$
   - **(2)** $t^2 + 5t + 10$
   - **(3)** $15t^2 + t + 10$
   - **(4)** $15t^2 + 5t - 10$
   - **(5)** $15t^2 - 5t - 10$

5. Which of the following expressions is equal to $5r - 2(2r + 6)$?
   - **(1)** $r + 12$
   - **(2)** $r - 12$
   - **(3)** $r - 6$
   - **(4)** $20r + 12$
   - **(5)** $20r + 6$

6. Which of the following expressions is equal to $2(3a + 5b) + 3(5a - 3b)$?
   - **(1)** $21a + b$
   - **(2)** $21a + 7b$
   - **(3)** $a + 7b$
   - **(4)** $a + b$
   - **(5)** $21a + 19b$

7. Which expression does $6(5a + 4b) + 2(2a - b)$ equal?
   - **(1)** $26a + 26b$
   - **(2)** $15a + 18b$
   - **(3)** $34a + 26b$
   - **(4)** $34a + 22b$
   - **(5)** $56ab$

8. Which of the following expressions is equal to $3a - 2(6a + 8)$?
   - **(1)** $-9a + 16$
   - **(2)** $15a - 16$
   - **(3)** $-15a - 16$
   - **(4)** $-9a - 16$
   - **(5)** $-9a + 6$

To check your answers, turn to page 418.

Evaluating Expressions

A **variable** is a letter used in place of a number. Within the same expression or equation, the variable must represent the same value.

In $n + n = 8$: both n's have the same value.

To simplify an algebraic expression when the values of the variables are given:

Step 1 Substitute the values given for the variables.

Step 2 Follow the rules for order of operations.

To evaluate algebraic expressions correctly, operations must be done in the following order:

$$8 + 5(6 - 4)^3$$
$$\downarrow$$

P Parentheses $8 + 5(2)^3$
$$\downarrow$$
E Exponents or roots $8 + 5(8)$
$$\downarrow$$
M D Multiplication or $8 + 40$
  Division from left to right
A S Addition or Subtraction from $\downarrow$
  left to right 48

Examples:

Find the value of the following:

$3x^2$ when $x = 7$ $2 + n^3$ when $n = 4$

Step 1 Substitute the values given for the variables.
$3(7)^2$ $2 + (4)^3$

Step 2 Follow the rules for order of operations.
  Exponents $3(7)^2$ Exponents $2 + (4)^3$
      $3(49)$ $2 + (64)$
  Multiply 147 Add 66

Unless there are parentheses grouping the values, only the number immediately in front of the exponent is raised to a power.

Example:

Find the value of $3x^2y$ when $x = 6$ and $y = 4$.

Step 1 Substitute the values given for the variables.
$3(6)^2(4)$

Step 2 Follow the rules for order of operations.
  Exponents $3(6)^2(4)$
      $3(36)(4)$
  Multiply 432

Example:

Find the value of $(2 + n)^3$ when $n = 4$.

Step 1 Substitute the values given for the variables.
$(2 + 4)^3$

Step 2 Follow the rules for order of operations.
  Parentheses $(2 + 4)^3$
      $(6)^3$
  Exponents 216

Exercise 8

Directions: Simplify the following expressions given $x = 2$, $y = 3$, and $z = 1$.

1. x^2
2. z^2
3. $5y^2$
4. xy^2
5. $\dfrac{x^2}{4}$
6. x^2y
7. $x^2 + y^2$
8. $(x + y)^2$
9. $x^2 + y$
10. x^2y^2

Directions: Choose the one best answer for each item.

11. What is the value of $\dfrac{t^2 + s^2}{s}$ when $t = 6$ and $s = -4$?

    (1) 13
    (2) 7
    (3) 2.5
    (4) −5
    (5) −13

12. What is the value of the expression $3.14r^2h$ when $r = 10$ and $h = 2$?

    (1) 6.28
    (2) 62.8
    (3) 452.16
    (4) 628
    (5) 1,256

13. What is the value of the expression $5s^3$ when $s = 2$?

    (1) 30
    (2) 40
    (3) 100
    (4) 300
    (5) 1,000

14. Which of the following will give the value of the expression prt, when $p = \$2,000$, $r = 0.06$, and $t = 4$?

    (1) $\$2,000(0.06 + 4)$
    (2) $\dfrac{\$2,000(0.06)}{4}$
    (3) $\$2,000(0.06)(4)$
    (4) $\$2,000 - (0.06)(4)$
    (5) $\$2,000 + (0.06) + (4)$

Check your answers on page 418.

Solving Equations

A father is ten times as old as his son. Their combined ages add to 33. Can you figure out their ages? One way to solve the problem is to guess ages and see if your guesses work. Trial and error is a legitimate way to solve a problem, but it does take time. You can most easily solve this problem by writing an equation and solving it.

An **equation** is a numerical statement in which one value is equal (=) to another.

$$2 + 2 = 4 \qquad 7(2) = 14 \qquad n + 7 = 9$$

Notice in the third equation n must equal 2 to make this statement true.

$m + 4 = 16$ What value for m will make this equation true? The variable m must equal 12. How do you get 12 using the numbers 16 and 4? Subtract: $16 - 4 = 12$.

$x - 8 = 10$ What value for x will make this equation true? The variable x must equal 18. How do you get 18 using the numbers 10 and 8? Add: $10 + 8 = 18$.

$3y = 30$ What value for y will make this equation true? The variable y must equal 10. How do you get 10 using the numbers 30 and 3? Divide: $30 \div 3 = 10$.

$\dfrac{r}{5} = 4$ What value for r will make this equation true? The variable r must equal 20. How do you get 20 using the numbers 5 and 4? Multiply: $5(4) = 20$.

To solve an equation:

   Step 1 Get the variable alone on one side by moving the number with it to the other (opposite) side of the equation.

   Step 2 Do the inverse (or opposite) operation.

Examples:

   Solve: $y + 3 = 9$

   Step 1 Move the 3 to the other side, and change its sign. $y + 3 = 9$ -3

   Step 2 **Subtract** it from 9. $y = 6$

You can check your answer by substituting it for the variable in the original equation.

   Check: $y + 3 = 9$
               $(6) + 3 = 9$

   Solve: $7m = 77$

   Step 1 Move the 7 to the other side, and apply the inverse operation. $7m = \dfrac{77}{7}$

369

Step 2 **Divide** 77 by it. $m = 11$

Check: $7m = 77$

$7(11) = 77$

Solve: $\dfrac{b}{2} = 16$

Step 1 Move the 2 to the other side, and apply the inverse operation. $\dfrac{b}{2} = 16(2)$

Step 2 **Multiply** it by 16. $b = 32$

Check: $\dfrac{b}{2} = 16$

$\dfrac{32}{2} = 16$

Exercise 9

Directions: Solve these equations using the inverse operation. Show each step.

	A.	B.	C.
1.	$n - 19 = 27$	$p + 27 = 46$	$7r = 56$
2.	$t + 15 = 19$	$\dfrac{c}{4} = 25$	$3f = 51$
3.	$\dfrac{a}{11} = 5$	$c + 26 = 32$	$n - 79 = 113$
4.	$\dfrac{x}{5} = 11$	$q + 9 = 97$	$\dfrac{n}{6} = 8$
5.	$9b = 90$	$72 = x - 48$	$\dfrac{s}{2} = 150$

6. Twelve people bought theater tickets for a total of $72. If t represents the price of each ticket, then the equation $12t = \$72$ can be used to find the price of one ticket. What does t, the price of one ticket, equal?

(1) $6
(2) $12
(3) $72
(4) $864
(5) Not enough information is given.

7. Lance plans to tile his kitchen floor. The area of the floor is 132 square feet, and the length of the room measures 12 feet. If w represents the width of the room, then the equation $12w = 132$ can be used to find the width. What is the width of the room?

(1) 8 feet
(2) 9 feet
(3) 10 feet
(4) 11 feet
(5) 12 feet

8. Ellen recently got a raise of $115 per month. She now earns $2,300 per month. If x represents her previous monthly salary, then the equation $x + \$115 = \$2,300$ can be used to find the amount she earned per month before her raise. What is that amount?

(1) $2,080
(2) $2,170
(3) $2,185
(4) $2,285
(5) $2,415

Check your answers on page 418.

Solving Multi-Step Equations

Some equations require more than one step to solve. Your task, however, is still the same. You need to find a way to isolate the variable on one side of the equation.

Test-Taking Tip:

For the multiple-choice questions, you can choose to guess and check to solve some algebra problems. Select one of the answer choices and substitute it into the equation in the problem. Try each choice until you find the correct one. The guess-and-check method is a good choice if an equation looks long or difficult to solve.

To isolate the variable:

Step 1 Remove any number added or subtracted by doing the inverse operation.

Step 2 Remove any number multiplied or divided by doing the inverse operation.

Example:

Solve: $3b + 7 = 28$

Step 1 Remove the 7 by **subtracting.** $3b + 7 = 28$
-7

Step 2 Remove the 3 by **dividing.** $3b = \dfrac{21}{3}$
$b = 7$

Substitute your answer into the original equation, and solve to check your answer.

Check: $3b + 7 = 28$
$3(7) + 7 = 28$
$21 + 7 = 28$

It may be necessary to simplify each side of an equation by combining like terms before solving by inverse operations. To simplify each side of the equation, remember to do the operation <u>as indicated</u> on the same side of the equation. You do the opposite or inverse operation only when you move a value to the opposite side of the equation.

Example:

Solve: $8y - 10 - 2y = 10 - 8$
On the same side, do the same (indicated) operation.

Step 1 **Combine** like terms on each side.
$8y - 10 - 2y = 10 - 8$
$6y - 10 = 2$
On the opposite side, do the opposite (inverse) operation.

Step 2 Remove the 10 by **adding.**
$6y - 10 = 2$
$+ 10$

Step 3 Remove the 6 by **dividing.**
$6y = 12$
6
$y = 2$

When a variable appears on both sides of the equation, use inverse operations to get the variables together on one side of the equation and the constants together on the other side.

Example:

Solve: $4(n - 6) = 3n$

Step 1 **Multiply** 4 times each number in the parentheses.
$4(n - 6) = 3n$
$4n - 24 = 3n$

Step 2 Move the $3n$ to the opposite side by **subtracting.**
$4n - 24 = 3n$
$-3n$

Step 3 Remove the 24 by **adding.**
$n - 24 = 0$
$+ 24$
$n = 24$

Exercise 10

Directions: Solve each equation using inverse operations.

1. $4w + 6 = 34$

2. $28 = 12y - 8$

3. $\dfrac{s}{4} - 13 = 2$

4. $3r + 6 + 2r = 21$

5. $3v - 42 = 100 - 2(20)$

6. $7(g - 6) = 42$

7. $8t = 2t + 6$

8. $13m + 7 = 11m + 21$

9. $14s + 11 = 13s + 17$

10. If $v - 6.8 = 3.4$, then what is the value of v?
    (1) 2
    (2) 3.4
    (3) 8.5
    (4) 10.2
    (5) 23.12

11. If $0.5k + 2 = 11$, then what does k equal?
    (1) 5
    (2) 18
    (3) 49
    (4) 60.5
    (5) 71

12. If $3x + 2(5x - 8) = 11x - 4$, then what does x equal?
    (1) 2
    (2) 3
    (3) 4
    (4) 5
    (5) 6

13. If $b^2 = 400$, then what is the value of b?
    (1) 10
    (2) 20
    (3) 30
    (4) 40
    (5) 50

371

14. If $6n + 6 = 5n + 6$, then what is the value of n?

   (1) 0
   (2) 2
   (3) 6
   (4) 10
   (5) 12

15. If $12k + 14 = 2(k + 22)$, then what does k equal?

   (1) 0
   (2) 3
   (3) 6
   (4) 12
   (5) 15

Check your answers on page 418.

Solving Inequalities

An **inequality** is a statement that two or more values are *unequal.*

The symbols of an inequality are:

> Greater than
< Less than
≥ Greater than **or** equal to
≤ Less than **or** equal to

In the statement $n - 3 = 10$, the only value that will satisfy the equation is $n = 13$.

In the statement $n - 3 > 10$, many values will satisfy the inequality. n can be 14, 15, 16, or any value greater than 13. The solution to the inequality can be written $n > 13$.

The solution set of an inequality consists of those values that will satisfy or make the statement true. The solution set can include whole numbers, fractions, and decimals.

Inequality	Solution Set
$x > 3$	x can be any number greater than 3
$y < 10$	y can be any number less than 10
$r \geq 7$	r can be 7 or any number greater than 7
$s \leq 5$	s can be 5 or any number less than 5

Inequalities, like equations, can be solved by inverse operations. The symbol of the inequality remains, unless a side is multiplied or divided by a negative quantity. Then the inequality symbol is reversed.

Example:

Solve: $3y - 7 \geq 11$

Step 1 Remove the 7 by **adding.** $3y - 7 \geq 11$
                                          $+ 7$

Step 2 Remove the 3 by **dividing.** $3y \geq 18$
                                            3

y can be 6 or any value $y \geq 6$
greater than 6.

Example:

Which of the following inequalities is true when x is replaced by 5?

   A. $2x + 3 \leq 15$
   B. $3x + 8 \geq 29$
   C. $-7x + 2 < -19$

To answer this question, you can solve each inequality and check to see if 5 is in the solution set. Note the sign reversal in **C.**

   A. $2x + 3 \leq 15$
        $2x \leq 12$
        $x \leq 6$ Yes $5 \leq 6$
   B. $3x + 8 \geq 29$
        $x \geq 21$
        $x \geq 7$ No $5 \geq 7$
   C. $-7x + 2 < -19$
        $-7x < -21$
        $x > 3$ Yes $5 > 3$

You may also answer the question by substituting 5 in each inequality to see if the statement is true.

   A. $2x + 3 \leq 15$ $2(5) + 3 \leq 15$
                             $10 + 3 \leq 15$
                             $13 \leq 15$ Yes
   B. $3x + 8 \geq 29$ $3(5) + 8 \geq 29$
                             $15 + 8 \geq 29$
                             $23 \geq 29$ No
   C. $-7x + 2 < -19$ $-7(5) + 2 < -19$
                             $-35 + 2 < -19$
                             $-33 < -19$ Yes

Exercise 11

Directions: Use inverse operations to solve the following inequalities.

1. Which of the following is true for $w - 15 < 12$?

   (1) $w < 3$
   (2) $w < 27$
   (3) $w > 3$
   (4) $w = 27$
   (5) $w < 180$

2. Which of the following is true for $2x \leq 100$?

   (1) $x = 25$
   (2) $x \leq 25$
   (3) $x \geq 50$
   (4) $x \leq 50$
   (5) $x = 200$

3. Which of the following is true for $3g + 17 > 140$?

   (1) $g = 37$
   (2) $g \geq 37$
   (3) $g > 41$
   (4) $g = 41$
   (5) $g > 52$

4. Which of the following values is in the solution set of $-3y - 7 \geq -28$?

   (1) 7
   (2) 8
   (3) 10
   (4) 12
   (5) 20

5. Which of the following values is *not* in the solution set of $8b - 4 > 28$?

   (1) 4
   (2) 5
   (3) 6
   (4) 7
   (5) 8

6. Which of the following inequalities is true when x is replaced by 10?

   (1) $2x + 3 \leq 15$
   (2) $3x + 8 \geq 29$
   (3) $7x - 2 < 19$
   (4) $4x - 8 < 30$
   (5) $2x + 9 > 35$

Check your answers on page 419.

Using Formulas

You have used formulas to find the perimeter and area of squares and rectangles. You can also use formulas as equations to solve for the length of a side when the perimeter or area is given.

Items A and B refer to the following figure.

12 in

Examples:

A. If the area of the rectangle is 84 square inches, what is the width of the rectangle?

Step 1 Substitute the values given for the variables in the appropriate formula

$A = lw$ ⬩ *Length = 12*
$84 = 12w$ ⬩ *Area = 84*

Step 2 Simplify each side of the equation, and use inverse operations to solve.

$$\frac{84}{12} = w$$

$7 = w$, the width of the rectangle

B. If the perimeter of the rectangle given is 36, what is the width of the rectangle?

Step 1 Substitute the values given for the variables in the appropriate formula.

$P = 2l + 2w$ ⬩ *Length = 12*
$36 = 2(12)$ ⬩ *Perimeter = 36*
$+ 2w$

Step 2 Simplify each side of the equation, and use inverse operations to solve.

$$36 = 24 + 2w$$
$$-24 \,\,\,\,\,\,\,$$
$$\frac{12 = 2w}{2 \,\,\,\,\,\,\,}$$

$6 = w$, the width of the rectangle

C. If the area of a square is 64 ft^2, what is the length of each side?

Step 1 Substitute the values given for the variables in the appropriate formula.

$A = s^2$ ⬩ *Area = 64*
$64 = s^2$

When the variable in an equation is squared, or taken to the second power, the inverse operation is finding the square root of the number on the other side of the equation.

Step 2 Simplify each side of the equation, and use inverse operations to solve.

$$\sqrt{64} = s$$
$$8 = s, \text{ the side of the square}$$

Exercise 12

Directions: Use the following formulas to solve items 1–7.

Area (A) of a square or a rectangle:

square $A = s^2$; where s = side
rectangle $A = lw$; where l = length,
          w = width

Perimeter (P) of a rectangle:

$P = 2l + 2w$; where l = length, w = width

Volume (V) of a rectangular container:

$V = lwh$; where l = length, w = width, h = height

1. How many inches is the length of a rectangle with an area of 68 cm² and a width of 4 cm?

   (1) 4
   (2) 9
   (3) 17
   (4) 34
   (5) 272

2. How many centimeters high is a rectangular container with a volume of 60 cm³, a length of 3 cm, and a width of 4 cm?

   (1) 2
   (2) 5
   (3) 6
   (4) 8
   (5) 10

3. Which equation below would be used to find the length of each side of a square with an area of 121 in²?

   (1) $121 = 4s$
   (2) $121 = s^3$
   (3) $121 = lw$
   (4) $121 = s^2$
   (5) Not enough information is given.

4. How many yards wide is Jill's front lawn with an area of 32 sq yd?

   (1) 4
   (2) 6
   (3) 8
   (4) 12
   (5) Not enough information is given.

5. Ron used 30 feet of fence to enclose a pen for his dog. If the pen is 5 feet wide, how many feet long is it?

   (1) 4
   (2) 6
   (3) 8
   (4) 10
   (5) Not enough information is given.

6. Which equation below would be used to find the width of a rectangular container with a volume of 600 cm³, a length of 10 cm, and a height of 10 cm?

   (1) $600 = s^3$
   (2) $600 = 10(10)w$
   (3) $600 = 10(10) + 10w$
   (4) $600 = 10w$
   (5) Not enough information is given.

7. A rectangular yard has a perimeter of 144 feet. What is the width of the yard in feet if the length of the yard is 42 feet?

   (1) 72
   (2) 60
   (3) 36
   (4) 30
   (5) 24

Check your answers on page 419.

Quadratic Equations

A **quadratic equation** is an equation in which the variable is raised to the second power or squared. Quadratic equations usually have two different solutions. There are two values for the variable that will **satisfy** the equation or make it true.

The two values that will satisfy $y^2 - 4y + 3 = 0$ are $y = 1$ and $y = 3$. When either of these values is substituted into the equation, it will be true.

$$y^2 - 4y + 3 = 0 \qquad\qquad y^2 - 4y + 3 = 0$$
$$(1)^2 - 4(1) + 3 = 0 \qquad (3)^2 - 4(3) + 3 = 0$$
$$1 - 4 + 3 = 0 \qquad\qquad 9 - 12 + 3 = 0$$

Since it is not likely that there will be more than one quadratic equation given on the GED Math Test, that one problem can be most easily solved by guessing and checking the multiple-choice answers in the equation. Use guess and check to solve this problem.

Example:

If $10t^2 - 15 = 235$, then t equals what numbers?

  (1)   0 and 5
  (2)   0 and −5
  (3)   5 and −5
  (4)   5 and 10
  (5)   −5 and 10

Perhaps you may notice that the problem contains several multiples of 5 so you can try choice (3), 5 and -5. Substitute each of these values into the equation.

$10t^2 - 15 = 235$	$10t^2 - 15 = 235$
$10(5)^2 - 15 = 235$	$10(-5)^2 - 15 = 235$
$10(25) - 15 = 235$	$10(25) - 15 = 235$
$250 - 15 = 235$	$250 - 15 = 235$

The correct answer is (3). Both of these values satisfy the equation.

Exercise 13

Directions: Solve the following.

1. If $p^2 - 5p = 14$, then p equals what numbers?
   (1)   0 and −2
   (2)   −2 and 7
   (3)   7 and −5
   (4)   −5 and 4
   (5)   4 and 10

2. If $2r^2 + 2r - 60 = 0$, then what does r equal?
   (1)   −5 and 6
   (2)   −5 and 7
   (3)   5 and −6
   (4)   7 and −6
   (5)   8 and −9

3. If $z^2 - z - 56 = 0$, then z equals what numbers?
   (1)   2 and −3
   (2)   −3 and 4
   (3)   4 and −5
   (4)   −5 and 8
   (5)   −7 and 8

Check your answers on page 419.

Using Algebra to Solve Word Problems

Earlier in this unit, you read a problem about a man and his son.

Example:

The father is ten times as old as his son. Their combined ages add up to 33. How old is the father?

Now let's see how an equation can be written to solve the problem.

Step 1 Use a variable to represent an unknown amount.

  x = son's age

Step 2 Write a variable expression to represent other unknown quantities.

  The father is ten times as old as his son.

  father's age = $10x$

Step 3 Write an equation that restates the information in the problem using these expressions.

  Their combined ages add to 33.

  $x + 10x = 33$

Unknown Amounts	Variable Expressions	Equation
Son's age	x	$x + 10x = 33$
Father's age	$10x$	

Step 4 Solve the equation to find the value of the variable.

  $x + 10x = 33$

  $11x = \dfrac{33}{11}$

  $x = 3$

Step 5 Use the value for the variable to *answer the question asked.*

  How old is the father?

  father = $10x$

  Therefore, the father is 10(3), or 30 years old.

A common kind of algebra word problem involves consecutive numbers. Consecutive numbers are numbers that follow each other in counting order. Examples: 5 and 6; 10 and 11; and 97, 98, and 99.

If one number is x, the next consecutive number is $x + 1$.

Example:

The sum of two consecutive numbers is 45. What are the numbers?

Steps 1–3 Make a table to represent the unknowns.

Unknown Amounts	Variable Expressions	Equation
First number x		
Next number $x + 1$	$x + x + 1 = 45$	

Step 4 Solve the equation.

$$x + x + 1 = 45$$
$$2x + 1 = 45$$
$$2x = 44$$
$$x = 22$$

Step 5 Answer the question asked.

What are the numbers?

First number = x, or 22
Next number = $x + 1$, or 23
The numbers are 22 and 23.

Writing inequalities is done in the same way as writing equations. However, a symbol of inequality, $>$, $<$, $\geq$, or $\leq$, is used in place of the equal sign ($=$).

Example:

The sum of three consecutive even numbers is less than 0. Find the three highest possible values for these numbers.

Unknown Amounts	Variable Expressions	Equation
First number	x	
Second number	$x + 2$	$x + x + 2 + x + 4 < 0$
Third number	$x + 4$	

$$x + x + 2 + x + 4 < 0$$
$$3x + 6 < 0$$
$$3x < -6$$
$$x < -2$$

If x must be an even number less than -2, the highest possible value for x is -4.

If $x = -4$, $x + 2 = -2$, and $x + 4 = 0$.

Exercise 14

Directions: For items 1–4, complete the following tables, solve the equations, and answer the questions asked.

1. Carl and his wife Mary drove to the lake in separate cars. Carl's car used twice as much gasoline as his wife's car. Together they used six gallons. How many gallons of gasoline did Carl's car use?

Unknown Amounts	Variable Expressions	Equation
Mary's car		
Carl's car		

How many gallons of gasoline did Carl's car use?_____

2. The high temperature today was 72°. That is 20° warmer than yesterday's high. What was yesterday's high temperature?

Unknown Amount	Variable Expression	Equation
Yesterday's temperature		

What was yesterday's high temperature?_____

3. Consecutive odd or even numbers are separated by 2. The sum of two consecutive odd numbers is 96. What is the first number?

Unknown Amounts	Variable Expressions	Equation
First number		
Next number		

What is the first number?_____

4. Debbie is three times as old as her daughter Aisling. In 10 years she will be twice as old as Aisling. How old is Debbie now?

Unknown Amounts	Now	In 10 Years	Equation
Aisling's age			
Debbie's age			

How old is Debbie now?_____

Directions: Choose the one best answer for each item.

5. Which of the following values is in the solution set for $5m + 15 > 30$?

   (1) 4
   (2) 3
   (3) 2
   (4) 1
   (5) 0

6. Twice as many women as men voted during the local election. If 3,600 individuals voted, how many women voted?

   (1) 1,200
   (2) 1,500
   (3) 2,000
   (4) 2,400
   (5) 3,000

7. An adult ticket to the movie cost $2 more than a child's ticket. A preschool spent $100 to pay for 10 children and 5 adults to see the movie. How much did each child's ticket cost?

   (1) $4
   (2) $6
   (3) $7.50
   (4) $8
   (5) $10

8. John wants to use a length of no more than 22 feet to install 3 bookshelves of equal length on a wall in his office. Which of the following lengths (in feet) of bookshelves can he use?

   (1) 7
   (2) 8
   (3) 9
   (4) 10
   (5) Not enough information is given.

9. Last week Carmen drove round-trip to work each day Monday through Friday. She also drove 74 miles round-trip on Wednesday evening to see a play. The car's odometer shows that Carmen drove a total of 324 miles last week. How many miles is her round-trip drive to work?

   (1) 12
   (2) 25
   (3) 50
   (4) 60
   (5) 72

10. The sum of three consecutive numbers is 159. What is the greater number?

   (1) 46
   (2) 47
   (3) 51
   (4) 52
   (5) 54

11. Sharon is 4 years younger than Kenny. In 5 years, three times Sharon's age will equal twice Kenny's age. How old is Sharon now?

   (1) 3
   (2) 7
   (3) 11
   (4) 15
   (5) 19

Check your answers on page 419.

Exercise 15

Directions: These are miscellaneous algebra problems. Treat these problems like an alternate-format question where you would need to fill out a standard grid. (*Calculator permitted.*)

1. Three consecutive numbers total 51. What is the second number?

2. The sum of two numbers is 87, and their difference is 13. What is the greater number?

3. A change-making machine contains $30 in dimes and quarters. There are 150 coins in the machine. Find the number of quarters in the machine.

4. Brian has scores of 88, 87, and 92 on his first three tests. What grade must he get on his next test to have an overall average of 90?

Check your answers on page 420.

Unit 10

GEOMETRY

Geometry (Greek: *geo* means 'earth'; *metrein*, means 'to measure') is the branch of mathematics that deals with measuring and exploring the properties of space. One form of geometry involves studying problems such as calculating the areas and diameters of two-dimensional figures and the surface areas and volumes of solids. The ancient Greeks Pythagorus and Euclid are given the honor of introducing the rudiments of plane and solid geometry. Then, in the seventeenth century, French mathematician and philosopher René Descartes combined algebra with geometry to create a new and useful branch of mathematics called analytic geometry, or coordinate geometry. This involves representing straight lines, curves, and other geometric figures by numerical and algebraic expressions using a set of axes and coordinates. Descartes introduced the Cartesian coordinate system, which states that any point in a plane may be located with respect to a pair of axes that are perpendicular to each other. This is done by specifying the distance of the point from each of these axes where the intersection of the axes acts as a reference or origin. More detailed explanation of the Cartesian (Rectangular) Coordinate system is given later in this unit.

Example:

The origin is always at (0,0). You want to find the point (3,−2). So count three units to the right for positive on the *x*-axis and two units down for negative on the *y*-axis. Remember, right (*x*-axis) and up (*y*-axis) is positive and left (*x*-axis) and down (*y*-axis) is negative.

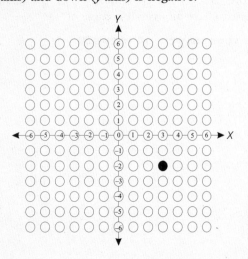

Lines and Angles

Parallel lines are lines on the same plane (a flat surface) that do not meet or intersect. Parallel lines remain an equal distance apart at every point. **Intersecting lines** are lines that *do* cross or intersect. Remember that when lines cross, they form angles. Those angles are measured in degrees (°).

A line that intersects two or more parallel lines is a **transversal**. In the figures below, lines A and B are parallel. Line C is a transversal. The intersecting lines form 8 angles.

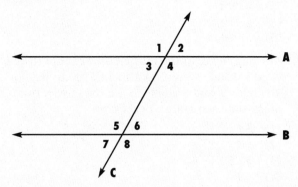

In the figure above, the following pairs of angles are equal:

Corresponding Angles	Vertical Angles	Alternate Angles
∠1 and ∠5	∠1 and ∠4	∠3 and ∠6
∠2 and ∠6	∠2 and ∠3	∠4 and ∠5
∠3 and ∠7	∠5 and ∠8	∠1 and ∠8
∠4 and ∠8	∠6 and ∠7	∠2 and ∠7

Another kind of angle is a straight angle. A **straight angle** is an angle whose sides lie on a straight line. A straight angle measures 180°.

If the sum of two angles is 180°, then the angles are **supplementary angles**. Angles 1 and 2 above are supplementary. If you know the measure of one of the angles, you can figure out the measure of the other.

Example:

If m∠1 = 100°, what is the measure of ∠2?
180° − 100° = 80°   m∠2 = 80°

When the sum of two angles is 90°, the angles are **complementary angles**. If you know the measure of one angle, you can find the measure of the other.

Example:

m∠A = 40°. What is the measure of ∠B?

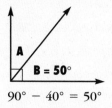

90° − 40° = 50°

Example:

Line AB is a transversal within two parallel lines.

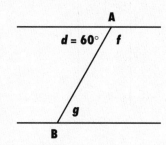

Find the measure of ∠g.

Angle g is an alternate angle to ∠d, so ∠g is also 60°.

Find the measure of ∠f.

Angle f is a supplementary angle to ∠d, so ∠f is 120°.

(180° − 60°) = 120°

Exercise 1

Directions: Items 1–4 refer to the following lines.

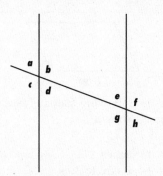

1. If m∠a is 70°, what is the measure of ∠b?

2. If m∠a is 70°, what is the measure of ∠e?

3. Name all the angles that are equivalent to ∠a.

4. Name all the angles that are equivalent to ∠b.

5. ∠X and ∠Y are complementary. If ∠X measures 35°, what is the measure of ∠Y?

(1) 55°
(2) 65°
(3) 90°
(4) 145°
(5) Not enough information is given.

Item 6 refers to the following diagram.

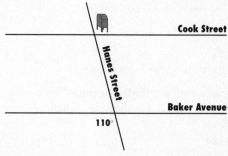

6. What is the angle of the intersection of Cook and Hanes Streets where the mailbox is to be installed?

(1) 70°
(2) 75°
(3) 80°
(4) 85°
(5) 110°

7. ∠3 and ∠4 are supplementary angles. ∠4 measures 90°. Which is a true statement?

(1) You cannot know the measure of ∠3.
(2) ∠3 and ∠4 are complementary angles.
(3) ∠3 and ∠4 are vertical angles.
(4) ∠3 measures 90°.
(5) The measures of ∠3 and ∠4 are not equal.

Check your answers on page 420.

Area of a Parallelogram

A **parallelogram** is a four-sided figure whose opposite sides are parallel and equal to each other. The longer side of the parallelogram is called the **base**, similar to the length of a rectangle. A line perpendicular to the bases is called the **height**. In the parallelogram below, the base is 8cm and the height is 4cm.

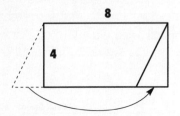

Use this formula to find the area:

> **Area (A) of a parallelogram:**
> $A = bh$, where b = base, h = height

Example:

Find the area of the parallelogram above.

Substitute 8 for b and 4 for h in $A = bh$.

> $A = 8(4)$
> $8(4) = 32$ square centimeters
> 32 sq cm, or 32cm^2

The area of the parallelogram is 32 sq cm.

Exercise 2

> **Directions:** Find the area of each parallelogram below.

1.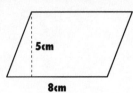

2.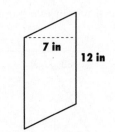

3.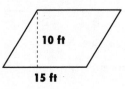

4.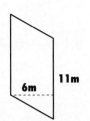

> **Directions:** Item 5 refers to the parallelogram below.

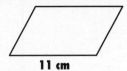

5. Which of the following statements is true for the parallelogram shown?

   (1) $P = 32$ inches
   (2) $P = 44$ inches
   (3) $A = 44$ square inches
   (4) $A = 56$ in^2
   (5) Not enough information is given.

Check your answers on page 420.

Types of Triangles

All **triangles** have 3 sides and 3 angles. The sum of the angles of any triangle is *always* equal to 180°. A triangle is defined by the measures of its angles and sides.

An **equilateral triangle** has 3 sides of equal length and 3 angles that measure 60° each. ΔABC is an equilateral triangle.

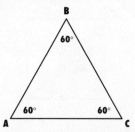

An **isosceles triangle** has two sides of equal length and two equal angles of equal measure called base angles. The third angle of an isosceles triangle is called the **vertex angle**. ΔJKL is an isosceles triangle.

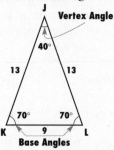

You know that a right angle measures 90°. A **right triangle** has one right (90°) angle. The longest side of a right triangle, called the **hypotenuse**, is directly across from the right angle. The other sides of a right triangle are called **legs**. ΔDEF and ΔGHI are right triangles.

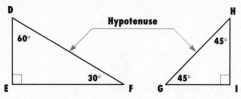

A **scalene triangle** has no sides of equal length and no angles of equal measure. ΔPQR is a scalene triangle.

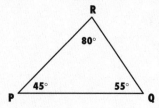

Exercise 3

Directions: Choose the <u>one best answer</u> for each item.

Item 1 refers to the following triangle.

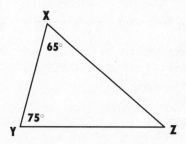

1. What kind of triangle is ΔXYZ?

    (1) Equilateral
    (2) Right
    (3) Scalene
    (4) Isosceles
    (5) Not enough information is given.

2. The measure of the angles of ΔRST are 30°, 60°, and 90°. What kind of triangle is ΔRST?

    (1) Equilateral
    (2) Right
    (3) Isosceles
    (4) Scalene
    (5) Not enough information is given.

Items 3 and 4 refer to the following triangle.

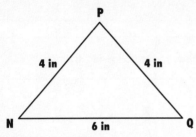

3. In $\triangle$NPQ, $\overline{NP}$ and $\overline{PQ}$ each measure 4 inches. What kind of triangle is $\triangle$NPQ?

    (1) Equilateral
    (2) Right
    (3) Scalene
    (4) Isosceles
    (5) Not enough information is given.

4. If $\angle$N and $\angle$Q each measure 65°, what is the measure of $\angle$P?

    (1) 30°
    (2) 50°
    (3) 65°
    (4) 130°
    (5) Not enough information is given.

Check your answers on page 420.

Perimeter and Area of a Triangle

What is the perimeter of the triangle below? The perimeter of any triangle can be found by adding the measure of all the sides.

Perimeter (P) of a triangle:

    $P = a + b + c$, where a, b, and c are the sides.

Example:

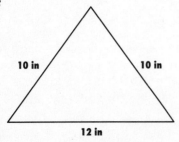

The perimeter of the triangle above is found by substituting the values given for the sides a, b, and c in $P = a + b + c$.

    $P = 10 + 10 + 12$

    $P = 32$ inches

When a rectangle, square, or other parallelogram is cut in half diagonally, two equal triangles are formed. How does this fact help you to find a triangle's area?

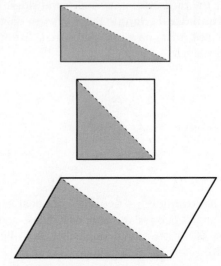

To find the area of each triangle in the figures above, you would find the area of the rectangle, square, or parallelogram and take half of it.

Area (A) of a triangle:

    $A = \dfrac{1}{2}bh$, where b = base, and h = height

As in a parallelogram, the height of the triangle must be perpendicular to the base. Sometimes the height of the triangle appears outside the triangle itself.

Examples:

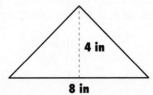

The height is shown within the triangle.

    $A = \dfrac{1}{2}bh$

    $A = \dfrac{1}{2}(8)(4)$

    $A = 16$ in^2

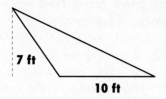

The height is shown outside of the triangle.

$A = \frac{1}{2}bh$

$A = \frac{1}{2}(10)(7)$

$A = 35$ sq ft

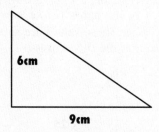

The height of a right triangle is the side that forms a right angle with the base.

$A = \frac{1}{2}bh$

$A = \frac{1}{2}(9)(6)$

$A = 27$cm^2

Exercise 4

Directions: Find the perimeter and area of each of the following triangles.

1.

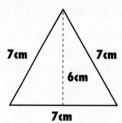

Perimeter = _____

Area = _____

2.

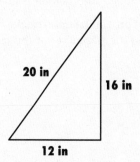

Perimeter = _____

Area = _____

Directions: Choose the <u>one best answer</u> for each item.

3. ΔGHJ is an equilateral triangle with a side of 6 inches. Which of the following statements is true based on the information given?

(1) The height of ΔGHJ is also 6 inches.

(2) The area of ΔGHJ can be found using
$A = \frac{1}{2}(6)(6)$.

(3) The base of ΔGHJ is the longest side.

(4) The perimeter of ΔGHJ can be found using
$P = 6 + 6 + 6$.

(5) The largest angle of ΔGHJ is a right angle.

4. How many square cm are enclosed in ΔMNO with a height of 14cm and a base of 20cm?

(1) 70

(2) 140

(3) 200

(4) 280

(5) Not enough information is given.

5. How many cm are needed to go around ΔMNO with a height of 14 cm and a base of 20cm?

　　(1)　28
　　(2)　34
　　(3)　47
　　(4)　54
　　(5)　Not enough information is given.

6. Smith City Hall has a triangular garden. The sides measure 6 ft, 10 ft, and 10 ft. The landscaper is going to install a trim around the edges. How many feet of trim does he need?

　　(1)　26
　　(2)　30
　　(3)　52
　　(4)　60
　　(5)　Not enough information is given.

7. One side of an equilateral triangle measures 12 inches. Find the perimeter of the triangle in inches.

　　(1)　24
　　(2)　36
　　(3)　48
　　(4)　72
　　(5)　144

8. Two sides of a scalene triangle measure 18 inches and 13 inches. What is the perimeter of the triangle in inches?

　　(1)　31
　　(2)　44
　　(3)　49
　　(4)　62
　　(5)　Not enough information is given.

Check your answers on page 420.

Right Triangles and the Pythagorean Theorem

A Greek mathematician, Pythagoras, discovered a relationship between the measure of the legs and the hypotenuse of a right triangle. The relationship known as the Pythagorean theorem is shown on the formula sheet.

Pythagorean theorem:

$$c^2 = a^2 + b^2,$$

where c = hypotenuse, a and b are legs of a right triangle.

The hypotenuse is the longest side of the right triangle. It is across from the right angle and is always represented in the formula by c. In the figure below, $c = 25$. Either leg may be a or b. When these values are substituted in the formula, you see that the theorem is true.

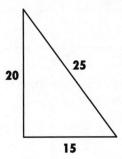

Example:

$$c^2 = a^2 + b^2$$
$$(25)^2 = (15)^2 + (20)^2$$
$$625 = 225 + 400$$

To find the unknown side of a right triangle, substitute the known values for the variables and solve the equation.

Example:

Find the hypotenuse of a right triangle with one leg = 9cm and the other leg = 12cm.

$$c^2 = a^2 + b^2$$
$$c^2 = (9)^2 + (12)^2$$
$$c^2 = 81 + 144$$
$$c^2 = 225$$

To solve for c, find $\sqrt{225}$. The value of c is 15.

Example:

Find the hypotenuse of a right triangle with legs that are 18 ft and 24 ft long.

Most Pythagorean problems on the GED Math Test utilize 3:4:5 or 5:12:13 ratios.

Look at the values for 3:4:5 right triangles shown in the table below.

Leg (a)	Leg (b)	Hypotenuse (c)
3	4	5
6 3(2)	8 4(2)	10 5(2)
9 3(3)	12 4(3)	15 5(3)
12 3(4)	16 4(4)	20 5(4)
15 3(5)	20 4(5)	25 5(5)

A shortcut to find the hypotenuse in the problem above is to check to see if the lengths given fit into a 3:4:5 ratio.

As 18 is 3(6) and 24 is 4(6), the hypotenuse must be 5(6), or 30.

You can check the answer using the Pythagorean formula.

$$c^2 = a^2 + b^2$$
$$30^2 = 18^2 + 24^2$$
$$900 = 324 + 576$$

Example:

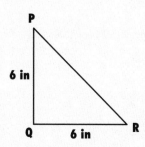

Find the length of the hypotenuse in ΔPQR.

The solution to some problems, such as this one, may require estimating the square root.

$$c^2 = a^2 + b^2$$
$$c^2 = (6)^2 + (6)^2$$
$$c^2 = 36 + 36$$
$$c = \sqrt{72}$$

The square root of 72 is not a whole number. It is between $\sqrt{64}$ and $\sqrt{81}$. The square root of 72 is between 8 and 9, so the length of the hypotenuse is between 8 and 9 inches long.

Exercise 5

Directions: Find the missing side of the following right triangles.

	Leg A	Leg B	Hypotenuse
1.	3	4	_____
2.	6	_____	10
3.	8	8	_____
4.	_____	40	50

Directions: Choose the one best answer for each item.

5. Which expression equals the length in centimeters of the second leg of a right triangle with a leg that equals 48cm and a hypotenuse that equals 60cm?

   (1) $\sqrt{1,024}$
   (2) $\sqrt{1,296}$
   (3) $\sqrt{1,600}$
   (4) $\sqrt{2,304}$
   (5) $\sqrt{2,916}$

6. Tammy placed a 20-foot ladder against the house to reach the second-floor windows. The bottom of the ladder was 6 feet away from the house. About how many feet above the ground were the second-floor windows?

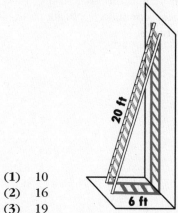

   (1) 10
   (2) 16
   (3) 19
   (4) 22
   (5) Not enough information is given.

Check your answers on page 420.

385

Congruent and Similar Triangles

Congruent triangles are identical figures. In congruent triangles, the three corresponding angles are equal in length and the three corresponding sides are equal in length.

    Similar triangles are the same shape, but they may not be the same size. In similar triangles, all three corresponding angles are equal in measure, and the corresponding sides are in proportion to one another.

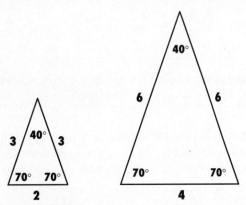

The triangles shown above are similar. All three corresponding angles are equal in measure and the proportion of *corresponding* sides is true.

$$\frac{2}{3} = \frac{4}{6}$$

$$3(4) = 2(6)$$

$$12 = 12$$

If you know that two triangles are similar, you can solve for a missing angle or side using ratio and proportion. Study these common applications of similar triangles in word problems.

Shadow of objects at the same time of day

    At 3 p.m. yesterday, a flagpole cast a shadow 10 feet long. At the same time, a 3-foot stick placed perpendicular to the ground cast a 1-foot shadow. How many feet tall is the flagpole?

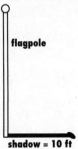

flagpole

shadow = 10 ft

yardstick

shadow = 1 ft

    Sketch the situation. Both figures make a right angle (90°) with the ground, and the sun shines on both objects at the same angle. Therefore, the situation described is about similar triangles with two equal angles.

    To find the length of the shadow, set up a proportion.

$$\frac{\text{object}}{\text{shadow}} \qquad \frac{3}{1} = \frac{x}{10} \qquad \frac{\text{object}}{\text{shadow}}$$

$$3(10) = 1(x)$$

$$30 = x$$

The flagpole is 30 feet tall.

Distance across a lake, pond, or river

What is the distance across the river?

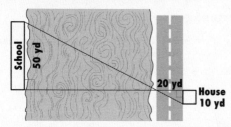

On the GED Math Test, a sketch is usually given with this type of problem. Notice that the lines form a large and small right triangle.

The intersection of the triangles are vertical angles. Vertical angles are equal, so those angles and the right angles are the two angles that prove that the triangles are similar.

To find the distance across the river, set up a proportion.

$$\frac{\text{long side}}{\text{base}} \quad \frac{20}{10} = \frac{x}{50} \quad \frac{\text{long side (across river)}}{\text{base}}$$

$$20(50) = 10(x)$$
$$1{,}000 = 10x$$
$$100 = x$$

It is 100 yards across the river.

Small triangle within a large triangle

What is the length of AB?

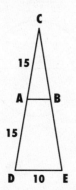

∠C is in both triangles. ∠A and ∠D are corresponding angles. They are in corresponding positions because a transversal (AD) crosses two parallel lines (AB and DE). Therefore, ΔDEC and ΔABC are similar.

To find the length of AB, set up a proportion.

$$\frac{\text{CD}(15 + 15)}{\text{DE}} \quad \frac{30}{10} = \frac{15}{x} \quad \frac{\text{AC}}{\text{AB}}$$

$$10(15) = 30(x)$$
$$150 = 30x$$
$$5 = x$$

AB is 5 inches.

Exercise 6

Directions: Choose the one best answer for each item.

Item 1 refers to the following diagram.

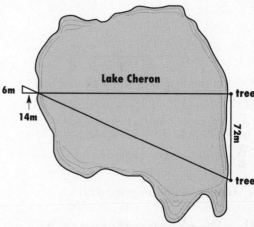

1. Surveyors are finding the distance in meters across Lake Cheron. First the distance between two trees on the opposite shore is measured. Then the surveyors stake out two similar right triangles. Using the measurements in the diagram, what is the distance in meters across the lake?

   (1) 84
   (2) 144
   (3) 168
   (4) 432
   (5) Not enough information is given.

2. At 5 p.m., an 8-foot signpost cast a shadow 12 ft long. At the same time, a tree cast a shadow 45 ft long. How tall in feet is the tree?

   (1) 20
   (2) 30
   (3) 45
   (4) 96
   (5) Not enough information is given.

Item 3 refers to the isosceles triangle below.

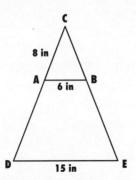

3. What is the length of side CE in inches?

   (1) 12
   (2) 14
   (3) 20
   (4) 27
   (5) 51

Check your answers on page 421.

Finding the Circumference of a Circle

A **circle** is a curved line in which every point on the curve is an equal distance from another point called the **center**.

The distance across a circle through its center is called the **diameter**. The distance around a circle is called the **circumference**. The ancient Greeks discovered a relationship between diameter and circumference. They used the Greek letter **pi** (π) to name the amount by which the diameter must be multiplied to find the circumference. They soon learned to use pi to find the area of a circle and the volume of a cylinder.

The circumference of a circle is a little more than 3 times the diameter. This value is called pi (π). Archimedes *approximated* π to be between $3\frac{1}{7}$ and $3\frac{10}{71}$. On the formula sheet given with your GED Math Test, π is rounded off to 3.14. Sometimes it is expressed as $\frac{22}{7}$.

The formula for finding the distance around a circle is as follows.

Circumference (*C*) of a circle:

$C = \pi d$, where $\pi = 3.14$ and $d =$ diameter

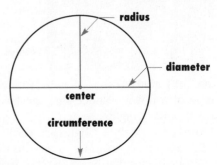

Example:

Find the circumference of a circle with a diameter of 5cm.

$C = \pi d$

$C = 3.14(5)$

$C = 15.7$cm

Exercise 7

Directions: Find the circumference of each of the following circles. Use the formula $C = \pi d$, where $\pi = 3.14$ and $d =$ diameter.

1.

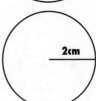

2.

3. How many feet long is the circumference of a circle with a diameter of 6 feet?

   (1) 3.14
   (2) 9.46
   (3) 12.0
   (4) 18.84
   (5) 37.68

Check your answers on page 421.

Finding the Area of a Circle

The area of a circle is also an estimate found by using 3.14 for the value of π.

The formula is:

Area (A) of a circle:

$A = \pi r^2$, where $\pi = 3.14$ and r = radius

To find the area of a circle, take the radius to the second power and multiply it by 3.14 for π.

Example:

Find the area of a circle with a radius of 8 in.

$A = \pi r^2$

Remember to simplify exponents first.

$A = 3.14(8)^2$

$A = 3.14(64)$

$A = 200.96$ square inches

Remember that the radius is half of the diameter. To find the radius when the diameter is given, divide the diameter by 2.

Exercise 8

Directions: Find the area of each of the following circles. Use the formula $A = \pi r^2$, where $\pi = 3.14$ and r = radius.

1.

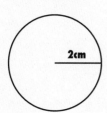

1 ft

2.

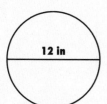

12 in

3.

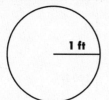

2 cm

4. Which of these expressions would be used to find the area of a circle with a radius of 2.5 m?

   (1) 3.14(2.5)

   (2) 3.14(5)

   (3) 3.14(5)(5)

   (4) 3.14(2.5)(2.5)

   (5) Not enough information is given.

5. J'lene is very proud of her circular garden. She arranged plants and flowers in the center and a stone walkway around them as shown.

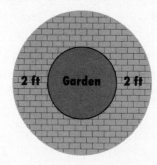

If the walkway is 2 feet wide, what is the area of the walkway?

   (1) 12.56

   (2) 15.7

   (3) 37.68

   (4) 50.24

   (5) Not enough information is given.

Check your answers on page 421.

Finding the Volume of a Cylinder

A three-dimensional figure with a circular base is a **cylinder**. To find the volume of a cylinder, you must find the area of the base and multiply it by the height of the cylinder.

The formula is:

Volume (V) of a Cylinder:

$V = \pi r^2 h$, where $\pi = 3.14$, r = radius, and h = height

Remember to simplify the exponent before completing the other multiplication.

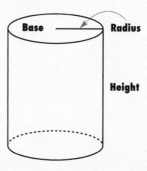

389

Example:

Find the volume of a cylinder with a height of 6 feet and a base with a 2-foot radius.

$$V = \pi r^2 h$$
$$V = 3.14(2)^2(6)$$
$$V = 3.14(4)(6)$$
$$V = 3.14(24)$$
$$V = 75.36$$

Volume is given in cubic units. The volume of the cylinder above is 75.36 cubic feet.

Example:

Which expression would be used to find how many cubic meters are contained in the cylinder below?

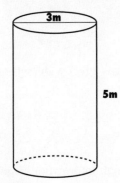

(1) $3.14(3)^2(5)$
(2) $3.14(1.5)^2(5)$
(3) $3.14(5)^2(3)$
(4) $3.14(5)^2(1.5)$
(5) Not enough information is given.

The formula uses the radius, so the diameter must be divided by 2. (3 ÷ 2 = 1.5) Then substitute this value for the radius (*r*) and 5 for the height (*h*) in the formula.

$3.14(1.5)^2(5)$

The correct answer is (2).

Exercise 9

Directions: Find the volume of the following figures. Use the formula $V = \pi r^2 h$, where $\pi = 3.14$, r = radius, and h = height.

1.

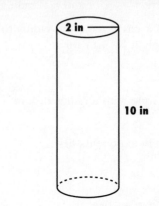

2.

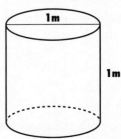

3.

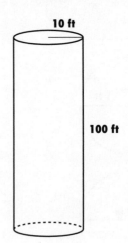

Directions: Choose the <u>one best answer</u> for each item.

4. Which expression would be used to find the volume of a cylinder with a height of 500cm and a radius of 100cm?

(1) $3.14(100)^2$
(2) $3.14(500)^2$
(3) $3.14(100)^2(500)$
(4) $3.14(500)^2(100)$
(5) $3.14(100)^2+(500)$

5. How many inches tall is a cylinder with a volume of 31.4 in³ and a radius of 1 inch?

(1) 1
(2) 5
(3) 8
(4) 10
(5) Not enough information is given.

Item 6 refers to the following cylinder.

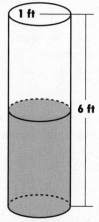

6. The water heater shown above is half full. How many cubic feet of water does it *now* hold?

(1) 6.00
(2) 9.42
(3) 18.84
(4) 37.68
(5) 54.99

Item 7 refers to the following figures.

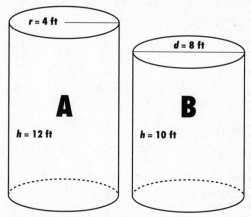

7. About how many more cubic feet does cylinder A hold than cylinder B?

(1) 20
(2) 100
(3) 200
(4) 230
(5) Not enough information is given.

Check your answers on page 421.

Coordinate Geometry

The **coordinate plane** is formed from two number lines. The ***x*-axis** is horizontal. The ***y*-axis** is the vertical number line. This lesson combines algebra and geometry to show how the positive and negative values for variables x and y in an equation can be graphed as a line.

All points on the coordinate plane can be identified by counting from the point where the *x*- and *y*-axes cross, called the **origin**. First count right or left, then count up or down. These directions are indicated by the coordinates of a point (x, y). Each line in the grid represents a whole number distance.

The *x*-coordinate, given first, tells how many places to count right or left along the *x*-axis. The *y*-coordinate, given next, tells how many places to count up or down from the *x*-value. Count right or up for positive values and left or down for negative ones.

To plot the point $(3, -1)$ on a coordinate plane, place your pencil at the origin. Then move your pencil 3 lines to the right along the *x*-axis. From there, move 1 line down parallel to the *y*-axis. This is point $(3, -1)$.

391

Exercise 10

Directions: Write the correct letter next to the coordinates of each point listed below.

1. (3, 4)
2. (3, −4)
3. (−3, −4)
4. (−3, 4)
5. (1, −2)
6. (−6, 0)
7. (0, 6)
8. (5, −4)
9. (−3, −3)
10. (5, 3)
11. (−1, 5)
12. (0, −4)

13. Plot the following points on the graph below, and label them with the correct letter name.

M (1, 1)
N (−2, −2)
P (5, −2)
Q (−5, 5)
R (0, −4)
S (3, 0)
T (−3, −1)
V (4, −3)
W (0, 1)
X (4, 4)
Y (−3, 0)
Z (−4, 3)

Check your answers on page 421.

Graphing a Line

You know that in the equation $10 = x + 2$, x must equal 8 to make the equation true. In the equation $y = x + 2$, what value for x will make the equation true?

The value of y in the equation $y = x + 2$ depends on the value of x.

If . . .	Then . . .	Therefore . . .	Coordinates . . .
$x = 0$	$y = 0 + 2$	$y = 2$	**(0, 2)**
$x = 1$	$y = 1 + 2$	$y = 3$	**(1, 3)**
$x = 2$	$y = 2 + 2$	$y = 4$	**(2, 4)**
$x = 3$	$y = 3 + 2$	$y = 5$	**(3, 5)**
$x = -1$	$y = -1 + 2$	$y = 1$	**(−1, 1)**
$x = -4$	$y = -4 + 2$	$y = -2$	**(−4, −2)**

The x and y values become coordinates of points. The coordinates in the table above are plotted on the graph below. What do you notice about these points?

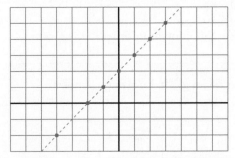

A straight line can be drawn through all of the points that satisfy the equation $y = x + 2$. Draw the line. This line, as other lines, goes on in both directions to infinity (with no end).

An equation with 2 variables is a **linear equation** because its solutions form a straight line. It is impossible to show all the possible combinations for x and y that would make this equation true, so the solution to the equation is a graph of the line.

Test-Taking Tip:
It is recommended that you find at least three points on the line. If you find only two and make a mistake with either one, the line will be incorrect. However, if you find three points on a straight line, then you can be confident that it is correct.

Example:

Graph the solution to $y = 2x - 4$.

To find the line that is the solution to any equation:

Step 1	Make a table with a column for *x*-val-		**x**	**y**
	ues and a column for *y*-values. List		0	
	any three values for x in the x col-		1	
	umn. Any numbers will do.		2	

Step 2 Substitute each value for x into the equation and solve for y. Write these values for y in the y-column. Be sure to keep them in the correct order.

$$y = 2x - 4$$

		x	y
when $x = 0$, $y = 2(0) - 4 = -4$		0	-4
when $x = 1$, $y = 2(1) - 4 = -2$		1	-2
when $x = 2$, $y = 2(2) - 4 = 0$		2	0

Step 3 Plot the points, and draw a line through them.

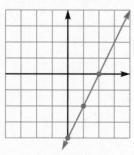

This is the graph of the equation $y = 2x - 4$.

Exercise 11

Directions: Complete a table for the following equation. Then plot the points to draw the graph of the line.

1. $y = x + 4$

x	y
-2	
-1	
0	
1	

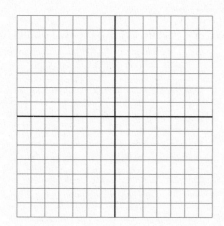

Directions: Choose the one best answer for each item.

Items 2 and 3 refer to the following graph.

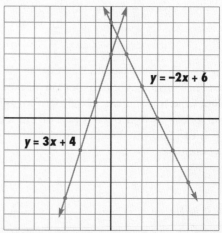

2. Benny was graphing the equation of the line $y = -2x + 6$. He made the following table for the coordinates.

Point	x	y
A	0	6
B	-1	4
C	-2	10

Which of the following statements is true?

   (1) His table is correct, and all three points are on the line $y = -2x + 6$.
   (2) Point A is incorrect. It will not fall on the line $y = -2x + 6$.
   (3) Point B is incorrect. It will not fall on the line $y = -2x + 6$.
   (4) Point C is incorrect. It will not fall on the line $y = -2x + 6$.
   (5) None of the points is correct.

3. Which of the following are coordinates of a point on the line $y = 3x + 4$?

   (1) $(0, -4)$
   (2) $(1, 7)$
   (3) $(1, 4)$
   (4) $(2, 2)$
   (5) None of the above

Check your answers on page 422.

393

Using a Formula to Find the Distance between Points

Example:

What is the distance between points *A* and *B* below?

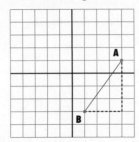

The dotted lines form a right triangle. The distance from *A* to *B* becomes the hypotenuse of the right triangle. If you count line spaces to find the lengths of the legs of the triangle, you can find the distance from *A* to *B* by solving for the hypotenuse.

$$c^2 = a^2 + b^2$$
$$c^2 = 3^2 + 4^2$$
$$c^2 = 9 + 16$$
$$c = \sqrt{25}$$
$$c = 5$$

Since the points are not on the same vertical or horizontal line, the distance cannot be counted simply by counting line spaces. To find the distance between any two points, you can use the formula given on the GED formula page.

The formula is stated:

Distance (*d*) between the two points in a plane:

$$d = \sqrt{(x_2 - x_1)^2 + (y_2 - y_1)^2}$$

where (x_1, y_1) and (x_2, y_2) are two points in a plane

Step 1 Use the coordinates of point *A* (4,1) as (x_2, y_2) and the coordinates of point *B* (1, −3) as (x_1, y_1).

Step 2 Substitute these into the formula.

$$d = \sqrt{(x_2 - x_1)^2 + (y_2 - y_1)^2}$$
$$d = \sqrt{(4 - 1)^2 + (1 - (-3))^2}$$

Step 3 Simplify and solve the equation.

$$d = \sqrt{(3)^2 + (1 + 3)^2}$$
$$d = \sqrt{(3)^2 + (4)^2}$$
$$d = \sqrt{9 + 16}$$
$$d = \sqrt{25}$$
$$d = 5$$

The distance between points *A* and *B* is 5.

Exercise 12

Directions: Find the distance between the points listed. Items 1–4 refer to the graph below.

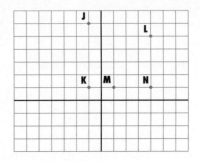

1. *J* (−1, 6) and *K* (−1, 1)

2. *M* (1, 1) and *N* (4, 1)

3. *L* (4, 5) and *N* (4, 1)

4. *L* (4, 5) and *M* (1, 1)

5. (5, 9) and (−1, 1)

Check your answers on page 422.

Slope of a Line

The **slope** of a line is the measure of the slant or incline of the line.

Slope is written as a ratio that compares

$$\frac{\text{change in } y\text{-units}}{\text{change in } x\text{-units}} \quad \frac{\text{up or down}}{\text{right or left}}$$

The slope can also be found by using a formula given on the formula sheet.

Slope (*m*) of a Line:

$$m = \frac{y_2 - y_1}{x_2 - x_1}$$

where (x_1, y_1) and (x_2, y_2) are two points in a plane

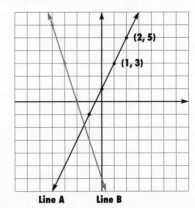

To use the formula to find the slope of Line A, *y* = 2*x* + 1:

Step 1 Choose any two points on the line.

x	y
1	3
2	5

Step 2 Substitute the values in the formula and subtract.

$$\frac{y_2 - y_1}{x_2 - x_1}$$

$$\frac{5 - 3}{2 - 1} = \frac{2}{1} = 2$$

The slope is 2.

each time count $\dfrac{\text{up 2 and}}{\text{over 1}}$

Lines that go up from left to right, such as Line A, have a *positive slope*. Lines that go down from left to right, such as Line B, have a *negative slope*.

Exercise 13

Directions: Find the slope in each of the following.

1. $y = 3x - 1$

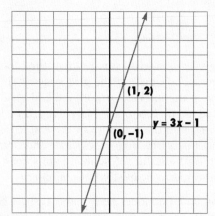

2. $y = 4$

3. Find the slope of the line that passes through the points $(4, 5)$ and $(8, 9)$.

4. Find the slope of the line that passes through the points $(-1, 3)$ and $(3, -1)$.

Check your answers on page 422.

Equation of the Line (Slope and *y*-intercept)

In the equation of the line $y = 2x + 1$, the numbers 2 and 1 have special significance; in the equation $y = -4x - 3$, the numbers -4 and -3 have special significance.

Look at the graph of these lines below.

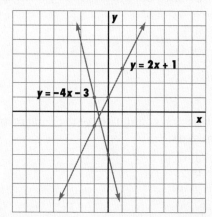

Notice that the line $y = 2x + 1$ crosses the *y*-axis at $(0, 1)$.

The line $y = -4x - 3$ crosses the *y*-axis at $(0, -3)$.

The point where the line crosses the *y*-axis is called the *y*-**intercept**. The value of x is 0 at the *y*-axis.

In any equation in the form $y = mx + b$, the value added or subtracted from the *x*-value is equal to the *y*-intercept.

Example:

What are the coordinates of the *y*-intercept of the line $y = -2x - 7$?

The value of x is 0 at the *y*-intercept.

The *y*-intercept of the line $y = -2x - 7$ is -7.

Therefore, the coordinates of the *y*-intercept are $(0, -7)$.

The slope of the line $y = 2x + 1$ is $\dfrac{2}{1}$.

The slope of the line $y = -4x - 3$ is $-\dfrac{4}{1}$.

In any equation in the form $y = mx + b$, m **(the coefficient of x) is equal to the slope of the line**. The formula for slope of a line uses m as slope.

$$m = \frac{y_2 - y_1}{x_2 - x_1}$$

Exercise 14

Directions: Find the slope and *y*-intercept as directed in the following.

1. What are the coordinates of the *y*-intercept of the line $y = 4x - 6$?

   (1) (0, 6)
   (2) (0, 4)
   (3) (−6, 0)
   (4) (4, 0)
   (5) (0, −6)

2. What are the coordinates of the *y*-intercept of the line $y = 3x + 2$?

   (1) (3, 0)
   (2) (0, 2)
   (3) (2, 0)
   (4) (0, 3)
   (5) (0, −2)

3. The point with the coordinates (0, −3) is the *y*-intercept of which of the following lines?

   (1) $y = -3x + 2$
   (2) $y = -2x + 3$
   (3) $y = -3x - 3$
   (4) $y = x$
   (5) Not enough information is given.

4. What is the slope of the line $y = 4x + 2$?

   (1) $\dfrac{2}{1}$

   (2) $-\dfrac{4}{1}$

   (3) $\dfrac{1}{4}$

   (4) $\dfrac{4}{1}$

   (5) Not enough information is given.

Check your answers on page 422.

Exercise 15

Directions: These are miscellaneous geometry problems. Treat these problems like an alternate-format question where you would need to fill out a standard grid. (*Calculator permitted.*)

1. Susan bought several containers of a special liquid building material for her class project. She wants to consolidate all the material into one big container. According to the picture, how many of the little containers of the liquid will she be able to fit into the big container? Round answer to nearest tenths.

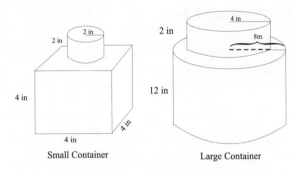

Small Container   Large Container

2. Mary lives in a small town where the blocks follow a coordinate plane grid system. There is a statue at the intersection of First and Main, which is used as the reference. Mary lives three blocks east and two blocks south of the statue, and her friend Tasha lives five blocks east and four blocks north of the statue. How many units apart do they live? Round to nearest whole number.

3. If you could connect Mary's and Tasha's houses (from the previous problem) with a straight line, what would be the slope of that line?

4. Find the area of this irregular shape. The corners have had quarter circles cut out. Round answer to nearest tenth.

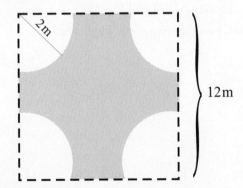

12m

Check your answers on page 422.

Exercise 16

Directions: The following are problems that require to be answered on a coordinate plane grid.

1. Mark the point $(-3, -2)$ on the coordinate plane grid.

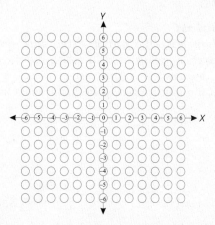

2. Justin lives in the same town as Mary and Tasha (see problem 2, ex. 15). Justin lives three blocks north and six blocks west of where Mary lives. Mark the coordinate plane grid where Justin lives.

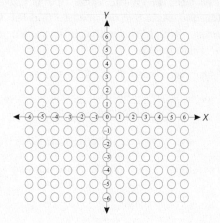

3. A circle is circumscribed around a square so that the diagonal of the square is the diameter of the circle. Look at the diagram. Mark the center of the circle on the coordinate plane grid.

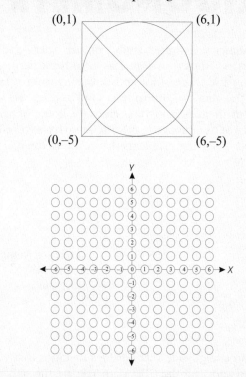

4. $\triangle ABC$ is an isosceles triangle. $\overline{BC}$ is the base. The altitude is 7 units. The coordinates of B and C are $B(-2, -5)$, $C(4, -5)$. Mark the coordinate of the vertex A on the coordinate plane grid.

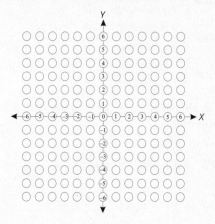

Check your answers on page 422.

Unit 11

TRIGONOMETRY

Trigonometry is the study of triangles and their properties. Numerous formulas have been derived from studying the three sides and three angles of a triangle. Since the time of Hipparchus (140 B.C.E.), an ancient Greek mathematician who is given the honor of being the founder of trigonometry, the discipline has evolved into a method of solving problems that relate to the real world.

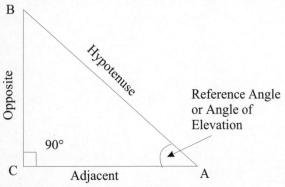

The three angle-side relationships or ratios that you will need to know for the GED Math Test are the sine, cosine, and tangent. We use the abbreviated form in the formulas.

$$sin\theta = \frac{Opposite}{Hypotenuse} = \frac{O}{H}$$

$$cos\theta = \frac{Adjacent}{Hypotenuse} = \frac{A}{H}$$

$$tan\theta = \frac{Opposite}{Adjacent} = \frac{O}{A}$$

You will also need to be able to find the reference angle given the ratios.

$$sin^{-1}\left(\frac{O}{H}\right) \equiv \arcsin\left(\frac{O}{H}\right) = \theta$$

$$cos^{-1}\left(\frac{A}{H}\right) \equiv \arccos\left(\frac{A}{H}\right) = \theta$$

$$tan^{-1}\left(\frac{O}{A}\right) \equiv \arctan\left(\frac{O}{A}\right) = \theta$$

A note of caution: Figures are not drawn to scale.

Finding Sides Given the Reference Angle

Examples:

Two ships leave the harbor at the same time. The first ship travels due north for 40 miles, and the second ship travels due east. Give the answer to the nearest tenth. Look at the following diagram for detailed information:

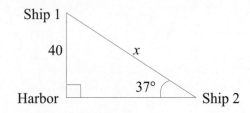

(a) How far apart are the ships?
(b) How far is the second ship from the harbor?

PART A

You have been given the value of the *opposite* side of the reference angle θ. You need to find the value of the *hypotenuse*, which we will call *x*. So we need to use the sine relationship.

$$Opposite = 40,\ \theta = 37,\ x = ?$$

$$sin\theta = \frac{Opposite}{Hypotenuse}$$

$$sin37° = \frac{40}{x};\ \text{multiply both sides by } x \text{ to get}$$

$$x \times sin37° = 40;\ \text{divide both sides by } sin37° \text{ to solve for } x$$

$$x = \frac{40}{sin37°}$$

$$x = 66.46 \approx 66.5$$

The two ships are approximately 66.5 miles apart.

PART B

By using the Pythagorean theorem $a^2 + b^2 = c^2$, we get

$$a^2 + (40)^2 = (66.5)^2$$
$$a^2 = (66.5)^2 - (40)^2$$
$$a^2 = 2822.25$$
$$a = \sqrt{2822.25} = 53.12 \approx 53.1$$

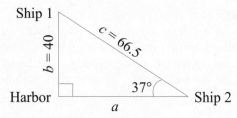

The second ship is approximately 53.1 miles away from the harbor.

ALTERNATE METHOD FOR PART B

You can also use the tangent relationship to find the distance from the harbor. Let's call it a.

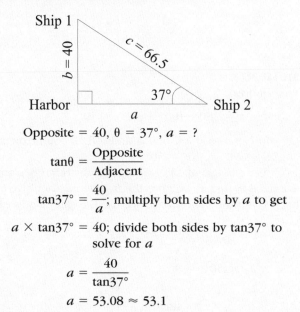

Opposite = 40, $\theta = 37°$, $a = ?$

$$\tan\theta = \frac{\text{Opposite}}{\text{Adjacent}}$$

$\tan 37° = \dfrac{40}{a}$; multiply both sides by a to get

$a \times \tan 37° = 40$; divide both sides by $\tan 37°$ to solve for a

$$a = \frac{40}{\tan 37°}$$
$$a = 53.08 \approx 53.1$$

Can you think of yet another way to arrive at this answer?

If you are thinking of solving the $\cos 37° = \dfrac{\text{Adjacent}}{\text{Hypotenuse}} =$

$\dfrac{a}{66.5}$ relationship, you are absolutely correct! Try it.

Finding Angle(s) Given the Sides

Examples:

Batman is standing 20 ft away from a 63-ft tall building and is contemplating a jump. Consider the given diagram. Round answer to nearest whole degree.

(a) What is the angle of elevation (reference angle) created from the point where he is standing to the roof of the building?

(b) What is the angle created by the building and Batman's line of sight?

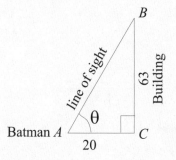

PART A

You have to find the reference angle θ given the information on the *opposite* and *adjacent* sides of the triangle. We can do this by using the inverse tangent ratio.

$$\text{opposite} = 63, \text{ adjacent} = 20, \theta = ?$$
$$\tan^{-1}\left(\frac{O}{A}\right) = \theta$$
$$\tan^{-1}\left(\frac{63}{20}\right) = 72.3° \approx 72°$$

The angle is approximately 72°.

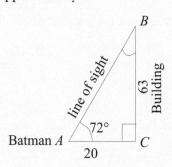

PART B

From Part A, you have found the value of θ or $\angle A$. You know that $\angle C$ is 90° and that all the angles of a triangle add up to 180°.

So, $180° - (90° + 72°) = 18°$

Or simply note that because $\angle C$ is 90°, the other two angles, $\angle A$ and $\angle B$, are complementary angles, and therefore, $90° - 72° = 18°$.

So the angle created by Batman's line of sight and the building is 18°.

Exercise 1

Directions: Given the necessary information, solve the following problems for the appropriate variables. Use the diagram for reference. Round the answers to the nearest tenth.

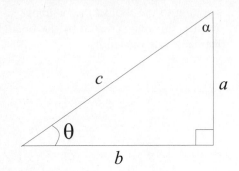

1. $\theta = 20°$, $b = 45$

2. $\theta = 51°$, $a = 70$

3. $\theta = 42°$, $c = 100$

4. $\alpha = 43°$, $b = 52$

5. $\alpha = 63°$, $a = 72$

6. $\alpha = 70°$, $c = 250$

7. $a = 30$, $b = 40$

8. $a = 20$, $c = 50$

9. $b = 82$, $c = 175$

10. $b = 15$, $c = 23$

Check your answers on page 422.

Application Problems

On the GED Test, you will sometimes be asked to find an approximate answer rounded off to a specified position, and at other times, you may be asked to provide an exact answer. An informal explanation for an exact answer is that you need not calculate decimal values for expressions that will give you irrational numbers for an answer.

Example:

A ladder is placed against a building. The distance from the point where the tip of the ladder touches the building to the ground is 8m. The angle created between the ladder and the building is 40°. What is the length of the ladder?

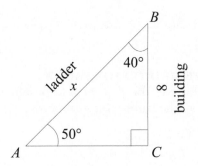

METHOD I

First find m∠A.

$$m\angle A = 180° - (90° + 40°) = 50$$

Or you can also think of ∠A and ∠B as complementary angles, so $90° - 40° = 50°$.

We can use m∠A = 50° to be our reference angle. We need to find *x*, which is the *hypotenuse*, and we have been given the *opposite*. So we use the sine relationship.

$$\sin 50° = \frac{8}{x}$$

$$x \times (\sin 50°) = 8$$

$$x = \frac{8}{\sin 50°}$$

If the answer is left as $x = \dfrac{8}{\sin 50°}$, then we call it an exact answer. We do not need a calculator to arrive at this answer. This would fall under a "set-up" category, and you would choose from multiple answers.

On the other hand, if we go ahead and calculate the approximate answer to two decimal places (hundredths), then we have $x = 10.443 \approx 10.44$.

This means the ladder is approximately 10.44m long. This problem requires a calculator and can be given to you as a multiple-choice or alternate-format problem where you will need to fill out the standard grid.

METHOD II
You could do this problem using m∠B = 40° as your reference angle. Then you would process the information as being *adjacent*, which has been given; we need to find the *hypotenuse*. So under this scenario, we use the cosine relationship.

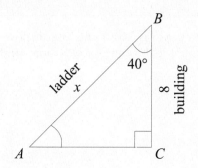

$$\cos 40° = \frac{8}{x}$$

$$x \times (\cos 40°) = 8$$

$$x = \frac{8}{\cos 40°}$$

$$x = 10.443 \approx 10.44$$

Note that the numerical answers are the same. The setup *appears* different but provides the same numerical answer. Remember, in any GED multiple-choice question, there is always *only* one correct answer.

Example:

Starting at a common point, Jack rides his bike 5 miles due south and Amala rides her bike 3 miles due east. Then they both stop for a break. What is the distance between them? Approximate answer to nearest whole number.

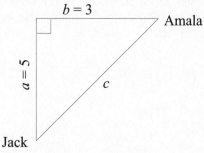

Pythagorean theorem: $a^2 + b^2 = c^2$

$$c^2 = (5)^2 = (3)^2$$

$$c^2 = 25 + 9$$

$$c^2 = 34$$

$$c = \sqrt{34}$$

Or, after using a calculator, we get an approximate answer of $c = 5.8 \approx 6$.

Here, your exact answer is $\sqrt{34}$ miles, and the problem can be done without a calculator.

However, 5.8, or roughly 6 miles, is the approximate answer, and you need a calculator to arrive at the answer. This could fall under the category of an alternate-format question where you calculate the answer and fill out a standard grid.

Solving Problems with a Calculator

Exercise 2

> **Directions:** Choose the one best answer for each item. You will need a calculator. Approximate all answers to the nearest tenth.

1. A ship sails 90 kilometers due west from the harbor. Another ship sails 120 miles due south. At this point in time, how far apart are the ships?

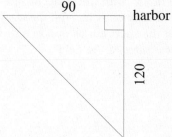

(1) 79.4
(2) 150
(3) 210
(4) 6,300
(5) 22,500

2. The external fuel tank of the space shuttle, which carries nearly a half million gallons of liquid hydrogen and liquid oxygen propellants, is 150 ft tall. If the fuel tank makes an angle of 88° with your line of sight, how far away from the shuttle are you?

(1) 5.2
(2) 1,909
(3) 4,063
(4) 4,295.4
(5) Not enough information is given.

401

3. You are standing 36 ft away from a 16-ft wall. What is the angle of elevation of your line of sight?

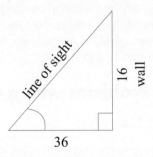

(1) 24°
(2) 26.4°
(3) 63.6°
(4) 66°
(5) Not enough information is given.

4. A cow cuts across a field to take a shortcut. She covers 60 meters, and the path she takes makes an angle of 35° with the adjacent side of the field. How many meters less did the cow travel by taking the short cut as opposed to walking around the two sides of the field?

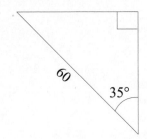

(1) 23.5
(2) 34.4
(3) 49.1
(4) 83.5
(5) Not enough information is given.

Check your answers on page 423.

Solving Set-up Problems
Exercise 3

Directions: Choose the one best answer for each item. No calculators permitted.

1. A radio tower is 110 ft tall. The shadow it casts is 200 ft. $\angle A$ is the angle of elevation. Find the value of $\angle A$.

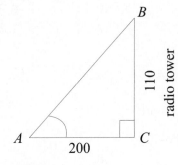

(1) $\theta = \tan\left(\dfrac{110}{200}\right)$

(2) $\theta = \tan^{-1}\left(\dfrac{200}{110}\right)$

(3) $\theta = \tan\left(\dfrac{200}{110}\right)$

(4) $\theta = \sin^{-1}\left(\dfrac{110}{200}\right)$

(5) $\theta = \tan^{-1}\left(\dfrac{110}{200}\right)$

2. Celine takes a shortcut through the parking lot. She walks 180 meters. One of the sides of the parking lot is 100 meters. What is the length of the other side?

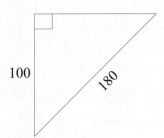

(1) $x = \sqrt{180^2 - 100^2}$
(2) $x = 180^2 + 100^2$
(3) $x = (180 - 100)^2$
(4) $x = (180 + 100)^2$
(5) $x = \sin^{-1}\left(\dfrac{100}{180}\right)$

3. Spiderman scales down a tall building and runs 150 yards from it. He then stops and measures the angle of elevation to be 26°. How tall is the building?

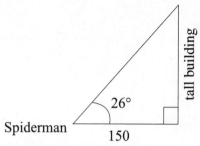

(1) $x = \dfrac{150}{\tan 26°}$

(2) $x = 150 \times (\cos 26°)$

(3) $x = 150 \times (\tan 26°)$

(4) $x = \dfrac{\tan 26°}{150}$

(5) $x = \dfrac{150}{\cos 26°}$

4. Starship A and Starship B are allies who are in formation. Starship A fires a torpedo at an alien craft at a 45° angle with respect to Starship B. The torpedo travels 1,500 kilometers and hits the alien vessel. How far apart are the two allied starships? (See diagram)

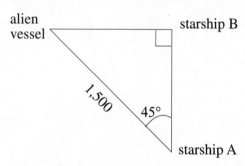

(1) $x = 1,500 \times (\sin 45°)$

(2) $x = 1,500 \times (\cos 45°)$

(3) $x = \dfrac{1,500}{\cos 45°}$

(4) $x = \dfrac{1,500}{\tan 45°}$

(5) Not enough information is given.

Check your answers on page 423.

Solving Alternate-Format Problems
Exercise 4

> **Directions:** Choose the one best answer for each item and fill out the standard grid. (Directions on how to fill out the standard grid are in the introduction of the Mathematics section). Calculator permitted. Round answers on the last step to nearest integer.

1. A flagpole casts a shadow of 33 ft. The angle of elevation, $\angle A$, is 43°. What is the height of the flagpole?

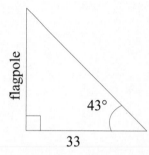

2. A child is looking up and waving at a helicopter pilot. The angle of elevation is 60°, and the line of sight created between the child and the pilot is 200 ft. What is the altitude of the helicopter?

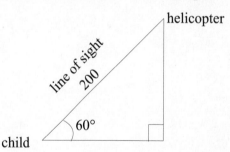

3. How many yards less will a goat walk if he takes a shortcut by cutting across a field with dimensions of 300 yards by 200 yards?

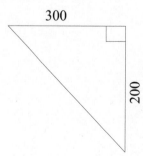

4. A laser 60 ft away from a wall is fired at an angle toward the wall. The distance it travels is 73 ft. Find the angle at which it was fired.

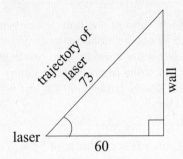

Check your answers on page 423.

FILLED-IN STANDARD GRIDS

Unit 1: Arithmetic, Exercise 7 (page 295)

1. 7 4   2. 4   3. 2 2 0   4. 2 4   5. 2 6

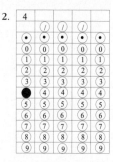

Unit 2: Understanding Word Problems, Exercise 5 (page 302)

1. 6 0 0   2. 1 2 8   3. 1 8 1   4. 2 0 4   5. 2 0 1

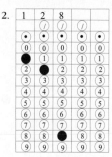

Unit 3: Decimals, Exercise 6 (page 309)

1. 4 . 4 3   2. 7 2 5   3. 1 0 . 5 0   4. 3 3 3

Unit 4: Fractions, Exercise 6 (page 319)

1. 5 / 7   2. 7 1 / 9 0   3. 1 1 2 5   4. 4 5 / 4

Unit 5: Ratio and Proportion, Exercise 4 *(page 325)*

1. 4 3 / 1 7
2. 3 0
3. 1 1 2 . 5
4. 1 4 0

Unit 6: Percent, Exercise 5 *(page 332)*

1. 7 7 1
2. 4 0
3. 5
4. 7 6 . 1 6

Unit 7: Data Analysis and Statistics, Exercise 8 *(page 345)*

1. 1 0 2 9
2. 0 . 0 7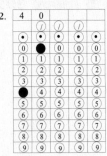
3. 3 1 0 8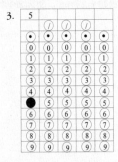
4. 1 7 . 7
5. 1 7 . 1

6. 9 . 7
7. 7 8 . 6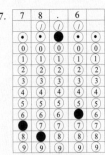
8. 7 9 . 4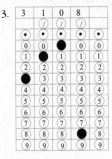
9. 6 9

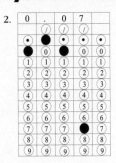

Unit 8: Measurement, Exercise 10 *(page 359)*

1. **40** 2. **9.8** 3. **33.7**

Unit 9: Algebra, Exercise 15 *(page 377)*

1. **17** 2. **50** 3. **100** 4. **93**

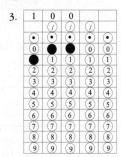

Unit 10: Geometry, Exercise 15 *(page 396)*

1. **28.2** 2. **6** 3. **3** 4. **131.4**

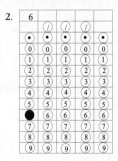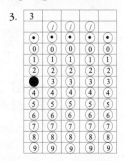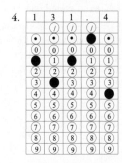

Unit 11: Trigonometry, Exercise 4 *(page 403)*

1. **31** 2. **173** 3. **139** 4. **35**

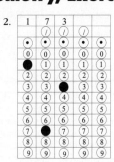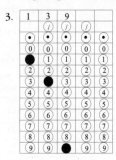

ANSWERS AND EXPLANATIONS

Unit 1: Arithmetic

Exercise 1 (page 290)

1. The correct answer is: Five hundred four
2. The correct answer is: One thousand, four hundred twenty
3. The correct answer is: Seven thousand, sixty
4. The correct answer is: Thirty-four thousand
5. The correct answer is: Two hundred one thousand, nine hundred
6. The correct answer is: One million, four hundred fifty thousand, three hundred twenty-three
7. The correct answer is: Two hundred fifty-seven million, five thousand, nine
8. The correct answer is: Six billion
9.

City	1990	> or <	1980
Phoenix	1,003,800	>	789,704
Chicage	2,852,041	<	3,005,072
Milwaukee	642,860	>	636,212
Philadelphia	1,608,942	<	1,688,210
Detroit	1,056,180	<	1,203,339
Jacksonville	649,437	>	540,920

10. The correct answer is: The Playroom Compare the four figures. The greatest is $1,805.

Exercise 2 (page 292)

1. The correct answer is: 600
2. The correct answer is: 5,000
3. The correct answer is (4): $100 Round 98 to the nearest 10.
4. The correct answer is (4): 290 Round 288 to the nearest 10.
5. The correct answer is (4): 44,000 Round 43,508 to the nearest thousand.
6. The correct answer is (5): 5,600,000 Round 5,641,000 to the nearest hundred thousand.

Exercise 3 (page 292)

1. The correct answer is: 1,841
2. The correct answer is: 3,061
3. The correct answer is: 100
4. The correct answer is: 1,463,675
5. The correct answer is: 135,670
6. The correct answer is: 650
7. The correct answer is: 2,825,050
8. The correct answer is: 170
9. The correct answer is: 4,885
10. The correct answer is: 1,306,245
11. The correct answer is (3): 1,053

Exercise 4 (page 293)

1. The correct answer is: 123
2. The correct answer is: 1,159
3. The correct answer is: 590
4. The correct answer is: 4,749
5. The correct answer is: 88
6. The correct answer is: 4,575
7. The correct answer is: 1,556
8. The correct answer is: 101,825
9. The correct answer is: 1,557,250
10. The correct answer is: 2,574,320
11. The correct answer is (2): 4,102

Exercise 5 (page 294)

1. The correct answer is: 216
2. The correct answer is: 3,500
3. The correct answer is: 2,160
4. The correct answer is: 87,464
5. The correct answer is (2): $650 $100 + ($55 × 10)
6. The correct answer is (5): $14,560 $280 × 52

Exercise 6 (page 295)

1. The correct answer is: 32
2. The correct answer is: 203
3. The correct answer is (5): 500 6,000 ÷ 12
4. The correct answer is (2): 20 200 ÷ 10

Exercise 7 (page 295)

1. The correct answer is: 74 First, find how many miles she traveled. 47,837 − 45,987 = 1,850 miles. Therefore, 1850 ÷ 25 = 74 gallons of gas. See page 405 for filled-in answer grid.
2. The correct answer is: 4 26 × 2 = 52 servings are allowed. 52 × 8 = 416 ounces of juice are needed. Therefore, 416 ÷ 128 = 3.25 ≈ 4 containers, because she cannot buy a partial container of juice. See page 405 for filled-in answer grid.
3. The correct answer is: 220 Basketball and concert tickets cost $30 + $25 = $55. For 4 people they will spend $55 × 4 = $220. See page 405 for filled-in answer grid.
4. The correct answer is: 24 4 − 2 = 2 more green paper cartons. 2 × 12 = 24 reams. See page 405 for filled-in answer grid.
5. The correct answer is: 26 Two tickets cost 2 × $9 = $18, one popcorn costs $4, two sodas cost 2 × $2 = $4. Therefore, total is $18 + $4 + $4 = $26. See page 405 for filled-in answer grid.

Unit 2: Understanding Word Problems

Exercise 1 (page 298)

1. The correct answer is (2): $68 Add the bills and divide by 3, the number of bills:

$$(\$64 + \$78 + \$62) \div 3 = \frac{\$204}{3} = \$68$$

2. The correct answer is (2): 260 Divide the number of videotapes by the number that will fit in a carton: $\frac{5,720}{22} = 260$

Exercise 2 (page 298)

1. The correct answer is (2): $17 You don't need to know the amount of the rent and the electric bill. Subtract: $42 − $25 = $17.
2. The correct answer is (5): Not enough information is given. You need to know the sale price of the changing table. You don't need the information about the crib.
3. The correct answer is (3): $52,584 You don't need to know the city manager's salary. Subtract to find the difference: $117,884 − $65,300 = $52,584. Using estimation, you can solve this item more quickly. Think: $120,000 − $65,000 = $55,000
4. The correct answer is (5): Not enough information is given. You know how many people did not have health coverage in California in 1990. You need the population of California in 1990 in order to find an answer.

Exercise 3 *(page 300)*

1. **The correct answer is:** $7(8 - 6)(5 + 7)$
   $7(2)(12)$
   $14(12) = 168$

2. **The correct answer is:** $\dfrac{36}{2} - 5 + 2(10)$
   $9 - 5 + 20$
   $4 + 20 = 24$

3. **The correct answer is:** $10(5 + 2) - \dfrac{36}{4}$
   $10(7) - \dfrac{36}{4}$
   $70 - 9 = 61$

4. **The correct answer is:** $10(5) + \dfrac{36}{2} - 4$
   $50 + 18 - 4$
   $68 - 4 = 64$

5. **The correct answer is (2): 10(12 + 30)** All the boxes have the same number of diskettes. You find the total number of boxes and then multiply by the number of diskettes in each box.

6. **The correct answer is (5): 2($8) + $12** Two pizzas cost $8 each and one cost $12. You could use addition: $8 + $8 + $12, but choice (5) has the same value.

7. **The correct answer is (5): $13(35) − $9(40)** To find out how much Linda earned at either job, multiply the number of hours by the hourly wage. Subtract the old job's wages from her weekly earnings on the new job.

Exercise 4 *(page 301)*

1. **The correct answer is (2): 9,081 feet. Subtract:** $20,320 - 11,239 = 9,081$. You can use estimation to solve this problem. **Think:** $20,000 - 11,000 = 9,000$. No other answer choice is close to the estimate.

2. **The correct answer is (1): Mount Everest** Use estimation to solve it. **Round** 14,491 to 14,000 and multiply by 2. $14,000(2) = 28,000$. Only the elevation of Mount Everest is close to the estimate.

3. **The correct answer is (5): Between 8,000 and 9,000. Add** the amounts from the graph: $3,000 + 3,500 + 2,000 = 8,500$.

4. **The correct answer is (2): Between 2,000 and 3,000. Subtract:** $5,000 - 2,500 = 2,500$

5. **The correct answer is (4): 3(2,000 + 1,500)** Probably the simplest way to solve the problem is to add the units sold for the two games and multiply by 3.

6. **The correct answer is (4): 1991** The line on the graph does not ascend from 1990 to 1991 so you know the price did not go up in 1991.

7. **The correct answer is (2): 1985** Find $12 on the scale, and follow it across to the line. The point on the line is directly over 1985.

8. **The correct answer is (1): 2($28) − 2($6)** One way to solve the problem is to find the total admission for the two adults for both years and then find the difference.

Exercise 5 *(page 302)*

1. **The correct answer is: $600** $10($24) + 20($18) = 600. See page 405 for filled-in answer grid.

2. **The correct answer is: $128** $24 \div 2 = 12$. $1536 \div 12 = 128. See page 405 for filled-in answer grid.

3. **The correct answer is: 181.** The week of highest input time is the week with the highest total time. By inspection we see that it is Week 2. $28 + 57 + 96 = 181$ hours. See page 405 for filled-in answer grid.

4. **The correct answer is: 204** $51 + 57 + 50 + 46 = 204$ hours. See page 405 for filled-in answer grid.

5. **The correct answer is: 201** $(84 + 96 + 86 + 68) - (22 + 28 + 34 + 49) = 201$ hours. See page 405 for filled-in answer grid.

Unit 3: Decimals

Exercise 1 *(page 305)*

1. **The correct answer is (2): 13.05**

2. **The correct answer is (2): 0.255, 0.25, 0.235, 0.23, 0.2**

3. **The correct answer is (5): 0.438** 0.43784786642
   $8 > 5$, so 1 is added to 7.

4. **The correct answer is (4): 1.60** 1.598
   $8 > 5$, so 1 is added to 9.

5. **The correct answer is (5): 23.5**

6. **The correct answer is (3): $0.47**

Exercise 2 *(page 306)*

1. **The correct answer is: 807.16**

2. **The correct answer is: 214.376**

3. **The correct answer is: $754.57**

4. **The correct answer is: 28.13166**

5. **The correct answer is: $6,349.07**

6. **The correct answer is: 1.8798**

7. **The correct answer is: 28.53**

8. **The correct answer is: 72.817**

9. **The correct answer is: 9,965.11**

10. **The correct answer is: $21.25**

11. **The correct answer is: $76.33**

12. **The correct answer is: 0.405**

13. **The correct answer is (4): $193.00** Add the amounts she spent to find the total.

14. **The correct answer is (1): 0.0016** Subtract 0.1849 from 0.1865 to find the difference.

15. **The correct answer is (4): $9.98** $2.59 + $3.89 + $1.32 + $0.89 + $1.29 = 9.98.

16. **The correct answer is (3): 0.75** $1.6 - 0.85 = 0.75$.

Exercise 3 *(page 307)*

1. **The correct answer is: 11.3184**

2. **The correct answer is: 28.782**

3. **The correct answer is: 466.2**

4. **The correct answer is: 0.0048**

5. **The correct answer is: $46.05**

6. **The correct answer is (5): $14,521** 52($279.25)

7. **The correct answer is (3): $8.26** 2.8($2.95)

8. **The correct answer is (3): $46.62**
   $3($0.42)(37) = 46.62

Exercise 4 *(page 307)*

1. **The correct answer is: 0.25**

2. **The correct answer is: 302**

3. **The correct answer is (3): 800** Divide $64 by $0.08.

4. **The correct answer is (1): $39.51 Divide:** $9,876.47 \div 250 = 39.50588
   Round to the nearest cent: $39.51

Exercise 5 *(page 308)*

1. **The correct answer is (4): $2,500.00** $2.50(1,000) Move the decimal point 3 places to the right.

2. **The correct answer is (3): $12.54** $125.40 \div 10$. Move the decimal 1 place to the left.

3. **The correct answer is (2): 250** $25,000 \div 100$. Move the decimal 2 places to the left.

4. **The correct answer is (2): $4.75** This problem contains extra information. You need to multiply $1 by 5. **Estimate:** $1(5) = $5.

Exercise 6 *(page 309)*

1. **The correct answer is: $4.43** 2 jars of sauce for $4.59 each (cost a total of $4.59 \times 2 = 9.18$) plus the coffee ($7.89) and kitchen towels ($8.50) all add up to a total of $25.57. The change from $30.00 is $30.00 - $25.57 = $4.43. See page 405 for filled-in answer grid.

2. **The correct answer is: $725** (Old balance + paycheck) = $509.67 + $2079.63 = $2589.30. Now subtract the total amount of bills from this amount. $2589.30 - ($988 + 256.79 + 273.65 + 345.78) = $725.08 ≈ $725. See page 405 for filled-in answer grid.

3. **The correct answer is: $10.50** Divide total earned by number of hours. $420 ÷ 40 = $10.50. See page 405 for filled-in answer grid.

4. **The correct answer is: $333** Add the deductions, then subtract from $420. $420 - ($37.70 + 21.00 + 18.90 + 9.25) = $333.05 ≈ $333. See page 405 for filled-in answer grid.

Unit 4: Fractions

Exercise 1 *(page 311)*

Name	Paint Used (in quarter gallons)	Total Gallons Used
1. Nancy	$\frac{9}{4}$	$2\frac{1}{4}$
2. Tyrone	$\frac{15}{4}$	$3\frac{3}{4}$
3. Pava	$\frac{6}{4}$	$1\frac{1}{2}$
4. Carmen	$\frac{12}{4}$	3
5. Hank	$\frac{17}{4}$	$4\frac{1}{4}$

6. **The correct answer is:** $\frac{1}{3} < \frac{7}{8}$

7. **The correct answer is:** $\frac{2}{3} = \frac{6}{9}$

8. **The correct answer is:** $\frac{7}{9} > \frac{4}{7}$

9. **The correct answer is:** $\frac{6}{7} > \frac{3}{8}$

10. **The correct answer is (2):** $\frac{1}{4}$

11. **The correct answer is (3): C**

12. **The correct answer is (4):** $\frac{3}{15}$ and $\frac{1}{5}$

13. **The correct answer is (3): $300 as part of Bun's $450 pay.**
$\frac{$300}{$450} = \frac{2}{3}$

14. **The correct answer is (2): 9 eggs as part of a dozen.**
$\frac{9}{12} = \frac{3}{4}$

Exercise 2 *(page 312)*

1. **The correct answer is (4):** $\frac{1}{3}$ $\frac{11}{30}$ can be rounded to $\frac{10}{30}$ and renamed.

2. **The correct answer is (5):** $\frac{1}{2}$ $\frac{52}{100}$ can be rounded to $\frac{50}{100}$ and renamed.

3. **The correct answer is (1):** $\frac{1}{8}$ $\frac{5}{42}$ can be rounded to $\frac{5}{40}$ and renamed.

4. **The correct answer is (5):** $\frac{7}{10}$ $\frac{72}{98}$ can be rounded to $\frac{70}{100}$ and renamed.

Exercise 3 *(page 314)*

1. **The correct answer is:** 1 $\frac{4}{4} = 1$

2. **The correct answer is:** $1\frac{1}{5}$
$\frac{12}{10} = 1\frac{2}{10}$, which can be renamed $1\frac{1}{5}$.

3. **The correct answer is:** $6\frac{2}{3}$

4. **The correct answer is:** $\frac{1}{2}$ $\frac{2}{4}$ can be renamed $\frac{1}{2}$.

5. **The correct answer is:** $\frac{1}{3}$ $\frac{4}{12}$ can be renamed $\frac{1}{3}$.

6. **The correct answer is:** $6\frac{1}{2}$ $6\frac{2}{2} - \frac{1}{2}$

7. **The correct answer is:** $4\frac{3}{5}$ $11\frac{7}{5} - 7\frac{4}{5}$

8. **The correct answer is (3):** $9\frac{1}{4}$

9. **The correct answer is (4):** $\frac{1}{2}$
She had $\frac{2}{4}$, which can be renamed $\frac{1}{2}$.

10. **The correct answer is (5):** $1\frac{1}{3}$

11. **The correct answer is (2): 7**

12. **The correct answer is (2):** $\frac{1}{2}$

Exercise 4 (page 316)

1. The correct answer is: $1\frac{1}{6}$

$$\frac{1}{2} \qquad \frac{3}{6}$$
$$\frac{+\frac{2}{3}}{\quad} = \frac{+\frac{4}{6}}{\frac{7}{6}} = 1\frac{1}{6}$$

2. The correct answer is: $1\frac{7}{20}$

$$\frac{3}{5} \qquad \frac{12}{20}$$
$$\frac{+\frac{3}{4}}{\quad} = \frac{+\frac{15}{20}}{\frac{27}{20}} = 1\frac{7}{20}$$

3. The correct answer is: $\frac{5}{12}$

$$\frac{3}{4} \qquad \frac{9}{12}$$
$$\frac{-\frac{1}{3}}{\quad} = \frac{-\frac{4}{12}}{\frac{5}{12}}$$

4. The correct answer is: $\frac{3}{8}$

$$\frac{7}{8} \qquad \frac{7}{8}$$
$$\frac{-\frac{1}{2}}{\quad} = \frac{-\frac{4}{8}}{\frac{3}{8}}$$

5. The correct answer is (3): $1\frac{5}{6}$

$$\frac{2}{3} + 1\frac{1}{6}$$

6. The correct answer is (4): $\frac{3}{16}$

$$5\frac{11}{16} - 5\frac{1}{2}$$

7. The correct answer is (2): $16\frac{1}{6}$

$$20\frac{2}{3} - 4\frac{1}{2}$$

8. The correct answer is (2): $26\frac{1}{4}$

$$12\frac{1}{2} + 13\frac{3}{4}$$

9. The correct answer is (1): $3\frac{1}{2}$

$$1\frac{1}{2} + \frac{1}{2} + 1\frac{1}{2}$$

10. The correct answer is (5): $\frac{1}{4}$

$$3\frac{3}{4} - 3\frac{1}{2}$$

Exercise 5 (page 318)

1. The correct answer is (3): $10\frac{1}{8}$

$$\frac{3}{4} \times \frac{27}{2} = \frac{81}{8} = 10\frac{1}{8}$$

2. The correct answer is (5): $23\frac{1}{3}$

$$\frac{5}{1} \times \frac{14}{3} = \frac{70}{3} = 23\frac{1}{3}$$

3. The correct answer is (1): $8\frac{1}{4}$

$$\frac{3}{1} \times \frac{11}{4} = \frac{33}{4} = 8\frac{1}{4}$$

4. The correct answer is (3): $\frac{15}{16}$

$$7\frac{1}{2} \div 8 = \frac{15}{2} \times \frac{1}{8} = \frac{15}{16}$$

5. The correct answer is (4): 16

$$12 \div \frac{3}{4} = \frac{12}{1} \times \frac{4}{3} = \frac{48}{3} = 16$$

6. The correct answer is (3): 12

$$3 \div \frac{1}{4} = \frac{3}{1} \times \frac{4}{1} = 12$$

Exercise 6 (page 319)

1. The correct answer is: **5/7** $78\frac{4}{7} \div 110 = \frac{550}{7} \times \frac{1}{110} = \frac{5}{7}$ pounds. See page 405 for filled-in answer grid.

2. The correct answer is: **71/90.** $180 - 38 = 142$ days are left. In fraction form this is $\frac{142}{180} = \frac{71}{90}$. See page 405 for filled-in answer grid.

3. The correct answer is: **1,125** $\frac{3}{10}$ of 5,000 is $\frac{3}{10} \times 5,000 = 1,500$ were defective. Therefore, $\frac{3}{4} \times 1,500 = 1,125$. See page 405 for filled-in answer grid.

4. The correct answer is: **45/4** For five days she jogs $1\frac{3}{4} \times 5 = \frac{7}{4} \times 5 = \frac{35}{4} = 8\frac{3}{4}$ miles. Add this to $2\frac{1}{2} = \frac{5}{2}$. Therefore, $\frac{35}{4} + \frac{5}{2} = \frac{35}{4} + \frac{10}{4} = \frac{45}{4}$. See page 405 for filled-in answer grid.

Unit 5: Ratio and Proportion

Exercise 1 (page 320)

1. The correct answer is: $\frac{5}{2}$

$$\frac{\text{water}}{\text{solution}}$$

2. The correct answer is: $\frac{59}{30}$

$$\frac{\text{win}}{\text{loss}}$$

3. The correct answer is: $\frac{25}{1}$

$$\frac{375 \text{ miles}}{15 \text{ gallons}}$$

4. The correct answer is: $\frac{3}{1}$

$$\frac{36 \text{ cars sold}}{12 \text{ months}}$$

5. The correct answer is (1): 3:16

$$\frac{\$75 \text{ savings}}{\$400 \text{ total pay}}$$

6. The correct answer is (4): 1:3

$$\frac{120 \text{ children's tickets}}{360 \text{ total tickets}}$$

7. The correct answer is (2): $\frac{2}{5}$

$$\frac{10,000 \text{ didn't vote}}{25,000 \text{ registered}}$$

8. The correct answer is (3): $\frac{2}{3}$

$$\frac{10,000 \text{ didn't vote}}{15,000 \text{ voted}}$$

Exercise 2 *(page 322)*

1. The correct answer is (3): $420

$$\frac{\$35}{100} = \frac{?}{1,200}$$

$$\frac{\$35(1,200)}{100} = \$420$$

2. The correct answer is (2): $4.17

$$\frac{12}{\$16.68} = \frac{3}{?}$$

3. The correct answer is (3): $11.25

$$\frac{2}{\$4.50} = \frac{5}{?}$$

4. The correct answer is (4): 2

$$\frac{\frac{1}{4}}{?} = \frac{1}{8}$$

5. The correct answer is (5): 14

$$\frac{1\frac{3}{4}}{?} = \frac{1}{8}$$

6. The correct answer is (1): 15

$$\frac{5}{\$77.50} = \frac{?}{\$232.50}$$

7. The correct answer is (3): 625

$$\frac{375}{15} = \frac{?}{25}$$

8. The correct answer is (3): 150

$$\frac{4}{20} = \frac{?}{750}$$

9. The correct answer is (4): 160

$$\frac{8}{2} = \frac{640}{?}$$

10. The correct answer is (2): 1,500

$$\frac{6}{20} = \frac{?}{5,000}$$

Exercise 3 *(page 324)*

1. The correct answer is (2): $\frac{4(500)}{5}$

2. The correct answer is (1): $\frac{1(460)}{23}$

3. The correct answer is (1): $\frac{23(2)}{\frac{1}{2}}$

4. The correct answer is (5): **Not enough information is given.** We are not told how many teachers are employed by the Milton schools at this time.

5. The correct answer is (1): $\frac{6(12)}{8}$

$$\frac{6 \text{ ounces}}{8 \text{ servings}} = \frac{x}{12 \text{ servings}}$$

$$\frac{6(12)}{8}$$

6. The correct answer is (5): $\frac{40(325)}{25}$

$$\frac{\$325}{25 \text{ hr}} = \frac{x}{40 \text{ h}}$$

$$\frac{40(325)}{25}$$

Exercise 4 *(page 325)*

1. The correct answer is: 43/17 Repair to finish is 86 to 34. So $\frac{86}{34} = \frac{43}{17} \Rightarrow 43/17$. Remember to reduce, and ratios are presented in improper form. See page 406 for filled-in answer grid.

2. The correct answer is: 30 ft Use a proportion.

	Shadow	Height
Gardener	4	6
Tree	20	x

$$\Rightarrow \frac{4}{20} = \frac{6}{x} \Rightarrow 4x = 6 \times 20 \Rightarrow x = \frac{120}{4}$$

Therefore, $x = 30$ ft. See page 406 for filled-in answer grid.

3. The correct answer is: 112.5 mm Use a proportion.

Years	Distance
4	18
25	x

$$\Rightarrow \frac{4}{25} = \frac{18}{x} \Rightarrow 4x = 18 \times 25 \Rightarrow = \frac{18 \times 25}{4}$$

Therefore, $x = 112.5$ millimeters. See page 406 for filled-in answer grid.

4. The correct answer is: 140 Use a proportion.

Ratio	Children
2	x
3	210

$$\Rightarrow \frac{2}{3} = \frac{x}{210} \Rightarrow 3x = 2 \times 210 \Rightarrow x = \frac{2 \times 210}{3}$$

Therefore, $x = 140$ children. See page 406 for filled-in answer grid.

Unit 6: Percent

Exercise 1 *(page 327)*

	Percent	Fraction
1.	$12\frac{1}{2}\%$	$\frac{1}{8}$
2.	25%	$\frac{1}{4}$
3.	40%	$\frac{2}{5}$
4.	50%	$\frac{1}{2}$
5.	60%	$\frac{3}{5}$
6.	70%	$\frac{7}{10}$
7.	75%	$\frac{3}{4}$

	Decimal	Percent
8.	0.07	7%
9.	0.1	10%
10.	0.18	18%
11.	0.65	65%
12.	1.25	125%
13.	1.8	180%
14.	2.5	250%

15. **The correct answer is (2): Divide the number by 4.**

16. **The correct answer is (4): Multiply by 2.**

Exercise 2 *(page 328)*

1. **The correct answer is: 162 is the missing part.**
$$\frac{90}{100} = \frac{x}{180}$$

2. **The correct answer is: 20%**
$$\frac{x}{100} = \frac{50}{250}$$

3. **The correct answer is: 20 is the missing whole.**
100% of any number is that number.
$$\frac{100}{100} = \frac{20}{x}$$

4. **The correct answer is: 50 is the missing whole.**
$$\frac{70}{100} = \frac{35}{x}$$

5. **The correct answer is (4): $292.50**
$$\frac{15}{100} = \frac{x}{\$1,950} \quad \frac{\text{discount}}{\text{total price}}$$

6. **The correct answer is (2): $1,200**
$$\frac{4.5}{100} = \frac{\$54}{x} \quad \frac{\text{interest}}{\text{account balance}}$$

7. **The correct answer is (4): $1,770**
$$\frac{6}{100} = \frac{x}{\$29,500} \quad \frac{\text{increase}}{\text{original salary}}$$

8. **The correct answer is (3): $31,270** Add his cost of living increase to his previous salary.

$$\begin{array}{r} \$29,500 \\ +\ 1,770 \\ \hline \$31,270 \end{array}$$

9. **The correct answer is (3): $103.40**
   Step 1 Find total of purchases.
   $$\begin{array}{r} \$\ 24.00 \\ 31.99 \\ +42.49 \\ \hline \$\ 98.48 \end{array}$$

   Step 2 Find 5% sales tax.
   $$\frac{5}{100} = \frac{tax}{\$98.48}$$
   tax = $4.924 or $4.92

   Step 3 Add tax to total.
   $$\begin{array}{r} \$\ 98.48 \\ +4.92 \\ \hline \$\ 103.40 \end{array}$$

10. **The correct answer is (5): Not enough information is given.** Commission is part of the total sales. To find the percent of commission, you need to know the amount of her total sales.

Exercise 3 *(page 329)*

1. **The correct answer is (4): 50%**
$$\frac{x}{100} = \frac{7,500}{15,000} \quad \frac{\text{change}}{\text{original number}}$$

2. **The correct answer is (5): Not enough information is given.** The original amount is not given.

3. **The correct answer is (3): 20%**
$$\frac{x}{100} = \frac{\$52}{\$264} \quad \frac{\text{change}}{\text{original amount}}$$
19.6% rounded to the nearest whole % is 20%.

4. **The correct answer is (2): 10%**
$$\frac{x}{100} = \frac{\$0.67}{\$6.70} \quad \frac{\text{change}}{\text{original amount}}$$

5. **The correct answer is (1): $486**

6. **The correct answer is (3): $14,000**

7. **The correct answer is (4): 220%**
$$\frac{x}{100} = \frac{64 - 20}{20} \quad \frac{\text{change}}{\text{original number}}$$

8. **The correct answer is (1): 14%**
$$\frac{x}{100} = \frac{\$28}{\$200} \quad \frac{\text{discount}}{\text{price}}$$
Since the problem asks for an approximation, round $199 to $200.

Exercise 4 *(page 331)*

1. **The correct answer is: $360** $2,000(0.09)(2)

2. **The correct answer is: $29.95**
$$\frac{\$599}{1} \times \frac{1}{10} \times \frac{1}{2}$$
6 months is ½ year or $599(0.1)(0.5)

3. **The correct answer is (3): $125,000(0.085)(25)**

4. **The correct answer is (4): $11,880**
$8,800(0.07)(5) = $3,080
$3,080 interest
$+8,800$ loan
$11,880 total to be repaid

5. **The correct answer is (3): $3,968** Angela borrowed $3,200.
$3,200(0.08)(3) = $768
$768 interest
$+3,200$ loan
$3,968 total to be repaid

Exercise 5 (page 332)

1. **The correct answer is: $771** 10% of $92,565 is 0.10 × $92,565 = $9256.50. Divide by 12 to get the monthly amount. $9256.50 ÷ 12 = $771.375 ≈ $771. See page 406 for filled-in answer grid.

2. **The correct answer is: 40 gb** Use a proportion.

Percent	Gigabyte
$3\frac{1}{2} = 3.5$	1.4
100	x

   $$\Rightarrow \frac{3.5}{100} = \frac{1.4}{x} \Rightarrow 3.5x = (1.4)100 \Rightarrow x = \frac{140}{3.5}$$

   Therefore, $x = 40$ gigabytes. See page 406 for filled-in answer grid.

3. **The correct answer is: 5** A raise is always compared to the previous year's wages, unless otherwise stated. Therefore, from 1998 to 1999, the difference is $10.5 - 10 = 0.5$. Compare this to the 1998 $\frac{0.5}{10} = 0.05 = 5\%$ raise. See page 406 for filled-in answer grid.

4. **The correct answer is: $76.16** 15% off means she has to pay $100\% - 15\% = 85\%$. Therefore, with the first discount, the price is $0.85 \times \$112 = \$95.20$. An additional 20% off of that means she has to pay 80% of $95.20. Therefore, $0.80 \times \$95.20 = \$76.16$. See page 406 for filled-in answer grid.

Unit 7: Data Analysis and Statistics

Exercise 1 (page 335)

1. **The correct answer is (1): 3–4 days** Look across the row labeled "Acute Bronchitis" to the column labeled "45–64 Years." The amount, 3.6 days, falls between 3 and 4 days.

2. **The correct answer is (5): 28–29 days** Look across the row labeled "Fractures/Dislocations" to the column labeled "18–24 Years." The amount, 28.7 days, falls between 28 and 29 days.

3. **The correct answer is (3): Pneumonia** Only 1.5 days are listed under the "25–44 Years" column.

4. **The correct answer is (2): Influenza** The number of sick days taken for influenza is the highest number listed in each column.

5. **The correct answer is (4): 742** Take 74.2% of 1,000.

6. **The correct answer is (3): Aero USA** Subtract 94 from 750 to find the number of WestAir flights that arrived on time. Divide the difference 656 by 750, the total number of flights. You need to carry out the division to only two places to see that Aero USA's percent is nearest.

7. **The correct answer is (2): $14,000** Look at the row for 10–14 years of service. Compare the two numbers, and find the difference.

8. **The correct answer is (4): 0.5($60,000) + $60,000** Find the amount of the raise by multiplying 0.5 by the current salary of $60,000. Then add the raise to the current salary.

9. **The correct answer is (1): $24,000** Add $90,000 and $75,000 to find the proposed salary for NHL referees with 20+ years of experience. Then subtract the NBA salary for the same range.

10. **The correct answer is (5): $\frac{4}{5}$**

    $$\frac{\$59,900}{\$75,500} \text{ rounded to } \frac{\$60,000}{\$75,000} = \frac{4}{5}$$

11. **The correct answer is (1): Two** Round each value.

    $$\frac{\$110,000}{\$50,000} = \text{about 2}$$

12. **The correct answer is (2): Boston and New York** Boston's price fell from $181,200 to $168,200, and New York's median price decreased from $183,800 to $169,300.

Exercise 2 (page 337)

1.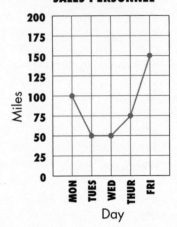

   AVERAGE WEEKDAY MILEAGE FOR DUNNE'S SALES PERSONNEL

2. **The correct answer is (3): 425**
   Add the miles from each day: $100 + 50 + 50 + 75 + 150$.

3. **The correct answer is (4): 125**
   $(50 + 75 + 150) - (100 + 50)$

4. **The correct answer is (5): $1.20** Beginning at 11/27 (November 27), look up the line to the corresponding point. Now look to the scale on the left where you see $1.20.

5. **The correct answer is (5): Not enough information is given.** You are not told how many gallons of gasoline were sold by each station.

Exercise 3 (page 339)

1. **The correct answer is (4): 300** 12% of 2,500 were men who take greater responsibility for shopping.

   $$\frac{12}{100} = \frac{x}{2,500}$$

   $$\frac{12(2,500)}{100} = 300$$

2. **The correct answer is (2): More than ten times as many women than men do the cleaning.** 7% of the cleaning is done by men. 78% done by the women is more than ten times that amount.

3. **The correct answer is (3): 710** 78% of the women take a greater responsibility versus 7% of the men. Subtract $78\% - 7\% = 71\%$; 71% of 1,000 is 710.

4. **The correct answer is (1): 63 million** 29.6% is about 30% of the 27 million homes with computers.

   $$\frac{10}{100} = \frac{27 \text{ million}}{x}$$

   $$\frac{100(27 \text{ million})}{30} = 90 \text{ million}$$

   The *total number of homes* in 1992 was about 90 million. If approximately 30% of the 90 million homes had computers, then approximately 70% of the homes *did not* have computers.

   $$\frac{70}{100} = \frac{x}{90 \text{ million}}$$

   $$\frac{70(90 \text{ million})}{30} = 63 \text{ million}$$

5. **The correct answer is (5): Not enough information is given.** You are not given the projected figures for the total number of homes in 1993.

Exercise 4 *(page 341)*

1. **The correct answer is (1):** $\frac{3}{10}$ 18% + 12% = 30%, or $\frac{3}{10}$ of the population.

2. **The correct answer is (5): 67,080,000 Estimate:** 26% is approximately 25%, so divide $\frac{258,000,000}{4}$, or solve by a proportion.

$$\frac{26}{100} = \frac{x}{258,000,000}$$

$$\frac{26(258,000,000)}{100} = 67,080,000$$

3. **The correct answer is (5):** $\frac{7}{10}$

$$\frac{\text{entertainment}}{\text{savings}} = \frac{\$70}{\$100} = \frac{7}{10}$$

4. **The correct answer is (1):** $\frac{1}{17}$

$$\frac{\text{savings}}{\text{total budget}} = \frac{\$100}{\$1,700} = \frac{1}{17}$$

5. **The correct answer is (4): 50** Multiply 800 by $\frac{1}{16}$.

6. **The correct answer is (3): 25%** The fraction in the section for glass and plastic bottles is $\frac{1}{4}$. The fraction $\frac{1}{4}$ is equal to 25%.

Exercise 5 *(page 342)*

1. **The correct answer is (3): 142** 710 ÷ 5

2. **The correct answer is (4): $15,700** $125,600 ÷ 8

Exercise 6 *(page 343)*

1. **The correct answer is (2): $6.50**

2. **The correct answer is (3): $9.75**

3. **The correct answer is (1): $63.35**

   Add the middle two values.

   $\begin{array}{r} \$\ 58.27 \\ +68.43 \\ \hline \$\ 126.70 \end{array}$

   Divide this sum by 2.

   $\begin{array}{r} \$63.35 \\ 2\overline{)\$126.70} \end{array}$

Exercise 7 *(page 344)*

1. **The correct answer is (5):** $\frac{1}{5}$ One correct answer out of five choices.

2. **The correct answer is (3):** $\frac{1}{25}$ Terry has 8 chances out of 200 to win. The fraction $\frac{8}{200}$ equals $\frac{1}{25}$.

3. **The correct answer is (4):** $\frac{1}{7}$ There are only seven possibilities, the seven days of the week. Tuesday is one of seven.

4. **The correct answer is (2):** $\frac{3}{250,000}$

5. **The correct answer is (1):** $\frac{1}{6}$ One of the six faces is a 6.

6. **The correct answer is (4):** $\frac{2}{3}$ Four of the six faces are *not 3 or 4*. Rename $\frac{4}{6}$ as $\frac{2}{3}$.

7. **The correct answer is (1):** $\frac{1}{2}$ How many guppies are in the tank is not important as long as there are the same number of males and females. There are 2 possible outcomes and 1 is male.

8. **The correct answer is (3):** $\frac{1}{3}$ Six of the 18 numbers are long-distance calls. $\frac{6}{18}$ equals $\frac{1}{3}$.

9. **The correct answer is (3):** $\frac{1}{2}$ Yellow and blue must each occupy $\frac{1}{4}$ of the spinner.

Exercise 8 *(page 345)*

1. **The correct answer is: $1,029** 15% of $82,350 is 0.15 × $82,350 = $12,352.5 in a year. ⇒ $12,352.5 ÷ 12 = $1,029.375 ≈ $1,029 in a month. See page 406 for filled-in answer grid.

2. **The correct answer is: 0.07** A probability is simply the percentage written in decimal form or fraction form. It is a number between 0 and 1, inclusive of the endpoints. ($0 \le p \le 1$). So in this problem, the answer is simply 7%, written in decimal form 0.07. See page 406 for filled-in answer grid.

3. **The correct answer is: $3,108** 0.36 × $8632 = $3107.52 ≈ $3,108. See page 406 for filled-in answer grid.

4. **The correct answer is: Team 3** Find the individual mean (averages) of each team. You will find that Team 3 had the highest average $\frac{17.4 + 18.2 + 17.1}{3} = \frac{52.7}{3} = 17.7$ See page 406 for filled-in answer grid.

5. **The correct answer is: 17.1** Arrange all the values in ascending order: 9.7, 9.7, 15.8, 16.2, 17.1, 17.4, 18.2, 19.2, 20.1. We have an odd number 9 of data points and the middle number 17.1 is the median. See page 406 for filled-in answer grid.

6. **The correct answer is: 9.7** The most frequently occurring number is the mode: 9.7. See page 406 for filled-in answer grid.

7. **The correct answer is: 78.6** *At least* translates to having no fewer than 3 toppings. Therefore, 38.7 + 19.3 + 20.6 = 78.6%. Omit the percent sign when filling out the grid. See page 406 for filled-in answer grid.

8. **The correct answer is: 79.4** *At most* translates to having no more than 4 toppings. So 19.3 + 38.7 + 11.0 + 10.4 = 79.4%. Omit the percent sign when filling out the grid. See page 406 for filled-in answer grid.

9. **The correct answer is: 69** 11 + 38.7 + 19.3 = 69%. Omit the percent sign when filling out the grid. See page 406 for filled-in answer grid.

Unit 8: Measurement

Exercise 1 *(page 348)*

1. **The correct answer is: j**
2. **The correct answer is: i**
3. **The correct answer is: f**
4. **The correct answer is: g**
5. **The correct answer is: h**
6. **The correct answer is: a**
7. **The correct answer is: k**
8. **The correct answer is: c**
9. **The correct answer is: l**

10. The correct answer is: b

11. The correct answer is: d

12. The correct answer is: e

13. The correct answer is: 3 ft

14. The correct answer is: 3 ft 11 in

15. The correct answer is: 1 lb 4 oz

16. The correct answer is: 2 lb 2 oz

17. The correct answer is: 1 d 12 hr

18. The correct answer is: 3 d 4 hr

19. The correct answer is: 86.4 oz

20. The correct answer is: 3 gal 2 qt, or $3\frac{1}{2}$ gal

21. The correct answer is: 2 T 1,000 lb, or $2\frac{1}{2}$ T

22. The correct answer is (4): ounces

Exercise 2 *(page 349)*

1. The correct answer is: a

2. The correct answer is: e

3. The correct answer is: d

4. The correct answer is: b

5. The correct answer is: c

6. The correct answer is: 500cm

$$\frac{1}{100} = \frac{5}{?}$$

$$\frac{5(100)}{1} = 500\text{cm}$$

7. The correct answer is: 60,000L

$$\frac{1}{1,000} = \frac{60}{?}$$

$$\frac{60(1,000)}{1} = 60,000 \text{ L}$$

8. The correct answer is: 8.762kg

$$\frac{1}{1,000} = \frac{?}{8,762}$$

$$\frac{1(8,762)}{1,000} = 8.762\text{kg}$$

9. The correct answer is (1): 1.5

10. The correct answer is (3): centimeters

Exercise 3 *(page 350)*

1. The correct answer is: 1 ft 7 in

2. The correct answer is: 10 in

3. The correct answer is: 36 min

4. The correct answer is: 18 ft

5. The correct answer is: 6 yd

6. The correct answer is: 19 lb 10 oz

7. The correct answer is: 2 qt

8. The correct answer is: 5 yd 1 ft

9. The correct answer is: 2 qt 2 c, or $2\frac{1}{2}$ qt

10. The correct answer is: 2 lb 10 oz

11. The correct answer is (3): 6 ft 6 in

12. The correct answer is (2): 4 hr 57 min

13. The correct answer is (5): 8 yd 2 ft

14. The correct answer is (5): **Not enough information is given.**
You need to know the weight allowance.

Exercise 4 *(page 351)*

1. The correct answer is: 19 ft 3 in, or 6 yd 1 ft 3 in

2. The correct answer is: 13 d 21 hr

3. The correct answer is: 87 lb 8 oz

4. The correct answer is: 54 gal 1 qt

5. The correct answer is: 21 qt

6. The correct answer is: 37 lb 4 oz

7. The correct answer is (4): 5

Exercise 5 *(page 352)*

1. The correct answer is: 1 mi 1,607 ft

2. The correct answer is: 4 hr 30 min

3. The correct answer is: 1 gal 2 qt, or $1\frac{1}{2}$ gal

4. The correct answer is: 4 ft 3 in

5. The correct answer is (1): 4 ft 10 in

6. The correct answer is (3): Four 8-hour days

Exercise 6 *(page 353)*

1. The correct answer is: 108.9L
   99.0
   +9.9
   ‾‾‾‾
   108.9

2. The correct answer is: 13mm
   5.8
   +7.2
   ‾‾‾‾
   13.0

3. The correct answer is: 12.9km   500m = 0.5km
   13.4
   −0.5
   ‾‾‾‾
   12.9

4. The correct answer is: 2.25km
   3.45
   −1.20
   ‾‾‾‾
   2.25

5. The correct answer is: 22.4cm

6. The correct answer is: 49.05kg

7. The correct answer is: 0.4km

8. The correct answer is: 1.34m

9. The correct answer is (1): 156   220 − 64 = 156

10. The correct answer is (4): 20

11. The correct answer is (3): $\frac{1,266}{2}$

12. The correct answer is (2): 5.25m
    Add: 185 + 340 = 525 cm
    Change to meters.

    $$\frac{525}{?} = \frac{100}{1}$$

    $$\frac{1(525)}{100} = 5.25 \text{ m}$$

13. The correct answer is (5): **Not enough information is given.**
    You would need to know how much the bottle holds to solve the problem. Don't waste time working with the numbers until you have read the whole problem. Make sure you have all the facts you need before you start any calculations.

14. **The correct answer is (4): 600mg**

    2 capsules
    × 4 times per day
    8 capsules daily
    × 3 days
    24 capsules in 3 days
    24 × 25mg = 600mg

15. **The correct answer is (2): 2.5g**

    25mg × 100 = 2,500mg = 2.5g

Exercise 7 *(page 355)*

1. **The correct answer is: 20cm** 2(7) + 2(3)

2. **The correct answer is: 66 ft**

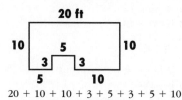

    20 + 10 + 10 + 3 + 5 + 3 + 5 + 10

3. **The correct answer is: 46cm**

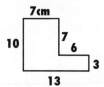

    7 + 7 + 6 + 3 + 13 + 10

4. **The correct answer is: 60 in**

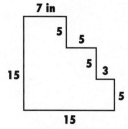

    7 + 5 + 5 + 5 + 3 + 5 + 15 + 15

5. **The correct answer is (4): 60**   perimeter of a square: 4(15)

6. **The correct answer is (3): 38**   perimeter of a rectangle: 2(11) + 2(8)

Exercise 8 *(page 357)*

1. **The correct answer is: 21cm²**   7(3)

2. **The correct answer is: 625 sq in**   25²

3. **The correct answer is: 12 sq ft**   12(1)

4. **The correct answer is: 130 in²**   13(10)

5. **The correct answer is (4): 370** Find the area of her backyard, and subtract the area of the patio. 22(20) − 10(7)

6. **The correct answer is (2): 15,604m²** Use the formula for finding the area of a rectangle.

    $A = lw$
    $A = 188(83)$
    $A = 15,604m^2$

    You can solve this problem more quickly using estimation.
    Instead of: 188(83)
    Think: 190(80) = 15,200
    Only choice (2) is close to the estimate.

7. **The correct answer is (5): 225**   15²

8. **The correct answer is (3): 12**   4(3)

Exercise 9 *(page 358)*

1. **The correct answer is: 12.167m³**   2.3(2.3)(2.3)

2. **The correct answer is: 560 ft³**   10(7)(8)

3. **The correct answer is: 253 cu in**   9.2(5)(5.5)

4. **The correct answer is (3): 8 cu ft** Use the formula for finding the volume of a cube.

    $V = s^3$
    $V = 2(2)(2) = 8$ cu ft

5. **The correct answer is (2): 60**   5(3)(4)

6. **The correct answer is (4): 3,200**   20(16)(10)

Exercise 10 *(page 359)*

1. **The correct answer is: 40** 1m = 100cm. ⇒ 4m = (4 × 100) = 400cm. Therefore, 400 ÷ 10 = 40. See page 407 for filled-in answer grid.

2. **The correct answer is: 9.8 lbs** First change all measures to ounces.

    10 lb 3oz = 10 × 16 + 3 = 163 oz.
    9 lb 11 oz = 9 × 16 + 11 = 155 oz.
    9 lb 9 oz = 9 × 16 + 10 = 154 oz.

    Total = (163 + 155 + 154) = 472. Average = $\frac{472}{3}$ = 157.33 oz. Change to lbs 157.33 ÷ 16 = 9.83 lb ≈ 9.8 lb average weight of each bag in pounds. Change 0.8 to oz 0.8 × 16 = 12.8 oz ≈ 13 oz. Therefore, 9 lb 13 oz average weight of each bag. See page 407 for filled-in answer grid.

3. **The correct answer is: 33.7 km** Change 55 miles to kilometers. Use a proportion.

Mile	Kilometer
0.62	1
55	x

    $\Rightarrow \frac{0.62}{55} = \frac{1}{x} \Rightarrow 0.62x\ 55 \times 1 \Rightarrow x = \frac{55}{0.062} = 88.70$km. Therefore, 88.70km − 75km = 33.7km. See page 407 for filled-in answer grid.

Unit 9: Algebra

Exercise 1 *(page 360)*

1. **The correct answer is (3): −6**

2. **The correct answer is (3): 3**

3. **The correct answer is (3): N < 5**

Exercise 2 *(page 361)*

1. **The correct answer is (2): −200 + 328** 200 feet below sea level is −200 and the lava shot up 328 (a positive).

2. **The correct answer is (1): −50**

3. **The correct answer is (3): 184 feet** You need to find the difference between the two numbers: 92 − (−92) = 184 feet.

4. **The correct answer is (2): 22 − (−4)** The second temperature (−4) is subtracted from the first (22).

5. **The correct answer is (4): −39**
   Add: 9 + (−10) + 11 + (−49) = −39

6. **The correct answer is (3): A and C**
   −(−3) changes to + 3.
   +(−2) is the same as − 2.

7. **The correct answer is (4): 10 − (5 − 10)** The operation in parentheses is used to find the temperature for Wednesday, which is subtracted from Thursday's temperature to find the change, or difference.

Exercise 3 *(page 363)*

1. The correct answer is: 60
2. The correct answer is: −60
3. The correct answer is: 42
4. The correct answer is: −5
5. The correct answer is: −5
6. The correct answer is: 5
7. The correct answer is (5): 24
8. The correct answer is (1): 14

Exercise 4 *(page 364)*

1. The correct answer is (3): $2b
2. The correct answer is (4): x + $35
3. The correct answer is (1): $20 − 3y
4. The correct answer is (5): $p^2 − 15$
5. The correct answer is (4): $\frac{g}{6}$
6. The correct answer is (3): 2(w + $1) The price of one pound of lobster this week is w + $1. Two pounds would be twice the sum of w + $1.
7. The correct answer is (2): 6(m − 3) Harry runs m − 3 each day. In six days he runs 6 times that amount.
8. The correct answer is (5): 43 − (x + 2y)

Exercise 5 *(page 365)*

1. The correct answer is: 10
2. The correct answer is: 15
3. The correct answer is: 14
4. The correct answer is: 12
5. The correct answer is: 7
6. The correct answer is: 20
7. The correct answer is (2): 8
8. The correct answer is (5): Between 14 and 15

Exercise 6 *(page 366)*

1. The correct answer is (3): 2.345×10^6 Move the decimal point behind the first digit, which is 6 places to the left.
2. The correct answer is (5): 3,600,000,000 Move the decimal point 9 places to the right to change back to standard notation.
3. The correct answer is (4): 4×10^3 is equal to 4,000 10^3 is equal to 1,000.
4. The correct answer is (2): 5.6×10^7

Exercise 7 *(page 367)*

1. The correct answer is (1): 19s
2. The correct answer is (4): 2.5h Add the coefficients 0.8 + 1.7.
3. The correct answer is (3): 4(t) − 4(7)
4. The correct answer is (4): $15t^2 + 5t − 10$
5. The correct answer is (2): r − 12   5r − 2(2r) − 2(6)
6. The correct answer is (1): 21a + b
7. The correct answer is (4): 34a + 22b

   6(5a + 4b) + 2(2a − b)
   30a + 24b + 4a − 2b
   34a + 22b
8. The correct answer is (4): −9a − 16

Exercise 8 *(page 368)*

1. The correct answer is: 4 $2^2 = 2(2)$
2. The correct answer is: 1 $1^2 = 1(1)$
3. The correct answer is: 45 $5(3)^2 = 5(9)$
4. The correct answer is: 18 $2(3)^2 = 2(9)$
5. The correct answer is: $1\frac{2^2}{4} = \frac{4}{4}$
6. The correct answer is: 12 $2^2(3) = 4(3)$
7. The correct answer is: 13 $2^2 + 3^2 = 4 + 9$
8. The correct answer is: 25 $(2 + 3)^2 = (5)^2$
9. The correct answer is: 7 $2^2 + 3 = 4 + 3$
10. The correct answer is: 36 $(2)^2(3)^2 = (4)(9)$
11. The correct answer is (5): −13

    $\frac{6^2 + (−4)^2}{−4} = \frac{36 + 16}{−4} = \frac{52}{−4}$
12. The correct answer is (4): 628 $3.14(10)^2(2) = 3.14(100)(2)$
13. The correct answer is: (2) 40
14. The correct answer is (3): $2,000(0.06)(4)

Exercise 9 *(page 370)*

1. A. n = 27 + 19 = 46
   B. p = 46 − 27 = 19
   C. r = 56 ÷ 7 = 8
2. A. t = 19 − 15 = 4
   B. c = 25(4) = 100
   C. f = 51 ÷ 3 = 17
3. A. a = 5(11) = 55
   B. c = 32 − 26 = 6
   C. n = 113 + 79 = 192
4. A. x = 11(5) = 55
   B. q = 97 − 9 = 88
   C. n = 8(6) = 48
5. A. b = 90 ÷ 9 = 10
   B. x = 72 + 48 = 120
   C. s = 150(2) = 300
6. The correct answer is (1): $6

   12t = $72

   $\frac{$72}{12} = 6
7. The correct answer is (4): 11 ft

   12w = 132

   $\frac{132}{12} = 11$
8. The correct answer is (3): $2,185

   x + $115 = $2,300
   x = $2,300 − $115 = $2,185

Exercise 10 *(page 371)*

1. The correct answer is: w = 7 $w = \frac{34 − 6}{4}$
2. The correct answer is: y = 3 $y = \frac{28 + 8}{12}$
3. The correct answers is: s = 60 $s = 4(2 + 13)$
4. The correct answer is: r = 3 $r = \frac{21 − 6}{5}$
5. The correct answer is: v = 34 $v = \frac{60 + 42}{3}$
6. The correct answer is: g = 12 $g = \frac{42 + 42}{7}$

7. **The correct answer is:** $t = 1$

$$8t - 2t = 6$$
$$6t = 6$$

8. **The correct answer is:** $m = 7$

$$13m - 11m = 21 - 7$$
$$2m = 14$$

9. **The correct answer is:** $s = 6$

$$14s - 13s = 17 - 11$$
$$s = 6$$

10. **The correct answer is (4): 10.2** $v = 3.4 + 6.8 = 10.2$

11. **The correct answer is (2): 18**

$$k = \frac{11 - 2}{0.5} = 18$$

12. **The correct answer is (5): 6**

$$3x + 10x - 16 = 11x - 4$$
$$13x - 11x = -4 + 16$$
$$2x = 12$$
$$x = 6$$

13. **The correct answer is (2): 20** $(20)^2 = 400$

14. **The correct answer is (1): 0**

15. **The correct answer is (2): 3**

Exercise 11 *(page 373)*

1. **The correct answer is (2):** $w < 27$ $w < 12 + 15$
2. **The correct answer is (4):** $x \leq 50$

$$x \leq \frac{100}{2}$$

3. **The correct answer is (3):** $g > 41$

$$g > \frac{140 - 17}{3}$$

4. **The correct answer is (1): 7**

$$-3y - 7 \geq -28$$
$$-3y \geq 21$$
$$y \leq 7$$

$7 = 7$ so it is in the solution set.

5. **The correct answer is (1): 4**

$$8h - 4 > 28$$
$$8h > 32$$
$$h > 4$$

4 is not greater than 4. 4 is not in the solution set.

6. **The correct answer is (2):** $3x + 8 \geq 29$

Exercise 12 *(page 374)*

1. **The correct answer is (3): 17** $68 = 4l$
2. **The correct answer is (2): 5** $60 = 3(4)h$
3. **The correct answer is (4):** $121 = s^2$
4. **The correct answer is (5): Not enough information is given.** The length of the yard is not given.
5. **The correct answer is (4): 10** $30 = 2l + 2(5)$
6. **The correct answer is (2):** $600 = 10(10)w$
7. **The correct answer is (4): 30** $P = 2l + 2w$

$$144 = 2(42) + 2(w)$$

Exercise 13 *(page 375)*

1. **The correct answer is (2): −2 and 7**

$$(-2)^2 - 5(-2) = 14$$
$$4 + 10 = 14$$
$$(7)^2 - 5(7) = 14$$
$$49 - 35 = 14$$

2. **The correct answer is (3): 5 and −6**

$$2(5)^2 + 2(5) - 60 = 0$$
$$2(25) + 10 - 60 = 0$$
$$50 + 10 - 60 = 0$$
$$2(-6)^2 + 2(-6) - 60 = 0$$
$$2(36) - 12 - 60 = 0$$
$$72 - 12 - 60 = 0$$

3. **The correct answer is (5): −7 and 8**

$$(-7)^2 - (-7) - 56 = 0$$
$$49 + 7 - 56 = 0$$
$$(8)^2 - 8 - 56 = 0$$
$$64 - 8 - 56 = 0$$

Exercise 14 *(page 376)*

1. **The correct answer is: 4 gallons** Carl's car is $2x$.

Unknown	Variable	Equation
Mary's car	x	$x + 2x = 6$
Carl's car	$2x$	

$$3x = 6$$
$$x = 2$$
$$2x = 4 \text{ Carl's car}$$

2. **The correct answer is: 52°** Yesterday's temperature was x.

Unknown	Variable	Equation
Yesterday's temperature	x	$72 = x + 20$

$$x = 52$$

3. **The correct answer is: 47**   The first number is x.

Unknown	Variable	Equation
1st no.	x	$x + x + 2 = 96$
2nd no.	$x + 2$	

$$2x + 2 = 96$$
$$2x = 94$$
$$x = 47 \text{ First number}$$

4. **The correct answer is: 30 years old** Debbie's age is $3x$.

Ages	Now	Now + 10	Equation
Aisling	x	$x + 10$	$3x + 10 = 2(x + 10)$
Debbie	$3x$	$3x + 10$	

$$3x - 2x = 20 - 10$$
$$x = 10$$
$$3x = 30 \text{ Debbie's age}$$

5. **The correct answer is (1): 4** Since the value of m must be greater than 3, only choice (1) can be correct.

6. **The correct answer is (4): 2,400** Women = $2x$

Unknown	Variable	Equation
Men	x	$x + 2x = 3,600$
Women	$2x$	

$$x = 1,200$$
$$2x = 2,400 \text{ Women}$$

7. **The correct answer is (2): $6** Child's ticket = t

$$10t + 5t = \$100 - \$10$$
$$15t = \$90$$
$$t = \$6 \text{ Child}$$
$$t + \$2 = \$8 \text{ Adult}$$

8. **The correct answer is: 7** $3s \leq 22$

9. **The correct answer is (3): 50** Round-trip distance = x

Unknown	Variable	Equation
Dist. to work	x	$5x + 74 = 324$
Trips to work	$5x$	

$$x = \frac{324 - 74}{5}$$

$$x = 50$$

10. **The correct answer is (5): 54** Largest number $= x + 2$

Nos.	Variable	Equation
1st no.	x	
2nd no.	$x + 1$	$x + x + 1 + x + 2 = 159$
3rd no.	$x + 2$	

$$3x + 3 = 159$$

$$x = \frac{159 - 3}{3}$$

$$x = 52$$

$x + 2 = 54$ Largest number

11. **The correct answer is (1): 3** Sharon $= a - 4$

Ages	Now	Now + 5	Equation
Kenny	a	$a + 5$	
Sharon	$a - 4$	$a - 4 + 5$	$2(a + 5) = 3(a + 1)$
		or $a + 1$	

$$2a + 10 = 3a + 3$$
$$2a - 3a = 3 - 10$$
$$-a = -7$$
$$a = 7$$

Exercise 15 (page 377)

1. **The correct answer is: 17** The three numbers are x, $(x + 1)$, $(x$ 2). Therefore, $x + (x + 1) + (x + 2) = 51 \Rightarrow 3x + 3 = 51 \Rightarrow x = 16$. Therefore, 17 is the second number. See page 407 for filled-in answer grid.

2. **The correct answer is: 50** Let x be the larger number, then $87 - x$ is the smaller number. Therefore, $x - (87 - x) = 13 \Rightarrow x - 87 + x = 13 \Rightarrow 2x = 13 + 87 \Rightarrow x = \frac{100}{2}$. Therefore, $x = 50$. See page 407 for filled-in answer grid.

3. **The correct answer is: 100**

	Quarters	Dimes	Total
Number of coins	x		150
Amount of money	$\$0.25x$	$\$0.10(150 - x)$	$\$30$

Therefore, $\$0.25x + \$0.10(150 - x) = \$30$.

$$\$0.25x + \$15 - \$0.10x = \$30$$
$$\$0.15x = \$15$$

Therefore, $x = 100$ quarters See page 407 for filled-in answer grid.

4. **The correct answer is: 93** Let x be the grade he needs on his next test. Then we have

$$\frac{88 + 87 + 92 + x}{4} = 90$$
$$267 + x = 90 \cdot 4$$
$$x = 360 - 267$$

Therefore, $x = 93$. See page 407 for filled-in answer grid.

Unit 10: Geometry

Exercise 1 (page 379)

1. **The correct answer is: $\angle b = 110°$** $180° - 70°$
2. **The correct answer is: $\angle e = 70°$** It corresponds with $\angle a$.
3. **The correct answer is: Angles d, e, and b**
4. **The correct answer is: Angles c, f, and g**
5. **The correct answer is (1): 55°** $90° - 35° = 55°$
6. **The correct answer is (5): 110°**
7. **The correct answer is (4): $\angle 3$ measures 90°**

Exercise 2 (page 380)

1. **The correct answer is: 40cm^2**
2. **The correct answer is: 84 in^2**
3. **The correct answer is: 150 ft^2**
4. **The correct answer is: 66m^2**
5. **The correct answer is (5): Not enough information is given.** The perimeter cannot be found without the length of the side. The area cannot be found without the length of the height.

Exercise 3 (page 381)

1. **The correct answer is (3): Scalene** A scalene triangle has no equal angles.
2. **The correct answer is (2): Right** Any triangle with a 90° angle is called a right triangle.
3. **The correct answer is (4): Isosceles** An isosceles triangle has two sides of equal length.
4. **The correct answer is (2): 50°** $180 - (65 + 65)$

Exercise 4 (page 383)

1. **The correct answer is: $P = 21$cm $A = 21$cm^2**
2. **The correct answer is: $P = 48$ in $A = 96$ in^2**
3. **The correct answer is (4): The perimeter of $\triangle$GHJ can be found using $P = 6 + 6 + 6$.** All three sides of an equilateral triangle have the same length.
4. **The correct answer is (2): 140** Square units are units of area. $\frac{1}{2}(20)(14)$
5. **The correct answer is (5): Not enough information is given.** You need the measure of all three sides to find the perimeter.
6. **The correct answer is (1): 26** $6 + 10 + 10$
7. **The correct answer is (2): 36** The sides of an equilateral triangle are equal. **Add:** $12 + 12 + 12 = 36$.
8. **The correct answer is (5): Not enough information is given.** Since all sides of a scalene triangle are different, there is no way to know the length of the missing side.

Exercise 5 (page 385)

Leg A	Leg B	Hypotenuse

1. **The correct answer is:**
   | 3 | 4 | **5** |

   $$c^2 = 3^2 + 4^2$$
   $$c = \sqrt{25}$$

2. **The correct answer is:**
   | 6 | 8 | 10 |

   $$(10)^2 = (6)^2 + b^2$$
   $$100 - 36 = b^2$$
   $$\sqrt{64} = b$$

3. **The correct answer is:**
   | 8 | 8 | **Between 11 and 12** |

   $$c^2 = 8^2 + 8^2$$
   $$c = \sqrt{128}$$

4. **The correct answer is:**
   | 30 | 40 | 50 |

   $$50^2 = a^2 + 40^2$$
   $$2,500 - 1,600 = a^2$$
   $$\sqrt{900} = a$$

5. **The correct answer is (2):** $\sqrt{1{,}296}$

$$60^2 = 48^2 + b^2$$
$$3{,}600 - 2{,}304 = b^2$$
$$\sqrt{1{,}296} = b$$

6. **The correct answer is (3): 19**

$$20^2 = 6^2 + b^2$$
$$400 - 36 = b^2$$
$$\sqrt{364} = b$$

Guess and check the answers.
$19(19) = 361$

Exercise 6 *(page 387)*

1. **The correct answer is (3): 168** Because the angles are the same, the two right triangles are similar. Use a proportion to find the missing side (the distance across the lake).

$$\frac{6\text{m (base)}}{14\text{m (height)}} = \frac{72\text{m (base)}}{x\text{m (height)}}$$

$$\frac{14(72)}{6} = 168$$

2. **The correct answer is (2): 30** The angle of the sun is the same on both the tree and the post, so you have two similar right triangles. Use a proportion to find the height of the tree.

$$\frac{8\text{ ft post}}{12\text{ ft shadow}} = \frac{x\text{ ft tree}}{45\text{ ft shadow}}$$

$$\frac{8(45)}{12} = 30\text{ ft}$$

3. **The correct answer is (3): 20** Side *CE* is proportional to side *AC*. Set up a proportion.

$$\frac{6\text{ in (base)}}{8\text{ in (side)}} = \frac{15\text{ in (base)}}{x\text{ in (side)}}$$

$$\frac{8(15)}{6} = 20\text{ in.}$$

Exercise 7 *(page 388)*

1. **The correct answer is: 31.4 in** $3.14(10)$
2. **The correct answer is: 12.56cm** $d = 2(2)$; then multiply by 3.14
3. **The correct answer is (4): 18.84 ft** $3.14(6)$

Exercise 8 *(page 389)*

1. **The correct answer is: 3.14 ft²** $3.14(1)^2 = 3.14(1)$
2. **The correct answer is: 113.04 in²**

$$r = \frac{1}{2}(12) = 6$$
$$3.14(6)^2 = 3.14(36)$$

3. **The correct answer is: 12.56cm²** $3.14(2)^2 = 3.14(4)$
4. **The correct answer is (4): 3.14(2.5)(2.5)**
5. **The correct answer is (5): Not enough information is given.** You need to know the diameter or radius of the garden to find the radius of the larger circle.

Exercise 9 *(page 390)*

1. **The correct answer is: 125.6 cubic inches**

$3.14(2)^2(10)$
$3.14(4)(10)$

2. **The correct answer is: 0.785 cubic meters** Half of the diameter is 0.5.

$3.14(0.5)^2(1)$
$3.14(0.25)(1)$

3. **The correct answer is: 31,400 ft³**

$3.14(10)^2(100)$
$3.14(100)(100)$

4. **The correct answer is (3):** $3.14(100)^2(500)$
5. **The correct answer is (4): 10**

$V = \pi r^2 h$
$31.4 = 3.14(1)^2 h$
Simplify the exponent and multiply.
$31.4 = 3.14h$
Divide by 3.14 to find *h*.

$$h = \frac{31.4}{3.14}$$

6. **The correct answer is (2): 9.42** $3.14(1)^2(6) \div 2$

$$\frac{3.14(1)(6)}{2} = 9.42$$

7. **The correct answer is (2): 100** The radius for both figures is the same. Find the volume of each, and subtract to find the difference.

Cylinder A: $(3.14)(4)^2(12) = 602.88$
Cylinder B: $(3.14)(4)^2(10) = 502.4$
The difference is nearly 100 cubic feet.

Exercise 10 *(page 392)*

1. **The correct answer is:** (3, 4) D
2. **The correct answer is:** (3, −4) K
3. **The correct answer is:** (−3, −4) H
4. **The correct answer is:** (−3, 4) C
5. **The correct answer is:** (1, −2) I
6. **The correct answer is:** (−6, 0) F
7. **The correct answer is:** (0, 6) A
8. **The correct answer is:** (5, −4) L
9. **The correct answer is:** (−3, −3) G
10. **The correct answer is:** (5, 3) E
11. **The correct answer is:** (−1, 5) B
12. **The correct answer is:** (0, −4) J
13.

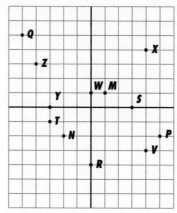

Exercise 11 (page 393)

1. **The correct answer is:** $y = x + 4$

x	y
−2	2
−1	3
0	4
1	5

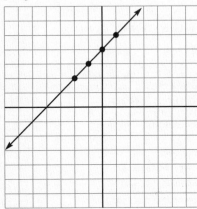

2. **The correct answer is (3): Point B is incorrect.** It will not fall on the line $y = -2x + 6$.

$$-2(-1) + 6 = 2 + 6 = 8$$

3. **The correct answer is (2): (1, 7)**

$$y = 3x + 4$$
$$7 = 3(1) + 4$$

Exercise 12 (page 394)

1. **The correct answer is: 5** Points on the same vertical line have the same x-coordinates. Count down from J (−1, 6) to K (−1, 1), or subtract the y-coordinates (6 − 1).

2. **The correct answer is: 3** Points on the same horizontal line have the same y-coordinates. Count over from M (1, 1) to N (4, 1), or subtract the x-coordinates (4 − 1).

3. **The correct answer is: 4** Points on the same vertical line have the same x-coordinates. Count down from L (4, 5) to N (4, 1), or subtract the y-coordinates (5 − 1).

4. **The correct answer is: 5** Substitute the coordinates of the points into the distance formula.

$$d = \sqrt{(x_2 - x_1)^2 + (y_2 - y_1)^2}$$
$$d = \sqrt{(4 - 1)^2 + (5 - 1)^2}$$
$$d = \sqrt{3^2 + 4^2}$$
$$d = \sqrt{9 + 16}$$
$$d = 5$$

5. **The correct answer is: 10** Substitute the coordinates of the points into the distance formula.

$$d = \sqrt{(x_2 - x_1)^2 + (y_2 - y_1)^2}$$
$$d = \sqrt{(5 - (-1))^2 + (9 - 1)^2}$$
$$d = \sqrt{36 + 64}$$
$$d = \sqrt{100}$$
$$d = 10$$

Exercise 13 (page 395)

1. **The correct answer is:** $\frac{3}{1}$**, or 3** Count up and over on the graph, or substitute the values for the points in the formula for slope.

$$m = \frac{2 - (-1)}{1 - 0} = \frac{2 + 1}{1} = \frac{3}{1} = 3$$

2. **The correct answer is: The slope of a horizontal line is zero.**

3. **The correct answer is: Slope = 1** Substitute the values for the points in the formula for slope.

$$m = \frac{9 - 5}{8 - 4} = \frac{4}{4} = 1$$

4. **The correct answer is: Slope = −1** Substitute the values for the points in the formula for slope.

$$m = \frac{-1 - 3}{3 - (-1)} = \frac{-4}{4} = -1$$

Exercise 14 (page 396)

1. **The correct answer is (5): (0, −6)** In the equation $y = 4x - 6$, **−6** is the y-intercept.

2. **The correct answer is (2): (0, 2)** In the equation $y = 3x + 2$, **2** is the y-intercept.

3. **The correct answer is (3): $y = -3x - 3$** In the equation $y = -3x - 3$, **−3** is the y-intercept.

4. **The correct answer is (4):** $\frac{4}{1}$ In the equation $y = 4x + 2$, the slope = 4.

Exercise 15 (page 396)

1. **The correct answer is: 28.2** Volume of small container: $(4 \times 4 \times 4) + (\pi \times 2^2 \times 2) = 89.12$. Volume of large container: $(\pi \times 8^2 \times 12) + (\pi \times 4^2 \times 2) = 2512$. Therefore, $2512 \div 89.12 = 28.12 \approx 28.2$. Note, you *can* fill a partial container of liquid. See page 407 for filled-in answer grid.

2. **The correct answer is: 6** Mary and Tasha live at points $(3, -2)$ and $(5, 4)$, respectively. The distance is
$$d = \sqrt{(5 - 3)^2 + (4 - (-2))^2} = \sqrt{2^2 + 6^2 rlx} = \sqrt{40} = 6.3 \approx$$
6. See page 407 for filled-in answer grid.

3. **The correct answer is: 3** $m = \frac{y_2 - y_1}{x^2 - x^1} = \frac{4 - (-2)}{5 - 3} = \frac{6}{2} = 3$. See page 407 for filled-in answer grid.

4. **The correct answer is: 131.4** The four quarter circles together become a whole circle. Therefore Area$_{Shape}$ = Area$_{Square}$ − Area$_{Circle}$ ⇒ $12^2 - \pi \times 2^2 = 144 - 4\pi = 131.44 \approx 131.4$. See page 407 for filled-in answer grid.

Exercise 16 (page 397)

1. **The correct answer is (−3,−2).** From the origin (0,0) move 3 units left, then 2 units down.

2. **The correct answer is (−3,1).** Use Mary's house as your reference. From $(3, -2)$, move 3 units north (up), then move 6 units west (left). This brings you to $(-3, 1)$.

3. **The correct answer is (3,−2).** The center of the circle is the midpoint of its diameter. Therefore,
$$\text{midpoint} = \left(\frac{x_1 + x_2}{2}, \frac{y_1 + y_2}{2}\right) = \left(\frac{6 + 0}{2}, \frac{1 - 5}{2}\right) = (3, -2).$$

4. **The correct answer is (1,2).** First find the midpoint of $\overline{BC}$. It is $(1, -5)$. Count 7 units up from here. You end up at $(1, 2)$.

Unit 11: Trigonometry

Exercise 1 (page 400)

1. $a = 16.4$, $b = 45$, $c = 47.9$, $\theta = 20°$, $\alpha = 70°$
2. $a = 70$, $b = 56.7$, $c = 90.1$, $\theta = 51°$, $\alpha = 39°$
3. $a = 66.9$, $b = 74.3$, $c = 100$, $\theta = 42°$, $\alpha = 48°$
4. $a = 55.8$, $b = 42$, $c = 76.2$, $\theta = 47°$, $\alpha = 43°$
5. $a = 72$, $b = 141.3$, $c = 158.6$, $\theta = 27°$, $\alpha = 63°$
6. $a = 85.5$, $b = 234.9$, $c = 250$, $\theta = 20°$, $\alpha = 70°$
7. $a = 30$, $b = 40$, $c = 50$, $\theta = 36.9°$, $\alpha = 53.1°$

8. $a = 50$, $b = 45.8$, $c = 20$, $\theta = 23.6°$, $\alpha = 66.4°$

9. $a = 154.6$, $b = 82$, $c = 175$, $\theta = 62.1°$, $\alpha = 27.9°$

10. $a = 17.4$, $b = 15$, $c = 23$, $\theta = 49.3°$, $\alpha = 40.7°$

Exercise 2 *(page 401)*

1. **The correct answer is (2): 150**

Distance $= \sqrt{90^2 + 120^2} = 150$.

2. **The correct answer is (4): 4,295.4**

$$\tan 88° = \frac{x}{150}$$
$$x = 150 \times (\tan 88°) = 4295.43 \approx 4295.4$$

3. **The correct answer is (1): 24.0°**

$$\theta = \tan^{-1}\left(\frac{16}{36}\right) = 23.96° \approx 24.0°$$

4. **The correct answer is (1): 23.5**

$$\cos 35° = \frac{x}{60}$$
$$x = 60(\cos 35°)$$
$$x = 49.14 \approx 49.1$$
$$\sin 35° = \frac{y}{60}$$
$$y = 60(\sin 35°)$$
$$y = 34.41 \approx 34.4$$
$$49.1 + 34.4 - 60 = 3.5$$

Exercise 3 *(page 402)*

1. **The correct answer is (5):** $\theta = \tan^{-1}\left(\frac{110}{200}\right)$

2. **The correct answer is (1):** $x = \sqrt{180^2 - 100^2}$

3. **The correct answer is (3):** $x = 150 \times (\tan 26°)$

4. **The correct answer is (2):** $x = 1500 \times (\cos 45°)$

Exercise 4 *(page 403)*

1. **The correct answer is: 31**

$$\tan 43° = \frac{x}{33}$$
$$x = 33 \times (\tan 43°) = 30.7 \approx 31$$

See page 407 for filled-in answer grid.

2. **The correct answer is: 173**

$$\sin 60° = \frac{x}{200}$$
$$x = 200 \times (\sin 60°) = 173.2 \approx 173$$

See page 407 for filled-in answer grid.

3. **The correct answer is: 139**

$$c = 360.6$$
$$(300 + 200) - 360.6 = 139.4 \approx 139$$

See page 407 for filled-in answer grid.

4. **The correct answer is: 35°**

$$\geq v = \cos^{-1}\left(\frac{60}{73}\right) = 34.7° \approx 35°$$

See page 407 for filled-in answer grid.

POSTTESTS

ANSWER SHEETS

- Use a #2 pencil.
- Mark one numbered space beside the number that corresponds to each question you are answering.
- Erase errors cleanly and completely.

Posttest 1: Language Arts, Writing
Part I

1. ① ② ③ ④ ⑤
2. ① ② ③ ④ ⑤
3. ① ② ③ ④ ⑤
4. ① ② ③ ④ ⑤
5. ① ② ③ ④ ⑤
6. ① ② ③ ④ ⑤
7. ① ② ③ ④ ⑤
8. ① ② ③ ④ ⑤
9. ① ② ③ ④ ⑤
10. ① ② ③ ④ ⑤
11. ① ② ③ ④ ⑤
12. ① ② ③ ④ ⑤
13. ① ② ③ ④ ⑤

14. ① ② ③ ④ ⑤
15. ① ② ③ ④ ⑤
16. ① ② ③ ④ ⑤
17. ① ② ③ ④ ⑤
18. ① ② ③ ④ ⑤
19. ① ② ③ ④ ⑤
20. ① ② ③ ④ ⑤
21. ① ② ③ ④ ⑤
22. ① ② ③ ④ ⑤
23. ① ② ③ ④ ⑤
24. ① ② ③ ④ ⑤
25. ① ② ③ ④ ⑤
26. ① ② ③ ④ ⑤

27. ① ② ③ ④ ⑤
28. ① ② ③ ④ ⑤
29. ① ② ③ ④ ⑤
30. ① ② ③ ④ ⑤
31. ① ② ③ ④ ⑤
32. ① ② ③ ④ ⑤
33. ① ② ③ ④ ⑤
34. ① ② ③ ④ ⑤
35. ① ② ③ ④ ⑤
36. ① ② ③ ④ ⑤
37. ① ② ③ ④ ⑤
38. ① ② ③ ④ ⑤

39. ① ② ③ ④ ⑤
40. ① ② ③ ④ ⑤
41. ① ② ③ ④ ⑤
42. ① ② ③ ④ ⑤
43. ① ② ③ ④ ⑤
44. ① ② ③ ④ ⑤
45. ① ② ③ ④ ⑤
46. ① ② ③ ④ ⑤
47. ① ② ③ ④ ⑤
48. ① ② ③ ④ ⑤
49. ① ② ③ ④ ⑤
50. ① ② ③ ④ ⑤

Posttest 2: Social Studies

1. ① ② ③ ④ ⑤
2. ① ② ③ ④ ⑤
3. ① ② ③ ④ ⑤
4. ① ② ③ ④ ⑤
5. ① ② ③ ④ ⑤
6. ① ② ③ ④ ⑤
7. ① ② ③ ④ ⑤
8. ① ② ③ ④ ⑤
9. ① ② ③ ④ ⑤
10. ① ② ③ ④ ⑤
11. ① ② ③ ④ ⑤
12. ① ② ③ ④ ⑤
13. ① ② ③ ④ ⑤

14. ① ② ③ ④ ⑤
15. ① ② ③ ④ ⑤
16. ① ② ③ ④ ⑤
17. ① ② ③ ④ ⑤
18. ① ② ③ ④ ⑤
19. ① ② ③ ④ ⑤
20. ① ② ③ ④ ⑤
21. ① ② ③ ④ ⑤
22. ① ② ③ ④ ⑤
23. ① ② ③ ④ ⑤
24. ① ② ③ ④ ⑤
25. ① ② ③ ④ ⑤
26. ① ② ③ ④ ⑤

27. ① ② ③ ④ ⑤
28. ① ② ③ ④ ⑤
29. ① ② ③ ④ ⑤
30. ① ② ③ ④ ⑤
31. ① ② ③ ④ ⑤
32. ① ② ③ ④ ⑤
33. ① ② ③ ④ ⑤
34. ① ② ③ ④ ⑤
35. ① ② ③ ④ ⑤
36. ① ② ③ ④ ⑤
37. ① ② ③ ④ ⑤
38. ① ② ③ ④ ⑤

39. ① ② ③ ④ ⑤
40. ① ② ③ ④ ⑤
41. ① ② ③ ④ ⑤
42. ① ② ③ ④ ⑤
43. ① ② ③ ④ ⑤
44. ① ② ③ ④ ⑤
45. ① ② ③ ④ ⑤
46. ① ② ③ ④ ⑤
47. ① ② ③ ④ ⑤
48. ① ② ③ ④ ⑤
49. ① ② ③ ④ ⑤
50. ① ② ③ ④ ⑤

Posttest 3: Science

1. ① ② ③ ④ ⑤
2. ① ② ③ ④ ⑤
3. ① ② ③ ④ ⑤
4. ① ② ③ ④ ⑤
5. ① ② ③ ④ ⑤
6. ① ② ③ ④ ⑤
7. ① ② ③ ④ ⑤
8. ① ② ③ ④ ⑤
9. ① ② ③ ④ ⑤
10. ① ② ③ ④ ⑤
11. ① ② ③ ④ ⑤
12. ① ② ③ ④ ⑤
13. ① ② ③ ④ ⑤

14. ① ② ③ ④ ⑤
15. ① ② ③ ④ ⑤
16. ① ② ③ ④ ⑤
17. ① ② ③ ④ ⑤
18. ① ② ③ ④ ⑤
19. ① ② ③ ④ ⑤
20. ① ② ③ ④ ⑤
21. ① ② ③ ④ ⑤
22. ① ② ③ ④ ⑤
23. ① ② ③ ④ ⑤
24. ① ② ③ ④ ⑤
25. ① ② ③ ④ ⑤
26. ① ② ③ ④ ⑤

27. ① ② ③ ④ ⑤
28. ① ② ③ ④ ⑤
29. ① ② ③ ④ ⑤
30. ① ② ③ ④ ⑤
31. ① ② ③ ④ ⑤
32. ① ② ③ ④ ⑤
33. ① ② ③ ④ ⑤
34. ① ② ③ ④ ⑤
35. ① ② ③ ④ ⑤
36. ① ② ③ ④ ⑤
37. ① ② ③ ④ ⑤
38. ① ② ③ ④ ⑤

39. ① ② ③ ④ ⑤
40. ① ② ③ ④ ⑤
41. ① ② ③ ④ ⑤
42. ① ② ③ ④ ⑤
43. ① ② ③ ④ ⑤
44. ① ② ③ ④ ⑤
45. ① ② ③ ④ ⑤
46. ① ② ③ ④ ⑤
47. ① ② ③ ④ ⑤
48. ① ② ③ ④ ⑤
49. ① ② ③ ④ ⑤
50. ① ② ③ ④ ⑤

Posttest 4: Language Arts, Reading

1. ① ② ③ ④ ⑤
2. ① ② ③ ④ ⑤
3. ① ② ③ ④ ⑤
4. ① ② ③ ④ ⑤
5. ① ② ③ ④ ⑤
6. ① ② ③ ④ ⑤
7. ① ② ③ ④ ⑤
8. ① ② ③ ④ ⑤
9. ① ② ③ ④ ⑤
10. ① ② ③ ④ ⑤

11. ① ② ③ ④ ⑤
12. ① ② ③ ④ ⑤
13. ① ② ③ ④ ⑤
14. ① ② ③ ④ ⑤
15. ① ② ③ ④ ⑤
16. ① ② ③ ④ ⑤
17. ① ② ③ ④ ⑤
18. ① ② ③ ④ ⑤
19. ① ② ③ ④ ⑤
20. ① ② ③ ④ ⑤

21. ① ② ③ ④ ⑤
22. ① ② ③ ④ ⑤
23. ① ② ③ ④ ⑤
24. ① ② ③ ④ ⑤
25. ① ② ③ ④ ⑤
26. ① ② ③ ④ ⑤
27. ① ② ③ ④ ⑤
28. ① ② ③ ④ ⑤
29. ① ② ③ ④ ⑤
30. ① ② ③ ④ ⑤

31. ① ② ③ ④ ⑤
32. ① ② ③ ④ ⑤
33. ① ② ③ ④ ⑤
34. ① ② ③ ④ ⑤
35. ① ② ③ ④ ⑤
36. ① ② ③ ④ ⑤
37. ① ② ③ ④ ⑤
38. ① ② ③ ④ ⑤
39. ① ② ③ ④ ⑤
40. ① ② ③ ④ ⑤

Posttest 5: Mathematics
Part I

1. ① ② ③ ④ ⑤

2. ① ② ③ ④ ⑤

3. ① ② ③ ④ ⑤

4.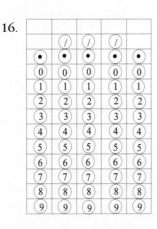

5. ① ② ③ ④ ⑤

6. ① ② ③ ④ ⑤

7. ① ② ③ ④ ⑤

8. ① ② ③ ④ ⑤

9.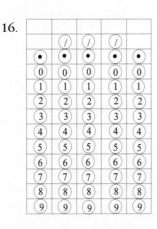

10.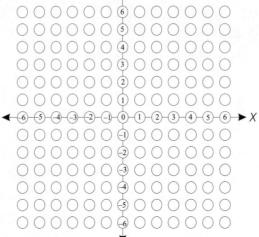

11. ① ② ③ ④ ⑤

12. ① ② ③ ④ ⑤

13. ① ② ③ ④ ⑤

14. ① ② ③ ④ ⑤

15. ① ② ③ ④ ⑤

16.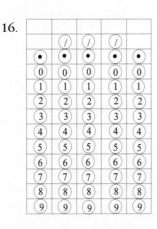

17. ① ② ③ ④ ⑤

18. ① ② ③ ④ ⑤

19. ① ② ③ ④ ⑤

20. ① ② ③ ④ ⑤

21.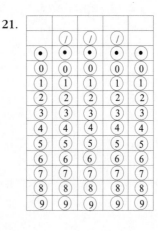

22.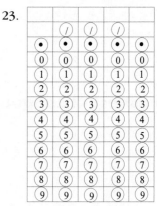

23.

24. ① ② ③ ④ ⑤

25. ① ② ③ ④ ⑤

Part II

1. ① ② ③ ④ ⑤
2. ① ② ③ ④ ⑤
3. ① ② ③ ④ ⑤
4. ① ② ③ ④ ⑤
5. ① ② ③ ④ ⑤
6. ① ② ③ ④ ⑤
7. ① ② ③ ④ ⑤
8. ① ② ③ ④ ⑤
9. ① ② ③ ④ ⑤
10. ① ② ③ ④ ⑤

11.

12. ① ② ③ ④ ⑤
13. ① ② ③ ④ ⑤
14. ① ② ③ ④ ⑤

15.

16. ① ② ③ ④ ⑤

17.

18. ① ② ③ ④ ⑤
19. ① ② ③ ④ ⑤
20. ① ② ③ ④ ⑤
21. ① ② ③ ④ ⑤
22. ① ② ③ ④ ⑤
23. ① ② ③ ④ ⑤
24. ① ② ③ ④ ⑤
25. ① ② ③ ④ ⑤

Posttest 1

LANGUAGE ARTS, WRITING
PART I: MULTIPLE CHOICE

75 Minutes ❖ 50 Questions

Directions: Choose the one best answer for each item.

Items 1–15 refer to the following paragraphs.

(1) *The topography in the Southwest encompasses a fascinating diversity of terrain from rugged mountains to vast deserts to deep canyons.* (2) *The Grand Canyon, which is located in Arizona, offers a particularly spectacular vista.* (3) *For miles the canyon twists and turns, evidence that something powerful carved it out of rock hundreds of years ago.* (4) *As far as the eye can see, the distinctive colors and shapes of the canyon stretches.* (5) *Available at the South and North Rims, especially beautiful in winter, visitors can stay at a choice of accommodations, but reservations must typically be made a year in advance because of the park's popularity.* (6) *Millions of visitors came every year in all seasons to experience the wonder and majesty of this national park.*

(7) *Watching the sun rise or set over Grand Canyon is a breathtaking experience because of the scene's beauty and splendor.* (8) *Such a photographer's paradise!* (9) *The hardy can hike to the bottom of the canyon and even camp overnight while others might choose to ride mules to the bottom.* (10) *Some visitors choose to see the canyon from a helicopter, other adventurous fearless souls ride the rapids of the Columbia River through this magnificent canyon.* (11) *Seeing this natural wonder for the first time is stunning.*

(12) *While Grand Canyon is by far the largest canyon, Arizona has others that have been homes to Native Americans such as Navajos, Hopi, and remnants of an earlier, well-developed civilization of the Anasazi, "the ancient ones," who's culture disappeared long ago.* (13) *Visiting a site some remnants of the two-thousand-year-old culture.* (14) *Canyon de Chelly is a small can-yon near Chinle in northeast Arizona, and it can be reached by hiking for perhaps an hour from a small road.* (15) *At the bottom, the hiker will find a little stream, just a vestige of a once-powerful river.* (16) *Looking across this diminished version of the Colorado River, visitors can see the remains of Anasazi homes carved into rock above, and tucked into caves.* (17) *Compared to the Grand Canyon, Canyon de Chelly is the smallest one.* (18) *Many Native American tribes, such as the Navajo, regard this canyon as central to their history and beliefs.* (19) *On the other hand, Chaco Canyon, another place that holds some of the mysteries of the Anasazi, is much larger.* (20) *Here archaeologists and other professionals interested in Native American history and culture are examining the site, trying not to disturb the ruins of this powerful place.* (21) *Arizonas unusual terrain can be the key to unlocking the past.*

1. Sentence 1: **The topography in the Southwest encompasses a fascinating diversity of terrain from rugged mountains to vast deserts to deep canyons.**

   What is the meaning of underline{topography} in this sentence?

   (1) Types of land surface
   (2) Plot of land
   (3) Density of plant life
   (4) Density of population
   (5) Method of depicting scenes in film

2. Sentence 2: **The Grand Canyon, which is located in Arizona, offers a particularly spectacular vista.**

Which is the most effective choice to revise this sentence concisely?

(1) The Grand Canyon that is located in Arizona offers a particularly spectacular vista.

(2) The Grand Canyon located in Arizona offers a particularly spectacular vista.

(3) Offering a particularly spectacular vista that is in Arizona is the Grand Canyon.

(4) The Grand Canyon in Arizona offers a particularly spectacular vista.

(5) Located in Arizona with a particularly spectacular vista is the Grand Canyon.

3. Sentence 4: **As far as the eye can see, the distinctive colors and shapes of the canyon stretches.**

What correction should be made to this sentence?

(1) Change can see to saw
(2) Change stretches to stretch
(3) Insert a comma after colors
(4) Omit the comma after see
(5) No correction is necessary

4. Sentence 5: **Available at the South and North Rims, which are especially beautiful in winter, visitors can stay at a choice of accommodations, but reservations must typically be made a year in advance because of the park's popularity.**

What correction should be made to the underlined part of this sentence?

(1) Available at the South and North Rims, visitors especially beautiful in winter can stay at a choice of accommodations

(2) Available at the South and North Rims, visitors can stay at a choice of accommodations especially beautiful in winter

(3) Visitors can stay at a choice of accommodations which are especially beautiful in winter available at the South and North Rims

(4) Visitors can stay at a choice of accommodations available at the South and North Rims, which are especially beautiful in winter

(5) No correction is necessary

5. Sentence 6: **Millions of visitors came every year in all seasons to experience the wonder and majesty of this national park.**

What correction should be made to this sentence?

(1) Insert a comma after seasons
(2) Change in all seasons to seasonally
(3) Change came to come
(4) Insert a comma after wonder
(5) No correction is necessary

6. Sentences 7 and 8: **Watching the sun rise or set over Grand Canyon is a breathtaking experience because of the scene's beauty and splendor. Such a photographer's paradise!**

What is the best way to combine these two?

(1) In this photographer's paradise, watching the sun rise or set over Grand Canyon is a breathtaking experience because of the scene's beauty and splendor.

(2) Because of the scene's beauty and splendor, such a photographer's paradise, watching the sun rise or set over Grand Canyon is a breathtaking experience.

(3) Such a photographer's paradise, watching the sun rise or set over Grand Canyon is a breathtaking experience because of the scene's beauty and splendor.

(4) Watching the sun rise or set over Grand Canyon, it is such a photographer's paradise, is a breathtaking experience because of the scene's beauty and splendor.

(5) Because of the scene's beauty and splendor, watching the sun rise or set over Grand Canyon is a breathtaking experience, such a photographer's paradise.

7. Sentence 9: **The hardy can hike to the bottom of the canyon and even camp overnight while others might choose to ride mules to the bottom.**

What correction should be made to this sentence?

(1) Insert a comma after canyon
(2) Change might choose to may choose
(3) Insert a comma after overnight
(4) Change can hike to hiked
(5) No correction is necessary

431

8. Sentence 10: **Some visitors choose to see the canyon from a helicopter, other adventurous fearless souls ride the rapids of the Columbia River through this magnificent canyon.**

What correction should be made to this sentence?

(1) Change the comma after <u>helicopter</u> to a semicolon
(2) Insert <u>but</u> after the comma following <u>helicopter</u>
(3) Place a period after <u>helicopter</u> and begin a new sentence with <u>other</u>
(4) All of the above are correct choices
(5) No correction is necessary

9. Sentence 12: **While Grand Canyon is by far the largest canyon, Arizona has others that have been homes to Native Americans such as Navajos, Hopi, and remnants of an earlier, well-developed civilization of the Anasazi, "the ancient ones" who's culture disappeared long ago.**

What correction should be made to this sentence?

(1) Change <u>largest</u> to <u>larger</u>
(2) Omit the comma after <u>canyon</u>
(3) Change <u>that have been homes</u> to <u>who have been homes</u>
(4) Change <u>who's</u> to <u>whose</u>
(5) No correction is necessary

10. Sentence 13: **Visiting a site some remnants of the two-thousand-year-old culture.**

What must be done to correct this sentence?

(1) Change <u>Visiting</u> to <u>Visit</u>
(2) Insert a comma after <u>remnants</u>
(3) Insert <u>can reveal</u> after <u>site</u>
(4) Insert <u>could reveal</u> after <u>remnants</u>
(5) No correction is necessary

11. Sentence 14: **Canyon de Chelly is a small canyon near Chinle in northeast Arizona, and it can be reached by hiking for perhaps an hour from a small road.**

How can this sentence be revised to reduce wordiness?

(1) Canyon de Chelly, a small canyon near Chinle in northeast Arizona, and it can be reached by hiking for perhaps an hour from a small road.
(2) Canyon de Chelly, a small canyon near Chinle in northeast Arizona, can be reached by hiking for perhaps an hour from a small road.
(3) Canyon de Chelly is a small canyon near Chinle in northeast Arizona reached by hiking for perhaps an hour from a small road.
(4) Canyon de Chelly, a small canyon near Chinle in northeast Arizona, reached by hiking for perhaps an hour from a small road.
(5) Canyon de Chelly, is a small canyon near Chinle in northeast Arizona, it can be reached by hiking for perhaps an hour from a small road.

12. Sentence 15: **At the bottom, the hiker will find a little stream, just a vestige of a once-powerful river.**

Given its use in the sentence, what is the most likely meaning of <u>vestige</u>?

(1) Remnant
(2) Gulch
(3) Lake
(4) Torrent
(5) Dry riverbed

13. Sentence 16: **Looking across this diminished version of the Colorado River, visitors can see the remains of Anasazi homes carved into rock above, and tucked into caves.**

What correction should be made to this sentence?

(1) Omit the comma after <u>River</u>
(2) Omit the comma after <u>above</u>
(3) Change <u>Looking</u> to <u>having looked</u>
(4) Change <u>carved</u> and <u>tucked</u> to <u>carving</u> and <u>tucking</u>
(5) No correction is necessary

14. Sentence 17: **Compared to the Grand Canyon, Canyon de Chelly is the smallest one.**

    What correction should be made to this sentence?

    (1) Move compared to the Grand Canyon to follow one
    (2) Omit the comma after Canyon
    (3) Change smallest to smaller
    (4) Change is to was
    (5) No correction is necessary

15. Sentence 21: **Arizonas unusual terrain can be the key to unlocking the past.**

    What correction should be made to this sentence?

    (1) Change unlocking to having unlocked
    (2) Change unusual to usual
    (3) Change can be to could be
    (4) Change Arizonas to Arizona's
    (5) No correction is necessary

    Items 16–27 refer to the following paragraphs.

    ---

(1) *In the early 1950s, American science fiction movies became popular because they transferred the pervasive fear of rapidly developing communism and the Cold War to a bazarre world where aliens invaded Earth.* (2) *After World War II ended with the dropping of the atomic bomb on Japan, America turned a fearful face to the Soviet Union.* (3) *Josef Stalin, who had been previously an American ally, now had changed into a foe.* (4) *Since both the U.S. and the Soviets had nuclear weapons, Americans dreaded that some reckless decision could be not only the end of the United States but also much of the world.*

(5) *These fears about the Soviets lead to the creation of U.S. Senator Joseph McCarthy's Un-American Activities Committee.* (6) *McCarthy actually accused the Department of State in 1950 of harboring communists.* (7) *President Harry Truman and his Secretary of State denied the assertions, the public began to believe McCarthy's charges.* (8) *Anxiety intensified when Alger Hiss, as well as the Rosenbergs, were arrested and convicted for being a Soviet spy.* (9) *The term "McCarthyism" described the widespread accusations and investigations of suspected Communist activities in the U.S. during the 1950s.* (10) *According to* The Crucible, *a play written by Arthur Miller in 1953, America had embarked on another "witch hunt" not unlike the Salem Witch Trials over three hundred years before.*

(11) *This exaggerated fear of "a communist hiding under every bed" terrified many Americans because of their uncertainty about how to identify these so-called communists.*

(12) *The fear of infiltration by enemies focused some attention especially on public figures.* (13) *Some businesses blacklisted, or refused to hire, those accused.* (14) *Many in the entertainment industry were called to testify before McCarthy's committee; McCarthy demanded the name of any entertainer who had connections to communism.* (15) *Surprising to Americans was the fact that some actors were actual members of the Communist Party attracted by the benefits that looked promising on paper.* (16) *The movie industry reacted by changing all work on movies about politics to cartoons.* (17) *As alarm spread quickly throughout the U.S., the movie industry took advantage of the tension and transferred the fear of communists to fear of aliens from outer space.* (18) *Even though movie aliens could adopt human form, Americans coped better with that invader in unrealistic films than with possibly real communists infiltrating American society.* (19) *Science fiction movies became very popular as an outlet for fear of communism as time passed.*

16. Sentence 1: **In the early 1950s, American science fiction movies became popular because they transferred the pervasive fear of rapidly developing communism and the Cold War to a bazarre world where aliens invaded Earth.**

    Where could this phrase be most logically located?

    such as the original "Invasion of the Body Snatchers"

    (1) After became popular
    (2) After communism
    (3) After science fiction movies
    (4) After In the early 1950s
    (5) After the Cold War

17. In Sentence 1, which of the following is the correct spelling of the word that means "weird"?

    (1) Bizare
    (2) Bazaar
    (3) Bazarre
    (4) Bizaar
    (5) Bizarre

18. Sentence 2: **After World War II ended with the dropping of the atomic bomb on Japan, America turned a fearful face to the Soviet Union.**

What correction should be made to this sentence?

(1) Omit <u>on Japan</u>
(2) Change <u>ended</u> to <u>had ended</u>
(3) Change <u>turned</u> to <u>had turned</u>
(4) Omit <u>ended with the dropping of the atomic bomb on Japan</u>
(5) No correction is necessary

19. Sentence 3: **Josef Stalin, who was previously an American ally, now changed into a foe**.

What correction should be made to this sentence?

(1) Omit the commas
(2) Change <u>ally</u> to <u>alley</u>
(3) Change <u>was</u> to <u>had been</u>
(4) Change <u>into</u> to <u>in</u>
(5) No correction is necessary

20. Sentence 4: **Since both the U.S. and the Soviets had nuclear weapons, Americans dreaded that some reckless decision could be not only the end of the United States but also much of the world.**

What correction should be made to this sentence?

(1) Change <u>Since</u> to <u>Cents</u>
(2) Change <u>reckless</u> to <u>wreckless</u>
(3) Omit <u>Since both the U.S. and the Soviet Union had nuclear weapons</u>
(4) Omit <u>the United States but also much</u>
(5) No correction is necessary

21. Sentence 5: **These fears about the Soviets lead to the creation of U.S. Senator Joseph McCarthy's Un-American Activities Committee.**

What correction should be made to this sentence?

(1) Change <u>lead</u> to <u>led</u>
(2) Change <u>McCarthy's</u> to <u>McCarthys</u>
(3) Change <u>McCarthy's</u> to <u>McCarthys'</u>
(4) Change <u>Activities</u> to <u>Activities'</u>
(5) No correction is necessary

22. Sentences 6 and 7: **McCarthy actually accused the Department of State in 1950 of harboring communists. President Harry Truman and his Secretary of State denied the assertions, the public began to believe McCarthy's charges.**

Which of the following can most logically combine these two sentences?

(1) Insert a comma plus <u>and</u> between the two sentences.
(2) As McCarthy actually accused the Department of State in 1950 of harboring communists, President Harry Truman and his Secretary of State denied the assertions, so the public began to believe McCarthy's charges.
(3) When McCarthy actually accused the Department of State in 1950 of harboring communists, President Harry Truman and his Secretary of State denied the assertions, but the public began to believe McCarthy's charges.
(4) McCarthy actually accused the Department of State in 1950 of harboring communists; however, President Truman and his Secretary State denied the accusations, and the public began to believe McCarthy's charges.
(5) McCarthy actually accused the Department of State in 1950 of harboring communists after President Truman and his Secretary of State denied the accusations before the public began to believe McCarthy's charges.

23. Sentence 8: **Anxiety intensified when Alger Hiss, as well as the Rosenbergs, were arrested and convicted for being a Soviet spy**.

What correction should be made to this sentence?

(1) Change <u>intensified</u> to <u>intensifies</u>
(2) Change <u>were</u> to <u>was</u>
(3) Insert a comma after <u>intensified</u>
(4) Insert a comma after <u>convicted</u>
(5) No correction is necessary

24. Which of the following will best serve as a concluding sentence for paragraph 2?

- **(1)** Innocent people were victimized and even executed in Salem's ordeal, and the quest begun by McCarthy had similar overtones.
- **(2)** The witches persecuted in Salem were like the communists because both were executed.
- **(3)** The search for communists begun by McCarthy yielded witches instead.
- **(4)** Innocent victims suffered from Salem's witch hunt.
- **(5)** Fear of communism spread like wildfire in America.

25. Which sentence in the fourth paragraph is irrelevant and should be removed?

- **(1)** Sentence 13
- **(2)** Sentence 14
- **(3)** Sentence 15
- **(4)** Sentence 16
- **(5)** Sentence 17

26. Sentence 15: **Surprising to Americans was the fact that some actors were actual members of the Communist Party attracted by the benefits that looked promising on paper.**

What correction should be made to this sentence?

- **(1)** Insert a comma after Americans
- **(2)** Change looked to look
- **(3)** Insert which after Party
- **(4)** Omit the fact that
- **(5)** No correction is necessary

27. Sentence 18: **Even though movie aliens could adopt human form, Americans coped better with that invader in unrealistic films than with possibly real communists infiltrating American society.**

What correction should be made to this sentence?

- **(1)** Change Even though to Because
- **(2)** Omit the comma after form
- **(3)** Change that invader to these invaders
- **(4)** Insert a comma after films
- **(5)** No correction is necessary

Items 28–37 refer to the following paragraphs.

(1) *When you prepare for a job interview, keep some key details in mind.* (2) *Foremost, your appearance is what the interviewer will notice first.* (3) *Be sure, then, that you are neatly groomed and dressed for success for the kind of job for which you are applying.* (4) *That adage that you never get a second chance too make a first impression is true, so be sure that yours is a positive one.* (5) *"Dress for success" is more than just a saying your choice of attire should be appropriate for the job you want.* (6) *Offer a firm handshake, too.*

(7) *It is also a good idea to research the company so that you will have some information about it to be able to ask your own questions.* (8) *As you are interviewed, respond with as much poise as you could.* (9) *Being frank about your experience and explaining your goals during this questioning process is also important.* (10) *However, if you do not know the answer to a question, be honest and say so.* (11) *You will be asked questions about your work experience and education so it is important that you prepare yourself for these inquiries.* (12) *The interview process is a key component in your job search.*

(13) *You should prepare a resume with information of your job skills relevant to the position for which you applied.* (14) *For instance, if you are interested in being employed as an administrative assistant or a data entry clerk, your resume should emphasize your computer skills and experience.* (15) *If you are being interviewed for a position as a nanny or teacher assistant, your resume should showcase your training and experience working with children.* (16) *An applicant for a delivery job should be able to prove a clean driving record.*

(17) *Be prepared to ask questions of your own about the company and the position.* (18) *These queries can include details about the jobs responsibilities and various company policies.* (19) *If you are encouraged to question further and you think the time is right, ask about salary and job benefits.* (20) *Above all before you leave the interview, be sure that you have spoken with as much as composure as you can and you have satisfied your questions about the job.* (21) *Leave your resume with the interviewer.*

28. Which sentences in the first paragraph are needlessly repetitive?

- **(1)** Sentences 1 and 3
- **(2)** Sentences 1 and 4
- **(3)** Sentences 1 and 5
- **(4)** Sentences 2 and 5
- **(5)** Sentences 2 and 6

29. Sentence 4: **That adage that you never get a second chance too make a first impression is true, so be sure that yours is a positive one.**

What correction should be made to this sentence?

- **(1)** Change adage to old adage
- **(2)** Change too to to
- **(3)** Change yours to your's
- **(4)** Change is to will be
- **(5)** No correction is necessary

30. Sentence 5: **"Dress for success" is more than just a saying your choice of attire should be appropriate for the job you want.**

What correction should be made to this sentence?

- **(1)** Omit the quotation marks around "Dress for success"
- **(2)** Change than to then
- **(3)** Insert a comma after saying
- **(4)** Insert a semicolon after saying
- **(5)** No correction is necessary

31. Sentence 8: **As you are interviewed, respond with as much poise as you could.**

What correction should be made to this sentence?

- **(1)** Omit the comma after interviewed
- **(2)** Insert a comma after poise
- **(3)** Change could to can
- **(4)** Change interviewed to interview
- **(5)** No correction is necessary

32. Sentence 9: **Being frank about your experience and explaining your goals during this questioning process is also important.**

What correction should be made to this sentence?

- **(1)** Change is to are
- **(2)** Change explaining to explain
- **(3)** Insert a comma after experience
- **(4)** Change is to was
- **(5)** No correction is necessary

33. Where would Sentence 11 be more logically located in the second paragraph?

- **(1)** After Sentence 7
- **(2)** After Sentence 8
- **(3)** After Sentence 9
- **(4)** Before Sentence 7
- **(5)** After Sentence 12

34. Sentence 13: **You should prepare a resume with information of your job skills relevant to the position for which you applied.**

What correction is needed for this sentence?

- **(1)** Change relevant to relevent
- **(2)** Change of to about
- **(3)** Insert a comma after resume
- **(4)** Change which to whom
- **(5)** No correction is necessary

35. Which of the following would serve most effectively as transition between Sentences 14 and 15?

- **(1)** Therefore
- **(2)** Because
- **(3)** On the other hand
- **(4)** As a result
- **(5)** Somehow or other

36. Sentence 18: **These queries can include details about the jobs responsibilities and various company policies.**

What correction should be made to this sentence?

- **(1)** Change These to Them
- **(2)** Change jobs to job's
- **(3)** Change company to companie's
- **(4)** Change company to companies'
- **(5)** No correction is necessary

37. Which of the following sentences would be the most effective concluding sentence for the final paragraph?

- **(1)** Leave your resume with the interviewer.
- **(2)** Being prepared for the interview is an important step in finding a job.
- **(3)** Do not ask too many questions.
- **(4)** The job interview is the only significant portion of the application process.
- **(5)** After the job interview is over, relax and wait for good news in a phone call.

Items 38–48 refer to the following paragraphs.

(1) *According to legend, the founding of the great city of Rome began with two brothers, Romulus and Remus, which were sired by the great hero Aeneas or the god Mars (the story varies), abandoned, and nursed by a she-wolf until they were rescued by a shepherd.* (2) *Mars, the god of war, is the figure for whom the candy bar is named.* (3) *They grew up, stole wives from neighboring tribes, and built a wall that represents the founding of Rome around 753 B.C.E.* (4) *In the process the brothers quarrel, and Romulus slayed Remus.* (5) *Hence the name of the city Rome.*

(6) *Very little of this folklore is credible.* (7) *More likely the area was originally settled by a variety of tribes that inhabited the area of the future city of Rome.* (8) *Evidence reveal that the Etruscans and the Latins, for instance, were early settlers.* (9) *Remains of Iron Age habitation on Palatine Hill, the most strategic location for a primitive settlement because it was easy to defend as well as close to a major river, also provides a more realistic beginning for Rome.* (10) *After the nearby tribes had been conquered and combined with the earliest settlers, the swampland between the Palatine and Capitoline Hills was drained and became known as the Forum.* (11) *Such a feat points to the elaborate engineering expertise of Etruscans.* (12) *A powerful monarchy under the next seven kings established Rome as a forceful presence in central Italy.*

(13) *The Roman Republic was established in 510 B.C.E., yet Rome soon set out to conquer the world.* (14) *Encounters with the more advanced Greeks quickly helped to transform Roman life with more interest focused on discussion and debate in the Forum and more energy directed to increasing the size and wealth of the Republic.* (15) *Hundreds of miles away various military expeditions conquered people such as those in Gaul, Carthage, Egypt, Spain, and the British Isles, and the Roman Empire grew to its maximum size under the Emperor Trajan, who ruled from 98–117 C.E.*

(16) *Attacks by barbarian tribes such as the Visigoths and Germanic peoples eventually weaken the empire, especially after it had been divided in half with Constantinople governing in the East.* (17) *Although this Eastern Empire was strong enough to endure another thousand years, the western half began to fall apart.* (18) *The "glory that was Rome," however, lives on with five languages based on Latin (French, Spanish, Italian, Romanian, and Portuguese), the twenty-six letter alphabet, use of Roman numerals, and the 365-day calendar used today.* (19) *A visitor to Rome now will see all kinds of sculptures, fountains, and buildings that commemorate ancient Rome.*

38. Sentence 1: **According to legend, the founding of the great city of Rome began with two brothers, Romulus and Remus, which were sired by either the great hero Aeneas or the god Mars (the story varies), abandoned, and nursed by a she-wolf until they were rescued by a shepherd.**

What correction should be made to this sentence?

(1) Change <u>began</u> to <u>begun</u>
(2) Omit the comma after <u>Remus</u>
(3) Change <u>which</u> to <u>who</u>
(4) Insert a comma after <u>she-wolf</u>
(5) No correction is necessary

39. Sentence 4: **In the process the brothers quarrel, and Romulus slayed Remus.**

What correction should be made to this sentence?

(1) Omit the comma after <u>quarrel</u>
(2) Change <u>quarrel</u> to <u>quarreled</u>
(3) Change <u>slayed</u> to <u>slaied</u>
(4) Change <u>slayed</u> to <u>slain</u>
(5) No correction is necessary

40. Sentence 5: **Hence the name of the city Rome.**

What correction needs to be made to this sentence?

(1) Insert a comma after <u>Hence</u>
(2) Insert <u>of</u> after <u>city</u>
(3) Add a predicate: <u>Hence the city was named Rome.</u>
(4) Add a predicate: <u>Hence Rome was named a city.</u>
(5) No correction is needed

41. Which sentence in the first paragraph should be removed because it is not relevant?

(1) Sentence 1
(2) Sentence 2
(3) Sentence 3
(4) Sentence 4
(5) Sentence 5

42. Sentence 8: **Evidence reveal that the Etruscans and the Latins, for instance, were early settlers.**

What correction should be made to this sentence?

(1) Change <u>reveal</u> to <u>reveals</u>
(2) Change <u>were</u> to <u>had been</u>
(3) Insert a comma after <u>reveal</u>
(4) Omit the commas around <u>for instance</u>
(5) No correction is necessary

437

43. Sentence 9: **Remains of Iron Age habitation on Palatine Hill, the most strategic location for a primitive settlement because it was easy to defend as well as close to a major river, also provides a more realistic beginning for Rome.**

What correction should be made to this sentence?

(1) Omit the comma after Palatine Hill
(2) Change because to thus
(3) Omit the comma after river
(4) Change provides to provide
(5) No correction is necessary

44. Which of the following would be a more logical arrangement of sentences in the second paragraph?

(1) Sentences 6, 7, 9, 8, 10, 11, 12
(2) Sentences 6, 7, 10, 8, 9, 11, 12
(3) Sentences 6, 7, 9, 10, 8, 12, 11
(4) Sentences 7, 6, 8, 9, 10, 11, 12
(5) Sentences 6, 7, 8, 9, 12, 11, 10

45. Sentence 13: **The Roman Republic was established in 510 B.C.E., yet Rome soon set out to conquer the world.**

What correction should be made to this sentence?

(1) Omit the comma after B.C.E.
(2) Change yet to therefore
(3) Change yet to and
(4) Change yet to since
(5) No correction is necessary

46. Which of the following would serve as an effective concluding sentence for the third paragraph?

(1) The Roman Empire knew no bounds in the world.
(2) Over time, the Roman Empire expanded to dangerous and burdensome proportions.
(3) Determined to outstretch all opponents, the Romans extended their empire to include much of the known world.
(4) Within a few centuries, Rome indeed tyrannized the world with its extensive empire.
(5) At the height of its growth, the Roman Empire reached remarkable proportions.

47. Sentence 16: **Attacks by barbarian tribes such as the Visigoths and Germanic peoples eventually weaken the empire, especially after it had been divided in half with Constantinople governing in the East.**

What correction should be made to this sentence?

(1) Change weaken to weakens
(2) Change weaken to weakened
(3) Insert a comma after tribes
(4) Change East to east
(5) No correction is necessary

48. In the final paragraph, which sentence if any should be omitted?

(1) Sentence 16
(2) Sentence 17
(3) Sentence 18
(4) Sentence 19
(5) No sentence should be omitted

Items 49–50 refer to the following paragraphs.

---

(1) *Early in life, before they learn to talk, children use sounds and body language to communicate. (2) Pointing and making nonsense sounds, communication begins. (3) Growing older, they learn to pronounce and use words correctly, but they continue to use body language throughout life to convey ideas and feelings.*

(4) *Many people, both adults and children, do not recognize the role of body language in communication, perhaps because body language is often subtle and may even be unconscious. (5) Frequently people do not realize that the way they feel may be communicated by their body language, not necessarily by their words. (6) Of course, a person's facial expression can also reveal attitude and interest.*

(7) *Sometimes the two kinds of communication even contradict each other. (8) Someone who is a careful "reader" of both languages can determine which response is the real one because often the body language portrays the truth. (9) For example, observing someone's eyes as the person makes a statement can oftentimes disclose whether that person is truthful. (10) Someone who deliberately equivocates may find it difficult, if not impossible, to maintain eye contact. (11) Instead, he consistently and unconsciously shifts his gaze to one side or the other. (12) The person who is untruthful may be completely unaware of what he or she reveals by body language.*

(13) *Other kinds of deliberate body language include some virtually universal gestures, while other types are specific to certain cultures. (14) Those in all*

branches of the military salute smartly. (15) *Asians typically bow to show respect in greeting one another Americans often greet one another with a handshake.* (16) *Many Europeans greet one another by kissing both cheeks.* (17) *Rubbing the thumb against the fingers on one hand and then offering an open palm is an almost worldwide request for money.* (18) *One should be careful, however, in using certain finger or hand gestures: a motion that can have positive meanings in one culture, such as a "thumbs up" or an "okay" signal, may have totally different, even offensive messages in other cultures.* (19) *To determine safe signals, a traveler, before visiting another country, should learn something about body language in that culture or should, upon arrival, observe native speakers before using that kind of abbreviated body language.*

(20) *Body language, like a twenty-four-hour sign with neon and blinking lights, can send messages constantly.* (21) *Knowing how to project the right ones and how to interpret those signals of others can be a rewarding experience.*

49. Sentence 2: **Pointing and making nonsense sounds, communication begins.**

What correction should be made to this sentence?

(1) Change communication begins to children begin to communicate
(2) Omit the comma after sounds
(3) After pointing insert at things
(4) After begins insert for them
(5) No correction is necessary

50. Sentence 3: **Growing older, they learn to pronounce and use words correctly, but they continue to use body language throughout life to convey ideas and feelings.**

Decide where the underlined phrase should most logically be located.

(1) At the beginning of the sentence as it is written
(2) After use words
(3) After body language
(4) After throughout life
(5) After ideas and feelings

PART II: ESSAY

45 Minutes

Directions: Imagine that the legislature in your state is considering this concept: Good, safe child-care options should be provided by the state in much the same way that kindergarten programs have been established as an essential step for children before first grade. Consider working parents and their quest for affordable, secure child care for their children under the age of 4 or 5. Think as well of problems you have become aware of because of licensing procedures and follow-up checks that may be haphazard and variable. If you were a parent looking for a good place for your baby or young child to stay while you are at work, what would you look for? What advice would you offer a legislator? On the other hand, if you disagree, what are your reasons?

Write an essay of around 200–250 words in which you explain your position on the following issue.

SCORED 4-3-2-1

SCORE = 4

I am a parent who has had to find a safe, clean daycare for my children, so I understand what other parents experience. Having state-provided daycare would be so helpful to parents because we wouldn't have to worry about whether a place was licensed.

When I looked for a daycare, I visited each one and talked to the people working there. I also checked out the facilities and watched the children. I wanted to see if everything was clean and orderly, if the children were happy and tended to, and if the workers cared about what they were doing. Fortunately, my choice has been a good one.

But I feel sorry for other parents who were not so lucky. Desperate decisions sometimes have to be made so that parents can go to work, so they have to find some place for their children. Stories in the newspaper and on TV time and time again point out deficiencies in the system. Daycare centers are not always inspected carefully, sometimes the facility isn't even licensed, and often the children are neglected because there are too many children there. When the centers are closed for these reasons, then parents have to start looking all over again. When can they look? They work all day, but I guess they could check out some on their lunch breaks. This idea would not work, however, for people without cars.

If the state could provide daycare centers that are clean, inspected regularly, and open to the public, then all citizens could benefit. I'm in favor of this proposal.

SCORE = 3

I think the idea of state-provided daycare is a good one because so many people have to find affordable, clean daycare for their children. There may seem to be plenty of places available, but not all of them are licensed. Some are overcrowded, and some simply are not clean. If people who run daycare centers knew that the state would regularly check their centers, I think that daycare would improve.

When a parent looks for a decent daycare, I think he or she wants to find a place that is bright and cheerful with lots of toys and books for the children. But more importantly, I think he or she wants to see that the people working there love to work with kids. A parent can also look for sanitary conditions because a lot of germs can be spread among children. The children ought to be happy with plenty of room to play and take naps. Babies should each have a bed.

If practices such as these were followed, the daycare center would probably be a good choice. If parents knew that the state would make sure everything was right, then their looking process could be eliminated and they could be sure that their children were safe. This suggestion makes sense to me.

SCORE = 2

Daycare provided by the state is a good idea as long as it doesn't cost to much. Parents sometimes have to spend a long time looking for a good daycare. And sometimes they have to use what they can find even if it isn't exactly what they were looking for. For example, some parents choose unlicensed daycare centers because they can't get their children in any other places. They try to do there best but these parents don't have much choice. If the state provided daycare centers, we could all be happier. Because we would know that all of the centers had to follow routine checks.

As for myself I have not had to find child care yet, but I know that when the time comes, I will need a clean place that doesn't try to have to many kids at once. But if I couldn't find a good place, then I would prolly have to choose somewhere that didn't meet all of my standards but did offer my child a place to stay. If the state provided daycare, I wouldn't have to worry.

SCORE = 1

If the state took care of solving the daycare problem, I for one would take advantage of the service. I have had to find daycare for my children, and its a hard job. Finding time to do it is one problem and then you have to visit some places to see for yourself what the place is like. I looked at the size of the center, how many kids were there, how many workers there were, what kind of toys and activities the kids could do. It takes some time to do all of this. And when can a working parent do this? Sometimes you just have to make due with what you can find.

If the state provided day centers, then parents wouldn't have to worry so much.

Posttest 2

SOCIAL STUDIES

75 Minutes ❖ 50 Questions

Directions: Choose the one best answer for each item.

Items 1–5 are based on the following three graphs.

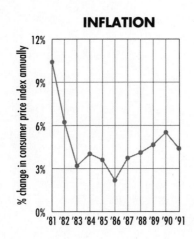

GROWTH

% change in real gross domestic product annually

9%

6%

3%

0%

−3%

'81 '82 '83 '84 '85 '86 '87 '88 '89 '90 '91

INFLATION

% change in consumer price index annually

12%

9%

6%

3%

0%

'81 '82 '83 '84 '85 '86 '87 '88 '89 '90 '91

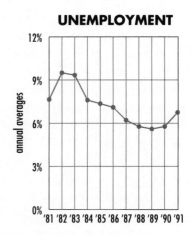

UNEMPLOYMENT

annual averages

12%

9%

6%

3%

0%

'81 '82 '83 '84 '85 '86 '87 '88 '89 '90 '91

1. The two-year period with the greatest percent change in the rate of inflation was the period from

   (1) 1989 to 1991.
   (2) 1981 to 1983.
   (3) 1984 to 1986.
   (4) 1988 to 1990.
   (5) 1985 to 1987.

2. Which statement best describes the relationship shown by the charts between the growth of the gross domestic product and the rate of unemployment?

   (1) A low rate of growth is often linked to high or rising unemployment.
   (2) A high rate of growth is often linked to high or rising unemployment.
   (3) A low or falling rate of unemployment is often linked to a low rate of growth.
   (4) A high or rising rate of unemployment is often linked to moderate growth.
   (5) A negative rate of growth is often linked to a low or falling rate of unemployment.

3. The greatest decrease in the growth of the gross domestic product was from

(1) 1981 to 1982.

(2) 1984 to 1985.

(3) 1988 to 1990.

(4) 1988 to 1991.

(5) 1985 to 1987.

4. These graphs could help a person determine the best time to look for a new job. Such a time would be when

(1) inflation is rising, unemployment is falling, and economic growth is rising.

(2) inflation is falling, unemployment is rising, and economic growth is falling.

(3) inflation is falling, unemployment is falling, and economic growth is rising.

(4) inflation is falling, unemployment is falling, and economic growth is falling.

(5) inflation is rising, unemployment is rising, and economic growth is rising.

5. The U.S. economy showed strong growth between 1983 and 1989. The most likely cause was

(1) an increase in the number of immigrants to the U.S. between 1981 and 1990.

(2) the falling rate of inflation between 1981 and 1986.

(3) the reelection of President Ronald Reagan in 1984.

(4) the falling rate of unemployment between 1983 and 1989.

(5) the strengthening of the European Common Market in the 1980s.

Items 6–10 refer to the following passage.

In June 1991, Mount Pinatubo in the Philippines began one of the most violent volcanic eruptions of the twentieth century. More than 200,000 acres were covered with a thick coat of volcanic ash, pumice, and debris. In some places the coating grew to 15 feet thick. More than 600 people died. Some were killed by the ash itself. Many others died from inhaling the deadly gases Mount Pinatubo gave off. Experts believe that the gases and ash thrown into the upper atmosphere were the cause of below-average worldwide temperatures the following year. Each year's monsoon season for the decade following the 1991 explosion is expected to cause avalanches. About half of the 7 billion cubic meters of volcanic material deposited on Mount Pinatubo's slopes is likely to wash down into the plains below.

6. What was the major worldwide effect of Mount Pinatubo's explosion in 1991?

(1) Avalanches

(2) A thick coat of ash

(3) Monsoons

(4) Cooling temperatures

(5) Deadly gases

7. According to the passage, avalanches were predicted during each monsoon season until at least what year?

(1) 1991

(2) 1992

(3) 1995

(4) 2000

(5) 2001

8. To prevent more death and destruction from Mount Pinatubo's mud slides, a reasonable policy would be to

(1) plant grasses and crops.

(2) blow up the mountain.

(3) pray for dry weather.

(4) do nothing.

(5) relocate people to a safe area.

9. The eruption created more than 60,000 refugees, many of them farmers and their families. The U.S. government sent $400 million in aid to help these people but criticized the way some of it was spent by the Philippine government. Philippine officials used much of the money to build four-lane highways and tall concrete buildings. What was the probable reason for American criticism of this use of the money?

(1) Not enough American contractors were used on the construction projects.

(2) The $400 million was not enough to build all the highways that the Philippine officials wanted to construct.

(3) The highways and tall buildings did not help the 60,000 refugees recover their lost farms and villages.

(4) The highways were poorly constructed and were damaged in the next monsoon season.

(5) American officials were not sure that the highways and tall buildings would withstand a possible future eruption of Mount Pinatubo.

10. According to the passage, people were killed by falling ash and

    (1) monsoons.
    (2) cooling temperatures.
    (3) avalanches.
    (4) falling buildings.
    (5) deadly gases.

Items 11–13 are based on the following passage.

In the summer of 1991, construction workers preparing the foundation of a new federal office building at the southern tip of Manhattan found an archaeological treasure. The construction workers uncovered some human skeletons just 20 feet below the surface. Archaeologists were called in, and they quickly realized the area was an old graveyard.

By studying colonial maps, the archaeologists determined the graveyard to be one called "Negroes' Burial Ground," which from 1710 to 1790 was used as a burial site for an untold number of African-American slaves and a few white paupers. Within a year of the start of archaeological work at the site, the remains of more than 400 bodies were unearthed.

The archaeologists found evidence to suggest that the burial site—the only such site with any pre-Revolutionary use now known in the United States—is one of the most significant archaeological discoveries of the twentieth century. For example, studies of the children's skeletons found there have indicated that as many as half of the area's slaves died at birth or within the first few years of life.

At first, federal officials refused to halt construction at the site. However, numerous groups and individuals, including people in Congress, New York's City Hall, and various African-American organizations, protested. The construction project was cancelled, and plans were made to include the ancient graveyard in a proposed historic district.

11. Which of the following sentences best summarizes the most important points of the passage?

    (1) In 1991, one of the most significant archaeological discoveries of the century was made in Manhattan.
    (2) In the early 1990s, the federal government started construction of a new office building in Manhattan but later abandoned the project after receiving complaints.
    (3) Archaeologists believe that as many as half of all African Americans born in the area of Manhattan in the 1700s died within the first few years of life.
    (4) The remains of more than 400 bodies in an old African-American graveyard were unearthed in the early 1990s.
    (5) Archaeologists often find items of great historical value at construction sites in major American cities.

12. Which of the choices below would be a good clue to the archaeologists that the graveyard was used during colonial times in America?

    (1) A Civil War sword
    (2) An engraved ring that says "for King and country"
    (3) A pair of plastic sandals
    (4) A map of the United States showing the transcontinental railroad
    (5) A family photograph

13. What does the death rate of newborns and young children say about life in the 1700s as compared with life today?

    (1) Life in the 1700s was much like it is today.
    (2) Medical care and nutrition in the 1700s were poor by today's standards.
    (3) Parents in the 1700s did not take very good care of their children.
    (4) About as many people in the 1700s lived to adulthood as do today.
    (5) Life in the 1700s was much easier than it is today.

Item 14 refers to the following cartoon.

'What it says isn't always what it means'

14. This cartoon refers to which principle of American government?

- **(1)** Separation of church and state
- **(2)** Checks and balances
- **(3)** Judicial review
- **(4)** Equality before the law
- **(5)** Bill of rights

15. The nine justices of the U.S. Supreme Court all receive lifetime appointments. In which of the following ways are their decisions probably most affected by this fact?

- **(1)** Because they have federal appointments, they probably favor the federal government over state governments when the two are on opposite sides of an issue.
- **(2)** They work more slowly and carefully than they might if some oversight group could set the pace.
- **(3)** They probably tend to follow the beliefs of the president who nominated them.
- **(4)** They probably tend to become independent thinkers because they are not accountable to any politician or party.
- **(5)** They probably rely more heavily on initial drafts of decisions that are written by their law clerks.

Items 16–19 refer to the following chart.

U.S. NATIONAL PARKS AND THEIR VISITORS

Year	No. of Parks	No. of Visitors (in thousands)
1970	35	45,879
1960	29	26,630
1950	28	13,919
1940	26	7,358
1930	22	2,775
1920	19	920
1910	13	119

16. How many visits were made to U.S. national parks in 1960?

- **(1)** 29
- **(2)** 26,630
- **(3)** 12,711
- **(4)** 26.63 million
- **(5)** 29 million

17. The number of national parks almost tripled between 1910 and 1970, but the number of visits increased at a much higher rate. Two of the oldest parks, Yellowstone and Yosemite, continue to have among the largest numbers of visitors per year. What factors probably best account for this great increase in visits?

- **(1)** A general increase in the U.S. population and more leisure time
- **(2)** A vastly improved transportation system and more leisure time
- **(3)** Creation of new parks close to large metropolitan areas and a general increase in U.S. population
- **(4)** Better advertising about improved park facilities and an increased interest nationally in ecology and the environment
- **(5)** Improved security services within the parks and an increase in the amount of disposable income available to most Americans

18. Between which two years did the smallest actual increase in visits take place?

- **(1)** 1960 and 1970
- **(2)** 1920 and 1930
- **(3)** 1910 and 1920
- **(4)** 1950 and 1960
- **(5)** 1930 and 1940

445

19. The factor that has contributed most to the growth in the number of national parks, as well as in the numbers of national historic sites, battlefields, and monuments, has been

    (1) the general growth of the federal government in the twentieth century.
    (2) the growth of the amount of leisure time for most Americans in the twentieth century.
    (3) a general American belief that national historic and natural sites of interest should be preserved for future generations to enjoy.
    (4) the increasing number of states in the western United States that were admitted to the Union in the first half of the twentieth century.
    (5) the inability of state governments to care adequately for various sites because of local financial problems.

Items 20–22 are based on the following table.

PROJECTED POPULATION OF SOME GROUPS OF PEOPLE WITHIN THE UNITED STATES
(number in millions)

Group	Year 2000	Year 2050	Year 2080
Male, White	108.8	105.6	103.6
Female, White	112.7	116.2	108.7
Male, Black	16.7	22.4	22.6
Female, Black	18.3	24.7	25.0

20. According to the chart, which group will be the largest in the year 2050?

    (1) All females
    (2) All males
    (3) Black males
    (4) White females
    (5) White males

21. Which group will show a decrease of 4 million between the years 2000 and 2080?

    (1) Black females
    (2) All females
    (3) White females
    (4) White males
    (5) All males

22. Which statement best summarizes the content of the table?

    (1) The number of blacks in the United States will increase between the years 2000 and 2080.
    (2) The number of blacks in the United States will show the greatest percentage of increase between the years 2000 and 2050.
    (3) The number of white females in the United States will increase between the years 2000 and 2050.
    (4) The number of whites in the United States will be greater than the number of blacks in the years between 2000 and 2080.
    (5) The total number of blacks in the United States will increase between the years 2000 and 2080 both in actual numbers and in relation to the total number of whites.

Items 23–28 refer to the following passage.

Andrew Jackson (1767-1845) was elected president of the United States in 1828. Following are some highlights of his colorful life:

- At age thirteen, Jackson joined the Continental Army and fought the British in the Revolutionary War. When taken prisoner, Jackson refused to clean a British officer's boots, and the officer struck him in the head with a sword. The permanent scar became a lifelong reminder of his hatred for the British.

- In 1787, Jackson was admitted to the bar in North Carolina, where he practiced law for several years.

- In 1791, he married Rachel Donelson Robards, believing, as she herself believed, that she was legally divorced at the time. Three years later, this proved to be untrue and the couple had to remarry. The resulting scandal followed the pair for the rest of their lives.

- In 1796, Jackson was elected without opposition as Tennessee's first representative to the U.S. House of Representatives.

- In 1798, Jackson was elected to Tennessee's highest court, where he was noted for dispensing quick, fair justice.

- In 1806, he fought a duel. Both men were shot, and his opponent died, although Jackson could have honorably prevented this death.

- In the War of 1812, Jackson rose to the rank of general and became a war hero through his successful leadership of American troops at the Battle of New Orleans. Later in his career, his political opponents charged him with murder for having approved the execution of several American soldiers for minor offenses during the war.

- As president, Jackson vetoed dozens of bills and grew powerful through the use of the spoils system.

- In 1835, he survived an assassination attempt. In 1837, he retired to his plantation after attending the inauguration of his handpicked successor, Martin Van Buren.

23. Jackson once said, "I believe that just laws can make no distinction of privilege between the rich and poor. . . ." What part of his life could he cite to prove that he followed this belief?

    (1) His marriage to Rachel Robards
    (2) His being charged with the murder of several American soldiers during the War of 1812
    (3) His time spent as a justice of the Tennessee Supreme Court
    (4) His use of the spoils system
    (5) His status as a hero of the War of 1812

24. Senator Henry Clay once described Jackson as "corrupt." What fact of Jackson's life might Clay have cited to prove his charge?

    (1) His manipulation of the spoils system
    (2) His joining of the Continental Army at age thirteen
    (3) The duel he fought in which both he and his opponent were shot
    (4) His almost lifelong hatred of the British
    (5) His election as Tennessee's first representative to the U.S. Congress

25. Jackson was known throughout his life for sometimes behaving in a rash manner. Which of his actions could be cited to support this point of view?

    (1) Studying law and being admitted to the bar
    (2) Marrying a woman whose marital status was later questioned
    (3) Retiring to his plantation after his two terms as president and hating the British
    (4) Joining the army at thirteen and fighting a duel
    (5) Becoming a hero of the War of 1812 and serving on the Tennessee Supreme Court

26. In which two American wars did Andrew Jackson participate?

    (1) Revolutionary War and the War of 1812
    (2) Civil War and the Spanish-American War
    (3) World War I and World War II
    (4) Korean War and the Vietnam War
    (5) Crimean War and the Russo-Japanese War

27. In the Battle of New Orleans, British casualties numbered 2,000 whereas American casualties were only 21. What might be inferred about Jackson's military skills from this fact?

    (1) The British troops were poorly trained.
    (2) The American troops had more and better weapons than the British did.
    (3) Jackson was an able military commander.
    (4) Jackson's infamous temper caused his chief military subordinates to do anything to win.
    (5) Jackson made a much better military leader than president.

28. President Jackson vetoed the bill to recharter the Bank of the United States. As a result, "pet" banks began to print money and make new loans with little backing. Issuing new money and making loans in this way most likely resulted in

    (1) a severe depression.
    (2) severe inflation.
    (3) more unemployment.
    (4) decreased spending.
    (5) a trade deficit.

Items 29–31 refer to the following passage.

What makes a good marriage? The collective efforts of numerous researchers are now beginning to develop an answer. A Florida study of marriages lasting twenty-five years or more showed that a key element of a successful relationship is the ability to solve problems jointly. The ability to listen constructively and nondefensively is another. The ability to have fun together—to be humorous and playful—is also important. The early results of a Michigan study point toward "affective affirmation" as a strong predictor of marital happiness. Affective affirmation is the unconditional approval of one's mate. This is such a powerful force in nonverbal communication, such as body language, that it can bring about a remarkable transformation in a relationship. In affective affirmation, each person moves toward his or her spouse's innermost ideal of a partner because of the existing positive indicators already being received.

29. Which sentence best summarizes this passage?

(1) People married for twenty-five years or more usually have happy marriages.

(2) Several basic factors seem to play important roles in determining how good a marriage is.

(3) Researchers in Florida and Michigan have studied the qualities that go into making a good marriage.

(4) The ability to have fun together is a key element needed to make a good marriage.

(5) Affective affirmation is the one essential quality needed to make a good marriage.

30. A married couple that argues a lot might best solve their problems by

(1) getting a divorce.

(2) seeking counseling to learn how to solve problems jointly.

(3) asking their friends for advice.

(4) setting aside a special time each day to try to work out their differences in a calm, nonconfrontational way.

(5) reading books that discuss how to deal with problems in relationships.

31. Many people believe that most marital problems are caused by differences between people and by problem areas such as money, children, and sex. However, a Denver researcher has discovered that it is not the differences and problems themselves that are most important but how these differences and problems are handled, especially early in the marriage. This finding confirmed the importance of which key factor?

(1) The ability to provide affective affirmation for each other

(2) The ability to solve problems jointly

(3) The ability to listen constructively

(4) The ability to be playful with each other

(5) The ability to limit arguments to 10 minutes or less

Items 32 and 33 refer to the following passage.

From 1848 to 1919, American women fought for a constitutional amendment giving them suffrage, or the right to vote. Year after year, more and more women attended rallies and marched in the streets. In one parade, a reporter noted that "women doctors, women lawyers, women architects, women artists, actresses and sculptors; women waitresses, domestics; a huge division of industrial workers . . . all marched with an intensity and purpose that astonished the crowds that lined the streets." In 1919, Congress passed the Nineteenth Amendment, giving women the right to vote. A year later, the states ratified it, and female suffrage became the law of the land.

32. Attending speeches, rallies, and marches are activities that

(1) are protected by the First Amendment.

(2) were unbecoming for women at the time.

(3) convinced lawmakers to pass the Nineteenth Amendment.

(4) did little to further the cause of suffrage.

(5) showed how determined all women were.

33. Which conclusion is best supported by the reporter's description of a suffragist parade?

(1) Only a handful of women wanted suffrage and were willing to take a stand.

(2) Only wealthy women had time to take part in marches and parades supporting suffrage.

(3) Voting was not a serious issue for most women.

(4) Women from many different walks of life took a stand in favor of women's suffrage.

(5) Working women were interested in voting because the stakes were higher for them.

Items 34–36 refer to the following passage.

The growth of industry and business led to several new ways of doing business. These new practices allowed owners of large companies to run their smaller competitors out of business by controlling supplies and prices. Once they had control of the market, these so-called "robber barons" could charge any prices they wished for their goods.

Trust: a combination of businesses in which one board of trustees controls the member companies

Monopoly: a business that has complete control over an industry or trade

Holding company: a combination of businesses in which one company owns stock in another company

Vertical integration: control of all steps of the production process in an industry

Horizontal integration: control of one area of production in an industry—for example, manufacturing or distribution

34. In 1873, John D. Rockefeller's Standard Oil Company bought several bankrupt oil refineries. This move, which gave Standard Oil control over the refining stage of oil production, is an example of

(1) a trust.
(2) a monopoly.
(3) a holding company.
(4) vertical integration.
(5) horizontal integration.

35. By 1879, Standard Oil controlled nearly all of the means of transporting oil. The company now had the power to control oil prices. This situation is an example of

(1) a trust.
(2) a monopoly.
(3) a holding company.
(4) vertical integration.
(5) horizontal integration.

36. Many Americans were against "big business" entities such as trusts, monopolies, and holding companies because they

(1) encouraged corruption and kept prices low.
(2) encouraged competition and kept prices high.
(3) killed competition and kept prices high.
(4) killed competition and kept wages high.
(5) kept prices low and wages high.

37. During the Cold War, many Americans believed that communism, if allowed to spread, would threaten democracy. To prevent the spread of communism, the United States pursued a policy of

(1) intervention in the affairs of communist countries.
(2) brinkmanship, or risking war to maintain peace.
(3) containment, or keeping communism within its current borders.
(4) massive retaliation against any threat or action by a communist country.
(5) covert operations, or secret activities aimed at undermining communist governments.

Items 38–40 refer to the following graph.

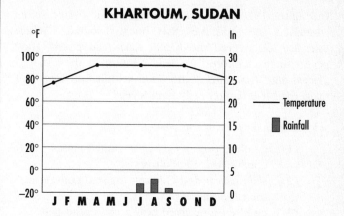

KHARTOUM, SUDAN

38. In what regions are you most likely to find a climate such as the one indicated in the graph?

(1) Tropics
(2) Polar regions
(3) Temperate zones
(4) Mountains
(5) Deserts

39. Which phrase best describes this climate?

(1) Hot and very rainy
(2) Hot, humid summers and mild winters
(3) Hot with very little rain
(4) Varying temperatures with very little rain
(5) Freezing temperatures with little or no precipitation

40. What kind of vegetation would you expect to find in this climate?

(1) Rain forests
(2) Forests
(3) Tall grasses
(4) Short grasses and shrubs
(5) Little or no vegetation

During the 1970s, gasoline processed in the United States contained lead additives that boosted octane. When scientists discovered the health risks lead posed, they began to test children for lead content in their blood. They found that those who lived within 500 feet of a main road had dangerously high levels.

41. The main idea of the passage is that

(1) gasoline processed in the United States contained lead additives.

(2) scientists tested children for lead content in their blood.

(3) children who lived near a main road had dangerously high levels of lead in their blood.

(4) location can put people at higher risk for lead poisoning.

(5) living near a main road is dangerous.

42. What conclusion can be reached from the passage?

(1) Gasoline processed in the United States is no longer dangerous.

(2) Location can put people at higher risk for lead poisoning.

(3) Location is often a vital factor in explaining health risk.

(4) Living too near a main road can cause lead poisoning.

(5) U.S. companies are responsible for the high levels of lead in children's blood.

43. George Washington set a precedent by not running for a third term as president. Later this practice became law. Why is a two-term limit a good policy for the country?

(1) Most people are too tired after two terms as president to be effective during a third term.

(2) Many people want to be president, and it's not fair to them if one person has the job too long.

(3) One person should not have so much power for such a long period of time.

(4) Members of Congress object to the predictable policies of one president.

(5) Most citizens get tired of listening to one leader after eight years and need to hear from someone else.

44. Whom do the men in the cartoon represent?

(1) The United Nations

(2) The secretaries of state, labor, and commerce and their aides

(3) American military leaders and policy makers

(4) Russian military leaders and policy makers

(5) Military leaders of several nations

45. What underlying point of view is the cartoonist presenting?

(1) The Defense Department has too many generals.

(2) Military leaders have too many tax dollars to spend as they choose.

(3) Leaders of the Air Force, Army, Navy, and Marines spend too much time having meetings and not enough time fighting wars.

(4) The legislative and executive branches of government have given too much power to military leaders.

(5) Military spending is important to the economic well-being of the United States.

46. U.S. senators are elected for six-year terms. They are expected to represent the interests of their states and to take a long-range view of the needs of the entire country. Which qualities or experiences would be least useful for a U.S. senator to have?

(1) An ability to reach compromises on important issues

(2) A clear understanding of the meaning of the Constitution

(3) Strong financial and business skills

(4) Strong ties to a foreign government

(5) A good public speaking style

47. Medicare, which provides health care to elderly Americans, is an example of

(1) government bureaucracy.
(2) Social Security.
(3) an independent agency.
(4) a political action committee.
(5) a government entitlement program.

Item 48 refers to the following cartoon.

48. What does this 1977 cartoon say about lobbyists?

(1) Lobbyists often drive expensive cars.
(2) Lobbyists have too strong a hold on Congress.
(3) Lobbyists are overpaid.
(4) Lobbyists are often former members of Congress.
(5) Lobbyists represent many different types of special interests.

49. For years, the United States took a hard-line stance against the communist Soviet Union. Now we are friendly and helpful toward Russia, the largest republic to result from the breakup of the Soviet Union. This change shows that U.S. foreign policy

(1) is flexible enough to change when circumstances change.
(2) reflects a wishy-washy attitude toward world events.
(3) is staunchly against communism.
(4) is subject to the whims of the president.
(5) has not changed for at least fifty years.

50. The secretary of state has been called the president's "right arm" in dealing with other nations. Which of the following is not a function of the State Department?

(1) Diplomacy
(2) Occupational health and safety
(3) Foreign policy
(4) Issue of passports
(5) Management of overseas bureaus

Posttest 3

SCIENCE

85 Minutes ❖ 50 Questions

Directions: Choose the <u>one best answer</u> for each item.

Items 1 and 2 refer to the following illustration.

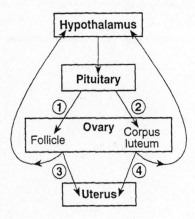

1. The substance secreted by the corpus luteum that acts upon the hypothalamus is

   (1) oxytocin.
   (2) progesterone.
   (3) estrogen.
   (4) epinephrine.
   (5) thyroxine.

2. The hormones that are released by the follicle (3) and the corpus luteum (4) are

   (1) oxytocin and follicle-stimulating hormone.
   (2) follicle-stimulating hormone and estrogen.
   (3) estrogen and progesterone.
   (4) progesterone and oxytocin.
   (5) estrogen and follicle-stimulating hormone.

3. Which of the following lists the taxonomic terms from the most to least inclusive?

   (1) Phylum, class, order, family, genus
   (2) Phylum, kingdom, class, order, family
   (3) Kingdom, phylum, order, class, family
   (4) Phylum, class, order, species, genus
   (5) Order, class, family, genus, species

4. Which of the following groups of vascular plants produces seeds?

   (1) Club mosses
   (2) Horsetails
   (3) Conifers
   (4) All of the above
   (5) None of the above

Items 5 and 6 refer to the following illustration.

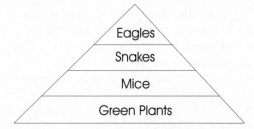

5. In the illustration above, the mice eat the green plants and are, in turn, eaten by the snakes. An ecologist would refer to the mice as either

   (1) herbivores or producers.
   (2) producers or primary consumers.
   (3) primary consumers or herbivores.
   (4) herbivores or secondary consumers.
   (5) herbivores or saprophytes.

6. If the amount of energy bound up in mice was determined to be 10,000 kcal/m²/yr, what amount would be bound up in the eagles?

 (1) 2500kcal/m²/yr
 (2) 1000kcal/m²/yr
 (3) 250kcal/m²/yr
 (4) 100kcal/m²/yr
 (5) 25kcal/m²/yr

7. Cinnabar is mercury sulfide, HgS. It is mined to produce mercury, which is separated from the sulfur by burning the cinnabar in the presence of oxygen, according to the following formula:

$$HgS + O_2 \rightarrow Hg + SO_2$$

Which of the following statements is not true?

 (1) The production of mercury can cause acid rain.
 (2) Sulfur is more electronegative than mercury.
 (3) Oxygen is more electronegative than sulfur.
 (4) One mole of cinnabar will yield one mole of mercury.
 (5) Two moles of oxygen atoms will yield 3 moles of sulfur dioxide atoms.

Item 8 refers to the following illustration and information.

In electrolysis, electrical energy is used to drive reactions in a solution that would not occur readily otherwise. The following illustration shows an electrolytic cell hooked to a battery or source of direct current. Oxidation is occurring at the anode and reduction at the cathode.

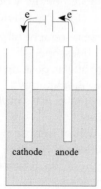

8. What will happen in a solution of molten sodium chloride (NaCl)?

 (1) Sodium ions will be attracted to the anode.
 (2) Sodium ions will be attracted to the cathode.
 (3) Chlorine ions will take up electrons at the anode.
 (4) Water will be formed at the anode.
 (5) Oxygen gas will be formed at the anode.

9. Which of the following functional groups is associated with fatty acids?

 (1) OH
 (2) COOH
 (3) CH_3OH
 (4) CCl
 (5) NH_2

Vapor Pressure of Water

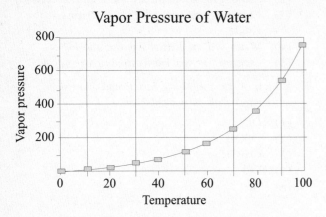

10. According to the graph, which of the following statements is not true?

(1) Food takes longer to cook at high altitudes because water boils at a lower temperature.

(2) All the water in a container will condense if held at 80° and 400mm Hg.

(3) The line represents the points where water vapor and liquid water are in equilibrium.

(4) If the conditions at point B are held for some time, all the water vapor will condense.

(5) Covering water before heating will decrease the time it takes to boil, because the pressure is increased.

11. Which of the following colors of light will be absorbed first as sunlight enters water?

(1) Red
(2) Orange
(3) Green
(4) Yellow
(5) Blue

One theory of the origin of the universe is the Big Bang. According to this theory, all of the matter in the universe was once in a massive ball. About 13 billion years ago, this ball exploded, sending matter in all directions. Scientists argue that this theory is supported by the fact that neighboring galaxies are moving away from one another. When light from objects moving away from the observer is analyzed, the wavelength appears as longer or redder than it actually is. This so-called red shift is referenced as primary evidence for the expansion of the universe.

12. Based on the information in the passage, which statement is correct?

(1) Shifting of light waves to the shorter wave-lengths, or a blue shift, would be evidence of a shrinking universe.

(2) The universe was actively contracting before the Big Bang, but it is not expanding.

(3) The universe will continue to expand indefinitely.

(4) The ancient Greek philosophers were correct in hypothesizing that the stars are eternal.

(5) Our solar system is near the center of the universe and serves as a model for the physical laws that account for all other systems.

13. Given the vastness of space, special techniques have been developed to measure the movement of galaxies. From the information in the passage, which method listed below would most likely reveal evidence of an expanding universe?

(1) Physical measurement of galactic movement through a telescope

(2) Plotting of stellar position change using time-lapse photography

(3) Spectroscopic analysis of light from near and distant stars

(4) Triangulation of galactic position by multiple observatories

(5) Comparison of Renaissance star charts with current positions

All ordinary materials offer some resistance to the flow of electrons, or electricity. Metals such as copper and silver are good conductors; that is, their resistance to the flow of electricity is low. A metal's resistance to the flow of electricity becomes even lower as the temperature decreases. The resistance of most metals does not decrease below a certain value, even at extremely cold temperatures.

Other materials, called superconductors, show an extraordinary drop in resistance at extremely cold temperatures. Lead, for example, gradually decreases in resistance until it reaches a certain temperature. At that point, the resistance of lead drops to zero.

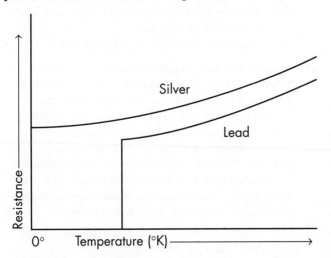

14. What is resistance?

   (1) The flow of electrons
   (2) A metal that conducts electricity
   (3) A substance that is a superconductor
   (4) The slowing down of the flow of electrons
   (5) A substance such as copper or silver

15. A material with extremely high resistance would most likely be used as

   (1) electrical wiring.
   (2) the filament in a light bulb.
   (3) a battery.
   (4) a covering for electrical wiring.
   (5) a lightning rod.

16. Which of the following statements is supported by the information given?

   (1) As the temperature decreases, the resistance of any material decreases until both values are zero.
   (2) As the temperature increases, the resistance of any material decreases.
   (3) The resistance of lead falls to zero at extremely low temperatures.
   (4) The resistance of conductors falls to zero at extremely low temperatures.
   (5) Resistance is measured in ohms.

17. All of the following statements about dicotyledons are true EXCEPT that

   (1) they have a fibrous root system.
   (2) their leaf venation is netted, not parallel.
   (3) their vascular bundles are not scattered randomly in the stem, but are aligned in a ring fashion.
   (4) they have two seed leaves, not one.
   (5) they possess floral parts in multiples of fours or fives.

18. Neurotransmitters are chemical substances released by cells that act on other cells. They could affect

   (1) nerve cells.
   (2) endocrine cells.
   (3) muscle cells.
   (4) All of the above
   (5) None of the above

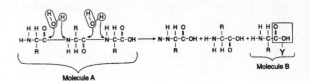

19. In molecule B, what type of group is contained in box Y?

   (1) An amino group
   (2) A variable group
   (3) A carboxyl group
   (4) A peptide group
   (5) A benzyl group

20. How may peptide bonds are present in molecule A?

   (1) 1
   (2) 2
   (3) 3
   (4) 4
   (5) 8

21. Which sequence represents the correct pathway for the removal of urine from the human body?

   (1) kidney→urethra→urinary bladder→ureter
   (2) ureter→kidney→urinary bladder→urethra
   (3) urethra→kidney→urinary bladder→ureter
   (4) kidney→ureter→urinary bladder→urethra
   (5) kidney→urinary bladder→ureter→urethra

Item 22 refers to the following information.

The second law of thermodynamics states that every time energy is transformed, it becomes less useful. For example, when electric energy runs a motor, no more than 80 percent of the energy is actually used. The rest becomes heat, which is given off by the machine. Waste heat is always generated by any use of energy. Even machines that use heat energy, such as a steam engine, take in very hot steam but discharge wastewater that is still warm.

22. Which of the following statements from the passage is a conclusion supported by the details given?

   (1) Every time energy is transformed, it becomes less useful.
   (2) When electric energy runs a motor, no more than 80 percent of the energy is actually used.
   (3) The rest becomes heat, which is given off by the machine.
   (4) Steam engines take in very hot steam.
   (5) Steam engines discharge wastewater that is still warm.

23. Nuclear fission is the process in which the nuclei of atoms are split by an additional neutron, resulting in a large release of energy. As a nucleus is split, it releases several neutrons, which in turn split other nuclei. The first neutron sets off a chain of fissions, called a chain reaction. Unless the chain reaction is controlled, enormous amounts of heat energy are produced in a fraction of a second, as in an atomic bomb.

What would be the result of slowing and controlling the chain reaction?

   (1) The amount of heat energy produced would increase sharply.
   (2) A more powerful bomb could be manufactured.
   (3) Additional neutrons would be released.
   (4) Heat production would take place at a decreased, steady pace.
   (5) The chain reaction would not begin.

24. In a photocopier, a metal drum has a negative electric charge. When an image of a document is projected onto the drum, the electric charge is deactivated wherever light hits the drum. The black toner powder is attracted to the areas of electric charge that remain. The photocopier deposits the toner powder on the paper, where it is melted in place. Which of the following is the most likely cause of getting blank pages instead of copies of a document from a photocopier?

   (1) The paper jams inside the machine.
   (2) The toner powder is melted unevenly.
   (3) Static electricity attracts the toner powder to the paper.
   (4) The supply of toner powder has run out.
   (5) The electric power has been disconnected.

25. A student was given 10ml of a 0.5 M NaCl solution. She was asked to prepare 100ml of a 0.01 M solution. How much of the 0.5 M NaCl solution will she use?

   (1) All of it
   (2) 5ml
   (3) 2ml
   (4) 1ml
   (5) 0.5ml

Item 26 refers to the following illustration and information.

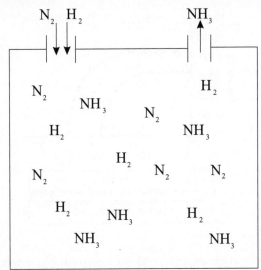

Ammonia is produced in the Haber process by the following reaction:

$$N_2 + 3H_2 \Leftrightarrow 2NH_3 + energy$$

26. Which of the following factors would not favor the production of ammonia (NH_3)?

(1) An increase of energy into the system
(2) An increase of nitrogen into the system
(3) An increase of hydrogen into the system
(4) A decrease of ammonia from the system
(5) An increase of pressure on the system

Items 27–29 refer to the following table.

MOHS SCALE OF RELATIVE HARDNESS

Relative Scale	Mineral	Hardness of Some Common Objects
Hardest		
10	Diamond	
9	Corundum	
8	Topaz	
7	Quartz	
6	Feldspar	
5	Apatite	5.5 Glass Pocketknife
4	Fluorite	
3	Calcite	3.5 Copper Penny
2	Gypsum	2.5 Fingernail
Softest		
1	Talc	

27. The Mohs scale of mineral hardness is a relative scale. This means that the hardness intervals between the different minerals on the scale are not necessarily equal. Using the information in the scale illustrated, which of the following statements are correct?

A. Gypsum is softer than Quartz.

B. Feldspar is harder than Corundum.

C. A penny is softer than glass.

(1) A only
(2) B only
(3) C only
(4) A and B
(5) A and C

28. Which of the following statements is incorrect?

(1) The hardest mineral is diamond.
(2) Talc can be scratched with a fingernail.
(3) Quartz is harder than topaz.
(4) Corundum is harder than fluorite.
(5) Quartz will scratch glass.

29. A sample of mineral X, a smoky, smooth crystal, will scratch feldspar, calcite, and fluorite. Which of the following statements must be correct?

(1) Mineral X must be diamond.
(2) Mineral X will scratch glass.
(3) Mineral X is not quartz.
(4) Mineral X is organic.
(5) Mineral X is gypsum.

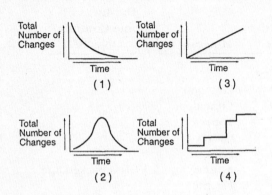

30. Which of the above graphs best illustrates the idea of punctuated equilibrium?

(1) 1
(2) 2
(3) 3
(4) 4
(5) None of the above

31. The HIV virus infects certain people and causes the disease known as AIDS. In which cells does the virus reproduce most of the time?

(1) Brain cells
(2) Kidney cells
(3) Liver cells
(4) Thyroid cells
(5) Blood cells

32. Soon after a building has been torn down and the ground cleared, grasses began to grow in that area. After 5 years, shrubs replaced the grasses. This pattern of plant growth is known as

(1) biological control.
(2) ecological succession.
(3) land-use management.
(4) cover cropping.
(5) biological magnification.

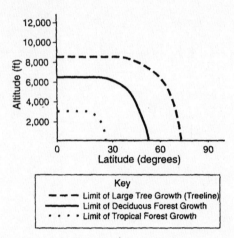

33. The diagram above shows a relationship among altitude, latitude, and tree growth. What valid inference can be made based on this graph?

(1) Deciduous trees cannot grow at an altitude of 5,000 feet.
(2) The effects of increasing altitude and latitude on tree growth are similar.
(3) There is less light available at 10,000 feet than at lower elevations.
(4) Trees do not grow rapidly in the tropics.
(5) Deciduous trees grow faster than tropical trees.

34. A boy whose blood type is O cannot have a father whose blood type is

(1) A
(2) B
(3) A or B
(4) AB
(5) O

35. How many different combinations of alleles can an animal that has the genotype AaBbCc have without crossing over?

(1) 2
(2) 4
(3) 6
(4) 8
(5) 12

36. In the early 1970s, Donald Johanson, Tim White, and others discovered a hominid skeleton they called Lucy. What is Lucy's correct scientific name?

(1) *Homo habilis*
(2) *Australopithecus africanus*
(3) *Australopithecus afarensis*
(4) *Homo erectus*
(5) *Homo neanderthalensis*

37. A pendulum is a weight suspended on a string that is attached to a fixed point, as illustrated in the following diagram.

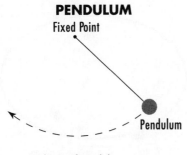

PENDULUM

Gravity causes a pendulum to move. Which type of energy conversion occurs in a pendulum?

(1) Electrical energy changes to light energy.
(2) Kinetic energy changes to heat energy.
(3) Chemical energy changes to electrical energy.
(4) Potential energy changes to kinetic energy.
(5) Sound energy changes to mechanical energy.

38. Water moves up and down when a wave passes. It does not move horizontally. Below, a toy boat is floating on the surface of a pond. A stone is thrown into the water.

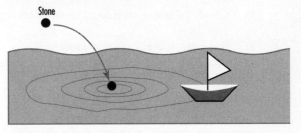

Which of the following statements best describes the resulting motion of the boat?

(1) It moves horizontally with each successive wave.
(2) It moves horizontally ahead of the waves.
(3) Its motion is related to the water temperature.
(4) It bobs up and down but does not move horizontally.
(5) It vibrates long after the waves have passed.

Items 39–41 refer to the following illustration.

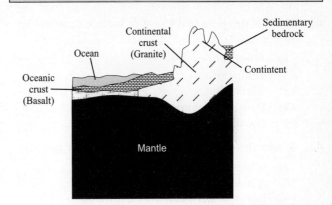

39. Based on the diagram of a cross-section of the earth's crust, which of the following statements is incorrect?

(1) The mantle is below the crust.
(2) The ocean crust is thinner than the continental crust.
(3) Sedimentary rock is present on top of sections of continental crust.
(4) Granite is denser than basalt.
(5) Sedimentary rock has formed on the ocean floor.

40. Based on the diagram, which statement is correct?

(1) Ocean depth is variable.
(2) Ocean crust is less dense than continental crust.
(3) A body of water existed at some point on the land mass.
(4) The mantle is in constant motion.
(5) Ocean depth and continental crust thickness are approximately equal.

41. Subduction zones are common where there is a convergence of ocean and continental crust. Usually, the thinner, denser ocean crust is forced under the thicker, less dense continental crust. Assuming that the boundary of ocean and continental crust shown in the illustration is a convergent tectonic boundary, what landform would most likely form there over time?

(1) Folded mountains as the crust segments collide
(2) A boundary unchanged from that pictured
(3) A trench, as the ocean crust was subducted under the continental crust
(4) A volcano, as magma reached the surface through the convergent boundary
(5) A rift, as the two plates moved away from each other

42. What is the principal cause of surface currents in the oceans?

(1) Wind action
(2) Temperature
(3) Coriolis effect
(4) Density differences
(5) Location of the thermoclines

43. Warm air tends to rise through cooler air because

(1) it contains more oxygen.
(2) it is less dense.
(3) heat transfer decreases.
(4) a convection cell is set up.
(5) heat transfer increases.

44. Which of the following represents the balanced equation for the following reaction?

iron plus oxygen yields iron(III) oxide

(1) $Fe + O \rightarrow FeO$
(2) $2Fe + O_2 \rightarrow Fe_2O$
(3) $2Fe + O_2 \rightarrow 2Fe_3O$
(4) $4Fe + 3O_2 \rightarrow 2Fe_2O_3$
(5) $2Fe + O_2 \rightarrow 2Fe_2O_2$

45. About how many molecules of water are in 1 microliter if there are 1 million microliters in a liter?

(1) About 3 million (3×10^6)
(2) About 3 billion (3×10^9)
(3) About 30 trillion (30×10^{12})
(4) About 30 million billion (30×10^{15})
(5) About 30 billion trillion (30×10^{18})

Item 46 refers to the following illustration.

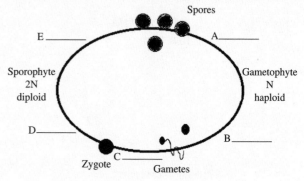

46. The life cycle illustrated above is known as the alternation of generations. Which position indicates where meiosis occurs?

(1) A
(2) B
(3) C
(4) D
(5) E

Items 47 and 48 refer to the following illustration of a flower.

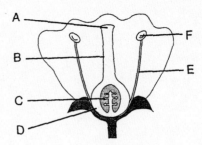

47. Pollen grains are produced in the structure labeled

(1) F
(2) E
(3) D
(4) C
(5) B

48. The stamen is composed of

(1) F and E
(2) D and C
(3) B and A
(4) D, C, and A
(5) F only

> Items 49 and 50 refer to the following paragraph.

A virus is a tiny organism, much smaller than a cell. A virus by itself is not really alive; it becomes active only after it has entered a living cell. Once inside the cell, the virus takes over the parts of the cell that direct the cell's activities, so that instead of producing the proteins it normally produces, the cell produces more viruses. Eventually, the host cell is destroyed. The new viruses invade other cells.

49. Which part of a cell would be the primary target of an invading virus?

(1) Cytoplasm
(2) Endoplasmic reticulum
(3) Mitochondria
(4) Nucleus
(5) Vacuole

50. In order to make the cell produce copies of a virus, the virus must contain something like one of the following cell components. Which one?

(1) Chromosome
(2) Golgi apparatus
(3) Nucleolus
(4) Organelle
(5) Ribosome

Posttest 4

LANGUAGE ARTS, READING

65 Minutes ❖ 40 Questions

Directions: Each excerpt from a longer work is followed by multiple-choice questions about the reading material. Read each excerpt and then answer the questions that follow. Choose the one best answer for each question. Refer to the reading material as often as necessary in answering the questions.

Each excerpt is preceded by a "purpose question." The purpose question gives a reason for reading the material. Use these purpose questions to help focus your reading. You are not required to answer these purpose questions. They are given only to help you concentrate on the ideas presented in the reading materials.

Items 1–5 refer to the following excerpt from a novel.

WHAT IS THE COLONEL'S STATE OF MIND?

Line The colonel took the top off the coffee can and saw that there was only one little spoonful left. He removed the pot from the fire, poured half the water onto the earthen floor, and scraped the
5 inside of the can with a knife until the last scrapings of the ground coffee, mixed with bits of rust, fell into the pot.

While he was waiting for it to boil, sitting next to the stone fireplace with an attitude of
10 confident and innocent expectation, the colonel experienced the feeling that fungus and poisonous lilies were taking root in his gut. It was October. A difficult morning to get through, even for a man like himself, who had survived so many mornings
15 like this one. For nearly sixty years—since the end of the last civil war—the colonel had done nothing else but wait. October was one of the few things which arrived.

His wife raised the mosquito netting when
20 she saw him come into the bedroom with the coffee. The night before she had suffered an asthma attack, and now she was in a drowsy state. But she got up to take the cup.

"And you?" she said.
25 "I've had mine," the colonel lied. "There was still a big spoonful left."

The bells began ringing at that moment. The colonel had forgotten about the funeral. While his wife was drinking her coffee, he unhooked the
30 hammock at one end, and rolled it up on the other, behind the door. The woman thought about the dead man.

"He was born in 1922," she said. "Exactly a month after our son. April 7th."
35 She continued sipping her coffee in the pauses of her gravelly breathing. She was scarcely more than a bit of white on an arched, rigid spine. Her disturbed breathing made her put her questions as assertions. When she finished her
40 coffee, she was still thinking about the dead man. "It must be horrible to be buried in October," she said. But her husband paid no attention. He opened the window. October had moved in on the patio. Contemplating the vegetation, which
45 was bursting out in intense greens, and the tiny mounds the worms made in the mud, the colonel felt the sinister month again in his intestines.

—From *No One Writes to the Colonel*,
by Gabriel Garcia Marquez

1. "She was scarcely more than a bit of white on an arched, rigid spine." This sentence suggests that

   (1) the colonel's wife is hard and unyielding.
   (2) the colonel's wife is very thin and ill.
   (3) the colonel dislikes his wife.
   (4) poisonous lilies are harming the colonel's wife.
   (5) the colonel's wife is dead.

2. What is the best way to describe the narrative structure of this story?

(1) It is made up of the impressions formed by small details.

(2) It is told by the colonel's interior monologue.

(3) It is told by the wife's interior monologue.

(4) It consists of a series of flashbacks.

(5) It consists of a series of exciting but disconnected incidents.

3. Which detail from the story is most important in telling you that the colonel is kind and considerate?

(1) He adds bits of rust to the coffee in the pot.

(2) He feels that fungus is taking root in his gut.

(3) He unhooks the hammock and rolls it up behind the door.

(4) He tells his wife that he has already had his coffee.

(5) He opens the window for this wife.

4. What is the best description of the general tone of this passage?

(1) Carefree

(2) Bittersweet

(3) Frenzied

(4) Cheerful

(5) Melancholy

5. "Contemplating the vegetation, which was bursting out in intense greens, and the tiny mounds the worms made in the mud, the colonel felt the sinister month again in his intestines."

This sentence is an example of

(1) alliteration.

(2) personification.

(3) satire.

(4) objectivity.

(5) simile.

Items 6–9 refer to the following excerpt from an autobiography.

WHAT ARE POSSIBLE CONSEQUENCES OF THE GERMANS' ADVANCE?

Line Spring 1944. Good news from the Russian front. No doubt could remain now of Germany's defeat. It was only a question of time—of months or weeks perhaps.

5   The trees were in blossom. This was a year like any other, with its springtime, its betrothals, its weddings and births.

        People said: "The Russian army's making gigantic strides forward . . . Hitler won't be able
10 to do us any harm, even if he wants to."

        Yes, we even doubted that he wanted to exterminate us.

        Was he going to wipe out a whole people? Could he exterminate a population so scattered
15 throughout so many countries? So many millions! What methods could he use? And in the middle of the twentieth century! . . .

        The following day, there was more disturbing news: with government permission, German
20 troops have entered Hungarian territory.

        Here and there, anxiety was aroused. One of our friends, Berkovitz, who had just returned from the capital, told us: "The Jews of Budapest are living in an atmosphere of fear and terror. There
25 are anti-Semitic incidents every day, in the streets, in the trains. The Fascists are attacking Jewish shops and synagogues. The situation is getting very serious."

        The news spread like wildfire through
30 Sighet. Soon it was on everyone's lips. But not for long. Optimism was revived.

        "The Germans won't get as far as this. They'll stay in Budapest. There are strategic and political reasons . . ."
35   Before three days had passed, German army cars had appeared on our streets.

—From *Night* by Elie Wiesel

6. Which of the following events occurs last in the passage?

(1) Berkovitz returns from the capital with frightening news.

(2) German troops enter Hungarian territory.

(3) German troops arrive at Sighet.

(4) Berkovitz's news spreads through Sighet.

(5) Good news arrives from the Russian front.

7. Which of the following can you assume from the last line of the passage?

    (1) A great number of army cars will soon be arriving.

    (2) The German army cars will not stay long in Sighet.

    (3) The townspeople will soon feel calm and relieved.

    (4) The atmosphere of fear and anxiety is warranted.

    (5) The Germans will cause no harm to the townspeople.

8. What was one cause of anxious feelings in Sighet?

    (1) The unusually long winter

    (2) News from the front that Germany would surrender

    (3) The number of betrothals that spring

    (4) The Russian army's steady advance

    (5) Berkovitz's account of events in the capital

9. Which of the following contrasting pairs adds irony to the passage?

    (1) The number of weddings and the beautiful spring

    (2) The cruelty of the Germans and the kindness of the Russians

    (3) Fire in Sighet and the warm spring weather

    (4) Berkovitz's fear and the news from the front

    (5) The quiet beauty of spring and the disturbing rumors

Items 10–14 refer to the following excerpt from an art history textbook.

HOW HAVE PAINTERS OF DIFFERENT AGES USED TEMPERA?

Line Until the end of the Middle Ages, most paintings were done in tempera, a medium made by combining water, pigment, and some gummy material, usually egg yolk. The paint was meticu-
5 lously applied with the point of a fine red sable brush. Colors could not readily be blended, and, as a result, effects of *chiaroscuro* were accomplished by means of careful and gradual hatching. In order to use tempera, the painting surface, often a wood
10 panel, had to be prepared with a very smooth ground not unlike the smooth plaster wall prepared for *buon fresco*. Gesso, made from glue and plaster of Paris or chalk, is the most common ground, and like wet plaster, it is fully absorbent,
15 combining with the tempera paint to create an

extremely durable and softly glowing surface unmatched by any other medium.

    Sandro Botticelli's *Primavera*, painted for a chamber next to the bedroom of his patron
20 Lorenzo di Pierfrancesco de'Medici, is one of the greatest tempera paintings ever made. As a result of its restoration in 1978, we know a good deal about how it was painted. The support consists of eight poplar panels, arranged vertically and
25 fastened by two horizontal strips of spruce. This support was covered with a gesso ground that hid the strips between the panels. Botticelli next outlined the trees and his human figures on the gesso and then painted the sky, laying blue
30 tempera directly on the ground. The figures and trees were painted on an undercoat, white for the figures, black for the trees. The transparency of the drapery was achieved by layering thin yellow washes of transparent medium over the white
35 undercoat. As many as thirty coats of color, transparent or opaque depending on the relative light or shadow of the area being painted, were required to create each figure.

    The kind of detail the artist is able to achieve
40 using egg tempera is readily apparent in *Braids* by Andrew Wyeth, one of the few contemporary artists to work almost exclusively in the medium. Wyeth's brushwork is so fine that each strand of hair escaping from his model's braids seems
45 caught individually in the light.

        —From *A World of Art*, by Henry M. Sayre

10. From the passage, you can tell that the greatest advantage of tempera is to allow painters to

    (1) show effects of light and shadow.

    (2) work slowly without worrying about the ground drying out.

    (3) produce vague and dramatic impressions.

    (4) show great detail.

    (5) blend colors.

11. After preparing and fastening the wood panels for *Primavera*, the next step was to

    (1) paint the sky.

    (2) outline the trees and human figures.

    (3) paint the drapery.

    (4) outline clouds and angels.

    (5) cover the support with gesso.

12. What is the author's overall purpose in this passage?

(1) To explain the technique of tempera painting

(2) To describe a variety of paintings in vivid language

(3) To compare the difference between Botticelli's and Wyeth's techniques

(4) To explain *Primavera*'s influence on later paintings

(5) To explain why *Primavera* is an excellent painting

13. According to the passage, tempera paint is made of

(1) poplar and spruce.

(2) layers of drapery.

(3) water, pigment, and a gummy material.

(4) glue and plaster of Paris or chalk.

(5) fine red sable.

14. According to the passage, as many as thirty coats of paint were required to create the

(1) sky in *Primavera*.

(2) figures in *Primavera*.

(3) hair in *Braids*.

(4) light in *Braids*.

(5) trees in *Primavera*.

Items 15–19 refer to the following excerpt from a book.

WHAT DOES THE SPEAKER SEE?

Line I swam out to Chinaman's Hat. We walked partway in low tide, then put on face masks. Once you open your eyes in the water, you become a flying creature. Schools of fish—zebra fish,
5 rainbow fish, red fish—curve with the currents, swim alongside and away; balloon fish puff out their porcupine quills. How unlike a dead fish an alive fish is. We swam through spangles of silver-white fish, their scales like sequins. Some-
10 times we entered cold spots, deserts, darkness under clouds, where the sand churned like gray fog, and sometimes we entered golden chambers. There are summer forests and winter forests down there. Sea cucumbers . . . rocked side to side. A
15 sea turtle glided by and that big shell is no encumbrance in the water. We saw no sharks, though they spawn in that area, and pilot fish swam ahead in front of our faces. The shores behind and ahead kept me unafraid.

20   Approaching Chinaman's Hat, we flew around and between a group of tall black stones like Stonehenge underwater, and through there, came up onto the land, where we rested with arms holding on to the island. We walked among
25 the palm trees and bushes that we had seen from the other shore. Large white birds were nesting on the ground under these bushes. We hurried to the unseen part of the island.

—From *China Men*, by Maxine Hong Kingston

15. In the passage, the speaker mentions all of the following EXCEPT

(1) zebra fish.

(2) rainbow fish.

(3) sharks.

(4) flying fish.

(5) sea cucumbers.

16. "How unlike a dead fish an alive fish is." (lines 7–8) Which of the following best restates the meaning of this statement?

(1) Whether alive or dead, all fish are beautiful.

(2) There is no easy way to describe the difficulty of fishing.

(3) Even dead, fish retain much of their natural beauty.

(4) To truly understand the beauty of fish, a person must go scuba diving.

(5) Seeing a fish in its natural environment is an enlightening experience.

17. From the descriptions in this passage, you can conclude that the speaker

(1) wants to become a professional deep-sea diver.

(2) enjoys observing fish more than she enjoys birdwatching.

(3) has never had a more successful diving expedition.

(4) feels as if she has entered another world.

(5) is afraid of the potential danger around her.

18. The speaker's comparison between fish scales and sequins in lines 8–9 emphasizes

(1) the deep, dark colors of the fish.

(2) the speaker's attraction to colorful things.

(3) the bright underwater sparkle of the fish.

(4) the sunlight that enters the ocean waters.

(5) the pale color of most of the fish's scales.

19. Which of the following series of events is most similar to the events in this passage?

   (1) A trip across the country, followed by a long vacation

   (2) A visit to a famous art museum, followed by the writing of an essay

   (3) An afternoon of swimming in the pool, followed by more exercise in the gym

   (4) A flight into space, followed by a return to Earth

   (5) A relaxing vacation in Jamaica, followed by a bumpy plane ride home

Items 20–25 refer to the following poem.

WHO IS THIS FELLOW?

Line A narrow Fellow in the Grass
      Occasionally rides —
      You may have met Him — did you not
      His notice sudden is —

5   The Grass divides as with a Comb —
      A spotted shaft is seen —
      And then it closes at your feet
      And opens further on —

      He likes a Boggy Acre,
10   A floor too cool for Corn —
      Yet when a Boy, and Barefoot —
      I more than once, at Noon,
      Have passed, I thought, a Whip lash
      Unbraiding in the Sun
15   When stooping to secure it
      It wrinkled, and was gone —

      Several of Nature's People
      I know, and they know me —
      I feel for them a transport
20   Of cordiality —

      But never met this Fellow,
      Attended, or alone,
      Without a tighter breathing
      And Zero at the Bone —
                    —Emily Dickinson

20. Which line from the poem contains a simile?

   (1) Line 5
   (2) Line 7
   (3) Line 13
   (4) Line 19
   (5) Line 24

21. Which line from the poem is an example of alliteration?

   (1) "Occasionally rides —"
   (2) "You may have met Him — did you not"
   (3) "A spotted shaft is seen —"
   (4) "Unbraiding in the Sun"
   (5) "It wrinkled, and was gone —"

22. The phrase "Nature's People" (line 17) refers to

   (1) other snakes.
   (2) other poets.
   (3) naturalists.
   (4) other animals.
   (5) scientists.

23. What does the author feel when she sees the narrow fellow in the grass?

   (1) Respect
   (2) Disgust
   (3) Cordiality
   (4) Joy
   (5) Fear

24. What is happening in the second stanza of the poem (lines 5–8)?

   (1) The poet is stepping on a snake.
   (2) The snake appears and reappears suddenly.
   (3) The poet tries to pick up the snake.
   (4) The snake moves to a wet area.
   (5) The snake suddenly bites the poet, who cries out.

25. The language in this poem can best be described as

   (1) old-fashioned.
   (2) highly poetic.
   (3) simple.
   (4) emotional.
   (5) unusual.

Items 26–30 refer to the following excerpt from a guide for job seekers.

HOW DO YOU APPLY FOR A JOB?

Line **Step 1—Find Out about Job Opportunities**
- Visit one of our Employment Service Offices to review our job listings.

5
- Review job announcements that cover positions in which you are interested. Job Announcements are the best source of information about the job. They describe the job, minimum qualifications required, type of test that will be used, and information on
10 where the job is located.

- Positions must be announced in order for applications to be accepted.

- Vacancies are announced for a minimum of 15 calendar days.

15 **Step 2—Submit Your Application**
- If you are interested in a job and believe that you meet the Minimum Qualifications, complete the application form.

- Each job announcement requires a separate
20 application. You may photocopy your completed application so that you can easily apply for other positions.

- Type or print clearly so the information can be easily read.

25
- Provide a Minimum Qualifications Summary with each job application. Number and discuss each Minimum Qualification. Describe your training and experience as accurately and completely as possible. The information
30 that you provide will help to establish your eligibility.

Note: *A listed* 'selective' *requirement on the job announcement is an additional required minimum qualification, which you have to meet*
35 *to qualify for the position. If there is a* 'preferential' *requirement, you do not have to meet this requirement to qualify for the position. A* 'preferential' *requirement is a desirable qualification.*

40
- Resumes are accepted. However, they often do not contain enough information to determine whether minimum qualifications are satisfied. Minimum Qualification summa-

ries are strongly encouraged.

45
- Mail, fax, or e-mail your completed application. Or hand Deliver your completed application to one of the addresses listed on the job announcement. Applications must be received by the close of business on the
50 closing date.

Step 3—Testing
- If a typing proficiency is required, schedule this test by calling one of our Employment Services Offices.

55
- Applications will be processed by the recruiting agency. The agency Personnel Office will determine whether you meet the Minimum Qualification.

- If you meet the Minimum Qualifications, you
60 will be mailed instructions on when and where to report for a written test.

- When a written test is not required, your application, will be rated on your training, education and/or work experience as it
65 relates to a particular job.

- If you are evaluated on your training and experience, your rating will vary for different types of jobs and may vary for positions with the same job title, depending on the require-
70 ments of the agency.

26. According to the passage, Job Announcements contain all of the following information EXCEPT

(1) a description of the job.
(2) a list of the minimum qualifications for the job.
(3) what type of test is required for the job.
(4) where the job is located.
(5) what the salary is.

27. According to the passage, if you wish to apply for three different jobs, you should

(1) fill out one application but list all three job titles on it.
(2) fill out one application and make a photocopy for each job.
(3) request permission to do this from an employment supervisor.
(4) fill out three separate applications by hand.
(5) submit a total of six applications, two for each job.

28. Suppose you wish to apply for a job that lists the following Preferential Requirement: Two years' experience using Quark Express for document design.

If you have used Quark Express for only one year, what should you do?

(1) Apply for the job anyway, because this is only a Preferential Requirement

(2) Apply for the job anyway, even though you will not be considered to be qualified

(3) Do not apply for the job, because you do not have the necessary Preferential Requirement

(4) Do not apply for the job, because you do not meet the Selective Requirement

(5) Request that the supervisor waive the Preferential Requirement

29. According to the passage, you cannot submit a job application by

(1) mail.

(2) fax.

(3) e-mail.

(4) telephone.

(5) hand delivery.

30. Why is it best to provide a Minimum Qualifications Summary instead of a resume?

(1) Resumes often do not provide enough detail.

(2) Resumes often include untrue statements and exaggerations.

(3) Resumes are often too long and detailed.

(4) A Minimum Qualifications Summary is submitted instead of an application.

(5) A Minimum Qualifications Summary can be submitted instead of taking a typing test.

Items 31–35 refer to the following excerpt from a play.

WHOSE DEATH IS BEING MOURNED?

Line CHARLEY: It's getting dark, Linda.

(LINDA *doesn't react. She stares at the grave.*)

BIFF: How about it, Mom? Better get some
5 rest, heh? They'll be closing the gate soon.

(LINDA *makes no move. Pause*)

HAPPY: (*Deeply angered*) He had no right to do that. There was no necessity for
10 it. We would've helped him.

CHARLEY: (*Grunting*) Hmmm.

BIFF: Come along, Mom.

LINDA: Why didn't anybody come?

CHARLEY: It was a very nice funeral.

15 LINDA: But where are all the people he knew? Maybe they blame him.

CHARLEY: Naa. It's a rough world, Linda. They wouldn't blame him.

LINDA: I can't understand it. At this time espe-
20 cially. First time in thirty-five years we were just about free and clear. He only needed a little salary. He was even finished with the dentist.

CHARLEY: No man only needs a little salary.

25 LINDA: I can't understand it.

BIFF: There were a lot of nice days. When he'd come home from a trip; or on Sundays, making the stoop; finishing the cellar; putting on the new porch;
30 when he built the extra bathroom; and put up the garage. You know something, Charley, there's more of him in that front stoop than in all the sales he ever made.

35 CHARLEY: Yeah. He was a happy man with a batch of cement.

LINDA: He was so wonderful with his hands.

BIFF: He had the wrong dreams. All, all, wrong.

40 HAPPY: (*Almost ready to fight* BIFF) Don't say that!

BIFF: He never knew who he was.

CHARLEY: (*Stopping* HAPPY'S *movement and re-*
ply. To BIFF) Nobody dast blame this
45 man. You don't understand: Willy was a salesman. And for a salesman, there is no rock bottom to the life. He don't put a bolt to a nut, he don't tell you the law or give you medicine. He's a
50 man way out there in the blue, riding on a smile and a shoeshine. And when they start not smiling back—that's an earthquake. And then you get yourself a couple of spots on your hat, and
55 you're finished. Nobody dast blame this man. A salesman is got to dream, boy. It comes with the territory.

—From *Death of a Salesman*, by Arthur Miller

31. The setting of this passage is

(1) the front stoop.
(2) a porch.
(3) the garage.
(4) a cemetery.
(5) a bathroom.

32. "He had no right to do that. There was no necessity for it. We would've helped him."

This speech of Happy's suggests that Willy

(1) committed suicide.
(2) stole money.
(3) was in debt.
(4) killed someone.
(5) caused an accident.

33. "No man only needs a little salary."

Which expression means the same thing as this speech of Charley's?

(1) A penny saved is a penny earned.
(2) Man does not live by bread alone.
(3) Penny wise but pound foolish.
(4) Neither a borrower nor a lender be.
(5) Waste not, want not.

34. According to the Charley, a salesman is a person who

(1) values money above everything else.
(2) has to face a difficult reality every day.
(3) lives on dreams and appearances.
(4) travels long distances every day.
(5) tries to fulfill the wrong dreams.

35. What type of play does this passage come from?

(1) A farce
(2) A comedy
(3) A satire
(4) A melodrama
(5) A tragedy

> Items 36–40 refer to this excerpt from a short story.

WHY WAS THE LESSON MEANINGFUL?

Line I rose from my desk and walked to the window.
The light made my skin look orange, and I started
thinking about what Wickham had told us once
about light. She said that oranges and apples,
5 leaves and flowers, the whole multi-colored world,
was not what it appeared to be. The colors we
see, she said, look like they do only because of the
light or ray that shines on them. "The color of the
thing isn't what you see, but the light that's
10 reflected off it." Then she shut out the lights and
shone a white light lamp on a prism. We watched
the pale spray of colors on the projector screen;
some people ooohed and aaahed. Suddenly, she
switched on a black light and the color of
15 everything changed. The prism colors vanished,
Wickham's arms were purple, the buttons of her
dress were as orange as hot coals, rather than the
blue they had been only seconds before. We were
all very quiet. "Nothing," she said after a while, "is
20 really what it appears to be." I didn't really
understand then. But as I stood at the window,
gazing at my orange skin, I wondered what kind
of light I could shine on Marvin, Oakley, and me
that would reveal us as the same.

—From "The Kind of Light That Shines on Texas,"
by Reginald McKnight

36. In lines 10-18, the narrator describes

(1) a disagreement between himself and Wickham.
(2) a science experiment using apples.
(3) the friendship between Marvin and Oakley.
(4) a science experiment using light and color.
(5) what it is like to be in school.

37. In lines 1-4, what event causes the narrator to remember Wickham's lesson?

(1) The light coming from the window makes his skin appear orange.
(2) He has an argument with Marvin and Oakley.
(3) Light hits a bucket of apples and oranges.
(4) He opens a picture album from school.
(5) He goes to a reunion and sees old friends.

38. ". . . Wickham's arms were purple, the buttons of her dress were as orange as hot coals, rather than the blue they had been only seconds before." (lines 16–18)

The author indicates these facts to show that

(1) Wickham has become very ill.
(2) the class is afraid of Wickham.
(3) heat can change the color of objects.
(4) Wickham's dress was ugly.
(5) colors can change under certain light.

39. ". . . I wondered what kind of light I could shine on Marvin, Oakley, and me that would reveal us as the same." (lines 22–24)

From this statement, you can conclude that the narrator

(1) realizes that, under the skin, people are the same.
(2) wants to perform an experiment with the light.
(3) didn't understand the science lesson.
(4) wishes he could be better friends with Marvin.
(5) enjoyed Wickham's science lesson.

40. Based on this passage, you can assume that Marvin, Oakley, and the narrator probably are

(1) from different ethnic backgrounds.
(2) first cousins.
(3) from different economic backgrounds.
(4) from similar ethnic backgrounds.
(5) best friends.

Posttest 5

MATHEMATICS FORMULAS

Use the following formulas to answer questions in the following posttest.

AREA of a:
square	Area = side^2
rectangle	Area = length × width
parallelogram	Area = base × height
triangle	Area = $\frac{1}{2}$ × base × height
trapezoid	Area = $\frac{1}{2}$ × (base$_1$ + base$_2$) × height
circle	Area = π × radius^2; π is approximately equal to 3.14

PERIMETER of a:
square	Perimeter = 4 × side
rectangle	Perimeter = 2 × length + 2 × width
triangle	Perimeter = side$_1$ + side$_2$ + side$_3$

CIRCUMFERENCE of a circle   Circumference = π × diameter; π is approximately equal to 3.14

VOLUME of a:
cube	Volume = edge^3
rectangular solid	Volume = length × width × height
square pyramid	Volume = $\frac{1}{3}$ × (base edge)^2 × height
cylinder	Volume = π × radius^2 × height; π is approximately equal to 3.14
cone	Volume = $\frac{1}{3}$ × π × radius^2 × height; π is approximately equal to 3.14

COORDINATE GEOMETRY   distance between points =

$$\sqrt{(x_2 - x_1)^2 + (y_2 - y_1)^2}; (x_1, y_1) \text{ and } (x_2, y_2) \text{ are two points in a plane.}$$

Slope of a line = $\dfrac{y_2 - y_1}{x_2 - x_1}$; (x_1, y_1) and (x_2, y_2) are two points on the line.

PYTHAGOREAN RELATIONSHIP $a^2 + b^2 = c^2$; a and b are legs and c the hypotenuse of a right triangle.

TRIGONOMETRIC RATIOS

$$\sin = \frac{\text{opposite}}{\text{hypotenuse}} \quad \cos = \frac{\text{adjacent}}{\text{hypotenuse}} \quad \tan = \frac{\text{opposite}}{\text{adjacent}}$$

MEASURES OF CENTRAL TENDENCY

mean = $\dfrac{x_1 + x_2 + ,,, + x_n}{n}$, where the x's are the values for which a mean is desired, and n is the total number of values for x.

median = the middle value of an odd number of *ordered* scores, and halfway between the two middle values of an even number of *ordered* scores.

SIMPLE INTEREST   interest = principal × rate × time

DISTANCE   distance = rate × time

TOTAL COST   total cost = (number of units) × (price per unit)

Posttest 5

MATHEMATICS
PART I

45 Minutes ❖ 25 Questions ❖ Calculator Permitted

1. Susan buys 3 cans of soup for 69 cents each, a loaf of bread for $1.29, and a paperback for $4.50. How much change will she receive if she uses a ten-dollar bill to pay for all her purchases?

   (1) $0.52
   (2) $2.14
   (3) $3.52
   (4) $6.48
   (5) $7.86

2. A consultant normally gives a 10% discount on large projects. She takes off an additional $\frac{1}{9}$ from the discount price because she is doing the job for a friend. How much did she earn if the original price for the job was $2,000?

   (1) $1,977.78
   (2) $1,800
   (3) $1,600
   (4) $200
   (5) $22.22

3. There are 2.2 pounds in 1 kilogram. Using this fact, how many kilograms make up a pound?

   (1) .455
   (2) 2.2
   (3) 22.2
   (4) 45.5
   (5) 91.818

4. Yasmin is working on a rag craft project. She needs 3 strands of red rag that are 3.6 meters long, 5 strands of blue rag that are 5.3 meters long, and 4 strands of white rag that are 2.7 meters long. What is the total amount of rags she will need for her project?

   Mark your answer on the standard grid in your answer sheet on page 428.

5. Justin has been given the enormous task of washing all of the windows in his house. It has taken him $\frac{3}{4}$ of an hour to wash 3 windows. At this rate, how much more time does he have to spend in order to finish washing all of the 20 windows in his house?

   (1) $2\frac{1}{4}$
   (2) $4\frac{1}{4}$
   (3) 5
   (4) 15
   (5) 20

6. The dimension of a box that contains 24 cans of cola is given below.

   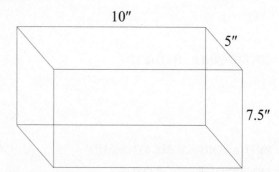

   What is the maximum number of these boxes that Margie can put into a cabinet with a capacity of 3,274 cubic inches?

   (1) 6
   (2) 7
   (3) 8
   (4) 8.7
   (5) 9

7. Mariana is a college student in Colorado who is trying to be frugal with her telephone bill. She wants to make a 50-minute telephone call to her best friend in California and wants to know how much she will save, to the nearest penny, if she took advantage of the evening rate and called her friend after 5 p.m. The day rate is $0.85 for the first two minutes and then $0.33 for each additional minute. The evening rate discounts the day rate by 35%.

(1) $5.84
(2) $8.75
(3) $10.85
(4) $16.69
(5) $25.00

8. Sonya withdrew amounts of $2,367.09 and $509.67 from her checking account. After the withdrawals, her balance was $1,089.34. What was her balance before the withdrawals?

(1) $768.08
(2) $1,277.75
(3) $1,787.42
(4) $2,876.76
(5) $3,966.10

9. Look at the chart below:

Time	3:00	4:00	5:00
Distance	73km	123km	173km

If the ship is traveling away from the harbor at a steady rate as shown in the table above, how far away from the harbor will it be at 4:36?

Mark your answer on the standard grid in your answer sheet on page 428.

10. *ABCD* is an isosceles trapezoid. The coordinates of vertex *A* is (0,4), *B* is (1,2), *D* is (6,4). On the coordinate plane on your answer sheet, mark the location of vertex *C*.

Mark your answer on the coordinate plane in your answer sheet page 428.

Items 11–15 refer to the following graph.

Percent distribution of voters in the last election by years of school completed.

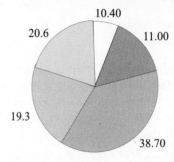

☐ Elementary, 0 to 8 years: 10.4%
▨ High School, 1 to 3 years: 11.0%
▨ High School, 4 years: 38.7%
▨ College, 1 to 3 years: 19.3%
▨ College, 4 years or more: 20.6%

11. Of the people who voted in the last election, what percentage had completed only high school?

(1) 11.0%
(2) 38.7%
(3) 49.7%
(4) 60.1%
(5) 78.6%

12. Of the people who voted in the last election, what percentage had at most a high school diploma?

(1) 11.0%
(2) 38.7%
(3) 49.7%
(4) 60.1%
(5) 78.6%

13. Of the people who voted in the last election, what percentage had at least some college education?

(1) 19.3%
(2) 20.6%
(3) 39.9%
(4) 60.1%
(5) 78.6%

14. Of the people who voted in the last election, what percentage went to graduate school?

(1) 19.3%
(2) 20.6%
(3) 39.9%
(4) 60.1%
(5) Not enough information is given.

15. Of the people who voted in the last election, what percentage had at least some high school education?

    (1) 89.6%
    (2) 78.6%
    (3) 58.0%
    (4) 38.7%
    (5) 11.0%

16. Lauren bought 5 videos during Buster Videos' summer sidewalk sale. Originally two of the videos were $19.99 each, and the other three were $14.99 each. For the sale, every video was discounted by 45%. How much did Lauren spend?

    Mark your answer on the standard grid in your answer sheet on page 428.

17. What is the mean weight of a sled dog in a team made up of Alaskan Malamutes that individually weigh 97 lb 8 oz, 102 lb 3 oz, 95 lb 11 oz, 107 lb 7 oz, and 93 lb 9 oz?

    (1) 496 lb 7 oz
    (2) 494 lb 38 oz
    (3) 99 lb 4.4 oz
    (4) 99 lb
    (5) 97 lb 8 oz

18. A laser is fired into a beam splitter that splits it into 3 beams. Each of these beams then hit another beam splitter that splits it into another three beams. If this happens 6 times, how many beams are there?

    (1) 729
    (2) 216
    (3) 18
    (4) 12
    (5) 9

Items 19 and 20 refer to the figure below.

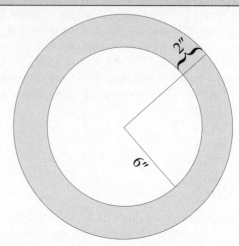

19. Find the area of a circular ring formed by two concentric circles. Look at the diagram for the necessary information. (Concentric circles are circles with the same center.)

    (1) 4π
    (2) 28π
    (3) 36π
    (4) 64π
    (5) 196π

20. What is the area of the larger circle?

    (1) 4π
    (2) 28π
    (3) 36π
    (4) 64π
    (5) 196π

21. You are standing 20 ft away from a 55-ft building. What is the angle of elevation of your line of sight with respect to the ground? Round your answer to the nearest hundredths.

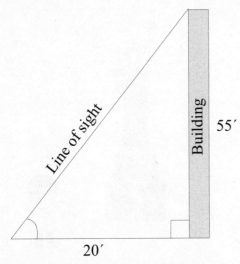

Mark your answer on the standard grid in your answer sheet on page 428.

22. For his fiancee, Alan buys a $\frac{3}{4}$-carat diamond to be set on a platinum band. He pays $920 for the diamond. At this price, what is the cost of one carat? Round to nearest dollar.

Mark your answer on the standard grid in your answer sheet on page 428.

23. Moe had $1,200 more in his checking account than he had in his savings account. His checking account paid 3% in interest, and his savings account paid 5% in interest. If he earned $96 in interest for the year, how much money does he have in his checking account?

Mark your answer on the standard grid in your answer sheet on page 428.

24. WeTutor.com, an Internet tutoring site, has the following billing system: Students who log on from 5 p.m. to midnight are charged $25 an hour. At any other time, the rate is $35 an hour. Over a period of one week, Sandra received 4.5 hours of tutoring between the hours of 5 p.m. and midnight and 2.75 hours in the morning. At this rate, how much will she spend on tutoring at the end of the month? (Assume a month has 4 weeks).

- **(1)** $208.75
- **(2)** $435
- **(3)** $835
- **(4)** $1,485
- **(5)** $1,740

25. If you were to fill the cone to the brim with water, how many cubic centimeters of water could it hold?

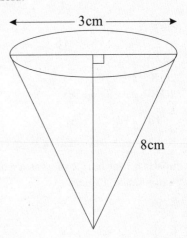

- **(1)** 5.89π
- **(2)** 6π
- **(3)** 24π
- **(4)** 138.94π
- **(5)** 185.25π

475

PART II

45 Minutes ❖ 25 Questions ❖ Calculator *Not* Permitted

1. An isosceles triangle has a base of 18 inches. The other leg is 3 less than twice the base. The perimeter of this triangle can be represented as

18

   (1) $18 \cdot 2 - 3$

   (2) $2(18 \cdot 2 - 3)$

   (3) $2(18 \cdot 2 - 3) + 18$

   (4) $\frac{1}{2} \cdot 18 \cdot (18 \cdot 2 - 3)$

   (5)   Not enough information is given.

2. If 2 cups is a pint and 2 pints is a quart, how many cups make a quart?

   (1)   2

   (2)   4

   (3)   6

   (4)   8

   (5)   10

3. A recipe calls for $\frac{1}{4}$ cup of sugar and serves four people. If you want to adjust the recipe to serve one person, how many cups of sugar should you use?

   (1) $\frac{1}{16}$

   (2) $\frac{1}{8}$

   (3) $\frac{1}{4}$

   (4) $\frac{1}{2}$

   (5)   1

4. The Statue of Liberty has a right arm length of 42 ft. A child is 4 ft tall, and her right arm is $1\frac{1}{2}$ ft long. If h represents the height of the statue, which of these equations would she use to find the height of the Statue of Liberty?

   (1) $\frac{x}{42} = \frac{1.5}{4}$

   (2) $\frac{1.5}{4} = \frac{x}{42}$

   (3) $\frac{x}{1.5} = \frac{42}{4}$

   (4) $\frac{1.5}{x} = \frac{42}{4}$

   (5) $\frac{1.5}{4} = \frac{42}{x}$

5. $879(96 - 32)$ has the same value as which of the following?

   (1) $879 - 96 - 32$

   (2) $879 \cdot 96 - 32$

   (3) $879 \cdot 96 + 879 \cdot 32$

   (4) $879 \cdot 96 - 879 \cdot 32$

   (5) $879 \cdot 96 \cdot (-32)$

6. On average, Sophea and Ivan spend 1.6 hours on each house they clean. At this rate, how many houses can they clean in an 8-hour workday?

   (1)   12.8

   (2)   5

   (3)   2

   (4)   0.5

   (5)   0.2

Items 7–9 refer to the graph below.

Millions of Workers in Selected Occupations

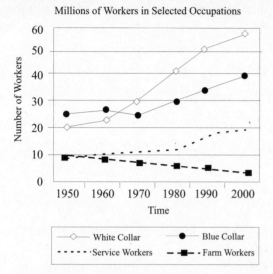

7. According to the graph, which group of workers had the largest increase?

(1) White Collar
(2) Blue Collar
(3) Service Workers
(4) Farm Workers
(5) Both White and Blue Collar Workers

8. In 1990, what was the total number of workers in millions in all four occupations?

(1) 63
(2) 68
(3) 88
(4) 112
(5) 121

9. In which year were the number of service workers and the number of farm workers approximately equal?

(1) 1950
(2) 1955
(3) 1960
(4) 1965
(5) 1970

10. The product of 5 and the sum of a number plus two is 11 less than the number times 8. If x represents the number, which of the following equations would provide the correct solution?

(1) $5(x + 2) = 11 - 8x$
(2) $2(5 + x) = 8x - 11$
(3) $5(x + 2) = 8x - 11$
(4) $5 \cdot x + 2 = 8x - 11$
(5) $5 \cdot 2 + x = 8x - 11$

11. The diameter of a circle has its end points at $(-3,2)$ and $(7,8)$. On the coordinate plane on your answer sheet, mark the center of the circle.

Mark your answer on the coordinate plane in your answer sheet on page 429.

12. Mary Beth just finished eating a piece of pecan pie that has 600 calories in it. If a casual stroll burns 150 calories in one hour, how many hours will it take Mary Beth to stroll off the pecan pie calories?

(1) 6
(2) 4
(3) 3
(4) 2
(5) $\frac{1}{4}$

13. If $3p^2 + 24p + 21 = 0$, then

(1) $p = -1$
(2) $p = 7$
(3) $p = -7, p = -1$
(4) $p = 7, p = 1$
(5) $p = -7, p = -1, p = 3$

14. Which of the following is the largest radius of a ball that will fit into the box?

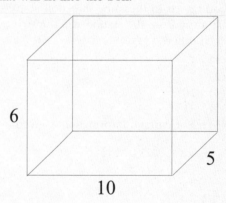

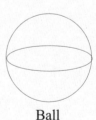

Ball

(1) 2.5
(2) 3
(3) 5
(4) 6
(5) 10

15. The energy of some photons emitted from certain atoms in a physics experiment fluctuates between $4\frac{2}{3}$ keV to $7\frac{1}{4}$ keV. What is the difference of the high and low temperature?

Mark your answer on the standard grid in your answer sheet on page 429.

16. What is the median of the following weights of puppies of several different breeds (weights are given in pounds): 4.6, 3.2, 6.2, 1.3, 2.1, .9, 2.7, 2.3.

(1) 2.3
(2) 2.5
(3) 2.7
(4) 2.9
(5) 5

17. Victor spent $23 to fill his car with 44 liters of gasoline. What is the cost of gasoline per liter in his town?

Mark your answer on the standard grid in your answer sheet on page 429.

18. A freight train leaves a station traveling at 35kph. A passenger train leaves the station 2 hours later and travels in the same direction at 105kph. How far away from the station will the two trains pass each other?

(1) 1
(2) 3
(3) 105
(4) 315
(5) Not enough information is given.

19. A computer manufacturer has a silicon plate with the following shape and dimensions measured in inches. If each chip they make is one square inch, then how many chips can they make from that sheet?

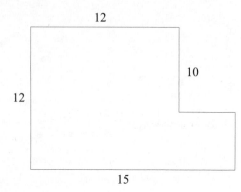

(1) 144
(2) 150
(3) 180
(4) 210
(5) 225

20. How much will Shirin pay to buy $\frac{5}{8}$ of a yard of velour fabric that is on sale for $6.40 per yard?

(1) $10.24
(2) $6.40
(3) $4.00
(4) $1.28
(5) $0.80

21. Tony is now three years older than Karen. If seven years from now, the sum of their ages is 79, how old is Karen now? If K represents Karen's age, then which of the following equations can be used to determine Karen's age?

(1) $(K + 3) + (K + 7) = 79$
(2) $(K - 7) + (K - 10) = 79$
(3) $(K - 3) + (K + 7) = 79$
(4) $(K + 3) + (K - 7) = 79$
(5) $(K + 7) + (K + 10) = 79$

22. Find the area of a square whose diagonal is 12 feet.

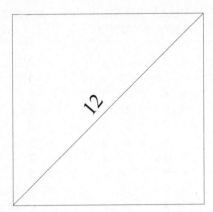

   (1) 144
   (2) 72
   (3) $\sqrt{72}$
   (4) $2\sqrt{6}$
   (5) $\sqrt{6}$

23. A printer and monitor together cost $356. The monitor cost $20 more than two times the printer. If *P* represents the cost of the printer, then solving which of the following equations will determine the cost of the printer?

   (1) $P + 2(20 + P) = 356$
   (2) $2P + (20 + 2P) = 356$
   (3) $2P + 2(20 + 2P) = 356$
   (4) $P + (20 + 2P) = 356$
   (5) $P + (20P + 2) = 356$

Items 24 and 25 refer to the following graph.

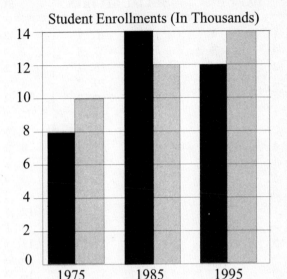

24. In 1985, 74% of the students attending State University were men. How many men attended State University in 1985?

   (1) 10,360
   (2) 9,620
   (3) 8,880
   (4) 7,400
   (5) 5,920

25. Find the percent increase in enrollment at Backwoods College from 1975 to 1985.

   (1) 17%
   (2) 20%
   (3) 43%
   (4) 44%
   (5) 75%

QUICK-SCORE ANSWERS

LANGUAGE ARTS, WRITING PART I

1. 1	26. 4
2. 4	27. 3
3. 2	28. 4
4. 4	29. 2
5. 3	30. 4
6. 1	31. 3
7. 2	32. 1
8. 4	33. 1
9. 4	34. 2
10. 3	35. 3
11. 2	36. 2
12. 1	37. 2
13. 2	38. 3
14. 3	39. 2
15. 4	40. 3
16. 3	41. 2
17. 5	42. 1
18. 2	43. 4
19. 3	44. 1
20. 5	45. 3
21. 1	46. 5
22. 3	47. 2
23. 2	48. 5
24. 1	49. 1
25. 4	50. 1

PART II
Turn to page 485.

SOCIAL STUDIES

1. 2	26. 1
2. 1	27. 3
3. 4	28. 2
4. 3	29. 2
5. 2	30. 2
6. 4	31. 2
7. 5	32. 1
8. 5	33. 4
9. 3	34. 5
10. 5	35. 2
11. 1	36. 3
12. 2	37. 3
13. 2	38. 5
14. 3	39. 3
15. 4	40. 5
16. 4	41. 4
17. 2	42. 3
18. 3	43. 3
19. 3	44. 3
20. 1	45. 2
21. 3	46. 4
22. 5	47. 5
23. 3	48. 2
24. 1	49. 1
25. 4	50. 2

SCIENCE

1. 2	26. 1
2. 3	27. 5
3. 1	28. 3
4. 3	29. 2
5. 3	30. 4
6. 4	31. 5
7. 5	32. 2
8. 2	33. 2
9. 2	34. 4
10. 4	35. 4
11. 1	36. 3
12. 1	37. 4
13. 3	38. 4
14. 4	39. 4
15. 4	40. 3
16. 3	41. 3
17. 1	42. 1
18. 4	43. 2
19. 3	44. 2
20. 2	45. 5
21. 4	46. 5
22. 1	47. 1
23. 4	48. 1
24. 4	49. 4
25. 3	50. 1

LANGUAGE ARTS, READING

1. 2	21. 3
2. 1	22. 4
3. 4	23. 5
4. 5	24. 2
5. 2	25. 3
6. 3	26. 5
7. 4	27. 2
8. 5	28. 1
9. 5	29. 4
10. 4	30. 1
11. 5	31. 4
12. 1	32. 1
13. 3	33. 2
14. 2	34. 3
15. 4	35. 5
16. 5	36. 4
17. 4	37. 1
18. 3	38. 5
19. 4	39. 1
20. 1	40. 1

MATHEMATICS, PART I

1. 2	14. 5
2. 3	15. 1
3. 1	16. $46.72
4. 48.1	17. 3
5. 2	18. 1
6. 3	19. 2
7. 1	20. 4
8. 5	21. 70.02
9. 153	22. $1227
10. (5,2)	23. $1950
11. 2	24. 3
12. 4	25. 1
13. 3	

MATHEMATICS, PART II

1. 3	14. 1
2. 2	15. 32/12
3. 1	16. 2
4. 5	17. 0.52
5. 4	18. 3
6. 2	19. 2
7. 1	20. 3
8. 4	21. 5
9. 2	22. 2
10. 3	23. 4
11. 2,5	24. 3
12. 2	25. 5
13. 3	

FILLED-IN STANDARD GRIDS AND COORDINATE PLANE GRIDS

Part I

4. 4 8 . 1

16. 4 6 . 7 2

22. 1 2 2 7

9. 1 5 3

21. 7 0 . 0 2

23. 1 9 5 0

10.

Part II

11.

15.

3	1	/	1	2

17.

0	.	5	2	

ANSWERS AND EXPLANATIONS

Posttest 1: Language Arts, Writing

1. **The correct answer is (1).** This is implied by the phrase "diversity of terrain." Choice (2) is too limited, while choices (3) and (4) pertain to plants and people rather than land. Choice (5) has no relevance because the passage does not pertain to filming.

2. **The correct answer is (4).** The key phrase is *in Arizona.* Choice (1) merely changes *which* to *that;* choice (2) still includes the unnecessary *located;* choice (3) rearranges the words in the original sentence, and choice (5) presents another rearranged version.

3. **The correct answer is (2).** There is a subject-verb agreement error. *Colors and shapes* is a compound subject; therefore, the predicate must also be plural. Choice (1) wrongly changes the tense; choice (3) incorrectly inserts a comma between parts of a compound subject, and choice (4) omits a comma that is required after an introductory adverb clause.

4. **The correct answer is (4).** The error is a misplaced modifier. Are the *visitors available?* Asking that question will help you eliminate choices (1) and (2). Choice (3) is an improvement, but *which are especially beautiful in winter* modifies *accommodations,* which changes the meaning of the sentence.

5. **The correct answer is (3).** This choice maintains the use of present tense. No comma is needed after *seasons,* choice (1), because a comma would incorrectly separate a prepositional phrase from the phrase that follows it. Choice (2) offers *seasonally,* which is an awkward form of adverb, while choice (4) would also incorrectly separate the parts of a compound object of *to experience.*

6. **The correct answer is (1).** This choice corrects the sentence fragment, *Such a photographer's paradise* and it arranges the words logically. Choice (2) is wrong because *such a photographer's paradise* has no function in the sentence. Likewise, in choice (3) the same problem appears in that *Such a photographer's paradise* has no function. Choice (4) attempts to correct the sentence fragment with *it is such a photographer's paradise,* but instead a comma splice is created because the correction is incorrectly inserted and interrupts the main sentence. Choice (5) also has a problem with the sentence fragment, merely adding it to the end of the sentence where it cannot logically modify anything.

7. **The correct answer is (2).** This choice maintains the use of present tense. Inserting a comma after *canyon,* choice (1), will interrupt the compound predicate, and inserting a comma after *overnight,* choice (3), is also unnecessary to separate the clauses of this complex sentence. Choice (4) will incorrectly shift to past tense.

8. **The correct answer is (4).** The first three choices are all proper ways to correct the main error here, which is a comma splice, a kind of error that occurs when two independent clauses are joined only by a comma.

9. **The correct answer is (4).** The possessive form *whose* is needed. Choice (1) is not a correct choice because *larger* is used to compare two things. Choice (2) will omit a comma required after an introductory adverb clause, and choice (3) is wrong because *who* is used to refer to people, not places.

10. **The correct answer is (3).** This choice maintains the use of present tense. Choice (1) will remedy the sentence fragment, but it will shift the perspective to second person with an understood subject, *you.* Choice (2) will incorrectly insert a comma between two prepositional phrases. Choice (4) will shift the tense from present to past.

11. **The correct answer is (2).** This choice reduces the first clause by converting it into an appositive phrase. Choice (1) creates the appositive phrase, but it fails to set up two independent clauses. Choice (3) seems like a good choice, but *reached by hiking . . .* is a misplaced modifier because it follows *Arizona,* which it cannot logically modify. Choice (4) offers the appositive, but it also creates a sentence fragment, which is a major error. Choice (5) creates a comma splice.

12. **The correct answer is (1).** Context clues should help you determine the answer to this kind of question. *Little stream* suggests something small. Choice (2), *gulch,* is a ditch; choice (3), *lake,* is a large body of water; choice (4), *torrent,* refers to a raging river with a lot of water in it; and choice (5), *dry riverbed,* would have no water in it.

13. **The correct answer is (2).** This needless comma separates parts of a compound predicate. Choice (1) is a necessary comma to follow an introductory participle phrase, choice (3) incorrectly changes the tense, and choice (4) illogically changes the form of these adjectives.

14. **The correct answer is (3).** Choice (3) is correct because only two things are being compared. *Smallest* is used for three or more. Choice (1) does not correct the error; choice (2) is not a good choice because the comma is needed to avoid confusion, and choice (4) wrongly shifts tense.

15. **The correct answer is (4).** The possessive form of *Arizona* is needed. Choice (1) presents a tense shift, while choice (2) changes the meaning of the sentence. Choice (3) offers another version of tense shift.

16. **The correct answer is (3).** This choice is the only one that will create a logical sequence, because *"Invasion of the Body Snatchers"* is the title of a movie.

17. **The correct answer is (5).** Choices (1), (3), and (4) are misspellings. Choice (2), *bazaar,* is correctly spelled, but it refers to a market.

18. **The correct answer is (2).** The error involves a tense sequence. Consider which action occurred first, the end of World War II or American's fears of the Soviet Union. The action that happened first should be in the "earliest" tense. In this sentence, the end of the war preceded fear of the Soviets; therefore, choice (2) corrects the error. Choice (1) changes the meaning of the sentence, choice (3) incorrectly shifts the tense of the wrong verb, and choice (4) also changes the meaning of the sentence.

19. **The correct answer is (3).** The commas, choice (1), are necessary to set off an adjective clause after a proper noun. Choice (2), changing the spelling of *ally* to *alley,* changes the meaning of the sentence. Choice (4) also presents a shift involving movement, as in *walking into a room* as opposed to *being in the room.*

20. **The correct answer is (5).** This sentence has no error. Choices (1) and (2) present spelling changes that are illogical; *cents* is a word about money, and *wreckless* is what is known as a back formation. We have the word *wreck,* so *wreckless* must mean without *wrecks.* Omitting the part of the sentence suggested in choice (3) changes the meaning of sentence, as does choice (4).

21. **The correct answer is (1).** Confusion about these two words is not unusual because lead can be pronounced as lead as in steer and lead as in pencil lead. *Lead* is the present tense form of the verb, while *led* is the past tense form. Choice (2) incorrectly changes the possessive form, while choices (3) and (4) unnecessarily change to possessive form.

22. **The correct answer is (3).** Choice (1) does not correct the comma splice in the second sentence. Choice (2) includes an illogical pair of conjunctions with *as* and *so.* Choice (3) provides the contrast essential in the final clause. Choice (4) also has a pair of illogical conjunctions with *however* and *and.* Choice (5) presents conjunctions of time that are illogical.

23. **The correct answer is (2).** The subject of the sentence, *Alger Hiss*, is singular. *As well as the Rosenbergs* is not part of the subject. Choice (1) changes the tense to past, and choices (3) and (4) insert a needless comma.

24. **The correct answer is (1).** It offers an accurate comparison of the similarities between what happened in Salem and during the McCarthy era. Choice (2) is not appropriate because the "communists" were not executed. Choice (3) has no evidence in the passage to prove it. Choice (4) presents an accurate comment about Salem, but it makes no mention of McCarthy, and choice (5) does not offer any similarities.

25. **The correct answer is (4).** *Cartoons* are not referred to at any other point in the passage. The other choices are relevant to the main idea of the paragraph.

26. **The correct answer is (4).** *The fact that* serves no grammatical function in the sentence. Choice (1), inserting a comma after *Americans,* interrupts the parts of the predicate, which is actually *was surprising*. Choice (2) changes the tense to present, and choice (3) changes the meaning of the sentence.

27. **The correct answer is (3).** It corrects the agreement problem. *Those invaders* refers to *movie aliens*. Choice (1) sets up an illogical statement; choice (2) omits a necessary comma after an introductory adverb clause, and choice (4) incorrectly inserts a comma in a complex sentence with an adverb clause of comparison.

28. **The correct answer is (4).** Both sentences refer to appearance and dress. The other choices are not logical pairs.

29. **The correct answer is (2).** Choice (2) is correct because *too* means *also*. In this sentence, *to* is needed for the infinitive form. Choice (1) is incorrect because *old adage* is redundant; choice (3) incorrectly inserts an apostrophe in the possessive form of *you*, and choice (4) changes the tense to future.

30. **The correct answer is (4).** This option will correct the run-on sentence. Choice (1) is not a good choice because the phrase is a quotation. Choice (2) is incorrect because *than* is the conjunction needed; *then* is an adverb. Choice (3) sets up a comma splice, which is a serious error.

31. **The correct answer is (3).** This choice maintains the use of the present tense. Choice (1) is incorrect because the comma is required after an introductory adverb clause; choice (2) is wrong because no comma is needed in the middle of an adverb clause of comparison, and choice (4) is not the right choice because the past participle form is needed.

32. **The correct answer is (1).** *Are* is correct because of the compound subject: *being frank* and *explaining your goals*. Choice (2) is incorrect because it will result in a lack of parallel form with *being* and *explaining*. No comma is needed after *experience*, choice (3), because it would interrupt the compound subject, and choice (4) changes the tense to past.

33. **The correct answer is (1).** This placement follows chronologically what is likely to happen during an interview. Sentence 8, choice (2), offers advice about trying to maintain your composure, and Sentence 9, choice (3), elaborates on this recommendation. Choice (4) fallaciously places the sentence out of chronological sequence.

34. **The correct answer is (2).** In this sentence, *about* means *refers to*. Choice (1) misspells a key term, while choice (3) improperly interrupts the connection between a noun and the prepositional phrase that modifies it. Choice (4) is wrong because *which* refers to things, not people.

35. **The correct answer is (3).** It is the only choice that sets up a needed contrast. Choices (1), (2), and (4) all set up logical consequences, while choice (5) is illogical.

36. **The correct answer is (2).** *Job's* is the possessive form needed to describe *responsibilities*. Choice (1) is incorrect because *them* is always an object, not a modifier. Choices (3) and (4) insert apostrophes when the possessive form is not needed.

37. **The correct answer is (2).** It is the most logical conclusion. Choice (1) is too limited; choice (3) offers negative advice that is absent from the passage as a whole; choice (4) is an exaggeration, and choice (5) is misleading.

38. **The correct answer is (3).** The pronoun refers to the *brothers*. *Who* is used in reference to people, while *which* refers to things. Choice (1) is not right because *begun* is the past participle form used for a tense like present perfect, *has begun*. Choice (2) is incorrect because the comma after *Remus* closes the appositive phrase for *brothers*. Choice (4) improperly separates the clauses in a complex sentence.

39. **The correct answer is (2).** This choice maintains the use of past tense. Choice (1) omits a comma required between the parts of a compound sentence. Choice (3) offers a misspelling, and choice (4) presents changes to the past participle form.

40. **The correct answer is (3).** It eliminates the sentence fragment, which has no predicate. Choices (1) and (2) do not remedy the problem, and choice (4) changes the meaning of the sentence.

41. **The correct answer is (2).** Although this sentence refers to Mars, whom some recognize as the father of the brothers, the Mars candy bar has nothing to do with the founding of Rome. The other sentences in the paragraph do pertain to the topic.

42. **The correct answer is (1).** There is a subject-verb agreement problem. The subject *evidence* is singular and needs a singular verb. *Were*, choice (2), is the correct tense. Choice (3) incorrectly separates the verb from its object, and choice (4) omits commas needed around a parenthetical expression.

43. **The correct answer is (4).** It eliminates the subject-verb agreement error. Choice (1) omits the comma that sets up the appositive phrase. Choice (2) will set up a run-on sentence because *thus,* when used as a conjunction, requires a semicolon before and a comma after it. Choice (3) omits the closing comma after the appositive phrase.

44. **The correct answer is (1).** This option allows Sentence 8 to serve as an example, just as the phrase *for instance* indicates. Although you may need to read the paragraph in the sequence of sentences offered in each possible answer, you should review all choices. For this question, only choice (1) sets up a logical arrangement of sentences.

45. **The correct answer is (3).** The original *yet* sets up an illogical contrast. *And* offers a more logical sequence: after the republic was established, Rome set out to conquer the world. Choice (1) is wrong because the comma is needed to separate the two clauses in this compound sentence. Choice (2) presents another misleading choice; just because the republic was founded, Rome did not necessarily set out to conquer the world. Choice (4) proposes yet another illogical conjunction.

46. **The correct answer is (5).** Choice (1) presents an exaggeration about the size of the Roman Empire; nothing in the paragraph suggests that it *knew no bounds*. Choice (2) is misleading because no evidence supports *dangerous and burdensome proportions*. Choice (3) is also deceptive, for there is no proof that Rome was *determined to outstretch all opponents*. The reference to *tyranny* in choice (4) also has no supporting evidence. Only choice (5) provides a factual statement.

47. **The correct answer is (2).** This choice maintains the use of past tense. Choice (1) is incorrect for two reasons: it is present tense and it is a singular verb even though the subject, *attacks*, is plural. Choice (3) is incorrect because there is no reason for inserting a comma after *tribes*; the phrase following it illustrates some tribes. Choice (4), *East*, is the correct form in this sentence because it refers to an area rather than to a direction, which is not capitalized.

48. **The correct answer is (5).** All of the sentences in the final paragraph are relevant and provide pertinent information. Look at the first sentence in the paragraph, and then read each of the following sentences to see if each one is connected to this topic sentence.

49. The correct answer is (1). This choice rectifies the modifier error because the sentence as written has nothing for the introductory phrase to modify logically. *Children* are the ones *pointing and making nonsense sounds.* Choice (2) is incorrect because a comma is needed after an introductory phrase like this one. Choice (3) is wrong because it does not solve the modifier problem, and choice (4) is not a correct choice because it does not amend the modifier.

50. The correct answer is (1). The phrase modifies *they*, which refers to the children. Choice (2) is incorrect because the phrase cannot logically modify *words*, nor does choice (3) correct the error because *body language* is not *growing older.* Choice (4) looks like a good possibility, but *life* is not what is *growing older.* Choice (5) also looks like a good choice, but the modifier will not be placed correctly here either.

Part II: Essay

The scoring information below will help you estimate a score for your essay. If you can, ask an instructor to read and score your essay. To help you decide which skills you need to work on, make a list of its strengths and weaknesses based on the checklist below.

With 6 as the top score and 1 at the bottom, rank your essay for each item on the checklist. Put a check in the box that you think reflects the quality of that particular part of your essay.

Does my essay . . .	1	2	3	4	5	6
discuss the topic?						
have a clear, controlling idea that is developed throughout?						
have a clear structure (introduction, body, and conclusion)?						
tell the reader in the introduction what the topic is and what I am going to say about it?						
use details and examples to support each point?						
sum up the essay in the conclusion?						
have few or no errors in sentence structure, usage, or punctuation?						

Posttest 2: Social Studies

1. **The correct answer is (2). (Application)** The greatest percent change in inflation was a decrease of approximately 7.5 percent from 1981 to 1983, making choice (2) the best answer.

2. **The correct answer is (1). (Analysis)** A low rate of growth often means that employers are not expanding their businesses and therefore not hiring additional employees, and the employers may actually be laying off some workers in response to sluggish sales.

3. **The correct answer is (4). (Application)** The greatest decrease—about 5 percent—was from 1988 to 1991.

4. **The correct answer is (3). (Evaluation)** The best time to look for a job would be when the economy was growing (so that businesses might be in need of additional workers), unemployment was falling (so that there would be fewer available workers for employers to choose from), and inflation was falling (so that businesses would not be afraid of future monetary problems).

5. **The correct answer is (2). (Analysis)** Falling inflation is good for both business and employment because business can better predict the costs of its materials and supplies, and people have a consistent amount of money to spend. Choice (4) was an effect, not a cause, of economic growth. Choices (1), (3), and (5) represent factors not included in the graph.

6. **The correct answer is (4). (Comprehension)** All of the choices describe the effects of the Mount Pinatubo eruption, but only choice (4) describes an effect that touched the whole world.

7. **The correct answer is (5). (Application)** Because the effects of the 1991 eruption were expected to last for a decade, avalanches were predicted until at least the year 2001.

8. **The correct answer is (5). (Analysis)** The safest plan would be to move people out of the danger zone. Planting grasses and crops (choice 1) is often a good long-term solution to prevent mudslides on slopes, but plants are not likely to grow in volcanic ash. Meanwhile, the destructive slides would continue. Choices (2), (3), and (4) are not reasonable options.

9. **The correct answer is (3). (Evaluation)** Because most of those who were displaced were farmers from small towns and villages, the creation of highways and tall buildings clearly did not help them regain what they had lost.

10. **The correct answer is (5). (Comprehension)** The passage states that deadly gases and falling ash were the elements that killed the most people.

11. **The correct answer is (1). (Evaluation)** The major emphasis in the passage is on the importance of the archaeological discovery, so choice (1) is correct.

12. **The correct answer is (2). (Analysis)** The reference to "King" links the graveyard to colonial times, when most residents of New York were subjects of the King of England.

13. **The correct answer is (2). (Evaluation)** Because medical care and nutrition greatly affect the span of life and because fewer than half of all newborns and young children die today in the United States, it can be surmised that today's levels of medical care and nutrition are superior to those of the 1700s.

14. **The correct answer is (3). (Application)** The power of the judicial system to review the constitutionality of laws is the principle of American government to which the cartoon refers.

15. **The correct answer is (4). (Evaluation)** This independence has led some justices, including some of the most famous, to follow their consciences, regardless of previous tilts toward liberal or conservative platforms.

16. **The correct answer is (4). (Comprehension)** The chart lists numbers of visits in thousands, and 26,630 times 1,000 equals 26.63 million.

17. **The correct answer is (2). (Evaluation)** The twentieth century has seen a great improvement in transportation systems world-wide. In addition, a shortened work week and more work-saving machines for both the home and the factory have led to an increase in leisure time. These two factors have allowed Americans to take more vacations and to visit national parks more frequently.

18. **The correct answer is (3). (Comprehension)** The smallest number of increased visits was 801,000, which occurred between 1910 and 1920.

19. **The correct answer is (3). (Analysis)** The belief in the preservation of valuable sites in America has contributed to the increase in the numbers of national parks, historic sites, battlefields, and monuments.

20. **The correct answer is (1). (Comprehension)** In the year 2050, the largest group will be females (white women and black women combined).

21. **The correct answer is (3). (Comprehension)** According to the chart, the number of white females will decrease from 112.7 million to 108.7 million, a difference of exactly 4 million.

22. **The correct answer is (5). (Analysis)** Choice (5) gives the most complete description of the relationship between the black population and the white population. Each of the other choices describes only one portion of the facts presented in the chart.

23. **The correct answer is (3). (Analysis)** Because the passage states that while a judge, Jackson was noted for his fairness, choice (3) is correct. None of the other choices is related to his beliefs about justice and fairness.

24. **The correct answer is (1). (Application)** Jackson's manipulation of the spoils system, which was in and of itself corrupt, would be a justification for Clay's description. The other four choices are in no way related to Jackson's corruptibility.

25. **The correct answer is (4). (Application)** Going off to fight a war as a youngster and becoming involved in a duel are clearly not well-thought-out actions. None of the other events, as described, could be called rash.

26. **The correct answer is (1). (Comprehension)** According to the passage, Jackson fought in the Revolutionary War in the late 1700s and in the War of 1812.

27. **The correct answer is (3). (Analysis)** The success of the Americans in the Battle of New Orleans and the extremely low number of American casualties are strong indicators that Jackson was a good military commander. Nothing in the passage supports any of the other four choices.

28. **The correct answer is (2). (Application)** Increasing the money supply and giving loans without increasing production would result in inflation.

29. **The correct answer is (2). (Comprehension)** Choice (2) best describes the overall meaning of the passage. All the other choices describe an individual part of the passage only.

30. **The correct answer is (2). (Analysis)** The passage points out the importance of joint problem solving, so seeking counseling to foster this ability would probably be the best way for the couple to reduce the number of arguments they have.

31. **The correct answer is (2). (Analysis)** The ability to solve problems jointly is directly tied to the Denver researcher's findings that the way in which problems are solved affects the likelihood of success in the marriage.

32. **The correct answer is (1). (Application)** The activities described are protected by the rights of free speech and assembly guaranteed in the First Amendment.

33. **The correct answer is (4). (Evaluation)** The description of the parade indicates that all sorts of women participated in pro-suffrage marches and other activities, so choice (4) is the best conclusion. The other choices assume that only certain groups of women marched or make incorrect assumptions about the womens' support of suffrage.

34. **The correct answer is (5). (Application)** By controlling at least one step in the oil production process—refining—Rockefeller had achieved horizontal integration.

35. **The correct answer is (2). (Application)** Standard Oil controlled nearly all of the oil production industry, making this a monopoly.

36. **The correct answer is (3). (Comprehension)** The passage states that the robber barons ran their competitors out of business and kept prices high.

37. **The correct answer is (3). (Analysis)** To prevent the spread of communism is to contain it, so containment, choice (3), is the only possible choice. In its fight against communism, the United States has since pursued the other policies listed, except choice (4), massive retaliation.

38. **The correct answer is (5). (Application)** The temperatures shown on the graph indicate an arid, desert climate.

39. **The correct answer is (3). (Application)** The place shown on the graph receives only a few inches of rain each year. It is therefore an arid or desert climate. Choice (1) describes a tropical climate, choice (2) a subtropical climate, choice (4) a semiarid climate, and choice (5) a polar climate.

40. **The correct answer is (5). (Analysis)** The climate is so dry that it is unlikely there would be much vegetation.

41. **The correct answer is (4). (Comprehension)** Choices (1), (2), and (3) are details that support the main idea. Choice (5) is a false generalization. Only choice (4) expresses the main idea.

42. **The correct answer is (3). (Analysis)** The passage provides no support for choices (1) and (5). Choice (2) is the main idea of the passage. Choice (4) is supported by the passage but is not broad enough to be a logical conclusion.

43. **The correct answer is (3). (Analysis)** The two-term limit is part of the system of checks and balances, which prevents any one group or individual from gaining too much power in the nation.

44. **The correct answer is (3). (Comprehension)** The figures in the cartoon represent U.S. military and political leaders.

45. **The correct answer is (2). (Analysis)** This cartoonist is pointing out the extremely high level of spending by the nation's military groups. Many Americans have criticized this level as being excessive and sometimes wasteful.

46. **The correct answer is (4). (Analysis)** Strong ties to a foreign government might make it impossible for an elected American official to operate with the best interests of the United States in mind.

47. **The correct answer is (5). (Application)** Medicare is an entitlement program that benefits millions of Americans over age 65.

48. **The correct answer is (2). (Analysis)** The cartoon's portrayal of lobbyists parking in spaces reserved for members of Congress expresses the idea that lobbyists may have too much influence over Congress.

49. **The correct answer is (1). (Analysis)** Foreign policy is meant to change with world events. After World War II, the United States allied itself with Japan and Germany, its enemies during that war, against the Soviet Union. Now that communism has collapsed, the United States can be friendly with the republics that once formed the Soviet Union.

50. **The correct answer is (2). (Application)** Occupational health and safety is the responsibility of the Labor Department. All other duties listed deal with foreign relations and therefore are part of the State Department.

Posttest 3: Science

1. **The correct answer is (2). (Fundamental understanding)** In this negative feedback loop, the pituitary is prohibited from releasing follicle-stimulating hormone.

2. **The correct answer is (3). (Fundamental understanding)** As long as both estrogen and progesterone levels remain high, the body will not begin another menstrual cycle.

3. **The correct answer is (1). (Unifying concepts and principles)** Kingdom would come before phylum and species would come after genus in this list to make a complete listing of the classification levels. Some people use mnemonics to help them memorize lists such as these. One that has been around a long time is King Phillip Came Over For Good Spaghetti.

4. **The correct answer is (3). (Fundamental understandings)** Conifers are trees such as pines and spruces, which produce seed-bearing cones. These trees are called gymnosperms or naked seeded plants.

5. **The correct answer is (3). (Fundamental understandings)** Primary consumers eat producers and are, in turn, eaten by secondary consumers, or carnivores.

6. **The correct answer is (4). (Fundamental understandings)** The general rule is that only 10% of the energy in one level can be gained by the next level. The other 90% is lost to the environment, mostly as heat.

7. **The correct answer is (5). (Science and technology)** Acid rain comes from both nitrates and sulfates in the air. The most electronegative elements are written at the right of a compound. Two moles of oxygen will yield 2 moles of sulfur dioxide.

8. **The correct answer is (2). (Fundamental understandings)** Sodium is a metal and forms positive ions. It will be attracted to the negative cathode.

9. **The correct answer is (2). (Science in personal and social perspective)** Fatty acids are hydrocarbon chains with a carboxyl (COOH) ending.

10. **The correct answer is (4). (Fundamental understandings)** All the water would vaporize, since conditions to the right of the curve go toward vaporization, and those to the left move toward condensation. The line represents a vapor pressure curve, which also gives the boiling points of a liquid if one assumes external pressure to be vapor pressure.

11. **The correct answer is (1). (Fundamental understandings)** Because water appears blue, it is absorbing the red wavelengths of light.

12. **The correct answer is (1). (Unifying concepts and processes)** Based on known physical laws, it would be reasonable to predict that if a red shift shows a lengthening of light waves and increasing distance, a blue shift (the opposite condition) indicates a compression of light waves and therefore closing distances. None of the other choices are supported by the passage.

13. **The correct answer is (3). (Fundamental understandings)** Spectroscopic analysis is the only listed choice that pertains to light or light waves.

14. **The correct answer is (4). (Fundamental understandings)** According to the passage, resistance is the degree to which the flow of electricity is slowed.

15. **The correct answer is (4). (Science as technology)** A material with extremely high resistance to electricity would be needed to cover electrical wires and protect people from shock. All the other choices have very low resistance and conduct electricity well.

16. **The correct answer is (3). (Unifying concepts and processes)** According to the passage and graph, lead reaches zero resistance at extremely low temperatures. Choices (1), (2), and (4) are contradicted by the graph. Choice (5) is true, but it is not supported by the information given.

17. **The correct answer is (1). (Fundamental understanding)** Monocots have fibrous root systems, and their floral structures are in multiples of three.

18. **The correct answer is (4). (Fundamental understandings)** Our bodies sense the environment with the nervous system and then respond. The nervous system controls other nerves, glands, and muscles.

19. **The correct answer is (3). (Fundamental understandings)** Amino acids, which make up proteins, are composed of four parts: the amine group (NH_2), the central carbon (CH), the variable group (R), and the carboxyl group (COOH).

20. **The correct answer is (2). (Fundamental understandings)** The peptide bonds were formed when the carboxyl group and the amine group joined together and water was released.

21. **The correct answer is (4). (Fundamental understandings)** Urine travels through the ureter to get to the bladder.

22. **The correct answer is (1): (Unifying concepts and processes)** Choice (1) is a conclusion, a general law. Choices (2) to (5) are all statements of facts that support this conclusion.

23. **The correct answer is (4): (Science as technology)** By slowing and controlling the fission chain reaction, the heat production can be decreased to a steady pace. In fact, this is what is done in nuclear reactors. Choices (1), (2), and (3) would be the result of speeding up the chain reaction. Choice (5) is incorrect because the reaction would be slowed, not prevented from starting.

24. **The correct answer is (4). (Science as technology)** Because the toner forms the image of the document on the copies, blank pages must result from the machine running out of toner. Choices (1) and (5) would result in no output at all. Choice (2) would result in uneven, poor quality copies. Choice (3) simply describes how the machine functions.

25. **The correct answer is (3). (Fundamental understandings)** A good equation to remember is $V_1M_1 = V_2M_2$, where V stands for volume and M for molarity. Solving, $V_1 = \frac{(V_2 \times M_2)}{M_1}$. Plugging in the numbers gives $\frac{(100 \times 0.01)}{0.5} = \frac{1}{0.5}$ or 2.

26. **The correct answer is (1). (Science and technology)** Adding reactants will drive the forward reaction, and adding the products (think of energy as a product in this case) will drive the reverse reaction. This is an application of Le Chatelier's Principle.

27. **The correct answer is (5). (Fundamental understandings)** Statements A and C are true. B is false. Corundum (hardness of 9) is harder than feldspar (hardness of 4). Since A and C are true, the correct choice is (5).

28. **The correct answer is (3). (Fundamental understandings)** Quartz has a hardness of 7 and topaz has a hardness of 8.

29. **The correct answer is (2). (Science as inquiry)** Choices (1) and (3) are incorrect. Based on the information given, mineral X could be either diamond or quartz. All minerals are inorganic, so choice (4) is incorrect. Choice (5) is incorrect because gypsum is softer than feldspar, calcite, and fluorite and therefore would not scratch them. Only choice (2) is a statement completely supported by the presented evidence.

30. **The correct answer is (4). (History and nature of science)** Punctuated equilibrium suggests that changes happen very quickly in geologic time, probably because of a major change in the environment.

31. **The correct answer is (5). (History and nature of science)** The T helper cells, a type of white blood cell, are most often invaded, which is very damaging because they play such an important role in the immune system.

32. **The correct answer is (2). (Fundamental understandings)** Succession is the replacement of species over time, not always in a predictable manner, but usually with some order each time it happens.

33. **The correct answer is (2). (Unifying concepts and principles)** Increasing altitude results in the colder temperatures, as does increasing latitude.

34. **The correct answer is (4). (Fundamental understandings)** The boy would inherit either the A allele or the B allele from his father, and therefore could not be an O, which is the absence of A or B.

35. **The correct answer is (4). (Fundamental understandings)** An organism that was AaBb could make the following sex cells: AB, Ab, aB, ab. If you add C to those four, or c to those four, you will end up with 8 possibilities.

36. **The correct answer is (3). (History and nature of science)** She was described as an African ground ape (*Australopithecus*) from the Afar triangle of Africa.

37. **The correct answer is (4). (Fundamental understandings)** A pendulum converts gravitational potential energy to kinetic energy. None of the other choices describes what a pendulum does.

38. **The correct answer is (4). (Fundamental understandings)** A wave will cause the boat to move up and down, but it will not push the boat horizontally. None of the other statements is true.

39. **The correct answer is (4). (Fundamental understandings)** All other statements are true and can be observed from the diagram presented. Choice (4) is incorrect, because basalt is actually denser than granite, but even if it were true, nothing in the diagram would indicate this. Evidence that would show differential density would be overlapping crust segments with the denser layer under the less-dense layer.

40. **The correct answer is (3). (Fundamental understandings)** The sedimentary rock layers on the land mass are direct evidence that a body of water existed on the continent at some point in the past. The other statements are not verifiable from the diagram.

41. **The correct answer is (3). (Unifying concepts and processes)** As ocean crust submerged under continental crust, trenching would occur at the boundary as materials form both sides of the boundary slowly moved down.

42. **The correct answer is (1). (Fundamental understandings)** Circulation at the surface of the ocean occurs primarily because of the action of the ocean/atmosphere interface. Of the listed choices, wind action occurs most often at this interface.

43. **The correct answer is (2). (Fundamental understandings)** When air is heated, it expands. As a result, its volume increases but its mass remains the same, making it less dense.

44. **The correct answer is (2). (Fundamental understandings)** The oxidation number of iron in this situation is +3. To make the atom neutral, there must be 2 iron atoms and 3 oxygen atoms (oxygen has an oxidation number of −2 most of the time). The number of atoms on the reactant side must equal the number on the product side.

45. **The correct answer is (5). (Unifying concepts and processes)** There are 6.02×10^{23} molecules in a mole of a substance (Avogadro's number). Convert 1 microliter to milliliters (1ml = 1,000 microliters), then to grams (1ml = 1g), then to moles of water (18g/mole), then multiply by the number of molecules in a mole.

46. **The correct answer is (5). (Fundamental understandings)** Meiosis produces the haploid spores.

47. **The correct answer is (1). (Fundamental understandings)** The pollen grains are produced in the anther.

48. **The correct answer is (1). (Fundamental understandings)** The anther and the filament make up the stamen, the male structure in a flower.

49. **The correct answer is (4). (Fundamental understandings)** The testes and the ovaries begin producing these hormones, which will cause changes around the time of puberty.

50. **The correct answer is (1). (Fundamental understandings)** The penis and the vagina are the reproductive organs in the two sexes.

Posttest 4: Language Arts, Reading

What Is the Colonel's State of Mind? *(page 462)*

1. **The correct answer is (2). (Analysis)** Other details in the story—the asthma attack, the gravelly breathing, the colonel's care of his wife—suggest that she is ill, in addition to this quoted sentence. There is no evidence for choice (1), and choice (3) is contradicted by the colonel's care of his wife. There is no support for choices (4) and (5) in the passage.

2. **The correct answer is (1). (Synthesis)** The narrator presents a series of small, insignificant details that together add up to an overall impression. There is no interior monologue; rather, we see the characters' actions but do not hear their thoughts, so choices (2) and (3) are incorrect. All the action takes place in the present, so choice (4) is incorrect. There are no exciting incidents, so choice (5) is incorrect.

3. **The correct answer is (4). (Analysis)** By doing this, the colonel gives his wife the last of the coffee and makes her think that their situation is not as bad as it really is. Choices (3) and (5) are also helpful acts, but not as considerate as choice (4). Choices (1) and (2) are not kind and considerate acts.

4. **The correct answer is (5). (Synthesis)** Many details add up to this answer: the colonel's poverty, the fact that he has been doing nothing for many years, that nothing but October ever arrives, that something is wrong in his gut, that his wife is sick. The other choices are not supported by the passage.

5. **The correct answer is (2). (Analysis)** Personification means that nonhuman objects, in this case the vegetation and the worms, are used to represent human conditions or characteristics, in this case the feeling in the colonel's stomach.

What Are the Possible Consequences of the Germans' Advance? *(page 463)*

6. **The correct answer is (3). (Comprehension)** The last event that occurs is the arrival of German troops in Sighet (lines 19–20). Choices (1), (2), (4), and (5) precede this event.

7. **The correct answer is (4). (Comprehension)** Throughout the passage, the speaker describes the anxiety over the thought that the German army may arrive. In lines 23–24, the fear and worry become reality. There is no evidence that more army cars are coming, as choice (1) suggests, or that they will stay only a brief time, as choice (2) suggests. The townspeople are afraid of what the Germans might do, so choices (3) and (5) are unlikely.

8. **The correct answer is (5). (Analysis)** Berkovitz's report in lines 23–28 causes anxiety among the townspeople. Choices (1), (2), (3), and (4) are all positive events or normal events that would not cause fear.

9. **The correct answer is (5). (Analysis)** The warm weather, weddings, and news of the Russian army's success (lines 5-7) are contrasted with the frightening rumors about the German's advance (lines 8-10). The events in choices (1) and (4) are not contrasted, but are paired together as evidence of positive events and negative events, respectively. The Russians' behavior is not described, so choice (2) is incorrect. Choice (3) can be eliminated because the "wildfire" in line 29 refers figuratively to the spread of the rumors.

How Have Painters of Different Ages Used Tempera? *(page 464)*

10. **The correct answer is (4). (Comprehension)** The passage states that color was meticulously applied with a fine brush and also emphasizes the detail shown in both paintings described. There is no support for the other choices in the passage.

11. **The correct answer is (5). (Comprehension)** The passage states that after preparing and fastening the panels, the next step was to hide the seams with the gesso. Only after that did Botticelli begin to paint.

12. **The correct answer is (1). (Analysis)** Most of the passage covers in detail the technique of tempera painting. Botticelli's technique in painting *Primavera* is used as a lengthy example of the overall topic. No comparisons between the two paintings are mentioned or comments on their value as works of art are provided.

13. **The correct answer is (3). (Comprehension)** The passage clearly states that tempera is made of water, pigment, and gummy material such as egg yolk. The other choices are all details from the passage, but they do not include the ingredients of tempera.

14. **The correct answer is (2). (Comprehension)** This fact is clearly stated in the passage.

What Does the Speaker See? *(page 465)*

15. **The correct answer is (4). (Comprehension)** The speaker states, "Once you open your eyes in the water, you become a flying creature" (lines 2-4). She does not mention "flying fish." She refers to "zebra fish" (line 4), "sharks" (line 16), and "sea cucumbers" (line 14), so choices (1), (2), (3) and (5) are incorrect.

16. **The correct answer is (5). (Comprehension)** Seeing the color and movement of the swimming fish shows the speaker how different a live fish is from one that is dead—and how much more beautiful. The speaker is contrasting live and dead fish, so choices (1) and (3) are incorrect. Observing fish while diving isn't fishing, so choice (2) is incorrect. There are other ways besides diving to observe fish, so choice (4) is incorrect.

17. **The correct answer is (4). (Synthesis)** The speaker describes a different world underwater of "cold spots, deserts, darkness under clouds . . . and golden chamber" (lines 10-12) and "summer forests and winter forests" (line 13). She does not mention becoming a professional diver or enjoying birdwatching, so choices (1) and (2) can be eliminated. There is no evidence that the speaker has gone diving before, so choice (3) is incorrect. The speaker mentions being "unafraid," so choice (5) is incorrect.

18. **The correct answer is (3). (Analysis)** Sequins are sparkly objects, so comparing the fish's scales to sequins means that the fish look bright and sparkling underwater. The fish are "silver-white" (lines 8-9), so choice (1) is incorrect. The primary characteristic of sequins is their sparkle, so the speaker is not describing her love of colorful objects, sunlight, or pale colors as choices (2), (4), and (5) suggest.

19. **The correct answer is (4). (Application)** The speaker journeys underwater and then returns to land, much like an astronaut flying into space and then returning to Earth. Choices (1), (2), (3), and (5) are not correct because they do not contrast two dramatically different places and experiences.

Who Is This Fellow? *(page 466)*

20. **The correct answer is (1). (Analysis)** A simile is a direct comparison that includes the word "like" or "as." The poet is comparing the way the snake moves through the grass to the way a person divides the hair in parting it with a comb. None of the other choices contain similes.

21. **The correct answer is (3). (Analysis)** Alliteration refers to repetition of the same consonant sound at the beginning of several words—in this case, the "s" sound in "spotted," "shaft," and "seen." None of the other choices contain this sound element.

22. **The correct answer is (4). (Analysis)** The poet says that she has gotten to know several other nature's people—other animals besides the fearsome snake—with cordiality, but she always meets a snake with fear. There is no support for the other choices in the poem.

23. **The correct answer is (5). (Analysis)** The answer is given in the last verse of the poem, where the poet says that when she meets a snake, she always feels "a tighter breathing" and "zero at the bone." In other words, her chest is tight and her bones are weak, both signs of fear. The other choices are not supported by the poem.

24. **The correct answer is (2). (Comprehension)** The grass divides because the snake suddenly appears there. The grass closes up again and the snake moves on, and the grass then opens up again in that spot. None of the other choices are supported by Stanza 2.

25. **The correct answer is (3). (Synthesis)** The language used is extremely simple and plain. It is neither poetic nor old-fashioned; although the poem was written in the mid-1800s, it could have been written yesterday. The other choices are not supported by the poem.

How Do You Apply for a Job? *(page 467)*

26. **The correct answer is (5). (Comprehension)** Choices (1), (2), (3), and (4) are clearly listed in lines 7-10. Choice (5) is not included in the description of the Job Announcement.

27. **The correct answer is (2). (Application)** The passage states that you should submit a separate application for each job, but that you may complete one and photocopy it. The other choices are not supported by the passage.

28. **The correct answer is (1). (Application)** The passage states that a Preferential Requirement is one that is not absolutely necessary in order for someone to apply for a job, although applicants who meet the requirement will receive preferred treatment. You have some experience with Quark, so you should apply, because it is possible that you will have more experience than the other applicants.

29. **The correct answer is (4). (Comprehension)** The passage clearly states that you may submit an application via mail, fax, e-mail, or hand delivery.

30. **The correct answer is (1). (Comprehension)** The passage states that resumes often do not provide enough detail and that Minimum Qualifications Summaries should be submitted instead. Choice (3) is contradicted by the passage. Choices (4) and (5) are not supported by the passage.

Whose Death Is Being Mourned? *(page 468)*

31. **The correct answer is (4). (Comprehension)** The opening stage direction mentions a grave, and the characters have just attended Willy's funeral. The other choices are mentioned in the dialogue but are unsupported by the passage.

32. **The correct answer is (1). (Analysis)** The speech suggests that Willy has taken some desperate action, and we know from Linda's speeches that Willy was not in financial distress, eliminating choices (2) and (3). Choices (4) and (5) are not supported by the passage.

33. The correct answer is (2). (Synthesis) The speech suggests that people need more than just money. Given the other information about Willy in the passage, particularly his love of building, this is the best explanation of the speech. The other choices are not supported by the passage.

34. The correct answer is (3). (Synthesis) According to Charley, a salesman is someone who rides "on a smile and a shoeshine"—on his outward appearance. Charley also denies Biff's statement that Willy never knew who he was, asserting instead that Willy fulfilled his nature. Choices (1), (2), and (4) are not supported by the passage. Choice (5) may actually be true, but it is not what Charley means, which is what the question asks for.

35. The correct answer is (5). (Synthesis) A tragedy is a play that leads inevitably toward the death of the major character. Also, the tone of this excerpt, which is dark and quiet, does not support any of the other choices.

Why Was the Lesson Meaningful? *(page 469)*

36. The correct answer is (4). (Comprehension) In lines 10–11, Wickham turns off the lights and shines a light on a prism. From this, you know that the class is watching an experiment with light and color. Apples and oranges are used as an example, but they are not the focus of the experiment; thus, choice (2) is incorrect. There is no evidence for the other choices.

37. The correct answer is (1). (Comprehension) When the narrator walks to the window, he notices the effect of light on his skin. Choice (3) can be eliminated because it refers to memories of the past. Choice (2) may be suggested, but only after the memory is shared. There is no evidence for choices (4) and (5).

38. The correct answer is (5). (Analysis) These details show how color can change when hit by a certain light. Choice (3) is incorrect because it states that heat, not light, causes the change. The other choices are not supported in the passage.

39. The correct answer is (1). (Synthesis) With this statement, the narrator shows his realization that skin color only makes people look different—it doesn't make them different. Choices (2) and (5) may be true, but they do not summarize the narrator's main point. Choice (3) contradicts the passage; choice (4) is not supported by it.

40. The correct answer is (1). (Synthesis) Because the narrator wonders what kind of light would make his and his friends' skin color look the same, you can conclude that they are from different ethnic or racial backgrounds. Choice (4) states the opposite. There is no evidence to suggest choices (2) or (3). Choice (5) may be true, but it is not relevant to the narrator's comment about skin tone.

Posttest 5: Mathematics

Part I

1. The correct answer is (2). 3 cans of soup for $0.69 each cost a total of $2.07 plus the bread ($1.29) and paperback ($4.50) all add up to a total of $7.86. The change from a $10 bill is $10 − $7.86 = $2.14.

2. The correct answer is (3). A 10% discount means you would pay 90%, so $0.9 \times 2000 = \$1{,}800$. Now, take another $\frac{1}{9}$ off of $1,800, which is $\frac{1}{9} \times 1800 = \$200$. So, the friend pays $1,800 − $200 = $1600.

3. The correct answer is (1). Use a proportion:

$$\frac{2.2\,\text{lb}}{1\,\text{lb}} = \frac{1\text{kg}}{x\text{kg}}$$

$$2.2x = 1$$

$$x = \frac{1}{2.2} = .455 \text{ or } .455\text{kg}$$

4. The correct answer is 48.1. $3(3.6) + 5(5.3) + 4(2.7) = 48.1$. Therefore, the number 48.1 should be coded in the standard grid. See page 481 for filled-in answer grid.

5. The correct answer is (2). Use a proportion:

$$\frac{\frac{3}{4}\,br}{x\text{hr}} = \frac{3\ \text{windows}}{20\ \text{windows}}$$

$$\frac{3}{4} \cdot 20 = 3x \text{ or } 3x = 15$$

Therefore $x = 5$.

Remember you were asked how much more time Justin has to spend to finish the job. So $5 - \frac{3}{4} = 4\frac{1}{4}$

6. The correct answer is (3). First, find the dimension of the cola box. $5 \times 10 \times 7.5 = 375$ cubic inches. The total capacity of the cabinet is 3,274 cubic inches. Therefore, $\frac{3{,}274}{375} = 8.7$. As you cannot fit a fraction of a box, the correct answer is 8 cola boxes.

7. The correct answer is (1). At the day rate for the first two minutes, she would pay $0.85. For the rest of the 50-minute call, $50 − 2 = 48$ minutes, she would pay $48(0.33) = \$15.84$. Her total day cost would be $15.84 + 0.85 = \$16.69$. The evening rate discounts the day rate by 35%. So her savings is 35% of $16.69 i.e., $(0.35)(16.69) = \$ 5.84$.

8. The correct answer is (5). The total amount that Sonya withdrew plus what was left over in her account *is* what she had originally, so $2367.09 + 509.67 + 1089.34 = \$3966.10$.

9. The correct answer is 153. From 3:00 to 4:00, that is in 1 hour, the ship has traveled $123 − 73 = 50$km. We notice the same distance covered in the next hour. Therefore, the ship is traveling at a steady rate. Note $d = r \cdot t$ or $50 = r \cdot 1$, so $r = 50$k/h. At 4:36 the ship will have traveled away from its previous location for 1 hour and 36 minutes. So now we need to find how far the ship will travel in 36 minutes. $d = 50 \cdot \frac{36}{60} = 30$km. Note that we need to express the 36 minutes in terms of hours, hence $\frac{36}{60}$. Now, we add 123 km, the distance the ship traveled away from the harbor until 4:00 to the 30 km it traveled in the next 36 minutes. So 123 + 30 =153 miles is how far away the ship will be from the harbor at 4:36. See page 481 for filled-in answer grid.

10. The correct answer is (5,2) First, mark all the given points: $A(0,4)$, $B(1,2)$, and $D(6,4)$. As $ABCD$ is an isosceles trapezoid, the two sides that are not parallel to each other will have to be the same length and the corresponding angles that are created between these sides and the parallel side must be equal. So the point is (5,2). See page 481 for filled-in answer grid.

11. The correct answer is (2). The portion on the pie chart that shows people who have actually completed high school is 38.7%.

12. The correct answer is (4). Mathematically speaking, *at most* translates to having at the highest (most) a high school diploma or anything less than that. Therefore, $38.7 + 11.0 + 10.4 = 60.1\%$

13. The correct answer is (3). Mathematically speaking, *at least* translates to having at the lowest (least) some college education or anything higher than that. Therefore, $19.3 + 20.6 = 39.9\%$.

14. The correct answer is (5). There is not enough information given to arrive at this fact. The 20.6% that had "4 years or more" could mean some just had 4 years and stopped whereas others went on to graduate school.

15. The correct answer is (1). *At least* translates to having at the lowest (least) some high school education or anything higher than that. Therefore, $11.0 + 38.7 + 19.3 + 20.6 = 89.6\%$.

16. The correct answer is $46.72. The price before the sale was $2(19.99) + 3(14.99) = \$84.95$. Everything was 45% off, so Lauren paid 100% − 45% = 55% of the original price. See page 481 for filled-in answer grid.

17. **The correct answer is (3).** To find the mean (average), we add all the values and divide by the total number of values. First, change all the pound values to ounces, then add all those values up, after which you divide by 5 (number of dogs) and then convert the ounces back to pounds and ounces.

97 lb	8 oz	=	$97 \times 16 + 8$	=	1560 oz
102 lb	3 oz	=	$102 \times 16 + 3$	=	1635 oz
95 lb	11 oz	=	$95 \times 16 + 11$	=	1531 oz
107 lb	7 oz	=	$107 \times 16 + 7$	=	1719 oz
93 lb	9 oz	=	$93 \times 16 + 9$	=	1497 oz
Add all the values					7942 oz

Now, divide by 5 $\quad \dfrac{7942}{5} \quad = \quad$ 1588.4 oz

Now, change to pounds $\quad \dfrac{1588.4}{16} \quad = \quad$ 99.275 lb

.275lbs $= .275 \times 16 = 4.4$ oz giving us 99 lbs 4.4 oz

18. **The correct answer is (1).** The first time (Time 1), a laser is fired through the beam splitter, it splits into 3. The second time (Time 2), each of those beams is split into 3 again, giving us $3 \times 3 = 3^2 = 9$ splits, which in turn, when split the third time (Time 3), will each split into 3 again, giving us $3 \times 3 \times 3 = 3^3 = 27$, and so on. Notice the pattern. The fourth time it should be $3 \times 3 \times 3 \times 3 = 3^4$. So we can predict that on the sixth time the beam is split, it will be $3 \times 3 \times 3 \times 3 \times 3 \times 3 = 3^6 = 729$.

19. **The correct answer is (2).** The area of the shaded region is the difference between the areas of the large circle and the small circle. So, we calculate the areas of the large circle whose radius is $(6 + 2) = 8$ and the small circle whose radius is 6.

$Area_{Large} = \pi r^2 = \pi(8)^2 = 64\pi$

$Area_{Small} = \pi r^2 = \pi(6)^2 = 36\pi$

Therefore, $Area_{Shaded\ Region} = 64\pi - 36\pi = 28\pi$

20. **The correct answer is (4).** The area of the large circle whose radius is $(6 + 2) = 8$ is $Area_{Large} = \pi r^2 = \pi(8)^2 = 64\pi$.

21. **The correct answer is 70.02.** Use the inverse tangent relationship to find the degree value. $tan^{-1}\left(\dfrac{55}{20}\right) = 70.016 \approx 70.02°$. See page 481 for filled-in answer grid.

22. **The correct answer is $1,227.** Use a proportion:

$$\dfrac{\frac{3}{4}\text{carat}}{1\ \text{carat}} = \dfrac{\$920}{x}$$

$\dfrac{3}{4}x = 920$ or $x = 920 \cdot \dfrac{4}{3}$

Therefore, $x = 1,226.67 \approx \$1,227$. See page 481 for filled-in answer grid.

23. **The correct answer is $1950.**

	Savings	Checking	Total
Amount Invested	x	$x + 1,200$	
Interest	0.05	0.03	96

Therefore, $0.05x + 0.03x(x + 1,200) = 96$

$0.05x + 0.03x + 36 = 96$

$0.08x = 60$

$x = \dfrac{60}{0.08} = 750$

$750 + 1200 = \$1,950$.

See page 481 for filled-in answer grid.

24. **The correct answer is (3).** From 5 p.m. to 12 p.m., she paid $4.5 \times 25 = 112.5$, and for the morning tutoring she paid $2.75 \times 35 = 96.25$. Her total expense for the week was $112.50 + 96.25 = \$208.75$. So, her monthly (4-week) expense was $208.75 \times 4 = \$835$.

25. **The correct answer is (1).** We need to find the volume of the cone: $V = \dfrac{1}{3}\pi r^2 h$. We need to find h, while the slant height s is given.

$V = \dfrac{1}{3}\pi r^2 h, r = \dfrac{3}{2} = 1.5, s = 8, h = ?$

$s^2 = h^2 + r^2 \qquad\qquad V = \dfrac{1}{3}\pi r^2 h$

$h^2 = s^2 - r^2$

$h^2 = 8^2 - (1.5)^2 \qquad V = \dfrac{1}{3}\pi(1.5)^2(7.858)$

$h = \sqrt{64 - 2.25} = 7.858 \qquad V = 5.89\pi$

Part II

1. **The correct answer is (3).** The other leg is 3 less than twice the base, which is means base times two minus three: $18 \cdot 2 - 3$. As the other two legs are equal in an isosceles triangle the perimeter, which is the sum of all sides is then $2(18 \cdot 2 - 3) + 18$.

2. **The correct answer is (2).**

1 pint $\Rightarrow$ 2 cups

2 pints $\Rightarrow 2 \times 2$ cups

3. **The correct answer is (1).**

4 People $\Rightarrow \dfrac{1}{4}$ cups

1 Person $\Rightarrow \dfrac{\frac{1}{4}}{4} = \dfrac{1}{4} \times \dfrac{1}{4} = \dfrac{1}{16}$ cups

4. **The correct answer is (5).** Use a proportion:

	Child	Statue
Arm	$1\frac{1}{2}$	42
Height	4	x

Therefore, $\dfrac{1.5}{4} = \dfrac{42}{x}$

5. **The correct answer is (4).** The distributive law has been applied: $879 \cdot 96 - 879 \cdot 32$.

6. **The correct answer is (2).** Use a proportion:

$\dfrac{1.6\ \text{hours}}{8\ \text{hours}} = \dfrac{1\ \text{house}}{x\ \text{houses}}$

$1.6x = 8 \times 1$

$x = \dfrac{8}{1.6} = 5$

7. **The correct answer is (1).** Calculate the range (difference between highest point and lowest point) of the different worker groups. Clearly $59 - 20 = 39$ is the biggest jump for the White Collar worker.

8. **The correct answer is (4).** Add up the number of workers from 1990: $6 + 18 + 35 + 53 = 112$.

9. **The correct answer is (2).** This is where the line for the Service Workers and Farm Workers intersect, which is around 1955.

10. **The correct answer is (3).** The sum of a number plus two translates to $x + 2$. The product of 5 and that quantity is then $5(x + 2)$. This is equal to 11 less than the number times 8, which is $8x - 11$. So we have $5(x + 2) = 8x - 11$.

11. **The correct answer is (2,5).** The mid-point of the diameter is the center: $\left(\dfrac{-3 + 7}{2}, \dfrac{2 + 8}{2}\right) = \left(\dfrac{4}{2}, \dfrac{10}{2}\right) = (2,5)$. See page 482 for filled-in answer grid.

12. **The correct answer is (2).** Use a proportion:

$\dfrac{1\ \text{hour}}{x\ \text{hours}} = \dfrac{150\ \text{calories}}{600\ \text{calories}}$

$600 \times 1 = 150x$

$x = \dfrac{600}{150} = 4$

13. **The correct answer is (3).** Factor and solve:

$$3p + 24p + 21 = 0$$
$$3(p^2 + 8p + 7) = 0$$
$$3(p + 7)(p + 1) = 0$$
$$p + 7 = 0 \quad \text{or} \quad p + 1 = 0$$
$$p = -7 \quad \text{or} \quad p = -1$$

14. **The correct answer is (1).** The largest ball that can fit into the box cannot have a diameter any larger than the smallest dimension of the box, which is 5. There the radius is $5 \div 2 = 2.5$.

15. **The correct answer is 32/12.** Calculate the range (difference between highest and lowest reading): $7\frac{1}{4} - 4\frac{2}{3} = 2\frac{7}{12} = \frac{31}{12}$. The standard grid *does not* allow mixed numbers. See page 482 for filled-in answer grid.

16. **The correct answer is (2).** Median is the middle number after you have ranked (put in ascending order) all your data points: .9, 1.3, 2.1, 2.3, 2.7, 3.2, 4.6, 6.2. Here, you have two middle numbers 2.3 and 2.7. So you take the average $(2.3 + 2.7) \div 2 = 2.5$.

17. **The correct answer is $0.52.** $23 \div 44 = .522 \approx \$0.52$. Remember monetary amounts need to be rounded to the nearest hundredth. See page 482 for filled-in answer grid.

18. **The correct answer is (3).** $d = r \cdot t$.

	r	t	d
Slow train	35	t	$35t$
Fast train	105	$t - 2$	$105(t - 2)$

Now we have:

$35t = 105(t - 2)$ The trains will pass each other after 3 hours

$35t = 105t - 210$ We need to find the distance

$-70t = -210$ $d = r \cdot t$

$t = 3$ $d = 35 \cdot 3 = 105$ miles from the station

19. **The correct answer is (2).** First, we find the area of the silicon plate, then we divide that by the area of the desired chip, which is 1 square inch. Look at the diagram:

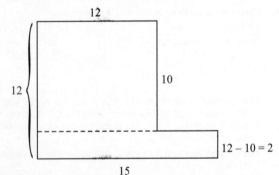

We need to find the areas of the two rectangles and add them to get the total area of the plate. $(12 \times 10) + (15 \times 2) = 150$. Now, $150 \div 1 = 150$.

20. **The correct answer is (3).**

1 yard $\Rightarrow$ \$6.40

$\frac{5}{8}$ yards $\Rightarrow 6.40 \times \frac{5}{8} = \$4.00$

21. **The correct answer is (5).** Karen is now K years old; therefore, Tony is now $(K + 3)$ years old. Seven years from now, Karen will be $(K + 7)$ years and Tony will be $(K + 3 + 7) = (K + 10)$ years old. The total of their age is $(K + 7) + (K + 10) = 79$. When we solve for K, we find Karen's age.

22. **The correct answer is (2).** If s is one side of a square, then

$$d^2 = s^2 + s^2$$
$$12^2 = 2s^2$$
$$s^2 = \frac{144}{2} = 72$$
$$A_{\text{Square}} = s^2 = 72$$

23. **The correct answer is (4).** The printer costs P. The monitor costs $(20 + 2P)$. Together they cost $P + (20 + 2P) = 356$. When we solve for P, we find the price of the printer.

24. **The correct answer is (3).** 74% of the 12,000 attending State U. were male. So, $0.74 \times 12,000 = 8,880$.

25. **The correct answer is (5).** Total increase at Backwoods College from 1975 to 1985 is $14,000 - 8,000 = \$6,000$. Compared to 1975, the percent increase is $\frac{6,000}{8,000} = .75 \equiv 75\%$.

PRACTICE TESTS

ANSWER SHEETS

- Use a #2 pencil.
- Mark one numbered space beside the number that corresponds to each question you are answering.
- Erase errors cleanly and completely.

Practice Test 1: Language Arts, Writing

1. ① ② ③ ④ ⑤	14. ① ② ③ ④ ⑤	27. ① ② ③ ④ ⑤	39. ① ② ③ ④ ⑤
2. ① ② ③ ④ ⑤	15. ① ② ③ ④ ⑤	28. ① ② ③ ④ ⑤	40. ① ② ③ ④ ⑤
3. ① ② ③ ④ ⑤	16. ① ② ③ ④ ⑤	29. ① ② ③ ④ ⑤	41. ① ② ③ ④ ⑤
4. ① ② ③ ④ ⑤	17. ① ② ③ ④ ⑤	30. ① ② ③ ④ ⑤	42. ① ② ③ ④ ⑤
5. ① ② ③ ④ ⑤	18. ① ② ③ ④ ⑤	31. ① ② ③ ④ ⑤	43. ① ② ③ ④ ⑤
6. ① ② ③ ④ ⑤	19. ① ② ③ ④ ⑤	32. ① ② ③ ④ ⑤	44. ① ② ③ ④ ⑤
7. ① ② ③ ④ ⑤	20. ① ② ③ ④ ⑤	33. ① ② ③ ④ ⑤	45. ① ② ③ ④ ⑤
8. ① ② ③ ④ ⑤	21. ① ② ③ ④ ⑤	34. ① ② ③ ④ ⑤	46. ① ② ③ ④ ⑤
9. ① ② ③ ④ ⑤	22. ① ② ③ ④ ⑤	35. ① ② ③ ④ ⑤	47. ① ② ③ ④ ⑤
10. ① ② ③ ④ ⑤	23. ① ② ③ ④ ⑤	36. ① ② ③ ④ ⑤	48. ① ② ③ ④ ⑤
11. ① ② ③ ④ ⑤	24. ① ② ③ ④ ⑤	37. ① ② ③ ④ ⑤	49. ① ② ③ ④ ⑤
12. ① ② ③ ④ ⑤	25. ① ② ③ ④ ⑤	38. ① ② ③ ④ ⑤	50. ① ② ③ ④ ⑤
13. ① ② ③ ④ ⑤	26. ① ② ③ ④ ⑤		

Practice Test 2: Social Studies

1. ① ② ③ ④ ⑤	14. ① ② ③ ④ ⑤	27. ① ② ③ ④ ⑤	39. ① ② ③ ④ ⑤
2. ① ② ③ ④ ⑤	15. ① ② ③ ④ ⑤	28. ① ② ③ ④ ⑤	40. ① ② ③ ④ ⑤
3. ① ② ③ ④ ⑤	16. ① ② ③ ④ ⑤	29. ① ② ③ ④ ⑤	41. ① ② ③ ④ ⑤
4. ① ② ③ ④ ⑤	17. ① ② ③ ④ ⑤	30. ① ② ③ ④ ⑤	42. ① ② ③ ④ ⑤
5. ① ② ③ ④ ⑤	18. ① ② ③ ④ ⑤	31. ① ② ③ ④ ⑤	43. ① ② ③ ④ ⑤
6. ① ② ③ ④ ⑤	19. ① ② ③ ④ ⑤	32. ① ② ③ ④ ⑤	44. ① ② ③ ④ ⑤
7. ① ② ③ ④ ⑤	20. ① ② ③ ④ ⑤	33. ① ② ③ ④ ⑤	45. ① ② ③ ④ ⑤
8. ① ② ③ ④ ⑤	21. ① ② ③ ④ ⑤	34. ① ② ③ ④ ⑤	46. ① ② ③ ④ ⑤
9. ① ② ③ ④ ⑤	22. ① ② ③ ④ ⑤	35. ① ② ③ ④ ⑤	47. ① ② ③ ④ ⑤
10. ① ② ③ ④ ⑤	23. ① ② ③ ④ ⑤	36. ① ② ③ ④ ⑤	48. ① ② ③ ④ ⑤
11. ① ② ③ ④ ⑤	24. ① ② ③ ④ ⑤	37. ① ② ③ ④ ⑤	49. ① ② ③ ④ ⑤
12. ① ② ③ ④ ⑤	25. ① ② ③ ④ ⑤	38. ① ② ③ ④ ⑤	50. ① ② ③ ④ ⑤
13. ① ② ③ ④ ⑤	26. ① ② ③ ④ ⑤		

Practice Test 3: Science

1. ① ② ③ ④ ⑤
2. ① ② ③ ④ ⑤
3. ① ② ③ ④ ⑤
4. ① ② ③ ④ ⑤
5. ① ② ③ ④ ⑤
6. ① ② ③ ④ ⑤
7. ① ② ③ ④ ⑤
8. ① ② ③ ④ ⑤
9. ① ② ③ ④ ⑤
10. ① ② ③ ④ ⑤
11. ① ② ③ ④ ⑤
12. ① ② ③ ④ ⑤
13. ① ② ③ ④ ⑤

14. ① ② ③ ④ ⑤
15. ① ② ③ ④ ⑤
16. ① ② ③ ④ ⑤
17. ① ② ③ ④ ⑤
18. ① ② ③ ④ ⑤
19. ① ② ③ ④ ⑤
20. ① ② ③ ④ ⑤
21. ① ② ③ ④ ⑤
22. ① ② ③ ④ ⑤
23. ① ② ③ ④ ⑤
24. ① ② ③ ④ ⑤
25. ① ② ③ ④ ⑤
26. ① ② ③ ④ ⑤

27. ① ② ③ ④ ⑤
28. ① ② ③ ④ ⑤
29. ① ② ③ ④ ⑤
30. ① ② ③ ④ ⑤
31. ① ② ③ ④ ⑤
32. ① ② ③ ④ ⑤
33. ① ② ③ ④ ⑤
34. ① ② ③ ④ ⑤
35. ① ② ③ ④ ⑤
36. ① ② ③ ④ ⑤
37. ① ② ③ ④ ⑤
38. ① ② ③ ④ ⑤

39. ① ② ③ ④ ⑤
40. ① ② ③ ④ ⑤
41. ① ② ③ ④ ⑤
42. ① ② ③ ④ ⑤
43. ① ② ③ ④ ⑤
44. ① ② ③ ④ ⑤
45. ① ② ③ ④ ⑤
46. ① ② ③ ④ ⑤
47. ① ② ③ ④ ⑤
48. ① ② ③ ④ ⑤
49. ① ② ③ ④ ⑤
50. ① ② ③ ④ ⑤

Practice Test 4: Language Arts, Reading

1. ① ② ③ ④ ⑤
2. ① ② ③ ④ ⑤
3. ① ② ③ ④ ⑤
4. ① ② ③ ④ ⑤
5. ① ② ③ ④ ⑤
6. ① ② ③ ④ ⑤
7. ① ② ③ ④ ⑤
8. ① ② ③ ④ ⑤
9. ① ② ③ ④ ⑤
10. ① ② ③ ④ ⑤

11. ① ② ③ ④ ⑤
12. ① ② ③ ④ ⑤
13. ① ② ③ ④ ⑤
14. ① ② ③ ④ ⑤
15. ① ② ③ ④ ⑤
16. ① ② ③ ④ ⑤
17. ① ② ③ ④ ⑤
18. ① ② ③ ④ ⑤
19. ① ② ③ ④ ⑤
20. ① ② ③ ④ ⑤

21. ① ② ③ ④ ⑤
22. ① ② ③ ④ ⑤
23. ① ② ③ ④ ⑤
24. ① ② ③ ④ ⑤
25. ① ② ③ ④ ⑤
26. ① ② ③ ④ ⑤
27. ① ② ③ ④ ⑤
28. ① ② ③ ④ ⑤
29. ① ② ③ ④ ⑤
30. ① ② ③ ④ ⑤

31. ① ② ③ ④ ⑤
32. ① ② ③ ④ ⑤
33. ① ② ③ ④ ⑤
34. ① ② ③ ④ ⑤
35. ① ② ③ ④ ⑤
36. ① ② ③ ④ ⑤
37. ① ② ③ ④ ⑤
38. ① ② ③ ④ ⑤
39. ① ② ③ ④ ⑤
40. ① ② ③ ④ ⑤

Practice Test 5: Mathematics
Part I

1. ① ② ③ ④ ⑤

2. ① ② ③ ④ ⑤

3. ① ② ③ ④ ⑤

4. ① ② ③ ④ ⑤

5.

6. ① ② ③ ④ ⑤

7. ① ② ③ ④ ⑤

8.

9. ① ② ③ ④ ⑤

10.

11. ① ② ③ ④ ⑤

12. ① ② ③ ④ ⑤

13. ① ② ③ ④ ⑤

14. ① ② ③ ④ ⑤

15. ① ② ③ ④ ⑤

16. ① ② ③ ④ ⑤

17. ① ② ③ ④ ⑤

18.

19. ① ② ③ ④ ⑤

20. ① ② ③ ④ ⑤

21. ① ② ③ ④ ⑤

22. ① ② ③ ④ ⑤

23.

24.

25.

Part II

1. ① ② ③ ④ ⑤
2. ① ② ③ ④ ⑤
3. ① ② ③ ④ ⑤
4. ① ② ③ ④ ⑤
5. ① ② ③ ④ ⑤

6.

7. ① ② ③ ④ ⑤
8. ① ② ③ ④ ⑤
9. ① ② ③ ④ ⑤
10. ① ② ③ ④ ⑤

11.

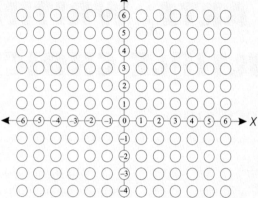

12. ① ② ③ ④ ⑤
13. ① ② ③ ④ ⑤
14. ① ② ③ ④ ⑤
15. ① ② ③ ④ ⑤
16. ① ② ③ ④ ⑤
17. ① ② ③ ④ ⑤
18. ① ② ③ ④ ⑤
19. ① ② ③ ④ ⑤

20. ① ② ③ ④ ⑤
21. ① ② ③ ④ ⑤
22. ① ② ③ ④ ⑤
23. ① ② ③ ④ ⑤

24.

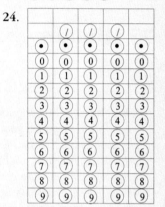

25. ① ② ③ ④ ⑤

Practice Test 1

LANGUAGE ARTS, WRITING
PART 1: MULTIPLE CHOICE

75 Minutes ❖ 50 Questions

Directions: The Language Arts, Writing test is intended to measure your ability to use clear and effective English. It is a test of English as it should be written, not as it might be spoken. This test includes both multiple-choice questions and an essay. These directions apply only to the multiple-choice section; a separate set of directions is given for the essay.

For Example:

Sentence 1:

We were all honored to meet governor Phillips.

What correction should be made to this sentence?

(1) Insert a comma after honored
(2) Change the spelling of honored to honered
(3) Change governor to Governor
(4) Replace were with was
(5) No correction is necessary

① ② ● ④ ⑤

In this example, the word "governor" should be capitalized; therefore, answer space 3 would be marked on the answer sheet.

The multiple-choice section consists of paragraphs with numbered sentences. Some of the sentences contain errors in sentence structure, usage, or mechanics (spelling, punctuation, and capitalization). After reading the numbered sentences, answer the multiple-choice questions that follow. Some of the sentences are correct as written. The best answer for other questions is the one that leaves the sentence as originally written. The best answer for some questions is the one that produces a sentence that is consistent with the verb tense and point of view used throughout the paragraph.

You should spend no more than 75 minutes on the multiple-choice questions and 45 minutes on your essay. Work carefully, but do not spend too much time on any one question. You may begin working on the essay part of this test as soon as you complete the multiple-choice section.

Do not mark in this test booklet. Record your answers on the separate answer sheet provided. Be sure that all requested information is properly recorded on the answer sheet. To record your answers, mark one numbered space on the answer sheet beside the number that corresponds to the question in the test booklet.

Do not rest the point of your pencil on the answer sheet while you are considering your answer. Make no stray or unnecessary marks. If you change an answer, erase your first mark completely. Mark only one answer space for each question; multiple answers will be scored as incorrect. Do not fold or crease your answer sheet.

Directions: Choose the <u>one best answer</u> for each item.

Items 1–13 refer to the following paragraphs.

(1) Standing proudly in New York Harbor, the Statue of Liberty, a gift from France to the United States, a symbol of freedom well-known throughout the world. (2) In 1884 the people of France presented this magnificent gift to express friendship and believing in political liberty shared by both the French and the Americans. (3) The idea of the statue was conceived by renowned French politician and historian Edouard-Rene Lefebvre de Laboulaye, what greatly admired the United States. (4) His friend, the French sculptor Frederic Auguste Bartholdi, set out to create the largest statue since ancient times. (5) Work commenced in 1875 as fund-raising began in both France and the United States, and American school children were important contributors.

(6) The process of creating the statue occurred in several stages. (7) First, Bartholdi made a small clay model to determine style and proportions, and then he followed that with several larger plaster versions. (8) The next step to construct a wooden framework to form a full-scale model for each part of the figure, and over that frame a layer of plaster was applied. (9) Metalworkers put thin sheets of copper on the forms and hammered them to fit the shape of the wooden and plaster forms. (10) When the forms were removed, the copper surface matched the figure of the plaster model exactly as Bartholdi had planned; now the statue required some kind of underpinning. (11) The framework that would provide a support system, designed by Alexandre Gustave Eiffel, the famous French engineer, was a central iron tower. (12) The copper exterior would be attached to this iron tower by a solid but resilient framework of iron bars. (13) After the completion of the statue, it was dismantled and packed in 214 wooden crates to be shipped to the U.S. to be reassembled soon after the pedestal for the statue was completed.

(14) Bartholdi had hoped to complete the statue in time for the Centennial Exposition, but only the right hand and torch were finished. (15) So these sent to America for this celebration in both Philadelphia and New York City. (16) The French helped the American colonies in the fight for independence. (17) The entire statue, officially named Liberty Enlightening the World, *and its pedestal was dedicated in 1886. (18) Since that time the Statue of Liberty has welcomed millions of immigrants to the United States it is a true symbol of America.*

1. What is a more chronological development of sentences in the first paragraph?
   - **(1)** Sentences 1, 3, 4, 5, 2
   - **(2)** Sentences 3, 2, 4, 5, 1
   - **(3)** Sentences 4, 3, 1, 2, 5
   - **(4)** Sentences 2, 1, 3, 4, 5
   - **(5)** Sentences 1, 2, 5, 3, 4

2. Sentence 1: **Standing proudly in New York Harbor, the Statue of Liberty, a gift from France to the United States, a symbol of freedom well-known throughout the world.**

   What correction should be made to this sentence?
   - **(1)** Omit the commas around <u>the Statue of Liberty</u>
   - **(2)** Insert <u>and</u> after <u>United States</u>
   - **(3)** Insert <u>is</u> after <u>United States</u>
   - **(4)** Move <u>a gift from France to the United States</u> to the beginning of the sentence
   - **(5)** No correction is necessary

3. Sentence 2: **In 1884 the people of France presented this magnificent gift to express friendship and believing in political liberty shared by both the French and the Americans.**

   What correction should be made to this sentence?
   - **(1)** Change <u>presented</u> to <u>present</u>
   - **(2)** Change <u>believing</u> to <u>belief</u>
   - **(3)** Omit <u>both . . . and</u>
   - **(4)** Insert a comma after <u>France</u>
   - **(5)** No correction is necessary

4. Sentence 3: **The idea of the statue was conceived by renowned French politician and historian Edouard-Rene Lefebvre de Laboulaye, what greatly admired the United States.**

   What correction should be made to this sentence?
   - **(1)** Omit <u>conceived by</u>
   - **(2)** Insert a comma after <u>renowned</u>
   - **(3)** Change <u>what</u> to <u>whoever</u>
   - **(4)** Change <u>what</u> to <u>who</u>
   - **(5)** No correction is necessary

5. Sentence 6: **The process of creating the statue occurred in several stages.**

   How can this sentence be most effectively revised?
   - **(1)** Creating the statue occurred in several stages.
   - **(2)** The process occurred in several stages.
   - **(3)** The process, creating the statue, occurred in several stages.
   - **(4)** In several stages, the process occurred.
   - **(5)** Creating the statue occurred.

6. Sentence 8: **The next step to construct a wooden framework to form a full-scale model for each part of the figure, and over that frame a layer of plaster was applied.**

What correction should be made to this sentence?

(1) Insert a comma after step
(2) Omit the comma after figure
(3) Insert was after step
(4) Insert is after step
(5) No correction is necessary

7. Sentence 9: **Metalworkers put thin sheets of copper on the forms and hammered them to fit the shape of the wooden forms.**

What correction should be made to this sentence?

(1) Change put to have put
(2) Move on the forms to follow metalworkers
(3) Change them to it
(4) Begin the sentence with After
(5) No correction is necessary

8. Sentence 9: **Metalworkers put thin sheets of copper on the forms and hammered them to fit the shape of the wooden and plaster forms.**

Which of the following will serve as effective transition to introduce this sentence and connect it to the previous one?

(1) However
(2) Last
(3) Then
(4) Finally
(5) As soon as

9. Sentence 11: **The framework that would provide a support system, designed by Alexandre Gustave Eiffel, the famous French engineer, was a central iron tower.**

Which is the most effective revision of this sentence without changing the meaning?

(1) The frame that provide a support system, designed by Alexandre Gustave Eiffel, the famous French engineer, was a central iron tower.
(2) The framework providing a support system was designed by Alexandre Gustave Eiffel, famous French engineer, was a central iron tower.
(3) Alexandre Gustave Eiffel, providing a support frame in a central iron tower, was a famous French engineer.
(4) Designed by Alexandre Gustave Eiffel, famous French engineer, the framework, a central iron tower, provided a support.
(5) Providing a support system with a central iron tower, framework designed Alexandre Gustave Eiffel was a famous French engineer.

10. Which of the following could be an effective concluding sentence for the second paragraph?

(1) Completing the statue and sending it to the U.S. took time.
(2) Completing the statue took place in several important steps because of the magnitude of the project.
(3) Completing this project was a complicated process.
(4) Attention to the details of the project produced a remarkable outcome.
(5) Two Frenchmen were produced the Statue of Liberty.

11. Sentence 15: **So these sent to America for this celebration in both Philadelphia and New York City.**

What correction should be made to this sentence?

(1) Insert a comma after America
(2) Insert were after these
(3) Omit these
(4) Insert kind of after this
(5) No correction is necessary

12. Which sentence in the final paragraph should be omitted?

(1) Sentence 15
(2) Sentence 16
(3) Sentence 17
(4) Sentence 18
(5) No sentence should be omitted

13. Sentence 18: **Since that time the Statue of Liberty has welcomed millions of immigrants to the United States it is a true symbol of America.**

What correction should be made to this sentence?

(1) Insert a comma after United States
(2) Insert which after Statue of Liberty
(3) Insert although after United States
(4) Insert because after United States
(5) No correction is necessary

Items 14–25 refer to the following paragraphs.

(1) *One of the most memorable short stories ever writen is famous for one feature, its ending.* (2) *Frank Stocktons "The Lady, or the Tiger?" is almost like a fairy tale with the usual characters of a king who is very protective of his daughter, who falls in love with a young man who is not of royal blood.* (3) *When the king discovers there love affair, he arranges a trial supposedly to test the young man, to see if he is worthy of his daughter.* (4) *The king, however, is described as "semi-barbaric" his notion of justice is not just at all because his real goal is to eliminate the princess' lover.* (5) *Kings have a reputation for being cruel.*

(6) *The young man is placed in an arena where he has to chose one of two doors that open into the arena.* (7) *Behind one door is a lovely young lady whom he would marry immediately, but behind the other door is a tiger savagely attacking him.* (8) *Regardless of his choice, neither of these options is fair to the young man or to the princess, who wants to marry him herself.* (9) *However, she is jealous of the young woman who is behind one of the doors.* (10) *Some how the princess manages to discover information that no one has ever found out before.* (11) *The princess learns the secret; she knows where the young woman is and where the tiger is.*

(12) *Just before the young man steps forward to select a door and looks at the princess sitting in the royal box.* (13) *Almost imperceptibly, she sends a small signal to direct his choice.* (14) *The reader who's interest has built during the story eagerly waits to see if the young man will live or die.* (15) *Much to*

everyone's surprise, the author ends his story with this question, "Who do you think came out of that door, the lady, or the tiger?" (16) *Stockton was at the time not a widely known writer, but once his remarkable story appeared, he was famous almost overnight.*

14. Sentence 1: **One of the most memorable short stories ever writen is famous for one feature, its ending.**

What correction should be made to this sentence?

(1) Change writen to written
(2) Change most to more
(3) Change its to it's
(4) Omit the comma after feature
(5) No correction is necessary

15. Sentence 2: **Frank Stocktons "The Lady, or the Tiger?" is almost like a fairy tale with the usual characters of a king who is very protective of his daughter, who falls in love with a young man who is not of royal blood.**

What correction should be made to this sentence?

(1) Insert commoner before young man
(2) Change tale to tail
(3) Insert princess before daughter
(4) Change Stocktons to Stockton's
(5) No correction is necessary

16. Sentence 3: **When the king discovers there love affair, he arranges a trial supposedly to test the young man, to see if he is worthy of his daughter.**

What correction should be made to this sentence?

(1) Omit the comma after affair
(2) Change there to their
(3) Change arranges to arranged
(4) Change is to was
(5) No correction is necessary

17. Sentence 4: **The king, however, is described as "semi-barbaric" his notion of justice is not just at all because his real goal is to eliminate the princess' lover.**

What correction should be made to this sentence?

(1) Change all instances of is to was
(2) Insert a comma after "semi-barbaric"
(3) Insert a comma and so after "semi-barbaric"
(4) Change his notion of justice to although his notion of justice
(5) No correction is necessary

18. Sentence 5: **Kings have a reputation for being cruel.**

Where should Sentence 5 be located in the first paragraph?

(1) After Sentence 1
(2) After Sentence 2
(3) After Sentence 3
(4) After Sentence 4
(5) Omit it from the paragraph

19. Sentence 6: **The young man is placed in an arena where he has to chose one of two doors that open into the arena.**

What correction should be made to this sentence?

(1) Change chose to choose
(2) Change is to was
(3) Insert When at the beginning of the sentence
(4) Insert a comma after arena
(5) No correction is necessary

20. Sentence 7: **Behind one door is a lovely young lady whom he would marry immediately, but behind the other door is a tiger savagely attacking him.**

What correction should be made to this sentence?

(1) Insert a comma after door
(2) Insert a comma after lady
(3) Change but to therefore
(4) Change savagely attacking him to that would savagely attack him
(5) No correction is necessary

21. Sentence 8: **Regardless of his choice, neither of these options is fair to the young man or to the princess, who wants to marry him herself.**

What correction should be made to this sentence?

(1) Change Regardless to Irregardless
(2) Omit the comma after choice
(3) Change is to was
(4) Change man or to the princess to man or the princess
(5) No correction is necessary

22. Sentence 10: **Some how the princess manages to discover information that no one has ever found out before.**

What correction should be made to this sentence?

(1) Change manages to managed
(2) Change Some how to Somehow
(3) Change ever to every
(4) Insert a comma after information
(5) No correction is necessary

23. Sentence 12: **Just before the young man steps forward to select a door and looks at the princess sitting in the royal box.**

What correction should be made to this sentence?

(1) Insert a comma after door
(2) Omit Just
(3) Omit Just before
(4) Insert a comma after princess
(5) No correction is necessary

24. Sentence 14: **The reader who's interest has built during the story eagerly waits to see if the young man will live or die.**

What correction should be made to this sentence?

(1) Change who's to whose
(2) Change will to would
(3) Insert a comma after story
(4) Insert a comma after live
(5) No correction is necessary

25. In the final paragraph, where is the best location for this sentence: "This surprise ending does not provide the answer."

(1) After Sentence 12
(2) After Sentence 13
(3) After Sentence 14
(4) After Sentence 15
(5) After Sentence 16

> Items 26–39 refer to the following paragraphs.

(1) *The earliest British settlers who came to what became the United States of America can be divided into two groups.* (2) *First those like Sir Walter Raleigh, who was intent on using the fertile soil of the area now known as Virginia to raise tobacco.* (3) *Some men who came with Raleigh were "second sons," according to British law, the eldest son would inherit the bulk of the estate.* (4) *Second and subsequent sons had to look elsewhere for livelihood.* (5) *Some chose to enter the ministry others came to Virginia, never intending to stay.* (6) *These men known as "planters" planned to turn tobacco into cash when they came back to Britain with their harvested crops.* (7) *Some even believed that they could easily turn the Native Americans into slaves.* (8) *The facts, of course, are that none of this fledgling tobacco business was easy.* (9) *While the area was remarkably rich, clearing the land required time and manpower.* (10) *Even though many of the planters did not plan to do the manual labor theirself, they tended to stake claims to huge*

acres of land. (11) Eventually, a work force of convicts, servants who were indentured, and natives from Africa were brought in. (12) The southern area of the New World would in time become the American South, and slavery already existed.

(13) The second group, the earliest arrivals in the North, were mostly British citizens seeking the freedom to practice religion as they wished. (14) This group had fled Great Britain and landed in the New England area, where the land was rocky and not very fertile. (15) These settlers tended to keep small communities in tack because they shared religious ties and sought to establish a theocracy, a society in which civil law is the same as religious law. (16) They also fear the wilderness, which was believed to be the home of Satan, so they settled in communities for protection. (17) With permanent homes as one of their objectives, they worked together to strengthen communities, and their settlements thrived.

(18) These two diverse groups of settlers with different motives and goals arrived in the New World within fifteen years of each other. (19) The basic differences in these two groups which did not occur until almost two hundred years later are among the factors responsible for the War Between the States.

26. Sentence 1: **The earliest British settlers who came to what became the United States of America can be divided into two groups.**

    What is the best way to revise the underlined portion of the sentence?

    (1) coming to the future United States of America
    (2) having come to the prospective United States
    (3) moving to the eminent United States of America
    (4) arriving in America
    (5) No correction is necessary

27. Sentence 2: **First those like Sir Walter Raleigh, who was intent on using the fertile soil of the area now known as Virginia to raise tobacco.**

    What correction should be made to this sentence?

    (1) Omit the comma after Raleigh
    (2) Insert a comma after First
    (3) Insert comes after Raleigh
    (4) Insert came after First
    (5) No correction is necessary

28. Sentence 3: **Some men who came with Raleigh were "second sons," according to British law, the eldest son would inherit the bulk of the estate.**

    What correction should be made to this sentence?

    (1) Insert who came because, after "second sons"
    (2) Insert they came, after "second sons"
    (3) Omit the comma after law
    (4) Insert because at the beginning of the sentence
    (5) No correction is necessary

29. Sentence 5: **Some chose to enter the ministry others came to Virginia, never intending to stay.**

    What correction should be made to this sentence?

    (1) Change chose to choose
    (2) Insert a comma after ministry
    (3) Omit the comma after Virginia
    (4) Insert while after ministry
    (5) No correction is necessary

30. Sentence 9: **While the area was remarkably rich, clearing the land required time and manpower.**

    What correction should be made to the underlined portion of this sentence?

    (1) Change was to is
    (2) Change While to When
    (3) Change While to Even though
    (4) Change While to If
    (5) No correction is necessary

31. Sentence 10: **Even though many of the planters did not plan to do the manual labor theirself, they tended to stake claims to huge acres of land.**

    What correction should be made to this sentence?

    (1) Change theirself to themselves
    (2) Change theirself to themself
    (3) Change theirself to hisself
    (4) Change theirself to himself
    (5) No correction is necessary

32. Sentence 11: **Eventually, <u>a work force of convicts, servants who were indentured, and natives from Africa</u> was brought in.**

What is the best way to revise the underlined portion of the sentence?

(1) convicts, servants who were indentured, and natives who were from Africa

(2) a work force of convicts, indentured servants and African natives

(3) workers who was convicts, indentured servants, and African natives

(4) a work force of men who were convicts, indentured servants, and natives from Africa

(5) No correction is necessary

33. Sentence 12: **The southern area of the New World would in time become the American South, <u>and</u> slavery already existed.**

What is the best way to revise the underlined portion of the sentence?

(1) Change <u>and</u> to <u>but</u>

(2) Change <u>and</u> to <u>because</u>

(3) Change <u>and</u> to <u>where</u>

(4) Change <u>and</u> to <u>although</u>

(5) Change <u>and</u> to <u>even though</u>

34. Which of the following is an effective concluding sentence for the first paragraph?

(1) Settlers in the South put slavery in place from the beginning.

(2) The southern planters' only goal was profit from slavery.

(3) Tobacco was an easily grown, lucrative crop.

(4) While the planters did not come to settle, they did seek to cultivate the land for tobacco.

(5) "Second sons" were the only planters who were willing to face the challenge of the South.

35. Sentence 13: **The second group, the earliest arrivals in the North, were mostly British citizens seeking the freedom to practice religion as they wished.**

How can this sentence be revised most effectively and concisely?

(1) The earliest arrivals in the North were mostly British citizens, the second group, who sought the freedom to practice religion as they wished.

(2) The second group, the earliest arrivals in the North, seeking freedom to practice religion as they wished, were mostly British.

(3) The earliest arrivals in the North were mostly British citizens seeking religious freedom.

(4) Arriving earliest in the North, the second group, mostly British, sought religious freedom.

(5) The second group, mostly British, sought religious freedom arriving earliest in the North.

36. Sentence 14: **This group had fled Great Britain landing in the New England area, where the land was rocky and not very fertile.**

How can this sentence be revised most effectively and concisely?

(1) This group had fled Great Britain and landed in the New England area with rocky, infertile land.

(2) Fleeing Great Britain and landing in the New England area with rocky and not fertile soil.

(3) Having fled Great Britain, this group landed in New England and rocky soil and infertile land.

(4) Having fled Great Britain, this group landed in New England with its rocky, infertile soil.

(5) In New England landed this group who fled Great Britain with its rocky, infertile soil.

37. Sentence 15: **These settlers tended to keep small communities in tack because they shared religious ties and sought to establish a theocracy, a society in which civil law is the same as religious law.**

What correction should be made to this sentence?

(1) Omit the comma after <u>theocracy</u>

(2) Change <u>in tack</u> to <u>intact</u>

(3) Insert a comma after <u>communities</u>

(4) Change <u>shared religious ties and sought to establish a theocracy</u> to <u>favored religiouslaw</u>

(5) No correction is necessary

38. Sentence 16: **They also fear the wilderness, which was believed to be the home of Satan, so they settled in communities for protection.**

What correction should be made to this sentence?

(1) Change so to because
(2) Change settled to settle
(3) Omit which was believed to be
(4) Change fear to feared
(5) No correction is necessary

39. Sentence 19: **The basic differences in these two groups which did not occur until almost two hundred years later are among the factors responsible for the War Between the States.**

What correction should be made to the underlined portion of this sentence?

(1) Move the clause to follow differences
(2) Move the clause to follow factors
(3) Place the clause at the beginning of the sentence
(4) Move the clause to follow States
(5) No correction is necessary

Items 40–50 pertain to the following paragraphs.

(1) *With his work on the peanut, scientist George Washington Carver made an enormous contribution to american agriculture.* (2) *During the 1800s and into the 1900s, cotton was the chief crop grown in the southern part of the United States.* (3) *However, cotton robs the soil of nutrients when it is planted in the same field year after year the yield dwindles yearly.* (4) *Southern farmers, therefore, especially those who farmed small plots, made little money growing this crop, and their future was precarious.* (5) *Rescued by a fellow Southerner, George Washington Carver, who wanted to help the southern farmer.* (6) *Employing students at Alabama's Tuskegee Institute to help carry out experiments on different crops and on products that could be made from those crops, he sought ways to help.* (7) *Carver was especially interested in the peanut and the sweet potato, two crops that harbor bacteria that add nutrients to the soil on their roots.* (8) *Carver discovered about 300 products that could be made from peanuts and more than 100 products that could be made from sweet potatoes.* (9) *These products included flour, cheese, milk, cosmetics, dyes, and rubber.* (10) *Southern farmers began to grow these crops, which were especially suited to the warm weather and the sandy*

soil of that region. (11) *In time, the soil-enriching peanut became the second-largest crop in the South.*

(12) *The peanut is a legume, a plant that bears fruit in the form of pods containing one or more seeds; in fact, this legume is more closely related to peas than to nuts.* (13) *Peanut seeds consist of almost 50 percent oil, which is commonly used to fry foods because it smokes only at high temperatures and does not absorb odors easily.* (14) *Peanuts are used as an ingredient in soaps, cosmetics, shaving creams, shampoos, paints, and even nitroglycerin.* (15) *Even the shells of peanuts have been used, sense they can be ground into powder to be used in plastics, cork substitutes, wallboard, and abrasives.*

(16) *Carver continued his research and publishes articles on practical matters such as improved farm techniques and food preservation.* (17) *His work was especially appreciated during the Great Depression of the 1930s, when many people were out of work and having little money to buy food.* (18) *Carver was an influential teacher, inspiring young people to find ways to make science work for the betterment of all.*

40. Which of the following is the best choice of a topic sentence for the first paragraph?

(1) George Washington Carver was a famous scientist.
(2) The development of new food crops is one of the most important ways that scientists benefit society.
(3) George Washington Carver discovered the peanut in the South.
(4) The planting of peanuts saved southern agriculture.
(5) The cotton crop was no longer the most productive in the twentieth century.

41. Sentence 1: **With his work on the peanut, scientist George Washington Carver made an enormous contribution to american agriculture.**

What correction should be made to this sentence?

(1) Omit his
(2) Capitalize scientist
(3) Change made to makes
(4) Capitalize american
(5) No correction is necessary

505

42. Sentence 2: **During the 1800s and into the 1900s, cotton was the chief crop grown in the southern part of the United States.**

What correction should be made to this sentence?

(1) Omit the comma after 1900s
(2) Capitalize cotton
(3) Change was to had been
(4) Insert a comma after crop
(5) No correction is necessary

43. Sentence 3: **However, cotton robs the soil of nutrients when it is planted in the same field year after year the yield dwindles yearly.**

What correction should be made to this sentence?

(1) Insert so after year
(2) Omit year after year
(3) Change robs to robbed
(4) Insert a semicolon after nutrients
(5) No correction is necessary

44. Sentence 4: **Southern farmers, therefore, especially those who farmed small plots, made little money growing this crop, and there future was full of risk.**

What correction should be made to this sentence?

(1) Omit the commas around therefore
(2) Omit the comma after plots
(3) Change who to which
(4) Change there to their
(5) No correction is necessary

45. Sentence 5: **Rescued by a fellow Southerner, George Washington Carver, who wanted to help the southern farmer.**

What correction should be made to this sentence?

(1) Omit the comma after Southerner
(2) Omit the comma after Carver
(3) Insert They were at the beginning of the sentence
(4) Omit who
(5) No correction is necessary

46. Sentence 6: **Employing students at Alabama's Tuskegee Institute to help carry out experiments on different crops and on products that can be made from those crops, he sought ways to help.**

What correction should be made to this sentence?

(1) Change Employing to Having been employed
(2) Omit the comma after crops
(3) Change can to could
(4) Change sought to seeked
(5) No correction is necessary

47. Sentence 7: **Carver was especially interested in the peanut and the sweet potato, two crops that harbor bacteria that add nutrients to the soil on their roots.**

Which of the following is the most effective way to revise this sentence to be more concise?

(1) Carver was especially interested in the peanut and the sweet potato that harbor bacteria adding nutrients to the soil on their roots.
(2) Carver was especially interested in the peanut and the sweet potato, two crops that harbor bacteria adding nutrients to the soil on their roots.
(3) Especially interested in the peanut and the sweet potato, two crops harboring bacteria to add nutrients to the soil on their roots.
(4) Carver was especially interested in the peanut and the sweet potato, two crops harboring bacteria that add nutrients to the soil on their roots.
(5) Carver was especially interested in two crops harboring bacteria and adding nutrients to the soil on their roots, the peanut and the sweet potato.

48. Sentences 8 and 9: **Carver discovered about 300 products that could be made from peanuts and more than 100 products that could be made from sweet potatoes. These products included flour, cheese, milk, cosmetics, dyes, and rubber.**

How can these sentences be most concisely combined?

(1) Carver discovered about 300 products that could be made from peanuts and more than 100 products that could be made from sweet potatoes, including flour, cheese, milk, cosmetics, dyes, and rubber.
(2) Carver discovered about 300 products made from peanuts and more than 100 products made from sweet potatoes, including flour, cheese, milk, cosmetics, dyes, and rubber.
(3) Carver discovered about 300 products from peanuts and more than 100 products from sweet potatoes included flour, cheese, milk, cosmetics, dyes, rubber, and peanut butter.
(4) Carver discover about 400 products from peanuts and sweet potatoes such as flour, cheese, milk, cosmetics, dyes, and rubber.
(5) Carver discovered about 300 products from peanuts and more than 100 products from sweet potatoes such as flour, cheese, milk, cosmetics, dyes, and rubber.

49. Sentence 10: **Southern farmers began to grow these crops, which were especially suited to the warm weather and the sandy soil of that region.**

Which is the most effective way to revise this sentence for conciseness?

(1) Southern farmers began to grow these crops especially suited to warm weather and sandy soil of that region.

(2) Southern farmers began to grow crops especially suited to the warm weather and the sandy soil of that region.

(3) Farmers began to grow these crops especially suited to weather and soil of the area.

(4) Southern farmers began to grow these crops suited to weather and soil of that region.

(5) These crops were especially suited to weather and soil of that region.

50. Sentence 12: **The peanut is a legume, a plant that bears fruit in the form of pods containing one or more seeds; in fact, this legume is more closely related to peas than to nuts.**

Which of the following is the best way to revise the underlined portion of the sentence?

(1) a plant bearing fruit in pods with seeds more closely related to peas than to nuts.

(2) a plant bearing fruit in pods containing one or more seeds more closely related to peas than to nuts.

(3) a plant that bears fruit in pods with seeds and is more closely related to peas than to nuts.

(4) a plant with fruit in pods more closely related to peas than to nuts.

(5) bearing fruit in pods containing one or more seeds more closely related to peas than to nuts.

PART II: ESSAY

45 Minutes

Directions: Write an essay of 200–250 words about the most influential person in your life. In your essay, explain why this person has deeply affected you. Keep in mind the important characteristics of a good essay. Include specific details.

SCORE = 1:2:3:4

SCORE = 4

The most influential person in my life has been my mother. She is the one who has consistently inspired me to do my best and supported me in everything I have done. Regardless of my decisions, which have sometimes been poorly chosen, my mother has stood behind me all the way. When I decided I was ready to live independently, she asked some key questions to help me determine if I could handle the expenses alone or if I needed a roommate to split the costs. She always offered that same kind of wisdom when I needed guidance.

More than her advice, however, my mother's values have molded my life. She has always stressed being kind to other people, telling the truth, doing the right thing, going to church, and aiming for the top. Whenever I have been faced with a tough choice, I knew that I could rely on what she has taught me. For example, when I worked for a fast-food restaurant as a cashier, I discovered that the manager was changing employees' time cards and giving them fewer hours than they had actually worked. I had to decide what to do with what I had found out. After talking with my mother, I concluded that I had to inform the district manager about what I had found. Because the district manager did not reveal my identity, I was lucky that I did not lose my job, but I figured that I did the right thing. I know what I did made my mother proud. She has made me what I am.

SCORE = 3

I have to say that the most influential person in my life was my grandfather. When my parents divorced, I went to live with my grandparents for a while. As it turned out, I spent most of my childhood on their farm. My grandpa taught me so much about farming, of course, especially about the hard work required to succeed as a farmer. He also inspired me to realize that success is a personal thing. I don't have to make a lot of money or have an important job to be a success. My grandpa was a simple tobacco farmer who also raised vegetables. He showed me that working hard brings satisfaction, knowing that you have done a good job. I learned that as long as I do the best I can, I can be satisfied and proud of myself.

Besides working hard on the farm, Grandpa was a man who looked out for his neighbors. When his friend on a nearby farm was in the hospital for a long time, my grandpa cut the man's tobacco and spiked it for the firing process. Both of these jobs are hot and dirty work, but Grandpa knew if they were not done, the man's crop would be lost. He didn't want or expect any payment because he figured he was just doing what he hoped someone would do for him. I admire him for his dedication, hard work, and compassion for others, and I'm happy to be his grandson. He is the person who influenced my life the most even though I don't plan to be a tobacco farmer, too.

SCORE = 2

The most influenccal person in my life has been my pastor. Since I am a member of a small church, I know all of the church members. And they all know me so I wasn't surprised when the pastor came to my house to visit with me and my family He said that he wanted to make sure that I had the right kind of raising to become a strong man with good values. After that visit I went to church more often and I got involved in more church activities. Such as youth fellowship, prayer meeting, Bible study, and Meals-on-Wheels. I found out that I could be a positive force in my church and my community due to my pastor's encouragement and support.

He has been a powerful inspiration to me. Inspiring me to do my best and to try new things has lead me to take this GED test in hopes that I can get a better job. I want to give back to my church and to my community. I am a Big Brother to a boy in a local foster home, and I try to encourage him the way my pastor did me. We go to places together on Saturday and we do things together to. Last week we went bowling and then to the new public library where we both got library cards and checked out some books. Even though we aren't big readers we want to try harder. My pastor is proud.

SCORE = 1

The most influential person in my life is my brother. He has taken care of me since our folks died. And he has always tried to do the best he can. Because he don't make a lot of money he has to be careful how he spends it. And he makes a budget every week to divide up the money. He has taught me how to handle money in this way.

He has taught me to work hard at my jobs and to try to do my best in everything. There's always something to do, my brother says, so just setting around and watching tv is no good way to spend your time. He has taught me how to do simple building tasks and repairs and to work on car engines which I enjoy.

I missed my parents when they died, but my brother has done his best to take there place. I love him for what he has done for me.

Practice Test 2

SOCIAL STUDIES

75 Minutes ❖ 50 Questions

Directions: The Social Studies test consists of multiple-choice questions intended to measure general social studies concepts. The questions are based on short readings that often include a graph, chart, or figure. Study the information given and then answer the question(s) following it. Refer to the information as often as necessary in answering the questions.

For Example:

Early colonists of North America looked for settlement sites that had adequate water supplies and were accessible by ship. For this reason, many early towns were built near

(1) mountains.
(2) prairies.
(3) rivers.
(4) glaciers.
(5) plateaus.

① ② ● ④ ⑤

The correct answer is "rivers"; therefore, answer space 3 would be marked on the answer sheet.

You should spend no more than 85 minutes answering the questions. Work carefully, but do not spend too much time on any one question. Be sure you answer every question. You will not be penalized for incorrect answers.

Do not mark in this test booklet. Record your answers on the separate answer sheet provided. Be sure all requested information is properly recorded on the answer sheet. To record your answers, mark the numbered space on the answer sheet beside the number that corresponds to the question in the test.

Do not rest the point of your pencil on the answer sheet while you are considering your answer. Make no stray or unnecessary marks. If you change an answer, erase your first mark completely. Mark only one answer space for each question; multiple answers will be scored as incorrect. Do not fold or crease your answer sheet.

Directions: Choose the one best answer for each item.

Items 1–6 refer to the following information.

The terms defined below are some basic terms of economics.

Balance of trade: the difference between the total values of the goods and services flowing into and out of a country in relation to a specific trading partner over a set period of time

Inflation: a general rise in the level of prices

Monopoly: control of the available supply of a specific product or service by a single producer or seller

National debt: the amount of money the federal government has borrowed over time as a result of expenditures in excess of its revenues

Profit: the difference between the total cost of making and marketing a product and the total revenue that it yields

1. The amount of money a publicly held company sometimes distributes to its shareholders usually comes from what source?

   (1) The national debt
   (2) Inflation
   (3) Profit
   (4) The balance of trade
   (5) A monopoly

2. In many years, Japanese businesses earn more money from American customers than American businesses earn from Japanese customers. This imbalance in Japan's favor describes what fact of American economic life today?

   (1) A rising national debt
   (2) Low inflation
   (3) High U.S. profits
   (4) An unfavorable balance of trade
   (5) An ineffectual monopoly

510

3. After World War I, defeated Germany saw its money become worthless. At one point, a person needed a wheelbarrow to carry all the currency required to purchase a single loaf of bread. In the early 1990s, the German government refused to lower the relatively high interest rate it paid to depositors. This policy negatively affected the economies of other nations in Europe and elsewhere, and many governments were very angry with the Germans. Nevertheless, the Germans continued the policy to protect themselves from the possibility of

(1) a large national debt.
(2) runaway inflation.
(3) lowered profitability.
(4) an unfavorable balance of trade.
(5) foreign monopolies.

4. The United States has laws to regulate monopolies. Some monopolies are forced to break up into several competing companies. Other monopolies—especially utilities, such as electric companies and gas companies—are allowed to operate but are carefully watched over by government officials. What is the advantage of allowing some monopolies to operate?

(1) Businesses are able to take advantage of certain economies of scale and distribution so that the general sale price to customers can be kept low.
(2) The government can control the basic supply of energy to citizens.
(3) Government bureaucrats can play a role in the daily lives of people.
(4) Businesses do not have to spend money on advertising and selling and can keep their costs to customers low.
(5) Some businesses can make large profits.

5. A company whose cost of production increased while the selling price of its products stayed the same would probably experience

(1) a favorable balance of trade.
(2) an unfavorable balance of trade.
(3) heightened profitability.
(4) lowered profitability.
(5) a monopoly.

6. Under communism, the government controlled the means of production. Which business goal did the Soviet Union say was bad and therefore illegal?

(1) Inflation
(2) Profit
(3) National debt
(4) Monopoly
(5) Balance of payments

Items 7–10 refer to the following circle graph.

IMMIGRATION TO THE UNITED STATES 1900–1910

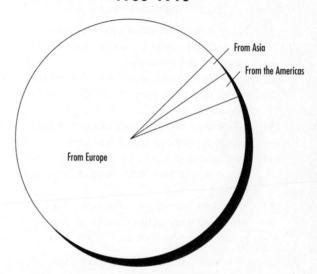

From Asia
From the Americas
From Europe

7. The period from the late 1800s to the early 1900s was a time of discrimination against people from Japan and China who wanted to immigrate to the United States. Which statement concerning the circle graph describes an effect of that discrimination?

(1) All of the immigrants to the United States came from Asia, the Americas, and Europe between 1900 and 1910.
(2) More immigrants came from Europe than from any other continent.
(3) According to the chart, no immigrants came from Africa or Australia.
(4) In the chart, "the Americas" refers to all those nations of the Western Hemisphere except the United States.
(5) Only a very small percentage of the total number of immigrants to the United States came from Asia, which includes China and Japan.

511

8. According to the graph, what percentage of the total number of immigrants came from Europe?

   (1) About 10 percent
   (2) About 30 percent
   (3) About 50 percent
   (4) About 70 percent
   (5) About 90 percent

9. The early 1900s were a time when most immigrants traveled by boat to the United States. European immigrants landed at and were processed through Ellis Island in New York Harbor. Asian immigrants landed at and were processed through Angel Island in San Francisco Harbor. Based on the information in the circle graph, which of the following statements is true?

   (1) Many more immigrants were processed through Ellis Island than through Angel Island in the early 1900s.
   (2) Asian immigrants were often forced to live at Angel Island for several months when they first arrived.
   (3) Ellis Island was the port of entry for passengers who did not travel first class.
   (4) Immigrants at both Ellis Island and Angel Island had to pass brief medical examinations.
   (5) Most immigrants from the rest of the Americas were refused entry to the United States between 1900 and 1910.

10. Racial tensions and the aftermath of the Civil War in the United States probably had what effect on immigration to the United States between 1900 and 1910?

   (1) They led to heavier immigration from Europe.
   (2) They led to virtually no immigration from Africa.
   (3) They caused Asian immigrants to reconsider their decisions to move to the United States.
   (4) They made available to immigrants from the Americas places for legal immigration to the United States.
   (5) They caused the United States to follow the foreign policy of isolationism.

Items 11–13 refer to the following map.

TIME ZONES IN THE CONTINENTAL UNITED STATES

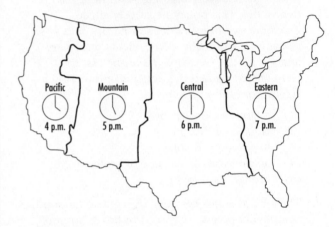

11. When it is 1:00 p.m. in San Francisco, what time is it in New York City?

   (1) 2 p.m.
   (2) 3 p.m.
   (3) 4 p.m.
   (4) 1 p.m.
   (5) 1 a.m.

12. A government worker in Washington, DC, has to make a phone call to a Portland, Oregon, business that opens at 9:00 a.m. What is the earliest time in Washington, DC, that the government worker can reach the Portland business?

   (1) 9 a.m.
   (2) 10 a.m.
   (3) 9 p.m.
   (4) 8 a.m.
   (5) Noon

13. Time zones came into use in the United States in the late 1800s. What event or invention was the greatest cause of this innovation?

   (1) The end of the Civil War
   (2) The completion of the transcontinental railroad
   (3) The widespread use of tin cans for preserving food
   (4) The inauguration of the Pony Express
   (5) The growth in the number of European immigrants to the United States

Items 14–16 refer to the following information and graph.

PROFITS FOR GARCIA'S GOODIES

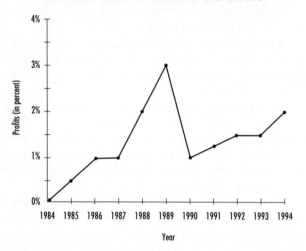

Mr. Antonio Garcia owns Garcia's Goodies, a gourmet grocery store he started in 1984. The line graph above shows the after-tax profits the store generated in each year of the first decade the store was in business.

14. According to the line graph, the year of highest profits was

(1) 1984.
(2) 1987.
(3) 1989.
(4) 1993.
(5) 1990.

15. When profits fell in 1990, Mr. Garcia could have successfully rectified the situation by

(1) reducing the number of full-time store employees.
(2) getting a large loan from a nearby bank.
(3) asking some of the store's managers to take long paid vacations.
(4) giving cost-of-living salary increases to minimum-wage employees only.
(5) working with owners of similar, nearby stores to raise prices on most items.

16. In which year did Mr. Garcia probably hire the most employees?

(1) 1986
(2) 1984
(3) 1989
(4) 1991
(5) 1993

Items 17 and 18 refer to the following illustration.

LATITUDE AND LONGITUDE

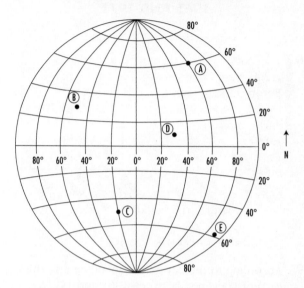

17. According to the illustration, which of the lettered points is found at 50 degrees south latitude and 20 degrees west longitude?

(1) A
(2) B
(3) C
(4) D
(5) E

18. What direction is point B from point D?

(1) West northwest
(2) East southeast
(3) East northeast
(4) West southwest
(5) South

Items 19 and 20 refer to the following bar graph.

FEDERAL SPENDING ON EDUCATION 1965 AND 1971

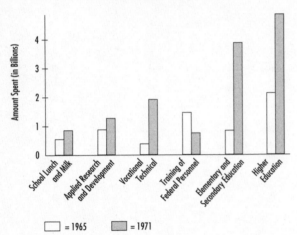

☐ = 1965   ▨ = 1971

19. According to the bar graph, spending for which category declined between 1965 and 1971?

   (1) School lunch and milk
   (2) Applied research and development
   (3) Vocational technical
   (4) Training of federal personnel
   (5) Elementary and secondary education

20. Which of the following statements can be verified by information in the graph?

   (1) The federal government spent a relatively small amount of its funds on education in both 1965 and 1971.
   (2) The food served in most school lunch rooms did not adequately meet federal nutrition guidelines.
   (3) Applied research and development was a relatively small part of the overall education budget in both 1965 and 1971.
   (4) In 1971, most Americans believed federal funds for education were not being wisely spent.
   (5) The number of Americans in college included a greater percentage of African Americans in 1971 than in 1965.

Items 21–24 refer to the following information.

Listed below are five major present-day forms of government.

   Aristocracy: government in which a small, privileged, hereditary group governs

   Constitutional monarchy: government in which the real power is held by an elected parliament or congress but documents recognize a hereditary ceremonial king or queen

   Dictatorship: government in which an individual and a small, trusted group of followers have all the power, usually to the detriment of the majority of citizens

   Direct democracy: government in which all eligible citizens are entitled to participate in the process of making laws and setting policy

   Representative democracy: government in which freely elected representatives of the great mass of citizens make laws and set policy

21. In Iraq, Saddam Hussein ruled what type of government?

   (1) Aristocracy
   (2) Constitutional monarchy
   (3) Dictatorship
   (4) Direct democracy
   (5) Representative democracy

22. Queen Elizabeth II of Great Britain and Northern Ireland is the head of a(n)

   (1) aristocracy.
   (2) constitutional monarchy.
   (3) dictatorship.
   (4) direct democracy.
   (5) representative democracy.

23. Although many others would disagree, the Irish Republican Army would probably describe the government of Northern Ireland as a(n)

   (1) aristocracy.
   (2) constitutional monarchy.
   (3) dictatorship.
   (4) direct democracy.
   (5) representative democracy.

24. People in the United States tend to oppose dictatorships because

    (1) most Americans have a basic belief in the rights of all people to have a say in their government.
    (2) most known dictatorships have operated to the detriment of the majority of their citizens.
    (3) most people in the United States know little about forms of government other than democracy.
    (4) dictatorships often deny equal trading rights in their nations to U.S. companies.
    (5) the United States has never been governed by a dictatorship.

Items 25–27 refer to the following information.

Violence has become a major concern of many Americans in the 1990s. This violence includes child abuse, spousal abuse, random shootings, assaults, and abuse of the elderly.

25. A member of a child welfare league would probably be most involved with finding solutions to which type of violence?

    (1) Child abuse
    (2) Spousal abuse
    (3) Abuse of the elderly
    (4) Random shootings
    (5) Assaults

26. A member of the American Association of Retired Persons would probably be most involved in finding solutions to which type of violence?

    (1) Child abuse
    (2) Spousal abuse
    (3) Abuse of the elderly
    (4) Random shootings
    (5) Assaults

27. Street gangs are most often associated with which type of criminal activity?

    (1) Anti-Semitic hate crimes
    (2) Thefts of information from computer systems
    (3) Retaliatory shootings
    (4) Rape
    (5) Credit card forgeries

Items 28–31 refer to the following map.

EXPANSION OF THE CONTINENTAL UNITED STATES

28. According to the map, the last part of the continental United States that was added was

    (1) the Louisiana Purchase.
    (2) the Mexican Cession.
    (3) Oregon Country.
    (4) the Gadsden Purchase.
    (5) Florida.

29. The Mexican War of 1846-1848 was ended by the Treaty of Guadalupe Hidalgo, which gave what large area of land to the United States?

    (1) The Louisiana Purchase
    (2) The Mexican Cession
    (3) Oregon Country
    (4) The Gadsden Purchase
    (5) Florida

30. The Louisiana Purchase was made during the presidency of which of the following men?

    (1) George Washington (1789-1797)
    (2) Millard Fillmore (1850-1853)
    (3) Thomas Jefferson (1801-1809)
    (4) James Polk (1845-1849)
    (5) Franklin Pierce (1853-1857)

515

31. Which sentence is the best summary of the map's content?

    (1) Texas was annexed before the Gadsden Purchase was made.

    (2) The Louisiana Purchase extended from the Gulf of Mexico to the Canadian border.

    (3) At the time of the Constitutional Convention, the territory of the United States was all east of the Mississippi River.

    (4) The Oregon Country is north and west of the Louisiana Purchase.

    (5) The expansion of the continental United States was made up of adjoining pieces of land that were added during the nineteenth century.

> Items 32 and 33 refer to the following information.

When the United States entered World War I in 1917, President Woodrow Wilson said, "The world must be made safe for democracy. Its peace must be planted upon the tested foundations of political liberty." Later he said, "The Americans who went to Europe . . . in World War I . . . . to die are a unique breed. Never before have men crossed seas to a foreign land to fight for a cause which they did not pretend was particularly their own, which they knew was the cause of humanity and mankind."

32. Of the following statements regarding potential U.S. courses of action in the early 1990s, which might Wilson have most strongly supported?

    (1) The United States should intervene militarily in the former Yugoslavia to stop the bloodshed there.

    (2) The United States should prevent the nations of Eastern Europe from joining NATO because such a situation could cause alarm in Russia.

    (3) The United States should launch surprise attacks against North Korea and Iraq to eliminate their dictatorial governments.

    (4) The United States should encourage the growth of economic groups like the European Common Market and the North American Free Trade Association.

    (5) The United States should ignore foreign affairs as much as possible and spend more of its funds and time on domestic affairs.

33. Which of the following beliefs or actions of Woodrow Wilson was consistent with his speeches about making the world safe for democracy?

    (1) His belief in white supremacy

    (2) His belief that God had foreordained him to be president of the United States

    (3) His eight-year tenure as president of Princeton University

    (4) His appointment of Louis D. Brandeis to be the first Jewish justice of the Supreme Court

    (5) His strong support for the League of Nations and U.S. participation in it

34. Which list below places the events of twentieth-century America in the correct chronological order?

    (1) The Roaring Twenties, the Great Depression, World War II, the assassination of John F. Kennedy, the Watergate scandal

    (2) The Great Depression, the assassination of John F. Kennedy, World War II, the Watergate scandal, the Roaring Twenties

    (3) World War II, the Watergate scandal, the Great Depression, the assassination of John F. Kennedy, the Roaring Twenties

    (4) The Watergate scandal, the assassination of John F. Kennedy, World War II, the Roaring Twenties, the Great Depression

    (5) The assassination of John F. Kennedy, World War II, the Great Depression, the Roaring Twenties, the Watergate scandal

35. Which of the following situations was not an outcome of World War I?

    (1) A drop in immigration from Italy, Austria-Hungary, and Russia to the United States between 1910 and 1920

    (2) The influenza epidemic of 1918

    (3) The creation of the American Expeditionary Force to Europe

    (4) The Treaty of Versailles

    (5) The League of Nations

Items 36 and 37 refer to the following information.

Clinical depression is a treatable, medical illness. Many Americans get the treatment they need. However, elderly people often fail to seek treatment even though statistically the elderly are more likely to suffer from clinical depression than any other age group in America.

36. Which choice would not be a reasonable cause of this low level of treatment among the elderly?

(1) They are of a generation that views depression not as an illness but as a symptom of weakness or laziness.

(2) They are already suffering from other illnesses, such as diabetes, heart disease, and kidney and liver disease, that sometimes alter the brain chemistry and set off depression.

(3) They are often taking numerous medications that may precipitate depression.

(4) They are in the age group most likely to develop other diseases, such as Alzheimer's, that may cause symptoms similar to depression and thus lead to misdiagnosis.

(5) They often lead such busy lives that it is difficult for them to find time to get a thorough diagnosis.

37. Someone who suspects that he or she may be suffering from clinical depression would do best to seek advice from a(n)

(1) friend who may also have the disease.

(2) X-ray technician.

(3) doctor.

(4) close relative.

(5) psychologist.

Item 38 refers to the following cartoon.

A WIDELY HELD VIEW OF AMERICAN TROOPS IN FOREIGN LANDS

38. Which statement is the best summary of the meaning of this 1993 cartoon?

(1) American troops are often not as well trained as their foreign enemies.

(2) American troops are often too lightly armed when they go into combat.

(3) Saddam Hussein failed to defeat America and its allies in the Gulf War.

(4) American troops often become targets themselves when they try to settle conflicts between two foreign adversaries.

(5) American troops are better at fighting wars at home than they are at fighting wars abroad.

Items 39–43 refer to the following information.

Below are some highlights of former President Herbert Hoover's career:

• He created the Wickersham Commission (in 1929), which concluded that Prohibition was a failure but nevertheless opposed its repeal.

• He signed into law the Smoot-Hawley Tariff, which set off a global trade war.

• He headed, at the end of World War I, the American Relief Administration, which distributed $5.2 billion in aid to Europe.

• He established the Hoover Institution on War, Revolution, and Peace at Stanford University.

• He ordered the clearing by force in 1932 of the Washington, DC, camp of the Bonus Army, which consisted of needy World War I veterans who came to the capital to seek early payment of a bonus Congress had promised them.

39. Which event in Hoover's career contributed to his sometimes being called the Great Humanitarian?

  (1) The Wickersham Commission
  (2) The Smoot-Hawley Tariff
  (3) The American Relief Administration
  (4) The Hoover Institution
  (5) The Bonus Army

40. Which situation showed Hoover's lack of understanding of the suffering of individuals during the Great Depression?

  (1) The Wickersham Commission
  (2) The Smoot-Hawley Tariff
  (3) The American Relief Administration
  (4) The Hoover Institution
  (5) The Bonus Army

41. At the end of World War II, President Harry S. Truman appointed Hoover as coordinator of Food Supply for World Famine. Which of Hoover's earlier experiences gave him the qualifications to head this group to alleviate world suffering?

  (1) The Wickersham Commission
  (2) The Smoot-Hawley Tariff
  (3) The American Relief Administration
  (4) The Hoover Institution
  (5) The Bonus Army

42. In 1917, Hoover said, "War is a losing business. . . . Its greatest compensation lies in the possibility that we may instill into our people unselfishness."

Which part of Hoover's own career might he have pointed to as an example of this unselfishness?

  (1) The Wickersham Commission
  (2) The Smoot-Hawley Tariff
  (3) The American Relief Administration
  (4) The Hoover Institution
  (5) The Bonus Army

43. In 1920, Franklin Roosevelt said of Hoover, "He is certainly a wonder and I wish we could make him president of the United States. There could not be a better one." However, in 1932 Roosevelt said, "I accuse the present [Hoover] administration [of having failed] to anticipate the dire needs of and the reduced earning power of the people." What may so drastically have changed Franklin Roosevelt's opinion of Hoover?

  (1) The fact that Roosevelt had contracted polio and had permanent paralysis in his legs by 1932
  (2) The fact that Roosevelt was running for president in 1932 against Hoover, the incumbent
  (3) The fact that both Hoover and Roosevelt had served in the administrations of previous presidents
  (4) The fact that Hoover was often associated with California whereas Roosevelt was associated with New York
  (5) The fact that Hoover opposed U.S. entry into World War II until after the Japanese attack on Pearl Harbor

---

Items 44–47 refer to the following information.

The World's Columbian Exposition was held in Chicago from May through October, 1893. It was held to celebrate (one year late) the 400th anniversary of Columbus's crossing of the Atlantic Ocean and to honor the progress of American civilization. Some facts concerning the fair are listed below.

- Some 28 million people visited the fair.

- Adults paid an entry fee of $0.50, a high price for the time.

- Nicknamed the White City, the fair's buildings were sheathed in a lightweight mixture of plaster, cement, and white paint.

- The fair had some 3,500 flush toilets, a new invention that, at the time, most fairgoers had never seen before.

- The world's first Ferris wheel (named for its inventor, George Washington Gale Ferris), which had thirty-six cars that could carry forty people each, was a highlight of the amusements.

- Countries that had their own official "government" buildings at the fair included Brazil, Canada, Ceylon, Colombia, France, Germany, Great Britain, Haiti, Japan, Norway, Siam, Spain, Sweden, Turkey, and Venezuela.

- The fair was illuminated by electric lights, which were first turned on by U.S. President Grover Cleveland when he tapped a gold-plated telegraph key.

- Speakers at the fair included feminist Susan B. Anthony, social reformer Ida B. Wells, politicians Theodore Roosevelt and Woodrow Wilson, historian Frederick Jackson Turner, scientist Booker T. Washington, African-American leader Frederick Douglass, and poet Paul Laurence Dunbar.

- The amusements included a toboggan ride, an exotic dancer known as Little Egypt, and ethnic villages from India, Java, Ireland, Lapland, Austria, and Turkey.

44. According to the passage, the greatest number of countries having official government buildings were from

   (1)   Asia.
   (2)   South America.
   (3)   Europe.
   (4)   North America.
   (5)   the Caribbean.

45. On the opening day of the fair, social reformer Jane Addams had her purse snatched, and on American Cities Day, October 28, Chicago mayor Carter Harrison, the day's triumphant host, was shot and killed by a deranged job seeker. What do these two events say about America of the late nineteenth century when compared to America of the early twenty-first century?

   (1)   American officials and notables have long received poor protection from their security forces.
   (2)   Criminals often prey on unsuspecting women.
   (3)   America has long been a violent society.
   (4)   America is more violent in the early twenty-first century than it was in the late nineteenth century.
   (5)   America was more violent in the late nineteenth century than it is now.

46. One way the Columbian Exposition honored American civilization was by

   (1)   the erection of ethnic villages.
   (2)   the fair's being nicknamed the White City.
   (3)   the great number of official "government" buildings.
   (4)   having the President of the United States open the fair.
   (5)   the inclusion of technological wonders of the times, such as the Ferris wheel, electric lights, and flush toilets.

47. One of the following statements is a conclusion about the Columbian Exposition. All of the others are supporting statements. Which one is the conclusion?

   (1)   The Columbian Exposition brought together a wide spectrum of nineteenth-century peoples, cultures, and technology to be seen by millions of Americans and others.
   (2)   Some 28 million people visited the fair over its six-month run in 1893, during which the fair took in almost $32 million in entrance and other fees.
   (3)   The 60 nations represented at the fair included Austria, Brazil, Ceylon, Germany, Haiti, Norway, Siam, and Venezuela.
   (4)   Many dignitaries visited the fair, and some—like Roosevelt, Wilson, Douglass, and Wells—spoke there also.
   (5)   Technology highlighted the fair with such novelties of the times as a Ferris wheel, flush toilets, and electric lights.

Items 48 and 49 refer to the following cartoon.

The NORTH ATLANTIC TEA and ORIGAMI Society

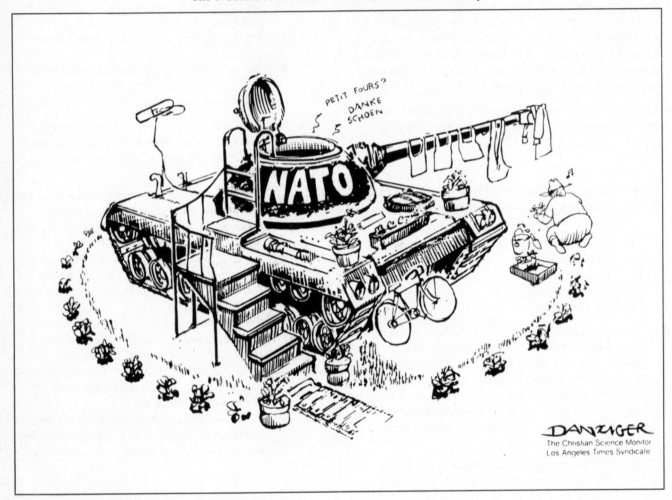

48. Which statement is the best summary of this 1990 cartoon's meaning?

   (1) NATO has become too involved in Japanese affairs.
   (2) NATO is not a well-managed organization.
   (3) NATO has become ineffectual since the fall of communism.
   (4) NATO needs to undertake joint training exercises with the former communist countries of Eastern Europe.
   (5) NATO was a better organization when it had a strong adversary.

49. With which of the following statements would the cartoonist probably most agree?

   (1) NATO needs a powerful enemy to be strong itself.
   (2) France needs to rejoin NATO before the organization can become strong again.
   (3) NATO has never been a useful organization for the United States to be a part of, and it never will be.
   (4) NATO should become a worldwide security group.
   (5) NATO's benefit to the West has ended, and it should be disbanded.

Item 50 refers to the following cartoon.

50. Which choice best summarizes the cartoonist's point?

(1) Poverty, drugs, and ignorance are root causes of gangs.

(2) Gangs are the root cause of poverty, drugs, and ignorance.

(3) Experts agree that poverty, drugs, and gangs are the major causes of ignorance.

(4) Drugs are the major cause of gang violence.

(5) Few people believe that poverty, drugs, and ignorance are root causes of gangs.

Practice Test 3

SCIENCE

85 Minutes ❖ **50 Questions**

Directions: The Science test consists of multiple-choice questions intended to measure the general concepts in science. The questions are based on short readings that often include a graph, chart, or figure. Study the information given and then answer the question(s) that follow. Refer to the information as often as necessary in answering the questions.

For Example:

Which of the following is the smallest unit in a living thing?

(1) Tissue
(2) Organ
(3) Cell
(4) Muscle
(5) Capillary

The correct answer is "Cell"; therefore, answer space 3 would be marked on the answer sheet.

You should spend no more than 85 minutes answering the questions in this booklet. Work carefully, but do not spend too much time on any one question. Be sure you answer every question. You will not be penalized for incorrect answers.

Do not mark in this test booklet. Record your answers to the questions on the separate answer sheet provided. Be sure all requested information is properly recorded on the answer sheet.

To record your answers, mark the numbered space on the answer sheet beside the number that corresponds to the question in the test booklet.

Do not rest the point of your pencil on the answer sheet while you are considering your answer. Make no stray or unnecessary marks. If you change an answer, erase your first mark completely. Mark only one answer space for each question; multiple answers will be scored as incorrect. Do not fold or crease your answer sheet.

Directions: Choose the one best answer for each item.

1. Which of the following represents the balanced equation for the following reaction?

   iron plus oxygen yields iron(II) oxide

   (1) $Fe + O \rightarrow FeO$
   (2) $2Fe + O_2 \rightarrow 2FeO$
   (3) $Fe + O_2 \rightarrow 2FeO$
   (4) $4Fe + 3O_2 \rightarrow 2Fe_2O_3$
   (5) $2Fe + 2O_2 \rightarrow Fe_2O_2$

2. What is the density of a piece of metal that displaces 50ml of water and weighs 75g?

   (1) 50ml/g
   (2) 0.67ml/g
   (3) 75g/ml
   (4) 1.5g/ml
   (5) 75g

Item 3 refers to the following illustration.

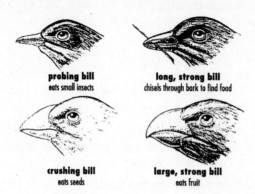

probing bill
eats small insects

long, strong bill
chisels through bark to find food

crushing bill
eats seeds

large, strong bill
eats fruit

3. Darwin observed several types of finches with different shapes and sizes of beaks on different islands in the Galapagos. Which of the following is the best explanation for the variance?

   (1) The different beaks allowed certain birds to capture more food than other birds.
   (2) Some birds born to one set of parents may forage for fruits, while others born to the same parents may forage for small insects.
   (3) When there is abundant rain and many fruits, the birds with large, strong bills will enjoy a reproductive success rate greater than those that find food using sticks.
   (4) Over time, beak shapes in the population diverged, with different beak types found on birds that depended on different food sources.
   (5) Only the strong survive.

4. Which of the following best summarizes the theory of natural selection?

   (1) All organisms are descended from prokaryotes.
   (2) Some organisms are better suited to the environment and produce more offspring.
   (3) Characteristics gained by the parents are passed directly to the offspring.
   (4) Some species are bound to go extinct.
   (5) Natural selection can be summed up in the phrase "survival of the fittest."

5. If 9 percent of all squirrels exhibit the homozygous recessive condition of curly fur, what is the gene frequency for that allele in the general population?

   (1) 0.90
   (2) 0.91
   (3) 0.09
   (4) 0.30
   (5) 0.03

6. In a very woody plant stem, which of the following tissues would be the most abundant?

   (1) Spongy mesophyll
   (2) Pallisade mesophyll
   (3) Phloem
   (4) Xylem
   (5) Cuticle

7. Which hormone causes the uptake of glucose and, therefore, lowers blood sugar?

   (1) Parathyroid hormone
   (2) Thyroid hormone
   (3) Thyroxin
   (4) Glucagon
   (5) Insulin

Items 8 and 9 refer to the following passage.

Establishing the exact age of geologic strata (rock layers) is difficult. Geologic processes can upset the original configuration of the rock layers. Index fossils can be helpful in establishing the age of a specific rock layer. Index fossils are fossils of organisms that were widely distributed geographically but were abundant for only a short period. Therefore, index fossils allow scientists to date a rock layer accurately. When index fossils are unavailable, geologists sometimes look for a particular mix of fossils that is known to have existed for only a short period.

8. Why are index fossils helpful in dating geologic strata?

   (1) The organism represented by the fossils lived for only a short period.
   (2) Sediments in the fossils are specifically helpful in dating the surrounding rock.
   (3) The sediments surrounding index fossils are unique.
   (4) Index fossil distribution is geographically specific.
   (5) Index fossils are found in association with many other types of fossils.

9. A geologist discovers a new fossil in a rock layer containing fossils of organisms known to have co-existed for about 50 million years. Based on this evidence, which of the following statements is incorrect?

   (1) Organisms based on all of the fossils lived at the same time.
   (2) The absolute age of the new fossil is unknown.
   (3) The species of organism represented by the new fossil existed for at long as 50 million years.
   (4) The organism represented by the new fossil probably evolved from the organisms represented by the new fossils.
   (5) The organisms represented by the fossils were not competing for the same food sources.

Items 10–12 refer to the following information.

A lever is a bar or rod that tilts on a fulcrum, or pivot. When you apply a force at one point on a lever, the lever tilts on the fulcrum to provide a force at another point. The force you apply is the effort, and the weight moved or resistance overcome is called the load. The effort times its distance from the fulcrum equals the load times its distance from the fulcrum.

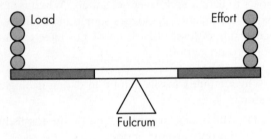

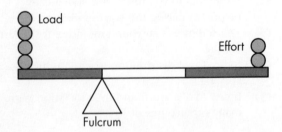

10. What would be the effect of moving the fulcrum from the center toward the effort?

    (1) The effort required to raise the load would decrease.
    (2) The effort required to raise the load would increase.
    (3) The weight of the load would increase.
    (4) The weight of the load would decrease.
    (5) The load and the effort would be equal.

11. The levers illustrated are first-class levers, in which the fulcrum is positioned between the load and the effort. In a second-class lever, the fulcrum is at one end, the effort is at the other, and the load is in the middle. Which of the following is a second-class lever?

    (1) A balance scale
    (2) A crowbar
    (3) The claw end of a hammer
    (4) A seesaw
    (5) A nutcracker

12. Which of the following statements is supported by the information given?

    (1) A fishing rod is a type of third-class lever in which one hand functions as the fulcrum and the other as the effort.
    (2) In a first-class lever, the farther the distance between the effort and the fulcrum, the less effort is needed to move a load.
    (3) The load and the effort are always equal in a first-class lever.
    (4) The greater the load, the less effort is required to move it.
    (5) All first-class levers have fulcrums equally distant from the load and the effort.

Items 13–15 refer to the following diagram.

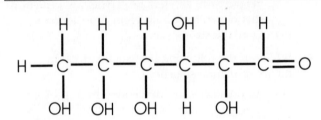

13. Which of the following types of compounds is illustrated above?

    (1) Protein
    (2) Lipid
    (3) Carbohydrate
    (4) Nucleic acid
    (5) Enzyme

14. How many oxygen atoms are there in each molecule of this compound?

    (1) 0
    (2) 2
    (3) 5
    (4) 6
    (5) 12

15. If two of the above molecules were combined in the body, what molecule would be formed?

   (1) Disaccharide
   (2) Water
   (3) Polypeptide
   (4) ATP
   (5) Glycerol

16. One volt of electricity is equal to 0.001 kilovolt. To convert volts to kilovolts, you should take the number of volts and

   (1) divide by 1,000.
   (2) divide by 100.
   (3) divide by 10.
   (4) multiply by 100.
   (5) multiply by 1,000.

17. George Ohm was a mathematician who studied electrical resistance. Ohm's law describes the following relationship among current, voltage, and resistance.

$$\text{current} = \frac{\text{voltage}}{\text{resistance}}$$

According to Ohm's law, what would happen if the resistance in a circuit remained the same and the voltage decreased?

   (1) The amount of current would remain constant.
   (2) The amount of current would increase.
   (3) The amount of current would decrease.
   (4) The circuit could not function.
   (5) The current would change direction.

18. When blood is pumped out of the left ventricle of the heart, it next goes to the

   (1) right pulmonary vein.
   (2) left pulmonary vein.
   (3) right pulmonary artery.
   (4) left pulmonary artery.
   (5) aorta.

Items 19 and 20 refer to the following illustration, which shows snacks consumed among U.S. children.

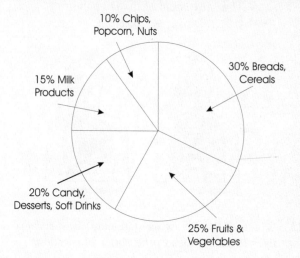

19. What percentage of snacks are derived from grains?

   (1) 10%
   (2) 15%
   (3) 20%
   (4) 30%
   (5) More than 30%

20. Which of the following snacks have the least nutritional value?

   (1) Chips, popcorn, and nuts
   (2) Milk products
   (3) Candy, desserts, and soft drinks
   (4) Fruits and vegetables
   (5) Breads and cereals

21. If there are 100 centimeters in a meter, 1,000 meters in a kilometer, and 1,000 millimeters in a meter, how many millimeters are in a kilometer?

   (1) 100
   (2) 1,000
   (3) 10,000
   (4) 100,000
   (5) 1,000,000

The Movement of the Diaphragm
During Respiration

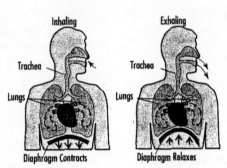

22. Which of the following statements best summarizes the main idea in the above illustration?

    (1) The diaphragm is posterior to the lungs.
    (2) The lungs are shaped like footballs.
    (3) When the diaphragm contracts, the volume of the chest cavity increases.
    (4) When the diaphragm contracts, the pressure on the lungs increases.
    (5) The organs in the respiratory system include the lungs and diaphragm.

23. Static electricity can be produced by rubbing two objects against each other, which transfers electrons from one object to another. Materials charged with static electricity attract each other if they have opposite electrical charges (positive and negative) and repel each other if they have like electrical charges (negative and negative). Stroking a piece of hard rubber with fur gives the rubber a negative charge and the fur a positive charge. Which of the following statements best explains how this happens?

    (1) The rubber gives up some electrons to the fur.
    (2) The fur gives up some electrons to the rubber.
    (3) The rubber gives up some protons to the fur.
    (4) The fur gives up some protons to the rubber.
    (5) The fur gives up some neutrons to the rubber.

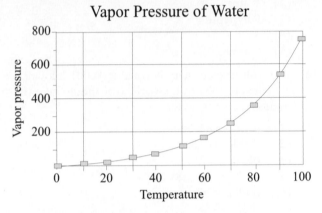

24. If the liquid water and the water vapor are in an equilibrium at 100°, which statement is correct?

    (1) There will be more water molecules leaving the liquid phase than entering it.
    (2) The water will be gone.
    (3) More water will be leaving during the vapor phase than during the liquid phase.
    (4) The pressure will be 760 mm Hg.
    (5) Fewer water molecules will be leaving during the liquid phase than entering.

$$2KClO_3 \rightarrow 2KCl + 3O_2$$

The molar mass of K is 39.1, Cl is 35.4, and O is 16.

25. If you had 60 grams of $KClO_3$, how much KCl could you expect to have upon completion of the reaction?

    (1) 0.61g
    (2) 1.64g
    (3) 16.4g
    (4) 36.5g
    (5) 48.0g

Item 26 refers to the following information.

The pH scale measures the concentration of an acid or base. Acids have a pH value less than 7. Bases, which have the ability to neutralize acids, have pH values of greater than 7. Neutralization reactions create salts. The pH scale, like the Richter scale, is logarithmic. Water is considered neutral and has pH of 7. The chart below lists the pH levels of several substances.

Substance	pH
Lime	1.9
Grapefruit juice	3.5
Human blood	7.5
Seawater	8.2
Magnesium hydroxide	10.5
Lye	13

26. The best substance to use to neutralize magnesium hydroxide would be

(1) 100 ml of seawater.
(2) 100 ml of lye.
(3) 100 ml of blood.
(4) 100 ml of grapefruit juice.
(5) 50 ml of lime.

Items 27–29 refer to the following illustration.

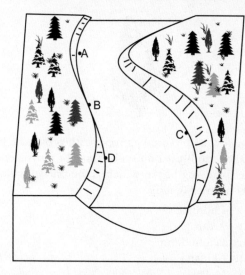

27. Based on the diagram, which of the following sediments is least likely to be carried in suspension when the stream passes point D?

(1) Clay
(2) Silt
(3) Sand
(4) Gravel
(5) Mud

28. At which point in the diagram would the deposition rate exceed the erosion rate?

(1) A
(2) B
(3) C
(4) D
(5) E

29. Note the erosion at point D in the diagram. This section of the riverbank would be least likely to be composed of

(1) uncompacted soil.
(2) sand.
(3) limestone.
(4) granite.
(5) sandstone.

30. Which of the following is the most pressing environmental problem today?

(1) The greenhouse effect
(2) Human population growth
(3) Habitat destruction
(4) Dependence on finite oil reserves
(5) Pollution

Item 31 refers to the following illustration.

31. The animal pictured above breathes by gills, has a mantle, and has a muscular foot for movement. Of the following phyla, which is the one to which it has been assigned?

(1) Chordate
(2) Arthropod
(3) Echinoderm
(4) Cnidaria
(5) Mollusk

32. A scientist conducts an experiment in which she varies the temperature and measures an organism's response. Which of the following statements about this experimental design is correct?

(1) The temperature is the independent variable, and the response is the dependent variable.
(2) The response is the independent variable, and the dependent variable should be controlled.
(3) The temperature is the independent variable, and the dependent variable should be controlled.
(4) The environmental variable should be the control, and the dependent variable is recorded as a response to that.
(5) One can determine the independent variable by seeing the control.

33. In order to be classified as a chordate, an organism must have which of the following at some time in its existence?

(1) Hair
(2) Mammary glands
(3) Teeth
(4) Pharyngeal gill slits
(5) Ventral nerve chord

34. The endosymbiotic theory proposed by Lynn Margulis argues that

(1) mitochondria are the descendants of prokaryotes.
(2) chloroplasts are the descendants of prokaryotes.
(3) mitochondria have DNA like that of prokaryotes.
(4) mitochondria reproduce on their own schedule.
(5) All of the above

35. Assume that there are 2 kilocalories in a peanut. If a student ignited the peanut and it all burned, how many grams of water could she heat 20°C?

(1) 1
(2) 10
(3) 20
(4) 100
(5) 200

36. Electricity ordinarily travels the shortest path between two points. A short circuit occurs when electricity takes the shortest path through an appliance and cuts out part of its intended route through a planned electrical circuit. Which of the following statements best explains why insulation can prevent a short circuit?

(1) Insulation prevents electricity from leaving its intended path.
(2) Insulation directs electricity in two directions at one time.
(3) Most appliances do not have insulation on their power cords.
(4) Insulation can cause static electricity to rest on the surface of an appliance.
(5) Insulation is a good conductor of electricity.

37. Because light is a wave, it does not strictly travel in straight lines. Waves are subject to diffraction, which means that they can bend around obstacles. This is shown in the figure below, where light rays near an obstacle are bent into the region behind the obstacle that would be considered the obstacle's shadow.

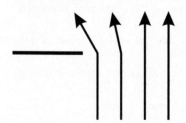

According to the wave theory of light, which statement is correct?

(1) Objects have distinct shadows.
(2) Some light shines in the geometrical shadow region.
(3) Light rays do not bend.
(4) Light cannot penetrate obstacles.
(5) Waves travel in straight lines.

Items 38–40 refer to the following illustration.

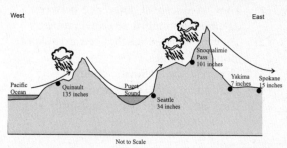

The diagram illustrates the concept of a rain shadow. The numbers given represent average annual precipitation for various locations in the state of Washington.

38. What is the best explanation for the differences in precipitation shown?

(1) It always rains more on the west side of a mountain range.
(2) The winds in the region blow north to south and block the eastward progress of the moisture.
(3) The region surrounding Yakima has always been arid.
(4) There is a dramatic difference in ambient temperature between the windward and leeward sides of the mountains
(5) By the time the winds reach the leeward side of the mountains, little moisture is left in the air.

39. Which of the following statements is not a reason for the high annual rainfall in the Cascade Mountains?

(1) The Cascade Mountains are near the Pacific Ocean.
(2) Mountains often produce unstable weather and copious rain.
(3) The Cascades act as a physical barrier and hold unstable air and storms on the windward side of the mountains.
(4) Canadian winds bring Alaskan moisture south through mountain passes.
(5) Rapid cooling in high elevations decreases the ability of the air masses to hold water vapor.

40. Yakima and Spokane are both located in a rain shadow desert. Which of the following factors are primarily responsible for this desert?

   (1) They have a small difference between daytime and nighttime temperatures.
   (2) They are located on the leeward side of mountain ranges.
   (3) They have arid climatic conditions.
   (4) They are at similar latitudes.
   (5) They are far from ocean moisture.

Item 41 refers to the following illustration.

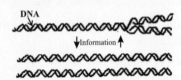

41. The above diagram is an illustration of

   (1) transcription.
   (2) translation.
   (3) replication.
   (4) transcription and translation.
   (5) translation and replication.

42. When did dinosaurs become extinct?

   (1) About 2.5 billion years ago
   (2) About 250 million years ago
   (3) About 60 million years ago
   (4) About 6 million years ago
   (5) About 25,000 years ago

43. Which of the following lists the steps in metamorphosis in the correct order?

   (1) Egg, nymph, pupa, adult
   (2) Egg, larva, pupa, adult
   (3) Egg, pupa, larva, adult
   (4) Egg, larva, nymph, adult
   (5) Egg, pupa, nymph, adult

44. If a strand of DNA read GGC AAT, what would the complementary strand of RNA read?

   (1) GGC UUT
   (2) AAT GGC
   (3) TTA CCU
   (4) CCG UUA
   (5) CCU TTA

45. The speed of sound in a gas depends on the temperature and molecular weight of the gas. Higher temperature or smaller mass results in greater speed. Which of the following will result in a lower speed of sound?

   (1) Increase in temperature and molecular weight
   (2) Decrease in temperature and molecular weight
   (3) Increase in weight and decrease in temperature
   (4) Decrease in weight and increase in temperature
   (5) Decrease in weight only

46. Which of the following is the best evidence of crustal movement?

   (1) Lava flow
   (2) A buried soil profile
   (3) Yilted sedimentary rocks
   (4) Sediments below sea level
   (5) Metamorphic rocks

47. The difference between oceanic and continental crust is one of

   (1) density.
   (2) structure.
   (3) uniformity.
   (4) composition.
   (5) placement.

Item 48 refers to the following chart.

Element	Molar Mass
Hydrogen	1
Carbon	12
Oxygen	16

48. A compound was analyzed and found to have the following composition:

72g Carbon 12g Hydrogen 96g Oxygen

What is the empirical formula for this compound?

   (1) CHO
   (2) C_2HO
   (3) CH_2O
   (4) C_2H_2O
   (5) CH_2O_2

Item 49 refers to the following diagram and information.

The U-shaped tube pictured below has a semipermeable membrane (designated by the arrow). Side A contains a 0.5 molar glucose solution, while Side B contains 0.3M glucose. The membrane has holes too small for the sugar to pass through.

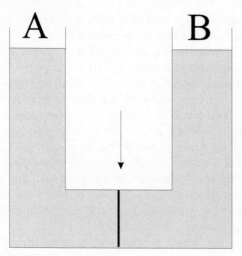

49. Which statement describes what will happen?
    (1) The membrane will eventually allow the sugar through because of water pressure.
    (2) The volume on side A will become higher than the volume on side B.
    (3) The two sides will remain equal for at least 24 hours.
    (4) The sugar will be evenly distributed within 24 hours.
    (5) The volume on side B will become higher than the volume on side A.

50. What is the pH of a solution of 0.01M HCl?
    (1) 1
    (2) 2
    (3) 5
    (4) 9
    (5) 91

Practice Test 4

LANGUAGE ARTS, READING

65 Minutes ❖ 40 Questions

Directions: The Language Arts, Reading test consists of excerpts from classical and popular literature and articles about literature or the arts. Each excerpt is followed by multiple-choice questions about the reading material.

For Example:

It was Susan's dream machine. The metallic blue paint gleamed, and the sporty wheels were highly polished. Under the hood, the engine was no less carefully cleaned. Inside, flashy lights illuminated the instruments on the dashboard, and the seats were covered by rich leather upholstery. The subject ("It") of this excerpt is most likely

(1) an airplane.
(2) a stereo system.
(3) an automobile.
(4) a boat.
(5) a motorcycle.

The correct answer is "an automobile"; therefore, answer space 3 would be marked on the answer sheet.

Read each excerpt first and then answer the questions that follow. Refer back to the reading material as often as necessary in answering the questions.

Each excerpt is preceded by a "purpose question." The purpose question gives a reason for reading the material. Use these purpose questions to help focus your reading. You are not required to answer these purpose questions. They are given only to help you concentrate on the ideas presented in the reading materials.

You should spend no more than 65 minutes answering the questions. Work carefully, but do not spend too much time on any one question. Be sure you answer every question. You will not be penalized for incorrect answers.

Do not mark in this test booklet. Record your answers on the separate answer sheet provided. Be sure all requested information is properly recorded on the answer sheet. To record your answers, mark the numbered space on the answer sheet beside the number that corresponds to the question in the test booklet.

Do not rest the point of your pencil on the answer sheet while you are considering your answer. Make no stray or unnecessary marks. If you change an answer, erase your first mark completely. Mark only one answer space for each question; multiple answers will be scored as incorrect. Do not fold or crease your answer sheet.

Directions: Each excerpt from a longer work is followed by multiple-choice questions about the reading material. Read each excerpt and then answer the questions that follow. Choose the one best answer for each question. Refer to the reading material as often as necessary in answering the questions.

Each excerpt is preceded by a "purpose question." The purpose question gives a reason for reading the material. Use these purpose questions to help focus your reading. You are not required to answer these purpose questions. They are given only to help you concentrate on the ideas presented in the reading materials.

Items 1–5 refer to the following excerpt from a novel.

WHAT IS THIS CHARACTER LIKE?

Line   "Walk up," hissed Cleo, somewhat fiercely.

    Judy was five, and her legs were fat, but she got up steam and propelled her small stout body along like a tired scow straining in the wake of a
5   racing sloop. She peeped at her mother from under the expansive brim of her leghorn straw. She knew what Cleo would look like. Cleo looked mad.

    Cleo swished down the spit-spattered street
10   with her head in the air and her sailor aslant her pompadour. Her French heels rapped the sidewalk smartly, and her starched skirt swayed briskly from her slender buttocks. Through the thin stuff of her shirtwaist her golden shoulders gleamed, and were
15   tied to the rest of her torso with the immaculate straps of her camisole, chemise, and summer shirt, which were banded together with tiny gold-plated safety pins. One gloved hand gave ballast to Judy, the other gripped her pocketbook.
20   This large patent-leather pouch held her secret life with her sisters. In it were their letters of obligation, acknowledging her latest distribution of money and clothing and prodigal advice. The instruments of the concrete side of her charity,
25   which instruments never left the inviolate privacy of her purse, were her credit books, showing various aliases and unfinished payments, and her pawnshop tickets, the expiration dates of which had mostly come and gone, constraining her to
30   tell her husband, with no intent of irony, that another of her diamonds had gone down the drain.

    The lesser items in Cleo's pocketbook were
. . . a lollipop for Judy in case she got tiresome, an
35   Irish-linen handkerchief for elegance, a cotton square if Judy stuck up her mouth, and a change purse with silver, half of which Cleo, clandestinely and without conscience, had shaken out of Judy's pig bank.
40   Snug in the bill compartment of the bag were forty-five dollars, which she had come by more or less legitimately after a minor skirmish with her husband . . .

    —From *The Living Is Easy,* by Dorothy West

1. In this passage, the writer describes Cleo mainly by telling about

  (1) her child.
  (2) the way she speaks.
  (3) the place she lives in.
  (4) the things in her pocketbook.
  (5) the way she moves.

2. What kind of narrative technique is used in this story?

  (1) The narrator is omniscient.
  (2) The narrator tells the story from Cleo's point of view.
  (3) The narrator tells the story from Judy's point of view.
  (4) The narrator speaks in the first person.
  (5) Cleo addresses the reader.

3. "Judy was five, and her legs were fat, but she got up steam and propelled her small stout body along like a tired scow straining in the wake of a racing sloop."

In this sentence, Judy is compared to

  (1) Cleo.
  (2) a boat.
  (3) a fat woman.
  (4) a little person.
  (5) a steam engine.

4. The overall picture of Cleo created in this passage is of a woman who is

  (1) beautiful and clever.
  (2) kind and generous.
  (3) vain and devious.
  (4) noble and selfless.
  (5) motherly and quiet.

5. Which detail from the passage indicates that this story takes place many years ago?

(1) Cleo's leather purse
(2) The amount of money in Cleo's pocketbook
(3) Cleo's diamonds
(4) Judy's bank
(5) Cleo's elaborate clothing

Items 6–11 refer to the following excerpt from a play.

WHY IS BECKY SURPRISED?

Line Becky: Tom, you frighten me! Eve has made you jealous again. (*goes to him and puts both arms around his neck*) Now, my darling, I give you my word
5   of honor I love only you and never have loved Fred Lindon and never could! Say you believe me!

      Warder: Haven't I always believed you?

      Becky: Ye—s.

10 Warder: But if I find your word of honor is broken in one thing, how can I ever trust it in another?

      Becky: Of course you can't—but you needn't worry, because it won't be broken.

15 Warder: Then, now that we're alone, tell me the truth, which you didn't tell me when you said you'd not seen Lindon often.

      Becky: (*turns away*) It was the truth. I
20   haven't—so very often.

      Warder: Not every day?

      Becky: (*sits in the chair by the writing table*) How could I?

      Warder: Nor telephoned him on Thursday,
25   breaking off an engagement after you told me absolutely you'd parted with him for good—and had no appointment?

      Becky: Of course not! The idea! (*But she
30   shows she is a little worried.*) Even Lindon could tell the truth!

      Warder: The telephone girl must have lied too or else the statement was made out of whole cloth. (*throwing the envelope
35   on the desk*)

      Becky: What statement?

      Warder: (*sitting on sofa*) From these detectives. (*He begins to look through the papers.*)

40 Becky: Detectives! (*stunned*) What detectives? (*picks up envelope and looks at it, puts it back on the desk*)

—From *The Truth* by Clyde Fitch

6. Based on lines 10–12, you can conclude that Warder

(1) is a well-respected man.
(2) always tells the truth.
(3) relies on a person's word of honor.
(4) doesn't believe what people say.
(5) has hired detectives to discover the truth.

7. Which of the following statements best summarizes the events in the passage?

(1) Becky confronts Warder about his adulterous behavior.
(2) Warder confronts Becky and then apologizes to her.
(3) Becky becomes angry at Warder for using detectives.
(4) Warder confronts Becky and discovers that she has lied.
(5) Becky admits to Warder that she is seeing Lindon.

8. The purpose of the stage directions in this passage (in *italics*) is to

(1) hide the fact that Becky has lied.
(2) show that Becky loves Warder.
(3) reveal Becky's increasing discomfort.
(4) describe the sofa, writing table, and desk.
(5) emphasize Warder's growing anger.

9. If Becky came to Warder two weeks after this discussion and promised never to see Lindon again, Warder probably would

(1) assume that she is lying.
(2) believe in her promise.
(3) be sorry he had doubted her.
(4) feel grateful to Becky and Lindon.
(5) leave Becky for good.

10. What will probably happen next in the play?

    (1) Becky will accuse Warder of infidelity.
    (2) Warder will read the detectives' report aloud.
    (3) Becky will make a full confession.
    (4) Warder will deny hiring detectives.
    (5) Becky will put her arms around Warder's neck again.

11. "Haven't I always believed you?" This question suggests that

    (1) Becky has been distrustful in the past.
    (2) Warder has only recently met Becky.
    (3) Warder is basically a distrustful person.
    (4) Becky is telling the truth.
    (5) Warder has trusted Becky until now.

Items 12–16 refer to the following excerpt.

WHAT MAKES THIS ARCHITECT'S WORK SPECIAL?

Line   In this age of high technology when construction
projects seem invariably to carry multimillion-
dollar price tags, it is refreshing to encounter the
work of Eladio Dieste. Working quietly for nearly a
5   half century, often in remote corners of his native
Uruguay, this structural engineer has designed
large buildings for communities and industries that
are at once inexpensive and of high aesthetic
quality. Avoiding costly steel or reinforced
10   concrete structural systems characteristic of so
many twentieth-century buildings, Dieste has
favored fired brick, a material both attractive and
easily produced locally. . . .

    Rooted in tradition yet futuristic in feeling,
15   Dieste's buildings are sturdy, easily maintained,
and possessed of genuinely beautiful lines. His
humane structures are so light and airy they
almost seem to flap in the wind.

    It is no accident that two of Dieste's best
20   known buildings are churches. He brings to all his
work (even industrial projects) a serious kind of
devotion that borders on the spiritual. As he has
said, "Besides its obvious functions, architecture
has in common with other arts the ability to help
25   us contemplate the universe. All the spiritual
activity of man is a conscious or unconscious
search for such contemplation. A building cannot
be as profound as art without serious and subtle
fidelity to the laws of the materials; only reverence
30   to this fidelity can make our works serious, lasting,
worthy companions for our daily contemplative
discourse."

       —From "Making Bricks Soar" by Caleb Bach

12. Which of the following best summarizes Dieste's opinions on architecture as expressed in lines 23–25?

    (1) Architecture is not a true art form.
    (2) The most important element of a building is its materials.
    (3) Architecture and spirituality are not related.
    (4) Good architecture helps us contemplate the universe.
    (5) The universe is unfathomable to humans.

13. Which of the following best describes why the reviewer admires Dieste's buildings?

    (1) They are beautiful and inexpensive.
    (2) Dieste has built beautiful churches.
    (3) Dieste often uses steel and concrete.
    (4) They seem a part of the natural environment.
    (5) They have many windows.

14. Comparing Dieste's buildings to flags being lifted by the wind (lines 15–18)

    (1) shows how flimsy and thin the walls are.
    (2) reveals Dieste's love of nature.
    (3) suggests the buildings' open, inspirational feel.
    (4) emphasizes that they seem full of motion.
    (5) illustrates how costly Dieste's work is.

15. If Dieste were a jewelry maker, which material would he most likely use?

    (1) Diamonds
    (2) Emeralds
    (3) Copper
    (4) Gold
    (5) Rubies

16. In lines 1–4, why does this reviewer emphasize the high cost of architecture today?

    (1) To highlight the low-cost simplicity of ancient buildings
    (2) To provide a contrast with Dieste's elegant, low-cost works
    (3) To praise Dieste's policy of working free of charge
    (4) To criticize the high cost of home insurance
    (5) To prove that, decades ago, materials were less expensive

535

Items 17–20 refer to this excerpt from a novel.

WHAT WILL HAPPEN ON THIS DAY?

Line When the rooster crowed, the moon had still not
left the world but was going down on flushed
cheek, one day short of full. A long thin cloud
crossed it slowly, drawing itself out like a name
5   being called. . . .

Then a house appeared on its ridge, like an
old man's silver watch pulled once more out of its
pocket. A dog leaped up from where he'd lain like
a stone and began barking for today as if he meant
10   never to stop.

Then a baby bolted naked out of the house.
She monkey-climbed down the steps and ran
open-armed into the yard, knocking at the walls of
flowers still colorless as faces, tagging in turn the
15   four big trees that marked off the corners of the
yard, tagging the gatepost, the well-piece, the
birdhouse, the bell post, a log seat, a rope swing,
and then, rounding the house, she used all her
strength to push over a crate that let a stream of
20   white Plymouth Rocks loose on the world. The
chickens rushed ahead of the baby, running
frantic, and behind the baby came a girl in a
petticoat. . . . She caught the baby and carried her
back inside, the baby with her little legs still
25   running like a windmill.

The distant point of the ridge, like the
tongue of a calf, put its red lick on the sky. Mists,
voids, patches of woods and naked clay, flickered
like live ashes, pink and blue. A mirror that hung
30   within the porch on the house wall began to
flicker as at the striking of kitchen matches.
Suddenly two chinaberry trees at the foot of the
yard lit up, like roosters astrut with golden tails.
. . . A figure was revealed, a very old lady seated
35   in a rocking chair with head cocked, as though
wild to be seen.

Then Sunday light raced over the farm as fast
as the chickens were flying. . . . Miss Beulah
Renfro came out of the passage at a trot and cried
40   in the voice of alarm which was her voice of
praise, "Granny! Up, dressed and waiting for 'em!
All by yourself! Why didn't you holler?" . . . She
folded the old lady very gently in her arms, kissed
her on the mouth, and cried, "And the birthday
45   cake's out of the oven!"

"Yes, I can still smell," said Granny.

—From *Losing Battles,* by Eudora Welty

17. Which of the following is an example of personification?

(1) "The moon was going down on flushed cheek . . ."
(2) "A dog leaped up from where he'd lain like a stone . . ."
(3) "She monkey-climbed down the steps . . ."
(4) "Two chinaberry trees lit up . . ."
(5) "Came out of the house at a trot . . ."

18. What general effect is this passage intended to have on the reader?

(1) Peacefulness and rest
(2) Anticipation
(3) Conflict
(4) Memories of a long time ago
(5) Fear of death

19. What effect does the writer achieve in the third paragraph?

(1) Mild anticipation
(2) Patient waiting
(3) Bright color and loud sound
(4) Rapid movement
(5) Extreme laziness

20. Which literary device does the writer rely on most in this passage?

(1) Personification
(2) Exaggeration
(3) Poetic language
(4) Metaphor
(5) Simile

WHAT IS HUMAN LIFE?

Line   Four Seasons fill the measure of the year
        There are four seasons in the mind of man:
   He has his lusty Spring, when fancy clear
        Takes in all beauty with an easy span:
5   He has his Summer, when luxuriously
        Spring's honied cud of youthful thought he loves
   To ruminate, and by such dreaming high
        Is nearest unto heaven: quiet coves
10   His soul has in its Autumn, when his wings
        He furleth close; contented so to look
   On mists in idleness—to let fair things
        Pass by unheeded as a threshold brook.
   He has his Winter too of pale misfeature,
15   Or else he would forego his mortal nature.

                —John Keats

21. What is the rhyme scheme of lines 1-4?

(1) AABB
(2) ABAB
(3) ABCA
(4) ABCD
(5) AAAB

22. The phrase "mortal nature" in line 15 refers to the fact that all people

(1) are born.
(2) live.
(3) think.
(4) write.
(5) die.

23. All the world's a stage,
And all the men and women merely players.
They have their exits and their entrances,
And one man in his time plays many parts,
His acts being as seven ages.

How are these lines by Shakespeare related to the poem by John Keats?

(1) Both state that human life has seven stages.
(2) Both compare humans to actors.
(3) Both divide human life into stages.
(4) Both compare death to winter.
(5) Both focus on childhood.

24. Lines 6-8 of Keats's poem compare a thoughtful young person to

(1) bees making honey.
(2) Cupid with his arrows.
(3) a daydreamer.
(4) a cow chewing on grass.
(5) a resting bird.

25. According to the poem, Autumn is a time of

(1) pleasure.
(2) beauty.
(3) quiet.
(4) decay.
(5) thought.

26. The poet's overall aim in writing this poem was most likely to

(1) express one central idea clearly.
(2) tie together four separate images.
(3) convey ideas in simple, everyday language.
(4) teach an important moral lesson.
(5) devise a striking and original image.

HOW DO YOU SEARCH FOR FILES?

Line   The Open dialog box displays a list of all files in the current folder. Searching for a specific file can be tedious if the folder is full of files with similar names, or if it's organized into many subfolders.
5   Office includes a powerful Find tool, available from the Open dialog box, that allows you to search for files by using almost any criteria. If you can remember a few scraps of information about the file—part of the name, a date, or even a word
10   or phrase you remember using in the document—you can probably find it. In workgroups, you can save and reuse searches to create a basic document management system.

     For example, a sales manager might look on
15   a shared network file server for all presentations that have been updated in the past week. Or a legal secretary might search for files that include a specific case number and are not marked completed. If space is at a premium on your local hard
20   drive, you can search for all Office files that were last modified more than six months ago, and then move them to a new location. You can save any custom search and use it later. . . .

     You construct a search by adding criteria to
25   a list. Each entry in the Criteria list consists of three pieces:

1. Property—Includes file system properties (name, date created, and file size, for instance), statistics (such as the number of

30   slides in a PowerPoint presentation or number of paragraphs in a Word document), and Office custom properties.

2. Condition—Defines the comparison you want Office to make. The list of available

35   conditions depends on the property you selected previously.

3. Value—Defines the specific text, number, or other data type for which you want Office to search.

40   A pair of buttons (And, Or) at the left of the criteria definition boxes allows you to combine criteria, and you can specify that Office search multiple folders and subfolders.

Criteria can be extremely simple—for
45   example, all files last modified this week. For more sophisticated searches, combine criteria to quickly filter a huge group of files into a manage-able list.

—From *Using Microsoft Office 2000*

27. The Find tool described in this passage is used to find
    (1) paper documents filed in a filing cabinet.
    (2) additional file folders in which to store paper documents.
    (3) specific computer files from among many with similar names.
    (4) employees who know how to keep track of documents.
    (5) additional space on your hard drive.

28. To get to the Find dialog box, you would click on
    (1) Open and then Tools.
    (2) Find and then Sort.
    (3) Tools and then Open.
    (4) Property and then Condition.
    (5) Condition and then Value.

29. According to the passage, which of the following is NOT a property of a file?
    (1) Name
    (2) Date
    (3) Size
    (4) Number of paragraphs
    (5) Range of dates

30. If a writer wanted to find all the articles she had written that included the word "evolution," she would search by
    (1) date.
    (2) size.
    (3) number of paragraphs.
    (4) number of slides.
    (5) contents.

31. Suppose an assistant must frequently find all files created for a specific client in the previous month. He could do this most easily by
    (1) searching individually for files created on each day in September.
    (2) creating a custom search and saving it.
    (3) finding all files created for that client and checking them for the right dates.
    (4) creating an alphabetical list of clients.
    (5) logging on to a workgroup.

Items 32–35 refer to the following excerpt from a novel.

HOW DOES MACON FEEL ABOUT BEING ALONE?

Line   After his wife left him, Macon had thought the house would seem larger. Instead, he felt more crowded. The windows shrank. The ceilings lowered. There was something insistent about the
5   furniture, as if it were pressing in on him.

Of course Sarah's personal belongings were gone, the little things like clothes and jewelry. But it emerged that some of the big things were more personal than he'd imagined. There was the
10   drop-leaf desk in the living room, its pigeonholes stuffed with her clutter of torn envelopes and unanswered letters. There was the radio in the kitchen, set to play 98 Rock. (She liked to keep in touch with her students, she used to say in the old
15   days, as she hummed and jittered her way around the breakfast table.) There was the chaise out back where she had sunbathed, planted in the only spot that got any sun at all.

He looked at the flowered cushions and
20   marveled at how an empty space could be so full of a person—her faint scent of coconut oil that always made him wish for a piña colada; her wide, gleaming face inscrutable behind dark glasses; her compact body in the skirted swimsuit she had
25   tearfully insisted on buying after her fortieth birthday. Threads of her exuberant hair showed up at the bottom of the sink. Her shelf in the medicine cabinet, stripped, was splashed with

liquid rouge in a particular plummy shade that
30   brought her instantly to Macon's mind. He had
always disapproved of the messiness, but now
those spills seemed touching, like colorful toys left
on the floor after a child has gone to bed.

—From *The Accidental Tourist* by Anne Tyler

32. What event is Macon adjusting to in this passage?

(1) A death
(2) A divorce
(3) A career change
(4) A new baby
(5) A new house

33. Based on the information in this passage, you can infer that Macon

(1) is glad that Sarah's personal belongings are finally gone.
(2) fought with Sarah when she lived there.
(3) did not expect to notice Sarah's absence so much.
(4) is a teacher, like Sarah was.
(5) enjoys being alone in a big house.

34. The structure of this passage could best be described as

(1) a list of a character's belongings.
(2) a series of causes and their effects.
(3) an interview with Macon.
(4) a series of letters to Sarah.
(5) a biography of Macon.

35. According to this passage, why did Sarah listen to 98 Rock?

(1) To win radio contests
(2) To practice her singing
(3) To learn how to dance
(4) To play music while she cooked
(5) To understand her students

Items 36–40 refer to the following excerpt from a novel.

HOW ARE THE MOTHERS AT GRAND ISLE DEPICTED?

Line It would have been a difficult matter for Mr.
Pontellier to define to his own satisfaction or any
one else's wherein his wife failed in her duty
toward their children. It was something which he
5   felt rather than perceived, and he never voiced the
feeling without subsequent regret and ample
atonement.

If one of the little Pontellier boys took a
tumble whilst at play, he was not apt to rush
10   crying to his mother's arms for comfort; he would
more likely pick himself up, wipe the water out of
his eyes and the sand out of his mouth, and go on
playing. Tots as they were, they pulled together
and stood their ground in childish battles with
15   doubled fists and uplifted voices, which usually
prevailed against the other mother-tots. The
quadroon nurse was looked upon as a huge
encumbrance, only good to button up waists and
panties and to brush and wash hair; since it
20   seemed to be a law of society that hair must be
parted and brushed.

In short, Mrs. Pontellier was not a mother-
woman. The mother-women seemed to prevail
that summer at Grand Isle. It was easy to know
25   them, fluttering about with extended, protecting
wings when any harm, real or imaginary, threatened their precious blood. They were women
who idolized their children, worshiped their
husbands, and esteemed it a holy privilege to
30   efface themselves as individuals and grow wings as
ministering angels.

Many of them were delicious in the role; one
of them was the embodiment of every womanly
grace and charm. If her husband did not adore
35   her, he was a brute, deserving of death by slow
torture. Her name was Adele Ratignolle. There are
no words to describe her save the old ones that
have served so often to picture the bygone
heroine of romance and the fair lady of our
40   dreams.

—From *The Awakening* by Kate Chopin

36. Based on lines 8–13 and 23–24, the setting of this passage is most likely a

   (1) steamy, hot city.
   (2) relaxed vacation site.
   (3) bustling, crowded train.
   (4) grand old mansion.
   (5) formal hotel.

37. Based on lines 8–13, which of the following best characterizes Mrs. Pontellier as a mother?

   (1) Warm and loving
   (2) Strict yet comforting
   (3) Cruel and abusive
   (4) Somewhat distant
   (5) Overprotective

38. ". . . since it seemed to be a law of society that hair must be parted and brushed." (lines 19–21) Which of the following best describes the tone of this statement?

   (1) Serious
   (2) Respectful
   (3) Social
   (4) Studious
   (5) Exaggerated

39. Based on lines 27–31, what is the meaning of *efface*?

   (1) Erase
   (2) Strengthen
   (3) Condemn
   (4) Praise
   (5) Support

40. What do lines 32–36 suggest about Adele Ratignolle?

   (1) She exemplified the "mother-woman" that summer.
   (2) She was frequently spoiled by her family and friends.
   (3) She was envied by the other women.
   (4) She cooked delicious meals for her family.
   (5) Her husband never treated her well.

Practice Test 5

MATHEMATICS FORMULAS

Use the following formulas to answer questions in the following practice test.

AREA of a:
square   Area = side^2
rectangle   Area = length × width
parallelogram   Area = base × height

triangle   Area = $\frac{1}{2}$ × base × height

trapezoid   Area = $\frac{1}{2}$ × (base$_1$ + base$_2$) × height

circle   Area = π × radius^2; π is approximately equal to 3.14

PERIMETER of a:
square   Perimeter = 4 × side
rectangle   Perimeter = 2 × length + 2 × width
triangle   Perimeter = side$_1$ + side$_2$ + side$_3$

CIRCUMFERENCE of a circle   Circumference = π × diameter; π is approximately equal to 3.14

VOLUME of a:
cube   Volume = edge^3

rectangular solid   Volume = length × width × height

square pyramid   Volume = $\frac{1}{3}$ × (base edge)^2 × height

cylinder   Volume = π × radius^2 × height; π is approximately
                equal to 3.14

cone   Volume = $\frac{1}{3}$ × π × radius^2 × height; π is approximately equal to 3.14

COORDINATE GEOMETRY   distance between points =

$$\sqrt{(x_2 - x_1)^2 + (y_2 - y_1)^2}; (x_1, y_1) \text{ and } (x_2, y_2) \text{ are two points in a plane.}$$

$$\text{Slope of a line} = \frac{y_2 - y_1}{x_2 - x_1}; (x_1, y_1) \text{ and } (x_2, y_2) \text{ are two points on the line.}$$

PYTHAGOREAN RELATIONSHIP $a^2 + b^2 = c^2$; a and b are legs and c the hypotenuse of a right triangle.

TRIGONOMETRIC RATIOS

$$\sin = \frac{\text{opposite}}{\text{hypotenuse}} \quad \cos = \frac{\text{adjacent}}{\text{hypotenuse}} \quad \tan = \frac{\text{opposite}}{\text{adjacent}}$$

MEASURES OF CENTRAL TENDENCY

$$\text{mean} = \frac{x_1 + x_2 + \ldots + x_n}{n}, \text{ where the } x\text{'s are the values for which a mean is desired, and } n \text{ is the total}$$
number of values for x.

median = the middle value of an odd number of *ordered* scores, and halfway between the two middle values of an even number of *ordered* scores.

SIMPLE INTEREST   interest = principal × rate × time

DISTANCE   distance = rate × time

TOTAL COST   total cost = (number of units) × (price per unit)

Practice Test 5

MATHEMATICS
PART I

45 Minutes ❖ 25 Questions ❖ Calculator Permitted

Directions: The Mathematical Understanding and Application test consists of multiple-choice and alternate-format questions intended to measure general mathematics skills and problem-solving ability. The questions are based on short readings, which often include a graph, chart, or figure. Study the information given and then answer the question(s) that follow. Refer to the information as often as necessary in answering the questions.

For Example:

If a grocery bill totaling $15.75 is paid with a $20 bill, how much change should be returned?

(1) $5.26
(2) $4.75
(3) $4.25
(4) $3.75
(5) $3.25

① ② ● ④ ⑤

The correct answer is "$4.25"; therefore, answer space 3 would be marked on the answer sheet.

You should spend no more than 45 minutes answering the questions for each section of this test. Work carefully, but do not spend too much time on any one question. Be sure you answer every question. You will not be penalized for incorrect answers.

Formulas you may need are given on page 541. Only some questions will require you to use a formula. Not all the formulas given will be used.

Some questions contain more information than you will need to solve the problem. Other questions do not give enough information to solve the problem. If the question does not give enough information to solve the problem, the correct answer choice is "Not enough information is given."

Do not mark in this test booklet. Use blank paper for your calculations. Record your answers on the separate answer sheet provided. Be sure all requested information is properly recorded on the answer sheet.

To record your answers, mark the numbered space on the answer sheet beside the number that corresponds to the question in the test booklet.

Do not rest the point of your pencil on the answer sheet while you are considering your answer. Make no stray or unnecessary marks. If you change an answer, erase your first mark completely. Mark only one answer space for each question; multiple answers will be scored as incorrect. Do not fold or crease your answer sheet.

1. Veronica went to the nearby drug store to buy medicine for her family. She needs to buy two bottles of Headache-gone and a bottle of aspirin. If the Headache-gone costs $2.37 a bottle and the aspirin costs $1.56, how much change will she receive if she pays with a $20 bill?

   (1) $3.93
   (2) $6.30
   (3) $13.70
   (4) $15.26
   (5) $16.07

2. James went to the nearby department store because he saw an advertisement that said all men's clothing was on sale. While he was there, a special sale started that said all clothes were an additional 10 percent off of the original price. If the advertisement promised that the men's wear would be 12 percent off at the checkout, how much will James have to pay at the checkout for a $53 suit?

   (1) 41.34
   (2) 41.98
   (3) 46.64
   (4) 47.70
   (5) 52.36

3. 0.453 kg. is equivalent to 1 lb. 0.001 metric tons is equivalent to a kg. Approximately how many pounds are equivalent to a metric ton?

  (1) 0.000453
  (2) 2.207
  (3) 453
  (4) 1000
  (5) 2207

4. AlphaHacker001 wants to back up his network data. His data is spread across three drives, and he wants to consolidate it onto a single set of CDs. He has 1,231MB on drive 1, another 3,452MB on drive 2, and 12,386MB on drive 3. If each CD can hold 800MB, how many CDs will he need to buy to create a complete backup set?

  (1) 2
  (2) 5
  (3) 16
  (4) 21
  (5) 22

5. A high-end fiber optics line can upload data at a rate of 37,500MB/s. How long (to the nearest tenth) will it take to upload a network hard drive that contains 4,000,000MBs of information?

Answer this question in the standard grid on your answer sheet on page 496.

6. Ralph bought several containers of sand so he could make sand paintings. He now wants to consolidate all the sand into one big container. According to the picture, how many of the little containers of sand will he be able to fit into the big container of sand?

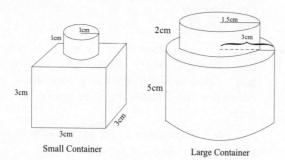

Small Container   Large Container

  (1) 7.32
  (2) 6.56
  (3) 5.81
  (4) 5.16
  (5) 4.56

7. Drew runs out of gas on the side of the interstate. He decides to make a collect call to his parents to let them know so that they can send help. He remembers that if he calls 10-10-232-122-127743-1772, he can save a few cents here and there. Their standard rate is $1.26 for the call and $0.04 for every minute of talking. If he can convince the operator that this is an emergency call and that he is stranded on the interstate, he may get a 12 percent discount! How much would he save by doing this on a 13-minute call?

  (1) $0.06
  (2) $0.15
  (3) $0.21
  (4) $0.52
  (5) $1.78

8. Mary deposited $1,325 in her checking account and soon after paid her bills as follows: She had to pay her mortgage, which was $935; her credit card, which was $136; her car payment, which was $432; and her utilities, which were $210. Afterward, her checking account had a balance of $513. How much money was in her checking account before she made the deposit or paid her bills?

Answer this question in the standard grid on your answer sheet on page 496.

9. A jet-fighter pilot is flying over a testing ground to determine how many windows in a specially designed building will break at certain speeds. According to the chart below, how many windows will break if a jet flies Mach 4?

Velocity	Mach 2	Mach 5	Mach 8
Windows Broken	124	310	496

Assume that the number of windows broken rises linearly with the velocity of the aircraft.

  (1) 124
  (2) 186
  (3) 248
  (4) 310
  (5) 384

10. Quadrilateral *QRST* is a kite. Three of the points are as follows: (1,1), (5,1), and (3,3). If the kite is 4 wide and 7 long, where is the fourth point?

Answer this question in the coordinate plane grid provided on your answer sheet on page 496.

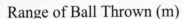

Questions 11–15 refer to the following chart.

Range of Ball Thrown (m)

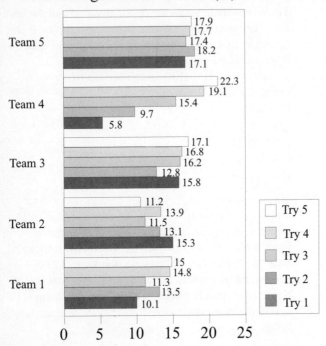

11. Which team would win if the average of the five throws were considered?

(1) Team 1
(2) Team 2
(3) Team 3
(4) Team 4
(5) Team 5

12. What was the range of throws for all the teams for all the tries?

(1) 4.10
(2) 4.30
(3) 4.72
(4) 12.20
(5) 16.50

13. If every time the pitcher had to walk to the ball and bring it back to the throwing line after every throw, how far would he have walked because of Team 3's throws?

(1) 157.40
(2) 78.70
(3) 15.74
(4) 8.60
(5) 4.30

14. What is the median of the third try?

(1) 14.35
(2) 15.40
(3) 15.74
(4) 15.80
(5) 16.2

15. What is the mode of all the throws?

(1) 11.5
(2) 17.1
(3) 18.2
(4) 19.1
(5) 22.3

16. Jay is playing a *Mental Math* game where he must collect points by doing certain tasks. For every second more that it takes him to complete a task, 1 percent of the points he gains is taken away. If he earns 162 points in 1 minute and 23 seconds when it is supposed to take 45 seconds, how many points will he receive?

(1) 134.46
(2) 100.44
(3) 89.10
(4) 61.56
(5) 27.54

17. A few metersticks are measured for quality control. The lengths of the sticks are 1001.12 mm, 998.95 mm, 1000.12 mm, 1003.14 mm, and 997.12 mm. What is the average length of the metersticks?

(1) 1001.13
(2) 1001.12
(3) 1000.12
(4) 1000.09
(5) 997.12

18. A bag contains 3 red balls, 2 green balls, 3 blue balls, 5 yellow balls, 9 orange balls, 4 brown balls, and 7 black balls. What is the probability of not drawing a green ball? Give your answer in fraction form.

Answer this question in the standard grid on your answer sheet on page 496.

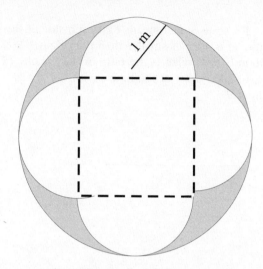

19. As shown in the figure, what is the area of the inner (white) figure in sq m?

   (1)   3.14
   (2)   6.28
   (3)   10.28
   (4)   12.56
   (5)   16.56

20. In the figure, what is the length of the side of the square?

   (1)   1
   (2)   2
   (3)   4
   (4)   8
   (5)   10

21. What is the area of the shaded region?

   (1)   12.56
   (2)   10.28
   (3)   6.28
   (4)   4.00
   (5)   2.28

22. A paperback book has 56 introduction pages, 1,226 reading pages, and another 18 index pages in it. If the book weighs 1.12 lbs, how many lbs does each page weigh?

   (1)   0.000862
   (2)   0.000913
   (3)   0.0151
   (4)   0.0200
   (5)   1160.714

23. Jimmy has a rabbit farm. He has a group of rabbits that reproduce at a rate of 11 percent and another group that reproduces at a rate of 15 percent. The second group of rabbits has 145 less rabbits than the first. After a year, he had 1,120 more rabbits than in the previous year. How many rabbits does Johnny have at the end of this year?

Answer this question in the standard grid on your answer sheet on page 496.

24. An Operations Research Consultant in a small firm makes $235.06 an hour. He works a 30-hour week, and his contract allows him to earn time and a half for anything over that. One week, he worked 38 hours. At this rate, how much money will he have made in a month? (Assume a month has 4 weeks.) Round answer to nearest dollar.

Answer this question in the standard grid on your answer sheet on page 496.

25. The following paint can has a small notch on its lid so that one can store small paint tools inside it. The basic design is a cylinder within a cylinder. How much paint could the following paint can hold? Round answer to nearest tenths.

Answer this question in the standard grid on your answer sheet on page 496.

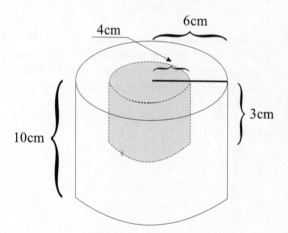

PART II

45 Minutes ❖ 25 Questions ❖ Calculator *Not* Permitted

1. Janet wants to enclose her ranch in a fence. Unfortunately, it is irregularly shaped. Using the diagram of the farm below, find how much fencing she needs.

   (1) 4,000
   (2) 1,000π + 4,000
   (3) 500π + 7,000
   (4) 3,750,000
   (5) 250,000π + 3,750,000

2. There is 1 mL in a cu. cm. There is 100cm in a m. How many mL are in a cu m?

   (1) 1,000,000
   (2) 100,000
   (3) 10,000
   (4) 1,000
   (5) 100

3. An investor wants to invest some money. He will put half of his money in stocks. The other half he wants to split equally between mutual funds, bonds, and trusts. How much of his money will go into stocks?

   (1) $\frac{5}{6}$

   (2) $\frac{1}{2}$

   (3) $\frac{1}{3}$

   (4) $\frac{1}{4}$

   (5) $\frac{1}{6}$

4. A 1:4 scale model means that each side of the model is 4 times smaller than the original. For the item below, what is the ratio of the volume of the 1:4 scale model of the figure with the actual figure?

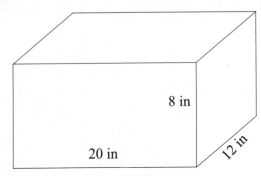

   (1) 1:4
   (2) 1:8
   (3) 1:16
   (4) 1:32
   (5) 1:64

5. (213 + 441)/112 is equivalent to which of the following?

   (1) (213 + 112) + (441 + 112)
   (2) (213 + 112)/(441 + 112)
   (3) (213 · 112)/(441 · 112)
   (4) (213/112) + (441/112)
   (5) (213 · 112 + 441 · 112)/112

6. For the sake of this problem, assume a 52-speed CD drive can copy a 4-minute song in about 0.7 seconds if it copies at maximum speed (unfortunately this never happens in real life). Assuming that the CD drive copies at maximum speed, how quickly can it copy a 10-song CD, if each song is 4 minutes long?

   Answer this question in the standard grid on your answer sheet on page 497.

Items 7–9 refer to the following graph.

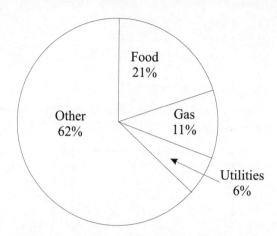

7. To the nearest 10%, if this person spent a total of $4,400 this month, how much did he spend on food?

(1) $264
(2) $440
(3) $484
(4) $880
(5) $924

8. To the nearest whole, how many times more money does this person spend on gas than on utilities?

(1) 1
(2) 1.90
(3) 2
(4) 3.5
(5) 4

9. To the nearest 10%, if the gas bill was $300, how much was his monthly spending?

(1) $5,000
(2) $3,000
(3) $2,727
(4) $1,500
(5) $1,429

10. Twice a number plus 2 is equal to 3 times the number minus 8. Which of the following equations can be used to properly solve for the number?

(1) $2n + 2 = 3n - 8$
(2) $2n + 8 = 3n - 2$
(3) $2n - 2 = 3n + 8$
(4) $2n + 2 = 3n + 8$
(5) $2n - 2 = 3n - 8$

11. Mark the average point of the following data set on your coordinate grid. (3,2), (1,5), (−3,5), (4,−6), (0,−1)

Answer this question in the coordinate plane grid provided on your answer sheet on page 497.

12. A paperboy can average 30 deliveries every half hour. How long would it take him to deliver papers to a housing tract that has 600 houses in it (in hours)?

(1) 300
(2) 150
(3) 20
(4) 10
(5) 5

13. Solve for x: $x^2 + 2x + 8$:

(1) +2 and +4
(2) +2 and −4
(3) −2 and +4
(4) −2 and −4
(5) It is not factorable.

14. What is the largest rod that can fit in this object?

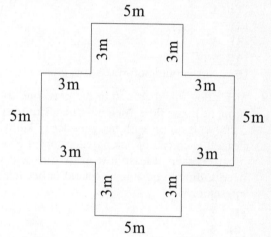

(1) $3\sqrt{2}$
(2) $\sqrt{34}$
(3) $5\sqrt{2}$
(4) $\sqrt{146}$
(5) $11\sqrt{2}$

15. What is the height difference between Mt. Whitney (14,495 ft above sea level) and Death Valley (282 ft below sea level)?

(1) −14,777
(2) −14,213
(3) 7,388
(4) 14,213
(5) 14777

16. The median test score for a class was 85.3%. Which one of the following data sets could possibly be the test scores for the class?

   (1) 76.3%, 78.8%, 85.3%, 88.2%, 89.1%, 99.2%
   (2) 79.1%, 81.2%, 83.1%, 84.1%, 85.3%, 89.1%
   (3) 54.6%, 61.3%, 84.3%, 89.1%, 90.5%, 92.4%
   (4) 58.1%, 69.2%, 83.8%, 86.8%, 89.1%, 99.9%
   (5) 81.5%, 84.1%, 84.5%, 86.1%, 87.4%, 88.2%

17. Ferdi wants to cut a 54-yd-long metal rod into two unequal pieces. One piece must be twice as long as the other. What will the length of the smaller rod be?

   (1) 13.5
   (2) 18
   (3) 27
   (4) 36
   (5) 51

18. Connie was playing music for 3 hours. She listened to the Backstreet Boys for 1 hour and listened to 'N Sync for the rest of the time. She also has a Britney Spears album. How long did she listen to 'N Sync?

   (1) 1
   (2) 2
   (3) 3
   (4) 5
   (5) Not enough information is given.

19. Meg's dog rolled around in the grass one day and brought home fleas. Meg now needs to dust her 3,200-sq ft house with flea powder to kill the fleas. If each can of flea powder covers 600 sq ft of space, then at least how many cans will she need to buy to be able to get rid of her flea infestation?

   (1) 3.2
   (2) 5
   (3) 5.3
   (4) 6
   (5) 7

20. For a dress, Irene needs 300 ft of thread. If she can buy a spool that has 125 ft in it for $1.50, how much will she have to pay to make her dress?

   (1) $6.00
   (2) $4.50
   (3) $3.60
   (4) $3.00
   (5) $1.50

21. Jimmy reaches into his pocket and finds $5.38 in change. There are 27 less nickels than pennies. Which of these equations can solve for the number of pennies in Jimmy's pocket.

   (1) $0.05(x - 27) = 5.38$
   (2) $0.01(x - 27) = 5.38$
   (3) $0.01x + 0.05(x - 27) = 5.38$
   (4) $0.01(x - 27) + 0.05 = 5.38$
   (5) $0.01x + 0.05(x - 27) + 5.38 = 0$

22. Find the area of this irregular shape. The corners have had quarter circles cut out.

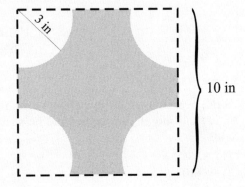

   (1) 100
   (2) $100 - \dfrac{9}{4}\pi$
   (3) $100 - 9\pi$
   (4) 9π
   (5) $\dfrac{9}{4}\pi$

23. In an undergraduate chemistry class, there are 206 more freshmen in the course than there are sophomores. If the total class enrollment was 816, how many sophomores were there? Only set the problem up.

   (1) $S + (S + 206) + 816 = 0$
   (2) $S + (S - 206) = 816$
   (3) $S + (S + 206) = 816$
   (4) $S - (S + 206) = 816$
   (5) $S - (S - 206) = 816$

Items 24 and 25 refer to the following graph.

A word processing company created a breakdown chart of the price of each component of their software.

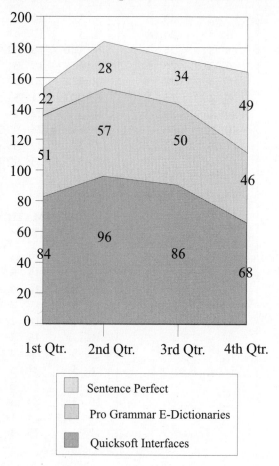

1st Qtr.   2nd Qtr.   3rd Qtr.   4th Qtr.

Sentence Perfect

Pro Grammar E-Dictionaries

Quicksoft Interfaces

24. What was the price of the software the quarter it was the most expensive?

Answer this question in the standard grid on your answer sheet on page 497.

25. On the average, which component cost the least?

(1) Sentence Perfect
(2) Pro Grammar E-Dictionaries
(3) Quicksoft Interfaces
(4) All the components were the same average price.
(5) Not enough information is given.

QUICK-SCORE ANSWERS

LANGUAGE ARTS, WRITING PART I		SOCIAL STUDIES		SCIENCE		LANGUAGE ARTS, READING		MATHEMATICS, PART I	
1. 1	26. 1	1. 3	26. 3	1. 2	26. 4	1. 4	21. 2	1. 3	14. 2
2. 3	27. 4	2. 4	27. 3	2. 4	27. 4	2. 1	22. 5	2. 2	15. 2
3. 2	28. 1	3. 2	28. 4	3. 4	28. 5	3. 2	23. 3	3. 5	16. 2
4. 4	29. 4	4. 1	29. 2	4. 2	29. 4	4. 3	24. 4	4. 5	17. 4
5. 1	30. 3	5. 4	30. 3	5. 4	30. 2	5. 5	25. 3	5. 106.7	18. 31/33
6. 3	31. 1	6. 2	31. 5	6. 4	31. 5	6. 3	26. 1	6. 4	19. 3
7. 5	32. 2	7. 5	32. 1	7. 5	32. 1	7. 4	27. 3	7. 3	20. 2
8. 3	33. 3	8. 5	33. 5	8. 1	33. 4	8. 3	28. 1	8. 901	21. 5
9. 4	34. 4	9. 1	34. 1	9. 4	34. 5	9. 1	29. 5	9. 3	22. 1
10. 4	35. 3	10. 2	35. 2	10. 2	35. 4	10. 2	30. 5	10. (3,−4)	23. 9757
11. 2	36. 4	11. 3	36. 5	11. 5	36. 1	11. 5	31. 2	11. 5	24. 39,490
12. 2	37. 2	12. 5	37. 3	12. 2	37. 2	12. 4	32. 2	12. 5	25. 979.7
13. 4	38. 4	13. 2	38. 4	13. 3	38. 5	13. 1	33. 3	13. 4	
14. 1	39. 4	14. 3	39. 3	14. 4	39. 4	14. 4	34. 1		
15. 4	40. 2	15. 1	40. 5	15. 1	40. 2	15. 3	35. 5		
16. 2	41. 4	16. 2	41. 3	16. 1	41. 3	16. 2	36. 2		
17. 3	42. 5	17. 3	42. 3	17. 3	42. 3	17. 1	37. 4		
18. 5	43. 4	18. 1	43. 2	18. 5	43. 2	18. 2	38. 5		
19. 1	44. 4	19. 4	44. 3	19. 5	44. 4	19. 4	39. 1		
20. 4	45. 3	20. 3	45. 3	20. 3	45. 3	20. 5	40. 1		
21. 5	46. 3	21. 3	46. 4	21. 5	46. 3				
22. 2	47. 1	22. 2	47. 1	22. 3	47. 4				
23. 3	48. 5	23. 3	48. 3	23. 2	48. 3				
24. 1	49. 4	24. 1	49. 1	24. 4	49. 2				
25. 4	50. 4	25. 1	50. 1	25. 4	50. 2				

PART II

Turn to page 508.

MATHEMATICS, PART II

1. 3	14. 4
2. 1	15. 5
3. 2	16. 4
4. 5	17. 2
5. 4	18. 2
6. 7	19. 4
7. 5	20. 2
8. 3	21. 3
9. 2	22. 3
10. 1	23. 3
11. (1,1)	24. 181
12. 4	25. 1
13. 5	

FILLED-IN STANDARD GRIDS AND COORDINATE PLANE GRIDS

Part I

5. 1 0 6 . 7

18. 3 1 / 3 3

24. 3 9 4 9 0

8. 9 0 1

23. 9 7 5 7

25. 9 7 9 . 7

10.

Part II

6.

7				
	/	/	/	
.	.	.	.	.
0	0	0	0	0
1	1	1	1	1
2	2	2	2	2
3	3	3	3	3
4	4	4	4	4
5	5	5	5	5
6	6	6	6	6
●	7	7	7	7
8	8	8	8	8
9	9	9	9	9

11.

24.

1	8	1		
	/	/	/	
.	.	.	.	.
0	0	0	0	0
●	1	●	1	1
2	2	2	2	2
3	3	3	3	3
4	4	4	4	4
5	5	5	5	5
6	6	6	6	6
7	7	7	7	7
8	●	8	8	8
9	9	9	9	9

ANSWERS AND EXPLANATIONS

Practice Test 1: Language Arts, Writing

1. **The correct answer is (1).** This choice sets up a reasonable, chronological development. Step-by-step presentation of ideas is the key factor.

2. **The correct answer is (3).** As written, the item is a sentence fragment because it lacks a predicate or verb. In choice (1), the commas around *the Statue of Liberty* are necessary to set off the introductory participle phrase and the appositive phrase that follows *Liberty*. Choice (2) is not correct because the item still has no verb, and the same is true for choice (4).

3. **The correct answer is (2).** It maintains parallel construction; *friendship* and *belief* are both nouns. Choice (1) is incorrect because it changes the tense sequence from past to present, while choice (3) will disrupt the meaning of the sentence. *Both . . . and* is a correlative conjunction; both parts are necessary. Choice (4) is wrong because the comma will separate the subject and the predicate.

4. **The correct answer is (4).** Choice (1) is wrong because removing this phrase will make the sentence illogical, while choice (2) is incorrect because the two adjectives, *renowned* and *French*, are not interchangeable nor can they meet the other test of inserting *and* between them. Choice (3) looks like a good choice, and you may be misled and select this one if you don't read all of the answers. *What* cannot be used as a reference to a person. *Whoever* implies a question.

5. **The correct answer is (1).** *Stages* implies a process. Choice (2) does not identify what kind of *process*; choice (3) is hardly a concise revision. Choice (4) is just the reversal of choice (2), and choice (4) does not include information about the *process* or *stages*. Choice (5) is a sentence fragment.

6. **The correct answer is (3).** The sentence as written is an incomplete construction because the first independent clause has no predicate or verb. Choice (1) is not right because no comma is needed between the noun and modifier. Choice (2) is incorrect because the comma is needed to separate two independent clauses. Choice (4) provides a verb, but it is in the wrong tense to maintain tense consistency.

7. **The correct answer is (5).** This sentence has no errors. Choice (1) incorrectly changes the tense; choice (2) illogically moves a modifier, and choice (3) sets up an agreement error between a pronoun and its antecedent (*them . . . sheets*). The subordinate conjunction, *After*, in choice (4) sets up a sentence fragment.

8. **The correct answer is (3).** *Then* indicates the step in time. Choice (1), *However*, implies a contrast that does not apply here. Choice (2) is not the right choice because it is not the *last* step; nor is choice (4), *finally*, a good answer. Choice (5), *As soon as*, sets up a sentence fragment.

9. **The correct answer is (4).** This is a difficult question because the sentence is complicated. Be sure that you read every answer before you make a choice. Choice (1) is incorrect because *provide* does not agree with *frame*, which is the antecedent for *that*. Choice (2) is not the answer because of the repetition of *was*. Choice (3) looks like a good choice, but it shifts the emphasis from the framework to the engineer. Choice (5) is another incomplete sentence.

10. **The correct answer is (4).** It most succinctly summarizes the paragraph. Choice (1) is true; however, it does not cover all of the main ideas. Choice (2) is wordy, while choice (3) states the obvious, and choice (5) is incomplete as its summary of the paragraph.

11. **The correct answer is (2).** The item is a sentence fragment. The comma in choice (1) is unneeded. Neither choice (3) nor choice (4) corrects the sentence fragment.

12. **The correct answer is (2).** This sentence is not about the statue, as the other choices are.

13. **The correct answer is (4).** The original item is a run-on sentence, and choice (4) provides a conjunction to connect the two clauses. Choice (1) is incorrect because it will merely create a comma splice. Choice (2) may look like a good choice, but it will not correct the run-on error. Choice (3) offers a conjunction that sets up an illogical contrast.

14. **The correct answer is (1).** The past participle form is needed to serve as an adjective here, and the correct spelling is *written*. Choice (2) is not correct because *more* is used to compare two items, while *most* is used for more than two. Choice (3) is wrong because *it's* is a contraction for *it is*, and the possessive form of *it* is needed. Choice (4) is also incorrect because the comma separates the appositive *its ending* from *feature*.

15. **The correct answer is (4).** The possessive form is needed. Choice (1) offers an unnecessary phrase to describe the *young man*. Choice (2) incorrectly changes the spelling of *tale*; a dog has a *tail*. Choice (3) offers needless information about the *daughter* because we know she is the king's daughter.

16. **The correct answer is (2).** The possessive form is needed. Choice (1) is wrong because the comma correctly separates the introductory adverb clause from the independent clause. Choice (3) changes the tense from present to past, and choice (4) does the same.

17. **The correct answer is (3).** Choice (1) incorrectly changes tense from present to past. Choice (2) looks like a good choice until you realize that it creates a comma splice. Choice (3) takes care of the run-on sentence by providing a suitable conjunction. A conjunction joining independent clauses must be preceded by a comma. Choice (4) offers an illogical change without correcting the run-on sentence.

18. **The correct answer is (5).** There is not enough evidence to support such a broad generalization. This king may be cruel, but not all kings are cruel.

19. **The correct answer is (1).** Choice (1) spells the present tense form of the verb correctly. Choice (2) changes the tense from present to past. Choice (3) presents a choice that will create a sentence fragment. The comma offered in choice (4) is needless because it will merely separate a noun from its modifier.

20. **The correct answer is (4).** The error in this sentence is a lack of parallelism, or balance. Look at the original item again. The pattern is established in the first part of the sentence: "lady whom he would marry." In the second part of the sentence, the construction should be the same: "tiger that would savagely attack him." Choice (1) is incorrect because no comma is needed to separate the prepositional phrase from what it modifies. Choice (2) is also wrong because inserting a comma would mean that *whom he would marry immediately* was not essential information. Choice (3) offers an illogical choice.

21. **The correct answer is (5).** This sentence has no errors. Choice (1) offers nonstandard usage with *irregardless*, a word that is never correct. Choice (2) is wrong because a comma is needed to separate the opening phrase. Choice (3) incorrectly changes the tense from present to past. Choice (4) makes a needless change.

22. **The correct answer is (2).** Choice (2) gives the correct spelling of *somehow*. Choice (1) incorrectly changes the tense from present to past; choice (3) offers a nonstandard use of *every*, and choice (4) provides a comma that is unnecessary.

23. **The correct answer is (3).** The item as written is a sentence fragment, so omitting *Just before* will eliminate the subordinate conjunction that sets up the fragment. Choice (1) inserts a comma between parts of the predicate. Choice (2) does not omit enough of that opening construction; the sentence fragment will remain. Choice (4) offers an incorrect comma after *princess* that separates a modifier from the word it is modifying.

24. The correct answer is (1). Choice (1) gives the correct spelling of the possessive form of *who*. Choice (2) incorrectly changes the verb form to past, and choice (3) inserts an incorrect comma between the subject and verb of the sentence. Choice (4) offers an incorrect comma between parts of the verb.

25. The correct answer is (4). The sentence will follow the question that surprises the reader who expects an answer to the question. The lack of an answer with such a novel is what made Stockton famous.

26. The correct answer is (1). Choice (2) is in the wrong tense, and choice (3) uses *eminent* instead of *imminent*, which means "future." Choice (4) reduces the clause too much because the territory is not yet known as America.

27. The correct answer is (4). The original item is a sentence fragment because it lacks a verb. Choice (1) removes a comma that needs to be there to separate the proper noun and the adjective clause following it. There is no reason to insert the comma offered in choice (2). Choice (3) will provide the needed verb, but *comes* is in the wrong tense.

28. The correct answer is (1). It explains why these *second sons* came with Raleigh: they had no inheritance. Choice (2) sets up a comma splice, and choice (3) omits a needed comma to set off a prepositional phrase. Choice (4) places *because* in the wrong place to develop a logical sentence.

29. The correct answer is (4). The original item is a run-on sentence: two sentences are combined without proper punctuation or conjunction. Choice (4) remedies the problem because *while* can connect the two sentences. Choice (1) is incorrect because it changes the tense from past to present. Choice (2) offers a comma that will create a comma splice instead of correcting the run-on sentence, and choice (3) incorrectly omits the comma needed to indicate that the phrase does not modify *Virginia*.

30. The correct answer is (3). It sets up the correct relationship of contrast between the introductory clause and the main clause. Choice (1) improperly shifts the tense from past to present. Choice (2) changes the conjunction and the meaning of the sentence. Choice (4) also offers a change in the relationship between the clauses and again sets up an illogical sequence.

31. The correct answer is (1). *Theirself* is nonstandard English and is never correct. Choice (2) offers a variation of the error; *themself* is also nonstandard usage. The same is true for choice (3) because *hisself* is also nonstandard; this answer is also wrong because it changes from plural to singular form of intensive pronoun. Choice (4) offers a correct form of pronoun, but this answer also shifts from plural to singular.

32. The correct answer is (2). This option presents a balanced phrase of three objects of the preposition *of*. Choice (1) is incorrect because the clause *who were indentured* upsets the balance necessary in the clause. Choice (3) in incorrect for the same reason except that in this option, the clause *who were convicts* is the problem, and an agreement error (workers . . . was) is created. Choice (4) is the wordiest of all of the choices.

33. The correct answer is (3). Understanding the relationship between the two clauses is the key to choosing the right answer. Choice (1) sets up a contrast that is illogical; choice (2) implies that the area that became the South did so because of slavery, another illogical conclusion; and choice (4) also sets up an invalid conclusion. Choice (5) is just a variation of the conjunction offered in choice (4).

34. The correct answer is (4). It is the only choice that is a valid statement. Choice (1) is incorrect because there is no evidence that slavery was put *in place from the beginning*. Choice (2) distorts the truth that the planters sought profit from tobacco. Choice (3) is incorrect because it is not broad enough to encompass the entire paragraph, and choice (5) is wrong because there is no evidence that these "second sons" were the only ones willing to face the challenge.

35. The correct answer is (3). This choice is the most concise version that does not distort information. Choice (1) is longer than the original sentence. Choice (2) presents a choppy version that interrupts the flow of ideas. Choice (4) is more concise but still choppy, and choice (5) implies that freedom arrived first.

36. The correct answer is (4). Choice (1) is choppy with phrases connected by *and*. Choice (2) is a sentence fragment rather than a complete sentence. Choice (3) looks like a better option until the final prepositional phrase, which has one too many *and*s. Choice (5) is shorter, but it is awkward because the final prepositional phrase modifies *Great Britain*.

37. The correct answer is (2). The misspelling is corrected. The comma in choice (1) is necessary to separate the appositive from *theocracy*. Choice (3) offers a needless comma to separate the clauses. Choice (4) presents an unnecessary change where there is no error.

38. The correct answer is (4). It is needed to maintain past tense. Choice (1) offers an illogical construction; choice (2) provides an improper tense shift, and choice (3) omits important information.

39. The correct answer is (4). The clause refers to the war. The other choices move the clause to set up invalid constructions.

40. The correct answer is (2). Choice (1) focuses entirely on Carver, not his accomplishments. Choice (3) is invalid because Carver did not *discover* the peanut. While choice (4) is true, it is not relevant to the first paragraph. Choice (5) contradicts the information in the paragraph indicating that cotton was the chief crop well into the twentieth century. Choice (2), therefore, provides the kind of general statement needed as a topic sentence.

41. The correct answer is (4). *American* is a proper adjective, meaning it is derived from a proper noun, which is always capitalized. Choice (1) disconnects Carver from his own work, while choice (2) wrongly capitalizes a common noun. Choice (3) shifts from past to present tense.

42. The correct answer is (5). There are no errors in this sentence. The comma in choice (1) is needed to separate an introductory preposition phrase. Although *cotton*, choice (2), is the subject of the sentence, it is a common noun that should not be capitalized. Choice (3) changes tenses incorrectly, and choice (4) inserts an unnecessary comma separating the modifier from the word it is modifying.

43. The correct answer is (4). The run-on sentence is eliminated by joining two clauses with a semicolon. Choice (1) is incorrect because it does not correct the run-on. Choice (2) is incorrect because it will remove essential information. Choice (3) improperly shifts the tense from present to past.

44. The correct answer is (4). It corrects the misspelling. The possessive form of the pronoun is required. Choice (1) needlessly omits commas that set off a parenthetical expression. Choice (2) omits a comma needed to separate parts of a compound predicate, and choice (3) misuses the relative pronoun *which*, for this pronoun form refers only to things, not people.

45. The correct answer is (3). It corrects the sentence fragment, which lacks a subject and predicate. Choice (1) is incorrect because the introductory phrase needs to be set off by a comma. Choice (2) is wrong because a comma is needed to follow a proper noun when it is followed by *who* or *whom*. Choice (4) seems to take care of the sentence fragment, but it changes the meaning of the sentence.

46. The correct answer is (3). It maintains tense consistency. Choice (1) shifts tense and voice from active to passive voice. Choice (2) omits a necessary comma following a long introductory phrase, and choice (4) changes to a nonstandard version of the verb *seek*.

47. The correct answer is (1). It is the most concise statement of ideas. Choice (2) eliminates only *that add* by changing it to *adding*. Choice (3) is a sentence fragment. Choice (4) changes *that harbor* to *harboring*, but that change is insufficient. Choice (5) revises *that harbor* and *that add*, but the sentence can be further reduced.

48. The correct answer is (5.) Read each choice carefully. Choice (1) combines the two sentences with *including*, but it achieves no conciseness. Choice (2) removes a few words, such as *that could*, but this option is not very concise either. Choice (3) looks much more concise until you reach *included*, where you should realize that the word is in the wrong form. Choice (4) has the wrong form of *discover*.

49. The correct answer is (4). Again, read each choice carefully. Choice (1) reduces the sentence by removing *which were*, and choice (2) also eliminates *these*; however, these choices are not as concise as the final three choices. Choice (3) removes much of the wordiness, but it also removes some essential details such as *Southern*. Choice (5) is by far the shortest sentence, but it loses virtually all of the necessary details.

50. The correct answer is (4). It provides the most concise revision. In the original item, no specific details like those in the previous item are included, so what is needed is to reduce clauses to phrases and phrases to words without changing the meaning of the sentence. Choice (4) does the best job of trimming unnecessary words.

Part II: Essay

The scoring information below will help you estimate a score for your essay. If you can, ask an instructor to read and score your essay. To help you decide which skills you need to work on, make a list of its strengths and weaknesses based on the checklist listed below.

With 6 as the top score and 1 at the bottom, rank your essay for each item on the checklist. Put a check in the box that you think reflects the quality of that particular part of your essay.

Does my essay . . .	1	2	3	4	5	6
discuss the topic?						
have a clear, controlling idea that is developed throughout?						
have a clear structure (introduction, body, and conclusion)?						
tell the reader in the introduction what the topic is and what I am going to say about it?						
use details and examples to support each point?						
sum up the essay in the conclusion?						
have few or no errors in sentence structure, usage, or punctuation?						

Language Arts, Writing Practice Test Analysis Chart

Use this table to determine your areas of strength and areas in which more work is needed. The numbers in boxes refer to the multiple-choice questions in the practice test.

Content Area	Sentence Correction	Sentence Revision	Construction Shift
Unit 1: Sentence Structure			
Fragment	27, 45		
Run-on	2, 13, 17, 29, 43		
Comma splice	28		
Coordination	20, 30	47, 50	
Subordination	23	26, 39	
Clarity, modification, and parallelism	3, 7, 20, 54	5, 32, 33,35, 36, 49	9
Unit 2: Usage and Grammar			
Agreement	4, 31		
Verbs	6, 11, 38, 46, 51, 53		
Unit 3: Mechanics			
Capitalization	41		
Punctuation	42		
Spelling, possessives, contractions, and homonyms	14, 15, 16, 19, 21, 22, 24, 37, 44, 52		
Unit 4: Organization			
Transitions		8, 55	
Topic sentence		40	25, 34
Coherence		48	1, 10, 12, 18

Practice Test 2: Social Studies

1. **The correct answer is (3). (Application)** Profit is the amount of money remaining after a company's bills have been paid. Frequently, a part of the profit is distributed to the company's shareholders on a quarterly basis.

2. **The correct answer is (4). (Application)** When more Japanese goods are sold in the United States than U.S. goods are sold in Japan, America has an unfavorable balance of trade with Japan. In recent years, this unfavorable balance of trade has become one of the major points of contention between the United States and Japan.

3. **The correct answer is (2). (Analysis)** Memories of the difficulties caused by galloping inflation led the German government to refuse to lower its interest rates.

4. **The correct answer is (1). (Analysis)** Monopolies are allowed to operate (under government supervision) so as to benefit the customers of the monopolies, so choice (1) is correct. Choice (4) is only a partial answer.

5. **The correct answer is (4). (Application)** If the cost of production rises but the selling price remains the same, the result is lower profitability.

6. **The correct answer is (2). (Comprehension)** One of the major beliefs of communism is that no enterprise should earn a profit. According to this view, profits are ill-gotten gains. Thus, choice (2) is the correct answer.

7. **The correct answer is (5). (Analysis)** Choice (5) is the only one that describes the situation regarding immigration from Japan and China to America.

8. **The correct answer is (5). (Comprehension)** More than 90 percent of the immigrants were from Europe.

9. **The correct answer is (1). (Evaluation)** The large number of immigrants from Europe, who, it must be assumed, were processed through Ellis Island, would indicate that choice (1) is the correct answer.

10. **The correct answer is (2). (Analysis)** The great racial tensions between African Americans and whites of European descent probably caused immigration from Africa to be almost nonexistent.

11. **The correct answer is (3). (Comprehension)** New York City is three time zones to the east of San Francisco, so it is 3 hours later in New York.

12. **The correct answer is (5). (Application)** Because Washington, DC, is in the Eastern time zone and Portland, Oregon, is in the Pacific time zone, the time difference is 3 hours, so when it is 9 a.m. in Portland, it is noon in Washington.

13. **The correct answer is (2). (Analysis)** Originally, each town across the country set its own time by the position of the sun, so it was impossible to figure the arrival and departure times of trains. The creation of time zones solved this problem.

14. **The correct answer is (3). (Comprehension)** According to the graph, the year of highest profits was 1989.

15. **The correct answer is (1). (Evaluation)** Reducing costs (i.e., salaries) would have helped increase profits. The other four choices would not have increased the profitability of the store; in fact, choices (2) and (3) would have actually added to the problem.

16. **The correct answer is (2). (Analysis)** The year the business opened, 1984, would have been the one during which the most employees would have been hired, because it can be assumed that a full staff would have been put in place that year.

17. **The correct answer is (3). (Comprehension)** This answer can be derived by looking only at the latitudes of the various options. Only choices (3) and (5), points C and E, are in the south latitudes, so the other three choices can be eliminated immediately. Choice (5) is at 60 degrees south latitude, so choice (3), point C, can be determined to be the correct answer by the process of elimination.

18. **The correct answer is (1). (Application)** By locating points B and D on the globe, it should become apparent that point B is both west and north of point D, so choice (1) is correct.

19. **The correct answer is (4). (Comprehension)** Between 1965 and 1971, spending declined for only one category—training of federal personnel—so choice (4) is correct.

20. **The correct answer is (3). (Analysis)** Choices (1), (2), (4), and (5) may or may not be true statements; they cannot be verified by the information in the bar graph. Only choice (3) contains information that can be verified by the bar graph.

21. **The correct answer is (3). (Application)** The Iraqi government under Saddam Hussein was a dictatorship.

22. **The correct answer is (2). (Application)** Great Britain and Northern Ireland are considered to be a model example of a constitutional monarchy. The current ruler is Queen Elizabeth II.

23. **The correct answer is (3). (Evaluation)** Because the Irish Republican Army strongly opposes British rule of Northern Ireland, the group would probably call the British government a dictatorship.

24. **The correct answer is (1). (Evaluation)** A belief in the right of people to have a say in their government is a traditional, strongly held American belief.

25. **The correct answer is (1). (Analysis)** Child abuse would probably be the major concern of someone involved in child welfare, so choice (1) is correct. The growth in the number of children who are involved in random shootings might also be a concern, particularly in terms of preventing such behavior, but this would still come under the overall heading of preventing child abuse.

26. **The correct answer is (3). (Analysis)** Of the types of violence listed, the AARP would probably be most interested in crimes directly targeted at its members, the elderly.

27. **The correct answer is (3). (Analysis)** Street gangs are most often associated with drive-by and random shootings of members of other such gangs, either in retribution for past incidents or as a way to gain territory.

28. **The correct answer is (4). (Application)** The Gadsden Purchase was added in 1853, making it the final acquisition to the continental United States.

29. **The correct answer is (2). (Application)** The Mexican Cession was added to the United States in 1848 as a result of the Mexican War, which ended that year.

30. **The correct answer is (3). (Analysis)** The Louisiana Purchase was made in 1803, during the presidency of Thomas Jefferson.

31. **The correct answer is (5). (Analysis)** Choice (5) summarizes the entire map; each of the other choices describes only one part of it.

32. **The correct answer is (1). (Evaluation)** Wilson's belief in the need for America to make the world safe for democracy would probably lead him to support military intervention in the former Yugoslavia, because that area's problems beginning in the early 1990s were heavily involved in the persecution of minority groups and the implementation of authoritarian rule.

33. **The correct answer is (5). (Evaluation)** Wilson's support for the League of Nations was directly tied to his belief that nations should, and could, talk together to settle differences in an open, fair, and democratic way.

34. **The correct answer is (1). (Comprehension)** The correct order of events is: the Roaring Twenties (1920-1929), the Great Depression (1929-1941), World War II (1939-1945), the assassination of John F. Kennedy (1963), and the Watergate scandal (1971-1974).

35. **The correct answer is (2). (Analysis)** The influenza epidemic was not tied to World War I; all the other choices were.

36. **The correct answer is (5). (Analysis)** Choices (1) through (4) describe situations that face many elderly Americans and may prevent them from receiving proper treatment for clinical depression. Choice (5) describes a situation that is not true for a large percentage of older people.

37. **The correct answer is (3). (Evaluation)** The most appropriate person to seek advice from would be a medical doctor. Only a person with medical training could determine if other illnesses are involved. Choice (5), a psychologist, might also be useful after diagnosis but would not have the training to rule out other medical problems such as Alzheimer's disease.

38. **The correct answer is (4). (Comprehension)** The cartoon's view of American soldiers in the sights of a gun indicates that the cartoonist believes U.S. troops often become targets when they go abroad to solve conflicts between other groups.

39. **The correct answer is (3). (Application)** The American Relief Administration, a humanitarian effort, led to Hoover's being called the Great Humanitarian.

40. **The correct answer is (5). (Application)** The Bonus Army was made up of needy veterans, and Hoover's handling of the affair indicated that he didn't understand the extent of their problems.

41. **The correct answer is (3). (Application)** Hoover's qualifications for leadership of world famine relief would be based mostly on his work with the American Relief Administration.

42. **The correct answer is (3). (Application)** The major career experience that showed Hoover's unselfishness among the choices was his leadership of the American Relief Administration.

43. **The correct answer is (2). (Evaluation)** The fact that Roosevelt was then running against Hoover for the presidency may be viewed as the major reason for the change in Roosevelt's opinion of Hoover.

44. **The correct answer is (3). (Application)** The greatest number of nations listed in the passage as having government buildings at the fair were European countries, so choice (3) is correct.

45. **The correct answer is (3). (Evaluation)** The passage shows that there was already much violence in America in the 1800s, as there is today.

46. **The correct answer is (4). (Comprehension)** Having the President of the United States open the fair was a way of honoring American civilization.

47. **The correct answer is (1). (Analysis)** Choice (1) is the only one that makes a broad statement about the fair.

48. **The correct answer is (3). (Comprehension)** The key word is *ineffectual*, because the drawing shows that the tank and its occupants have little to do except decorate a garden.

49. **The correct answer is (1). (Evaluation)** The cartoon implies that NATO's reason for existence (the Soviet Union) has disappeared. Therefore, the cartoonist would probably agree that a powerful enemy once again would lead to a stronger NATO.

50. **The correct answer is (1). (Comprehension)** The drawing shows gangs growing out of poverty, drugs, and ignorance.

Social Studies Practice Test Analysis Chart

Use this table to determine your areas of strength and areas in which more work is needed. The numbers in the boxes refer to the multiple-choice questions in the practice test.

Content Area	Comprehension	Application	Analysis	Evaluation	Score
Unit 1: History	8, 34, 46, 48	39, 40, 41, 42, 44	7, 10, 47	9, 43, 45, 49	_____ of 16
Unit 2: Geography	11, 17	12, 18	13		_____ of 5
Unit 3: Political Science	19, 48	21, 22, 28, 29, 31	20, 30, 35	23, 24, 32, 33	_____ of 14
Unit 4: Economics	6, 14	1, 2, 5	3, 4, 16	15	_____ of 9
Unit 5: Behavioral Science	50		25, 26, 27, 36	37	_____ of 6
Score	_____ of 11	_____ of 15	_____ of 14	_____ of 10	_____ of 50

Practice Test 3: Science

1. **The correct answer is (2). (Fundamental understandings)** Iron's oxidation state is given as $+2$. Oxygen, except under certain circumstances, such as in peroxides, has an oxidation number or state of -2. Therefore, FeO is a neutral compound that satisfies the oxidation states. The answer cannot be choices (1) or (3) because the number of atoms must be equal on the reactant and product sides.

2. **The correct answer is (4). (Fundamental understandings)** Density is defined as mass divided by volume.

3. **The correct answer is (4). (History and nature of science)** Darwin's hypothesis was that many of the birds he saw had been in severe competition for resources. Those that were best suited to their environment enjoyed more reproductive success.

4. **The correct answer is (2). (Unifying concepts and processes)** See item number 3. Choice (3) is a statement of Lamarkian evolution, termed the theory of acquired characteristics, which is false. Choice (5) is a popular conception of evolution, but the key phrase would actually be "reproduction of the fittest," not "survival of the fittest."

5. **The correct answer is (4). (Unifying concepts and processes)** Using the Hardy-Weinberg Equilibrium, $p^2 + 2pq + q^2 = 1$, we know that $q^2 = 9$ percent or 0.09. To find the allele frequency, q^2, take the square root of 0.09.

6. **The correct answer is (4). (Fundamental understandings)** Each year, a tree makes new xylem and phloem with its vascular cambium. The preceding years' xylem makes up most of the rings in a tree.

7. **The correct answer is (5). (Fundamental understandings)** Insulin causes the uptake of glucose through the capillaries, while glucagon causes the liver to turn glycogen into glucose, raising the blood glucose level.

8. **The correct answer is (1). (Unifying concepts and processes)** Index fossils have been extensively studied, and very close parameters are known regarding when these organisms populated the earth. Sediments surrounding or within index fossils, choices (2) and (3), are much less important than the fossil in determining dates. Choice (4) is inaccurate, since the passage states that index fossils are widely distributed. Although the passage mentions associations of fossils, choice (5), this is not the main reason that index fossils are useful for dating.

9. **The correct answer is (4). (Unifying concepts and processes)** Given that all of the fossils discussed are in the same strata and therefore the organisms were contemporaries, it is unlikely that an evolutionary connection could be shown. It is much more likely that similar organisms found in successive strata would be so associated.

10. **The correct answer is (2). (Fundamental understandings)** As the distance to the fulcrum decreases, the effort required to lift the load increases. When the fulcrum is in the center, effort and load are equal. When the fulcrum is moved toward the load, as shown in the second diagram, the effort required decreases. Choices (3) and (4) are incorrect because the load does not change.

11. **The correct answer is (5). (Fundamental understandings)** In a second-class lever, the load is between the fulcrum and the effort. Of the choices listed, only the nutcracker fits this description. The fulcrum is the hinged end; the effort is your hand at the other end, and the load is the nut in the middle. All the other choices are first-class levers.

12. **The correct answer is (2). (Fundamental understandings)** The diagrams show that as the distance between the fulcrum and the effort increases, the effort decreases. Choice (1) happens to be true, but the information provided does not support it. Choices (3), (4), and (5) are contradicted by the information given.

13. **The correct answer is (3). (Fundamental understandings)** The structure fits the general formula for a monosaccharide, $C_nH_{2n}O_n$, and is glucose.

14. **The correct answer is (4). (Unifying concepts and processes)** The formula is $C_6H_{12}O_6$. The subscripts describe the number of atoms in that molecule, and the coefficient (in this case understood to be 1) describes the number of molecules.

15. **The correct answer is (1). (Fundamental understandings)** A disaccharide is made up of two monosaccharides. Some well-known examples are sucrose and maltose.

16. **The correct answer is (1). (Fundamental understandings)** If 1 volt is equal to 0.001 kilovolt, conversion of volts to kilovolts requires division by 1,000.

17. **The correct answer is (3). (Fundamental understandings)** The amount of current would decrease. None of the other choices would be in accordance with Ohm's law.

18. **The correct answer is (5). (Fundamental understandings)** The aorta receives the blood from the biggest chamber of the heart.

19. **The correct answer is (5). (Science in social and personal perspectives)** Breads and cereals are made from grains, but so are popcorn and some chips.

20. **The correct answer is (3). (Science in social and personal perspectives)** This group has lots of calories, but it lacks fiber and minerals and is digested quickly.

21. **The correct answer is (5). (Fundamental understandings)** If there are 1,000 millimeters in 1 meter and 1,000 meters in a kilometer, then $1,000 \times 1,000 = 1,000,000$.

22. **The correct answer is (3). (Science in social and personal perspectives)** When the volume increases, the pressure decreases, and air enters the trachea.

23. **The correct answer is (2). (Unifying concepts and processes)** The addition of electrons gives the rubber a negative electrical charge. If choice (1) were true, the rubber would become positively charged. None of the other choices describes a transfer of electrons.

24. **The correct answer is (4). (Unifying concepts and processes)** The line represents the equilibrium points between vapor and liquid when there are as many molecules going to one phase as the other. The line represents a vapor pressure curve, which also gives the boiling points of a liquid if one assumes external pressure to be vapor pressure. By the process of elimination, most of the answers are wrong, so the pressure of 760mm Hg can be surmised from the chart.

25. **The correct answer is (4). (Fundamental understandings)** Begin by converting 60g of $KClO_3$ to moles of $KClO_3$. Since $KClO_3$ and KCl are in a 1:1 ratio, that's also the number of moles of KCl that will be formed. Then convert that number of moles to grams. Without the units, the solution would look like this:

    $(60) (1/122.5) (2/2) (34.5/1) = 36.5$

26. **The correct answer is (4). (Fundamental understandings)** Grapefruit juice is 3.5 pH units away from neutral, and so is magnesium hydroxide.

27. **The correct answer is (4). (Fundamental understandings)** Gravel, choice (4), is the largest sediment listed and therefore the first to become deposited on the riverbank. Sand, choice (3), is next largest in size and therefore the next sediment to be deposited.

28. **The correct answer is (5). (Fundamental understandings)** Location E, choice (5), shows a beach of sorts extending into the river. River flow would be slowest here, and sediment would be most likely to collect.

29. **The correct answer is (4). (Fundamental understandings)** Granite is by far the toughest material listed. All others are sedimentary rocks or sediments and therefore much more easily broken down and carried away.

30. **The correct answer is (2). (Science in social and personal perspectives)** The increase in human population growth is the driving force behind most of the other problems.

31. **The correct answer is (5). (Unifying concepts and processes)** Not all mollusks breathe by gills, but only mollusks have mantles and muscular feet.

32. **The correct answer is (1). (Science as inquiry)** As an example, think about heat as the independent variable. As the temperature increases, you can watch or measure the response of an organism, such as a dog's respiration rate.

33. **The correct answer is (4). (Fundamental understandings)** In addition to pharyngeal gill slits, chordates also have a dorsal nerve chord and a notochord. The first two choices are characteristics of mammals, which are a group contained within the phylum Chordata.

34. **The correct answer is (5). (History and nature of science)** Her theory is based on all the observations listed.

35. **The correct answer is (4). (Fundamental understandings)** There are 1,000 calories in a kilocalorie. One calorie will raise one gram of water one degree. Therefore, 2,000 calories will raise 200 grams 10 degrees or 100 grams 20 degrees.

36. **The correct answer is (1). (Science as technology)** Insulation can prevent electricity from taking unwanted paths. Choices (2), (3), and (5) are all untrue. Choice (4) is true, but it does not explain why insulation can prevent a short circuit.

37. **The correct answer is (2). (Fundamental understandings)** The main point of the passage is that diffraction causes light to bend around obstacles, resulting in illumination in the shadow region behind an object. While it is true that light does not penetrate obstacles, choice (4), this was not the point of the passage.

38. **The correct answer is (5). (Fundamental understandings)** Dramatic temperature shifts, obstruction of storm patterns, and direct physical barrier are all reasons that moisture may not reach the leeward side of a mountain range. All other choices listed are fabrications.

39. **The correct answer is (4). (Fundamental understandings)** Regional winds over North America generally travel west to east. Canada is north of Seattle. All other choices list legitimate reasons for the rainfall differential between windward and leeward sides of a mountain range.

40. **The correct answer is (2). (Fundamental understandings)** Both cities are on the leeward side of a mountain range. Choices (1) and (3) are effects, not causes. Choices (4) and (5) are not correct.

41. **The correct answer is (3). (Unifying concepts and principles)** The double-stranded molecule will have complementary copies made of both strands. In the bottom, there is one old strand and one new strand in each double helix.

42. **The correct answer is (3). (Fundamental understandings)** Earth is about 4.5 billion years old, and the first land plants and fish showed up about 400 million years ago. The dinosaurs date back to about 250 million years ago and went extinct about 60 million years ago. The oldest hominids found to date are about 4.5 million years old.

43. **The correct answer is (2). (Fundamental understandings)** Insects can undergo incomplete metamorphosis (egg, nymph, adult) or complete metamorphosis (egg, larva, pupa, adult).

44. **The correct answer is (4). (Fundamental understandings)** Guanine (G) is complementary to cytosine (C), and thymine (T) is complementary to adenine (A). When DNA is transcribed to RNA, uracil (U) takes the place of thymine (T).

45. **The correct answer is (3). (Fundamental understandings)** Since the speed increases with decreasing mass, then higher mass results in a lower speed. Likewise, raising the temperature causes the speed to increase, so lowering the temperature causes the speed to decrease.

46. **The correct answer is (3). (Fundamental understandings)** Sedimentary rocks are formed from material settling at the bottom of a body of water in layers that are generally parallel to the horizon. Tilted sedimentary strata would be very good evidence that the original layers had moved.

47. **The correct answer is (4). (Fundamental understandings)** Choices (1), (2), (3), and (5) are true only some of the time, and all have exceptions when comparing oceanic to continental crust. Composition is the most consistent difference between oceanic and continental crust. Oceanic crust is generally basaltic, and continental crust is generally granitic.

48. **The correct answer is (3). (Fundamental understandings)** Converting each mass to moles gives the ratio $C_6H_{12}O_6$, which can be reduced to CH_2O.

49. **The correct answer is (2). (Unifying concepts and processes)** Water is the only molecule that is moving through this semipermeable membrane. It will always move from a higher to lower concentration, and since there are more water molecules (because there are less sugar molecules) in B, the water molecules will move toward A.

50. **The correct answer is (2). (Fundamental understandings)** pH is the negative log of the hydrogen ion concentration. HCl ionizes completely; therefore, take the negative log of 1/0.01.

Science Practice Test Analysis Chart

Use this table to determine your areas of strength and areas in which more work is needed. The numbers in the boxes refer to the multiple-choice questions in the practice test.

Content Area	Fundamental Under-standings	Unifying Concepts and Processes	Science as Inquiry	Science as Technology	Science in Personal and Social Perspectives	History and Nature of Science
Unit 1: Life Science	6, 7, 13, 15, 18, 22, 33, 43, 44	4, 5, 8, 9, 14, 31, 41, 49			19, 20	3, 34
Unit 2: Physical Science	1, 2, 10, 11, 12, 16, 17, 21, 25, 26, 35, 37, 45, 48, 50	23, 24	32	36		
Unit 3: Earth and Space Science	27, 28, 29, 38, 39, 40, 46, 47				30	

Practice Test 4: Language Arts, Reading

What Is This Character Like? *(page 533)*

1. **The correct answer is (4). (Analysis)** Although the passage mentions Cleo's daughter and the way she walks, the main information in it is about the contents of Cleo's pocketbook. By reading about that, we learn how Cleo feels about her sisters, her husband, and her daughter, as well as her general saucy attitude toward life.

2. **The correct answer is (1). (Analysis)** The narrator tells us what is going on in both Judy's and Cleo's thoughts and also knows what is in Cleo's pocketbook, which "held her secret life." Choices (2) and (3) are incorrect, because we hear the thoughts of both these characters, not just one. The narrator does not use the first-person "I," choice (4), and Cleo does not address the reader herself, choice (5); instead, we hear the omniscient narrator's account of them.

3. **The correct answer is (2). (Analysis)** Judy is compared to a "tired scow" and Cleo to a "racing sloop." The comparison means that compared to the quick, sleek Cleo, Judy is slow and plodding. The other choices are not supported by the passage.

4. **The correct answer is (3). (Synthesis)** In this passage, the narrator describes Cleo's careful attention to her appearance and her many financial intrigues, shown by the contents of her purse. This shows that she is both vain about her appearance and devious in her financial transactions. Although there is some support for choice (1), choice (3) is far better supported in the passage as a whole. There is no support in the passage for the other choices.

5. **The correct answer is (5). (Synthesis)** The description of Cleo's clothing and hair—her hat, her pompadour, starched skirt, shirtwaist, camisole, and chemise—indicate that the story does not take place in the present. The other choices all indicate details that do not date the story to any particular time period.

Why Is Becky Surprised? *(page 534)*

6. **The correct answer is (3). (Analysis)** Warder's questioning whether he can trust Becky's word of honor if she breaks it (lines 10–12) suggests that he relies on a person's word of honor. There is no evidence for choices (1) and (2). Although Warder may not believe Becky, there is no evidence that he doesn't believe what people say in general, so choice (4) can be eliminated. Choice (5) is supported by lines 37–38 but not by lines 10–12.

7. **The correct answer is (4). (Comprehension)** Throughout the passage, Warder asks Becky questions about her actions. In lines 10–12, Warder has divulged that he knows Becky to be lying to him. Choice (1) states the opposite. The passage does not end with an apology from Warder, so choice (2) is incorrect. The fact that Warder has hired detectives worries Becky (lines 40–42), so choice (3) is incorrect. Becky denies seeing Lindon, so choice (5) can be eliminated.

8. **The correct answer is (3). (Analysis)** The stage directions first show Becky comfortably hugging Warder (lines 2–3) and then describe her as "worried" (line 30). They help reveal that she is lying, so choice (1) is incorrect. Becky says that she loves Warder, but since the stage directions do not reveal this, choice (2) can be eliminated. The stage directions refer to the furniture but do not describe it, as choice (4) suggests. Choice (5) is incorrect because Warder's emotions are not made clear.

9. **The correct answer is (1). (Application)** In lines 10–12, Warder asks, ". . . if I find your word of honor is broken in one thing, how can I ever trust it in another?"; thus, after discovering that Becky is lying, he probably would assume she is lying again. Choice (2) states the opposite. He would be angry, so choices (2) and (4) are incorrect. Choice (5) is a possibility, but Warder might leave Becky after this first lie. Also, choice (1) applies more directly to his statement in lines 15–18.

10. **The correct answer is (2). (Synthesis)** The entire passage, as Becky has grown increasingly uncomfortable and Warder has grown increasingly angry, has led up to the disclosure of the detectives' report, in which Becky will be confronted with proof of her deceit. The other choices are not supported by the passage.

11. **The correct answer is (5). (Analysis)** These words imply that Warder has always believed Becky in the past and has become distrustful only recently. Choice (1) can be eliminated because the speech is Warder's, not Becky's. Choice (2) can be eliminated because the entire passage suggests that Warder and Becky have known each other for some time. Choice (3) and (4) are contradicted by the passage.

What Makes This Architect's Work Special? *(page 535)*

12. **The correct answer is (4). (Comprehension)** In lines 23–25, Dieste states that "architecture has in common with other arts the ability to help us contemplate the universe." Dieste considers architecture to be both an art and something spiritual; thus, choices (1) and (3) can be eliminated. Although Dieste might agree with choices (2) and (5), the ideas in those choices are not related to this question.

13. **The correct answer is (1). (Comprehension)** In lines 8–9, the reviewer states that Dieste's buildings "are at once inexpensive and of high aesthetic quality." Though choices (2) and (4) are true, they are not the main reason the reviewer admires Dieste. Choice (3) is incorrect because Dieste avoids "costly steel" (line 9). There is no mention of windows, so choice (5) can be eliminated.

14. **The correct answer is (4). (Analysis)** The correct response is reinforced by the author's frequent reminders of the spiritual quality of Dieste's buildings. Dieste's buildings are "sturdy" (line 15), so choice (1) is incorrect. There is no mention of nature or openness, as choices (2) and (3) suggest. Dieste's buildings are "inexpensive" (line 8), so choice (5) is incorrect.

15. **The correct answer is (3). (Application)** Since Dieste favors inexpensive materials, he would probably use copper, the least expensive of the choices.

16. **The correct answer is (2). (Analysis)** The reviewer contrasts the "multimillion-dollar price tags" of most architects with Dieste's work. Choices (1) and (3) are incorrect because Dieste's work is modern and low in cost, not free. The reviewer does not discuss home insurance or prices decades ago, so choices (4) and (5) can be eliminated.

What Will Happen on This Day? *(page 536)*

17. **The correct answer is (1). (Analysis)** Personification means describing something that is not human in human terms. Choice (1) describes the moon as if it were a person with flushed cheeks. Choices (2) and (4), the first comparing the sleeping dog to the stone, the second comparing the bright-colored trees to roosters' tails, use nonhuman terms. Choices (3) and (5) are descriptive phrases but not figures of speech.

18. **The correct answer is (2). (Synthesis)** The passage describes the slow coming of the day. All the details—the trees lighting up, the wild rushing of the baby around the yard, the birthday cake in the oven—indicate that something important is going to happen. This is confirmed by the old lady's attitude when we first see her—sitting waiting, "as though wild to be seen." There is no indication of conflict or death in the passages, so the other choices are not supported.

19. **The correct answer is (4). (Analysis)** The writer achieves an effect of rapid movement by using active verbs (bolted, ran, rushed) and short, rhythmic phrases (the well-piece, the birdhouse, the bell post . . .). The other choices are not supported by the paragraph.

20. The correct answer is (5). (Analysis) A simile is a figure of speech in which something is compared to something else, using the word "like" or "as." Almost every sentence in the passage contains a simile. Although there are a few examples of personification and metaphors, choices (1) and (4), particularly in the first paragraph, there are far more similes in the passage. The passage does not employ exaggeration, choice (2), or flowery poetic language, choice (3).

What Is Human Life? *(page 537)*

21. The correct answer is (2). (Analysis) The rhyme scheme is ABAB: the last word of lines 1 and 3 (year and clear) rhyme, as do the last words of lines 2 and 4 (man and span).

22. The correct answer is (5). (Comprehension) The last two lines of the poem state that a person must go through winter, a time of "pale misfeature," because otherwise we would forego our mortal nature, or death. Although the other choices are things that all or most people do, the term "mortal" refers to a creature that will die.

23. The correct answer is (3). (Synthesis) Both poems divide human life into stages: four for the Keats poem and seven for the short excerpt (from Shakespeare's *As You Like It*). Choices (1) and (2) are wrong because they refer only to the short excerpt. Choices (4) and (5) are not supported by either text.

24. The correct answer is (4). (Analysis) The poetic image is that of a ruminant, a cow or sheep, that is chewing its cud, playing on the double meaning of "ruminate," which means both to chew and to think long and deeply. Choice (1) is wrong, because although the word "honied" appears, there is no allusion to bees; choice (3) is wrong because although the young person is dreaming, there is no allusion to daydreaming; and choice (5) is used in the description of autumn in the next lines, not in lines 6–8. There is no support for choice (2) in the poem.

25. The correct answer is (3). (Analysis) In autumn, the person is like a bird with furled wings, at rest and contented merely to observe. The other choices are all suggested by different parts of the poem but not by the part about autumn.

26. The correct answer is (1). (Synthesis) The poem clearly conveys one central idea, that human life is divided into stages. Choice (2) is incorrect because the poem does not clearly convey four images—for summer, for example, two distinct images are used. Choice (3) is incorrect because the language is not simple but rather highly poetic. Choice (4) is incorrect because the poem does not teach a moral lesson. Choice (5) is incorrect because the image used is not original but rather commonplace, as shown in the quotation from Shakespeare.

How Do You Search for Files? *(page 537)*

27. The correct answer is (3). (Comprehension) The passage states that this is one typical use of this feature. Choices (1) and (2) are about storing paper documents, whereas the passage is about storing computer files. Choices (4) and (5) are not supported by the passage.

28. The correct answer is (1). (Comprehension) The passage states that the Find tool is available from the Open dialog box. Choices (2) and (3) are not supported by the passage. Choices (4) and (5) are search criteria listed in the passage.

29. The correct answer is (5). (Comprehension) All of the other choices are specifically listed in the passage as properties of files.

30. The correct answer is (5). (Application) The writer wants all files about a specific topic, so she would search by content. The other choices include criteria that would not be helpful in this search.

31. The correct answer is (2). (Application) The assistant should create a custom search and save it, since he conducts the same search repeatedly. Choices (1) and (3), which involve searching through files one by one, would take much longer than using a custom search. Choices (4) and (5) are not supported by the passage.

How Does Macon Feel about Being Alone? *(page 538)*

32. The correct answer is (2). (Comprehension) This passage describes a separation or divorce rather than a death, as choice (1) indicates; the passage begins "After his wife left him . . ." Choice (5) is incorrect because Macon has clearly stayed in the house that he and Sarah shared. There is no evidence for choices (3) and (4).

33. The correct answer is (3). (Synthesis) Macon's focus on Sarah's belongings, and the fact that the house seems smaller when he expected it to feel larger, show that he is surprised to be feeling her absence so keenly. Choices (1) and (5) suggest the opposite, and there is no evidence to support choice (4). It is possible that Macon and Sarah fought, but the passage does not mention this; therefore, choice (2) can be eliminated.

34. The correct answer is (1). (Analysis) The second and third paragraphs list Sarah's personal belongings. Macon is thinking, not being interviewed or writing to Sarah, as choices (3) and (4) suggest. The passage does not discuss events in Macon's life, so choice (5) is incorrect. Although Sarah's belongings influence Macon's emotions, the cause-and-effect relationship is not the main focus of the passage, so choice (2) can be eliminated.

35. The correct answer is (5). (Comprehension) Lines 13–14 state directly that "She liked to keep in touch with her students . . ." There is no evidence for choices (1), (2), or (4). Choice (3) is incorrect because, though the passage suggests that she is dancing, it does not indicate that she is learning to dance.

How Are the Mothers at Grand Isle Depicted? *(page 539)*

36. The correct answer is (2). (Synthesis) Lines 8–13 and 23–24 mention sand, water, and summer, so the setting is probably a vacation site—a seashore or an island. Choices (1) and (3) can be eliminated because they describe crowded, stressful situations. Although the families may be staying in large old homes or even hotels, there is no evidence to support these ideas; therefore, choices (4) and (5) can be eliminated.

37. The correct answer is (4). (Synthesis) Since Mrs. Pontellier's child is "not apt to rush crying to his mother's arms for comfort" (lines 9–10), she is probably a somewhat distant mother. Choices (1) and (5) suggest the opposite, whereas choice (3) is too strongly negative a description based on the passage. There is no evidence that Mrs. Pontellier is or is not strict, but the speaker does indicate that she is not comforting, so choice (2) is incorrect.

38. The correct answer is (5). (Analysis) Since hair parting cannot be an actual law, the speaker is humorously exaggerating its importance to the characters in this passage. Choices (1), (2), and (4) all suggest that the speaker is serious. Although the speaker is describing a social custom or standard, her tone could not be characterized as social, so choice (3) can be eliminated.

39. The correct answer is (1). (Analysis) The point of this statement is that the women direct so much of their energy toward their husbands and children that their own personalities are nearly erased, or *effaced*. Choices (2), (4), and (5) are incorrect because they suggest that the women are building up, not erasing, their own personalities. Choice (3) is not the best choice because the women are not criticizing or condemning themselves—they simply aren't paying any attention to their own needs.

40. The correct answer is (1). (Synthesis) As the "embodiment of every womanly grace and charm" (lines 33–34), Adele is the model, or perfect example, of the "mother-woman." Choices (2), (3), and (4) may be true, but they are not supported by the passage. Adele's husband is not described, so choice (5) is incorrect.

Language Arts Reading Practice Test Analysis Chart

Use this table to determine your areas of strength and areas in which more work is needed. The numbers in the boxes refer to the multiple-choice questions in the practice test.

Content Area	Comprehension	Application	Analysis	Synthesis
Unit 1: Fiction	32, 35		1, 2, 3, 17, 19, 20, 34, 38, 39	4, 5, 18, 33, 36, 37, 40
Unit 2: Poetry	22		21, 24, 25	23, 26
Unit 3: Drama	7	9	6, 8, 11	10
Unit 4: Nonfiction	12, 13, 27, 28, 29	15, 30, 31	14, 16	

Practice Test 5: Mathematics

Part I

1. **The correct answer is (3).** Two bottles of Headache-gone at $2.37 cost $4.74, and one bottle of Aspirin at $1.56 add up to a total of $6.30. The change from a $20 bill is $20 − $6.30 = $13.70.

2. **The correct answer is (2).** A 12% discount means you would pay 88%, so $0.88 \times 53 = \$46.64$. Now, take another 10% off of $46.64, which is $0.10 \times 46.64 = \$4.664$. So James pays $46.64 − $4.664 = $41.96 \approx \$41.98$.

3. **The correct answer is (5).**

   0.453kg = 1 lb   0.001MT = 1kg

   $1\text{kg} = \dfrac{1}{0.453}\text{ lb}$ $0.001\text{MT} = \dfrac{1}{0.453}\text{ lb}$

   $1\text{MT} = \dfrac{1}{0.453} \div 0.001 = 2207\text{ lb}$

4. **The correct answer is (5).** $(1{,}231 + 3{,}452 + 12{,}386) \div 800 = 21.3 \approx 22$. He needs to buy complete CDs.

5. **The correct answer is 106.7.** $4{,}000{,}000 \div 37{,}500 = 106.66 \approx 106.7$ seconds. See page 551 for filled-in answer grid.

6. **The correct answer is (4).** Volume of small container: $(3 \times 3 \times 3) + (\pi \cdot 1^2 \cdot 1) = 30.14$. Volume of large container: $(\pi \cdot 3^2 \cdot 5) + (\pi \cdot 1.5^2 \cdot 2) = 155.43$. Therefore, $155.43 \div 30.14 = 5.156 \approx 5.16$.

7. **The correct answer is (3).** For making the call, he pays $1.26. For talking for 13 minutes he pays $0.04 \times 13 = \$0.52$. In total, he pays $1.26 + + 0.52 = \$1.78$. If there is a 12% discount on this amount, he will save $0.12 \times 1.78 = 0.2136 \approx \$0.21$. Money should be appropriately rounded.

8. **The correct answer is 901.** If she had x dollars before any transactions, then $(x + 1{,}325) − (935 + 136 + 432 + 210) = 513$. Therefore, $x = \$901$. See page 551 for filled-in answer grid.

9. **The correct answer is (3).** Make a proportion: For every $5 − 2 = 3$ Mach rise in velocity, the number of broken windows rises by $310 − 124 = 186$. So, we write the proportion

Velocity	Broken Windows
3	186
4	x

   so we have $\dfrac{3}{4} = \dfrac{186}{x}$ or $3 \times x = 4 \times 186$.

   Therefore, $x = \dfrac{744}{3} = 248$.

10. **The correct answer is (3,-4).** First mark all the points of the kite (1,1), (5,1), and (3,3). Notice that the "4 wide" is across from (1,1) to (5,1). So count 7 down from (3,3) and you end up at (3,−4). See page 551 for filled-in answer grid.

11. **The correct answer is (5).** Add up the scores and divide by 5:
    $\dfrac{17.9 + 17.7 + 17.4 + 18.2 + 17.1}{5} = 17.66$. Notice, you only need to compare Teams 5 and 4, because the rest of the teams are explicitly lower in their scores.

12. **The correct answer is (5).** The range is the difference between the highest and the lowest score: $22.3 − 5.8 = 16.5 = 16.50$.

13. **The correct answer is (4).** Add all the throws: $17.1 + 16.8 + 16.2 + 12.8 + 15.8 = 78.7 = 78.70$.

14. **The correct answer is (2).** Order all the values pertaining to Try 3, and the middle number is the median. 11.3, 11.5, [15.4], 16.2, 17.4.

15. **The correct answer is (2).** The mode is the most frequently occurring number, therefore 17.1

16. **The correct answer is (2).** 1 min 23 seconds = $60 + 23 = 83$ seconds. Therefore, $83 − 45 = 38$ seconds over. For every second over, he loses 1%; therefore, he loses 38%—i.e., he receives $100 − 38 = 62\%$ of the total points. Therefore, $0.62 \times 162 = 100.44$.

17. **The correct answer is (4).** To find the mean (average), we add all the values and divide by the total number of values.

    $\dfrac{1001.12 + 998.95 + 1000.12 + 1003.14 + 997.12}{5}$

    $= \dfrac{5000.45}{5} = 1000.09$.

18. **The correct answer is 31/33.** Probability is the ratio between the number of ways a particular event can occur and the total number of outcomes there possibly could be. Therefore, the probability of drawing a green ball is $P(Green) = \dfrac{2}{3 + 2 + 3 + 5 + 9 + 4 + 7} = \dfrac{2}{33}$. But you are asked to find the probability of *not* getting a green. Therefore, $1 − \dfrac{2}{33} = \dfrac{31}{33}$. See page 551 for filled-in answer grid.

19. **The correct answer is (3).** The radius of the semicircle is 1. Therefore, the side of the square is equal to the diameter of these semicircles, which is 2. So the "white" area is the sum of the area of all the semicircles, which are simply two whole circles and the area of the square. $A = 2^2 + 2 \cdot \pi^2 = 4 + 2\pi = 10.28$.

20. **The correct answer is (2).** Side is 2. Explanation provided in number 19.

21. **The correct answer is (5).** The radius of the big circle is 2.
    $\text{Area}_{\text{Shaded Region}} = \text{Area}_{\text{Big Circle}} − \text{Area}_{\text{White Region}}$
    $\text{Area}_{\text{Shaded Region}} = \pi 2^2 − 10.28 = 12.56 − 10.28 = 2.28$.

22. **The correct answer is (1).** $1.12 \div (56 + 1226 + 18) = 0.0008615 \approx 0.000862$ pounds.

23. The correct answer is 9757.

	11% (slow) reproduction rate rabbits	15% (fast) reproduction rate rabbits	Total
Number of rabbits from last year	x	$x - 145$	$2x - 145$
Rabbits born at the end of this year	$0.11x$	$0.15(x - 145)$	$2x - 145 + 1120$ or $2x + 975$

Therefore,

$$0.11x + 0.15(x - 145) = 1,120$$
$$0.11x + 0.15x - 21.75 = 1,120$$
$$0.26x = 1,141.75$$
$$x = \frac{1,141.75}{0.26} = 4,391.3 \text{ slow reproducing rabbits.}$$

Remember, you cannot have a fraction of a rabbit, so using $x = 4,391$ and substituting in $2x + 975$ gives 9,757 rabbits at the end of this year. See page 551 for filled-in answer grid.

24. The correct answer is 39,490. For the first 30 hours, he gets paid $.30 \times 235.06 = 7,051.8$. For the next 8 hours, he is paid time and a half: $8 \times \left(235.06 + \frac{235.06}{2}\right) = 2,820.72$. At the end of the week, he has earned $7,051.80 + 2,820.72 = 9,872.52$. In a month, he makes $9,872.52 \times 4 = 39,490.08 \approx \$39,490$. See page 551 for filled-in answer grid.

25. The correct answer is 979.7. We need to find the difference of the volumes of the two cylinders: $V = \pi r^2 h$, $V_{Big} - V_{Small} = 3.14(6)^2(10) - 3.14(4)^2(3) = 979.68 \approx 979.7$. See page 551 for filled-in answer grid.

Part II

1. The correct answer is (3). The perimeter of the farm is the sum of the circumference of the half-circle and the three sides of the rectangle plus the left-over portions of the fourth side, which is $2,500 - 2 \times 500 = 1,500$. Entire perimeter is $\frac{1}{2} \times 2\pi r + 2w + l + 1,500 = \pi \cdot 500 + 3,000 + 2,500 + 1,500 = 500\pi + 7,000$.

2. The correct answer is (1). Use the following conversion: $1\text{cu.cm} = 1\text{mL}$, $1\text{m} = 100\text{cm}$, $(1\text{m})^3 = (100\text{cm})^3 \Rightarrow 1\text{cu.m.} = 1,000,000\text{cu.cm}$. Therefore, $1,000,000\text{cu.cm.} = 1,000,000\text{mL}$.

3. The correct answer is (2). $\frac{1}{2}$ the money goes to stocks.

4. The correct answer is (5). The ratio of the volume is simply the cubes of the original ratios. $1^3 : 4^3 \Rightarrow 1:64$.

5. The correct answer is (4). The distributive law has been applied: $(213/112) + (441/112)$.

6. The correct answer is 7. $10 \times 0.7 = 7$ seconds. See page 552 for filled-in answer grid.

7. The correct answer is (5). Find 21% of 4,400—i.e., $0.21 \times 4,400 = \$924$.

8. The correct answer is (3). Round off 11 to 12 and compare to 6—i.e., $12 \div 6 = 2$.

9. The correct answer is (2). First, round off to the nearest 10% for the gas allotment, which is 10%. 10% = $300. Therefore, 100% = $300 \times 10 = \$3,000$.

10. The correct answer is (1). Twice a number ($2n$) plus ($+$) two gives $2n + 2$, which is equal ($=$) to three times the number $3n$ minus ($-$) eight $3n - 8$. Therefore, $2n + 2 = 3n - 8$.

11. The correct answer is (1,1). Find the average of the x-values and the y-values. $\left(\frac{3 + 1 - 3 + 4 + 0}{5}, \frac{2 + 5 + 5 - 6 - 1}{5}\right) = (1,1)$. See page 552 for filled-in answer grid.

12. The correct answer is (4). Use a proportion:

Deliveries/Houses	Time
30	$\frac{1}{2}$
600	x

Therefore, $\dfrac{30}{600} = \dfrac{\frac{1}{2}}{x}$

$$30x = 600 \times \frac{1}{2}$$
$$x = \frac{300}{30} = 10$$

13. The correct answer is (5). This problem cannot be factored.

14. The correct answer is (4). The largest rod that can fit into this shape must be its longest diagonal, which is the line drawn from the upper right-hand corner to the lower left-hand corner. This creates a right triangle with a height of $3 + 5 + 3 = 11$ and a base of 5. Therefore, the length of the diagonal is $(\text{diagonal})^2 = 11^2 + 5^2 \Rightarrow \text{diagonal} = \sqrt{121 + 25} = \sqrt{146}$.

15. The correct answer is (5). Calculate the range (difference between highest and lowest). $14,495 - (-282) = 14,777$. Remember, "below sea-level" means a negative number.

16. The correct answer is (4). Median for the six data points is the average of the two middle data points. $\frac{83.8 + 86.8}{2} = 85.3\%$.

17. The correct answer is (2). If the small piece is x, then the long piece is $2x$. Therefore, $x + 2x = 54 \Rightarrow 3x = 54$. Thus, $x = 18$.

18. The correct answer is (2). $3 - 1 = 2$ hours.

19. The correct answer is (4). $3200 \div 600 = 5.3$. She needs to buy 6 cans because she cannot buy a partial can.

20. The correct answer is (2). $300 \div 125 = 2.4$. But she needs to buy 3 spools. So she pays $1.50 \times 3 = 4.50$.

21. The correct answer is (3).

	Pennies	Nickels	Total
Number of coins	x	$x - 27$	
Amount of money	$0.01x$	$0.05(x - 27)$	5.38

Therefore, $0.01x + 0.05(x - 27) = 5.38$.

22. The correct answer is (3). The four quarter circles together become a whole circle. Therefore, $\text{Area}_{Shape} = \text{Area}_{Square} - \text{Area}_{Circle} \Rightarrow 10^2 - \pi \cdot 3^2 = 100 - 9\pi$.

23. The correct answer is (3).

	Sophomore	Freshmen	Total
Number of students	S	$S + 206$	816

Therefore, the equation is $S + (S + 206) = 816$.

24. The correct answer is 181. Add up peak prices: $28 + 57 + 96 = 181$. See page 552 for filled-in answer grid.

25. The correct answer is (1). Calculate the mean (average) of each component and compare: $\frac{22 + 28 + 34 + 49}{4} = 33.25$. Therefore, it is Sentence Perfect.

Credits

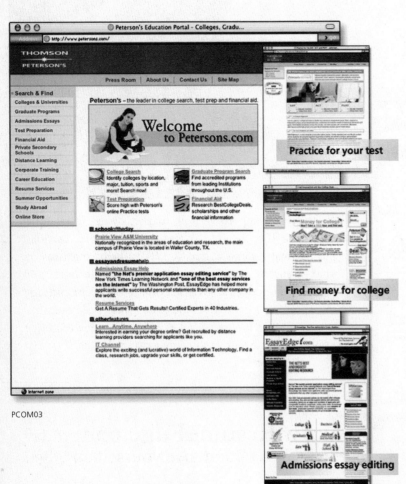